Dearborn

Series 7

General Securities Representative

License Exam Manual
15th Edition

Dearborn
PASSTRAK™

At press time, this edition of Series 7 contains the most complete and accurate information currently available for the NASD Series 7 license examination. Owing to the nature of securities license examinations, however, information may have been added recently to the actual test that does not appear in this edition.

This publication is designed to provide accurate and authoritative information in regard to the subject matter covered. It is sold with the understanding that the publisher is not engaged in rendering legal, accounting, or other professional service. If legal advice or other expert assistance is required, the services of a competent professional person should be sought.

©2004 by Dearborn Financial Publishing, Inc.
Published by Dearborn Financial Institute, Inc.

All rights reserved. The text of this publication, or any part thereof, may not be reproduced in any manner whatsoever without written permission from the publisher.

Printed in the United States of America.

04 05 06 10 9 8 7 6 5 4 3 2 1

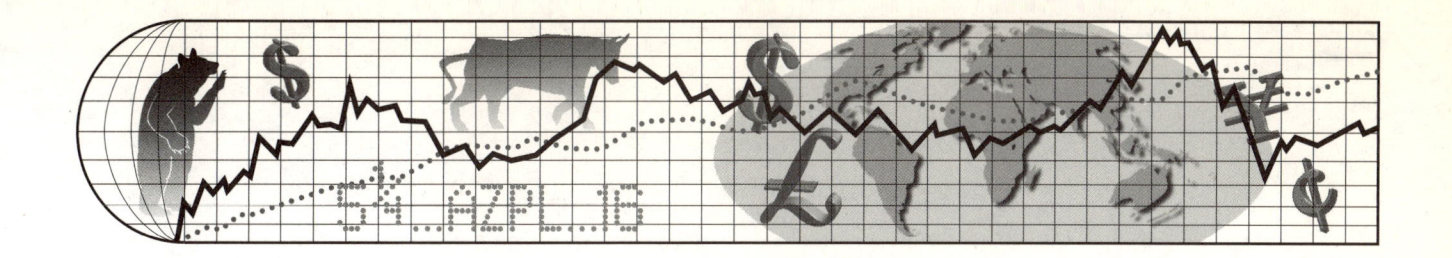

Table of Contents

Series 7 Introduction   ix

1. Equity Securities   1
   What Is a Security?   2
   Stock   3
   Preferred Stock   16
   Return on Investment   19
   Transferability of Ownership   20
   Tracking Equity Securities   22
   Rights and Warrants   29
   American Depositary Receipts   33
   Real Estate Investment Trusts (REITs)   34
   Equity Securities HotSheet   36
   Series 7 Unit Test 1   39
   Series 7 Unit Test 1 Answers & Rationale   41

2. Debt Securities   43
   Characteristics of Bonds   44
   Bond Yields   56
   Corporate Bonds   66
   The Trust Indenture   70
   Trading Corporate Bonds   71
   US Government & Agency Securities   79
   Accrued Interest Calculations   90
   Money Market Securities and Interest Rates   100
   Tracking Debt Securities   109

Debt Securities HotSheet   112

Series 7 Unit Test 2   115

Series 7 Unit Test 2 Answers & Rationale   118

3. **Municipal Securities   121**
   Municipal Debt Characteristics   122
   Issuing Municipal Securities   137
   Analysis of Municipal Securities   151
   Municipal Trading and Taxation   160
   Municipal Securities Rules and Regulations   171
   Tracking Municipal Securities   178
   Municipal Securities HotSheet   178
   Series 7 Unit Test 3   181
   Series 7 Unit Test 3 Answers & Rationale   186

4. **Options   189**
   The Options Contract   190
   Basic Option Transactions   209
   Using Options to Protect a Position   224
   Multiple Option Transactions   234
   Nonequity Options   251
   How the Options Market Functions   261
   Tax Rules for Options   269
   Options HotSheet   273
   Series 7 Unit Test 4   277
   Series 7 Unit Test 4 Answers & Rationale   281

5. **Customer Accounts   285**
   New Accounts   286
   Types of Accounts   295
   Uniform Gifts to Minors Act (UGMA) Accounts   301
   Customer Accounts HotSheet   306
   Series 7 Unit Test 5   309
   Series 7 Unit Test 5 Answers & Rationale   312

6. **Margin Accounts   315**
   Extension of Credit in the Securities Industry   316
   Margin Accounting   322
   Special Memorandum Account   345
   Pledging Customer Securities for Loans   346

Margin Accounts HotSheet 348
Series 7 Unit Test 6 351
Series 7 Unit Test 6 Answers & Rationale 353

7. Issuing Securities 355
The Regulation of New Issues 356
The Three Phases of an Underwriting 357
The Underwriting Process 364
The Underwriting Syndicate 369
Types of Underwriting Commitments 370
Exemptions from the Securities Act of 1933 376
Hot Issues 382
Issuing Securities HotSheet 384
Series 7 Unit Test 7 387
Series 7 Unit Test 7 Answers & Rationale 390

8. Trading Securities 393
The Regulation of Trading 394
Securities Markets and Broker/Dealers 395
The New York Stock Exchange (NYSE) 399
The Specialist 402
Long and Short Sale Rules 418
Other Domestic and International Exchanges 421
Computerized Order Routing 422
The Consolidated Tape 423
The Over-the-Counter Market 425
Quotations 427
NASD 5% Markup Policy 430
NASD Automated Quotation System 434
Trading Securities HotSheet 438
Series 7 Unit Test 8 441
Series 7 Unit Test 8 Answers & Rationale 444

9. Brokerage Support Services 447
Processing an Order 448
Rules of Good Delivery 461
Brokerage Support Services HotSheet 467
Series 7 Unit Test 9 469
Series 7 Unit Test 9 Answers & Rationale 471

10. Investment Company Products   473
Investment Company Purpose   474
Investment Company Registration   480
Management of Investment Companies   483
Information Distributed to Investors   486
Characteristics of Mutual Funds and the Mutual Fund Concept   488
Comparing Mutual Funds   493
Mutual Fund Marketing and Pricing   496
Mutual Fund Distributions and Taxation   506
Mutual Fund Purchase and Withdrawal Plans   511
Tracking Investment Company Securities   515
Investment Company Products HotSheet   518
Series 7 Unit Test 10 521
Series 7 Unit Test 10 Answers & Rationale 523

11. Retirement Plans   525
Retirement Plans   526
Individual Retirement Accounts (IRAs)   528
Keogh (HR-10) Plans   535
Tax-Sheltered Annuities (403(b) Plans)   538
Corporate Retirement Plans   538
The Employee Retirement Income Security Act of 1974 (ERISA)   540
Retirement Plans HotSheet   543
Series 7 Unit Test 11 545
Series 7 Unit Test 11 Answers & Rationale 547

12. Variable Annuities   549
Types of Annuity Contracts   550
Purchasing Annuities   557
Receiving Distribution from Annuities   558
Variable Annuities HotSheet   565
Series 7 Unit Test 12 567
Series 7 Unit Test 12 Answers & Rationale 569

13. Direct Participation Programs   571
Characteristics of Limited Partnerships   572
Types of Limited Partnership Programs   583
Direct Participation Programs HotSheet   595
Series 7 Unit Test 13 597
Series 7 Unit Test 13 Answers & Rationale 599

14. Economics & Analysis 601
Economics 602
Economic Policy 608
Technical Analysis 615
Fundamental Analysis 622
Corporate Analysis 624
Financial Ratios and Analyzing Corporate Equity 635
Economics & Analysis HotSheet 640
Series 7 Unit Test 14 643
Series 7 Unit Test 14 Answers & Rationale 645

15. Ethics, Recommendations & Taxation 647
Ethics in the Securities Industry 648
Investment Considerations and Suitability 658
Suitability: Analyzing Financial Risks and Rewards 662
Portfolio Management 667
Federal and State Taxation 672
Ethics, Recommendations & Taxation HotSheet 685
Series 7 Lesson Exam 15 689
Series 7 Lesson Exam 15 Answers & Rationale 692

16. US Government & State Rules & Regulations 695
Overview of Federal and Securities Legislation 696
State Securities Regulations 706
US Government and State Rules & Regulations HotSheet 708
Series 7 Unit Test 16 711
Series 7 Unit Test 16 Answers & Rationale 714

17. Other SEC & SRO Rules & Regulations 715
Registration and Regulation of Broker/Dealers 716
The National Association of Securities Dealers (NASD) 717
Investigation: Code of Procedure & Code of Arbitration Procedure 726
SROs: The NYSE Constitution and Rules 735
Communications with the Public: Advertising and Sales Literature 738
Other SEC & SRO Rules & Regulations HotSheet 754
Series 7 Unit Test 17 757
Series 7 Unit Test 17 Answers & Rationale 760

Glossary 763

Index 825

HotSheets 833
  Equity Securities HotSheet 833
  Debt Securities HotSheet 835
  Municipal Securities HotSheet 837
  Options HotSheet 839
  Customer Accounts HotSheet 843
  Margin Accounts HotSheet 845
  Issuing Securities HotSheet 847
  Trading Securities HotSheet 849
  Brokerage Support Services HotSheet 851
  Investment Company Products HotSheet 853
  Retirement Plans HotSheet 855
  Variable Annuities HotSheet 857
  Direct Participation Programs HotSheet 859
  Economics & Analysis HotSheet 861
  Ethics, Recommendations & Taxation HotSheet 863
  US Government and State Rules & Regulations HotSheet 865
  Other SEC & SRO Rules & Regulations HotSheet 867

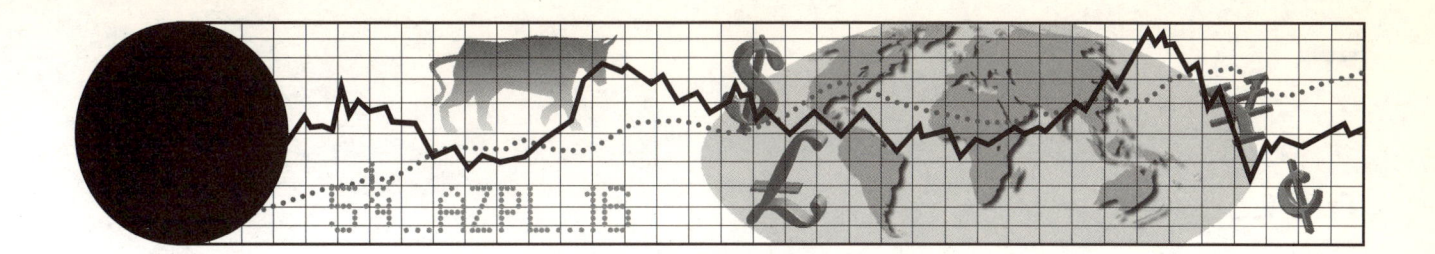

Series 7 Introduction

Thank you for choosing Dearborn's PASSTRAK exam preparation system for your educational needs and welcome to the Series 7 License Exam Manual. This system has been designed with applied adult learning principles to give you the tools you'll need to pass your exam on the first attempt.

Some of these special features include:

- exam-focused questions and content to maximize test preparation;
- an interactive design for the License Exam Manual that integrates content with questions to increase retention; and
- integrated Drill & Practice exam preparation tools to sharpen test-taking skills.

Is there someone I can contact if I have questions as I study?

Dearborn is here to help you with every step of your study process. If you have questions about your study materials, please contact Dearborn's **AnswerPhone** at:

1-800-621-9621 x3598

between 8:00 am and 6:00 pm CT, Monday through Friday. **AnswerPhone's** staff of content experts will answer your questions and clarify the material as needed. If your inquiry is regarding a particular question in the practice exams or in the Drill & Practice, please note the QID number (Question Identifier) as this will allow us to find your question within our testing database.

In addition, visit **www.dearborn.com** for industry updates and current exam information.

The Course

How is the License Exam Manual organized? Dearborn's Series 7 License Exam Manual consists of 17 units, unit tests, and 10 practice exams. When an additional point will be valuable to your comprehension, special notes are embedded in the text.

✓ ***Take Note:*** Tips and examples to amplify important test points.

💡 **Test Topic Alert!** Each Test Topic Alert highlights content that is likely to appear on the Series 7 exam.

✓ ***For Example:*** Provides situations and numerical instances of the material.

You will also see **Quick Quizzes,** which will help you understand and retain the material covered in that particular section. Quick Quizzes aren't difficult—just a brief interactive review of what you just read.

In addition, **Unit HotSheets** at the end of each unit summarize the key points in bullet-point format. For your convenience and use as review notes, Hot-Sheets are reprinted at the end of the book on perforated pages.

If your study packet included Dearborn's Drill & Practice CD-ROM, the Drill & Practice includes a large bank of questions that are similar in style and content to those you will encounter on the Series 7 exam. You may use it to generate exams by a specific topic or create 125-question practice finals that are similar in difficulty and proportionate mixture to the Series 7 examination.

If you prefer to complete written exams, the print Practice Finals will provide similar practice. Note that the questions on the print exams are included in the CD-ROM. Devote a significant amount of your study time to the completion of practice questions and review of rationales.

How Much Time Should I Spend Studying? Plan to spend approximately 90–120 hours reading the material and working through the questions. Your actual time may vary depending on your study habits and professional background.

Spread your study time over 6–8 weeks before the date on which you are scheduled to take the exam. Select a time and place for studying that will allow you to concentrate. There is a lot of information to learn, so be sure to give yourself enough time to understand the material.

Do I Need to Take All of the Dearborn Practice Exams? The exams test the same knowledge you will need in order to answer the questions on the NASD Series 7 exam. By completing all the exams and checking your answers against the rationales, you should be able to pinpoint areas of difficulty. Review any questions you miss, paying particular attention to their rationale. If a subject still seems troublesome, go back and review the section(s) covering those topics.

What Topics are Covered in the Course?

The *License Exam Manual* consists of 17 units, each devoted to a particular area of general securities sales and regulation that you will need to know to pass the General Securities Registered Representative Exam (the Series 7). Each unit is divided into study sections devoted to more specific areas with which you need to become familiar.

The Series 7 exam and PASSTRAK Series 7 address the following topics:

Unit	Topic	Estimated # of Exam Questions
1	Equity Securities	10–15
2	Debt Securities	15–25
3	Municipal Securities	50–55
4	Options	40–45
5	Customer Accounts	10–20
6	Margin Accounts	5–10
7	Issuing Securities	10–15
8	Trading Securities	15–20
9	Brokerage Support Services	10–15
10	Investment Company Products	10–15
11	Retirement Plans	5–10
12	Variable Annuities	5–10
13	Direct Participation Programs	10–12
14	Economics and Analysis	10–15
15	Ethics, Recommendations & Taxation	10–20
16	US Government and State Rules & Regulations	10–15
17	Other SEC and SRO Rules & Regulations	10–15

Why do I Need to Pass the Series 7 Exam?

Your employer is a member of the New York Stock Exchange (NYSE) or another self-regulatory organization that requires its members and employees of its members to pass a qualification exam to become registered. To be registered as a representative qualified to sell all types of securities, you must pass the Series 7 exam.

Are There Any Prerequisites?

There are no prerequisite exams to pass before taking the Series 7.

What Is the Series 7 Exam Like?

The Series 7 is a two-part, six-hour, 250-question exam administered by the National Association of Securities Dealers (NASD). The exam is given in two three-hour sessions, each covering different areas of general securities sales and regulation. It is offered as a computer-based test at Prometric testing sites around the country.

Series 7 Introduction

What Score Must I Achieve to Pass?
You must score at least 70% on the Series 7 exam to pass and become eligible for registration as a general securities representative.

What Topics Will I See on the Exam?
The questions you will see on the Series 7 exam do not appear in any particular order. The computer is programmed to select a new, random set of questions for each test taker, selecting questions according to the preset topic weighting of the exam. Each Series 7 candidate will see the same number of questions on each topic, but a different mix of questions. The Series 7 exam is divided into seven critical function areas:

	# of Questions	% of Exam
1. Prospecting for and qualifying customers	9	3.6%
2. Evaluating customer needs and objectives	4	1.6%
3. Providing customers with investment information and making suitable recommendations	123	49.2%
4. Handling customer accounts and account records	27	10.8%
5. Understanding and explaining the securities markets' organization and participants to customers	53	21.2%
6. Processing customer orders and transactions	13	5.2%
7. Monitoring economic and financial events, performing customer portfolio analysis, and making suitable recommendations	21	8.4%

When you complete your exam, you will receive a printout that identifies your performance in each area.

Additional Trial Questions
During your exam, you will see up to 10 extra trial questions. These are potential exam-bank questions that the NASD is testing by having examinees answer them during the course of an exam. These questions are not included in your final score, and you will be given extra time to answer them.

How Do I Enroll for the Exam?
To obtain an admission ticket to the Series 7 exam, your firm must file an application form with the NASD, along with processing fees. The NASD will then send you a directory of Prometric centers and an enrollment valid for a stated number of days. To take the exam during this period, you should make an appointment with a center as far in advance as possible of the date on which you would like to take the test. You may contact the Prometric NASD Registration Center at 1-800-578-6273.

What Should I Take to the Exam?	Take one form of personal identification with your signature and photograph as issued by a government agency. You cannot take reference materials or anything else into the testing area. Calculators are available upon request. Scratch paper and pencils will be provided by the testing center, although you cannot take them with you when you leave.
How Well Can I Expect to Do?	If you study and complete all of the sections of this course, and consistently score at least 80% on the review and practice final exams, you should be well prepared to pass the Series 7.
Examination Results and Reports	At the end of the exam, your score will be displayed, indicating whether you passed. The next business day after your exam, your results will be mailed to your firm and to the self-regulatory organization and state securities commission specified on your application.

Successful Test Taking

Passing the Series 7 exam depends not only on how well you learn the subject matter, but also on how well you take tests. You can develop your test-taking skills—and improve your score—by learning a few test-taking techniques:

- Read the full question
- Avoid jumping to conclusions—watch for hedge clauses
- Interpret the unfamiliar question
- Look for key words and phrases
- Identify the intent of the question
- Recognize synonymous terms
- Memorize key points
- Eliminate/short-list Roman numeral choices
- Use a calculator
- Beware of changing answers
- Pace yourself

Each of these pointers is explained below, including examples that show how to use them to improve your performance on the exam.

Read the Full Question	You cannot expect to answer a question correctly if you do not know what it is asking. If you see a question that seems familiar and easy, you might anticipate the answer and mark it before you finish reading it. Be sure to read the full question before answering it—questions are often written to trap people who assume too much. Here is an example of a question in which an assumption could produce a wrong answer.

1. What is the term for a divided underwriting of municipal securities that is priced through a bidding process involving more than one investment banking firm?

    A. Eastern
    B. Western
    C. Negotiated
    D. Competitive

The answer is D—the question describes a situation in which competitive bidding sets the price, and therefore the spread, of the offering. This is an easy question to answer only for someone who has read the full question, because the point is made in the second half. If you read the question too quickly, you might get to the word *divided* and assume that you are being asked to remember whether a *divided* underwriting is also called an Eastern underwriting or a Western underwriting.

Avoid Jumping to Conclusions—Watch for Hedge Clauses

The questions on the Series 7 are often embellished with deceptive distractors as choices. To avoid being taken in by seemingly obvious answers, be sure to read each question and each answer twice before selecting your choice. Doing so will provide you with a better chance of doing well on the test.

Watch out for hedge clauses embedded in the question. Examples of hedge clauses include the terms *if, not, all, none* and *except*. In the case of *if* statements, the question can be answered correctly only by taking into account the qualifier. If you ignore the qualifier, you will not answer correctly.

Qualifiers are sometimes combined in a question. Some that you will frequently see together are *all* with *except* and *none* with *except*. In general, when a question starts with *all* or *none* and ends with *except*, you are looking for an answer that is opposite to what the question appears to be asking. For example:

2. All of the following are characteristics of T-bills EXCEPT that they

    I. mature in more than one year
    II. are sold at a discount
    III. pay interest semiannually
    IV. are very safe investments

    A. I and II
    B. I and III
    C. II and III
    D. II and IV

If you neglect to read the *except*, you will look for choices that are characteristics of T-bills. In fact, the question asks which choices are *not* characteristics of T-bills (the exceptions). T-bills mature in six months or less and do not pay periodic interest; therefore, choices I and III are incorrect and the answer is B.

Interpret the Unfamiliar Question Do not be surprised if some questions on the test seem unfamiliar at first. If you have studied your material, you will have the information to answer all the questions correctly. The challenge may be a matter of understanding *what* the question is asking. Very often, questions present information indirectly. You may have to interpret the meaning of certain elements before you can answer the question. The following two examples concerning bond yields and prices highlight this point.

3. What is the effect of a decline in purchasing power on the current yields of outstanding bonds?

   A. The yields decrease.
   B. The yields increase.
   C. The yields stay the same.
   D. This cannot be determined with the information given.

This question is asking you to apply your knowledge of economics, investment recommendations, and the relationship between bond prices and yields. Consumer purchasing power declines during periods of inflation. Inflation causes interest rates to rise, and this in turn causes prices of outstanding bonds to decrease. You will learn that when a bond declines in price or sells at a discount, the current yield increases (answer B).

This same content could have been tested in a different way, as illustrated by the next example.

4. What is the effect of tight money on bond prices?

   A. Bond prices decrease.
   B. Bond prices increase.
   C. Bond prices stay the same.
   D. This cannot be determined with the information given.

When you study the sections on economics, you will see that tight money is closely related to high interest rates. When money is scarce (tight), interest rates rise. When interest rates rise, prices of outstanding bonds decrease (answer A).

At first glance, the two questions appear very different, but in fact they test the same relationship—the relationship between a bond's price and its yield. Be aware that the exam will approach a concept from different angles.

Look for Key Words and Phrases Look for words that are tip-offs to the situation presented. For example, if you see the word *prospectus* in the question stem, you know the question is about a new issue.

Sometimes a question will even supply you with the answer if you can recognize the key words it contains. The following is an example of how a key word can help you answer correctly.

5. Whose Social Security number must appear on an account under the Uniform Gifts to Minors Act?

   A. Minor
   B. Donor
   C. Legal guardian
   D. Parent

Looking at the answers, answer A is a likely candidate. Under UGMA, the minor is the owner of the securities. As the owner, the minor's Social Security number must be listed on the account. Few questions provide clues as blatant as this one, but many offer key words that can help you select the correct answer if you pay attention. Read all instructional phrases carefully.

6. Rank the following persons in descending order of their claims against a corporation's assets when the corporation is forced into liquidation.

   I. General creditors
   II. Preferred stockholders
   III. Bondholders
   IV. Common stockholders

   A. I, II, III, IV
   B. I, III, II, IV
   C. III, I, II, IV
   D. III, II, IV, I

The most important aspect of this question is identifying the key word—*descending*. A descending order ranks a list from highest to lowest—in this question, the highest claim on assets to the lowest claim on assets. (The answer is C: bondholders, general creditors, preferred stockholders, common stockholders.) The question could have asked for the ascending order—lowest to highest. Or it could have asked you to rank the choices from junior claim to senior claim or vice versa. Take time to identify the key words to answer this type of question correctly.

Identify the Intent of the Question

Many questions on the Series 7 exam supply so much information that you lose track of what is being asked. This is often the case in story problems. Learn to separate the story from the question. For example:

7. You have decided to buy 100 shares of ABC Mutual Fund, which prices its shares at 5:00pm every business day. You turn in your order at 3:00 pm. when the shares are priced at $10 NAV, $10.86 POP. The sales load is 7.9%. What will your 100 shares cost?

   A. $1,000
   B. $1,079
   C. $1,086
   D. 100 times the offering price that will be calculated at 5:00 pm

A clue to the answer is presented in the first sentence—the fund price at 5:00 pm. Orders for mutual funds are executed based on the next price calculated (forward pricing); therefore, the answer to this question is D. You do not need to calculate anything.

Take the time to identify what the question is asking. Of course, your ability to do so assumes you have studied sufficiently. There is no magic method for answering questions if you don't know the material.

Recognize Synonymous Terms

The securities industry has a tendency to abbreviate terms and use acronyms. Several terms may be used interchangeably throughout the test, and you should be able to recognize them. Examples include the following.

- NAV = net asset value = bid price
- POP = public offering price = ask price
- periodic payment plan = contractual plan
- buy = long = own
- sell = short = owe
- registered representative (RR) = account executive (AE)
- tax-sheltered annuity (TSA) = tax-deferred annuity (TDA)
- Uniform Gifts to Minors Act (UGMA) = Uniform Transfers to Minors Act (UTMA)

Memorize Key Points

Reasoning and logic will help you answer many questions, but you will have to memorize a good deal of information. The HotSheets summarize some of the most important key points for memorization.

Eliminate/Short-List Roman Numeral Choices

Roman numeral (or multiple-multiple) questions are common on the Series 7 exam; they require you to distinguish between several likely answers. When you are confronted with Roman numeral choices, try to eliminate one or two of them to help narrow your choices. For example, if you can eliminate choice II in a Roman numeral question, and three of the four answers contain choice II, you have narrowed down your options to the correct answer by the process of elimination. For example:

8. An owner of common stock has the right to

   I. determine when dividends will be issued
   II. vote at stockholder meetings or by proxy
   III. determine the amount of any dividends issued
   IV. buy redeemed shares before they are offered to the public

   A. I, III and IV only
   B. II only
   C. II, III and IV only
   D. II and IV only

The answer to this question is B. Stockholders have the right to vote on certain corporate matters and the right to dividends if and when declared. Stockholders do not vote on when a dividend is to be paid, nor on the amount of dividend to be paid. Knowing this, you can eliminate answers A and C. You are now left with only two answers to choose from.

Use a Calculator

For the most part, the Series 7 exam will not require the use of a calculator. Most of the questions are written so that any math required is simple. However, if you have become accustomed to using a calculator, you will be provided with one by the testing center staff.

Avoid Changing Answers

If you are unsure of an answer, your first hunch is most likely to be correct. Do not change answers on the exam without good reason. In general, change an answer only if you:

- discover that you did not read the question correctly; and/or
- find new or additional helpful information in another question.

Pace Yourself

Some people finish the exam early; some use the entire time allowed; and some do not have time to finish all the questions. Watch the time carefully (time remaining will be displayed on your screen) and pace yourself.

Do not waste time by dwelling on a question if you simply do not know the answer. Make the best guess you can, mark the question for *Record for Review*, and return to the question if time allows. Make sure that you have time to read all the questions so that you can record the answers you do know.

To give yourself an indication of how much time you need to answer a 250-question exam, time yourself on a practice final in the CD ROM or print set. Remember that your ability to take an exam within an allotted time will improve with practice.

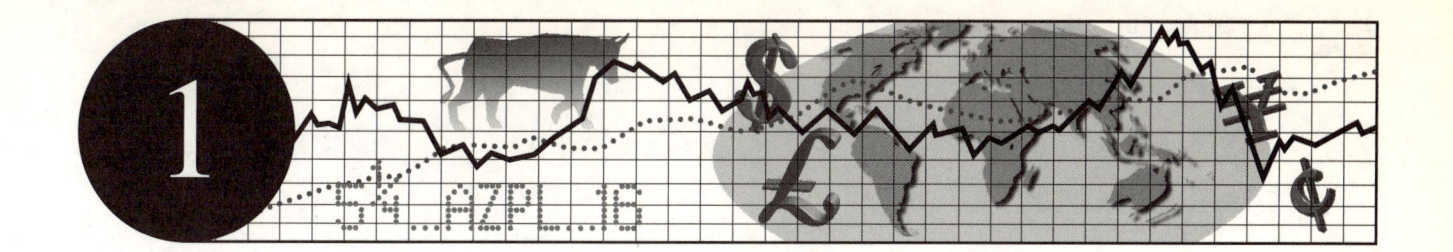

Equity Securities

INTRODUCTION

Because equity is such an important capital market security, the fundamentals that you learn in this unit will lay the groundwork for your success in future units. This unit will cover common stock, preferred stock, and related equity securities.

The investment world is divided between owners (stock or equity) and lenders (bonds or debt). Owning equity in a company is perhaps the most visible and accessible means by which wealth is created. Individual investors become owners of a publicly traded company by buying stock in that company. In so doing, they can participate in the company's growth over time.

This unit will cover information that will account for approximately 10–15 questions on the Series 7 exam.

UNIT OBJECTIVES

When you have completed this unit, you should be able to:

- describe the basic features of a security;
- compare and contrast the four classifications of common stock;
- identify and describe the three methods of common stock valuation;
- list rights, benefits, and risks of common stock ownership;
- describe six types of preferred stock and the unique features of each;
- calculate return on investment in common stock;
- describe the process of transferring stock ownership;
- interpret financial charts that report performance of equity securities;
- compare and contrast the features of rights and warrants; and
- identify and describe the features of ADRs and REITs.

Equity Securities

What Is a Security?

In the simplest terms, a **security** is an investment that represents either an ownership stake or a debt stake in a company. An investor becomes part owner in a company by buying shares of the company's stock. A **debt security** is usually acquired by buying a company's bonds. A **debt investment** is a loan to a company in exchange for interest income and the promise to repay the loan at a future maturity date. It does not confer ownership.

Stocks and bonds are normally purchased and sold on a stock exchange or in the **over-the-counter** (**OTC**) market. A stock exchange, such as the **New York Stock Exchange** (**NYSE**), is an auction market where buyers and sellers are matched by a specialist who maintains a fair and orderly market for a particular set of stocks.

The OTC market is an interdealer market linked by computer terminals to **National Association of Securities Dealers** (**NASD**) member firms across the country. The OTC market has no physical location, and traders do not transact business face-to-face as they do on stock exchange floors.

Equity and Debt

Stock represents **equity** or ownership in a company, and bonds are a loan to a company (a debt). A company discloses the composition of its total capitalization—equity and debt—by publishing a balance sheet.

The Balance Sheet The **balance sheet** summarizes the company's:

- **assets**—what the company **owns**: cash in the bank, accounts receivable (money it is owed), investments, property, inventory, and so on;
- **liabilities**—what the company **owes**: accounts payable (current bills it must pay), short- and long-term debt and other obligations; and
- **equity**—the excess of the value of assets over the value of liabilities (the company's net worth).

Net Worth A company's **net worth** is computed by subtracting all liabilities from the value of total assets. This computation is summarized by the basic balance sheet equation: **assets − liabilities = net worth**.

✓ **Take Note:** Other ways to express this same equation are as follows:

Assets = liabilities + net worth
Assets − liabilities = net worth

Stock

A company issues **stock** as its primary means of raising business capital. Investors who buy the stock buy a share of ownership in the company's net worth. Whatever a business owns (its assets) less its creditors' claims (its liabilities), belongs to the business owners (its stockholders).

Each share of stock entitles its owner to a portion of the company's profits and dividends and an equal vote on directors and other important matters. Most corporations are organized in such a way that their stockholders regularly vote for and elect candidates to a **board of directors** (**BOD**) to oversee the company's business. By electing a board of directors, stockholders have some say in the company's management but are not involved with the day-to-day details of its operations.

✓ *Take Note:* An individual's stock ownership represents his proportionate interest in a company. If a company issues 100 shares of stock, each share represents an identical 1/100—or 1%—ownership position in the company. A person who owns 10 shares of stock owns 10% of the company; a person who owns 50 shares of stock owns 50% of the company.

Common Stock

Corporations may issue two types of stock: **common** and **preferred**. When speaking of stocks, people generally refer to common stock. **Preferred stock** represents equity ownership in a corporation, but it usually does not have the same voting rights or appreciation potential as common stock. Preferred stock normally pays a fixed semi-annual dividend and has priority claims over common stock; that is, the preferred is paid first if a company declares bankruptcy.

Common stock can be classified in four ways:

- authorized;
- issued;
- outstanding; and
- treasury.

Authorized Stock **Authorized stock** refers to a specific number of shares the company has authorization to issue or sell. This is laid out in the company's original charter. Often, a company sells only a portion of the authorized shares to raise enough capital for its foreseeable needs. The company may sell the remaining authorized shares in the future or use them for other purposes. Should the company decide to sell more shares than are authorized, the charter must be amended through a stockholder vote.

Issued Stock Issued stock has been authorized and distributed to investors. When a corporation issues (sells) fewer shares than the total number authorized, it normally reserves the unissued shares for future needs, including:

- raising new capital for expansion;
- paying stock dividends;
- providing stock purchase plans for employees or stock options for corporate officers;
- exchanging common stock for outstanding convertible bonds or preferred stock; or
- satisfying the exercise of outstanding stock purchase warrants.

Authorized but unissued stock does not carry the rights and privileges of issued shares and is not considered in determining a company's total capitalization.

Outstanding Stock Outstanding stock includes any shares that a company has issued but has not repurchased—that is, stock that is investor-owned.

Treasury Stock Treasury stock is stock a corporation has issued and subsequently repurchased from the public. The corporation can hold this stock indefinitely or can reissue or retire it. A corporation could reissue its treasury stock to fund employee bonus plans; distribute it to stockholders as a stock dividend; or under certain circumstances, redistribute it to the public in an additional offering. Treasury stock does not carry the rights of outstanding common shares, such as voting rights and the right to receive dividends.

By buying its own shares in the open market, the corporation reduces the number of shares outstanding. If fewer shares are outstanding and operating income remains the same, earnings per share increase. A corporation buys back its stock for a number of reasons, such as to:

- increase earnings per share;
- have an inventory of stock available to distribute as stock options, fund an employee pension plan, and so on; or
- use for future acquisitions.

Test Topic Alert! Expect to see a question on outstanding stock similar to the following.

ABC company has authorized one million shares of common stock. It issued 800,000 shares one year ago. It then purchased 200,000 shares for its treasury. How many shares of ABC stock are outstanding?

The solution requires that you know a basic formula:

Issued stock – treasury stock = outstanding stock

In applying this formula to our sample question, the solution is as follows:

800,000 − 200,000 = 600,000

Alternatively, treasury stock equals issued shares minus outstanding shares.

✓ **Take Note:** This question illustrates a point about NASD exams. The question provided information about the number of shares of authorized stock but that information was not necessary for you to solve the problem. Prepare for questions that give you more information than you need. The Series 7 exam expects you to know concepts so well that you can determine both what is and what is not essential to the solution of a problem.

Common Stock Values

The laws of **supply and demand** (based largely on the perception of a company's profitability and business prospects) determine the company's stock price in the market. Although a stock's **market price** is the most meaningful measure of its value, other measures include **par value** and **book value**.

Par Value For investors, a common stock's **par value** is meaningless. It is an arbitrary value the company gives the stock in the company's articles of incorporation and has no effect on the stock's market price. If a stock has been assigned a par value for accounting purposes, it is usually printed on the face of the stock certificate.

When the corporation sells stock, the money received exceeding par value is recorded on the corporate balance sheet as **capital in excess of par**, also known as **paid-in surplus**, **capital surplus**, or **paid-in capital**.

Book Value A stock's **book value** per share is a measure of how much a common stockholder could expect to receive for each share if the corporation were liquidated. Most commonly used by analysts, the book value per share is the difference between the value of a corporation's tangible assets and its liabilities divided by the number of shares outstanding. The book value per share can—and usually does—differ substantially from a stock's market value.

Market Value Market price—the price investors must pay to buy the stock—is the most familiar measure of a stock's value. Market value is influenced by a company's business prospects and the consequent effect on **supply** (the number of shares available to investors) and **demand** (the number of shares investors want to buy).

Equity Securities

Test Topic Alert! The three methods of common stock valuation do not result in the same amount.

Par value = an arbitrary value
Book value = current liquidation value of a share
Market value = supply and demand value

The market value is most meaningful and familiar to the typical investor.

Quick Quiz 1.1

Match each of the following terms with the appropriate description below.

A. Outstanding stock
B. Authorized stock
C. Book value
D. Par value

___ 1. Number of shares that a corporation is permitted to issue
___ 2. Dollar amount assigned to a share of stock by its issuer
___ 3. Liquidation value of each share of common stock
___ 4. Issued stock – treasury stock

Answers 1. **B.**   2. **D.**   3. **C.**   4. **A.**

Rights of Common Stock Ownership

Stockholders are owners of a company and therefore have certain rights that protect their ownership interests.

Voting Rights Common stockholders use their **voting rights** to exercise control of a corporation by electing a board of directors and by voting on important corporate policy matters at annual meetings, such as:

- issuance of convertible securities (dilutive to current stockholders) or additional common stock;
- substantial changes in the corporation's business, such as mergers or acquisitions; and
- declarations of stock splits.

Stockholders have the right to vote on the issuance of convertible bonds because they will dilute current stockholders' proportionate ownership when converted (changed into shares of common).

Statutory vs. Cumulative Voting

EXAMPLE ONE : Mr. X owns 100 Shares

STATUTORY VOTING	
Board of Directors Seat 1	100 ✓
Board of Directors Seat 2	100 ✓
Board of Directors Seat 3	100 ✓

EXAMPLE TWO : Mr. X owns 100 Shares

CUMULATIVE VOTING	
Board of Directors Seat 1	175 ✓
Board of Directors Seat 2	50
Board of Directors Seat 3	75 ✓

OR

CUMULATIVE VOTING	
Board of Directors Seat 1	300 ✓
Board of Directors Seat 2	0
Board of Directors Seat 3	0

Calculating the Number of Votes

A stockholder can cast one vote for each share of stock owned. Depending on the company's bylaws and applicable state laws, a stockholder may have either a **statutory** or **cumulative** vote.

Statutory Voting. Statutory voting allows a stockholder to cast one vote per share owned for each item on a ballot, such as candidates for the BOD. A board candidate needs a simple majority to be elected.

Cumulative Voting. Cumulative voting allows stockholders to allocate their total votes in any manner they choose.

✓ *For Example:* XYZ Corp. will be electing 3 directors at its annual meeting. Each XYZ shareholder has a number of votes equal to the number of shares owned times the number of directorships up for election. Assume a shareholder owns 100 shares. Under statutory voting, the shareholder may use a maximum of 100 votes for any one seat on the board.

Equity Securities

Under cumulative voting, the shareholder may allocate all 300 votes to one director, giving the shareholder a greater impact.

✓ **Take Note:** Cumulative voting benefits the smaller investor while statutory voting benefits larger shareholders.

Test Topic Alert! Shareholders do not vote on dividend-related matters, such as when they are declared and how much they will be. They do vote on stock splits, board members, and issuance of additional equity-related securities like common stock, preferred stock, and convertible securities.

Proxies Stockholders often find it difficult to attend the annual stockholders' meeting, so most vote on company matters by means of a **proxy** (a form of absentee ballot). After it has been returned to the company, a proxy can be automatically cancelled if the stockholder attends the meeting, authorizes a subsequent proxy, or dies. When a company sends proxies to shareholders, usually for a specific meeting, it is known as a **proxy solicitation**.

Sample Proxy Ballot

DATAWAQ, INCORPORATED

Proxy for Annual Meeting of Stockholders, August 24, 2002

The undersigned, having received the Notice of Meeting and Proxy statement dated July 24, 2002, hereby appoints Maurice Saltzman and Gerald Kurland, and each of them, proxies of the undersigned, with full power of substitution and revocation, to attend the annual meeting of the stockholders of the Company, to be held at the Company's executive offices at 6000 Data Place, Chula Vista, California, on Thursday, August 24, 2002, at 10:00 am (Pacific Time), and any adjournment thereof, and thereat to vote all the shares of stock of the undersigned in the Company which the undersigned would be entitled to vote if personally present, upon the following:

(1) The election of seven (7) Directors;   _____ For _____ Abstain

(2) The adoption of the Employees'
    Savings Plan of Datawaq, Inc.;   _____ For _____ Against
(3) The ratification of the appointment
    of Max Leveth & Co. as
    independent auditors;   _____ For _____ Against
(4) In their discretion, on any matters
    coming before the meeting, or any
    adjournment thereof;

hereby ratifying and confirming all that said proxies may lawfully do or cause to be done by virtue hereof, and hereby revoking any proxies heretofore given by the undersigned to vote at said meeting or any adjournment thereof.

This proxy will be voted as directed or, if no direction is indicated, will be voted in favor of the proposals listed as items (1), (2) and (3).

THIS PROXY IS SOLICITED BY THE MANAGEMENT.

(To be signed on the reverse side.)

Companies that solicit proxies must supply detailed and accurate information to the shareholders about the proposals to be voted on. Before making a proxy solicitation, companies must submit the information to the **Securities and Exchange Commission (SEC)** for review.

If a proxy vote could change control of a company (a **proxy contest**), all persons involved in the contest must register with the SEC as participants or face criminal penalties. This registration requirement includes anyone providing unsolicited advice to stockholders about how to vote. However, brokers who advise customers who request advice are not considered participants. A stockholder may revoke a proxy at any time before the company tabulates the final vote at its annual meeting.

Nonvoting Common Stock

Companies may issue both **voting** and **nonvoting** (or limited voting) common stock, normally differentiating the issues as Class A and Class B respectively. Issuing nonvoting stock allows a company to raise additional capital while maintaining management control and continuity without diluting voting power.

Preemptive Rights When a corporation raises capital through the sale of additional common stock, it may be required by law or its corporate charter to offer the securities to its common stockholders before the general public; this is known as an **antidilution provision**. Stockholders then have a **preemptive right** to purchase enough newly issued shares to maintain their proportionate ownership in the corporation.

✓ *Take Note:* Preemptive rights give investors the right to maintain a proportionate interest in a company's stock.

✓ *For Example:* ABC has 1 million shares of common stock outstanding. Mr. X owns 100,000 shares of ABC common stock, or 10%. If ABC issues an additional 500,000 shares, Mr. X will have the opportunity to purchase 50,000 of those shares.

	Original		*New*		
ABC:	1,000,000 shares	+	500,000	=	1,500,000 shares
Mr. X:	100,000 shares	+	50,000	=	150,000 shares
	10%		10%		10%

Limited Liability Stockholders cannot lose more than the amount they have paid for a corporation's stock. Limited liability protects stockholders from having to pay a corporation's debts in bankruptcy.

Inspection of Corporate Books Stockholders have the right to receive annual financial statements and obtain lists of stockholders. Inspection rights do not include the right to examine detailed financial records or the minutes of BOD's meetings.

Equity Securities

Residual Claims to Assets If a corporation is liquidated, the common stockholder (as owner) has a **residual right to claim corporate assets** after all debts and other security holders have been satisfied. The common stockholder is at the bottom of the liquidation priority list.

✓ **Take Note:** Because common stock is last in line in a corporate liquidation, it is known as the **most junior security**.

Stock Splits

Although investors and executives are generally delighted to see a company's stock price rise, a high market price may inhibit trading of the stock. To make the stock price attractive to a wider base of investors—that is, retail versus institutional investors—the company can declare a **stock split**.

Forward Splits A forward stock split increases the number of shares and reduces the price without affecting the total market value of shares outstanding—an investor will receive more shares, but the value of each share is reduced. The total market value of the ownership interest is the same before and after the split.

✓ **Take Note:** More shares, less value = same total ownership interest before and after

✓ **For Example:** If an investor has 100 shares at $60 per share, the total value is $6,000 [100 × $60 = $6,000].

Assume a 2-for-1 split. To find the new number of shares, multiply the original number by 2 (the first number of the split), and then divide by 1 (the second number of the split) [100 × 2 = 200; 200 / 1 = 200]. Because the total value of the shares is the same before and after the split, determine the new per share value as follows:

200 × ? = 6,000 (6,000 / 200 = 30). The new per share value is $30.

Assume a 5-for-4 split this time (original position is 100 shares at $60):

100 × 5 = 500; 500 / 4 = 125. The new number of shares is 125.
125 × ? = 6,000 (6,000 / 125 = 48). The new value per share is $48.

Reverse Splits A **reverse split** has the opposite effect on the number and price of shares. After a reverse split, investors own fewer shares worth more per share.

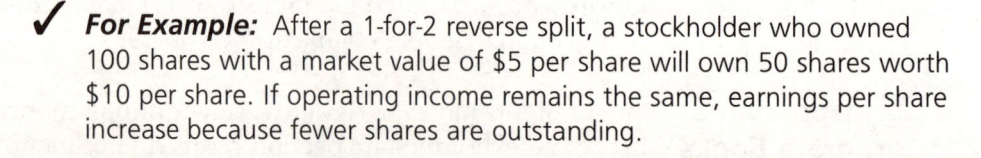

✓ **For Example:** After a 1-for-2 reverse split, a stockholder who owned 100 shares with a market value of $5 per share will own 50 shares worth $10 per share. If operating income remains the same, earnings per share increase because fewer shares are outstanding.

The rule for reverse splits is as follows:

Less shares, more value = same total interest before and after

Assume the original interest of 100 shares at $5:

100 × $5 = $500

After a 1-for-4 reverse split, what is the new number and value of shares?

100 × <u>1</u> = 100, 100 / <u>4</u> = 25. The new number of shares is 25.
25 × ? = 500 (500 / 25 = 20). The new value per share is $20.

Not all questions on splits involve calculations. If you remember that there are more or fewer shares at lower or greater value as a result of the split, you might be able to answer the question without using math.

Benefits and Risks of Owning Common Stock

Generally, and throughout this course, it is assumed an investor buys or owns shares of stock with the intent of selling them at a higher price in the future—buy low, sell high later. An investor who buys shares is considered **long** the stock.

An investor may also sell shares before he owns them, with the intent of buying them back at a lower price in the future—sell high, buy low later. Such a transaction, known as a **short sale**, involves borrowing shares to sell that the investor must eventually replace. An investor who sells borrowed shares is considered **short** the stock until he buys and returns the shares to the lender.

Benefits of Owning Stock People generally expect to receive financial growth, income, or both from common stock investments.

Growth

An increase in the market price of shares is known as **capital appreciation**. Historically, owning common stock has provided investors with high real returns.

Income

Many corporations pay regular quarterly **cash dividends** to stockholders. A company's dividends may increase over time as profitability increases. Dividends, which can be a significant source of income for investors, are a major reason many people invest in stocks. Issuers may also pay **stock dividends** (additional shares in the issuing company) or **property dividends** (shares in a subsidiary company or a product sample).

Equity Securities

Test Topic Alert! Stock dividends are frequently paid by companies that wish to reinvest earnings for research and development. Technology companies, aggressive growth companies, and new companies are examples of companies likely to pay stock dividends. Property dividends are the least common form of dividend payment.

Tax Effects of Selling and Owning Stock

Buying low and selling high is one of the main objectives of stock investors. When this is accomplished, investors experience **capital gains**. If the investor sells the stock at the higher price, the investor has a **realized gain**, and will be responsible for taxes on the gain. If the investor does not sell the stock, the investor has an **unrealized gain**, which is not taxed. Stock gains are taxable only when they are realized.

Another reason people buy stock is to generate income from the **dividends** paid. Investors who receive dividends must generally pay income taxes on them. The IRS makes no exceptions for individuals; corporations, however, receive a 70% exclusion on dividend income received from investments in other companies.

Risks of Owning Stock

Regardless of their expectations, investors have no assurance of receiving the returns they expect from their investments.

Market Risk

The chance that a stock will decline in price at a time the investor needs his money is one risk of owning common stock. A stock's price fluctuates daily as perceptions of the company's business prospects change and affect the actions of buyers and sellers. Investors have no assurances that they will be able to recoup their investment in a stock at any time.

✓ *Take Note:* A long investor's losses are limited to his total investment in a stock. A short seller's losses are theoretically unlimited because there is no limit to how high a stock's price may climb.

Decreased or No Income

Another risk of stock ownership is the possibility of dividend income decreasing or ceasing entirely if the company loses money.

Low Priority at Dissolution

If a company declares bankruptcy, the holders of its bonds and preferred stock have priority over common stockholders, making a company's debt and preferred shares considered as **senior securities**. Common stockholders have only residual rights to corporate assets upon dissolution.

Long and Short Positions

When a customer purchases stock to open a position, the customer is said to be long the stock. In order to close the position, the customer would sell the stock (a long sale). The risk of a long position is that the price of the stock falls. Maximum loss occurs if the stock becomes worthless.

When a customer sells short to open a position, the customer is selling the stock he does not own. He does this by borrowing stock from a stock lender and selling the borrowed shares. The customer is taking the view that the stock will decline in price, enabling him to buy the shares back at a lower price for return to the stock lender. In this scenario, the customer profits by the difference between the short sale price and the price at which the shares are bought back. A customer who sells short is said to be short the stock. The risk to a short seller is that the price of the borrowed shares increases, forcing him to buy back at a higher price. As there is no limit on how high a stock's price may rise, a short seller has unlimited loss potential.

Quick Quiz 1.2 Multiple Choice

1. Which of the following represent(s) ownership (equity) in a company?

    I. Corporate bonds
    II. Common stock
    III. Preferred stock
    IV. Mortgage bonds

    A. I and IV only
    B. II only
    C. II and III only
    D. I, II, III and IV

2. Treasury stock

    I. has voting rights and is entitled to a dividend when declared
    II. has no voting rights and no dividend entitlement
    III. has been issued and repurchased by the company
    IV. is authorized but unissued stock

    A. I and III
    B. I and IV
    C. II and III
    D. II and IV

3. Stockholders' preemptive rights include the right to

   A. serve as an officer on the board of directors
   B. maintain proportionate ownership interest in the corporation
   C. purchase treasury stock
   D. a subscription price on stock

4. At the annual meeting of ABC Corporation, 5 directors are to be elected. Under the cumulative voting system, an investor with 100 shares of ABC would have a total of

   A. 100 votes to be cast for each of 5 directors
   B. 500 votes to be cast in any way the investor chooses for 5 directors
   C. 500 votes to be cast for each of 5 directors
   D. 100 votes to be cast for only 1 director

5. A client has 100 shares of XYZ. The stock undergoes a split. After the split, the client will have

   A. a proportionately decreased interest in the company
   B. a proportionately increased interest in the company
   C. no effective change in value
   D. a greater exposure

6. Cumulative voting rights

   A. benefit the large investor
   B. aid the corporation's best customers
   C. give preferred stockholders an advantage over common stockholders
   D. benefit the small investor

7. Stockholders must approve

   A. declaration of a cash dividend
   B. a 3-for-1 stock split
   C. repurchase of 100,000 shares for the treasury
   D. declaration of a 15% stock dividend

8. What is the basic formula of the balance sheet?

   A. Assets = liabilities − net worth
   B. Assets + liabilities = net worth
   C. Assets = net worth
   D. Assets = liabilities + net worth

9. If a stock undergoes a 1-for-5 reverse split, which of the following are TRUE?

   I. Market price per share increases.
   II. The number of shares outstanding increases.
   III. Earnings per share typically increase.

   A. I and II only
   B. I and III only
   C. II and III only
   D. I, II, and III

Answers

1. **C.** Owning either common or preferred stocks represents ownership (or equity) in a corporation. The other two choices represent debt instruments. Clients purchasing corporate or mortgage bonds are considered lenders, not owners.

2. **C.** Treasury stock is stock a corporation has issued but subsequently repurchased from investors in the secondary market. The corporation can either reissue the stock at a later date or retire it. Stock that has been repurchased by the corporation has no voting rights and is not entitled to any declared dividends.

3. **B.** Preemptive rights enable stockholders to maintain their proportionate ownership when the corporation wants to issue more stock. If a stockholder owns 5% of the outstanding stock and the corporation wants to issue more stock, the stockholder has the right to purchase enough of the new shares to maintain a 5% ownership position in the company.

4. **B.** With cumulative voting rights, this investor may cast 500 votes for the 5 directors in any way the investor chooses.

5. **C.** When a stock splits, the number of shares each stockholder has increases. However, the value of each share decreases proportionately. The customer, therefore, experiences no effective change in position or proportionate interest.

6. **D.** The cumulative method of voting gives an investor one vote per share owned, times the number of directorships to be elected. For example, if an investor owns 100 stock shares and there are 5 directorships to be elected, the investor will have a total of 500 votes. The stockholder may cast all of his votes for one candidate, thereby giving the small investor more voting power.

7. **B.** Shareholder approval is required to change the stated value of stock, which occurs with a stock split. Decisions regarding payment of dividends or repurchase of stock are made by the board of directors (management only) since these are considered operational decisions.

8. **D.** The basic formula of the balance sheet is: assets = liabilities + net worth.

9. **B.** After a reverse split, there will be fewer shares outstanding. As a result, market price and earnings per share should increase.

Preferred Stock

Preferred stock has features of both equity and debt securities. Preferred stock is an **equity security** because it represents ownership in the corporation. However, it does not normally offer the appreciation potential associated with common stock.

Like a bond, preferred stock is usually issued as a **fixed-income security** with a fixed dividend. Its price tends to fluctuate with changes in interest rates rather than with the issuing company's business prospects unless, of course, dramatic changes occur in the company's credit quality. Unlike common stock, most preferred stock is nonvoting.

Although preferred stock does not typically have the same growth potential as common stock, preferred stockholders generally have the following two advantages over common stockholders:

- When the BOD declares dividends, owners of preferred stock receive their dividends before common stockholders.
- If a corporation goes bankrupt, preferred stockholders have a priority claim over common stockholders on the assets remaining after creditors have been paid.

Preferred Stock Characteristics

Fixed Rate of Return A preferred stock's **fixed dividend** is a key attraction for income-oriented investors. Normally, a preferred stock is identified by its annual dividend payment stated as a percentage of its par value, usually $100. (A preferred stock's par value is meaningful, unlike that of a common stock.)

✓ **For Example:** A preferred stock with a par value of $100 that pays $6 in annual dividends is known as a 6% preferred.

The dividend of preferred stock with no par value is stated in a dollar amount, such as a $6 no-par preferred.

✓ **Take Note:** Preferred stock dividends, like common stock dividends, are not guaranteed. They are often paid semiannually as declared by the BOD.

Adjustable-Rate Preferred Some preferred stocks are issued with **adjustable**, or **variable**, dividend rates. Such dividends are usually tied to the rates of other interest rate benchmarks, such as Treasury bill and money market rates, and can be adjusted as often as semi-annually. The date of dividend adjustment is sometimes referred to as the **reset date**.

Limited Ownership Privileges Except for rare instances, preferred stock does not have voting or preemptive rights.

No Maturity Date or Set Maturity Value Although a fixed-income investment, preferred stock (unlike bonds) has no preset date at which it matures and no scheduled redemption date.

> ✓ ***Take Note:*** Although preferred stock is an equity instrument, it fluctuates in price more like a debt instrument. The fixed rate of dividend payment causes preferred stock to trade like bonds.

> ✓ ***For Example:*** Consider a 6% preferred. If interest rates are currently 8% and you want to sell your preferred, you will have to sell at a discounted price. Who would be willing to pay full value for an investment that is not paying a competitive market rate?
>
> But if interest rates fall to 5%, the 6% preferred will trade at a premium. Because it is offering a stream of income above the current market rate, it will command a higher price.

When interest rates rise, the preferred price falls. Conversely, when interest rates fall, the preferred stock's price rises. This exact relationship occurs in bonds, and is known as the **inverse relationship** between price and interest rates.

Categories of Preferred Stock

Separate categories of preferred stock may differ in the dividend rate, in profit participation privileges, or in other ways. All, however, maintain a degree of preference over common stock. Preferred stock may have one or more of the following characteristics.

Straight Preferred **Straight preferred** (**noncumulative**) has no special features beyond the stated dividend payment. Missed dividends are not paid to the holder.

Cumulative Preferred Buyers of preferred stock expect fixed semi-annual dividend payments. The directors of a company in financial difficulty can reduce or suspend dividend payments to both common and preferred stockholders. Most likely, the corporation will never make up any dividends common stockholders miss. In contrast to this, all dividends due cumulative preferred stock accumulate on the company's books until the corporation can pay them.

When the company can resume full payment of dividends, cumulative preferred stockholders receive their current dividends plus the total accumulated dividends—dividends in arrears—before any dividends may be distributed to common stockholders. Therefore, cumulative preferred stock is safer than straight preferred stock.

For Example: RST Corporation has both common stock and cumulative preferred stock outstanding. Its preferred stock has a stated dividend rate of 5% (par value $100). Because of financial difficulties, no dividend was paid on the preferred stock in 2001 and 2002.

If RST wished to declare a common stock dividend in 2003, RST is required to first pay $15 in dividends to the cumulative preferred shareholders. This amount includes the dividends in arrears for 2001 ($5) and 2002 ($5), plus the $5 dividend for 2003.

Convertible Preferred

A preferred stock is **convertible** if the owner can exchange each preferred share for shares of common stock.

The price at which the investor can convert is a preset amount and is noted on the stock certificate. Because the value of a convertible preferred stock is linked to the value of the issuer's common stock, the convertible preferred's price fluctuates in line with the common, providing the common stock's value is high enough to make conversion attractive.

Convertible preferred is often issued with a lower stated dividend rate than nonconvertible preferred because the investor may have the opportunity to convert to common shares and enjoy capital gains. In addition, the conversion of preferred stock into shares of common increases the total number of common shares outstanding, which decreases earnings per common share and may decrease the common stock's market value.

Participating Preferred

In addition to fixed dividends, **participating preferred** stock offers its owners a share of corporate profits that remain after all dividends and interest due other securities are paid. The percentage to which participating preferred stock participates is noted on the stock certificate.

For Example: If a preferred stock is described as "XYZ 6% preferred participating to 9%," the company pays its holders up to 3% in additional dividends in profitable years if the BOD declares so.

Callable Preferred

Corporations often issue **callable**, or **redeemable**, preferred, which a company can buy back from investors at a stated price after a specified date. The right to call the stock allows the company to replace a relatively high fixed dividend obligation with a lower one.

When a corporation calls a preferred stock, dividend payments and conversion rights generally cease on the call date. In return for the call privilege, the corporation usually pays a premium exceeding the stock's par value at the call, such as $103 for a $100 par value stock.

Test Topic Alert!

Which type of preferred stock typically has the highest stated rate of dividend (all other factors being equal)?

Callable preferred. When the stock is called, dividend payments are no longer made. To compensate for that possibility, the issuer pays a higher dividend.

Of straight and cumulative preferred, which would you expect to have the higher stated rate?

Straight preferred. Cumulative preferred is safer, and there is always a risk-reward trade-off. Because straight preferred has no special features, it will pay a higher stated rate of dividend.

Return on Investment

An investment's total return is a combination of the dividend income and price appreciation or decline over a given period.

Dividends

Dividends are distributions of a company's profits to its stockholders. Investors who buy stock are entitled to dividends only when the company's board of directors votes to make such distributions. Stockholders are automatically sent any dividends to which their shares entitle them.

Cash Dividends

Cash dividends are normally distributed by check if an investor holds the stock certificate or are automatically deposited to a brokerage account if the shares are held in **street name** (held in a brokerage account in the firm's name to facilitate payments and delivery). Cash dividends are taxed in the year they are received.

Stock Dividends

If a company uses its cash for business purposes rather than to pay cash dividends, its board of directors may declare a **stock dividend**. This is typical of many growth companies that invest their cash resources in research and development. Under these circumstances, the company issues shares of its common stock as a dividend to its current stockholders. A stock's market price declines after a stock dividend, as with a stock split, but the company's total market value remains the same.

✓ **Take Note:** Stock dividends, like splits, are not taxable. The only effect of a stock dividend or a stock split is to reduce the investor's cost basis per share.

✓ **For Example:** An investor buys 200 shares of XYZ at $60 per share for a total cost of $12,000. If XYZ were to declare and pay a 20% stock dividend, the investor would have 240 shares. Dividing $12,000 by 240 shares results in a cost basis per share of $50.

Equity Securities

Calculating Current Yield

The **current yield** (dividend yield) is the annual dividend (normally four times the quarterly dividend) divided by the current market value of the stock.

Test Topic Alert! You will probably be asked to calculate dividend yield on your exam.

$$\frac{\text{Annual dividend}}{\text{Current market value of the stock}}$$

✓ **For Example:** RST stock has a current market value of $50. Total dividends paid during the year were $5. What is the dividend yield?

The solution is found by dividing $5 by $50 (5 / 50 = .10). The yield is 10%.

Be alert for a slightly "tricky" approach to this question. The question might state that RST has a current market value of $50. The most recent quarterly dividend paid was $1.25. What is the dividend yield?

The solution is found by annualizing the dividend (multiplying by 4) first. $1.25 × 4 = $5. $5 / $50 = a 10% dividend yield. Remember to use annual dividends in calculating yield.

Transferability of Ownership

The ease with which stocks and other securities can be bought and sold contributes to the smooth operation of the securities markets. When an investor buys or sells a security, the exchange of money and ownership requires little or no additional action on his part.

Features of Transferable Securities

The Stock Certificate A **stock certificate** indicates the shares of a corporation a person owns. The vast majority of stock transactions are for round lot numbers of shares—that is, share amounts evenly divisible by 100. Odd-lot transactions are share amounts of fewer than 100 shares, such as 4 or 99. Individual stock certificates may be issued for any number of shares.

✓ **For Example:** An investor who buys 100 shares receives one certificate for 100 shares.

Among other things, stock certificates identify the company's name, number of shares, and the investor's name. In addition, each certificate is printed with the security's CUSIP number.

Transferability of Ownership   21

CUSIP Numbers A **Committee on Uniform Securities Identification Procedures (CUSIP)** number is a universal security identification number. Each issue of common stock, preferred stock, corporate bond, and municipal bond has its own CUSIP number, which helps identify and track the certificate if it is lost or stolen. The CUSIP number is also used in trade confirmations, correspondence regarding specific securities, and tracking lost or stolen securities.

Negotiability Shares of stock are negotiable; that is, a stockholder can give, transfer, assign, or sell shares he owns with few or no restrictions.

To transfer ownership of a stock, the registered owner must sign the stock certificate or a **stock power** (a form that duplicates the back of a stock certificate for transfer purposes). When securities are held in a brokerage account but registered in the owner's name, the stock power facilitates the transfer of securities upon sale. Once a certificate or stock power has been signed, an NYSE member firm or commercial bank must **guarantee the signature.**

Transfer Procedures

The **transfer** and **registration** of stock certificates are two distinct functions that, by law, cannot be performed by a single person or department operating within the same institution. Issuers typically use commercial banks and trust companies to handle these functions.

Transfer Agent The **transfer agent** for a corporation is responsible for:

- ensuring that its securities are issued in the correct owner's name;
- cancelling old and issuing new certificates;
- maintaining records of ownership; and
- handling problems relating to lost, stolen, or destroyed certificates.

The transfer agent distributes additional shares in the event of a stock split or new certificates in the event of a reverse split. If a stock dividend or stock split results in fractional shares, under most circumstances the transfer agent sends the beneficial owner a check for a fractional share's value.

✓ *Take Note:* In a stock split, par value changes, as does the market price of a stock. In the event of a stock split, the customer will receive the additional shares directly from the transfer agent. In addition, the investor will receive a sticker to put on his existing certificate to change its par value.

Registrar Any stock or bond transaction requiring the registration and issuance of new certificates is routed through a **registrar** as well as the transfer agent. The registrar does not, however, keep a list of the names of the owners of the company's securities.

Equity Securities

The registrar ensures that a corporation does not have more shares outstanding than have been authorized. The registrar is also responsible for certifying that a bond represents a legal debt of the issuer. Unlike the transfer agent, the registrar must be independent of the issuing corporation and is usually a bank or trust company.

Quick Quiz 1.3 Match each of the following terms with the appropriate item below.

A. CUSIP number
B. Preemptive right
C. Current yield
D. Registrar
E. Transfer agent

___ 1. Party responsible for recording security owners' names and holdings and delivering new securities

___ 2. Assigned to each security for identification

___ 3. Stockholders may maintain proportionate ownership by purchasing newly issued shares before they are offered to the public

___ 4. Party responsible to account for all of an issuer's outstanding stock

___ 5. Annualized dividend divided by current market price

Answers 1. **E.** 2. **A.** 3. **B.** 4. **D.** 5. **C.**

Tracking Equity Securities

Common and preferred stock prices are listed in the financial sections of daily newspapers and other financial publications. A stock's market price is quoted in whole dollars, also known as **points**, plus cents.

Test Topic Alert! The test will probably require you to determine the cost of a round lot of stock in whole dollars from its quoted price. For instance, if ABC stock is quoted at 83.13, how much does the investor pay for 100 shares?

To determine the price of a round lot, simply multiply by 100 (move the decimal point two places to the right). The investor will pay $8,313.00 for a round lot of ABC stock.

Tracking Equity Securities 23

NYSE Composite Transactions

New York Stock Exchange Composite Transactions

Tuesday, September 13, 1999
Quotations include trades on the Chicago, Pacific, Philadelphia, Boston and Cincinnati Stock Exchanges and reported by the National Association of Securities Dealers and INSTINET.

52 Weeks High	Low	Stock	Div	Yld %	PE Ratio	Sales 100s	High	Low	Close	Net Chg.
80	40	ABCorp	.75	1	12	3329	78	71	73	- 1.50
n 8.38	6.50	ACM IncFd	1.01	12.4	...	178	8.25	8.13	8.13	- .13
42.63	26.88	ALFA	2.40	5.6	12	x 1265	42.63	41.25	42.63	+1.25
35	24.63	Anchor	1.48	4.9	36	1960	30	29.75	30	+ .25
27.25	25	ANR pf	2.67	10.3	...	6	26	26	26	...
6	1.88	ATT Cap wt	...	...	...	20	5.88	5.75	5.75	- .25
s 22.75	14	AVEMCO	.40	1.9	17	6	21.50	21.38	21.50	...
84.25	40	BrlNth	2.20	3.7	13	2701	59.38	58.25	58.75	+ .50
4.75	.50	Brooke rt	...	...	...	26	4.63	4.63	4.63	...
7	2.50	CV REIT	.25	4.0	...	10	6.38	6.25	6.25	...
3.13	2.25	CalifREIT	.40	13.9	...	3	2.88	2.88	2.88	...
39.38	17.88	Circus wi	...	...	...	14	39.25	38.88	39.25	+ .63
82.50	39.63	Dsny	.32	.6	17	6211	53.75	52	53.25	+1.25
38.38	19.50	Febar	.24	.9	13	z 1454	28	26.88	27.38	+ .25
8.75	3.63	Navistr	...	...	...	6484	4.50	4.13	4.25	...

EXPLANATORY NOTES
The following explanations apply to New York and American Exchange listed issues and the National Association of Securities Dealers Automated Quotations system's over-the-counter securities. The 52-week high and low columns show the highest and lowest price of the issue during the preceding 52 weeks. Dividend rates, unless noted, are annual disbursements. Yield is the dividends paid by a company on its securities, expressed as a percentage of price. The PE ratio is determined by dividing the price of a share of stock by its company's earnings. Sales figures are quoted in 100s (00 omitted). a-Extra dividend. b-Annual rate of the cash dividend and a stock dividend was paid. n-Newly issued in the past 52 weeks. pf-Preferred. rt-Rights. s-Stock split or dividend greater than 25% in the past 52 weeks. vi-In bankruptcy or receivership. wd-When distributed. wi-When issued. wt-Warrants. ww-With warrants. x-Ex-dividend or ex-rights. xw-Without warrants. z-Sales in full, not in hundreds.

Exchange-Listed Stocks

The previous table is an example of an NYSE composite transactions listing as it might be printed in a financial publication. These consolidated stock tables present the most complete information available and report activity for the previous business day.

Range of Prices   The range of prices is shown for the previous 52 weeks, but does not include the latest trading day.

✓ **For Example:** ALFA has had a 52-week high of $42.63 and a low of $26.88 per share.

Stock Name and Dividend   The stock name and annual dividend follow the 52-week price range. The dividend is quoted as an annual dollar amount based on the most recent quarter. ALFA is paying an annual dividend of $2.40 per share. The *Yld* column reports the security's current yield. For ALFA, the yield is 5.6% ($2.40 / 42.63 = 5.6%).

PE Ratio The **PE ratio (price/earnings ratio)** column follows the *Yld* column. It gives the ratio of the stock's current price to its most recent 12 months earnings per share. ALFA's PE ratio is 12.

Number of Shares The **Sales** column reports the number of shares traded during the day. Trading is reported in round lots of 100 shares. The entry for ALFA is 1265, which means that 126,500 shares of stock were traded.

Ex-Dividend The *x* before the sales volume indicates that the stock is selling **ex-dividend**, or **ex-rights**, meaning that a buyer will not receive the next dividend check.

High and Low The two columns after **Sales** list the daily range of prices—the stock's high and low prices for the day. ALFA sold for a high of 42.63, and a low of 41.25. The column labeled **Close** shows the final price for the day. ALFA closed at 42.63, at the top of its 52-week range.

Net Change in Price The final column reports the **net change in price**. The net change is the difference between the closing price on the trading day reported and the previous day's closing price. ALFA closed up 1.25 points from the previous day's close.

Over-the-Counter Stocks

Thousands of securities trade in the **over-the-counter (OTC)** market. OTC stocks that have national interest are listed on the **National Association of Securities Dealers Automated Quotation system** (**Nasdaq**). Nasdaq-listed stocks can be placed in two distinct categories: Nasdaq National Market (NNM) and SmallCap.

National Market stocks are the more well known, more heavily traded stocks such as Microsoft. Nasdaq SmallCap stocks are smaller, less heavily traded stocks. Over-the-counter stocks that do not qualify for a Nasdaq listing are referred to as Non-Nasdaq stocks. These issues trade on the over-the-counter Bulletin Board (OTCBB) or in the electronic Pink Sheets.

✓ *Take Note:* These trading markets are discussed in more detail later in this unit.

Tracking Equity Securities

Nasdaq Small Cap Transactions

Nasdaq Small Cap Issues
Quotations as of 4 pm Eastern Time
Tuesday, September 13, 2002

Stock & Div	Sales 100s	Last	Net Chg.	Stock & Div	Sales 100s	Last	Net Chg.
A&A Fd g	29	4.63	- .07	FtnPh un	5	15	...
ACS En	12	1.38	...	Frnchtx .03e	118	5.50	+ .13
ACTV	14	1.88	...	FrntAd .04e	20	2.50	...
ACTV wt	86	.75	...	FutCm	472	6.75	- .07
AFN s	390	1.88	...	BG Fds	209	4.50	+ .07
AGBag	162	4.63	...	GTEC 56pf .90	6	10.50	...
APA	40	4.50	...	GTEC 5pf 1.00	z65	11.50	...

The listing shows the stock name, dividend, sales volume in round lots, execution price of the day's last transaction, and the net change from the previous day's last transaction.

Nasdaq National Market (NNM) Stocks

OTC stocks with very high national interest are listed on the **Nasdaq National Market** (**NNM**). Although these securities may be eligible for listing on an exchange, the companies have chosen to trade OTC instead. Intel is an example of a well-known company that does not list its stock on an exchange. NNM listings contain similar information as is supplied for exchange-listed securities.

NNM Transactions

Nasdaq National Market Issues
Quotations as of 4 pm Eastern Time
Tuesday, September 13, 2002

52 Weeks High	Low	Stock	Symbol	Div	Yld %	PE Ratio	Sales 100s	High	Low	Close	Net Chg.
37.75	20	A&W Brands	SODA	.40	1.1	26	237	36.75	35.75	36	- .50
8.50	5.13	Acme Steel	ACME	.32	5.1	20	3	6.25	6	6.25	+ .25
13.50	4.13	Adobe Sys	ADBE	.16	1.6	20	59	10.25	9.75	10.25	+ .50
43.50	15.25	AdvMktg	ADMS	...	...	21	226	41.25	40.25	40.25	- .25
30	7.63	AffBkshCo	AFBK	t	...	3	x 3764	11.50	9.13	10.88	+1.88
7.25	4	Aldus	ALDS	...	...	18	3211	6.50	6.13	6.50	...
41.50	26.63	AmGreetgs	AGREA	.70	2.1	13	1511	34.50	33.38	33.38	- 1

Nasdaq Symbol Explanation

Securities in the Nasdaq system are identified by a four or five letter symbol. The fifth letter, as described below, indicates issues that aren't common stock, or which are subject to restrictions or special conditions. A-Class A. B-Class B. C-Exempt from Nasdaq listing qualifications for a limited period. D-New issue. E-Delinquent J-Voting. K-Nonvoting. L-Miscellaneous. M-Fourth preferred. N-Third preferred. O-Second preferred. P-First preferred. Q-In bankruptcy. R-Rights. S-Shares of beneficial interest. T-With warrants or rights. U-Units. V-When issued or when in required SEC filings. F-Foreign. G-First convertible bond. H-Second convertible bond. I-Third convertible bond. distributed. W-Warrants. Y-American Depositary Receipt. Z-Miscellaneous situations.

Dividend Department

The **dividend department** collects and distributes cash dividends for stocks held in street name. In addition to processing cash dividends, the department handles registered bonds' interest payments, stock dividends, stock splits, rights offerings, warrants, and any special distributions to stockholders or bondholders.

Dividend Disbursing Agent

Stockholders are sent cash, property or stock dividends, or new shares after a split. If the broker/dealer holds the securities in street name, the **dividend disbursing agent (DDA)** (in the case of dividends) or the **transfer agent** (in the case of stock splits) makes the appropriate distributions or transfers directly to the broker/dealer. The broker/dealer's dividend department then distributes the dividends or additional shares to the appropriate accounts. If a stockholder has possession of the shares, the DDA or the transfer agent contacts him directly.

Dividend Disbursing Process

Declaration Date

When a company's board of directors approves a dividend payment, it also designates the payment date and the dividend record date. The SEC requires any corporation that intends to pay cash dividends or make other distributions to notify the NASD or the appropriate exchange at least 10 business days before the record date. This enables the NASD or exchange to establish the ex-date.

Ex-Dividend Date

Based on the dividend record date, the NASD Uniform Practice Committee or the exchange (if the stock is listed) posts an ex-date. The **ex-date** is two business days before the record date. Because most trades settle regular way—three business days after the trade date—a customer must purchase the stock three business days before the record date to qualify for the dividend.

✓ *Take Note:* Customers are at risk for securities transactions when the trade is executed. However, for dividends only, the buyer is considered the owner as of the settlement date, not the trade date.

The word "ex" is Latin and it means "without." If the investor wishes to purchase the stock "with" the dividend, they must purchase the stock before it is "without" the dividend—the "ex"-date.

On the ex-date, the stock's opening price drops to compensate for the fact that customers who buy the stock that day do not qualify for the dividend. Trades executed regular way on or after the ex-date do not settle until after the record date.

Tracking Equity Securities

The customer who buys the stock before the ex-date receives the dividend, but pays a higher price for the stock. The customer who buys the stock after the ex-date does not receive the dividend, but pays a lower price for the stock.

Dividend Record Date. The stockholders of record on the record date receive the dividend distribution.

Payable Date. Three or four weeks after the record date, the dividend disbursing agent sends dividend checks to all stockholders whose names appear on the books as of the record date.

Cash Trades. Cash trades settle the same day, so they go ex-dividend on the day after the record date because no lag occurs between the trade date and the transaction settlement.

✓ **Take Note:** *DERP* will help you remember the order in which the dates involving dividend distributions occur.

Order of dates is **D**eclaration, **E**x, **R**ecord, **P**ayable.

Test Topic Alert!

Declaration, Record, and Payment are determined by the board of directors, and the NASD, or the exchange, determines Ex-date.

Ex-Date and Record Date Relationship

The NASD sets an ex-date for trading purposes two business days before the record date.

✓ **For Example:** If RST declares a cash dividend of $.75 to stockholders of record on Wednesday, June 21, the ex-date is Monday, June 19.

Test Topic Alert!

Let's work through some scenarios involving the ex-date. The calendar below assumes a record date of June 21. Will an investor who purchases the stock on Friday, June 16, receive the dividend?

June

Sun	Mon	Tue	Wed	Thu	Fri	Sat
				1	2	3
4	5	6	7	8	9	10
11	12	13	14	15	16	17
18	19	20	**21**	22	23	24
25	26	27	28	29	30	

Record Date → 21

28 Equity Securities

In this situation, the investor would receive the dividend because regular way settlement takes place 3 business days after the trade. Monday, Tuesday, and Wednesday are the 3 business days that must be counted. The investor settles on Wednesday, June 21, which means he owns the stock on the record date, and is entitled to the dividend. When is the ex-date? June 19.

But, what if the transaction had taken place on Monday, June 19, instead? Counting the 3 business days required, regular way settlement would take place on June 22. The investor would own the stock on the business day after the record date—too late to receive the dividend.

This example illustrates that the 19th is the first day the investor buys the stock without the dividend (the ex-date) when the record date is June 21. An investor must buy the stock before the ex-date to get the dividend. The seller receives the dividend if the transaction takes place on or after the ex-date.

The ex-date is 2 business days before the record date in transactions executed with regular way settlement.

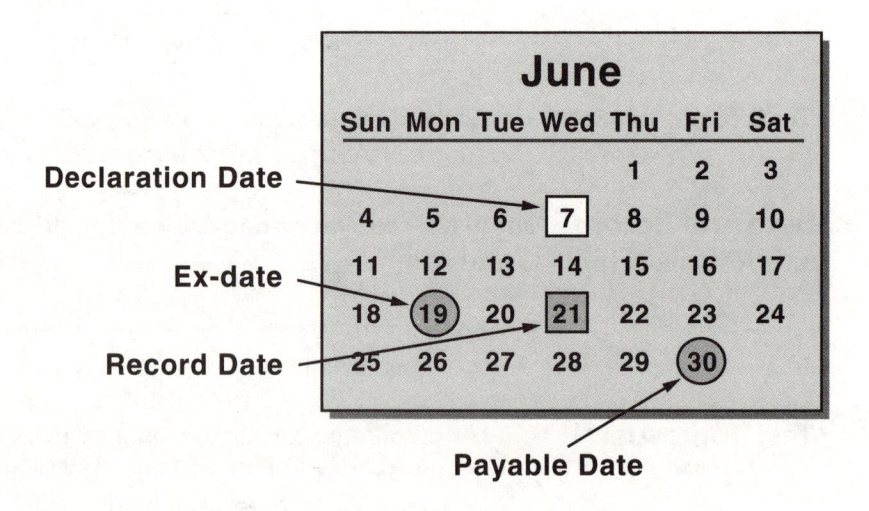

June

Sun	Mon	Tue	Wed	Thu	Fri	Sat
				1	2	3
4	5	6	**7** (Declaration Date)	8	9	10
11	12	13	14	15	16	17
18	(19) Ex-date	20	[21] Record Date	22	23	24
25	26	27	28	29	(30) Payable Date	

Referring to the calendar again, assume the investor purchased the stock on Wednesday, June 21, in a cash settlement transaction. Because the settlement takes place the same day, the investor receives the dividend, and he owns the stock on the record date of the 21st. The ex-date in this circumstance is the business day after the record date.

On the ex-date, the stock's opening price is adjusted downward by the amount of the dividend.

Stock Dividends and Splits Normal stock dividends are handled the same as cash dividends. A stock distribution of 25% or more of the shares outstanding is subject to **special handling**. The same is true of stock splits where total shares outstanding increase by 25% or more. The ex-date on stock dividends of 25% or more and stock splits of 5 for 4 or better is the first business day following the payable date.

Due Bills A **due bill** is a printed statement showing a buyer's right to a dividend. If securities are purchased before the ex-date but, for whatever reason, settle after the record date, the wrong party (the seller) will receive the dividend from the issuer. In this case the buyer's firm will send a due bill to the seller's firm demanding remittance of the dividend.

Rights and Warrants

Characteristics of Rights

Issuance Existing stockholders have **preemptive rights** that entitle them to maintain their proportionate ownership in a company by buying newly issued shares before the company offers them to the general public. A **rights offering** allows stockholders to purchase common stock below the current market price. The rights are valued separately from the stock and trade in the secondary market during the subscription period.

A stockholder who receives rights may:

- exercise the rights to buy stock by sending the rights certificates and a check for the required amount to the rights agent;
- sell the rights and profit from their market value (rights certificates are negotiable securities); or
- let the rights expire and lose their value.

Approval of Additional Stock The board of directors must approve decisions to issue additional stock through a rights offering. If the additional shares will increase the stock outstanding beyond the amount authorized in the company charter, the stockholders must vote to amend the charter.

Subscription Right Certificate A **subscription right** is a certificate representing a short-term (typically 30 to 45 days) privilege to buy additional shares of a corporation. One right is issued for each common stock share outstanding.

Terms of the Offering The **terms** of a rights offering are stipulated on the subscription right certificates mailed to stockholders. The terms describe how many new shares a stockholder may buy, the price, date the new stock will be issued, and the final date for exercising the rights.

✓ *For Example:* ABC Co. plans to raise capital by issuing additional stock and, on April 1, declares a rights offering. Common stockholders as of May 1 can subscribe to one new share, at a price of $70, for each 5 shares of stock they own. ABC stock trades in the open market for $100 per share. The rights will expire on June 18.

Equity Securities

The corporation will issue rights on May 8 to stockholders of record May 1. Stock is traded **cum rights** until the ex-date. An investor who buys stock **cum rights** receives the right. An investor who buys stock **ex-rights** does not.

The number of rights required to buy one new share is based on the number of shares outstanding and the number of new shares offered.

✓ *For Example:* Associated Industries has 5 million shares outstanding and will issue 1 million additional shares. Because each existing share is entitled to 1 right, the company will issue 5 million rights. Because 5 million rights entitle stockholders to buy 1 million shares, it will require 5 rights to buy 1 new share. Between April 1 and June 18, the stock tables in newspapers and other publications will show two entries for Associated Industries:

- price of the stock with rights (**cum rights**) or, after the rights distribution ex-date, without rights (**ex-rights**); and
- price of the rights, either on a when issued basis—before they are issued—or after they have been issued.

Test Topic Alert!

Rights have a theoretical value based on the savings to investors, who then purchase stock below the market price.

Before the ex-date, when the stock is trading with rights, the value of a right is found using the cum rights formula. Consider the following: ABC's price per share is $41; the subscription per share is $30. 10 rights are needed to purchase one share of stock. The value of one right is found as follows:

$$\frac{\text{Market price} - \text{subscription price}}{\text{Number of rights to purchase 1 share} + 1}$$

$$\frac{41 - 30}{10 + 1} = \frac{11}{11} = \$1$$

After the ex-date, the market price typically drops by the value of the right. Use the ex-rights formula to determine the value of a right after the ex-date. The ex-rights formula is:

$$\frac{\text{Market price} - \text{subscription price}}{\text{Number of rights to purchase 1 share}}$$

If ABC had dropped after ex-date to $40 (reduced by the $1 value of the right) the solution is:

$$\frac{41 - 30}{10} = \frac{10}{10} = \$1$$

You may see an exam question on either of these formulas.

The Rights Agent The **rights agent** keeps a record of who owns each right, just as a transfer agent records each stockholder's name. When a right is sold, the rights agent records the new owner's name. The rights agent may or may not be the same individual or trust that acts as transfer agent.

Standby Underwriting If the current stockholders do not subscribe to all the additional stock, the issuer may offer unsold rights to an investment banker in a standby underwriting. A **standby underwriting** is done on a firm commitment basis, meaning the underwriter buys all unsold shares from the issuer then resells them to the general public.

Characteristics of Warrants

A **warrant** is a certificate granting its owner the right to purchase securities from the issuer at a specified price (normally higher than the current market price) as of date of issue of the warrant. Unlike a right, a warrant is usually a long-term instrument, giving the investor the choice of buying shares at a later date at the exercise price.

✓ **Take Note:** Warrants typically have a life of 5 years, but in the past perpetual warrants have been issued, which do not expire.

Origination of Warrants Warrants are usually offered to the public as **sweeteners** (inducements) in connection with other securities, such as bonds or preferred stock, to make those securities more attractive. Such offerings are often bundled as **units**.

After issuance, the warrants are detachable and trade separately from the bond or preferred stock. When first issued, a warrant's exercise price is set well above the stock's market price. As the stock's price increases above the exercise price, the owner can exercise the warrant and buy the stock below the market price or sell the warrant in the market.

Rights	*Warrants*
Short term	Long term
On issuance, exercise price below market price	On issuance, exercise price higher than market price
May trade with or separate from the common stock	May trade with or separate from the units
Offered to existing share holders with preemptive rights	Offered as a sweetener for another security

Equity Securities

✓ *Take Note:* The long-term nature of warrants is said to be attractive to speculators because of the leverage it offers. Warrants also allow issuers to offer bonds or preferred stock at an interest or dividend rate lower than the market rate as the issuer is offering investors something extra; the long term right to buy stock at a fixed price.

Quick Quiz 1.4   Multiple Choice

1. Which of the following statements regarding warrants is TRUE?

   A. Warrants are offered to current shareholders only.
   B. Warrants have longer terms than rights.
   C. Warrants do not trade in the secondary market.
   D. At the time of issuance, the exercise price of a warrant is typically below the market value of the underlying stock.

2. Which of the following statements regarding rights is TRUE?

   A. Common stockholders do not have the right to subscribe to rights offerings.
   B. Preferred stockholders do not have the right to subscribe to rights offerings.
   C. Both common and preferred stockholders have the right to subscribe to rights offerings.
   D. Neither common nor preferred stockholders have the right to subscribe to rights offerings.

3. ABC Co. is attempting to sell new shares through a rights offering. A shareholder who chooses to exercise his rights sends his check to the

   A. company
   B. underwriter
   C. customer's broker
   D. rights/transfer agent

4. An investor owns 100 shares of MTN common stock. After MTN splits 2-for-1, the investor receives

   A. another certificate for 100 shares
   B. another certificate for 200 shares
   C. notice that the investor's 100-share certificate now represents 200 shares
   D. notice to send in the current certificate to be replaced by a new certificate for 200 shares

Answers 1. **B.** *Warrants are issued with long-term maturities. They may be used as sweeteners in an offering of the issuer's preferred stock or bonds and are not offered only to current shareholders. The exercise price of a warrant is typically above the market value of the stock at the time of issue.*

2. **B.** *Preferred stockholders have no right to maintain a percentage of ownership when new shares are issued (no preemptive rights). However, they do receive preference in dividend payment.*

3. **D.** *The rights (or transfer) agent receives the checks for a rights offering. The agent can be the company's transfer agent or special rights agent for the rights offering only.*

4. **A.** *The issuer will send the investor another certificate for 100 shares. The investor is not required to send back the existing stock certificate.*

American Depositary Receipts

American depositary receipts (ADRs), also known as **American depositary shares (ADSs)**, facilitate the trading of foreign stocks in US markets. An ADR is a negotiable security that represents a receipt for shares of stock in a non-US corporation, usually from 1 to 10 shares. ADRs are bought and sold in the US securities markets like stock.

Characteristics of ADRs

Rights of ADR Owners ADR owners have most of the rights common stockholders normally hold. These include the right to receive dividends when declared. ADR holders do not normally have preemptive rights or voting rights.

Delivery of Foreign Security

ADR owners have the right to exchange their ADR certificates for the foreign shares they represent. They can do this by returning the ADRs to the depository banks, which cancel the ADRs and deliver the underlying stock.

Currency Risk In addition to the normal risks associated with stock ownership, ADR investors are subject to **currency risk**, the possibility that an investment denominated in one currency could decline if the value of that currency declines in its exchange rate with the US dollar. Currency exchange rates are an important consideration because ADRs represent shares of stock in companies located in foreign countries.

Custodian Bank Foreign branches of large commercial US banks issue ADRs. A custodian, typically a bank in the issuer's country, holds the shares of foreign stock that

Equity Securities

the ADRs represent. The stock must remain on deposit as long as the ADRs are outstanding because the ADRs are the depository bank's guarantee that it holds the stock.

Registered Owner ADRs are registered on the books of the US banks responsible for them. The individual investors in the ADRs are not considered the stock's registered owners. ADRs are registered on the books of US banks, so dividends are sent to the custodian banks as registered owners. The banks collect the payments, convert them into US funds for US owners and withhold any required foreign tax payments.

✓ *Take Note:* Although dividends may be withheld to pay local taxes, owners of ADRs can claim a US tax credit for these withholdings. Also, dividends are declared in the foreign currency but payable in US dollars.

Real Estate Investment Trusts (REITs)

A **REIT** is a company that manages a portfolio of real estate investments in order to earn profits for shareholders. REITs are normally traded publicly and serve as a source of long-term financing for real estate projects. A REIT pools capital in a manner similar to an investment company, and shareholders receive dividends from investment income or capital gains distributions.

REITs are organized as trusts where investors buy shares or certificates of beneficial interest either on stock exchanges or in the OTC market. Under the guidelines of Subchapter M of the Internal Revenue Code, a REIT can avoid being taxed as a corporation by receiving 75% or more of its income from real estate and distributing 90% or more of its net investment income to its shareholders.

Test Topic Alert!

ADRs:
- No preemptive rights
- Dividends in dollars
- Investors do not have voting rights

REITs:
- Not a limited partnership
- Not an investment company
- Pass through income, not losses
- 75% of income must come from real estate-related activity
- Must distribute 90% or more of income to shareholders to avoid taxation as a corporation
- Trade on exchanges or OTC
- Dividends received from REITS are taxed as ordinary income

Real Estate Investment Trusts (REITs)

There might be up to 5 questions on REITs on the exam.

You should be feeling confident in your knowledge of equity instruments at this point. If you're struggling with any of these concepts, review them now to achieve a firm grasp of these basic industry concepts.

Quick Quiz 1.5   Multiple Choice

1. ADRs are used to facilitate the

    A. foreign trading of domestic securities
    B. foreign trading of US government securities
    C. domestic trading of US government securities
    D. domestic trading of foreign securities

2. Which of the following are characteristics of a REIT?

    I. It is traded on an exchange or over the counter.
    II. It is professionally managed.
    III. It passes through both gains and losses to investors.
    IV. It is a type of limited partnership

    A. I and II only
    B. I, II, and III only
    C. III and IV only
    D. I, II, III, and IV

3. All of the following characteristics are advantages of a REIT investment EXCEPT

    A. liquidity
    B. tax deferral
    C. diversification
    D. professional management

4. To avoid taxation at the corporate level, REITs must derive at least 75% of their income from real property, and must distribute to shareholders

    A. 75% of net income
    B. 90% of net income
    C. 95% of net income
    D. 98% of net income

Equity Securities

Answers

1. **D.** ADRs are tradable securities issued by banks, with the receipt's value based on the underlying foreign securities held by the bank.

2. **A.** REITs are traded on exchanges and OTC, and they are professionally managed. REITs share some features with a limited partnership, but they are a different type of business entity. Both REITs and limited partnerships provide pass-through of gains to investors, but REITs do not provide pass-through of losses.

3. **B.** A REIT is a professionally managed company that invests in a diversified portfolio of real estate holdings. Many REITs are actively traded on exchanges and OTC, thereby providing liquidity. REIT portfolio losses are not passed through to investors.

4. **B.** REITs must distribute at least 90% of their net investment income to shareholders to avoid corporate taxation.

Equity Securities HotSheet

Stock Classifications:
- Authorized: number of shares corporation is permitted to issue
- Issued: has been sold to the public
- Treasury: repurchased by corporation; no voting rights, receives no dividends, cannot be traded on the open market
- Outstanding: number of shares held by the public
- Treasury = issued – outstanding
- Outstanding = issued – treasury

Stock Valuations:
- Par: assigned accounting value
- Book: liquidation or net worth value
- Market: value determined by supply and demand

Preemptive Rights:
- Allow shareholders to maintain proportionate interest

Voting Rights:
- Directors, issuance of convertible bonds or preferred stock; *not* on dividend payment or amount

Stock Splits:
- Forward: more shares, less value per share, same total value before and after
- Reverse: less shares, more value per share, same total value before and after

Preferred Stock:
- Par value = $100
- Stated (fixed) dividend rate
- Priority over common stock in liquidation and dividend payment
- Typically no voting rights

Current Yield:
- Annual dividends divided by current market price

Rights:
- 30–45 day duration
- Exercise price is below market on issuance
- Trade as a separate security
- Available to existing shareholders only
- One right per share outstanding

Warrants:
- Long term
- Exercise price above market when issued
- Trade as separate security
- Offered as sweeteners

ADRs:
- No preemptive rights
- Dividends in dollars
- No voting rights

REITs:
- Not a limited partnership
- Not an investment company
- Pass through income, not losses
- 75% of income must come from real estate
- Must distribute 90% or more of income to shareholders to avoid taxation as a trust
- Trade on exchanges or OTC

Dividends:
- Ex-date 2 business days prior to record date
- Ex-date set by NASD or Exchange
- Price of stock reduced at the opening by the amount of the dividend

Series 7 Unit Test 1

1. The board of directors is responsible for setting all of the following EXCEPT

   A. declaration date
   B. payable date
   C. ex-dividend date
   D. record date

2. ABC common stock is currently selling for $150 per share with a quarterly dividend of $1.50. The current yield for ABC common stock is

   A. 1%
   B. 4%
   C. 12.5%
   D. 25%

3. ABC Corporation has declared a record date of Thursday, May 17, for its next quarterly cash dividend. When is the last day the investor could purchase the stock regular way and receive the dividend?

   A. Monday, May 14
   B. Tuesday, May 15
   C. Wednesday, May 16
   D. Thursday, May 17

4. Which of the following statements regarding warrants is TRUE?

   A. Warrants give the holder a perpetual interest in the issuer's stock.
   B. The term of a warrant is generally shorter than the term of a right.
   C. Warrants are issued with other securities to make the offering more attractive.
   D. Warrants are safer than corporate bonds.

5. Which of the following have equity positions in a corporation?

   I. Common stockholders
   II. Preferred stockholders
   III. Convertible bondholders
   IV. Mortgage bondholders

   A. I and II only
   B. I and III only
   C. II and III only
   D. I, II, III and IV

6. Five directors will be elected at the annual meeting of CDE. Under the cumulative voting system, an investor with 100 shares of CDE would have

   A. 100 votes that he could cast for each of 5 directors
   B. 100 total votes that he could cast in any way he chooses among 5 directors
   C. 500 votes that he could cast for each of 5 directors
   D. 500 total votes that he could cast in any way he chooses among 5 directors

7. The following chart shows the capital transactions of ABC Corporation.

Date	Event	Amount
10-19-96	Initial offering	6 million shares
4-1-00	Treasury purchase	500,000 shares

   ABC wants to raise additional capital by selling 2 million shares through a rights offering and engages an underwriter on a standby basis. By expiration date, ABC was only able to sell 1 million shares to existing shareholders. After expiration, how many shares does ABC have outstanding?

   A. 6.5 million
   B. 7.0 million
   C. 7.5 million
   D. 8.0 million

8. An ADR represents a
   A. US security in a foreign market
   B. foreign security in a domestic market
   C. US security in both a domestic and a foreign market
   D. foreign security in both a domestic and a foreign market

9. If a corporation attaches warrants to a new issue of debt securities, which of the following would be a resulting benefit?
   A. Dilution of shareholders' equity
   B. Reduction of the debt securities' interest rate
   C. Reduction of the number of shares outstanding
   D. Increase in earnings per share

10. Treasury stock
    I. has voting rights and is entitled to a dividend when declared
    II. has no voting rights and no dividend entitlement
    III. has been issued and repurchased by the company
    IV. is authorized but unissued stock

    A. I and III
    B. I and IV
    C. II and III
    D. II and IV

11. REITs must
    I. invest at least 75% of their assets in real estate-related activities
    II. distribute at least 90% of their net investment income
    III. be organized as trusts
    IV. pass along losses to shareholders

    A. I and II only
    B. I and IV only
    C. I, II and III only
    D. II and III only

12. In a portfolio containing common stock, preferred stock, convertible preferred stock, and guaranteed common stock, changes in interest rates would be most likely to affect the market price of the
    A. common
    B. preferred
    C. convertible preferred
    D. guaranteed

13. Holders of both XYZ preferred stock and common shares are paid an annual dividend of $5 per share and then share equally in further dividends up to $1 per share in any one year. In these circumstances, the preferred stock is known as
    A. cumulative
    B. adjustable
    C. participating
    D. convertible

14. ABC Corp. has outstanding a 10% noncumulative preferred stock. Two years ago, ABC omitted its preferred dividend. Last year, it paid a dividend of $5 per share. In order to pay a dividend to common shareholders, each preferred share must be paid a dividend of
    A. $5
    B. $10
    C. $15
    D. $25

15. Shareholder approval is required for all of the following corporate events EXCEPT
    A. stock splits
    B. the acceptance of a tender offer
    C. stock dividends
    D. the issuance of convertible bonds

Series 7 Unit Test 1 Answers & Rationale

1. C. The ex-date for a distribution is set by the appropriate self-regulatory organization. The issuer determines the other dates listed.
QID: 29634

2. B. To calculate current yield, the quarterly dividend must be annualized ($1.50 × 4 = $6). The $6 annual dividend / $150 market price = 4%.
QID: 27770

3. A. In order to receive a cash dividend, an investor must be owner of record as of the close of business on record date. Because regular way settlement is three business days, the customer must purchase the stock no later than Monday, May 14. If the investor waited until Tuesday, May 15, to purchase the stock, the investor would not receive the dividend as the trade would settle on Friday, May 18. Tuesday, May 15, is the ex-date which is the first day the stock trades without the dividend. For regular way trades, the ex-date is two business days before the record date.
QID: 36478

4. C. Warrants are generally issued with bond offerings as a sweetener. Warrants are long-term options to buy stock and because they are equity securities, warrants are junior in safety to bonds.
QID: 32139

5. A. Common and preferred stockholders have equity positions, or ownership positions. Bondholders (mortgage or otherwise) are creditors, not stockholders.
QID: 28816

6. D. With cumulative voting rights, this investor may cast 500 votes for the 5 directors in any way he chooses. Cumulative voting gives an investor one vote per share owned times the number of directorships to be voted on.
QID: 27758

7. C. Before the rights offering, the company had 5.5 million shares outstanding (6 million issued – 500,000 treasury shares). In connection with the offering, ABC engages a standby underwriter, which commits to purchasing any unsold shares. Therefore, regardless of the number of shares initially subscribed to, all 2 million shares will be sold.
QID: 35068

8. B. ADR stands for American depositary receipt. ADRs are receipts issued by US banks, represent ownership of a foreign security, and are traded in US securities markets.
QID: 29616

9. B. Usually, a warrant is issued as a sweetener to make the debt instrument more marketable. This enhancement allows the issuer to pay a slightly lower rate of interest. A warrant may be issued together with an issue of bonds or preferred stock, entitling the owner to purchase a given number of common shares at a specific price for a certain number of years.
QID: 27777

10. C. Treasury stock is stock a corporation has issued and subsequently repurchased from the public in the secondary market. It does not carry the rights of other common shares, such as voting rights, rights to dividends, or preemptive rights.
QID: 27762

11. C. Real Estate Investment Trusts (REITs) engage in real estate activities and can qualify for favorable tax treatment if they pass through at least 90% of their net investment income to their shareholders. While they can pass through income, they cannot pass through any losses; they are not DPPs.
QID: 34847

12. B. Preferred stock most closely resembles bonds; therefore, it would be the most sensitive to interest rates among the alternatives listed. Convertible preferred stock is influenced by the common stock because it is convertible into the underlying security. Guaranteed common stock is common stock whose dividends are guaranteed by another corporation.
QID: 28818

13. C. Participating preferred stock allows for an increase in the stated dividend when the common dividend is increased. Cumulative preferred requires that dividends in arrears must be paid before the current dividend can be paid. Adjustable refers to an adjustable dividend rate. Convertible preferred can be converted into the issuer's common shares. QID: 30632

14. B. The company must pay the full stated dividend of $10 per preferred share in order to pay any dividends to the common shares. Note that this is straight, or noncumulative, preferred. QID: 35140

15. C. Shareholder approval is not required for the payment of dividends. Shareholder approval is normally required for actions that increase (or potentially increase) the number of shares outstanding, such as stock splits and the issuance of convertible bonds. A corporation's acceptance of a tender offer requires shareholder approval. QID: 36482

Debt Securities

INTRODUCTION

This unit reviews the process of issuers borrowing money from investors through the sale of bonds. When an investor loans money to the issuer, the issuer must make regular interest payments for the use of the funds. Because of the fixed interest payments that an investor receives, debt securities are also known as fixed-income securities.

Corporations, municipalities, and the US government are issuers of debt securities. Each issuer has unique features, but overall they share many characteristics.

The Series 7 exam asks approximately 15–25 questions on the features of corporate and government debt, money market instruments, and interest rates.

UNIT OBJECTIVES

When you have completed this unit, you should be able to:

- list and describe basic characteristics of all debt instruments;
- discuss the inverse relationship between bond prices and yields;
- define and explain the relationship between current yield, yield to maturity, and yield to call;
- identify unique features of corporate debt instruments;
- calculate conversion parity;
- compare three different types of marketable government securities;
- name and describe the most common agency issues;
- identify the features and risks of CMOs;
- list and describe money market instruments;
- name the benchmark interest rates in our economy;
- describe Eurodollars and foreign exchange risk;
- interpret debt instrument quotations from financial charts and tables; and
- accrued interest.

Characteristics of Bonds

Unlike stockholders, **bondholders** have neither ownership interest in the issuing corporation nor voice in management. As creditors, bondholders receive preferential treatment over common and preferred stockholders if a corporation files for bankruptcy. Bonds are considered senior securities because creditor claims are settled before the claims of stockholders. Therefore, stockholders' interests are subordinate to those of bondholders.

Issuers

Corporations issue bonds to raise working capital or funds for capital expenditures such as plant construction or equipment and other major purchases. Corporate bonds with maturities of five years or more are commonly referred to as **funded debt**.

The federal government is the nation's largest borrower and the most secure credit risk. Treasury bills (six months or less), notes (2- to 10-year maturities), and bonds (maturities of more than 10 years) are backed by the full faith and credit of the government and its unlimited taxing powers.

✓ **Take Note:** As of October 2001, the Treasury Department discontinued issuing 30-year Treasury bonds. The maximum maturity of newly issued Treasury securities is now 10 years. The 30-year Treasury bonds will continue to trade until they mature or are refunded by the US Treasury Department.

Municipal securities are the debt obligations of state and local governments and their agencies. Most are issued to raise capital to finance public works or construction projects that benefit the general public.

Interest

Both the interest rate an issuer pays its bondholders and the timing of payments are set when a bond is issued. The interest rate, or **coupon**, is calculated from the bond's par value. **Par value**, also known as **face value**, is normally $1,000 per bond, meaning each bond will be redeemed for $1,000 when it matures. Interest on a bond accrues daily and is paid in semiannual installments over the life of the bond.

The final semiannual interest payment is made when the bond matures, and it is combined with repayment of the principal amount. If a bondholder has been receiving semiannual payments of $350 from 10 bonds, he will receive a check for $10,350 when the bonds mature.

Test Topic Alert!

Be prepared to solve a question similar to the following:

An investor purchases 5M ABC J&J 15 8s of '09. What will the investor receive at maturity of the bond?

To solve the problem, decode the bond quote first.

5M: Five – $1,000 bonds, or a total principal amount of $5,000

ABC: The issuer of the bond; it is a corporate bond because of its three-letter name (corporate stock and bond symbols are from 1 to 5 letters).

J&J 15: The bond pays interest on January 15 and July 15 each year. If there is no 15, assume interest is paid on the first of the month. The interest dates are six months apart. An M&S bond pays interest on March 1 and September 1.

8s: The bond pays a stated rate of interest of 8% annually. This is known as the coupon or nominal or stated rate of interest.

'09: The investor will receive the principal at the bond's maturity in 2009.

Now back to the original question. The investor will receive the full principal plus the last semiannual interest payment when the bond matures.

Bond principal:	$5,000	(Annual interest is $80 per thousand; with $5,000 face value the semiannual interest is $200)
Semiannual interest:	+ 200	
Total at maturity:	$5,200	

Maturities

On the **maturity date**, the loan principal is repaid to the investor. Each bond has its own maturity date. The most common maturities fall in the 5- to 30-year range. Three basic types of bond maturity structures are term, serial, and balloon.

Term Maturity — A **term bond** is structured so that the principal of the whole issue matures at once. Because all of the principal is repaid at one time, issuers may establish a sinking fund account to accumulate money to retire the bonds at maturity.

Serial Maturity — A **serial bond issue** schedules portions of the principal to mature at intervals over a period of years, until the entire balance has been repaid.

Balloon Maturity — An issuer sometimes schedules its bond's maturity using elements of both serial and term maturities. The issuer repays part of the bond's principal before the final maturity date, as with a serial maturity, but pays off the major portion of the bond at maturity. This bond has a **balloon**, or **serial and balloon**, maturity.

Series Issues Instead of placing all of its bonds in the hands of investors at one time, any bond issuer may spread out its borrowing over several years as its needs dictate by issuing the bonds in separate series.

Bond Certificate

Bonds were traditionally issued as **certificates**—physical evidence that designates the bond's ownership and characteristics—in essence, an IOU. All bond certificates contain basic information including the following:

- name of issuer;
- interest rate and payment date;
- maturity date;
- call features;
- principal amount;
- CUSIP number for identification;
- dated date—the date that interest starts accruing; and
- reference to the bond indenture.

Registration of Bonds Bonds are **registered**, in varying degrees, to record ownership should a certificate be lost or stolen. Tracking a bond's ownership through its registration has only been common in the United States since the early 1970s.

Coupon (Bearer) Bonds Though no longer issued, in past years most bonds were issued in coupon, or bearer, form. Issuers kept no records of purchasers, and securities were issued without an investor's name printed on the certificate. Coupon bonds are not registered, so whoever possesses them can collect interest on, sell, or redeem the bonds.

Interest coupons are attached to bearer bonds, and holders collect interest by clipping the coupons and delivering them to an issuer's paying agent. Individual coupons are payable to the bearer. When a bond matures, the bearer delivers it to the paying agent and receives his principal.

No proof of ownership is needed to sell a bearer bond. Even though bearer bonds are not issued today, the term *coupon* is still used to describe interest payments received by bondholders.

Registered Bonds A common form of bond issued today is the **registered bond**. When a registered bond is issued, the issuer's transfer agent records the bondholder's name. The buyer's name appears on the bond certificate's face.

Fully Registered

When bonds are registered as to both principal and interest, the transfer agent maintains a list of bondholders and updates this list as bond ownership changes. Interest payments are automatically sent to bondholders of record. The transfer agent transfers a registered bond whenever a bond is sold by canceling the seller's certificate and issuing a new one in the buyer's name. Most corporate bonds are issued in fully registered form.

Registered as to Principal Only

Principal-only registered bonds have the owner's name printed on the certificate, but the coupons are in **bearer form.** When bonds registered as to principal only are sold, the names of the new owners are recorded (in order) on the bond certificates and on the issuer's registration record. Like coupon bonds, bonds registered as to principal only are no longer issued.

Book-Entry Bonds **Book-entry** bond owners do not receive certificates. Rather, the transfer agent maintains the security's ownership records. While the names of buyers of both registered and book-entry bonds are recorded (registered), the book-entry bond owner does not receive a certificate, but the registered bond owner does. The trade confirmation serves as evidence of book-entry bond ownership. Most US government bonds are available only in book-entry form.

Denominations Bearer bonds were only issued in denominations of $1,000 and $5,000. Registered bonds are available in $1,000 denominations or multiples of $1,000 ($5,000, $10,000, $20,000, etc.) up to $100,000 per certificate.

Test Topic Alert! The exam might ask which form a bond must be in for an investor to receive interest and principal payments by mail. Bonds must be fully registered or in book-entry form.

New bonds are only issued in fully registered and book entry form. Even though bonds with coupons attached have not been issued since 1983, they are still available in the secondary market.

Pricing

Once issued, bonds are bought and sold in the secondary market. Bond prices are determined primarily by interest rates. Additional influences may be unique to the issuer.

Par, Premium, and Discount Bonds are generally issued with a **face value**, or par value, of $1,000. **Par** represents the dollar amount of the investor's loan to the issuer, and it is the amount repaid when the bond matures.

In the secondary market, bonds can sell for any price—**at par, below par** (at a **discount**) or **above par** (at a **premium**). The two primary factors affecting a bond's market price are the issuer's financial stability and overall trends in interest rates. If an issuer's credit rating remains constant, interest rates are the only factor that affect the market price.

Corporate bond quotes are commonly stated as percentages of par in increments of ⅛. A bid of 100 means 100% of par, or $1,000. A bond quote of 98⅛, means 98 and ⅛% (98.125%) of $1,000, or $981.25. Bond price changes are quoted in newspapers in points. One point is 1% of $1,000, or $10; ¼ point = $2.50. The minimum variation for most corporate bond quotes is ⅛, (.125%, or $1.25). In addition, there are 100 basis points in each point.

✓ **For Example:** If one point equals $10, one basis point equals 10 cents.

Test Topic Alert!

1. Expect a question similar to the following.

    80 basis points equals

    I. $8.00
    II. $80.00
    III. 0.8%
    IV. 8.0%

    A. I and III
    B. I and IV
    C. II and III
    D. II and IV

    Answer: **A**. We know that 100 basis points = $10 = 1% of a bond's face value. Therefore, 80 basis points = .8% and is worth $8.00 (80 × 10 cents).

Rating and Analyzing Bonds

Rating services, such as Standard & Poor's (S&P) and Moody's, evaluate the credit quality of bond issues and publish their ratings. Standard & Poor's and Moody's rate both corporate and municipal bonds. Both base their bond ratings primarily on an issuer's creditworthiness—that is, the issuer's ability to pay interest and principal as they come due.

A plus or minus sign in a Standard & Poor's rating indicates that the bond falls within the top (+) or bottom (−) of that particular category. Moody's uses A1 and Baa1 to indicate the highest quality bonds within those two categories. Moody's also provides ratings for short-term municipal notes, designating MIG-1 as the highest quality and MIG-4 as the lowest.

The rating organizations rate those issues that either pay to be rated or have enough bonds outstanding to generate constant investor interest. The fact that a bond is not rated does not indicate its quality; many issues are too small to justify the expense of a bond rating.

Basis for Bond Ratings

Bond ratings are based on an issuer's financial stability. The rating services apply a series of financial tests to assess a corporation's financial strength.

Specific criteria used to rate corporate and municipal bonds include:

- the amount and composition of existing debt;
- the stability of the issuer's cash flow;
- the issuer's ability to meet scheduled payments of interest and principal on its debt obligations;
- asset protection; and
- management capability.

A bond's rating may change over time as the issuer's ability to make interest and principal payments changes.

Bond Ratings

Standard & Poor's	Moody's	Interpretation
Bank grade (investment grade) bonds		
AAA	Aaa	Highest rating. Capacity to repay principal and interest judged high.
AA	Aa	Very strong. Only slightly less secure than the highest rating.
A	A	Judged to be slightly more susceptible to adverse economic conditions.
BBB	Baa	Adequate capacity to repay principal and interest. Slightly speculative.
Speculative (non-investment grade) bonds		
BB	Ba	Speculative. Significant chance that issuer could miss an interest payment.
B	B	Issuer has missed one or more interest or principal payments.
C	Caa	No interest is being paid on bond at this time.
D	D	Issuer is in default. Payment of interest or principal is in arrears.

Investment Grade

The **Comptroller of the Currency**, the **Federal Deposit Insurance Corporation (FDIC)**, the **Federal Reserve**, and state banking authorities have established policies determining which securities banks can purchase. A municipal bond must be **investment grade** (a rating of BBB/Baa or higher) to be suitable for purchase by banks. Investment-grade bonds are also known as **bank-grade bonds**.

✓ **Take Note:** An easy way to distinguish between Moody's and S&P ratings is to remember that "Mood swings are Up and Down." This phrase reminds you that Moody's uses upper and lower case letters while S&P uses capital letters only for its ratings. For Moody's, investment grade is Baa and above, while with S&P, investment grade is BBB and above.

Relationship of Rating to Yield

Generally, the higher a bond's rating, the lower its yield. Investors will accept lower returns on their investments if their principal and interest payments are safe. Bonds with low ratings due to the issuer's instability pay higher rates because of the risks to principal and interest associated with such uncertainties.

Qualitative Analysis

In addition to financial statistics, qualitative factors such as an industry's stability, the issuer's quality of management, and the regulatory climate may be considered when bonds are rated.

Comparative Safety of Debt Securities

Although there are exceptions to the rule, a hierarchy exists in the degree of safety associated with different categories of debt securities. Normally, the higher the degree of safety, the lower the yield relative to other investments at the same time.

US Government Securities

The highest degree of safety is in securities backed by the full faith and credit of the US government. These securities include: US Treasury bills, notes, and bonds (and savings bonds like Series EE and HH bonds).

Government Agency Issues

The second highest degree of safety is in securities issued by government agencies and government-sponsored corporations, although the US government does not back the securities (GNMA is the exception). These organizations include:

- Government National Mortgage Association bonds (GNMAs or **Ginnie Maes**);
- Federal Farm Credit Banks (FFCBs);
- Federal Home Loan Mortgage Corporation (FHLMC or **Freddie Mac**); and
- Federal National Mortgage Association (FNMA or **Fannie Mae**).

Municipal Issues

Generally, the next level of safety is in securities issued by municipalities. **General obligation bonds (GOs)**, backed by the taxing power of the issuer,

Characteristics of Bonds

are usually safer than revenue bonds. Revenue bonds are backed by revenues from the facility financed by the bond issue.

Corporate Debt

Corporate debt securities cover the safety spectrum, from very safe (AAA corporates) to very risky (**junk bonds**). Corporate bonds are backed, in varying degrees, by the issuing corporation. Usually, these securities are ranked from safe to risky, as follows:

- Secured bonds
- Debentures
- Subordinated debentures
- Income bonds

However, these rankings serve only as a rough guideline.

Liquidity **Liquidity** is the ease with which a bond or any other security can be sold. Many factors determine a bond's liquidity, including:

- size of the issue;
- quality;
- rating;
- maturity;
- call features;
- coupon rate and current market value;
- issuer; and
- existence of a sinking fund.

✓ **Take Note:** The terms *liquidity* and *marketability* are synonymous. Either term refers to how quickly a security can be converted into cash.

Debt Retirement

The schedule of interest and principal payments due on a bond issue is known as the **debt service**.

Redemption When a bond's principal is repaid, the bond is **redeemed**. Redemption usually occurs on the maturity date.

The four redemption features are:

- sinking fund;
- call;
- refunding; and
- prerefunding.

Sinking Fund

To facilitate the retirement of its bonds, a corporate or municipal issuer may establish a **sinking fund** operated by the bonds' trustee. The trust indenture often requires a sinking fund, which can be used to call bonds, redeem bonds at maturity, or buy back bonds in the open market.

To establish a sinking fund, the issuer deposits cash in an account with the trustee. Because a sinking fund makes money available for redeeming bonds, it can aid the bonds' marketability.

✓ **Take Note:** As a general rule, highly rated issuers do not establish sinking funds. Lower-rated issuers do so to make their issues more marketable.

Calling Bonds

Bonds are often issued with a **call feature**, or **call option**. A call feature allows the issuer to redeem a bond issue before its maturity date, either in whole or in part (in-whole or partial calls).

The issuer does this by notifying bondholders that it will call the bonds at a particular price on a certain date.

In a partial call, the issuer will call selected bonds, not the entire issue, at a particular call date and call price. The bonds called in a partial call are selected by lottery; that is, randomly.

Call Premium

The right to call bonds for early redemption gives issuers flexibility in their financial management. In return, an issuer usually pays bondholders a premium, a price higher than par, known as a **call premium**. Various municipal bonds, corporate bonds and preferred stocks are callable at some point over their terms.

💡 **Test Topic Alert!**   A call premium is the difference between the call price and par.

✓ **For Example:** If a bond were callable at 102, the call premium would be two points, or $20.00 per bond.

Advantages of a Call to the Issuer

Callable bonds can benefit the issuer in many ways.

- If general interest rates decline, the issuer can redeem bonds with a high interest rate and replace them with bonds with a lower rate.
- The issuer can call bonds to reduce its debt any time after the initial call date.

- The issuer can replace short-term debt issues with long-term issues, and vice versa.
- The issuer can call bonds as a means of forcing the conversion of convertible corporate bonds.

Term bonds are generally called by random drawing. **Serial bonds**, on the other hand, are usually called in inverse order of their maturities because longer maturities tend to have higher interest rates. Calling the long maturities lowers the issuer's interest expense by the largest amount.

If a bond issue's trust indenture does not include a call provision, the issuer normally can buy bonds in the open market, known as **tendering**, to retire a portion of its debt.

Call Protection

Bonds are called when general interest rates are lower than they were when the bonds were issued. Investors, therefore, are faced with having to replace a relatively high fixed-income investment with one that pays less; this is known as **call risk**. A newly issued bond normally has a noncallable period of 5 or 10 years to provide some protection to investors. During this period, the issuer cannot call any of its bonds.

When the call protection period expires, the issuer may call any or all of the bonds, usually at a premium. A **call protection feature** is an advantage to bondholders in periods of declining interest rates.

Effects of a Call on Trading

After a call notice is issued, but before the call date, called bonds continue to trade in the open market. When bonds are called, a bondholder can turn in the bonds to the issuer on the call date or sell them in the open market. The bonds will trade at a slight discount to the call price during this period. By selling at the small discount, the investor does not have to wait until the call date to get his money.

Test Topic Alert!   Following are three test points pertaining to bond call features.

2. Under what economic circumstances do issuers call bonds?

   Answer: Calls occur when interest rates are declining. Put yourself in the issuer's shoes. Would you want to pay more interest for the use of money than you need to?

3. 2.Investors who purchase callable bonds face what type(s) of investment risk?

   Answer: Call risk is the risk that the bonds will be called and the investor will lose the stream of income from the bond. Remember that bonds do not pay interest after they have been called. The call feature also causes reinvestment risk. If interest rates are down when the call takes place, what likelihood does the investor have of investing the principal received at a comparable rate?

Both call risk and reinvestment risk also apply to callable preferred stock.

4. Which of the following would an issuer most likely call?

   A. High interest bond, callable at a premium
   B. High interest bond, callable at par
   C. Low interest bond, callable at a premium
   D. Low interest bond, callable at par

Answer: **B**. Issuers want to call bonds that are costly to them at as low a price as possible. A high interest bond with no call premium is the best combination. The issuer would be least likely to call a low interest bond with a high call premium.

Refunding Bonds **Refunding** is the practice of raising money to call a bond. Specifically, the issuer sells a new bond issue to generate funds to retire an existing issue. Refunding, like a call, can occur in full or in part. Generally, an entire issue is refunded at once. Refunding is common for bonds approaching maturity. An issuer may not have enough cash to pay off the entire issue, or it may choose to use its cash for other needs.

✓ *Take Note:* Refunding can be thought of as issuer refinancing. Homeowners know that when interest rates drop, it makes sense to replace a high interest mortgage with a new mortgage at a more competitive rate. An issuer can accomplish the same thing by refunding.

Prerefunding When a bond issue is **prerefunded**, also known as **advance refunding,** a new issue is sold at a lower coupon before the original bond issue can be called. An issuer prerefunds a bond issue to lock in a favorable interest rate. The proceeds from the new issue are placed in an escrow account and invested in US government securities. Interest received from the investment is used to pay interest on the original or prerefunded bonds, called at the first call date using the escrowed funds.

Prerefunded bonds are generally rated AAA or Aaa, the highest rating available. Advance refunding is a form of **defeasance**, or termination, of the issuer's obligation; prerefunded bonds are considered defeased and no longer count as part of the issuer's debt.

✓ *Take Note:* Prerefunding often occurs where there is a call protection period. The issuer cannot legally call the bonds until a future date, but if interest rates are low, a low rate can be locked in by issuing the new bonds in advance of the call date.

Know these facts about prerefunded bonds:

- AAA rated (cannot get any safer)
- Considered defeased
- Funds escrowed in government securities
- The marketability of the prerefunded bond increases
- Once prerefunded, the issue is no longer considered part of the outstanding debt of the issuer

Tender Offers When general interest rates are down, companies may wish to redeem callable and noncallable bonds and replace them with bonds paying less interest. A bond issuer may make a **tender offer** for its outstanding bonds, most likely at a premium price as an inducement to bondholders to tender their securities.

Puttable Bonds (Bonds with Put Options) Bonds issued with put options are known as **put**, or **puttable**, bonds. In return for accepting a slightly lower interest rate, an investor receives the right to put (sell) the bond to the issuer at full face value. Once the bond becomes puttable, the investor has the right, generally once a year, to force the issuer to buy back the bonds at par.

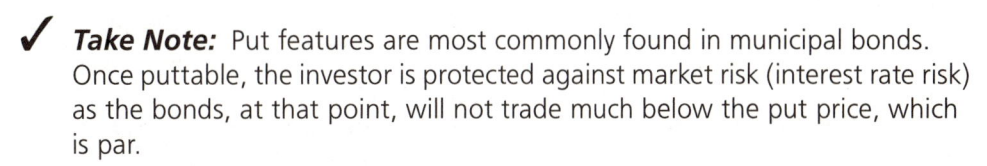

✓ *Take Note:* Put features are most commonly found in municipal bonds. Once puttable, the investor is protected against market risk (interest rate risk) as the bonds, at that point, will not trade much below the put price, which is par.

Quick Quiz 2.1

Match each of the following terms with the appropriate description below.

A. Call protection
B. Call premium
C. Term maturity
D. Sinking fund

___ 1. Account established so that an issuer has the money to redeem its bonds

___ 2. Contractual promise stating that the bond issue is not callable for a certain period

___ 3. Large number of an issuer's bonds come due at a specific time, typically the final maturity date

___ 4. Difference between the higher price paid for a bond and the bond's face amount

Answers 1. ***D.***   2. ***A.***   3. ***C.***   4. ***B.***

Bond Yields

A bond's **yield** expresses the cash interest payments in relation to the bond's value. Yield is determined by the issuer's credit quality, prevailing interest rates, time to maturity, and call features. Bonds can be quoted and traded in terms of their yield as well as a percentage of par dollar amount.

Comparing Yields

Bonds most frequently trade for prices other than par, so the price discount or premium from par is taken into consideration when calculating a bond's overall yield. You can look at a bond's yield in several ways.

Nominal Yield A bond's coupon yield is set at issuance and printed on the face of the bond. The **nominal yield** (a.k.a. **coupon**) is a fixed percentage of the bond's par value.

> ✓ **For Example:** A coupon of 6% indicates the bondholder is paid (6% of the face amount of $1,000), or $60 in interest annually until the bond matures.

Current Yield **Current yield** (CY) measures a bond's coupon payment relative to its market price, as shown in the following equation:

$$\text{Coupon payment} / \text{market price} = \text{current yield}$$

Bond prices and yields move in opposite directions: as interest rates rise, bond prices fall and vice versa. When a bond trades at a discount, its current yield increases; when it trades at a premium, its current yield decreases.

💡 **Test Topic Alert!** *Current Yield, Yield to Maturity, and Yield to Call*

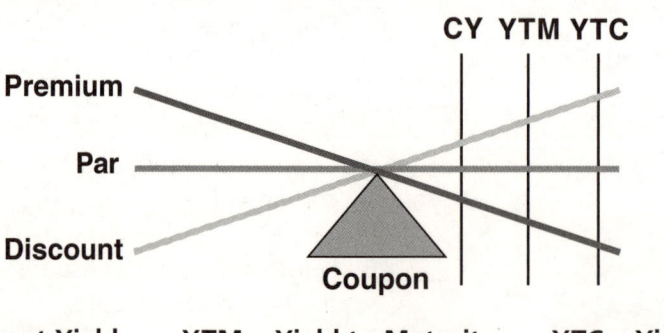

CY = Current Yield   YTM = Yield to Maturity   YTC = Yield to Call

Bond Yields

1. What is the current yield of a 6% bond trading for $800?

   Current yield (CY) = Annual income / Current market price

   Find the solution as follows: $60 / $800 = 7.5%. This bond is trading at a discount. When prices fall, yields rise. The current yield is greater than the nominal yield when bonds are trading at a discount.

2. What is the current yield of a 6% bond trading for $1,200?

   Find the solution as follows: $60 / $1,200 = 5%. This bond is trading at a premium. Price is up so the yield is down. The current yield is less than the nominal yield when bonds are trading at a premium.

   It is critical to understand the inverse relationship between price and yield. An effective way to visualize it is through the chart. When bonds are at par, coupon and current yield are equal. When bonds are at a premium, the CY is less than the coupon. When bonds are at a discount, the CY is greater than the coupon.

CMV of Bond with 10 Years to Maturity

Current market value (CMV) of bond with 10 years to maturity

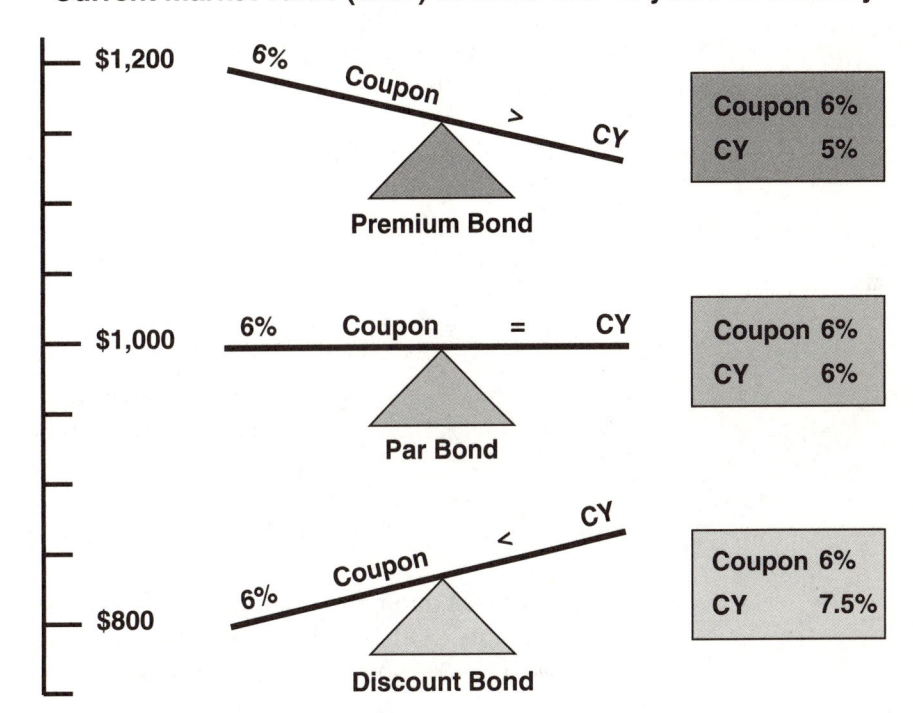

CMV	Diagram	Coupon	CY
$1,200	6% Coupon > CY — Premium Bond	6%	5%
$1,000	6% Coupon = CY — Par Bond	6%	6%
$800	6% Coupon < CY — Discount Bond	6%	7.5%

Debt Securities

Yield to Maturity A bond's **yield to maturity (YTM)** reflects the annualized return of the bond if held to maturity. In calculating yield to maturity, the bondholder takes into account the difference between the price paid for a bond and par value. If the bond's price is less than par, the discount amount increases the return. If the bond's price is greater than par, the premium amount decreases the return.

✓ *For Example:* An investor who buys a 10% coupon bond at 105 ($1,050 per bond) with 10 years remaining to maturity can expect $100 in interest per year. If he holds the bond to maturity, the bondholder loses $50, the amount of the premium. This loss is included in the YTM approximation.

The actual YTM calculation for this premium bond is shown below:

$$\frac{\text{Annual interest} - (\text{Premium} / \text{Years to Maturity})}{\text{Average price of the bond}}$$

A bond's average price is the price paid plus the amount received at maturity (par) divided by two. Alternatively, the average price is that price midway between the purchase price and par.

$$\frac{100 - (50 \div 10)}{1025} = \frac{95}{1025} = .093, \text{ or } 9.3\%$$

The YTM of a bond bought at a premium is always lower than both the coupon rate (nominal yield) and the current yield. In this example, the nominal yield is 10% and the current yield is 9.52% (100 divided by 1,050).

If an investor buys a 10-year bond with a 10% coupon for 95 ($950 per bond), he receives $100 per year in coupon interest payments and a gain of $50 (the amount of the discount) at maturity. This gain is included in the YTM approximation.

The actual YTM calculation for this discount bond is shown below:

$$\frac{\text{Annual interest} + (\text{Discount} / \text{Years to Maturity})}{\text{Average price of the bond}}$$

$$\frac{100 - (50 \div 10)}{975} = \frac{105}{975} = .1077, \text{ or } 10.77\%$$

The YTM of a bond bought at a discount is always higher than both the coupon rate (nominal yield) and the current yield. In this example, the nominal yield is 10% and the current yield is 10.53% (100 divided by 950).

If these calculations seem complicated, don't worry. You will have at most one question requiring a YTM calculation. Focus on the relationship between YTM and CY based on the price of the bond.

✓ **Take Note:** Another term for yield to maturity is basis. A 4% bond trading on a 5% basis is trading at a price to yield 5% to maturity.

Yield to Call   A bond with a call feature may be redeemed before maturity at the issuer's option. Unless the bond was bought at par and is callable at par, **yield to call (YTC)** calculations reflect the early redemption date and consequent acceleration of the discount gain or premium loss from the purchase price.

An investor who buys a callable bond at a premium loses the premium faster when the bond is called at par than if it were held to maturity. Because a bond sells for a premium when its coupon rate is higher than current market rates, premium bonds are likely to be called so the issuer can save on interest expenses. The sooner the bonds are called, the sooner the premium the investor paid is lost.

The YTC for a premium bond called at par, therefore, is always lower than the nominal yield, current yield, and YTM. If a premium bond is called at a premium, the yield relationship is determined by the difference between the purchase price and the call price.

For a bond bought at a discount, YTC is always higher than the nominal yield, current yield, and YTM. If a discount bond is bought at par, the gain is earned faster than if the bond were held to maturity.

Relationship between Bond Prices and Yields to Maturity

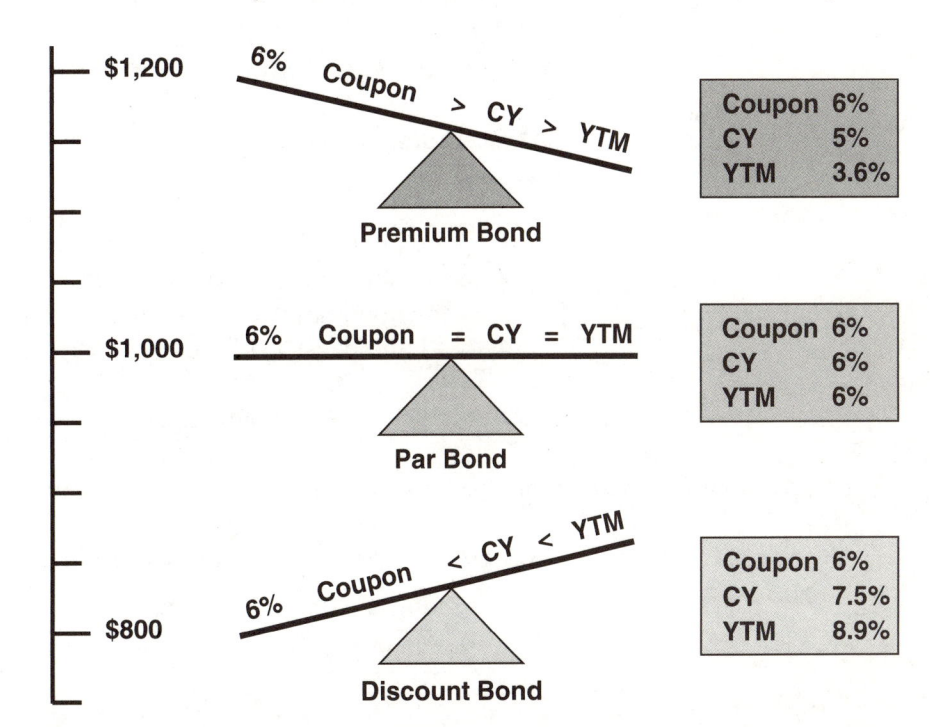

$1,200 — 6% Coupon > CY > YTM — **Premium Bond**

Coupon	6%
CY	5%
YTM	3.6%

$1,000 — 6% Coupon = CY = YTM — **Par Bond**

Coupon	6%
CY	6%
YTM	6%

$800 — 6% Coupon < CY < YTM — **Discount Bond**

Coupon	6%
CY	7.5%
YTM	8.9%

Debt Securities

Relationship between Bond Prices, Yields to Maturity, and Yields to Call

Current market value (CMV) of bond with 10 years to maturity

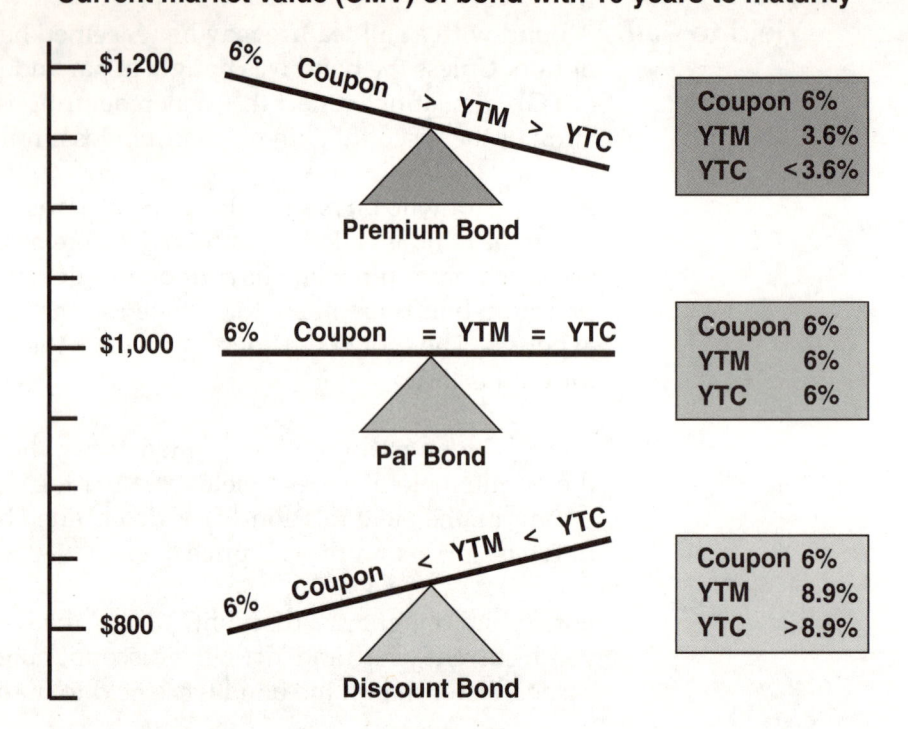

$1,200 — 6% Coupon > YTM > YTC (Premium Bond)	Coupon 6% YTM 3.6% YTC <3.6%
$1,000 — 6% Coupon = YTM = YTC (Par Bond)	Coupon 6% YTM 6% YTC 6%
$800 — 6% Coupon < YTM < YTC (Discount Bond)	Coupon 6% YTM 8.9% YTC >8.9%

Test Topic Alert! When you sit down to take the exam, draw charts for your reference on a piece of scratch paper provided by the testing center. The chart will help you answer yield questions without hesitation.

✓ *For Example:* Answer the following questions with **premium**, **par**, or **discount**.

1. If the bond has a YTC lower than its CY, it is trading at:
2. If the bond has a YTM and CY that are equal, the bond is trading at:
3. If the bond has a YTM less than its YTC, the bond is trading at:
4. If a bond has a YTM greater than its coupon, the bond is trading at:

The answers are: 1. premium; 2. par; 3. discount; 4. discount.

Test Topic Alert! Memorize the following chart for the exam:

Ranking Yields from Lowest to Highest

Discounts	Premiums
Nominal	YTC
CY	YTM
YTM	CY
YTC	Nominal

Bond Yields

Once you understand the yield ranking for discounts, the ranking for premium is easy—it is the exact opposite.

Yield Curve Bond prices and yields have an **inverse relationship**: as interest rates rise, prices decline. In addition, under normal circumstances the longer a bond's maturity, the greater its yield. The increased yield reflects the potential for credit quality or inflation risks over time.

The difference in yields between short-term and long-term bonds of the same quality is known as the **yield curve**. In a **normal yield curve**, the difference between short-term and long-term rates is about three percentage points (300 basis points), but may be much larger or smaller at any given time.

Normal (Positive) Yield Curve

Normal (Positive) Yield Curve

As the term of the security <u>increases</u>, the yield <u>increases</u>.

(Yield axis: 4%–7%; Years to Maturity axis: 0–25)

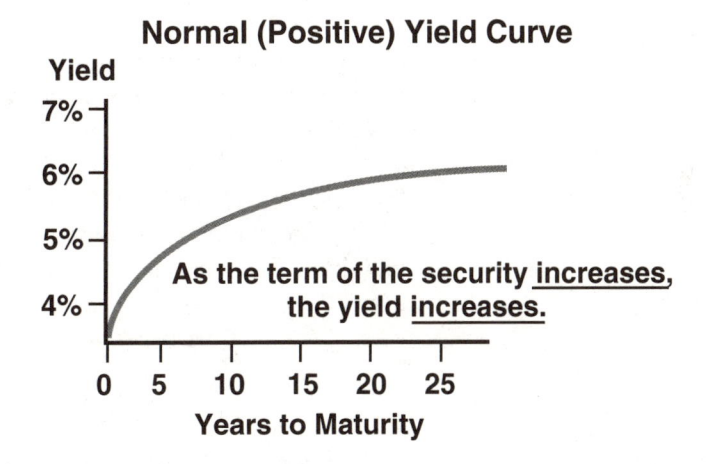

When interest rates are high and expected to begin declining, long-term bond yields can be lower than short-term yields as their market price anticipates the declining rates. When long-term interest rates are lower than short-term rates, the yield curve is considered **inverted**.

Inverted (Negative) Yield Curve

Inverted (Negative) Yield Curve

As the term of the security <u>increases</u>, the yield <u>decreases</u>.

(Yield axis: 4%–7%; Years to Maturity axis: 0–25)

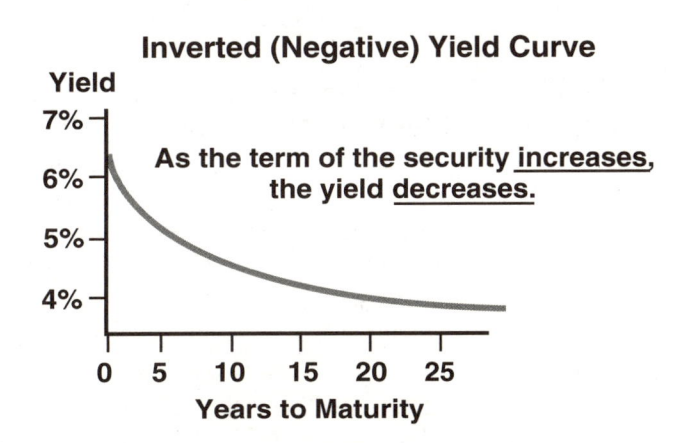

When short-term and long-term rates are the same, the yield curve is flat.

✓ **Take Note:** The shape of the yield curve varies with changes in the economic cycle.

- A normal (ascending) yield curve occurs during periods of economic expansion—it generally predicts interest rates will rise in the future.
- A flat yield curve occurs when the economy is peaking, no change in interest rates is expected.
- An inverted (descending) yield curve occurs when the Federal Reserve Board has tightened credit in an overheating economy; it predicts rates will fall in the future.

Yield curves for issuers with different risk levels can be compared to make economic predictions.

- If the yield curve spread between corporate bonds and government bonds is widening, a **recession** is expected. Investors have chosen the safety of government bonds over higher corporate yields, which occurs when the economy slows down.
- If the yield curve between corporate bonds and government bonds is narrowing, an economic **expansion** is expected and investors are willing to take risks. They will sell government bonds to buy higher yielding corporates.

Corporate and Government Bonds

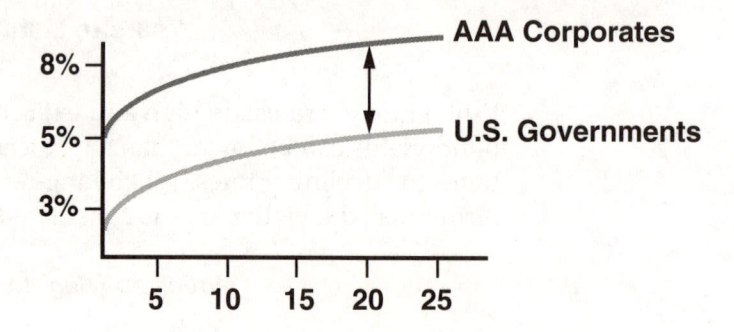

Rate Changes and Bond Prices

As interest rates change, long-term bond prices move more in price than short-term bonds. As rates rise, long-term bond prices decline more than short-term bond prices. As rates fall, long-term bond prices appreciate more than short-term bond prices. Where two bonds have the same time to maturity, the bond with the lower coupon will move more in price. In other words, given a change in interest rates, discounts tend to move more in price than premiums.

💡 **Test Topic Alert!**

If you are given two discount bonds and asked which will appreciate the most if rates fall, choose the bond trading at the deeper discount; i.e., the one with the lower coupon.

Bond Yields

Quick Quiz 2.2

Match each of the following terms with the appropriate description below.

A. Nominal yield
B. Investment grade
C. Book entry
D. Current yield
E. Yield to call

___ 1. Percentage return factoring the difference between a bond's acquisition costs and proceeds, including annual interest, calculated to the earliest date when the issuer may call the bond

___ 2. Stated on the face of the bond certificate

___ 3. Annual interest divided by today's market price

___ 4. Bond owner's name is stored in records kept by the transfer agent

___ 5. Bonds rated BBB/BAA or above

Answers   1. **E.**   2. **A.**   3. **D.**   4. **C.**   5. **B.**

Quick Quiz 2.3

Multiple Choice

1. Which of these bond features is the most attractive to a corporate issuer?

    A. Low call premium
    B. High interest rate
    C. Nonrefundable
    D. High sinking fund requirement

2. An investor purchased a 6½% bond to yield 5½%. If the company calls the bond at par before maturity, the YTC would be

    A. less than 5½%
    B. 5½%
    C. 6½%
    D. greater than 6½%

3. A new convertible bond contains a provision that it cannot be called for five years after the date of issuance. This call protection would be most valuable to a recent purchaser of the bond if interest rates are

   A. falling
   B. rising
   C. stable
   D. fluctuating

4. What is the calculation for determining the current yield on a bond?

   A. Annual interest / par value
   B. Annual interest / current market price
   C. Yield to maturity / par value
   D. Yield to maturity / current market price

5. A customer purchased a 5% US.government bond yielding 6%. A year before the bond matures, new US government bonds are being issued at 4%, and the customer sells the 5% bond. The customer

   I. bought it at a discount
   II. bought it at a premium
   III. sold it at a discount
   IV. sold it at a premium

   A. I and III
   B. I and IV
   C. II and III
   D. II and IV

6. Which yield to maturity would be higher?

   A. 5% nominal yield bond with a premium price
   B. 5% nominal yield bond with a discount price
   C. 5% nominal yield bond with a price at par
   D. YTM is the same for all of the above

7. A corporation issues 9% AAA rated debentures at par. Two years later, similar AAA issues are being offered in the primary market at 9½%. Which of the following statements regarding the outstanding 9% issue are TRUE?

   I. The current yield on the issue will be higher.
   II. The current yield on the issue will be lower.
   III. The dollar price per bond will be higher than par.
   IV. The dollar price per bond will be lower than par.

   A. I and III
   B. I and IV
   C. II and III
   D. II and IV

8. In a comparison of long-term bonds with short-term bonds, all of the following are characteristics of long-term bonds EXCEPT that they

    A. usually have higher yields than short-term bonds
    B. usually provide greater liquidity than short-term bonds
    C. are more likely to be callable
    D. will fluctuate in price more than short-term bonds in response to interest rate changes

9. When interest rates are falling or rising, the price fluctuations of which of the following will be the greatest?

    A. Short-term bonds
    B. Long-term bonds
    C. Money market instruments
    D. Common stock

10. In a scenario of falling inflation and a positive yield curve, which of the following bonds will appreciate the most?

    A. 20-year bond selling at a premium
    B. 20-year bond selling at a discount
    C. 1-year bond selling at a premium
    D. 1-year bond selling at a discount

11. An inverted yield curve is the result of

    A. investors buying long-term bonds and selling short-term bonds
    B. investors buying short-term bonds and selling long-term bonds
    C. rising interest rates
    D. declining interest rates

Answers

1. **A.** A low call premium means that the bond may be called at a low premium before maturity. This feature is attractive to corporations because it provides flexibility in managing their capital structure. For example, it allows a corporation to discontinue debt financing or to replace it with equity financing. The other answers would place burdens on a corporation and so are not attractive.

2. **A.** The bond with a 6½% coupon is priced to yield 5½% and is selling at a premium. Any bond bought at a premium called prior to maturity will have a yield less than the YTM, which is 5½%. Keep in mind that for a bond trading at a premium, YTC is less than YTM.

3. **A.** Call protection is most valuable to a purchaser when interest rates are falling. Bonds tend to be called when rates fall. In this case, the call protection period protects the investor.

4. **B.** Annual interest / current market price = current yield

5. **B.** The customer purchased the 5% bond when it was yielding 6%, therefore at a discount. The customer sold the bond when other bonds of like kind, quality

66 Debt Securities

     and maturity were yielding 4%. The bond is now at a premium because the 5% coupon is attractive to investors.

6. **B**. *With the same nominal yield, the discount bonds will generate higher yields. In addition to the interest payments received on an ongoing basis, the investor receives the amount of the discount at maturity.*

7. **B**. *Because interest rates in general have risen since the issuance of the 9% bond, the bond's price will now be discounted to give a higher current yield on the bond—making it competitive with new issues now being sold at 9½%.*

8. **B**. *Long-term bonds are not as liquid as short-term obligations.*

9. **B**. *Long-term debt prices fluctuate more than short-term debt prices as interest rates rise and fall. Common stock prices are not directly affected by interest rates.*

10. **B**. *In general, prices of long-term bonds are more volatile than prices of short-term bonds. Therefore, the 20-year bonds will appreciate more than the one-year bonds when interest rates fall. Also, prices of bonds with low coupon rates tend to be more volatile than prices of bonds with high coupon rates. A bond sells at a discount when its coupon is lower than prevailing interest rates. Because of its lower coupon, therefore, the 20-year discount bond will appreciate more than the 20-year premium bond.*

11. **A**. *When investors believe that interest rates soon may decline, they seek to lock in the current rate of return by buying long-term bonds. Increased demand increases the price and causes the yields on long-term debt instruments to fall below short-term yields. As a result, the yield curve takes on a negative slope.*

Corporate Bonds

Corporate bonds are issued to raise working capital or capital for expenditures such as plant construction and equipment purchases. The two primary types of corporate bonds are **secured** and **unsecured**.

Secured Bonds

A bond is **secured** when the issuer has identified specific assets as collateral for interest and principal payments. A trustee holds the title to the assets that secure the bond. In a **default**, the bondholder can lay claim to the collateral.

Mortgage Bonds   **Mortgage bonds** have the highest priority among all claims on assets pledged as collateral. While mortgage bonds, in general, are considered relatively safe, individual bonds are only as secure as the assets that secure them and are rated accordingly.

Corporate Bonds

When multiple classes of a mortgage bond exist, the first claim on the pledged property goes to first-mortgage bonds, second claim to second-mortgage bonds and so on.

Open-End Indentures

An open-end trust indenture permits the corporation to issue more bonds of the same class later. Subsequent issues are secured by the same collateral backing the initial issue and have equal liens on the property.

Closed-End Indentures

A closed-end indenture does not permit the corporation to issue more bonds of the same class in the future. Any subsequent issue has a subordinated claim on the collateral.

Prior Lien Bonds

Companies in financial trouble sometimes attract capital by issuing mortgage bonds that take precedence over first-mortgage bonds. Before issuing prior lien bonds, however, a corporation must have the consent of first-mortgage bondholders (which is unlikely).

Collateral Trust Bonds

Collateral trust bonds are issued by corporations that own securities of other companies as investments. A corporation issues bonds secured by a pledge of those securities as collateral. The trust indenture usually contains a covenant requiring that a trustee hold the pledged securities. Collateral trust bonds may be backed by one or more of the following securities:

- another company's stocks and bonds;
- stocks and bonds of partially or wholly owned subsidiaries;
- pledging company's prior lien long-term bonds that have been held in trust to secure short-term bonds; or
- installment payments or other obligations of the corporation's clients.

Equipment Trust Certificates

Railroads, airlines, trucking companies and oil companies use **equipment trust certificates** (**ETCs**) (or equipment notes and bonds) to finance the purchase of capital equipment. ETCs are issued serially so that the amount outstanding goes down year-to-year in line with the depreciating value of the collateral (e.g., aircraft, railroad cars, etc.).

Title to the newly acquired equipment is held in trust, usually by a bank, until all certificates have been paid in full. Because the certificates normally mature before the equipment wears out, the amount borrowed is generally less than the full value of the property securing the certificates.

Unsecured Bonds

Unsecured bonds have no specific collateral backing and are classified as either **debentures** or **subordinated debentures**.

Debentures Debentures are backed by the general credit of the issuing corporation, and a debenture owner is considered a general creditor of the company. Debentures are below secured bonds and above subordinated debentures and preferred and common stock in the priority of claims on corporate assets.

Subordinated Debentures The claims of subordinated debenture owners are subordinated to the claims of other general creditors. Subordinated debentures generally offer higher yields than either straight debentures or secured bonds due to their subordinate (thus riskier) status, and they often have conversion features.

Guaranteed Bonds

Guaranteed bonds are backed by a company other than the issuer, such as a parent company. This effectively increases the issue's safety.

Income Bonds

Income bonds, also known as **adjustment bonds**, are used when a company is reorganizing and coming out of bankruptcy. Income bonds pay interest only if the corporation has enough income to meet the interest payment and the board of directors declares a payment. Because missed interest payments do not accumulate for future payment, these bonds are not suitable investments for customers seeking income.

Liquidation In the event a company goes bankrupt, the hierarchy of claims on the company's assets are as follows:

- unpaid wages;
- IRS (taxes);
- secured debt (bonds and mortgages);
- unsecured liabilities (debentures) and general creditors;
- subordinated debt;
- preferred stockholders; and then
- common stockholders.

Test Topic Alert! Be ready for a question on liquidation priority. Secured is safest, followed by unsecured or general creditors, then subordinated. Common stock is always last in line. Bonds are frequently called senior securities because of their priority in this hierarchy.

Zero-Coupon Bonds

Bonds are normally issued as interest-paying securities. **Zero-coupon bonds** are an issuer's debt obligations that do not make regular interest payments. Instead, zeros are issued (sold) at a deep discount to their face value and mature at par. The difference between the discounted purchase price and the full face value at maturity is the return (accreted interest) the investor receives.

The price of a zero-coupon bond reflects the general interest rate climate for similar maturities.

Zero-coupon bonds are issued by corporations, municipalities, the US Treasury, and may be created by broker/dealers from other types of securities.

Advantages and Disadvantages

A zero-coupon bond requires a relatively small investment—perhaps $300 to $400 per bond—and matures at $1,000. Zero-coupon bonds offer investors a way to speculate on interest rate moves. Because they sell at deep discounts and offer no cash interest payments to the holder, zeros are substantially more volatile than traditional bonds; their prices fluctuate wildly with changes in market rates. Moreover, the longer the time to maturity, the greater the volatility. When interest rates change, a zero's price changes much more as a percentage of its market value than an ordinary bond's price.

Taxation of Zero-Coupon Bonds

Although zeros pay no regular interest income, investors in zeros owe income tax each year on the amount by which the bonds have accreted, just as if the investor had received it in cash. The income tax is due regardless of the direction of the market price.

✓ **For Example:** A customer buys a 10-year zero at a cost of $400. At maturity, the customer will realize $600 of interest income. Each year, however, the customer must accrete the discount and pay income tax on this "phantom" income. Here's how it works:

The IRS requires the customer to accrete the discount annually on a straight line basis. The total discount is $600. As there are 10 years to maturity, the customer must accrete $60 annually ($600 divided by 10 years). Each year, the customer pays income tax on $60 of interest income. The good news is that each year, the customer is permitted to adjust the cost basis of the zero upward by the amount of the annual accretion. After one year, the customer's cost basis is $460. After two years, the cost basis is $520. After three years, it is $580 and so on. At maturity, the cost basis will be adjusted to par. Therefore, if held to maturity, there is no capital gain (cost basis is par; redeemed at par).

However, if the customer sells the zero prior to maturity, there may be a capital gain or a capital loss, depending on the difference between sales proceeds and the cost basis at time of sale.

Consider the prior example. If the 10-year zero bought at $400 is sold five years later for $720, the customer would realize a $20 per bond gain. At that point, the customer's cost basis is $700 ($400 plus 5 years of annual accretion of $60 per year).

Test Topic Alert! If the exam asks you to choose the security that has no reinvestment risk, the answer to look for is a zero, because with no interest payments to reinvest, the investor has no reinvestment risk. Further, because there is no reinvestment risk, buying a zero is the only way to "lock in" a rate of return.

The Trust Indenture

The **Trust Indenture Act of 1939** requires corporate bond issues of $5 million or more sold interstate to be issued under a trust indenture, a legal contract between the bond issuer and a trustee representing bondholders. Although the face of a bond certificate mentions the trust indenture, it is not automatically supplied to bondholders.

The trust indenture specifies the issuer's obligation and bondholders' rights, and it identifies the trustee.

The Trustee The Trust Indenture Act of 1939 requires a corporation to appoint a **trustee**—usually a commercial bank or trust company—for its bonds. The trustee monitors compliance with the covenants of the indenture and may act on behalf of the bondholders if the issuer defaults.

Exemptions Federal and municipal governments are exempt from the Trust Indenture Act provisions, although municipal revenue bonds are typically issued with a trust indenture to make them more marketable.

Protective Covenants In the trust indenture for a mortgage bond, the debtor corporation agrees to:

- pay the interest and principal of its bonds;
- specify where bonds can be presented for payment;
- defend the legal title to the property;
- maintain the property to ensure that business can be conducted;
- insure the mortgaged property against fire and other losses;
- pay all taxes and assessments (property, income, franchise); and
- maintain its corporate structure and the right to do business.

Other covenants might include provisions for a sinking fund, a replacement fund, minimum working capital, or other requirements.

Mortgage bonds may be issued with either closed- or open-end covenants. Bonds issued with **closed-end covenants** have senior claim on the underlying assets, even if the corporation issues other bonds secured by the same assets. An **open-end covenant** permits subsequent issues to be secured by the same property and have equal liens on it.

Test Topic Alert!

The test sometimes refers to closed-end indenture bonds as **senior lien bonds**.

Remember that a trust indenture is a contract between the issuer and the trustee for the benefit of the bondholders. It is easy to mistakenly identify the contract as one between the issuer and the bondholders.

Trading Corporate Bonds

NYSE-Listed Bonds

The **New York Stock Exchange** (**NYSE**) provides a central marketplace for trading bonds. Unlike stocks traded on the exchange, listed corporate bonds trade sporadically. Trading in listed bonds is extremely thin. Most bonds are traded in the OTC market, and as long-term investments, bonds are not traded as frequently as stocks. Many institutional investors (e.g., banks and insurance companies) are legally restricted in their investments and tend to be long-term holders.

Most brokerage firms do not maintain regular floor brokers to execute bond orders; they enlist **bond brokers** to execute the orders on their behalf. A bond broker charges a small fee (a **give-up commission**) for each order executed. The NYSE bond market operates under the same principles and auction procedures used on the stock trading floor.

Bids and Offers Unlike bids and offers for stocks, bids to buy and offers to sell bonds are stated as a percentage of the bond's par value.

✓ *For Example:* A bid of 100 means 100%, not $100. For a $1,000 bond, it means the bidder will pay $1,000.

Convertible Bonds

Convertible bonds are corporate bonds that may be exchanged for a fixed number of shares of the issuing company's common stock. They are convertible into common stock, so convertible bonds pay lower interest rates than nonconvertible bonds and generally trade in line with the common stock. Convertible bonds have fixed interest payments and maturity dates, so they are less volatile than common stock.

Advantages of Convertible Securities to the Issuer

A corporation adds a conversion feature to its bonds or preferred stock to make it more marketable. Other reasons corporations issue convertible securities include the following.

- Convertibles can be sold with a lower coupon rate than nonconvertibles because of the conversion feature.
- A company can eliminate a fixed interest charge as conversion takes place, thus reducing debt.
- Because conversion normally occurs over time, it does not have an adverse effect on the stock price (as may occur after a subsequent primary offering).
- By issuing convertibles rather than common stock, a corporation avoids immediate dilution of primary earnings per share.
- At issuance, conversion price is higher than market price of the common stock.

Disadvantages of Convertible Securities to the Issuer

On the other hand, convertibles have potential disadvantages for a corporation and its stockholders:

- When bonds are converted, shareholders' equity is diluted; that is, more shares are outstanding, so each share now represents a smaller fraction of ownership in the company.
- Common stockholders have a voice in the company's management, so a substantial conversion could cause a shift in the control of the company.
- Reducing corporate debt through conversion means a loss of leverage.
- The resulting decrease in deductible interest costs raises the corporation's taxable income; therefore, the corporation pays increased taxes as conversion takes place.

The Market for Convertible Securities

Convertible bonds offer the safety of the fixed-income market and the potential appreciation of the equity market, providing investors with several advantages.

- As a debt security, a **convertible debenture** pays interest at a fixed rate and is redeemable for its face value at maturity, provided the debenture is not converted. As a rule, interest income is higher and surer than dividend income on the underlying common stock. Similarly, convertible preferred stock usually pays a higher dividend than does common stock.
- If a corporation experiences financial difficulties, convertible bondholders have priority over common stockholders in the event of a corporate liquidation.

- In theory, a convertible debenture's market price tends to be more stable during market declines than the underlying common stock's price. Current yields of other competitive debt securities support the debenture's value in the marketplace.
- Because convertibles can be exchanged for common stock, their market price tends to move upward if the stock price moves up.
- Conversion of a senior security into common stock is not considered a purchase and a sale for tax purposes. Thus, the investor incurs no tax liability on the conversion transaction.
- Stable interest rates tend to result in a stable bond market. When rates are stable, the most volatile bonds tend to be those with a conversion feature because of their link to the underlying common stock. Therefore, in a stable rate environment, a convertible bond can be volatile if the underlying stock is volatile.

Conversion Price and Conversion Ratio

The **conversion price** is the stock price at which a convertible bond can be exchanged for shares of common stock. The **conversion ratio**, also called **conversion rate**, expresses the number of shares of stock a bond may be converted into.

✓ *For Example:* A bond with a conversion price of $40 has a conversion ratio of 25-to-1 ($1,000 / $40 = 25).

Conversion terms are stated in the indenture agreement, either as a conversion ratio or as a conversion price.

✓ *Take Note:* Although the conversion ratio of a bond is always stated on the bond certificate and the investor's confirmation, it is not stated directly in the number of shares, but in terms of the price at which a conversion can occur.

✓ *For Example:* If a bond has a conversion price of $40 per share, you can determine that an investor is entitled to convert it into 25 shares. Always start with the par value of the instrument: par of $1,000 divided by conversion price of $40 results in a conversion ratio of 25 shares.

The same concept applies to convertible preferred stock. An investor bought a share of preferred that converts at $20. By starting with an assumed par of $100, you can derive that the investor is entitled to five shares of common. $100 / the conversion price of $20 = conversion ratio of 5 shares.

Stock Splits and Dividends

Conversion prices are adjusted if stock splits and stock dividends are declared on the underlying common stock during the life of the bond.

Mergers, Consolidations, and Dissolutions

If the corporation ceases to exist because of any of these situations, convertible bondholders may lose their conversion privileges.

Calculating Conversion Parity

Parity means that two securities are of equal dollar value (in this case a convertible bond and the common stock into which it can be converted).

✓ **For Example:** If a corporation issues a bond convertible at $50, the conversion ratio is 20-to-1. If a bond selling for 104 ($1,040) is convertible into 20 shares of common, the common stock price would have to be $52 to be at parity with, or equal to, the convertible bond price ($1,040 / 20 = 52). If the common stock is selling below 52, the convertible bond is worth more than the stock. If the stock is selling above 52, the investor can make more money by acquiring the bond, converting to common and selling the shares.

The following formulas calculate the parity prices of convertible securities and their underlying common shares:

$$\frac{\text{Market price of the bond}}{\text{Conversion ratio (\# of shares)}} = \text{Parity price of common stock}$$

Market price of common × conversion ratio = parity price of convertible

Test Topic Alert!

On the Series 7 exam, there will most likely be questions on parity. Here are two methods to help you solve the problem:

RST bond is convertible to common at $50. If RST bond is currently trading for $1,200, what is the parity price of the common?

Method One: Parity means equal. Solve for the conversion ratio as follows:

Par value:	$1,000
Conversion price:	$ 50
Conversion ratio:	20

The parity stock price is found by dividing $1,200 by 20. The parity price of the common is $60.

Method Two: If you prefer to think in percentages, identify that the new bond price of $1,200 is 20% greater than the original $1,000 price. To be at equivalence, the stock price must also increase by 20%. So add 20% to 50 and the problem is solved. 20% of 50 is 10; 10 + 50 = parity price of $60.

Here is another style of parity question:

RST bond is convertible to common at $50. If the common is trading for $45, what is the parity price of the bond? Start by solving for the conversion ratio.

Par value:	$1,000
Conversion price:	$ 50
Conversion ratio	20

The bond price is found by multiplying 20 × 45. The parity price of the bond is $900. Using the percentage method, you can determine that the market price of the common stock is 10% below that of the conversion price (5 / 50 = 10%). Reducing the bond price of $1,000 by 10% results in a parity price of the bond of $900.

In a **rising** market, the convertible's value rises with the common stock's value. In a **declining** market, the convertible's market price tends to level off when its yield becomes competitive with the yield on nonconvertible bonds, and it may not decline in price as much as the common stock. Convertible bonds normally sell at a premium above parity, which is why they are not constantly exchanged for common stock when the stock price is rising.

Anti-Dilution Covenant

Dilution of an investor's ownership interest occurs when the percentage of ownership is lessened. Convertible bondholders are protected by an **anti-dilution covenant** found in the trust indenture. This covenant requires an adjustment to the conversion price for stock splits, stock dividends and the issuance of new shares.

✓ **For Example:** A convertible bond has a conversion price of $25. The investor is currently entitled to 40 shares. If the issuer declares a stock dividend of 25%, the convertible bondholder's 40 shares are adjusted to 50 shares (40 × 1.25 = 50). The conversion price is adjusted to $20 as a result (25 / 1.25).

✓ **For Example:** A convertible bond is issued with a conversion price of $40. If the issuer declares and pays a 10% stock dividend, what is the new conversion price? Before the stock dividend is declared and paid, the customer would receive 25 common shares ($1000 / $40). With the stock dividend paid, the customer would need to receive 10% more shares, or 27.5 shares to stay even. Dividing $1000 by 27.5 equals 36.36, the new conversion price. Alternatively, divide the existing conversion price of $40 by 110%, which equals 36.36. To make sure this is correct, you can divide the new conversion price into $1000 to see how many shares the customer will now receive if the bond is converted: $1000 divided by 36.36 equals 27.5 shares.

Forced Conversion

A **forced conversion** occurs when an issuer calls its convertible bonds and it is clearly in the best interest of bondholders to convert their bonds rather than let them be called away.

✓ **For Example:** XYZ Corp. has 7% callable convertible debentures outstanding currently trading at 113. The conversion price is $25 and the bonds are callable at 104. The price of XYZ common stock is $28. If XYZ announces a call, a bondholder has three options:

- tender bonds to the call receiving $1,040;
- sell the bonds in the open market receiving $1,130; or
- convert the bonds and sell the stock receiving $1,120.

Given these choices, selling the bonds on the open market would appear to be the most advantageous choice. However, as soon as the call is announced, the price of the bond will move quickly to the conversion value of $1,120. As a result of announcing the call, the issuer has forced bondholders to either convert or sell the bonds.

Quick Quiz 2.4

Match each of the following terms with the appropriate description below.

A. Zero-coupon bonds
B. Parity
C. Guaranteed bonds
D. Subordinated debenture

___ 1. Claims are junior to those of other creditors

___ 2. Party other than the issuing corporation promises to maintain payments of principal and interest

___ 3. Dollar amount at which a convertible security is equal in value to its corresponding stock

___ 4. Investor receives Form 1099 and reports interest for tax purposes even though no interest income has been received

Answers   1. D.   2. C.   3. B.   4. A.

Quick Quiz 2.5

Match each of the following items with the appropriate description below.

A. Collateral trust bond
B. Income bond
C. Mortgage bond
D. Convertible bond

___ 1. Debt obligation secured as a property pledge

___ 2. Debenture that can be exchanged for common stock at specified prices or rates

___ 3. Secured bond backed by stocks or bonds of another issuer

___ 4. Interest payment must be declared by issuer's board of directors

Answers   1. **C.**   2. **D.**   3. **A.**   4. **B.**

Quick Quiz 2.6

Multiple Choice

1. A trust indenture spells out the covenants between

    A. trustee and underwriter
    B. issuer and underwriter
    C. issuer and bondholders
    D. issuer and a trustee for the benefit of a bondholder

2. ABC, Inc. has filed for bankruptcy. Interested parties will be paid off in which order?

    I. Holders of secured debt
    II. Holders of subordinated debentures
    III. General creditors
    IV. Preferred stockholders

    A. I, III, II, IV
    B. III, I, II, IV
    C. I, II, III, IV
    D. IV, I, II, III

3. Moody's Bond Page lists the following: GMAC ZR '12 54-¼ Ogden 5s '08. The annual interest on 50 Ogden bonds is

   A. $93
   B. $500
   C. $930
   D. $2,500

4. Which of the following statements regarding convertible and callable bonds are TRUE?

   I. If called, the owners have the option of retaining the bonds and will continue to receive interest.
   II. After the date it is called, interest will cease to be paid.
   III. Upon conversion, there will be dilution.
   IV. The coupon rate would be less than the rate for a nonconvertible bond.

   A. I and III only
   B. I, III, and IV only
   C. II, III, and IV only
   D. II and IV only

5. Which of the following statements regarding convertible bonds is NOT true?

   A. Coupon rates are usually higher than nonconvertible bond rates of the same issuer.
   B. Convertible bondholders are creditors of the corporation.
   C. Coupon rates are usually lower than nonconvertible bond rates of the same issuer.
   D. If the underlying common stock should decline to the point where there is no advantage to convert the bonds into common stock, the bonds will sell at a price based on their inherent value as bonds, regardless of the convertible feature.

6. A bond is convertible to common stock at $20 per share. If the market value of the bond falls to $800, what is the new parity price of the stock?

   A. $12
   B. $16
   C. $25
   D. $40

7. A convertible bond is purchased at its face value and convertible at $125. What is the conversion ratio?

   A. 2
   B. 8
   C. 12
   D. 20

Answers

1. **D.** *The trust indenture is a contract between the issuer and a trustee for the benefit of a bondholder. It spells out the covenants to be honored by the issuer and gives the trustee the power to monitor compliance with the covenants and the ability to take action on behalf of the bondholder(s) if a default of the covenants is found.*

2. **A.** *The order in a liquidation is as follows: IRS (and other government agencies), secured debt holders, unsecured debt holders, general creditors (in most cases, unsecured debt holders are given a slight priority over all but the largest creditors), holders of subordinated debt, preferred stockholders, and common stockholders.*

3. **D.** *Ogden 5s means 5% bonds. 5% of $1,000 par equals $50 interest per bond annually. For 50 bonds, the annual interest is $2,500.*

4. **C.** *When a bond is called and the owner does not redeem, the interest payments cease. Conversion causes dilution, and generally interest rates on convertible bonds are less than straight debt issues.*

5. **A.** *Coupon rates are not higher; they are lower because of the value of the conversion feature. The bondholders are creditors, and if the stock price falls, the conversion feature will not influence the bond's price.*

6. **B.** *The calculations are: $1,000 / $20 = 50 shares for one bond. $800 bond price ÷ 50 shares = $16 parity price.*

7. **B.** *$1,000 par / $125 conversion price = 8 shares per bond.*

US Government & Agency Securities

The US Treasury Department determines the quantity and types of government securities it must issue to meet federal budget needs. The marketplace determines the interest rates those securities will pay. In general, the interest government securities pay is exempt from state and municipal taxation, but subject to federal taxation.

The federal government is the nation's largest borrower as well as the best credit risk. Securities issued by the US government are backed by its full faith and credit, based on its power to tax.

Most government securities are issued in **book-entry form**, meaning no physical certificates exist.

Marketable Government Securities

Treasury securities are classified as **bills**, **notes**, and **bonds** to distinguish an issue's term to maturity.

Treasury Bills (T-bills)

T-bills are short-term obligations issued at a discount from par. Rather than making regular cash interest payments, bills trade at a discount from par value; the return on a T-bill is the difference between the price the investor pays and the par value at which the bill matures.

Maturities and Denominations

Treasury bills are issued in denominations of $1,000 to $1 million and have original maturities of 4, 13, and 26 weeks.

Pricing

T-bills are quoted on a yield basis and sold at a discount from par. They are zero-coupon securities.

✓ *For Example:*

Issue	Bid	Ask
T-bills maturing 03/15/03	1.15	1.12

The bid reflects the yield buyers want to receive. The ask reflects the yield sellers are willing to accept.

✓ *Take Note:* The exam will not require you to calculate the bid and ask prices of T-bills.

Because T-bills are quoted in yield, a T-bill quote has a bid higher than its asked, which is the reverse of bid-ask relationships for other instruments. Higher yield on the bid side translates into a lower dollar price.

Treasury Notes (T-notes)

Unlike Treasury bills, **T-notes** pay interest every six months. They are sold at auction every four weeks.

Maturities and Denominations

Issued in denominations of $1,000 to $1 million, T-notes are intermediate-term bonds maturing in 2 to 10 years. T-notes mature at par, or they can be **refunded**. If a T-note is refunded, the government offers the investor a new security with a new interest rate and maturity date as an alternative to a cash payment for the maturing note.

Pricing

T-notes are issued, quoted and traded as a percent of par in 1/32s.

✓ **For Example:** A quote of 98.24, which can also be expressed as 98-24 or 98:24, on a $1,000 note means that the note is selling for 98-24/32% of its $1,000 par value. In this instance, .24 designates 24/32 of 1%, not a decimal. A quote of 98.24 equals 98.75% of $1,000, or $987.50.

Pricing of T Notes

A bid of...	Means...	Or...
98.01	98 1/32% of $1,000	$980.3125
98.02	98 2/32% of $1,000	$980.6250
98.03	98 3/32% of $1,000	$980.9375
98.10	98 10/32% of $1,000	$983.1250
98.11	98 11/32% of $1,000	$983.4375
98.12	98 12/32% of $1,000	$983.7500

Treasury Bonds (T-Bonds) **T-bonds**, which are no longer issued, are long-term securities that pay interest every six months.

Maturities and Denominations

Treasury bonds were issued in denominations of $1,000 to $1 million that matured in more than 10 years from issuance.

Pricing

T-bonds are quoted exactly like T-notes.

✓ **Take Note:** The Treasury Department has not offered a T-bond since its October 2001 decision to suspend issuance of the 30-year bond.

Testable Features of T Bills, Notes, and Bonds

MARKETABLE GOVERNMENT SECURITIES			
Type	**Maturity**	**Pricing**	**Form**
T Bills	4 weeks – 26 weeks	Issued at a discount; priced on discount basis	Book entry
T Notes	2 –10 years (intermediate-term)	Priced at percentage of par	Book entry
T Bonds	10 – 30 years	Priced at percentage of par	Book entry

Treasury Receipts   Brokerage firms can create **Treasury receipts** from US Treasury notes and bonds. Broker/dealers buy Treasury securities, place them in trust at a bank and sell separate receipts against the principal and coupon payments. The Treasury securities held in trust collateralize the Treasury receipts. Unlike Treasury securities, Treasury receipts are not backed by the full faith and credit of the US government.

✓ **For Example:** To illustrate how Treasury receipts are created, think of a $1,000 10-year Treasury note with a 6% coupon as 21 separate payment obligations. The first 20 are the semiannual $30 interest payment obligations until maturity. The 21st is the obligation to repay the $1,000 principal at maturity. An investor may purchase a Treasury receipt for any of the 20 interest payments or the principal repayment.

Each Treasury receipt is priced at a discount from the payment amount, like a zero-coupon bond.

STRIPS

In 1984, the Treasury Department entered the zero-coupon bond market by designating certain Treasury issues as suitable for stripping into interest and principal components. These securities became known as **STRIPS**, which stands for **Separate Trading of Registered Interest and Principal of Securities**. While the securities underlying Treasury STRIPS are the US government's direct obligation, major banks and dealers perform the actual separation and trading.

💡 **Test Topic Alert!**   STRIPS are backed in full by the US government. Receipts are not. Treasury receipts are sold under names like CATS (Certificates of Accrual on Treasury Securities) and TIGRS (Treasury Income Growth Receipts).

Treasury Inflation Protection Securities (TIPS)   A relatively new type of treasury issue, **Treasury Inflation Protection Securities (TIPS)**, helps protect investors against purchasing power risk. These notes are issued with a fixed interest rate, but the principal amount is adjusted semiannually by an amount equal to the change in the **Consumer Price Index (CPI)**, the standard measurement of inflation.

The interest payment the investor receives every six months is equal to the fixed interest amount times the newly adjusted principal. In times of inflation, the interest payments increase, while in times of deflation the interest payments fall. These notes are sold at lower interest rates than conventional fixed rate Treasury notes because of their adjustable nature.

Like other Treasury notes, TIPS are exempt from state and local income taxes on the interest income generated, but are subject to federal taxation. However, in any year when the principal is adjusted for inflation, that increase is considered reportable income for that year even though the increase will not be received until the note matures.

Test Topic Alert!

The Series 7 exam may ask a question similar to the following:

1. A customer wishes to buy a security providing periodic interest payments, safety of principal and protection from purchasing power risk. The customer should purchase

   A. TIPs
   B. TIGRs
   C. CMOs
   D. STRIPs

   Answer: **A**. TIPs offer inflation protection and safety of principal because they are backed by the US government.

Agency Issues

Congress authorizes the following agencies of the federal government to issue debt securities:

- Farm Credit Administration
- Government National Mortgage Association (GNMA or Ginnie Mae)

Other agency-like organizations operated by private corporations include:

- Federal Home Loan Mortgage Corporation (FHLMC or Freddie Mac)
- Federal National Mortgage Association (FNMA or Fannie Mae)
- Student Loan Marketing Association (SLMA or Sallie Mae)

The term *agency* is sometimes used to refer to entities that are not technically government agencies, but that do have ties to the government. Fannie Mae is privately owned but government-sponsored.

Yields and Maturities

Agency issues have higher yields than direct obligations of the federal government, but lower yields than corporate debt securities. Their maturities range from short to long term. Agency issues are quoted as percentages of par and trade actively in the secondary market.

Taxation Government agency issues that are backed by mortgages are taxed at the federal, state, and local levels. Other agency securities (such as Sallie Mae) are taxed at the federal level only.

Government National Mortgage Association (Ginnie Mae) The **Government National Mortgage Association (GNMA)** is a government-owned corporation that supports the Department of Housing and Urban Development. Ginnie Maes are the only agency securities backed by the full faith and credit of the government.

Types of Issues

GNMA buys **Federal Housing Administration (FHA)** and **Department of Veteran Affairs (VA)** mortgages and auctions them to private lenders, which pool the mortgages to create pass-through certificates for sale to investors. Monthly principal and interest payments from the pool of mortgages pass through to investors. Like the principal on a single mortgage, the principal represented by a GNMA certificate constantly decreases as the mortgages are paid down. GNMA pass-throughs pay higher interest rates than comparable Treasury securities, yet are guaranteed by the federal government.

GNMA also guarantees timely payment of interest and principal. GNMAs are backed directly by the government so risk of default is nearly zero. Prices, yields, and maturities fluctuate in line with general interest rate trends. If interest rates fall, homeowners tend to pay off their mortgages early, which accelerates the certificates' maturities. If interest rates rise, certificates may mature more slowly.

GNMAs are issued in minimum denominations of $25,000. Because few mortgages last the full term, yield quotes are based on a 12-year prepayment assumption—that is, a mortgage balance should be prepaid in full after 12 years of normally scheduled payments.

In addition to interest rate risk (the risk that rates rise causing the value of the underlying mortgages to fall), there are two other types of risk associated with mortgage-backed securities. The first is **pre-payment risk**, the risk that the underlying mortgages will be paid off earlier than anticipated. This will occur if interest rates fall, causing homeowners to refinance their mortgages at lower rates.

The second is **extended maturity risk**, the risk that the underlying mortgages will remain outstanding longer than anticipated. This will occur if interest rates rise, virtually eliminating any refinancings.

Taxation

Interest earned on GNMA certificates is taxable at the federal, state, and local levels.

Test Topic Alert! The Series 7 exam expects you to know that mortgage-backed instruments are susceptible to reinvestment risk. The reasons are outlined below.

When interest rates fall, mortgage holders typically refinance at lower rates. This means that they pay off their mortgages early, which causes a prepayment of principal to holders of mortgage-backed securities. The early principal payments cannot be reinvested at a comparable return.

Sometimes the test asks which instruments are not subject to reinvestment risk. Of the ones listed, the best answer to choose is typically a zero-coupon bond. No interest is paid on a current basis, so the investor has no reinvestment risk.

Farm Credit System

The **Farm Credit System** (**FCS**) is a national network of lending institutions that provides agricultural financing and credit. The system is a privately owned, government-sponsored enterprise that raises loanable funds through the sale of Farm Credit Securities to investors. These funds are made available to farmers through a nationwide network of eight banks and 225 Farm Credit lending institutions. The Farm Credit Administration (FCA), a government agency, oversees the system.

The Federal Farm Credit System issues discount notes, bonds, and master notes. The maturities range from one day to 30 years. The proceeds from the sale of securities are used to provide farmers with real estate loans, rural home mortgage loans, and crop insurance. Interest paid on these securities is exempt from state and local taxation.

Federal Home Loan Mortgage Corporation (Freddie Mac)

The **Federal Home Loan Mortgage Corporation** (**FHLMC**) is a public corporation whose stock trades on the NYSE. It was created to promote the development of a nationwide secondary market in mortgages by buying residential mortgages from financial institutions and packaging them into mortgage-backed securities for sale to investors.

Pass-Through Certificates

A pass-through security is created by pooling a group of mortgages and selling certificates representing interests in the pool. The term **pass-through** refers to the mechanism of passing homebuyers' interest and principal payments from the mortgage holder to the investors. Fannie Mae, Ginnie Mae, and Freddie Mac function this way.

FHLMC sells two types of pass-through securities: **mortgage participation certificates** (**PCs**) and **guaranteed mortgage certificates** (**GMCs**). PCs make principal and interest payments once a month; GMCs make interest payments twice a year and principal payments once a year.

Taxation

Income from FHLMC securities is subject to federal, state, and local income taxes.

Federal National Mortgage Association (Fannie Mae)

The **Federal National Mortgage Association (FNMA)** is a publicly held corporation that provides mortgage capital. FNMA purchases conventional and insured mortgages from agencies such as the FHA and the VA. The securities it creates are backed by FNMA's general credit, not by the US government. FNMA stock also trades on the NYSE.

Types of Issues

FNMA issues debentures, short-term discount notes, and mortgage-backed securities. The notes are issued in denominations of $5,000, $25,000, $100,000, $500,000, and $1 million. Debentures with maturities from three to 25 years are issued in minimum denominations of $10,000 in increments of $5,000. Interest is paid semiannually. They are issued in book-entry form only.

Taxation

Interest from FNMA securities is taxed at the federal, state, and local levels.

Test Topic Alert!

GNMAs are backed in full by the US government; other agency instruments are not—they are backed by their own issuing authority.

GNMA features are heavily tested. Know the following features.

- $25,000 minimums
- Monthly interest and principal payments
- Taxed at all levels
- Pass-through certificates
- Significant reinvestment risk

Sallie Mae

The **Student Loan Marketing Association (Sallie Mae)** issues discount notes and short-term floating rare notes. The floaters have six-month maturities. The proceeds from the securities sales are used to provide student loans for higher education. Interest paid on Sallie Mae securities is exempt from state and local taxation.

Quick Quiz 2.7

Match each of the following items with the appropriate description below.

A. Treasury bill
B. Treasury receipt
C. GNMA
D. Separate Trading of Registered Interest and Principal of Securities (STRIPS)

___ 1. Zero-coupon bond issued and backed by the Treasury Department

___ 2. Marketable US government debt with a maturity of 6 months or less

___ 3. Zero-coupon bond issued by investment bankers

___ 4. Government agency that issues mortgage-backed securities

Answers   1. **D.**   2. **A.**   3. **B.**   4. **C.**

Quick Quiz 2.8

Match each of the following terms with the appropriate description below.

A. Farm Credit System
B. Federal National Mortgage Association (FNMA)
C. GNMA Pass-Through Certificate
D. Treasury Receipt

___ 1. Government-sponsored corporation that purchases conventional mortgages and government agency mortgages

___ 2. Privately owned banks that provide credit and mortgage services to farmers

___ 3. Zero-coupon bond issued by a brokerage firm and collateralized by Treasury securities

___ 4. Security representing an interest in a pool of mortgages guaranteed by the full faith and credit of the US government

Answers   1. **B.**   2. **A.**   3. **D.**   4. **C.**

Quick Quiz 2.9 — Multiple Choice

1. Which of the following statements regarding T-bills are TRUE?

    I. T-bills trade at a discount to par.
    II. T-bills have six months or less to maturity.
    III. Most T-bill issues are callable.
    IV. T-bills are a direct obligation of the US government.

    A. I and II only
    B. I, II, and III only
    C. I, II, and IV only
    D. I, II, III and IV

2. You buy 10 8% T-notes at 101–16. What is the dollar amount of this purchase?

    A. $1,001.50
    B. $1,011.60
    C. $10,150.00
    D. $10,812.00

3. Which of the following statements regarding US government agency obligations are TRUE?

    I. They are all direct obligations of the US government.
    II. They generally have higher yields than yields of treasury securities.
    III. The FNMA is a publicly traded corporation.
    IV. Securities issued by GNMA trade on the NYSE floor.

    A. I and II
    B. I and III
    C. II and III
    D. II and IV

Answers

1. **C.** T-bills trade at a discount to par, are six months or less to maturity, and are a direct obligation of the US government. T-bills are noncallable.

2. **C.** Government notes and bonds are quoted in 1/32nds. Therefore, a quote of 101–16 means 101-16/32nds. To find the price of one of the bonds, multiply the price by 10 points: 101.5 × 10 = $1,015; $1,015 × 10 bonds = $10,150.

3. **C.** US government agency debt is an obligation of the issuing agency. This causes agency debt to trade at higher yields reflecting this greater risk. FNMA was created as a government agency but was spun off in 1968 and is now an NYSE-listed corporation. GNMA pass-through certificates trade OTC.

Issuance of Government Securities

Like municipal securities, US government securities are exempt securities which means they are exempt from the registration provisions of the Act of 1933. Treasury bills and Treasury notes are sold through an auction conducted on behalf of the US Treasury by the Federal Reserve.

In Treasury auctions, there are two types of bids that can be placed: competitive and non-competitive. **Competitive bids** are those placed by primary dealers in US government securities. There are over 20 banks and broker/dealers which have been designated as primary dealers by the Federal Reserve. Examples include HSBC, J.P. Morgan, Citigroup, and Banc One. These primary dealers are the largest banks and brokerage firms. Primary dealers are required to bid at Treasury auctions.

Non-competitive bids are placed by other market participants: smaller banks and broker/dealers, insurance companies, and individuals. Non-competitive bids are always filled, but the price these bidders pay is the lowest accepted competitive bid called the **stop out price**.

Competitive bids are made in yield, not dollar, price.

✓ *For Example:* The Treasury is planning to auction $25 billion of 10-year notes. By noon on the day of the auction, the Fed has received $5 billion in non-competitive bids. This leaves $20 billion to be auctioned to the primary dealers. By 1:00 pm, the Fed receives $30 billion in competitive bids as follows:

Dealer	Dollar Amount	Bid (Yield)
#1	$4 billion	3.98
#2	$5 billion	3.99
#3	$3 billion	4.00
#4	$5 billion	4.02
#5	$3 billion	4.03
#6	$4 billion	4.05
#7	$6 billion	4.06

The highest bid (lowest yield) is accepted first and on down the line until $20 billion has been accepted. The lowest accepted bid (4.03) is the stop out price; the price that all bidders will pay, both competitive and non-competitive. This type of auction is called a **dutch auction**. Note that some bidders will pay less than they bid. Also note that the bids of Dealers #6 and #7 were not filled.

✓ *Take Note:* Non-competitive bids are always filled; competitive bids are not always filled.

Settlement of winning bids takes place on Thursday of that week for T-bills and the Thursday of the following week for T-notes.

US government agency securities, on the other hand, are issued through underwriting groups who buy the securities directly from the agency, at par less a spread, and are sold to the public at par.

Accrued Interest Calculations

Most bonds trade "and interest," meaning a buyer pays a seller a bond's market price, plus any accrued interest since the last interest payment. The buyer receives the full amount of the next interest payment, including interest that accrued while the seller owned the bond.

Most bonds pay interest every six months on either the 1st or the 15th of the specified months. The payment dates are known as **coupon dates**. Accrued interest affects bond transactions when settlement occurs between coupon dates. Some examples of coupon dates follow.

If the interest dates are:	The bonds are known as:
January 1 and July 1	J&J bonds
February 15 and August 15	F&A 15 bonds
March 1 and September 1	M&S bonds
April 1 and October 1	A&O bonds
May 15 and November 15	M&N 15 bonds
June 15 and December 15	J&D 15 bonds

Accrued Interest and the Dated Date

For a new bond issue, the date from which interest accrual begins is called the **dated date**. Even if a bond is issued at a later date, the bond starts accruing interest on the date designated as the dated date.

✓ *Take Note:* The accrued interest amount is calculated to add to the price that the buyer pays and the seller receives when the bond trades between its coupon payment dates. Assume a bond with interest payments on January 1 and July 1. If a trade is made in April, the seller is entitled to some of the July interest payment. Specifically, the seller will receive interest up to, but not including, the settlement date of the transaction as shown here:

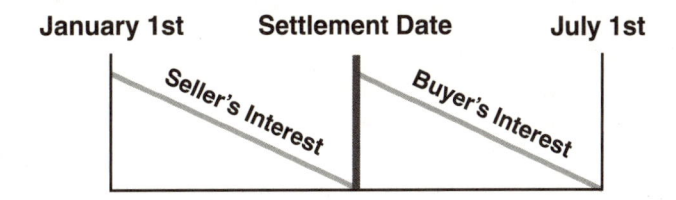

January 1st   Settlement Date   July 1st

Seller's Interest   *Buyer's Interest*

Corporate and Municipal Bonds

Unless the settlement date on a bond transaction coincides with the bond's most current interest payment date (only two days per year), the bond cost to the buyer and the proceeds to the seller include accrued interest. Accrued interest increases the bond cost to the buyer and the proceeds to the seller.

Accrued interest is calculated from the last interest payment date up to, but not including, the settlement date. The buyer owns the bond on the settlement date, which means that the interest for that day belongs to the buyer.

Accrued Interest Calculations Two methods are used to calculate accrued interest. The 30-day-month (360-day-year) method is used on all corporate and municipal bonds. The actual-calendar-days (365-day-year) method is used on all US government bonds.

Accrued Interest Calculation: 360-Day-Year

Accrued interest on corporate and municipal bonds is calculated for a 360-day-year of 30-day months.

Principal × Interest rate × Elapsed days / 360 days = Accrued bond interest

✓ **For Example:** If an F&A municipal bond is traded regular way on Monday, March 5, the number of days of accrued interest is calculated as follows:

February	30 days
March 5 trade	7 days (settles March 8)
Days of accrued interest	37 days

Because the trade settles on March 8, seven days of interest accrue for March.

Debt Securities

If an A&O corporate or municipal bond is bought or sold in a cash trade on August 16, the number of days of accrued interest is calculated as follows:

April	30 days
May	30 days
June	30 days
July	30 days
August	15 days (day before trade date)
Days of accrued interest	135 days

Accrued Interest Calculation: 365-Day-Year

For calculating time elapsed since the most recent interest payment on a government bond, an actual-days-elapsed method is used instead of the 30-day-month, 360-day-year method used for corporate and municipal bonds.

✓ **For Example:** If an F&A government bond is traded regular way on Monday, March 5, the number of days of accrued interest would be calculated as follows:

February	28 days
March	5 days
Days of accrued interest	33 days (up to but not including the March 6 settlement date)

If an A&O government bond is traded for cash on August 16, the number of days of accrued interest would be calculated as follows:

April	30 days
May	31 days
June	30 days
July	31 days
August	15 days
Days of accrued interest	137 days (actual days elapsed)

Accrued Interest Calculations

Summary of Accrued Interest Calculations

	Corporate or Municipal Bonds	U.S. Government Bonds
Regular way settlement	Third business day from trade date	Next business day after trade date
Monthly interest days	30-day months (including February)	Actual calendar days per month
Accrued interest meter starts	Last interest payment date is DAY ONE for accrued interest purposes	Same
Accrued interest meter stops	Bond interest accrues up to, but does not include, settlement date	Same

Test Topic Alert!

An ABC J&J 15 8s of '09 is purchased on Monday, April 15, in a regular way transaction. How many days of accrued interest are owed to the seller?

You must determine that ABC is a corporate bond (three letter names are corporate instruments) that pays interest on January 15 and July 15. To set up the calculation, first determine the settlement date. Then count the number of days up to, but not including the settlement date, to determine the accrued interest owed to the seller.

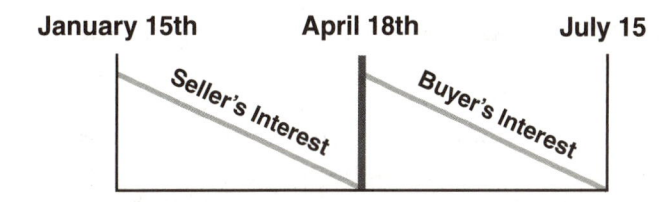

January 15th — April 18th — July 15
Seller's Interest | Buyer's Interest

The seller receives interest through April 17. The number of days are calculated based on a corporate month of 30 days as follows:

- January: 16 days (You must *include* the 15th, which makes 16 days.)
- February: 30 days
- March: 30 days
- April: 17 days

The total is 93 days of accrued interest payable to the seller.

If you were asked to calculate the dollar amount of interest, take the number of days divided by 360 × the coupon amount. 93 / 360 = .2583 × $80 = $20.67.

94 Debt Securities

The Series 7 exam is probably more likely to ask the number of days rather than the dollar amount on accrued interest calculations.

Let's change the situation slightly. Assume a US Treasury bond, J&J 15 8s of '09 is purchased on Monday, April 15, in a regular way transaction. How many days of accrued interest are owed to the seller?

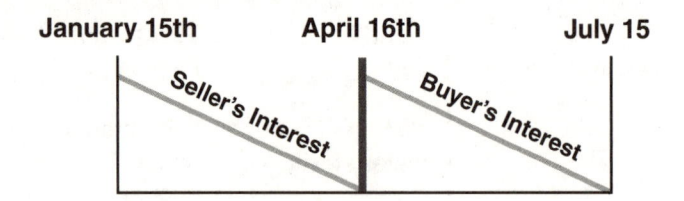

```
January 15th          April 16th          July 15
       \                    |\                 
        \ Seller's           | \ Buyer's       
         \ Interest          |  \ Interest     
```

This calculation involves the settlement rule of T+1 and actual day months.

- January: 17 days (You must include the 15th, which makes 17 days.)
- February: 28 days (Always assume no leap years)
- March: 31 days
- April: 15 days

The total is 91 days of accrued interest payable to the seller.

Read the questions carefully so that all significant details are included in your accrued interest calculations. You are likely to see a concept and a calculation question about accrued interest.

Collateralized Mortgage Obligations (CMOs)

CMOs are mortgage-backed securities like the pass-through obligations that Ginnie Mae and Fannie Mae issue. CMOs pool a large number of mortgages, usually on single-family residences. A pool of mortgages is structured into maturity classes called **tranches**. CMOs are issued by private sector financing corporations and are often backed by Ginnie Mae, Fannie Mae, and Freddie Mac pass-through securities. As a result, these CMOs are rated AAA.

A CMO pays principal and interest from the mortgage pool monthly; however, it repays principal to only one tranche at a time. In addition to interest payments, investors in a short-term tranche must receive all of their principal before the next tranche begins to receive principal repayments. Principal payments are made in $1,000 increments to randomly selected bonds within a tranche. Changes in interest rates affect the rate of mortgage prepayments, and this, in turn, affects the flow of interest payment and principal repayment to the CMO investor.

✓ **Take Note:** This type of CMO, also referred to as a **plain vanilla CMO**, pays interest on all tranches simultaneously. However, it only pays principal to one tranche at a time until it is retired. Subsequent principal payments are made to the next tranche in line until it is paid off, and so on.

A CMO's yield and maturity are estimates based on historical data or projections of mortgage prepayments from the **Public Securities Association (PSA)**. The particular tranche an investor owns determines the priority of his principal repayment. The time to maturity, amount of interest received, and amount of principal returned are not guaranteed.

Sample CMO Tranche Structure

Tranche	Interest Rate	Estimated Life in Years
1	5.125%	1.5
2	5.25%	3.5
3	5.5%	6.0
4	5.875%	8.5
5	6.125%	11.0

Classes of CMOs In addition to the standard CMOs discussed, some CMOs have been structured to suit specific needs of investors. Common CMO types include:

- principal-only;
- interest-only;
- planned amortization class; and
- targeted amortization class.

Principal-Only CMOs (POs)

The flow of income from underlying mortgages is divided into principal and interest streams and directed to the owners of **principal-only CMOs (POs)** and **interest-only CMOs (IOs)**, respectively. For a PO, the income stream comes from principal payments on the underlying mortgages—both scheduled mortgage principal payments and prepayments. Thus, the security ultimately repays its entire face value to the investor.

A PO sells at a discount from par; the difference between the discounted price and the principal value is the investor's return. Its market value, like all deeply discounted securities, tends to be volatile. POs, in particular, are affected by fluctuations in prepayment rates. The value of a PO rises as interest rates drop and prepayments accelerate, and its value falls when interest rates rise and prepayments decline.

Interest-Only CMOs (IOs)

IOs are by-products of POs. Whereas POs receive the principal stream from underlying mortgages, IOs receive the interest. An IO also sells at a discount, and its cash flow declines over time, just as the proportion of interest in a mortgage payment declines over time. Unlike POs, IOs increase in value when interest rates rise and decline in value when interest rates fall because the number of interest payments changes as prepayment rates change. Thus, they can be used to hedge a portfolio against interest rate risk.

When prepayment rates are high, the owner of an IO may receive fewer interest payments than anticipated. Because the entire CMO series receives more principal sooner and, therefore, less overall interest, the IO owner does not know how long the stream of interest payments will last.

Planned Amortization Class CMOs (PACs)

PACs have targeted maturity dates; they are retired first and offer protection from **prepayment** risk and **extension** risk (the chance that principal payments will be slower than anticipated) because changes in prepayments are transferred to companion tranches, also called support tranches.

Targeted Amortization Class CMOs (TACs)

A TAC structure transfers prepayment risk only to companion tranches and does not offer protection from extension risk. TAC investors accept the extension risk and the resulting greater price risk in exchange for a slightly higher interest rate.

Zero-Tranche CMO (Z-Tranche)

A Z-Tranche receives no payment until all preceding CMO tranches are retired (the most volatile CMO tranches).

CMO Characteristics Because mortgages back CMOs, they are considered relatively safe. However, their susceptibility to interest rate movements and the resulting changes in the mortgage repayment rate mean CMOs carry several risks.

- The rate of principal repayment varies.
- If interest rates fall and homeowner refinancing increases, principal is received sooner than anticipated (prepayment risk).
- If interest rates rise and refinancing declines, the CMO investor may have to hold his investment longer than anticipated (extended maturity risk).

Accrued Interest Calculations

Yields

CMOs yield more than Treasury securities and normally pay investors interest and principal monthly. Principal repayments are made in $1,000 increments to investors in one tranche before any principal is repaid to the next tranche.

Taxation

Interest from CMOs is subject to federal, state, and local taxes.

Liquidity

There is an active secondary market for CMOs. However, the market for CMOs with more complex characteristics may be limited or nonexistent. Certain tranches of a given CMO may be riskier than others and some CMOs in certain tranches carry the risk that repayment of principal may take longer than anticipated.

Denominations

CMOs are issued in $1,000 denominations.

Suitability

Some varieties of CMOs, such as PAC companion tranches, may be particularly unsuitable for small or unsophisticated investors because of their complexity and risks. The customer is required to sign a **suitability statement** before buying any CMO. Potential investors must understand that the rate of return on CMOs may vary due to early repayment. Also note that the performance of CMOs may not be compared to any other investment vehicle.

Test Topic Alert! Expect to see about three test questions on CMOs.

- CMOs are not backed by the US government—they are corporate instruments.
- Interest paid is taxable at all levels.
- CMOs are backed by mortgage pools.
- CMOs yield more than US Treasury securities.
- CMOs are considered relatively safe, but are subject to interest rate risks.
- CMOs are issued in $1,000 denominations and trade OTC.
- PACs have reduced prepayment and extension risk.
- TACs are protected against prepayment risk, but not extension risk.

Non-Marketable US Government Securities The US Treasury issues non-marketable securities in the form of savings bonds. These bonds are non-marketable because no secondary market exists. Buying and selling these bonds is affected directly between the investor and agents of the US Treasury such as commercial banks.

Series EE Bonds

Series EE bonds are issued at 50% of their face value and reach final maturity 30 years from issuance. Interest is paid semi-annually and added to the current value of the bond. They are designed to reach face value in approximately 17 years although an investor can hold them for up to 30 years and continue to accrue interest. The rate of interest is recomputed every six months at 90% of the average five-year Treasury yield for the preceding six months.

Interest is taxable at the federal level only. Investors can elect to defer taxation until the bond ceases to pay interest (30 years after issuance) or until it is redeemed. At maturity, investors have the option of exchanging their EE bonds for Series HH bonds.

Series HH Bonds

These bonds can only be obtained in exchange for EE bonds. If an investor has elected to defer taxation of interest on EE bonds, this deferral can continue until the HH bonds mature in 20 years or are redeemed.

HH bonds are issued at face value and pay interest every six months at a fixed rate. they are current income securities; i.e., interest is paid to the bondholder and it is taxable at the federal level in the year received.

Series I Bonds

I bonds are designed for investors seeking to protect the purchasing power of their investment and earn a real rate of return. I bonds are an accrual security—meaning interest is added to the bond monthly and paid when the bond matures or is redeemed. I bonds are sold at face value and they grow in value with inflation-indexed interest for up to 30 years.

The interest on an I bond is a combination of two separate rates; a fixed rate and a variable semi-annual inflation rate. The semi-annual inflation rate is based on changes in the Consumer Price Index.

I bonds increase in value each month and interest is compounded semi-annually. I bonds earn interest for up to 30 years and interest is exempt from state and local taxation. Federal income taxes can be deferred for up to 30 years or until redemption, whichever comes first.

✓ **Take Note:** As long as investors fall within annual income guidelines, the interest income on I bonds as well as that on EE bonds, can be tax free as long as the proceeds from redemption are used to pay tuition and related fees at eligible colleges or universities. This incentive is not available to high income individuals.

Quick Quiz 2.10 Multiple Choice

1. CMOs are backed by

   A. mortgages
   B. real estate
   C. municipal taxes
   D. the full faith and credit of the US government

2. The term tranche is associated with which of the following investments?

   A. FNMA
   B. CMO
   C. GNMA
   D. SLMA

3. Interest received from a CMO investment is taxable at which levels?

   I. Federal
   II. State
   III. Local

   A. I only
   B. II and III only
   C. III only
   D. I, II, and III

4. When selling a CMO to a customer, the registered representative must make which of the following disclosures?

   A. Repayment of principal is guaranteed by the federal government.
   B. Rate of return may vary owing to early repayment.
   C. Minimum investment is $15,000.
   D. Certificate is issued in the name of the beneficial owner.

5. Which of the following debt securities does not have a fixed maturity date?

   A. Collateralized mortgage obligation
   B. General obligation bond
   C. Treasury STRIPS
   D. Subordinated debenture

6. A registered representative may compare the performance of a CMO investment to the performance of a security issued by which of the following agencies?

   A. GNMA
   B. FDIC
   C. SLMA
   D. None of the above

Answers

1. **A.** Collateralized mortgage obligations are collateralized by mortgages on real estate. They do not own the underlying real estate, so they are not considered to be backed by it.

2. **B.** CMOs are a type of mortgage-backed security. A CMO issue is divided into several tranches, which set priorities for payments of principal and interest.

3. **D.** Interest received from CMOs is fully taxable at federal, state, and local levels.

4. **B.** Prepayment risk is one of the important risks associated with CMOs and must be disclosed to prospective investors. All of the other statements are false.

5. **A.** Collateralized mortgage obligations (CMOs) are mortgage-backed securities. Because mortgages are often paid off ahead of the scheduled maturity, the maturity date of a CMO is not certain.

6. **D.** The performance of CMOs may not be compared to any other investment vehicle.

Money Market Securities and Interest Rates

In the financial marketplace, a distinction is made between the **capital market** and the **money market**. The capital market serves as a source of intermediate-term to long-term financing usually in the form of equity or debt securities with maturities of more than one year.

The money market, on the other hand, provides very short-term funds to corporations, banks, broker/dealers, and the US government. Money market securities are debt issues with maturities of one year or less.

The Money Market

Liquidity and Safety Money market instruments are fixed-income securities with short-term maturities—typically one year or less. Money market securities are highly liquid because they are short-term instruments. Money market securities also provide a relatively high degree of safety because they are short-term and have little chance of default.

Money market securities include:

- Treasury bills
- repurchase agreements (repos);
- reverse repurchase agreements;
- bankers' acceptances (time drafts);
- commercial paper (prime paper);
- negotiable certificates of deposit; and
- federal funds.

Money Market Instruments

Repurchase Agreements

In a **repurchase agreement** (**repo**), a financial institution, such as a bank or broker/dealer, raises cash by temporarily selling some of the securities it holds with an agreement to buy back the securities at a later date. Thus, a repo is an agreement between a buyer and a seller to conduct a transaction (sale), then to reverse that transaction (repurchase) in the future.

A repo contract includes both a **repurchase** price and a **maturity date**. If the agreement sets a specific date, the repo is considered a fixed agreement. If the maturity date is left to the initial buyer's discretion, the repo is known as an **open repo** and becomes a demand obligation callable at any time.

Though technically a sale of securities, a repo is similar to a fully collateralized loan. Instead of borrowing money and putting up securities as collateral for the loan, the dealer sells the securities and agrees to buy them back later at a higher price. The interest on the loan is the difference between the sale price and the repurchase price. The loan's interest rate (called the **repo rate**) is negotiated between the two parties and is generally lower than bank loan rates.

If the dealer defaults on the agreement to buy back the securities, the lender can sell the securities in the secondary market. If interest rates have risen sharply causing bond prices to fall, the lender, in selling out, may experience a loss. Therefore, the major risk in a repo, assuming the underlying security has no credit risk (a US government security, for example) is interest rate risk.

Reverse Repurchase Agreements

In a repo, a dealer agrees to sell its securities to a lender and buy them back at a higher price in the future. In a **reverse repurchase agreement** (**reverse repo**), a dealer agrees to buy securities from an investor and sell them back later at a higher price.

Bankers' Acceptances

A **banker's acceptance** (**BA**) is a short-term time draft with a specified payment date drawn on a bank—essentially a postdated check or line of credit. The payment date of a banker's acceptance is normally between 1 and 270 days. American corporations use bankers' acceptances extensively to finance international trade—that is, a banker's acceptance typically pays for goods and services in a foreign country.

A banker's acceptance is a secured money market instrument because the holder has a lien against the trade goods in the event the accepting bank fails. Banks frequently use bankers' acceptances as collateral against **Federal Reserve Bank** (**FRB**) loans. Banker acceptances are sold at a discount and mature at par. They are quoted in yield.

Commercial Paper

Corporations issue short-term, unsecured **commercial paper**, or **promissory notes**, to raise cash to finance accounts receivable and seasonal inventory gluts. Commercial paper interest rates are lower than bank loan rates.

Commercial paper maturities range from 1 to 270 days, although most mature within 90 days, and is normally issued in book entry form. Typically, companies with excellent credit ratings issue commercial paper. The primary buyers of commercial paper are money market funds, commercial banks, pension funds, insurance companies, corporations, and nongovernmental agencies. Commercial paper is sold at a discount and matures at par. It is quoted in yield.

Direct Paper

Direct paper is commercial paper sold by finance companies directly to the public without the use of dealers. General Motors Acceptance Corporation (GMAC) is a well-known issuer. High-quality commercial paper is sometimes called prime paper.

Dealer Paper

Dealer paper is commercial paper sold by issuers through dealers rather than directly to the public.

Tax-Exempt Commercial Paper

Municipal commercial paper is similar to corporate paper, but the municipality usually has acquired a credit line or letter of credit for the issue.

Certificates of Deposit (CDs)

Banks issue and guarantee **CDs** with fixed interest rates and minimum face values of $100,000, although face values of $1 million and up are more common. Some can be traded in the secondary market.

Nonnegotiable CDs

Most investors are familiar with the CD time deposits having set maturities and fixed interest rates and offered by banks and savings and loans. Nonnegotiable CDs are not traded in the secondary market and are not money market securities.

Negotiable CDs

Negotiable CDs are time deposits banks offer. They have minimum face values of $100,000, but most are issued for $1 million or more. A negotiable CD is an unsecured promissory note guaranteed by the issuing bank. Most negotiable CDs mature in one year or less, with the maturity date often set to suit a buyer's needs. CDs can be traded in the secondary market before their maturity because they are negotiable. Accrued interest is included in the price of a negotiable CD.

Interest Rates

The cost of doing business is closely linked to the cost of money; the cost of money is called **interest**. The money supply and inflation levels within the economy determine the level of general interest rates. The level of a specific interest rate can be tied to one or more benchmark rates, such as the federal funds rate, the prime rate, the discount rate, and the broker loan rate.

Federal Funds Rate The **federal funds rate** is the rate the commercial money center banks charge each other for overnight loans of $1 million or more. It is considered a barometer of the direction of short-term interest rates, which fluctuate constantly. The federal funds rate is listed in daily newspapers. It is the most volatile rate in the economy.

Prime Rate The **prime rate** is the interest rate that large US money center commercial banks charge their most creditworthy corporate borrowers for unsecured loans. Each bank sets its own prime rate, with larger banks generally setting a rate other banks use. Banks lower their prime rates when the Federal Reserve Board (FRB or Fed) eases the money supply and raise rates when the Fed contracts the money supply.

Discount Rate The **discount rate** is the rate the Federal Reserve charges for short-term loans to member banks. The discount rate also indicates the direction of FRB monetary policy: a decreasing rate indicates an easing of FRB policy; an increasing rate indicates a tightening of FRB policy.

Broker Loan Rate The **broker loan rate** is the interest rate banks charge broker/dealers on money they borrow to lend to margin account customers. The broker loan rate is also known as the **call loan rate** or **call money rate**. The broker loan rate usually is a percentage point or so above other short-term rates. Broker call loans are callable on 24-hour notice.

Interest Rate Summary Interest rates reflect the cost of money, and therefore, the cost of doing business. The key interest rates people monitor include the following.

- **Federal Funds Rate**—The interest rate charged on reserves traded among member banks for overnight use in amounts of $1 million or

more. The federal funds rate changes daily in response to the borrowing banks' needs. Considered the most volatile rate. The fed funds rate is a market rate of interest. Unlike the discount rate, it is not set by the Federal Reserve. The effective fed funds rate is the daily average of selected money center banks throughout the country.
- **CD Rate**—Bank rate offered on nonnegotiable CDs. Considered the least volatile of the rates listed.
- **Prime Rate**—The base rate on corporate loans at large US money center commercial banks. The prime rate changes when banks react to changes in FRB policy.
- **Discount Rate**—The charge on loans to depository institutions by the Federal Reserve. It is set by the Federal Reserve.
- **Call Money Rate**—The charge on loans to broker/dealers.
- **Commercial Paper**—The rate on commercial paper placed directly by finance companies or the rate on high-grade unsecured notes that major corporations sell through dealers.

Test Topic Alert!

You will see several money market/interest rate questions. These are basically definition questions, so review the significant features of each instrument. Also note that of the four major rates—prime, discount, fed funds, and call loan—the prime rate is the highest and the fed funds rate is the lowest. From high to low, they are ranked as follows: prime rate, call loan rate, discount rate, and fed funds rate.

Quick Quiz 2.11 Multiple Choice

1. All of the following are money market instruments EXCEPT

   A. Treasury bills
   B. municipal notes
   C. commercial paper
   D. newly issued Treasury notes

2. The maximum maturity of commercial paper is how many days?

   A. 90 days
   B. 180 days
   C. 270 days
   D. 360 days

3. Negotiable certificates of deposit

   I. are backed by the issuing bank
   II. are callable
   III. have minimum denominations of $1,000
   IV. can be traded in the secondary market

   A. I, II, and III only
   B. I and IV only
   C. II and III only
   D. I, II, III, and IV

4. Commercial paper is

   A. a secured note issued by a corporation
   B. a guaranteed note issued by a corporation
   C. a promissory note issued by a corporation
   D. none of the above

5. Which of the following money market instruments finances imports and exports?

   A. Eurodollars
   B. Bankers' acceptances
   C. ADRs
   D. Commercial paper

6. A US government bond dealer sells bonds to another dealer with an agreement to buy back the securities in a specified time. This is a(n)

   A. repurchase agreement
   B. reverse repurchase agreement
   C. open market certificate
   D. open market note

7. The federal funds rate is calculated from the

   A. daily average rate charged by the largest money center banks
   B. daily average rate charged by the Federal Reserve
   C. weekly average rate charged by the largest money center banks
   D. weekly average rate charged by the national Federal Reserve member banks

8. Which of the following interest rates is considered the most volatile?

   A. Discount rate
   B. Federal funds rate
   C. Prime rate
   D. Broker call rate

9. Which of the following securities trades with accrued interest?

   A. Negotiable certificates of deposit
   B. Bankers' acceptances
   C. Commercial paper
   D. Treasury bills

Answers

1. **D.** *Newly issued Treasury notes have a minimum maturity of 2 years. Money market instruments have a maximum maturity of 1 year.*

2. **C.** *Commercial paper is normally issued for a maximum period of 270 days.*

3. **B.** *Negotiable certificates of deposit are issued primarily by banks and are backed by the issuing bank. Minimum denomination is $100,000.*

4. **C.** *Commercial paper is a short-term unsecured promissory note issued by a corporation.*

5. **B.** *Bankers' acceptances are used in international trade to finance imports and exports. Eurodollars are not money market instruments.*

6. **A.** *The question defines a repurchase agreement.*

7. **A.** *The federal funds rate reflects the rate charged by member banks lending funds to member banks that need to borrow funds overnight to meet reserve requirements.*

8. **B.** *The federal funds rate is considered the most volatile rate in our economy. It fluctuates on a daily basis.*

9. **A.** *Negotiable CDs are traded with interest. The other securities are issued at a discount and are traded without accrued interest (flat). They are zeros.*

Eurodollars and the Foreign Currency Markets

The cost of raising money and doing business is not restricted by national boundaries. International monetary factors (such as changes in foreign currency exchange rates, Eurodollars, Eurosecurities, and the interbank market) can also affect US money markets and businesses.

Eurodollars **Eurodollars** are US dollars deposited in banks outside the United States; that is, the deposits remain denominated in US dollars rather than the local currency.

> ✓ **For Example:** Euroyen are Japanese yen deposited in banks outside Japan. In other words, when a currency is preceded by the prefix "Euro," it refers to a bank deposit outside of the currency's home country.

Eurodollar time deposits tend to be short term, ranging from overnight to 180 days. European banks lend Eurodollars to other banks in much the same way that US banks lend federal funds. The interest rate is usually based on the **London Interbank Offered Rate (LIBOR)**.

Eurobonds and Eurodollar Bonds

A **Eurobond** is any long-term debt instrument issued and sold outside the country of the currency in which it is denominated. A US dollar-denominated Eurobond (Eurodollar bond) is a bond issued and sold outside the United States, but for which the principal and interest are stated and paid in US dollars. Foreign corporations, foreign governments, domestic corporations, and domestic governments (including municipalities) can issue Eurodollar bonds. The US government does not issue Eurodollar bonds

The Eurobond market is largely unregulated, and investors usually demand a higher return because they enjoy few safeguards. Eurobonds are sometimes used by investors to diversify domestic portfolios.

Test Topic Alert!

Test questions sometimes ask you to contrast Eurobonds and Eurodollar bonds. The name of the instrument tells you how principal and interest is paid. Eurodollar bonds pay in US dollars; Eurobonds pay in foreign currency. Note that these instruments must be issued outside of the United States. Also note that Eurodollar bonds are issued in bearer form.

Interbank Market

The **interbank market** developed as a means of transacting business and trading, lending, and consolidating foreign currency deposits. It is an unregulated, decentralized international market that deals in the various major world currencies. The Federal Reserve buys and sells US dollars in an attempt to influence the dollar's exchange rate in the interbank market.

If the Fed decides that the US dollar is priced too high in the interbank market, it can sell US dollars in the market. As the supply of dollars in the market increases, the price should decrease and the exchange rate should drop. Conversely, if the Fed decides that exchange rates for the US dollar are too low, it can buy dollars in the market.

Two types of trades are: **spot trades**, which settle and are delivered in one or two business days (sometimes referred to as the **cash market** or **spot market**); and forward trades, which settle later than spot, generally months in the future

✓ **Take Note** Spot trades in actively traded currencies settle in one business day while trades of less actively traded currencies settle in 2 business days.

Exchange Rates

An exchange rate is the rate at which one currency can be converted into another. Affected by many factors, exchange rates fluctuate daily. Exchange rates are usually quoted in terms of the currency of the country in which the quote is published.

A currency is **appreciating** if it is rising in value compared to other currencies on the foreign exchange market. A currency is **depreciating** when it falls in value on the foreign exchange market. In this case, it will buy fewer units of another country's currency. A declining US dollar means that US dollars are becoming cheaper for citizens of other countries, and American goods and services are becoming less expensive abroad.

Valuation

The exchange rate between currencies changes, or **floats**, constantly. The devaluation or revaluation in relationship to the currencies of other countries can result from market factors or central bank intervention.

Speculating in Foreign Currencies Foreign currencies provide speculative opportunities for sophisticated investors. Risks of foreign currency speculation include that the interbank market is unregulated and decentralized; and changes in a country's economic, governmental, or social policies could have immediate and dramatic impact on its currency's value.

Quick Quiz 2.12 Multiple Choice

1. A valid reason for investing in Eurobonds would be because Eurobonds

   A. can provide diversification to a portfolio
   B. can be purchased more inexpensively than comparable US bonds
   C. are traded in an unregulated market free from government intervention
   D. can provide an exchange rate hedge against fluctuations in the US dollar

2. An international, unregulated, decentralized market for trading currencies and in which prices are affected by economic policies and conditions is the

   A. Federal Reserve Board
   B. interbank market
   C. London Stock Exchange
   D. International Monetary Fund

3. All of the following are true regarding a Eurodollar deposit EXCEPT that

   A. the interest rate is set by the Federal Reserve Board
   B. the deposit is dollar-denominated but is held in a foreign bank
   C. it carries higher risk than a domestic certificate of deposit
   D. it pays a higher rate of interest than a domestic certificate of deposit

4. What does the abbreviation *LIBOR* stand for?

   A. Limited Industrial Bond Ordinance Regulation
   B. Legal Interest Bond Opinion Rule
   C. London Interbank Offered Rate
   D. Letter of Intent Backdate Order Rule

5. A floating exchange rate for a nation's currency

   A. is set by the nation's central bank
   B. is tied to the current market price of gold
   C. fluctuates based on the values of other currencies
   D. fluctuates based on the London Interbank Offered Rate

Answers

1. **A.** Eurobonds may provide a sophisticated investor with a means of adding diversification to a portfolio. All of the other answers are either untrue statements or represent disadvantages of investing in Eurobonds.

2. **B.** The interbank market system is an international, unregulated, decentralized market involved in trading currencies. As with any market, changes in economic policies and conditions will influence prices.

3. **A.** The FRB has no authority to set interest rates on Eurodollar deposits, dollar-denominated deposits held in banks outside the United States.

4. **C.** LIBOR is the acronym for the London Interbank Offered Rate. The LIBOR is the average of interbank offered rates for dollar deposits in the London market, and it is the basis for many international interest rates.

5. **C.** Most of the world's currencies go up and down in value in relation to one another. The fluctuations are caused by the relationship of supply and demand in the marketplace.

Tracking Debt Securities

Corporate Bonds

Bonds are listed in daily newspapers and other financial publications.

✓ **For Example:** *See AlaP (Alabama Power) in the graphic.*

The description of its 9s 2003 bond indicates that the bond pays 9% interest and matures in the year 2003. Current yield is given as 8.9%, indicating that the bond is selling at a premium.

The **Vol** (volume, or sales) column states how many bonds traded the previous day (day being reported). Eighteen bonds, or $18,000 par value, were traded in AlaP 9s of 2000. The next three columns explain the high, low, and closing prices for the day. For AlaP, the high was 100¾, low was 100⅝ and the bonds closed at (last trade) 100¾.

Net change (last column) refers to how much the bond's closing price was up or down from the previous day's close. Alabama Power 9s of 2003 closed up ¼ of a point, or $2.50. AlaP closed yesterday at 100½ (100¾ – ¼). Note that the Allied Chemical (AlldC) zr bonds have "..." in the current yield column. This indicates that these are zero-coupon bonds that do not pay interest.

Corporate Bond Quotations

New York Exchange Bonds
Quotations as of 4 pm Eastern Time
Friday, July 16, 2002
Corporation Bonds
Volume $45,198,000

Bonds	Cur Yld	Vol	High	Low	Close	Net Chg
AForP 5s 30r	9.6	50	52 1/4	51 7/8	52	+3/4
AbbtL 7 5/8s 09	7.6	21	99 3/4	99 3/4	99 3/4	...
Advst 9s 08	cv	72	103 1/2	103	103	...
AetnLf 8 1/8s 07	8.5	15	95 3/4	95 3/4	95 3/4	–1
AirbF 7 1/2s 11	cv	32	114	112	114	+1
AlaP 9s 2003	8.9	18	100 3/4	100 5/8	100 3/4	+1/4
AlaP 8 1/2s 01	8.6	13	98 3/8	98 3/8	98 3/8	–3/8
AlaP 8 7/8s 03	8.5	65	102 7/8	102 1/2	102 1/2	–3/8
AlldC zr 12	...	10	91 1/2	91 1/8	91 1/2	–1/8
viAmes 7 1/2s 14f	cv	79	15 1/2	14 3/4	15	+1
Ancp 13 7/8s 02f	cv	10	91	89 3/8	91	+2

EXPLANATORY NOTES
Yield is current yield. cld–Called. cv–Convertible bond. dc–Deep discount. f–Dealt in flat. m–Matured bonds, negotiability impaired by maturity. na–No accrual. r–Registered. zr–Zero coupon. vi–In bankruptcy or receivership or being reorganized.

Tracking US Government Securities

Quotes for Treasury bonds, notes, and bills are listed in the graphic. Reading from left to right under "Govt. Bonds & Notes," you can determine the coupon rate, maturity date, bid and asked prices, bid change from the previous trading day, and the yield to maturity.

Treasury Securities Quotations

Treasury Bonds, Notes & Bills
Quotations as of mid-afternoon
Monday, August 1, 1999

Govt. Bonds & Notes

Rate	Maturity Mo/Yr	Bid	Asked	Chg	Ask Yld
7 1/2	Aug 99n	100:02	100:04	....	7.37
7 1/4	Aug 00	100:26	100:30	....	6.30
9 1/2	Oct 02	105:31	106:01	....	7.35
8 1/2	Apr 03	102:18	102:20	+1	7.92
9	May 04	104:24	104:26	....	8.07
3 1/2	Nov 04	94:05	95:05	-1	4.28
13 3/8	Aug 07	134:26	135:02	....	8.19
10 3/4	Feb 09	117:27	118:03	-1	8.28

U.S. Treasury STRIPS

Maturity	Type	Bid	Asked	Chg	Bid Yld
Nov 00	np	78:19	78:22	+1	7.46
Aug 01	ci	73:15	73:18	+1	7.78
Feb 07	ci	45:06	45:10	-2	8.50
Nov 10	bp	32:19	32:23	....	8.62
Feb 11	ci	31:22	31:26	-1	8.67
Nov 15	bp	20:19	20:22	....	8.83
May 21	ci	13:09	13:12	....	8.67
Aug 26	ci	9:11	9:14	....	8.33

EXPLANATORY NOTES

Colons in bid and asked quotes represent 1/32nds. 99:01 means 99 1/32. Net changes are in 1/32nds. n-Treasury note. Treasury bill quotes in hundredths, quoted on terms of a rate of discount. Yields are to maturity or to earliest call date.

U.S. Treasury STRIPS quotes are based on transactions of $1,000,000 or more. Colons represent 1/32nds. Abbreviations: ci-stripped coupon interest. bp-Treasury bond, stripped principal. np-Treasury note, stripped principal.

Treasury Bills

Maturity	Days to Maturity	Bid	Asked	Chg	Ask Yld
Aug 08 99	7	5.54	5.44	-0.05	5.52
Oct 24 99	84	5.55	5.53	-0.02	5.68
Dec 26 99	147	5.60	5.58	....	5.81
Apr 23 00	266	5.82	5.80	....	6.10
May 07 00	280	5.81	5.79	-0.01	6.10

Treasury Bonds and Notes

T-bonds and notes are quoted at percentages of par. The first note shown pays a rate of 7½% and matures in August 1999. (An "n" after the year indicates that the security is a Treasury note; no letter after the year indicates a bond.) The bid and ask prices reflect the most recently reported OTC market prices; the bid change indicates how much the price has changed from the last report. At the current ask, this particular note would yield 7.37%.

Other government and agency issues are quoted in a similar fashion. In the second listing under "Govt. Bonds & Notes," the bonds have a 7½% coupon rate and mature in August 2000. The bid was 100:26 (100 and 26/32); the ask price was 100:30 (100 and 30/32). The bonds have a YTM of 6.30%.

Treasury Bills

Treasury bills are quoted at their annualized discount rates (or yields). The maturity date is given in the first column of the Treasury bills quotation in the graphic. The second column shows the number of days remaining until the bills' maturity. The third column shows the discount rate that results from the bid prices dealers will pay to buy the bills. The fourth column is the ask price. The number reflects the discount from par, and the discount on the ask side is smaller than that on the bid side.

The first bill in the table matures August 8, 1999. It is being offered for sale at par less a discount computed at a rate of 5.44%, to yield 5.52%. On August 8, 1999, the bill is redeemed at par.

Debt Securities HotSheet

Maturities:
- Term: matures at one date in the future
- Serial: matures over period of years; Balloon: large lump payment at end; Series: spread out issue, not a maturity

Investment Grade:
- Baa or BBB and above; based on default risk; ability to pay interest and principal when due

Call Features:
- Called by issuer when interest rates are falling; no interest after call
- Issuer cannot call during call protection period

Interbank Market:
- Establishes rates of exchange for foreign currency; decentralized; unregulated

Bond Yields:

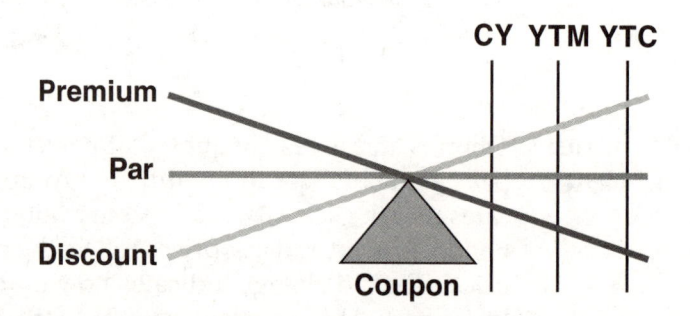

CY YTM YTC

Premium

Par

Discount

Coupon

Refunding:
- Refinancing at a lower rate
- Pre-refunded bonds are Triple A rated, considered defeased, funds escrowed in Treasuries

Corporate Bonds:
- Called *funded debt* if 5 or more years to maturity
- **Secured:** mortgage, collateral trust (backed by securities), equipment trust certificates
- **Unsecured:** backed by full faith and credit, debentures and subordinated debentures

Trust Indenture:
- Covenants between issuer and trustee for the benefit of bondholders

Convertibles:
- Par / conversion price = conversion ratio
- Market price / conversion ratio = parity price of common
- Conversion ratio × common stock price = parity price of bond

Governments:
- Bills quoted at a discount; notes and bonds in 32nds; notes and bonds are callable, bills are not
- Treasury STRIPS are backed in full by the US government

Debt Securities HotSheet

- TIPs provide inflation protection, safety of principal
- Interest is taxed at federal level, exempt from state and local taxation

Agencies:
- Ginnie Maes are backed in full by US government
- Interest fully taxable on mortgage-backed securities

CMOs:
- Corporate instrument with tranches; taxable monthly interest
- PACs protect from prepayment risk
- TACs— no protection from extension risk; subject to interest rate risk

Money Markets:
- Commercial paper: most heavily traded; corporate issue; issued at a discount, 270-day max maturity
- Negotiable CD: minimum face of $100,000, trade with accrued interest
- BAs: time draft, letter of credit for foreign trade; 270-day max maturity

Interest Rates:
- Fed funds rate most volatile, established by market; discount rate set by FRB; short-term rates more volatile than long-term rates

Rate Changes and Bond Prices:
- Long-term bonds react more than bonds to interest rate changes
- Discounts react more than premiums to rate changes
- In comparing two discount bonds, the one with the deeper discount (lower coupon) will react more
- Long-term zeroes react the most to rate changes

Savings Bonds:
- EE bonds issued at 50% of face value; interest is added to value of bond; investors can defer tax until maturity or redemption
- HH bonds issued at face value and pay fixed rate of interest which is taxable in year of receipt; can only be obtained in exchange for EE bonds
- I bonds have a fixed rate of interest plus inflation-adjusted rate; interest is added to the value of bond; taxable on redemption are used to pay tuition etc. at eligible colleges.

TIPS:
- Issued with fixed rate, principal is adjusted for inflation

Insurance of Government Securities:
- T-bills and T-notes are sold at auction
- Competitive bids by primary dealers are not always filled
- Non-competitive bids are always filled
- Competitive bid made in yield
- All winning bids filled at stop out price
- Agency securities sold through underwriting groups

Accrued Interest:
- Corp. and Muni–30/360
- T-notes and T-bonds—actual days
- Prior interest payment date up to but not including SD

Series 7 Unit Test 2

1. A customer buys a 6% T-bond, maturing in 10 years, at a price of 91.07. The YTM is
   A. less than nominal yield
   B. greater than nominal yield
   C. less than current yield
   D. same as current yield

2. Identify the sequence that correctly orders the claim of the obligations below (from first to last) on the assets of a corporation in bankruptcy.
   I. Taxes
   II. Unpaid wages
   III. Preferred stock
   IV. Subordinated debt

   A. I, II, III, IV
   B. II, I, IV, III
   C. III, IV, I, II
   D. IV, III, II, I

3. Debt obligations of which of the following are directly guaranteed by the federal government?
   A. Federal Home Loan Banks
   B. Federal Housing Loan Guarantee Corporation
   C. Federal National Mortgage Association
   D. Government National Mortgage Association

4. Which of the following bonds trade flat?
   A. Revenue bonds
   B. Income bonds
   C. GO bonds
   D. Mortgage bonds

5. Which of the following regarding US government agency obligations are TRUE?
   I. They are direct obligations of the US government.
   II. They generally have higher yields than direct US obligations.
   III. The Federal National Mortgage Association is a publicly traded corporation.
   IV. Securities issued by GNMA trade on the NYSE floor.

   A. I and II
   B. I and III
   C. II and III
   D. II and IV

6. When a customer purchases a new municipal bond, the accrued interest is calculated
   I. from the trade date
   II. from the dated date
   III. up to the interest payment date
   IV. up to, but not including, the settlement date

   A. I and III
   B. I and IV
   C. II and III
   D. II and IV

7. Which of the following mortgage-backed securities would provide investors with the most predictable maturity date?
   A. PACs
   B. TACs
   C. Ginnie Maes
   D. Fannie Maes

8. A corporate bond is quoted at 102⅝. A customer buying 10 bonds would pay
   A. $10,025.80
   B. $10,258.00
   C. $10,262.50
   D. $10,285.00

9. Interest rates have been rising for the past few days which means that the price of bonds traded in the secondary market has

    A. increased
    B. decreased
    C. stayed the same
    D. Bond prices are not affected by interest rates.

10. A client acquires a newly-issued $1,000 par, 5% convertible corporate bond convertible into common at $40 per share. The common stock increases 20% from initial parity due to a hopeful earnings projection. What is the parity price of the bond after the rise in the common stock's price?

    A. $800
    B. $1,000
    C. $1,200
    D. $1,250

11. A 10-year bond, callable in five years at par, is sold at a discount. Rank the following yields from lowest to highest.

    I. Nominal yield
    II. Current yield
    III. Yield to call
    IV. Yield to maturity

    A. II, I, IV, III
    B. I, II, IV, III
    C. IV, II, III, I
    D. I, II, III, IV

12. All of the following statements regarding convertible bonds are true EXCEPT

    A. holders may share in the growth of the common stock
    B. holders receive a higher rate of interest
    C. issuer pays a lower rate of interest
    D. holders have a fixed rate of interest

13. On February 13, your customer buys 10M of an 8% Treasury bond maturing in 2009, for settlement on February 14. The bonds pay interest on January 1 and July 1. How many days of accrued interest are added to the buyer's price?

    A. 14
    B. 43
    C. 44
    D. 45

14. Which of the following statements regarding Eurodollar bonds are TRUE?

    I. US issuers are not subject to currency risk.
    II. Non-US issuers are not subject to currency risk.
    III. They are issued outside of the US.
    IV. Interest and principal are paid in US dollars.

    A. I and III only
    B. I, III and IV only
    C. II and III only
    D. II and IV only

15. Below which of the following ratings would a bond be considered speculative?

    A. A
    B. B
    C. BB
    D. BBB

16. Bonds

    I. represent a loan to the issuer
    II. give the bondholder ownership in the entity
    III. are issued to finance capital expenditures or to raise working capital
    IV. are junior securities

    A. I and II only
    B. I and III only
    C. II and III only
    D. I, II, III and IV

17. Which of the following would most likely be found in a money market fund's portfolio?

    I. T-bills
    II. T-bonds with a short time to maturity
    III. Negotiable CDs
    IV. Common stock

    A. I and II only
    B. I, II and III only
    C. III and IV only
    D. I, II, III and IV

18. The term *trading flat* means

    A. the bond is in default
    B. there is no accrued interest
    C. the price of the bond has remained level
    D. the bond is sold without markup or commission

19. During periods when the yield curve is normal, as market interest rates change, which is TRUE?

    A. Both short-term and long-term bond prices move equally.
    B. Short-term bond prices move more sharply.
    C. Long-term bond prices move more sharply.
    D. There is no relationship between the relative price movements of short-term and long-term bonds.

20. Accrued interest on a bond confirmation is

    I. added to the buyer's contract price
    II. added to the seller's contract price
    III. subtracted from the buyer's contract price
    IV. subtracted from the seller's contract price

    A. I and II
    B. I and IV
    C. II and III
    D. III and IV

21. A convertible corporate bond has been issued with an anti-dilution covenant. If the issuer declares a 5% stock dividend, which of the following statements are TRUE as of the ex-date?

    I. Conversion ratio increases.
    II. Conversion ratio decreases.
    III. Conversion price increases.
    IV. Conversion price decreases.

    A. I and III
    B. I and IV
    C. II and III
    D. II and IV

22. Which of the following statements regarding Treasury bills are TRUE?

    I. They are sold in minimum denominations of $10,000.
    II. They mature in 4, 13, or 26 weeks from issuance.
    III. Their interest is exempt from taxation at the state level.
    IV. They are callable by the US Treasury at any time prior to maturity.

    A. I and II
    B. I and III
    C. II and III
    D. II and IV

Series 7 Unit Test 2 Answers & Rationale

1. **B.** A bond whose price is below par, or at a discount, has a yield to maturity that is higher than current yield, which in turn is higher than the nominal yield. QID: 34992

2. **B.** When a corporation's assets are liquidated, all unpaid wages are paid first; then taxes must be paid; then all other liabilities must be satisfied; finally, shareholders are paid from what remains. Preferred shareholders have priority over common shareholders and subordinated debenture holders have a lower claim than other debenture holders. QID: 30634

3. **D.** GNMA is the only agency whose securities are direct obligations of the US government. QID: 35209

4. **B.** Bonds that trade flat do not trade with accrued interest. These include income bonds (also known as adjustment bonds), zeroes, bonds in default, and bonds that settle on an interest payment date. QID: 35037

5. **C.** US government agency debt is an obligation of the issuing agency. This causes agency debt to trade at slightly higher yields reflecting this greater risk. FNMA was created as a government agency but was spun off in 1968 and is now an NYSE-listed corporation. GNMA pass-through certificates trade OTC. GNMAs are the only agency whose securities are direct US government obligations. QID: 32153

6. **D.** Interest accrues from the bond's dated date up to but not including the settlement date. QID: 28175

7. **A.** PACs are planned amortization class CMOs and have established maturity dates. Prepayment risk is transferred to the PAC companion, or support, class bonds. QID: 35117

8. **C.** 102 5/8% of par ($1,000 for bonds) = $1,026.25. [10 × $1,026.25 = $10,262.50.] 1/8 point equals $1.25 when quoting corporate bonds. QID: 35002

9. **B.** When interest rates rise, bond prices fall. QID: 30543

10. **C.** $1,000 × 120% = $1,200. At par, conversion price and market price are the same. Therefore, the common stock is in essence, trading at parity, ($40 per share). If the stock rises to $48 per share, on conversion a holder receives 25 shares: 25 shares × $48 = $1,200. QID: 35195

11. **B.** The lowest of all yields for a discount bond is the nominal yield (coupon rate) which is a fixed percentage of par. The highest possible return to the owner of a bond purchased at a discount would occur if the bond were called prior to maturity, since less time needs to elapse for the investor to receive the discount. QID: 35071

12. **B.** Because of the possibility of participating in the growth of the common stock through an increase in the market price of the common, the convertible can be issued with a lower rate of interest. QID: 32150

13. **C.** Accrued interest for government bonds is figured on an actual-days-elapsed basis. The number of days begins with the previous coupon date and continues up to, but not including, the settlement date. In this question, the bonds pay interest on January 1; the number of days of accrued interest for January equals 31. The bonds settle February 14; the number of days of accrued interest for February equals 13. Remember, do not count the settlement date (31 + 13 = 44 days). QID: 28167

14. **B.** Eurodollar bonds are issued outside the US, but principal and interest are paid in US dollars. Therefore, an American issuer or investor bears no currency risk although a foreign issuer or investor does. QID: 35104

15. **D.** A rating of BBB is the lowest investment-grade rating assigned by Standard & Poor's. Any rating beneath this is considered speculative.
QID: 34912

16. **B.** Bonds are debt securities; as such, they represent loans to the issuer. As senior securities, they take precedence over common and preferred stock in claims against an issuer. They are issued to finance capital expenditures or to raise working capital.
QID: 32144

17. **B.** Money market instruments are short-term, high quality debt securities. This includes treasuries with less than 1 year to maturity and negotiable CDs. Because common stock is equity, it is not found in money market funds. Negotiable CD's (over $100,000) are considered money market securities. Treasuries due to mature in less than a year are money market securities, but common stock is not.
QID: 28566

18. **B.** When a bond trades flat, the buyer does not owe accrued interest to the seller.
QID: 35095

19. **C.** Long-term bond prices are more volatile than similar short-term prices, in large part due to the added risk of owning a longer term debt security.
QID: 34906

20. **A.** The accrued interest calculation is made to determine the seller's share of the upcoming interest payment. It is added to the buyer's contract price (the buyer pays), and it is added to the seller's contract price (the seller receives).
QID: 35011

21. **B.** The bond will be convertible into an additional 5% more shares, so the conversion price will decrease in proportion. If the conversion price is lowered, the conversion ratio must increase.
QID: 35142

22. **C.** Treasury bills are sold in minimum denominations of $1,000 and are not callable prior to maturity. They mature in 4, 13, or 26 weeks (from issuance) and are sold at a discount. Interest on Treasury bills is taxable at the federal level only.
QID: 36480

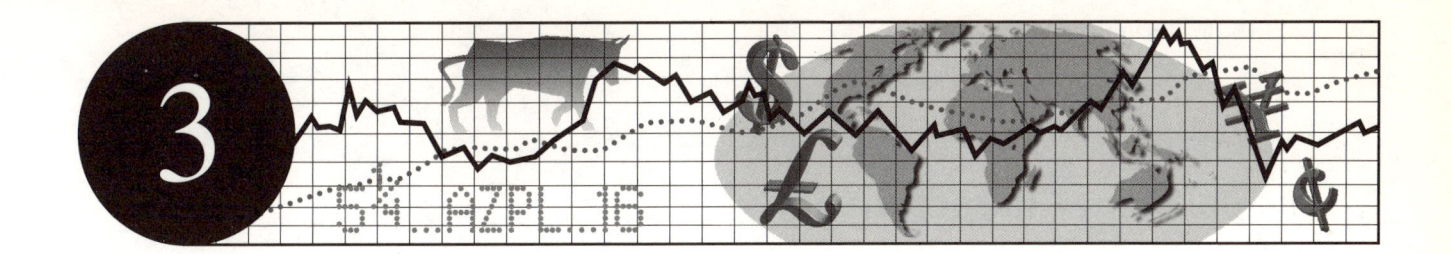

Municipal Securities

INTRODUCTION

The municipal securities unit is a critical section for success on the Series 7 exam. Learn the language of the municipal industry and pay attention to definitions and industry rules. There are very few calculations in this unit—the primary emphasis is on knowing the industry.

Municipal securities offer investors a relatively safe means of investing for tax-free income. Because the interest municipal securities pay is not taxable by the federal government, the yield is lower than that of taxable corporate or government bonds. The two primary types of municipal securities are general obligation bonds (almost always issued in a competitive bid offering) and revenue bonds (normally issued in a negotiated offering).

The exam will ask approximately 55 questions on municipal securities and Municipal Securities Rulemaking Board (MSRB) rules—this may be the most heavily-tested topic on the entire exam.

UNIT OBJECTIVES

When you have completed this unit, you should be able to:

- differentiate municipal bonds from government and corporate bonds;
- compare and contrast general obligation (GO) and revenue bonds;
- identify documentation associated with a new issue of municipals;
- define the steps involved in municipal securities underwriting;
- describe the role of the syndicate and specific rules that apply to the syndicate manager;
- identify unique features of municipal securities trading;
- discuss available sources of municipal industry information;
- describe the tax treatment of municipal securities; and
- identify the role of the MSRB and list significant rules that affect the municipal securities industry.

Municipal Debt Characteristics

Municipal bonds are securities issued either by state or local government or US territories, authorities, and special districts. Investors that buy such bonds are loaning money to the issuers for the purpose of public works and construction projects (e.g., roads, hospitals, civic centers, sewer systems, airports). Municipal securities are considered second in safety of principal only to US government and US government agency securities. The safety of a particular issue is based on the issuing municipality's financial stability.

Municipal securities are exempt from the filing requirements of the Act of 1933. However, like all other securities, they are subject to the antifraud provisions of the **Securities Exchange Act of 1934**.

Tax Benefits Purchasers of municipal debt often benefit from favorable tax treatment on the interest payments. The federal government does not generally tax the interest payments. This tax treatment originated from the **Doctrine of Reciprocal Immunity (Doctrine Of Mutual Reciprocity)**, established by a Supreme Court decision in 1895.

The doctrine specifies that a level of government can only tax the interest of its own issues. Interest on municipal securities may be taxed by the municipal level (state and local governments), but not by the federal government. Interest on issues of the federal government (Treasury bills, notes, and bonds) is taxed by the federal government but is exempt from taxation at the state and local levels. Interest on issues of US territories is subject to a triple exemption (federal, state, local).

✓ *Take Note:* Two important municipal tax issues must be clarified:

- The interest on municipal debt is largely exempt from taxation, but not capital gains. Muni investors who buy low and sell high will have capital gains to report.
- Investors that purchase municipal bonds issued by the state in which they live often receive a special tax exemption; they may not be required to pay taxes on interest to the federal *or* state government. For instance, if you live in Los Angeles, CA, and buy a State of California muni bond, the interest will not be subject to taxation on your federal or State of California return. However, if you live in Tempe, AZ and buy a California municipal bond, the interest will be exempt from taxation by the federal government, but will be taxed by the State of Arizona.

As a result of the tax-advantaged status of municipal bond interest, municipalities generally pay lower interest rates than do corporate issuers. The amount of tax savings experienced by an investor will determine if a municipal bond is a better investment choice than a corporate bond. Investors should be aware of the tax-equivalent yield when assessing the merits of a municipal bond investment. In general, tax-free municipal securities are more appropriate for investors in high tax brackets, and are not suitable for investors in low tax brackets.

Issuers The following three entities are legally entitled to issue municipal debt securities:

- territorial possessions of the United States (US Virgin Islands, Puerto Rico, Guam);
- state governments; and
- legally-constituted taxing authorities (county and city governments, agencies created by these governments, and authorities that supervise ports and mass transit systems, like port authorities and special districts).

Maturity Structures Municipal notes and bonds are issued with maturities that range from less than one year to more than 30 years. There are three types of maturity schedules common to municipal and corporate debt issues.

Term Maturity

All principal matures at a single date in the future.

✓ *For Example:* $200 million Illinois GO 5% Debentures due November 1, 2008.

Some issuers establish a **sinking fund account** to accumulate funds to pay off term bonds at or prior to the established maturity date. Term bonds are quoted by price (like corporate bonds) and are called dollar bonds.

Serial Maturity

Bonds within an issue mature on different dates according to a predetermined schedule. The Sample Serial Maturity Structure table shows an example of a $100 million state of Illinois GO serial issue.

Municipal Securities

Sample Serial Maturity Structure

Amount	Coupon	Maturity	Price/Yield
$10,000,000	6%	11-1-08	5.80%
$10,000,000	6%	11-1-09	5.90%
$10,000,000	6%	11-1-10	100%
$10,000,000	6%	11-1-11	6.10%
$20,000,000	6%	11-1-12	6.20%
$20,000,000	6%	11-1-13	6.30%
$20,000,000	6%	11-1-14	6.40%

Serial bonds are quoted based on their yield-to-maturity, called basis, to reflect the difference of maturity dates within one issue. A price/yield of 100% indicates the yield-to-maturity is equal to the coupon rate, which means the bond is being offered at par.

Balloon Maturity

An issuer pays part of a bond's maturity before the final maturity date but the largest portion is paid off at maturity. The Sample Balloon Maturity table shows an example of a $100 million state of Illinois GO balloon maturity issue due November 1, 2011.

Sample Balloon Maturity

Amount	Coupon	Maturity	Price/Yield
$10,000,000	6%	11-1-08	5.80%
$10,000,000	6%	11-1-09	5.90%
$10,000,000	6%	11-1-10	100%
$70,000,000	6%	11-1-11	6.10%

✓ **Take Note:** A balloon maturity is a type of serial maturity. Also note that most municipal bonds are issued serially.

Types of Municipal Issues

Two categories of municipal securities exist. **General obligation bonds (GOs)**, backed by the full faith, credit, and taxing powers of the municipality, and **revenue bonds**, backed by the revenues generated by the municipal facility the bond issue finances.

General Obligation Issues (GOs)

GOs are municipal bonds issued for capital improvements that benefit the entire community. Typically, these projects do not produce revenues, so principal and interest must be paid by taxes collected by the municipal issuer. Because of this backing, general obligation bonds are known as **full faith and credit issues**.

Sources of Funds

GOs are backed by the issuing municipality's taxing power. Bonds issued by states are backed by income taxes, license fees, and sales taxes. Bonds issued by towns, cities, and counties are backed by property (**ad valorem**) taxes, license fees, fines, and all other sources of revenue to the municipality. School, road, and park districts may also issue municipal bonds backed by property taxes.

Statutory Debt Limits

The amount of debt a municipal government may incur can be limited by state or local statutes to protect taxpayers from excessive taxes. Debt limits can also make a bond safer for investors. The lower the debt limit, the less risk of excessive borrowing and default by the municipality.

Voter Approval. If an issuer wishes to issue GO bonds which would put it above its statutory limit, a public referendum is required.

Tax Limits. Some states limit property taxes to a certain percentage of the assessed property value or to a certain percentage increase in any single year. The tax rate is expressed in mills; one mill equals $1 per $1,000, or $.001.

Limited Tax GO. A limited tax GO is a bond secured by a specific tax, (e.g., income tax). In other words, the issuer is limited as to what tax or taxes can be used to service the debt. As a result, there is more risk with a limited tax GO than with a comparable GO backed by the full taxing authority of the issuer.

Overlapping Debt. Several taxing authorities that draw from the same taxpayers can issue debt. Bonds issued by different municipal authorities that tap the same taxpayer wallets are known as **coterminous debt**.

Test Topic Alert! The term *coterminous* is derived from a Latin word that means "living together." In the context of municipal securities, it refers to two or more taxing agencies that share the same geographic boundaries and are able to issue debt separately. Overlapping debt occurs when two or more issuers are taxing the same property to service their respective debt.

✓ **For Example:** Take the town of Smithville, located in Jones County. If Smithville issues GO debt, it will tax property in Smithville to service that debt. If Jones County issues GO debt, it will tax property in the county, which includes Smithville, to service its debt. As a result, there are two issuers taxing the same property.

✓ **Take Note:** Coterminus debt only occurs in property taxing situations. As states do not generally tax real estate, state debt never overlaps.

Double-Barreled Bonds. **Double-barreled bonds** are revenue bonds that have characteristics of GO bonds. Interest and principal are paid from a specified facility's earnings. However, the bonds are also backed by the taxing power of the state or municipality and, therefore, have the backing of two sources of revenue. Although they are backed primarily by revenues from the facility, double-barreled bonds are rated and traded as GOs.

Test Topic Alert

You might see questions on GOs similar to the following:

A taxpayer's home is currently valued at $400,000. For property tax purposes, it is assessed a value equal to 50% of its market value. If the annual tax rate is 7 mill, what is the taxpayer's annual property tax liability?

Calculate the tax liability by multiplying the mill rate by the property's assessed value.

$200,000 (50% of $400,000) × .007 (a mill is 1 one-thousandth) = $1,400.

To simplify the calculation, drop the last three zeros off the property's assessed value (200) and multiply by the number of mill (7). 200 × 7 = $1,400.

1. Which is not included in the calculation of coterminous debt?

   A. County
   B. City
   C. School district
   D. State

The best answer is **D**. Coterminous, or overlapping, debt occurs when property taxes from one property are used in support of debt issued by various municipal issuers. For instance, property taxes on a home might support county, city, and school district debt obligations. Property taxes are not assessed by states, so states are not included in the definition of coterminous or overlapping debt.

2. All of the following are used to pay debt service on GOs EXCEPT

   A. sales taxes
   B. license fees
   C. tolls
   D. ad valorem taxes

   The best answer is **C**. Generally, associate GOs with taxes. There will be some exceptions, but GOs are predominately backed by tax collections.

Revenue Bonds

Revenue bonds can be used to finance any municipal facility that generates sufficient income. Revenue bonds are not subject to statutory debt limits and do not require voter approval. A particular revenue bond issue, however, may be subject to an additional bonds test before subsequent bond issues with equal liens on the project's revenue may be issued. The additional bonds test assures the adequacy of the revenue stream to pay both the old and new debt.

Feasibility Study

Prior to issuing a revenue bond, an issuer will engage various consultants to prepare a report detailing the economic feasibility and the need for a particular project, (for example, a new bridge or airport). The study will include estimates of revenues that will be generated and details of the operating, economic, or engineering aspects of the proposed project.

Sources of Revenue

Revenue bonds' interest and principal payments are payable to bondholders only from the specific earnings and net lease payments of revenue-producing facilities, such as:

- utilities (water, sewer, electric);
- housing;
- transportation (airports, toll roads);
- education (college dorms, student loans);
- health (hospitals, retirement centers);
- industrial (industrial development, pollution control); and
- sports facilities.

Debt service payments do not come from general or real estate taxes and are not backed by the municipality's full faith and credit. Revenue bonds are considered self-supporting debt as principal and interest payments are made exclusively from revenues generated by the project for which the debt was issued.

Protective Covenants

The face of a revenue bond certificate may refer to a **trust indenture** (or **bond resolution**). This empowers the trustee to act on behalf of the bondholders.

In the trust indenture, the municipality agrees to abide by certain protective covenants, or promises, meant to protect bondholders. A trustee appointed in the indenture supervises the issuer's compliance with the bond covenants.

Bond Covenants

The trust indenture's provisions can vary, but a number of standard provisions are common to most bond issues, including the following.

- **Rate covenant**—a promise to maintain rates sufficient to pay expenses and debt service
- **Maintenance covenant**—a promise to maintain the equipment and facility(ies)
- **Insurance covenant**—a promise to insure any facility built so bondholders can be paid off if the facility is destroyed or becomes inoperable
- **Additional bonds test**—whether the indenture is **open-ended** (allowing further issuance of bonds with the same status and equal claims on revenues) or **closed-ended** (allowing no further issuance of bonds with an equivalent lien on earnings; with a closed-end provision, any additional bonds issued will be subordinated to the original issue)
- **Sinking fund**—money to pay off interest and principal obligations
- **Catastrophe clause**—a promise to use insurance proceeds to call bonds and repay bondholders if a facility is destroyed
- **Flow of funds**—the priority of disbursing the revenues collected
- **Books and records covenant**—requires outside audit of records and financial reports
- **Call features**

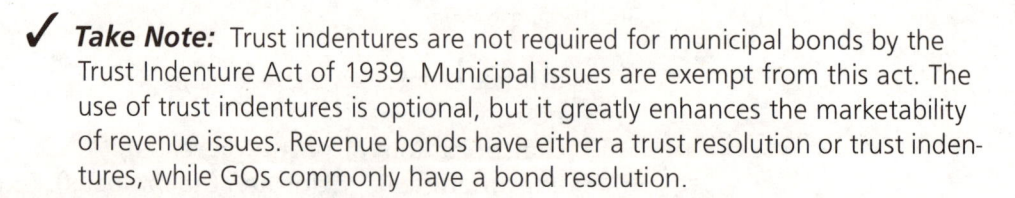

✓ *Take Note:* Trust indentures are not required for municipal bonds by the Trust Indenture Act of 1939. Municipal issues are exempt from this act. The use of trust indentures is optional, but it greatly enhances the marketability of revenue issues. Revenue bonds have either a trust resolution or trust indentures, while GOs commonly have a bond resolution.

Types of Revenue Bonds

There are a number of categories of revenue bonds, depending on the type of facility the bond issue finances.

Industrial Development Revenue Bonds. A municipal development authority issues **industrial development revenue bonds (IDRs or IDBs)** to construct facilities or purchase equipment, which is then leased to a corporation. The municipality uses the money from lease payments to pay the principal and interest on the bonds. The ultimate responsibility for the payment of principal and interest rests with the corporation leasing the facility; therefore, the bonds carry the corporation's debt rating.

Technically, industrial revenue bonds are issued for a corporation's benefit. Under the **Tax Reform Act of 1986**, the interest on these nonpublic purpose bonds may be taxable because the act reserves tax exemption for public purposes. Due to the fact that these bonds are used for a nonpublic purpose, the interest income may be subject to the alternative minimum tax (AMT) discussed later in this text.

Lease Rental Bonds. Under a typical lease-rental (or lease-back) bond arrangement, a municipality issues bonds to finance office construction for itself or its state or community.

✓ *For Example:* An example of a lease-back arrangement follows.

> A municipality might issue bonds to raise money to construct a school and lease the finished building to the school district. The lease payments provide backing for the bonds.
>
> Lease payments come from funds raised through special taxes or appropriations, from the lessor's revenues, such as the school's tuition or fees, or from the municipality's general fund.

Special Tax Bonds. These are bonds secured by one or more designated taxes other than ad valorem (property) taxes. For example, bonds for a particular purpose might be supported by sales, tobacco, fuel, or business license taxes. However, the designated tax does not have to be directly related to the project purpose. Such bonds are not considered self-supporting debt.

Special Assessment Bonds (or Special District Bonds). Special assessment bonds are issued to finance the construction of public improvements such as streets, sidewalks, or sewers. The issuer assesses a tax only on the property that benefits from the improvement and uses the funds to pay principal and interest.

New Housing Authority Bonds. Local housing authorities issue **New Housing Authority bonds (NHAs)** to develop and improve low-income housing. NHAs are backed by the full faith and credit of the US government. NHAs are sometimes called **Public Housing Authority Bonds (PHAs)**. Because of their federal backing, they are considered the most secure of all municipal bonds. PHAs are backed by the rental income from the housing. If the rental income is not sufficient to service the debt, the federal government makes up any shortfall. For this reason, PHAs have AAA rating. Note that these bonds are not considered to be double-barreled. To be double-barreled, a bond must be backed by more than one municipal revenue source. In this case, the second backing is the federal government.

> **Test Topic Alert!** PHAs (or NHAs) are the only municipal issues backed in full by the US government. They are also called **Section 8** bonds.

Moral Obligation Bonds. A **moral obligation** bond is a state (or local) issued, or state (or local) agency-issued bond. If revenues or tax collections backing the bond are not sufficient to pay the debt service, the state legislature has the authority to appropriate funds to make payments. The potential backing by state revenues tends to make the bond more marketable, but the state's obligation is not established by law; it is a moral obligation only.

✓ **Take Note:** Moral obligation bonds are revenue bonds only. For instance, a state may take on the moral obligation to service debt on city-issued general obligation bonds when the city has surpassed its statutory debt limit. This situation occurred in New York City's financial crisis of 1975. Typically, moral obligation bonds are issued in times of financial distress and have increased credit risk.

Issuer Default. If a GO bond goes into default, bondholders have the right to sue to compel a tax levy to pay off the bonds. If a moral obligation bond goes into default, the only way bondholders can be repaid is through "legislative apportionment." The issuer's legislature would have to apportion money to satisfy the debt but is not legally obligated to do so. Remember, the issuer has the moral, but not legal obligation to service the debt.

> **Test Topic Alert!** Following are typical questions on revenue bonds:

1. Which is backed by the full faith and credit of the US government?

   A. Moral obligation bonds
   B. PHAs
   C. IDRs
   D. Special tax bonds

   B. PHAs or NHAs are issued to construct, maintain, and improve low-income housing. The US government guarantees the rent on these properties, and they are considered the most secure of all municipal revenue bonds.

2. All of the following are used to provide debt service for revenue bonds EXCEPT

   A. excise taxes
   B. business license taxes
   C. ad valorem taxes
   D. alcohol taxes

C. Property taxes, or *ad valorem* taxes, are associated with GOs. Special taxes are used to back revenue bonds. Examples include hotel, tobacco, liquor, and gasoline taxes. These are the exceptions to the rule that taxes should be associated with GO issues.

Be ready for 5 to 7 questions that require you to differentiate between the features of GOs and revenue bonds. If you're not confident about the basic features of these instruments, review before continuing. It's important to be extremely familiar with these basics.

Quick Quiz 3.1

Label each description below with the appropriate letter.

G. General Obligation Bond
R. Revenue Bond
B. Both
N. Neither

____ 1. Interest generally exempt from federal tax

____ 2. Trust indenture is typical, though not required

____ 3. Feasibility study

____ 4. Voter approval

____ 5. Debt limit

____ 6. Full faith and credit bonds

____ 7. Special tax bond

____ 8. Additional bonds test

____ 9. Limited tax bond

____ 10. Coterminous debt

____ 11. IDR

____ 12. Self-supporting

____ 13. Generally safer than corporates

____ 14. Generally safer than US government securities

Answers	1.	**B.**	2.	**R.**	3.	**R.**	4.	**G.**	5.	**G.**	6.	**G.**
	7.	**R.**	8.	**R.**	9.	**G**	10.	**G.**	11.	**R.**	12.	**R.**
	13.	**B.**	14.	**N.**

Municipal Notes

Municipal anticipation notes are short-term securities that generate funds for a municipality that expects other revenues soon. Usually municipal notes have less than 12-month maturities, although maturities may range from three months to three years. They are repaid when the municipality receives the anticipated funds. Municipal notes fall into several categories.

- Municipalities issue **tax anticipation notes** (**TANs**) to finance current operations in anticipation of future tax receipts.
- **Revenue anticipation notes** (**RANs**) are offered periodically to finance current operations in anticipation of future revenues.
- **Tax and revenue anticipation notes** (**TRANs**) are a combination of the characteristics of both TANs and RANs.
- **Bond anticipation notes** (**BANs**) are sold as interim financing that will eventually be converted to long-term funding through a sale of bonds.
- **Tax-exempt commercial paper** is often used in place of BANs and TANs, up to 270 days though maturities are most often 30, 60, and 90 days.
- **Construction loan notes** (**CLNs**) are issued to provide interim financing for the construction of housing projects.
- **Variable rate demand notes** have a fluctuating interest rate and are usually issued with a put option.

Variable Rate Municipals (Variable Rate Demand Obligations)

Some municipal bonds and notes are issued with **variable**, or **floating**, rates of interest. A **variable-rate municipal bond** offers interest payments tied to the movements of another specified interest rate, much like an adjustable rate mortgage. Because the coupon rate of the bond changes with the market, the price of these bonds remains relatively stable.

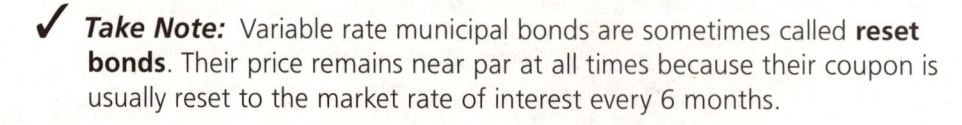

✓ ***Take Note:*** Variable rate municipal bonds are sometimes called **reset bonds**. Their price remains near par at all times because their coupon is usually reset to the market rate of interest every 6 months.

Quick Quiz 3.2   Multiple Choice

1. The main advantage of a variable-rate municipal bond investment is that the

   A. bond is likely to increase in value
   B. bond's price should remain relatively stable
   C. bond is noncallable
   D. bond's interest is exempt from all taxes

2. If a municipality wants to even out its cash flow, it is most likely to issue which of the following securities?

   A. TANs
   B. BANs
   C. RANs
   D. CLNs

3. All of the following are true of a municipality's debt limit EXCEPT that

   A. the purpose of debt restriction is to protect taxpayers from excessive taxes
   B. revenue bonds are not affected by statutory limitations
   C. the debt limit is the maximum amount a municipality can redeem in a year
   D. a public referendum is required if an issuer wishes to issue GO debt which would put the issuer above its statutory debt limit

4. Which of the following is a double-barreled bond?

   A. New Housing Authority bond
   B. Project note
   C. Hospital bond backed by revenues and taxes
   D. GO bond to construct a new grade school

5. Your customer, a resident of Minnesota, is in the 28% federal tax bracket and the 14% state tax bracket. She must pay both federal and state taxes on which of the following investments?

   A. Minneapolis Housing Authority bonds
   B. Series HH bonds
   C. Ginnie Mae pass-throughs
   D. Treasury bills

Answers

1. **B.** A variable-rate bond has no fixed coupon rate. The interest rate is tied to a market rate (for example, T-bill yields) and is subject to change at regular intervals. Because the interest paid reflects changes in overall interest rates, the price of the bond remains relatively close to its par value.

2. **A.** *Property taxes are a primary source of cash flow for most municipalities, but property taxes are collected at established intervals. Issuing tax anticipation notes (TANs) backed by future tax revenues can help a municipality maintain an even cash flow throughout its fiscal year.*

3. **C.** *The debt limit is the maximum amount of debt a municipality can incur. Such restrictions have made revenue bonds increasingly popular because they are normally not subject to statutory debt limitations.*

4. **C.** *A double-barreled bond is backed by a defined source of revenue, other than property taxes, plus the full faith and credit of an issuer with taxing authority.*

5. **C.** *The interest income from most US government and agency securities is exempt from state and local taxes, but not federal taxes. The interest on municipal issues (like the Minneapolis Housing Authority bonds) is exempt from both federal taxes and, because this investor is a Minnesota resident, state taxes. Ginnie Maes are subject to taxation on all levels*

Municipal Security Documents

Bond Contract A municipal issuer enters into a **bond contract** with the underwriters of, and prospective investors in, its securities. The bond contract is a collection of legal documents that includes a bond resolution (or trust indenture), applicable state and federal law, and other legal documents pertaining to that particular issue and issuer. By issuing its securities, the issuer has agreed to abide by the terms and covenants in the documents that compose the bond contract.

Authorizing Resolution The municipality authorizes the issue and sale of its securities through the **bond resolution**. The authorizing resolution contains a description of the issue.

Bond Resolution Indenture On the face of most municipal revenue bond certificates is a reference to the bonds' **underlying trust indenture**, also known as a **protective covenant**. Although it is not required by law, most municipal issuers use indentures to make the issue more marketable. The indenture serves as a contract between the bond's issuer and a trustee appointed on behalf of the bond's investors.

Normally, the indenture includes a flow of funds statement establishing the priority of payments made from a facility's revenues. The indenture is too long to supply to all bondholders, although the issuer must make a complete copy available upon request. The official statement outlines the indenture's covenants.

Official Statement (OS) The **official statement** is the municipal securities industry's equivalent of the corporate prospectus. The official statement serves as a disclosure document and contains any material information an investor might need about an issue. Prepared by the issuer, the official statement identifies the issue's purpose, the source from which the interest and principal will be repaid, and the issuer's and community's financial and economic backgrounds. The official statement also has information relating to the issue's creditworthiness.

A typical official statement includes all of the following information:

- offering terms;
- summary statement;
- purpose of issue;
- authorization of bonds;
- security of bonds;
- description of bonds;
- description of issuer, including organization and management, area economy, and a financial summary;
- construction program;
- project feasibility statement;
- regulatory matters;
- specific provisions of the indenture or resolution, including funds and accounts, investment of funds, additional bonds, insurance, and events of default;
- legal proceedings;
- tax status;
- appropriate appendixes, including consultant reports, the legal opinion, and financial statements; and
- credit enhancements.

Preliminary Official Statement

Municipal issuers may also prepare preliminary official statements. The preliminary official statement discloses most of the same material information as the official statement, with the exception of the issue's interest rate(s) and offering price(s). Underwriters use a preliminary official statement to determine investors' and dealers' interest in the issue.

Any municipal securities dealer involved in the sale of a new issue must deliver a final **official statement** to every customer who has purchased the issue, at or prior to settlement date.

Legal Opinion Printed on the face of every bond certificate (unless the bond is specifically stamped *Ex-Legal*) is a legal opinion written and signed by the **bond counsel,** an attorney specializing in tax-exempt bond offerings. The legal opinion states that the issue is legally binding on the issuer and conforms with applicable laws. If interest from the bond is tax exempt, that too is stated in the legal opinion.

The legal opinion is issued either as a **qualified opinion** (there may be a legal uncertainty of which purchasers should be informed) or as an **unqualified opinion** (issued by the bond counsel unconditionally).

Some issuers, normally smaller municipalities, choose not to obtain a legal opinion. In such a case, the bond certificate must clearly state that the bonds are **ex-legal**. The ex-legal designation allows a bond to meet good delivery requirements without an attached legal opinion.

The Underwriter's Counsel

The managing underwriter may choose to employ another law firm as underwriter's counsel. This firm is not responsible for the legal opinion and is employed to represent the underwriter's interests.

✓ *Take Note:* Issuers desire an unqualified legal opinion.

Quick Quiz 3.3   Multiple Choice

1. All of the following statements are true about qualified legal opinions EXCEPT that they

    A. are issued by bond counsel that specializes in tax-exempt issues
    B. state that counsel has no reservations about the issue
    C. state whether the interest on the issue will be considered tax exempt
    D. are issued by attorneys not affiliated with the issuer

2. Which of the following documents are furnished to potential municipal bond buyers as a disclosure document?

    A. Official statement
    B. Legal opinion
    C. Indenture
    D. All of the above

3. The Trust Indenture Act of 1939 requires trust indentures to include all of the following EXCEPT

    A. trustee's name
    B. protective covenants
    C. responsibilities of the trustee
    D. investors' names

4. Who renders an opinion as to the validity and legality of a municipal issue?

    A. Bond counsel
    B. Underwriter's counsel
    C. MSRB
    D. Managing underwriter

Answers   1. **B.**   *A qualified legal opinion means that bond counsel has some reservation about the issue or is trying to inform potential buyers of the existence of a certain condition. An unqualified opinion is what the issuer ideally wants—it means the counsel has no reservations about any aspects of the issue. The bond counsel that issues the legal opinion must be completely independent of the issuer.*

2. **A.**   *The official statement is the muni industry's equivalent of a prospectus and is used as disclosure to potential buyers. The indenture is too long to provide to all bondholders, but it must be made available to investors upon request. The legal opinion is a part of each bond certificate.*

3. **D.**   *The Trust Indenture Act of 1939 requires trust indentures to include clauses protecting the bondholders. It does not include names of investors.*

4. **A.**   *An independent bond attorney is hired by the issuer to render an opinion as to the validity, legality, and tax-exempt status of a municipal bond issue before it is issued. The bond counsel should not be confused with the underwriter's counsel (employed by the managing underwriter to protect the interests of the underwriters).*

Issuing Municipal Securities

A uniform sequence of events leads to a new municipal issue. The issuer must first obtain a **legal opinion**, which determines whether and how the bonds may be offered. Then, the terms of the municipal bond offering may be set by either **negotiation** or **competitive bidding**.

Negotiated Underwriting

In a **negotiated underwriting**, the municipality appoints an investment banker to underwrite the offering. The underwriter works with the issuer to establish the interest rate and the offering price in light of the issuer's financial needs and market conditions.

Most revenue bonds are issued through negotiated underwritings, and the issue can be distributed as either a public offering or a private placement.

Competitive Bidding

With few exceptions, municipal GOs are awarded to an underwriter through **competitive bidding**. When a municipality publishes an invitation to bid, investment bankers respond in writing to the issuer's attorney or another designated official requesting information on the offering.

✓ **Take Note:** The bid representing the lowest net interest cost to the issuer is the winner in a competitive bid.

Official Notice of Sale The notice of bond sale to solicit bids for the bonds is usually published in *The Bond Buyer* and local newspapers and includes:

- date, time, and place of sale;
- name and description of issuer;
- type of bond;
- bidding restrictions (usually requiring a sealed bid);
- interest payment dates;
- dated date (interest accrual date) and first coupon payment date;
- maturity structure;
- call provisions (if any);
- denominations and registration provisions;
- expenses to be borne by purchaser or issuer;
- amount of good faith deposit that must accompany bid;
- paying agent or trustee;
- name of the firm (the **bond counsel**), providing the legal opinion;
- details of delivery;
- issuers right of rejection of all bids;
- criteria for awarding the issue; and
- issuers obligation to prepare the final official statement and deliver copies to the successful bidder.

The bond's rating and the underwriter's name are not included in a notice of sale because they have yet to be determined.

Investment bankers prepare bids for the securities based on information in the notice of sale, comparable new issue supply and demand, and general market conditions.

✓ **Take Note:** All new municipal debt is issued in fully-registered form or in book-entry form.

Sources of Municipal Securities Information

A number of publications and services offer information on proposed new issues and secondary market activity for municipal issues. These include *The Bond Buyer* and *Munifacts*.

The Bond Buyer *The Bond Buyer* is published every business day and serves as an authoritative source of information on primary market municipal bonds. The Friday edition publishes the **30-day visible supply** (the total dollar volume of municipal offerings (not including short-term notes) expected to reach the market in the next 30 days) and the **placement ratio indexes** (the percentage of new issues sold versus new issued offered for sale the prior week).

✓ *Take Note:* If the visible supply is exceptionally large, interest rates are likely to rise to attract investors to the larger number of bonds available. A small visible supply is an indication that interest rates are likely to fall.

If the placement ratio is high, the market for municipal bonds is strong. If it is low, dealers will be likely to exhibit concern about bidding on new issues. A placement ratio of 90% means that market has absorbed 90% of the dollar volume of bonds issued for the week, with 10% left in the dealer's inventory.

The Bond Buyer also compiles the 40 Bond Index, 20 Bond Index, 11 Bond Index, and the Revdex 25.

Bond Buyer Compiled Indexes

40 Bond Index
Daily price index of 40 GO and revenue bonds with an average maturity of 20 years. A rise in the index indicates bond prices are rising and yields are falling.

20 Bond Index
Weekly index of 20 GO bonds with 20 years to maturity, rated A or better.

11 Bond Index
Weekly index of 11 of the 20 bonds from the 20 Bond Index; rated AA or better.

Revdex 25
Weekly index of 25 revenue bonds with 30 years to maturity, rated A or better.

✓ *Take Note:* The yields on the Revdex are always higher than the yields on the GO 20 Bond Index because revenue bonds have higher risk. The yields on the 11 Bond Index are lower than the yields on the 20 Bond Index because the 11 Bond Index is more highly rated.

Munifacts *Munifacts* is a subscription wire service of *The Bond Buyer* that supplies prices, information about proposed new issues, and general news relevant to the municipal bond market.

Test Topic Alert! Test your knowledge of information sources on the municipal bond market.

1. Which municipal publication includes the 30-day visible supply index?

2. Which municipal publication provides the most up-to-the-minute information relevant to the bond market?

The answers: 1. *The Bond Buyer*; 2. *Munifacts*

Municipal Securities

Quick Quiz 3.4

Match each of the following items with the appropriate description below.

A. *The Bond Buyer*
B. *Munifacts*
C. Official Notice of Sale

___ 1. News wire service for the municipal bond industry

___ 2. Publication in which dealers find official notices of sale

___ 3. Invitation to prospective underwriters to bid on a municipal issue

Answers   1. **B**.   2. **A**.   3. **C**.

Glass-Steagall Act of 1933

The **Glass-Steagall Act of 1933** erected a wall between commercial banking and investment banking activities—a wall that was being slowly dismantled in the 1990s. The act was intended to protect bank customers by preventing banks from engaging in the investment banking, brokerage, or underwriting business.

The Glass-Steagall Act prohibits commercial banks from underwriting corporate securities and most municipal revenue bonds—but does allow commercial banks to underwrite general obligation bonds and New Housing Authority bonds without restriction. Banks also can underwrite housing and education revenue bonds and moral obligation bonds. The revenue bonds that commercial banks are permitted to underwrite are known as **bank eligible** bonds.

Gramm-Leach-Blily Act

With its enactment on November 12, 1999, the **Gramm-Leach-Blily Act** repealed certain sections of the Glass-Steagall Act. Banks and securities or insurance firms are now allowed to affiliate, and bank affiliates may engage in a full range of securities and mutual funds business. This act has made the concept of "one-stop financial shopping" a closer reality. Gramm-Leach-Blily permits the affiliation of these firms, but does not alter their traditional roles.

Formation of the Underwriting Syndicate

Once an issuer's notice of sale has circulated, those investment bankers interested in placing competitive bids for an issue form **syndicates**. A syndicate is an account that helps spread the risk of underwriting an issue among a number of underwriters. Although the bidding process is competitive, successive offerings of a particular municipality are often handled by the same syndicate, comprised of the same members.

✓ *Take Note:* To acquire relevant details about a new issue, the syndicate manager typically orders the New Issue Worksheet from *The Bond Buyer.* This worksheet provides, in an organized format, all information presented in the Official Notice of Sale. It shows a schedule of year-by-year maturities and their corresponding dollar amounts and also a computation of bond years. Bond years are the number of $1,000 bonds of a maturity multiplied by the number of years the bonds are outstanding. This computation is used to calculate the average life of an issue and its total interest cost.

Sample Computation of Bond Years and Average
Life of a $3.5 million Issue dated 9/01/00

Maturity	Years to Maturity	Number of Bonds	Bond Years
9/1/10	10	1,000	10,000
9/1/11	11	1,000	11,000
9/1/12	12	1,000	12,000
9/1/13	13	500	6,500
		Total 3,500	Total 39,500

$$\text{Average life} = \frac{\text{Total bond years}}{\text{Total number of bonds}} = \frac{39,500}{3,500} = 11.286 \text{ years}$$

A firm makes the decision to participate as a syndicate member after it considers the following factors:

- potential demand for the security;
- existence of presale orders;
- determination and extent of liability;
- scale and spread; and
- ability to sell the issue.

Participants formalize their relationship by signing a **syndicate letter** or **syndicate agreement** in a competitive bid or a **syndicate contract** or **agreement**

among underwriters in a negotiated underwriting. About two weeks before the issue is awarded, the syndicate manager sends the syndicate letter or contract to each participating firm for an authorized signature. The member's signature indicates its agreement with the offering terms. Syndicate letters include the following:

- each member firm's level of participation or commitment;
- priority of order allocation;
- duration of the syndicate account;
- appointment of the manager(s) as agent(s) for the account;
- fee for the managing underwriter and breakdown of the spread; and
- other obligations, such as member expenses, good faith deposits, observance of offering terms, and liability for unsold bonds.

✓ *Take Note:* Syndicate letters are not legally binding until the syndicate's submission of the bid. Firms may drop from the group until this point.

Types of Syndicate Accounts

The financial liability each underwriter is exposed to depends on the type of syndicate account. Underwriting syndicates use two arrangements: Western accounts and Eastern accounts.

Western Account

The **Western account** is a divided account. Each underwriter is responsible only for its own underwriting allocation.

Eastern Account

An **Eastern account** is an **undivided** account. Each underwriter is allocated a portion of the issue. After the issue has been substantially distributed, each underwriter is allocated additional bonds representing its proportionate share of any unsold bonds. Thus, an underwriter's financial liability might not end when it has distributed its initial allocation.

✓ *Take Note:* When it comes to remembering the difference between Western and Eastern, divided and undivided accounts, try this phrase: "The continental *divide* is in the *west*." It helps remind you that Western accounts and divided accounts are the same, as are Eastern and undivided.

✓ *For Example:* A syndicate is underwriting a $5 million municipal bond issue. There are five syndicate members, each with equal participation, including your firm. Your firm sells its entire allocation, but bonds worth $1 million remain unsold by the other syndicate members.

If this is a Western account, what is your firm's liability?

In a Western account, your firm would have no remaining liability because its entire share was sold. However, if your firm had sold only $700,000 of its

$1 million allocation, it would have to purchase the remaining $300,000 for its own inventory.

If this is an Eastern account, what is your firm's liability?

In an Eastern account, the unsold amount is divided among all syndicate members based on their initial participation. In this example, your firm would be allocated 20% of the remaining amount, or $200,000. The responsibility for any unsold bonds continues until the entire bond issue is sold.

Due Diligence Municipal underwriters must investigate an issuer's financing proposals thoroughly. With revenue bonds, this due diligence investigation is conducted through a feasibility study, which focuses on the projected revenues and costs associated with the project and an analysis of competing facilities.

Establishing the Syndicate Bid

A **syndicate** arrives at its competitive **bid** over a series of meetings during which member dealers discuss the proposed reoffering scale and spread for the underwriters. Their goal is to arrive at the best price to the issuer while still making a profit. At a preliminary meeting, the manager seeks tentative agreement from members on the prices or yields of all maturities in the issue, as well as the gross profit or underwriting spread.

A final bid price for the bond is set at a meeting conducted just before the bid is due. If the member dealers cannot all agree on a final bid, the syndicate can go ahead with its bid as long as the syndicate members agree to abide by the majority's decision.

✓ *Take Note:* To win the bid, the syndicate must resolve this question: What is the lowest interest rate that can both win the bid and provide a competitive investment to public buyers as well as provide a profit for the underwriter?

The process of establishing the reoffering yield (or price) for each maturity is called **writing the scale**. A scale is the list of the bond issue's different maturities. If the coupon rate has already been determined, each maturity listed is assigned a yield. If the rate has not been set, each maturity is assigned a coupon. A normal scale has higher yields for long-term bonds.

Once the underwriters have written a scale that allows them to resell the bonds, they prepare the final bid. Put another way, writing the scale is first determining what prices (yields) are necessary in order to be able to sell the various serial maturities and then backing off a little to arrive at a bid. Before they submit the bid, the underwriters ensure that they have met any unique specifications the issuer has set.

Firm Commitment

Competitive bids are submitted as firm commitments. Therefore, bids must be carefully written to be competitive, yet still profitable. Underwriters receive no profit guarantee. Note that syndicates bidding on the proposed issue must bid on the entire amount being offered for sale.

Disclosure of Fees

Fees to be paid to a clearing agency and the syndicate manager must be disclosed to syndicate members in advance. Normally, this disclosure is part of the syndicate letter or the agreement among underwriters. Management fees include any amount in the gross spread that is paid to the manager alone and not shared with syndicate members.

Awarding the Issue

After the issuer meets with its attorneys and accountants to analyze each bid, it awards the municipal bond issue to the syndicate that offers to underwrite the bonds at the lowest **net interest cost** (**NIC**) or **true interest cost** (**TIC**) to the issuer.

Net interest cost is a common calculation used for comparing bids and awarding the bond issue. It combines the amount of proceeds the issuer receives with the total coupon interest it pays. True interest cost provides the same type of cost comparison adjusted for the time value of money.

$$\text{NIC} = \frac{\text{total interest payments} + \text{discount} (- \text{premium})}{\text{Bond years}}$$

In **split-rate bids** (bids with more than one interest rate), interest is determined by the lowest average interest cost to the issuer. If each bid calls for one rate for the whole issue, the award goes to the syndicate with the lowest rate.

✓ **Take Note:** NIC is a straight mathematical interest rate calculation. The lowest net interest cost is the winner. TIC weights more heavily early interest payments to give greater value to dollars of today over dollars to be paid in the future, consistent with present value calculations.

When the issuer makes its choice, it announces the successful bidder and returns the good faith deposits to the remaining syndicates.

The successful syndicate has a firm commitment to purchase the bonds from the issuer and reoffer them to the public at the offering price the members agreed on. The issuer keeps the successful bidder's good faith deposit to ensure that the syndicate carries out its commitment.

Issuing Municipal Securities

✓ **Take Note:** The difference between the winning bid on a new issue and the next best bid is called the **cover** which may be expressed in basis points or dollars per bond. The next best bid is termed the **cover bid**.

Syndicate Account The **syndicate account** is created when the issue is awarded. The syndicate manager is responsible for keeping the books and managing the account. All sale proceeds are deposited to the syndicate account, and all expenses are paid out of the account.

Breakdown of the Spread

The price at which the bonds are sold to the public is known as the **reoffering price** (or **reoffering yield**). The syndicate's compensation for underwriting the new issue is the **spread**, the difference between the price the syndicate pays the issuer and the reoffering price. Each participant in the syndicate is entitled to a portion of the spread, depending on the role each member plays in the underwriting.

✓ **Take Note:** The term *production* refers to the total dollar sales earned from a municipal issue. The production less the amount bid for the issue results in the spread.

Syndicate Management Fee The syndicate manager receives a per-bond fee for its work in bringing the new issue to market.

✓ **For Example:** The manager might receive ⅛ point ($1.25) as a management fee from a total spread of 1 point ($10).

Total Takedown The portion of the spread that remains after subtracting the management fee is called the **total takedown**. Members buy the bonds from the syndicate manager **at the takedown**.

In the example, out of a spread of 1 point with a management fee of ⅛ point, the takedown is ⅞ point ($8.75). A member that has purchased bonds at the takedown can either sell its bonds to customers at the offering price or sell them to a dealer in the selling group below the offering price.

Firms that are part of the selling group, unlike syndicate members, do not assume financial risk. They are engaged to help the syndicate members sell the new issue. Their compensation for each bond sold is termed the concession.

Selling Concession and Additional Takedown A syndicate member can buy bonds from the manager for $991.25, sell them to the public for $1,000 and earn the takedown of ⅞ point ($8.75). If the firm chooses instead to sell bonds to a member of the selling group, it does so at a price less than $1,000, in this case $995.00. The discount the selling group receives from the syndicate member is called the **concession**—½ point (5.00).

Selling group members buy bonds from syndicate members at the concession. The syndicate member keeps the remainder of the total takedown, called the **additional takedown**. The additional takedown in this example is ⅜ point ($3.75).

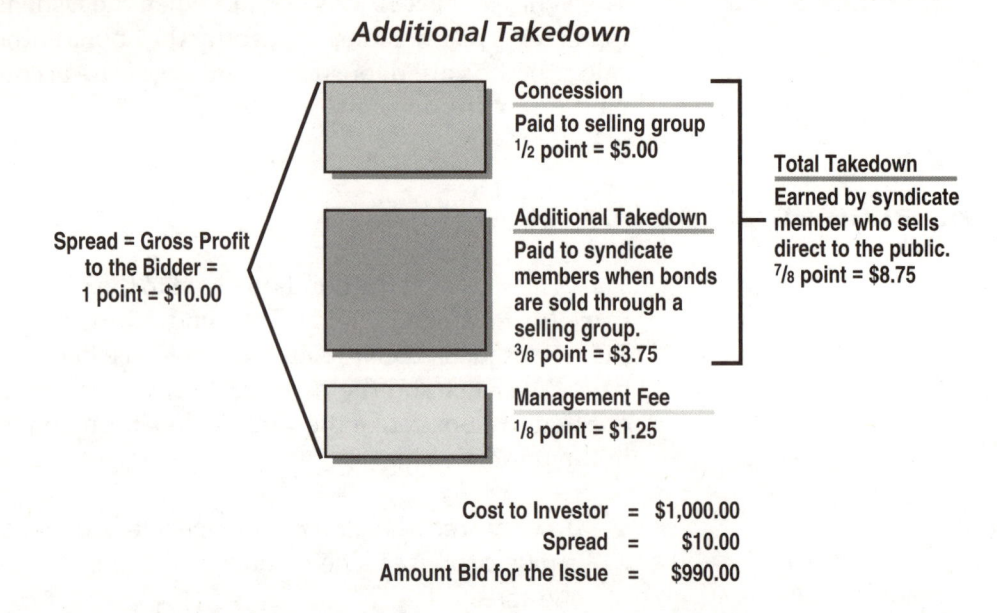

Additional Takedown

Spread = Gross Profit to the Bidder = 1 point = $10.00

Concession
Paid to selling group
½ point = $5.00

Additional Takedown
Paid to syndicate members when bonds are sold through a selling group.
⅜ point = $3.75

Total Takedown
Earned by syndicate member who sells direct to the public.
⅞ point = $8.75

Management Fee
⅛ point = $1.25

Cost to Investor = $1,000.00
Spread = $10.00
Amount Bid for the Issue = $990.00

The syndicate manager may notify other firms who are not syndicate or selling group members of the new issue through *The Bond Buyer*. Interested firms may buy the bonds from the syndicate at a small discount from the reoffer price. This discount is termed a **reallowance** which is generally 1/2 of the concession amount.

💡 **Test Topic Alert!** Municipal spread questions are generally asked in terms of points, not dollars. One bond point equals $10.

Be ready for a question that asks you to rank parts of the spread in order of their size. Remember that the manager's fee is typically the smallest and the total takedown is the largest. The additional takedown is actually a part of the total takedown amount—even though the name is a bit misleading.

You may see a question that asks under what circumstances a syndicate member can receive the full spread when a bond is sold. The answer is that the syndicate member receives the full spread if the member is also the syndicate manager. Also, be ready to define total takedown as the concession plus the additional takedown.

Order Allocation

Municipal bond orders are allocated according to priorities the syndicate sets in advance. The **Municipal Securities Rulemaking Board (MSRB)** requires

Issuing Municipal Securities

syndicates to establish **priority allocation provisions** for orders. The managing underwriter must submit these provisions to all syndicate members in writing. Normally, the manager includes allocation priorities and confirmation procedures in the syndicate agreement.

The syndicate must establish a definite sequence in which orders will be accepted and may not simply state that the order priority will be left to the manager's discretion.

Syndicate members must signify in writing their acceptance of the allocation priorities. In addition, the manager must notify the members in writing of any change to the set priorities.

Order Period The MSRB has established a time line for municipal underwritings. The **order period** is the time set by the manager during which the syndicate solicits customers for the issue and all orders are allocated without regard to the sequence in which they were received. The order period usually runs for an hour on the day following the award of the bid.

Allocation Priorities A syndicate's **allocation priorities** become especially important when a bond issue is oversubscribed. The normal priority follows.

Presale Order

A **presale order** is entered prior to the date that the syndicate wins the bid, which means that a customer is willing to place an order without knowing the final price or if the syndicate will even win the bid. A presale order takes priority over other types of orders and individual syndicate members are not credited with any takedown on presale orders. The takedown is split among all syndicate members according to participation.

Group Net Order

A group order is placed after the bid is awarded. A syndicate member that wants a customer's order to receive priority enters the order as a **group net order**. The takedown on a group net order is deposited in the syndicate account, and upon completion of the underwriting, it is split among all syndicate members according to participation.

Designated Order

The next highest priority for orders received during the order period is assigned to designated orders. These orders are usually from institutions who wish to allocate the takedown to certain syndicate members.

Member Order and Member-Related Order

The lowest priority for orders goes to member and member-related orders. A member firm enters such an order for its own inventory or related accounts, such as for a dealer-sponsored **unit investment trust (UIT)**. The easiest way to remember the priority of the various types of orders is that the highest priority is given to those orders that benefit the most members. The lowest priority is given to orders that benefit a single member.

Under MSRB rules, a syndicate member placing an order for a related account must disclose this fact to the syndicate manager when the order is placed. Therefore, the manager knows to accord these orders the lowest priority.

Within two business days of the sale date, the syndicate manager must send a written summary of how orders were allocated to the other syndicate members.

✓ **Take Note:** A simple way to remember the normal order allocation priority found is in the syndicate letter: "Pro Golfers Don't Miss." PGDM stands for Presale, Group, Designated, and Member.

Quick Quiz 3.5   Multiple Choice

1. Your manager notifies you that a new municipal bond issue that you have been working on has been oversubscribed. How is the priority for acceptance of orders for this issue determined?

    A. On a first-come, first-served basis
    B. As outlined in the official statement
    C. As outlined in the official notice of sale
    D. As outlined in the syndicate agreement

2. Who signs the syndicate agreement for a municipal bond issue?

    A. Managing underwriter and the issuer
    B. Managing underwriter and the trustee
    C. Managing underwriter and the bond counsel
    D. All members of the underwriting syndicate

3. In a municipal underwriting, the scale is

    A. the first thing determined by the underwriting syndicate in calculating its bid
    B. the yield at which the syndicate plans to reoffer the bonds to the public
    C. both A and B
    D. neither A nor B

4. Your firm is bidding on a new general obligation bond issue. As the issuer weighs and evaluates the competitive bids, what will be the most important factor in deciding who will be awarded the winning bid?

    A. Net interest cost
    B. Scale
    C. Takedown
    D. Concession

5. An order confirmed for the benefit of the entire underwriting syndicate placed after the bid is awarded is called a

    A. group net order
    B. net designated order
    C. presale order
    D. member at the takedown order

6. A dealer should consider all of the following factors when determining the spread on a new issue EXCEPT

    A. prevailing interest rates in the marketplace
    B. amount bid on the issue
    C. type and size of the issue
    D. amount of the good faith check

7. An unqualified legal opinion means that the

    A. issue is legal, but certain contingencies may limit the flow of funds in the future
    B. interest is not exempt from state or local taxes
    C. bond counsel has rendered an opinion without any qualifying limitations
    D. underwriter has failed to disclose sufficient information to qualify the issue

8. The reoffering yield on a new municipal bond issue is the

    A. coupon rate on the new issue
    B. tax-equivalent yield of the new issue
    C. interest rate less any premiums that underwriters are willing to pay
    D. yield at which the bonds are offered to the public

Municipal Securities

Answers

1. **D.** The priority of filling municipal orders is established by the managing underwriter in the release terms letter sent to the syndicate once the bid is won. This letter is an amendment to the syndicate agreement.

2. **D.** The syndicate agreement is signed by all members of the syndicate including the managing underwriter. It is not signed by the issuer, the bond counsel, or the trustee.

3. **C.** The scale (or reoffering scale) is the yield(s) to maturity at which the syndicate will reoffer the bonds to the public. Syndicate participants consider the market for bonds of similar quality in deciding at what yields to market the issue on which they are bidding.

4. **A.** Net interest cost (NIC) measures an issuer's overall cost of borrowing for a particular bond issue. It is therefore the most important item considered by an issuer when evaluating competing bids. Coupon rate, par value, and maturity length are elements of the net interest cost calculation. The reoffering scale is the arrangement of yields at which the bonds will be sold to the public and is unrelated to the issuer's cost of borrowing. Takedown and concession refer to the arrangements for allocating bonds and assigning underwriting profit to the various underwriters once the winning bid has been awarded. These do not affect the net interest cost.

5. **A.** A municipal group net order is credited to syndicate members according to their percentage participation in the account. This order type is given priority over designated or member takedown orders (but not over presale orders). By placing this type of order, syndicate members are stipulating that they want those bond orders to have the highest priority still available. Note that pre-sale orders are also confirmed for the benefit of the entire syndicate but these are placed prior to the time the winning bid is awarded.

6. **D.** The spread is the difference between the reoffering price and the amount bid on an issue in competitive bidding. MSRB rules state that a dealer is entitled to make a profit in an underwriting. Therefore, the dealer can take into account such factors as market conditions, the type and size of the issue, the dollar volume of the transaction, and any extraordinary costs incurred by the syndicate. The amount of the good faith check deposited before bidding on the issue has no relevance to the bid or to the reoffering price.

7. **C.** An unqualified legal opinion means that the bond counsel found no problems with the issue. A qualified opinion means that the issue is legal, but some qualification is necessary because certain contingencies exist. For example, the bond counsel might render a qualified opinion because competing facilities may restrict the flow of funds in the future. Or if the issuer does not have clear title to the property, the legal opinion may be qualified. The legal opinion has nothing to do with broker/dealer disclosure.

8. **D.** In a competitive bidding situation, each syndicate submits a sealed written bid. The price the bonds are sold at is called the reoffering yield.

Payment and Delivery

New municipal bond issues are usually sold on a **when-issued** basis, meaning the securities are authorized, but not yet issued. After awarding an issue to a syndicate, the issuer has the bond certificates printed and finalizes any other legal matters. If the bonds are to be eligible for automated comparison and clearing, the managing underwriter must register the securities with a registered clearing agency, providing the agency with notice of the securities' coupon rate and settlement date as soon as they are known.

When the bonds are ready, the syndicate manager gives notice of the **settlement date**. The syndicate members, in turn, give notice of the settlement date to the purchasers. On the settlement date, the newly issued bonds are delivered to the underwriters with a final legal opinion, and the underwriters pay for the bonds on delivery.

Confirmations of Sales to Customers

On or before the completion of the transaction (settlement date), final confirmations must be sent to investors who purchased bonds from the underwriters. The investors' confirmations disclose the purchase price and settlement date for the transaction. The underwriters then deliver the bonds, accompanied by the legal opinion, to the investors.

The settlement date should not be confused with the **dated date** the issuer assigns to the bond issue. The dated date is the date on which interest begins to accrue. An investor must pay any interest that has accrued from the dated date up to, but not including, the settlement date. The investor starts receiving interest on the settlement date.

Analysis of Municipal Securities

Different criteria are used to evaluate the merits of general obligation and revenue bonds. When analyzing GOs, investors assess the municipality's ability to raise enough tax revenue to pay its debt. Revenue bond debt service depends on the income generated from a specific facility to cover its operating costs and pay its debt.

General Obligation Bonds

General Wealth of the Community

Because GOs are backed primarily by tax revenues, their safety is determined by the community's general wealth, which includes its:

- property values;
- retail sales per capita;

- local bank deposits and bank clearings;
- diversity of industry in its tax base; and
- population growth or decline.

A GO issuer's taxing power enables it to make principal and interest payments through all but the most unusual economic circumstances.

Characteristics of the Issuer

A **quantitative analysis** focuses on objective information regarding a municipality's population, property values, and per capita income. A **qualitative analysis** focuses on subjective factors that affect a municipality's securities. The community's attitude toward debt and taxation, population trends, property value trends, and plans and projects being undertaken in the area are all relevant considerations.

Debt Limits

To protect taxpayers from excessive taxes, statutory limits may be placed on the overall amount of debt a municipality can have. If a city's total debt is limited to 5% of the estimated market value of all taxable property within the city limits, this is the city's statutory debt limit. A bond's official statement discloses how close total outstanding debt, including newly issued debt, comes to its statutory debt limit.

A state constitution or city charter can also limit the purposes for which a city may issue bonds. Often, a city may issue bonds to finance capital improvements only if those bonds mature within the expected lifetimes of the improvements. This provision ensures that the city will not owe money on a facility when it becomes obsolete.

Income of the Municipality

The primary sources of municipal income are discussed below.

- Income and sales taxes are major sources of state income.
- Real property taxes are the principal income source of counties and school districts; real property taxes are the largest source of city income.
- City income can include fines, license fees, assessments, sales taxes, hotel taxes, city income taxes, utility taxes, and any city personal property tax.

Ad Valorem Taxes

Property taxes are based on a property's assessed valuation, a percentage of the estimated market value. That percentage is established by each state or county and varies substantially. The market value of each piece of property in a county is determined by the county assessor, who relies on recent sale prices of similar properties, income streams, replacement costs, and other information.

Because the real property tax is based on the property's value, it is said to be an **ad valorem**, or per value, tax. The tax is a lien on the property, which means the property can be seized if the tax is not paid. GOs, backed by the power to tax and seize property, are considered safer than revenue bonds of the same issuer and, therefore, can be issued with a lower interest rate.

Analyzing the Official Statement

Analysts study the documents included in the official statement to determine the issuer's financial condition at the present and in the foreseeable future.

Future Financial Needs

The municipality's financial statements should be scrutinized for signs of future debt requirements. The municipality might need to issue more debt if:

- its annual income is not sufficient to make the payments on its short-term (or floating) debt;
- principal repayments are scheduled too close together;
- sinking funds for outstanding term bonds are inadequate;
- pension liabilities are unfunded; or
- it plans to make more capital improvements soon.

Issuing more debt in the near future could damage an issuer's credit rating, which would cause the current issue to trade at a lower price.

The Debt Statement

The **debt statement** is used in the analysis of GO debt. It includes the estimated full valuation of taxable property, the estimated assessed value of property, and the assessment percentage.

To evaluate the municipality's debt structure, an analyst calculates **total debt**, the sum of all bonds issued by the municipality, and subtracts **self-supporting debt** from this figure. Although revenue bond debt is included in total debt, it is backed by revenues from the facility it financed and is not a burden on the municipality's taxpayers.

The result is the municipality's **net direct debt**, which includes GOs and short-term notes issued in anticipation of taxes or for interim financing. To net direct debt the analyst adds **overlapping debt.**

Overlapping debt disclosed on the debt statement is the city's proportionate share of the county's, school district's, park district's and sanitary district's debts. The city's **net total debt**, also called **net overall debt**, is the sum of the overlapping debt and the net direct debt.

Calculating a Municipality's Net Total Debt

A municipality's net total debt can be calculated as follows:

```
  Total Debt
− Self-supporting debt
− Sinking fund accumulations
= Net direct debt
+ Overlapping debt
= Net total debt
```

Test Topic Alert! A question might ask about what is or is not included in the various categories on the debt statement. A good rule of thumb: any category that uses the word *net*, self-supporting debt and sinking fund accumulations are not included. For instance, net total debt includes all GOs and overlapping debt but does not include the self-supporting and sinking fund accumulations.

Do not expect a calculation question on this topic—the exam is more interested in an understanding of the concept.

Revenue Bonds

Revenue bonds are rated according to a facility's potential to generate sufficient money to cover operating expenses and principal and interest payments. Revenue bonds are not repaid from taxes, so they are not subject to statutory debt limits. Revenue bonds are meant to be self-supporting, and if the facility they finance does not make enough money to repay the debts, the bondholders, not the taxpayers, bear the risk. When assessing the quality of revenue bonds, an investor should consider the following factors:

- **Economic justification:** the facility being built should be able to generate revenues
- **Competing facilities:** a facility should not be placed where better alternatives are easily available
- **Sources of revenue:** should be dependable
- **Call provisions:** with callable bonds, the higher the call premium, the more attractive a bond is to an investor
- **Flow of funds:** revenues generated must be sufficient to pay all of the facility's operating expenses and to meet debt service obligation

Applications of Revenues Principal and interest on revenue bonds are paid exclusively from money generated by the facility the issue finances. The issuer pledges to pay expenses in a specific order, called the **flow of funds**.

In most cases, a **net revenue pledge** is used, meaning operating and maintenance expenses are paid first. The remaining funds (or net revenues) are used to pay debt service and meet other obligations.

Flow of Funds in a Net Revenue Pledge

In a **net revenue pledge**, total receipts from operating the facility are usually deposited in the **revenue fund**, and funds are disbursed as follows.

- **Operations and maintenance**—used to pay current operating and maintenance expenses; remaining funds are called net revenues
- **Debt service account**—used to pay the interest and principal maturing in the current year and serving as a sinking fund for term issues
- **Debt service reserve fund**—used to hold enough money to pay one year's debt service
- **Reserve maintenance fund**—used to supplement the general maintenance fund
- **Renewal and replacement fund**—used to create reserve funds for major renewal projects and equipment replacements
- **Surplus fund**—used for a variety of purposes, such as redeeming bonds or paying for improvements

If the issuer has not pledged to pay operating and maintenance expenses first, debt service is the priority expense. When debt service is paid first, the flow of funds is called a **gross revenue pledge**.

The debt service includes current principal and interest due, plus any sinking fund obligations. If revenues exceed operating and other obligations, the money is usually placed in a surplus fund.

Gross and Net Revenue Pledges

Gross Revenue Pledge	Net Revenue Pledge
Issuer pays debt service first from gross revenues.	Issuer pays expenses first from gross revenues.
User pays operations and maintenance.	Issuer pays debt service second from net revenues.

Test Topic Alert! If you see questions that require differentiating gross revenue and net revenue pledges, maybe this will help: the name of the pledge tells you how debt service is paid. In a gross revenue pledge, debt service is paid first, from gross revenues. Operations and maintenance expenses are paid after debt service. In a net revenue pledge, debt service is paid from the net revenues, meaning operations and maintenance costs are paid first. This is the more common of the two pledges.

Municipal Debt Ratios

A community's ability to meet its debt service is reflected in the following mathematical ratios based on information in the debt statement and other documents.

- **Net debt to assessed valuation:** A ratio of 5% ($5,000 of debt per $100,000 of assessed property value) is considered reasonable for a municipality.
- **Net debt to estimated valuation:** Assessed valuation varies among municipalities, so most analysts prefer to use **estimated valuation** of property.
- **Taxes per person or per capita:** This ratio equals the city's tax income divided by the city population; it is used to evaluate the population's tax burden.
- **Debt per capita:** Larger cities can assume more debt per capita because their tax bases are more diversified.
- **Debt trend:** This number indicates whether the ratios are rising or falling. Bonds can be long-term investments, so it is important to anticipate the community's future financial position.
- **Collection ratio:** Equals the taxes collected divided by the taxes assessed; can help detect deteriorating credit conditions.
- **Coverage ratio:** Also called the **times interest earned ratio**, shows how many times annual revenues will cover debt service. A coverage of 2:1 is considered adequate for a typical municipal revenue bond. For utility revenue bonds (sewer, water, electricity), a coverage of 5:4 (125%) of fixed charges is considered adequate.

Basic demographic information (such as average age, average income, number of children in or expected to be in public schools, etc.) for a population living in a particular area is also used to evaluate GO bonds.

Test Topic Alert! Memorizing the ratios is less important than understanding them. A question might ask if a ratio is used to analyze GOs or revenues. Associate all ratios with GOs, except for debt service coverage ratio, which analyzes revenues.

1. A municipal revenue bond indenture contains a net revenue pledge. The following are reported for the year: $30 million of gross revenues, $18 million of operating expenses, $4 million of interest expense and $2 million of principal repayment. What is the debt service coverage ratio?

    A. 2:1
    B. 3:1
    C. 5:1
    D. 9:1

    A. Under a net revenue pledge, bondholders are paid from net revenue, which equals gross revenue minus operating expenses. Net revenue is

Analysis of Municipal Securities

$12 million ($30 million – $18 million). Debt service is the combination of interest and principal repayment. The debt service is $6 million ($4 million + $2 million). To compute the debt service ratio, divide net revenue by debt service: $12 million / $6 million = a ratio of 2-to-1.

Other Sources of Information for Municipal Bond Analysis

Interest Rate Comparisons In addition to issuer-specific information, the value of any bond is affected by trends in the overall bond market. Municipal bond prices tend to fluctuate more than government and corporate bond prices because each issue is unique and may have few regular market makers. Because fewer market makers exist in the municipal bond market than exist in the OTC equity market, the market for any specific municipal bond is typically thinner than the market for comparable corporate or government bonds.

Municipal Bond Insurance Municipal bond issuers can insure their securities' principal and interest payments by buying insurance from the **Municipal Bond Investors Assurance Corporation (MBIA)**, **AMBAC Indemnity Corporation (AMBAC)**, or **Financial Guaranty Insurance Company (FGIC)**. Insured bonds can be issued with lower coupon rates because investors will accept lower rates of return for the added safety insurance affords. Insured bonds are typically rated AAA.

Bond Ratings Rating services, such as Standard & Poor's, and Moody's and Fitch's, evaluate the credit quality of municipal bonds and publish their ratings. They also provide ratings for short-term municipal notes.

Moody's short-term MIG ratings are from MIG 1 (the best) through MIG 4 (acceptable). If a note is speculative, it is listed as S6. S&P's rates notes SP-1, SP-2, SP-3, and Fitch rates notes F-1, F-2, and F-3.

Quick Quiz 3.6   Multiple Choice

1. If an insured municipal bond defaults, the insurance company must pay

    A. interest only
    B. principal only
    C. both principal and interest
    D. neither principal nor interest

2. Which of the following are considered sources of debt service for GO bonds?

   I. Personal property taxes
   II. Real estate taxes
   III. Fees from delinquent property taxes
   IV. Liquor license fees

   A. I and IV only
   B. II and III only
   C. II, III, and IV only
   D. I, II, III and IV

3. In rating a general obligation bond, an analyst must consider

   I. debt per capita
   II. total outstanding debt
   III. tax collection ratio
   IV. political attitude

   A. I and II only
   B. I and III only
   C. II, III, and IV only
   D. I, II, III and IV

4. Which of the following is not considered when evaluating municipal revenue bond credit risk?

   A. Competing facilities
   B. Quality of management
   C. Coverage ratios
   D. Interest rate movements

5. A municipal bond issue would be nonrated when the

   A. municipality's credit is not good
   B. municipality's debt is too small to be rated
   C. issue is a term bond
   D. municipality has an outstanding bond in default

6. A qualitative analysis of a general obligation bond that is to be issued would take into consideration all of the following factors EXCEPT the

   A. tax base of the community
   B. economic character of the community
   C. dollar denominations of the bonds to be issued
   D. makeup of the community's population

Analysis of Municipal Securities

7. Which of the following would a customer examine to evaluate the credit quality of a new municipal security?

   A. Official statement
   B. Legal opinion
   C. Prospectus
   D. Trust indenture

8. All of the following would indicate deteriorating credit conditions EXCEPT an increase in

   A. bankruptcies
   B. consumer debt
   C. bond defaults
   D. assessed valuations

9. Which of the following could insure payment of principal and interest on a municipality's outstanding debt?

   I. MBIA
   II. AMBAC
   III. SIPC
   IV. FDIC

   A. I and II only
   B. I, II, and III only
   C. III and IV only
   D. I, II, III and IV

Answers

1. **C.** Municipal bond insurance is purchased to insure the payments of principal and interest in the event the issuer defaults.

2. **D.** All of the fees and taxes listed are payments received by the municipality that are not the result of a revenue-producing facility. General revenues of the municipality may be used to pay the debt service on a general obligation bond.

3. **D.** General obligation bonds are backed by the full faith and credit of an issuer, which is based on its ability to levy and collect taxes. While these quantitative factors are important to an analyst, qualitative factors such as a community's attitude toward borrowing and repaying debt are also important considerations.

4. **D.** Interest rate movements have no bearing on determining the quality of revenue bond issues.

5. **B.** The size of the municipality does not count, but the size of the debt outstanding for a municipality does. A municipality with a small amount of debt will not have enough activity in those debt instruments to warrant a rating by a rating agency.

Municipal Securities

6. **C.** The dollar denomination of bonds to be issued has no bearing on a GO bond analysis. The tax base, economic character, and population makeup would all be considered.

7. **A.** The official statement is an offering document that discloses material information on a new issue of municipal securities. Because it commonly includes information concerning the purpose of the issue, how the securities will be repaid, and the financial, economic, and social characteristics of the issuer, it is an appropriate place to review the creditworthiness of an issue. The legal opinion reviews the legality of the issue (including certain legal exemptions). A prospectus is the document that provides material information about a nonexempt security being publicly distributed. The trust indenture is the basic bond contract between the issuer and the trustee.

8. **D.** When credit conditions deteriorate, bankruptcies rise, bond defaults increase, and consumer debt increases (answers A, B, and C). An increase in assessed valuation (property value) would indicate a strengthening economy.

9. **A.** MBIA and AMBAC insure municipal bonds.

Municipal Trading and Taxation

Quotations

Municipal bonds are bought and sold in the over-the-counter (OTC) market. Most large brokerages maintain trading departments that deal exclusively in municipal bonds. Many of the rules governing the trading of other OTC securities also apply to municipal bond transactions.

Muni dealers are called upon regularly to provide current quotations for municipal securities. The term **quotation** means any bid for or offer of municipal securities. Any indication of interest or solicitation by a muni dealer (such as **bid wanted** or **offer wanted**) would be considered a quotation request.

Municipal bonds are usually priced and offered for sale on a **yield to maturity (YTM)** basis rather than a dollar price. This is called a **basis quote**. Municipal bonds with serial maturities are quoted in basis (YTM).

Dollar Bonds Some municipal revenue bonds are quoted on a percentage of par dollar basis rather than basis. Such bonds are commonly called dollar bonds. Dollar bonds are usually term bonds callable before maturity.

Test Topic Alert! If a question talks about a 6% bond quoted on a 6.5 basis, you should be able to determine that the coupon of the bond is 6% and its YTM is 6.5%. Because the YTM is higher than the coupon, the bond is trading at a discount.

Municipal Trading and Taxation

YTM/YTC and Premium and Discount

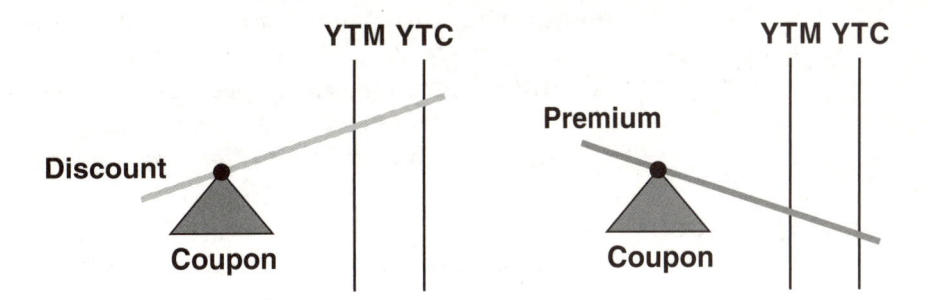

Are the following bonds trading at premium or a discount?

1. 7% bond, 6.25% basis
2. 7% bond, 7.64% basis
3. 5% bond, 4.85% basis
4. 6% bond, 6.45% basis

The answers: 1. Premium; 2. Discount; 3. Premium; 4. Discount

Be sure to recognize that a bond quoted at 104 is known as a dollar bond. For test questions, always associate dollar bonds with term maturities and basis bonds with serial maturities.

Bona Fide   If a muni dealer gives, distributes or publishes a quotation for a security, that quote must be **bona fide**. For a quote to be considered bona fide, or firm, the dealer must be prepared to trade the security at the price specified in the quote and under the conditions and restrictions (if any) accompanying the quote. A bona fide quote:

- must reflect the dealer's best judgment and have a reasonable relationship to the fair market value for that security; and
- may reflect the firm's inventory and expectations of market direction.

In other words, a quotation need not represent the best price but it must have a reasonable relationship to fair market value. A quotation may take into consideration such other factors as the dealer's inventory position and any anticipated market movement.

If the dealer distributes or publishes the quotation on behalf of another dealer, it must have reason to believe that the quote is bona fide and based on the other dealer's best judgment of fair market value. Dealers cannot knowingly misrepresent a quote made by another municipal securities dealer.

Quotations are always subject to prior sale or change in price. Any means of communication, including print, voice, and electronic media, can be used to disseminate, distribute, or publish quotations.

✓ **Take Note:** Municipal dealers can make offers to sell securities by providing quotes without owning the bonds. The dealer, however, must know where to obtain the bonds if such offers are accepted.

Types of Quotations A municipal securities dealer can give several types of quotations in addition to firm quotes. The most common are bona fide and nominal. Bona fide is a firm quote, meaning that the dealer is prepared to act.

- A **workable indication** reflects a bid price at which a dealer will purchase securities from another dealer. A dealer giving a workable indication is always free to revise its bid for the securities as market conditions change.
- A **nominal (or subject) quotation** indicates a dealer's estimate of a security's market value. Nominal quotations are provided for informational purposes only and are permitted if the quotes are clearly labeled as such. The rules on nominal quotes apply to all municipal bond quotes distributed or published by any dealer.

Holding a Quote A municipal securities dealer may quote a bond price that is firm for a certain time.

An **out firm with recall** quote is an example of this type of quote. Generally, these quotes are firm for an hour (or half hour) with a five-minute recall period. This provides time for the firm that received the quote to try to sell the bonds. If during this period, the firm that gave the quote has another buyer interested in the same bonds, the firm can contact the dealer and give him five minutes to confirm his order. If the order is not confirmed, the dealer loses the right to buy the bonds at the quoted price.

✓ **Take Note:** Receiving an out-firm quote allows a dealer to try to sell bonds that it does not own, knowing that if it finds a buyer within the allotted time, it can buy the bonds at a fixed price from the firm providing the out-firm quote.

Reports of Sales

MSRB rules prohibit dealers from distributing or publishing any report of a municipal security's purchase or sale unless they know or have reason to believe that the transaction took place. Broker/dealers reporting the sale must believe that the reported trade is real and not fictitious, fraudulent, or deceitful.

Municipal Trading and Taxation

Municipal securities dealers must report trades with other dealers to the **National Securities Clearing Corporation (NSCC)**. The report must include the two executing firms' names and the amount of accrued interest, if known.

✓ **Take Note:** A round lot for municipal bonds is usually $100,000 face amount.

Broker's Broker — Some municipal brokers specialize in trading only with institutional customers such as banks and other municipal brokers, not with the retail public. These firms are called **broker's brokers** because their business focuses on helping other muni dealers place unsold portions of new bond issues. They do not disclose the identity of the customers they represent. Further, they act solely as agents and do not maintain an inventory of bonds.

💡 **Test Topic Alert!** Broker's brokers protect the identity of their customers.

Broker/Dealer Regulation

Reciprocal Dealings (Antireciprocal Rule) — A dealer cannot solicit trades in municipal securities from an investment company in return for sales by the dealer of shares or units in the investment company (**antireciprocal rule**).

✓ **For Example:** If a municipal bond fund makes a large number of trades every month in its portfolio, a muni dealer cannot be selected to execute the fund's portfolio trades based only on the firm's promise that its account executives will increase sales of the bond fund's shares. The firm can be selected to execute those trades based on the services the dealer offers to the fund, such as prompt execution and research.

Customer Recommendations — MSRB rules require municipal securities brokers and dealers to make suitable recommendations to customers. Before making a recommendation, a municipal securities firm must make a reasonable effort to learn the customer's financial status, tax status, investment objectives, and other holdings. The **suitability test** applies to discretionary accounts as well as to other accounts. The practice of increasing commissions through excessive trading, or **churning**, is specifically prohibited. Before an account is opened it must be approved in writing by a principal.

✓ **Take Note:** If a customer refuses to disclose net worth and/or income, the account can still be opened. However, in this situation recommendations cannot be made.

Protecting Customer Accounts

Municipal securities dealers cannot misuse securities or funds held for another person. Dealers also may not guarantee customers against loss (put options and repurchase agreements are not considered guarantees against loss) or share in the profits or losses of a customer's account. An exception to this rule applies in the case of an associated person who establishes a personal joint account with a customer and obtains written permission from the firm. In this situation, the associated person may share in the account's profits and losses only in proportion to the amount of capital contributed to the account.

Disclosure of Control

A municipal securities firm that has a **control relationship** with respect to a municipal security is subject to additional disclosure requirements. A control relationship exists if the dealer controls, is controlled by, or is under common control with that security's issuer.

✓ **For Example:** An officer of a municipal dealer sits on the Board of Directories of an issuer.

The dealer must disclose the control relationship to the customer before it can effect any transaction in that security for that customer. While initially this disclosure can be verbal, the dealer must make a written disclosure at or before the transaction's completion. The disclosure is normally made on the confirmation. If the transaction is for a discretionary account, the customer must give express permission before the transaction can be executed.

Markups and Commissions

A dealer acts as an agent when it arranges trades for customers and charges **commissions**. A dealer acts as a principal when it buys for or sells securities from its own inventory. The dealer charges a **markup** for principal transactions when it sells securities to customers and a **markdown** when it buys securities from customers.

Principal Transactions Each **principal transaction** is executed at a net price, which includes the markup or markdown. Some of the factors taken into consideration include the:

- dealer's best judgment of fair market value;
- expense of effecting the transaction;
- fact that the dealer is entitled to a markup or markdown (profit);
- total dollar amount of the transaction; and
- value of any security exchanged or traded.

✓ **Take Note:** Markups or markdowns are not disclosed separately on a customer's confirmation.

Agency Transactions Each agency transaction is executed for a commission that is not in excess of a fair and reasonable amount, considering all relevant factors. For an agency commission calculation, a dealer takes into consideration the:

- security's availability;
- expense of executing the order;
- value of services the dealer renders; and
- amount of any other compensation received or to be received in connection with the transaction.

Best Execution

When executing an order as an agent, a dealer must make a reasonable effort to obtain a fair and reasonable price.

✓ *Take Note:* Commissions are disclosed on customer confirmations.

Confirmations

Customers must receive a written **confirmation** of each municipal securities transaction they have entered. The confirmation must describe the security; list the trade date, settlement date, and amount of accrued interest; state the firm's name, address, and phone number; and indicate whether the firm acted as agent or principal in the trade. A confirmation that does not include the time of execution must indicate that this information will be provided if the customer requests it.

Disclosing Yield In disclosing yield on a customer confirmation, the following rules apply. If the bond is non-callable, the actual life of the bond is known with certainty. Therefore, the yield shown is the yield to maturity.

If the bond is callable, the problem is the uncertainty surrounding a possible call. Will the bond be called? The answer is we do not know. If interest rates have risen since the bond's issuance (causing the price to fall and trade at a discount), the issuer is not likely to call the bonds since any refunding bonds would have to be sold at higher yields. If rates have fallen since the bond's issuance (causing the price to rise and trade at a premium), the issuer is more likely to call the bonds since any refunding bonds can be sold at lower yields.

Therefore, the result is that discount bonds are not likely to be called while premium bonds are likely to be called.

To deal with all of this, the MSRB requires that the yield shown on a customer confirmation be the lower of YTM or YTC. For discount bonds, the lower is YTM. For premium bonds the lower is YTC. If a premium bond has a number of call dates and prices, rather than computing yield to all of the possible call dates and prices to determine which is the lowest, the MSRB permits firms to show yield to the near-term (closest in) in-whole call.

Further, if the issuer has announced an in-whole call, there is no longer any uncertainty. Therefore, the confirmation should show yield computed to the announced call date and price which is the "new maturity" of the bond. If an issue is subject to a partial call, there is uncertainty as to whether the bond being sold to the customer will be one of the bonds selected for the call. In this situation, the basic rule applies: show the lower of YTM or YTC.

There are three cases where no separate yield disclosure is required:

- Variable rate bonds (**re-set bonds**). As the coupon is adjusted periodically, a yield computation is impossible.
- Bonds in default. If a bond is no longer paying interest, a yield computation is impossible.
- Bonds sold at par. For bonds sold at par, no separate yield disclosure is required because the yield cannot be anything other than the coupon rate. Remember: at par, all yields are the same.

Zero-Coupon Municipal Securities

A zero-coupon bond is issued at a deep discount from par and pays no current interest. The confirmation must indicate an interest rate of 0% and state that accrued interest is not calculated.

Required Information on Confirmations

Each confirmation must also include the following information.

- In an agency transaction, the name of the party on the other side of the transaction and the source and amount of any commission must be included (the name of the other party must be disclosed on request if it is not listed on the confirmation)
- The dated date if it affects the interest calculation
- Whether the securities are fully registered, registered as to principal only, in book-entry form, or in bearer form.
- Whether the securities are called or prerefunded, as well as the date of maturity fixed by the call notice and the amount of the call price
- Any special qualification or factor that might affect payment of principal or interest
- Whether the bond interest is taxable or subject to the alternative minimum tax (AMT)

Since 1983, any confirmation sent to a customer must include the security's **Committee on Uniform Securities Identification Procedures (CUSIP) number** (if available). The Committee on Uniform Securities Identification Procedures assigns a unique number to each **class** of common and preferred stock and to each **issue** of corporate and municipal bonds; the number is used to identify and track a particular security.

Advertising

Any material designed for use in the public media is considered **advertising**. This includes abstracts and summaries of the official statement; offering circulars; reports; market letters; and form letters, including professional, product, and new issue advertisements.

A municipal securities principal or general securities principal of the dealer must approve all advertising before use, and a copy of each advertisement must be kept on file for three years.

✓ **Take Note:** Preliminary and final official statements are not considered advertising because they are prepared by or on behalf of an issuer. Also note that copies of advertising are never filed with the MSRB.

The Broker/Dealer as Financial Adviser

Financial Advisers The MSRB has established ethical standards and disclosure requirements for municipal securities dealers that act as **financial advisers** to municipal securities' issuers. A financial advisory relationship exists when a muni dealer provides financial advisory or consulting services to an issuer with respect to a new issue for a fee or other compensation. This includes advice regarding the structure, timing and terms of, as well as other matters concerning, the issue or issuer.

Basis of Compensation

Each financial advisory relationship must be documented in writing before, upon, or promptly after its inception. This document establishes the basis of compensation for the advisory services to be rendered.

Conflicts of Interest Potential **conflicts of interest** arise if a firm acts as both underwriter and financial adviser for the same issue. The MSRB has the following requirements.

In the case of a **competitive bid**, a dealer that has a financial advisory relationship with the issuer can purchase all or part of the new issue if the issuer has consented in writing before the bid to such participation. There is no conflict of interest in this situation as the issuer will select the winning bidder based on NIC or TIC considerations.

In a **negotiated sale**, a muni dealer that has a financial advisory relationship can buy all or part of a new issue if it meets the following two conditions:

- it expressly discloses in writing to the issuer at or before the termination of the relationship that a conflict of interest may exist and the

issuer expressly acknowledges in writing to the broker/dealer receiving such disclosure; and
- the broker/dealer discloses in writing at or before termination the source of the anticipated amount of all remuneration to the broker/dealer with respect to the issue, in addition to compensation received for financial advisory services, and the issuer acknowledges in writing receiving such disclosure.

Purchasers of the new issue securities must be informed if an advisory relationship exists at or prior to confirmation of sale.

Assistance with Official Statement

As part of its financial advisory services to an issuer, a municipal securities dealer may help prepare the final official statement for a new issue. If it prepares the official statement, the adviser must make a copy of that statement available to the managing underwriter promptly after the award is made and at least two days before the syndicate manager delivers the securities to the syndicate members.

Use of Ownership Information

While acting in a fiduciary capacity for an issuer, a municipal securities dealer often obtains confidential information about its bondholders. The dealer cannot use this information to solicit purchases or sales of municipal securities or to pursue other financial gain without the issuer's consent.

Examples of fiduciary capacities include, but are not limited to, acting as paying agent, transfer agent, registrar, or indenture trustee for an issuer.

Quick Quiz 3.7   Multiple Choice

1. According to the MSRB, a control relationship would exist between a municipal broker/dealer and an issuer when

   A. senior officers of the municipal dealer live in the municipality
   B. the firm recently completed a negotiated underwriting for the municipality
   C. an officer of the underwriter is in a position of authority over the issuer of the municipal bonds
   D. the dealer has an inventory of the issuer's bonds that are trading at a premium

2. A municipal bond is issued with five years of call protection. The bonds are callable after that date with a scale of declining premiums. The bond has been prerefunded and the proceeds of the refunding issue deposited in an escrow account and invested in direct federal debt issues. The bonds are sold at a dollar price, so the confirmation must show the

   A. lowest yield to maturity or yield to call
   B. yield to the maturity date established by the refunding
   C. yield to the longer call with the lower resulting yield
   D. yield to the longer call with the higher resulting yield

3. MSRB rules prohibit municipal securities firms from engaging in which of the following activities with investment companies?

   A. Accepting a presale order for a new municipal issue
   B. Hiring investment company officers
   C. Soliciting municipal transactions from the investment company as compensation for shares sold of the investment company
   D. Any transactions in municipal securities by investment companies

4. If a firm prepares a summary official statement for a new issue of municipal bonds, before it is distributed to customers it must have the written approval of which of the following?

   A. MSRB
   B. Issuer
   C. Firm's municipal securities principal
   D. Bond attorney

Answers

1. **C.** The officer of the broker/dealer has control over both the broker/dealer and the issuer.

2. **B.** The bond has been refunded; the money is in the escrow account, and the outstanding bonds will be called as soon as possible. With these conditions, the date and the price at which the bonds will be called are known. The maturity date is established by the refunding. The yield that is to be shown on the confirmation is the yield to call established by that refunding.

3. **C.** The idea behind the municipal antireciprocal rule is that investment companies should not attempt to induce municipal broker/dealers to sell shares of the fund. This could be done if the investment company ran its portfolio trades only through those broker/dealers that sold the most fund shares. This practice is prohibited under MSRB rules. Of course, presale orders for new municipal issues may be accepted and transactions between investment companies and municipal broker/dealers are allowed. Otherwise, how could the fund's portfolio be traded?

4. **C.** A person qualified as a general securities or municipal securities principal must give prior written approval to muni securities advertising. Abstracts and summaries of official statements are included in the MSRB definition of advertising.

Taxation of Municipal Issues

Tax-Exempt Interest Payments The **Tax Reform Act of 1986** restricted the federal income tax exemption of interest for municipal bonds to public purpose bonds, bonds issued to finance projects that benefit citizens in general rather than particular private interests. If a bond channels more than 10% of its proceeds to private parties, it is considered a private activity bond and is not automatically granted tax exemption.

Calculating Tax Benefits

An investor considering the purchase of a tax-exempt bond should compare its yield carefully with that of taxable securities. The tax savings of the tax-free bond may be more attractive than a taxable bond with a higher interest rate. This depends, in part, on the investor's tax bracket: the higher the tax bracket, the greater the tax exemption's value.

To determine a municipal bond investment's tax benefit, an investor must calculate the tax-equivalent yield. To do so, divide the tax-free yield by 100% less the investor's tax rate.

Test Topic Alert! When answering a tax equivalent yield question, keep in mind that the muni yield will always be less than the corporate yield.

An investor is in the 30% tax bracket. A municipal bond currently yields 7%. To offer an equivalent yield, what must a corporate bond yield?

Divide the municipal yield by 100%—the investor's tax bracket.

This is known as the tax-equivalent yield formula.

$$7\% / (100\% - 30\%) = 10\%$$

Assume the same investor is in the 30% tax bracket. If a corporate bond currently yields 11%, what would be the equivalent muni yield?

To find the answer, multiply the corporate yield by 100%—the investor's tax bracket. This is known as the tax-free equivalent yield formula.

$$11\% \times (100\% - 30\%) = 7.7\%$$

No Interest Deductions The expenses associated with purchasing or holding municipal bonds are not deductible. This includes interest on loans to acquire bonds (such as margin loans) and safe deposit box rental. These rules apply because of the tax-free nature of the interest income at the federal government level.

Exception for Banks

When banks purchase certain issues of GO bonds (limited to a maximum face amount of $10 million), they are allowed to deduct 80% of the interest carrying cost of the deposits funding the purchase of the bonds.

✓ **For Example:** A bank buys municipal bonds with $1 million of deposits paying 3% interest. Because these bonds are bank qualified, the bank can deduct 80% of the interest paid (1 million × .03 × .8 = $24,000). The bank also receives interest on the newly purchased municipal bonds free of federal income tax.

Municipal Securities Rules and Regulations

Municipal Securities Rulemaking Board (MSRB)

The Securities Acts Amendments of 1975 established the **Municipal Securities Rulemaking Board** as an independent SRO. The MSRB governs the issuing and trading of municipal securities. The rules require municipal securities underwriters and dealers to protect investors' interests, be ethical in offering advice, and be responsive to complaints and disputes. The MSRB rules apply to all firms and individuals engaged in the conduct of municipal securities business.

Rule Enforcement

The MSRB has no authority to enforce the rules it makes. The rules concerning municipal securities dealers are enforced by the NASD; the Office of the Comptroller of the Currency enforces those rules that apply to national banks.

The **Federal Reserve Board (FRB)** enforces MSRB rules governing any non-national banks that are members of the Federal Reserve System. The **Federal Deposit Insurance Corporation (FDIC)** enforces MSRB rules for non-national banks that are not members of the Federal Reserve System.

✓ **Take Note:** This final section of the Municipal Securities unit addresses the rules of the MSRB. Each rule is identified with a G-number, such as G-12. It is unnecessary to memorize these rules by their numbers; instead, know the context of these rules thoroughly. About 10 to 15 of the muni questions will probably be from these MSRB rules.

General Regulations The three categories of MSRB rules include (1) rules that provide consistent legal definitions of terms used in the business of trading municipal securities, (2) administrative rules that cover the organization and functions of the MSRB, and (3) general rules and regulations that describe MSRB policies. The following sections highlight the important MSRB rules.

Rule G-1. A bank that has a separately identifiable department or division engaged in any activity related to the municipal securities business is classified as a municipal securities dealer and must comply with MSRB regulations. A separately identifiable division is one under the direct supervision of an officer of the bank responsible for the day-to-day conduct of municipal securities business.

Municipal securities-related activity includes underwriting, trading or selling municipal securities, or serving as an issuer's financial adviser. In addition, a firm that provides research or advisory services for municipal securities investors or that communicates with the public in any way about investing in municipal securities is considered a municipal securities dealer and must register with the MSRB.

Rules G-2 and G-3. Those who must qualify by examination under MSRB rules include municipal securities principals, financial and operations principals, and municipal securities representatives. A municipal securities rep is any person who gives financial advice to municipal securities issuers or investment advice to investors. Anyone who communicates with the public about municipal securities acts as a representative.

A person must pass the Municipal Securities Representative Qualification Exam (Series 52) or the General Securities Registered Representative Exam (Series 7) to be qualified as a municipal securities representative. To qualify as a municipal securities principal, a person must pass the Municipal Securities Principal Qualification Exam (Series 53).

✓ *Take Note:* Excluded from the licensing requirements are persons acting in a clerical or ministerial capacity who:

- read approved quotes;
- provide trade reports; or
- record or enter orders.

Persons who take a qualification exam and fail cannot retake the exam for 30 days. After failing the exam three or more times, a six-month wait is imposed before another attempt is allowed. The NYSE and NASD have adopted this rule.

A 90-day apprenticeship is required of people entering the securities industry, and during this period they may not engage in any municipal securities business with the public. An apprentice may engage in municipal business with other dealers, but may not receive commissions for such transactions, although the apprentice can receive a salary during this period. The MSRB counts time spent as a general securities representative toward the 90-day requirement.

If a new municipal representative has not passed the appropriate exam within 180 days, he must stop performing all functions of a municipal representative.

Rule G-6. The MSRB requires municipal broker/dealers to maintain blanket fidelity bonds as mandated by the SRO to which a broker/dealer belongs. The dollar amount of coverage required varies according to the firm's size. Banks are not affected by this rule.

Rule G-7. A municipal securities dealer must obtain and keep on file specific information about its associated persons. Most of the required information (e.g., employment history, disciplinary actions, residence, personal data) is contained on the U-4 and U-5 forms.

Rule G-10. Any time a municipal securities firm receives a written complaint from a customer, the firm must enter the complaint in a complaint file, indicating what action, if any, the firm has taken, and it must deliver a copy of the MSRB's *Investor Brochure* to that customer.

Rule G-11. During the underwriting period, a syndicate must establish a priority for allocating orders and identify conditions that might alter the priority.

Rule G-12. This rule outlines the procedures (**uniform practices**) for settling transactions between municipal securities firms. The MSRB uniform practices include regulations regarding settlement dates, which are the same for municipal securities firms as they are for the rest of the securities industry.

- **Cash trades** settle on the trade date.
- **Regular way** trades settle on the third business day after the trade date.

Rule G-12 also discusses **good delivery requirements**. Securities that are not in good delivery form are rejected (buyer does not accept delivery) or reclaimed (buyer accepts delivery only to find the bonds are not good delivery). This does not invalidate the trade—the seller is still obligated to sell the securities.

Delivery is made in denominations of $1,000 or $5,000 for bearer bonds. Registered bonds are delivered in multiples of $1,000 par value, with a maximum par value on any one certificate of $100,000.

Mutilated certificates are not good delivery unless the transfer agent or some other acceptable official of the issuer validates the security. The issuer or a commercial bank must endorse mutilated coupons for them to be considered good delivery. Coupon bonds must have all unpaid coupons attached in proper order.

In the case of an issue's **partial call**, the called securities are not good delivery unless they are identified as called when traded. Municipal securities without legal opinions attached are not good delivery unless it is specified on the trade date that the transaction is ex-legal.

Rule G-13. Dealers can publish quotations only for bona fide bids or offers. Nominal quotes (informational only) are permissible if identified as such. No dealer participating in a joint account may distribute a quotation indicating more than one market for that security.

Rule G-15. Confirmations of trades must be sent or given to customers at or before a transaction's completion. Each confirm must include the following:

- broker/dealer's name, address, and telephone number;
- customer's name;
- detailed description of the security, including issuer, interest rate and maturity, whether it is callable, etc.;
- trade date and time of execution;
- settlement date;
- CUSIP number, if any;
- yield and dollar price;
- amount of accrued interest;
- extended principal amount (the total principal of all securities the information covers);
- total dollar amount (the extended principal plus any accrued interest);
- whether the firm acted as broker or dealer (if it acted as broker, the name of the person on the other side of the trade must be given, if requested, and the dollar amount of commission earned from both parties must be disclosed);
- dated date, if it affects the interest calculation and the first interest payment date;
- level of registration of the security (fully registered, registered as to principal only, or book-entry);
- whether the bonds are called or prerefunded; and
- any other special fact about the security traded (escrowed to maturity, ex-legal trade, federally taxable, odd denominations, etc.).

Rule G-16. Each municipal broker/dealer must be examined at least once every two calendar years to ensure that the firm is in compliance with MSRB regulations, SEC rules, and the Securities Exchange Act of 1934. Because the MSRB does not enforce its own rules, it does not examine municipal securities firms. The appropriate enforcement agency (NASD, FDIC, Comptroller of the Currency, FRB) administers the examinations.

Rule G-17. Municipal securities dealers must deal fairly with everyone in transacting municipal securities business and must not engage in deceptive, dishonest, unfair, or manipulative practices.

Rule G-18. Dealers must try to obtain prices for customers that are reasonable and fairly related to the market. This rule also applies to brokers' brokers, which regularly effect trades for the accounts of other municipal brokers and dealers.

Rule G-19. A municipal securities firm, through its reps, must obtain extensive financial, personal, and investment information about a client to ensure suitable recommendations and transactions. A representative must obtain and use as much information as possible when making recommendations and must have reasonable grounds for recommending any particular security or transaction.

The MSRB prohibits broker/dealers from recommending municipal securities to a customer if a broker/dealer has not obtained the customer's financial information, tax status, and investment objectives, even if the broker/dealer has reasonable grounds to believe that the recommendation is suitable for the customer.

Rule G-20. Municipal securities dealers cannot give gifts valued at more than $100 to any person in one year other than their employees. Payments for services rendered are allowed. Gifts of occasional meals or tickets to sporting events or concerts (not season passes) are permitted. Sponsorship of legitimate business functions is also permissible.

Rule G-21. Municipal securities firms must be truthful in their advertising. They must not publish advertisements that are false or misleading in regard to their services, skills, or products. An advertisement for a new issue can show the original reoffering price, even though it may have changed, if the advertisement contains the sale date. A firm's municipal or general securities principal must approve each advertisement in writing before first use.

Rule G-22. Clients must be informed if a **control relationship** exists between a municipal firm and an issuer. A control relationship means the dealer or one of its officers is in a position to influence the issuer or is in a position to be influenced by the issuer. The phrase "...controls, is controlled by or is under common control with..." allows the broadest interpretation of *control*. Verbal disclosure is required before the trade is effected, with written disclosure following no later than at the time of the confirmation.

> ✓ ***Take Note:*** Particular care must be taken in a discretionary account. If a control relationship exists, no transaction is permitted without prior authorization from the customer.

Rule G-23. If a firm acting in a financial advisory capacity wants to participate in the issue on which it has advised, it must get written consent from the issuer to submit a competitive bid. For a negotiated bid, the advisory contract must be terminated in writing, and the issuer must give written consent. The former financial adviser must tell the issuer of the possible conflict of interest and disclose to the issuer the source and anticipated amount of money received, if participating in the issue. Also, if a financial advisory relationship exists or did exist between the dealer and issuer, the dealer must inform buyers of the securities of this fact.

For a competitive bid, the advisory contract need not be terminated. The issuer, however, must consent to the underwriter's participation in writing.

Rule G-24. In the normal course of business, dealers gain access to confidential, nonpublic information about their customers. Municipal securities firms may not use this confidential information to solicit trades of municipal securities except with an issuer's express consent.

Rule G-25. Like other types of broker/dealers, municipal securities firms and their representatives may not misuse securities or money held for other people. They must not guarantee a customer against loss or share in the profits or losses of a customer's account, although joint accounts in a private capacity are allowed. Bona fide put options and repurchase agreements are not considered guarantees against loss.

Rule G-27. Each municipal securities firm must designate a principal to supervise the firm's representatives and must create and maintain a written supervisory procedures manual. The designated principal for the firm must approve in writing:

- the opening of new customer accounts;
- every municipal securities transaction;
- actions taken on customer complaints; and
- correspondence regarding municipal securities trades.

Every broker/dealer, but not bank-dealers, must have a **financial and operations principal (FinOp)** who maintains the financial books and records.

Rule G-28. If a municipal securities dealer employee opens an account with another municipal securities firm, MSRB rules require the firm opening the account to notify the employer in writing and to send duplicate confirmations to the employer. The firm opening the account must comply with any other requests the employer makes.

Rule G-29. Every municipal securities dealer's office must keep a copy of MSRB regulations so that it may provide a copy of these rules for review to any customer upon request.

Rule G-30. The markups or markdowns that municipal securities dealers charge must be fair and reasonable, taking into account all characteristics of a trade, such as:

- fair market value of the securities at trade time;
- total dollar amount of the transaction;
- any special difficulty in doing the trade; and
- the fact that the dealer is entitled to a profit.

Rule G-31. A municipal securities broker/dealer may not solicit business from an investment company based on the broker/dealer's record of sales of the investment company's shares.

Rule G-32. When a new issue of municipal securities is delivered to a customer, a copy of the official statement must accompany or precede the delivery.

If the issue is a negotiated underwriting, the municipal firm must disclose in writing to the customer the amount of the spread, the amount of any fee received if the firm acted as an agent in the sale, and the initial offering price for each maturity in the issue. There is no requirement to disclose the spread in competitive underwritings.

It is the underwriter's responsibility to supply offering documents upon request to any broker/dealer to which it sells new municipal securities.

Rule G-33. Municipal dealers must calculate accrued interest when a municipal security trades "and interest." Municipal bonds, like corporates, use a 360-day year with 30-day months.

Rule G-37. Rule G-37 prohibits municipal firms from engaging in municipal securities business with an issuer for two years after any political contribution is made to an official of that issuer. In this context, municipal securities business refers to negotiated underwritings, not to competitive underwritings. The idea is to prevent firms from making large political contributions in return for being selected as underwriter for that issuer.

The rule applies to contributions by the firm, its municipal finance professionals (representatives) and by Political Action Committees controlled by the firm or its representatives. Contributions of up to $250 per election, are permitted by municipal finance professionals as long as these individuals are eligible to vote for the issuer official. This exemption does not apply to firms.

Rule G-39. Telemarketers calling on behalf of a firm may not call a person before 8:00 am or after 9:00 pm in the called person's time zone. The caller must disclose his name and the firm's name, the firm's telephone number or address, and the fact that he is calling to solicit the purchase of municipal bonds or investment services.

The requirements do not apply if the person called is an established customer who has an account and has made a transaction within the previous year. Calls made to other brokers or dealers are also exempt.

Tracking Municipal Securities

Tax-exempt bonds are listed in financial publications such as *The Bond Buyer* and *The Wall Street Journal*.

Tax-Exempt Bond Transactions

Tax-Exempt Bonds

Representative prices for tax-exempt revenue and GO bonds based on institutional trades. Changes rounded to nearest 1/8th. Yield is YTM.

Issue	Coupon	Maturity	Price	Chg	Bid Yld
Alaska Hsg Fin Corp	6.600	12-01-23	97 1/2	- 1/4	6.79
Cal Dept of Wtr Res	6.125	12-01-13	95 3/4	- 1/2	6.50
Charlotte Hosp Auth	6.250	01-01-20	95 3/8	+ 1/2	6.62
Farmington NM Util Sys	5.750	05-15-13	91 1/4	- 1/8	6.53
Ill State Toll Hwy Auth	6.375	01-01-15	96	+ 3/8	6.72
Kenton Co KY Airport	6.300	03-01-15	95 1/4	- 1/2	6.71

✓ **For Example:** Look at the Kenton County, Kentucky Airport bond. The name of the bond appears in the left column under "Issue." The entries in the "Coupon" and "Maturity" columns indicate that the bond pays 6.300% interest and matures on March 1, 2015. The bond was traded at 95-1/4, or $952.50 per $1,000 bond.

The price represents a half-point ($5) decrease from the last trade, as reported under the "Chg" (change) column. The 6.71 yield is the bid yield and the yield to maturity. Because the bond is selling at a discount, the yield to maturity is higher than the coupon yield.

Municipal Securities HotSheet

GOs:
- "Full faith and credit bonds"
- Backed primarily by taxes

- Generally safer than revenues
- Voter approval required
- Debt limits may restrict issuance
- Generally competitive bid underwriting
- Generally firm commitment underwriting
- Generally serial maturities with basis quotes
- Analysis based on taxes, debt statement, ratios, demographics

Revenues:
- Self-supporting bonds
- Backed by user fees
- Generally less safe than GOs
- No voter approval, may be subject to additional bonds test
- Feasibility study to determine economic viability
- Generally negotiated underwriting
- May be serial maturities with basis quotes or term maturities with dollar quotes
- Analysis based on feasibility study, debt service coverage ratio

IDRs:
- Backed by corporations; leaseback payments; interest may be taxable

PGDM:
- Presale, Group, Designated, Member: order allocation priority in syndicate letter

Bond Buyer:
- Mostly primary market info
- Includes 30-day visible supply, placement ratios, official notices of sale

Munifacts:
- Wire service, provides general information relevant to muni market
- Owned by the *Bond Buyer*

Spread:
- Compensation to syndicate
- Smallest portion is manager's fee
- Largest portion is takedown (concession plus additional takedown)

Three Years:
- Required time for keeping advertising records
- 2 years in readily accessible location
- Advertising may be approved by muni or general securities principal

90 Days:
- Muni apprenticeship period; no commissions, no dealing with customers

Confirmations:
- No later than settlement date for final confirmations

Unqualified:
- Most desirable legal opinion; no reservations by bond counsel

$100:
- Maximum gift allowed to persons other than employees

TIC:
- Includes time value of money; NIC method more commonly used for determining winning bid

Commissions:
- Markups/commissions must be fair and reasonable; no 5% guideline for MSRB

Tax-Equivalent Yield:
- Muni yield / (100% − Investor's tax bracket)

Tax-Free Equivalent Yield:
- Corp yield × (100% − Investor's tax bracket)

Rule G-37:
- 2-year prohibition on municipal securities business
- Exemption allowed for contributions of $250 or less by municipal finance professionals

Series 7 Unit Test 3

1. The call premium on a municipal bond trading above par is best described as the difference between

   A. the market price and par
   B. the market price and the call price
   C. par and the call price
   D. the amortized premium and the annual interest

2. The interest from which of the following bonds is exempt from federal income tax?

   I. State of California
   II. City of Anchorage
   III. Treasury bonds
   IV. GNMA

   A. I and II
   B. I, II and IV
   C. III and IV
   D. I, II, III and IV

3. A couple's home has an assessed valuation of $40,000 and a market value of $100,000. What will the tax be if a rate of 5 mills is used?

   A. $200
   B. $500
   C. $2,000
   D. $5,000

4. The document that establishes the municipal syndicate as either Eastern or Western and establishes the terms for operation of the syndicate is known as the

   A. underwriting agreement
   B. trust indenture
   C. agreement among underwriters
   D. bond resolution

5. All of the following deal with the secondary market EXCEPT

   A. dealer quotes
   B. broker's broker
   C. notice of sale
   D. Munifacts

6. The MSRB is authorized to adopt rules concerning all of the following EXCEPT the

   A. form and content of price quotations
   B. sale of new issues to related portfolios
   C. information to be provided by municipal issuers
   D. records to be maintained by municipal dealers

7. Which of the following have authority to enforce MSRB rules?

   I. SEC
   II. NASD
   III. Comptroller of the Currency
   IV. Federal Reserve Board

   A. I and II only
   B. I, II and IV only
   C. III and IV only
   D. I, II, III and IV

8. Municipal broker's brokers deal with all of the following EXCEPT

   A. bank dealers
   B. municipal dealers
   C. individuals
   D. institutions

9. Which of the following projects is most likely to be financed by a general obligation rather than a revenue bond?

   A. Municipal hospital
   B. Expansion of an airport
   C. New high school
   D. Public golf course

10. All of the following characteristics regarding industrial development bonds are true EXCEPT

    A. the bonds are issued by municipalities or other governmental units
    B. the funds are used to construct a facility for a private corporation
    C. these bonds are normally backed by the full faith and credit of the municipality
    D. funds from the lease are used to pay the principal and interest on the bonds

11. Which of the following statements regarding the good faith deposit submitted by interested bidders are TRUE?

    I. It is usually 1 to 2% of the total par value of the bonds offered.
    II. It is usually 10% of the total par value of the bonds offered.
    III. If the bid is unsuccessful, it is returned to the underwriting syndicate.
    IV. If the bid is unsuccessful, it is retained by the issuer.

    A. I and III
    B. I and IV
    C. II and III
    D. II and IV

12. If IDB bonds are called because of condemnation, this would be covered under which of the following clauses in the bond indenture?

    A. Defeasance
    B. Refunding
    C. Catastrophe
    D. Refinancing

13. Which of the following would be found in the agreement among underwriters for a municipal bond offering?

    I. Legal opinion
    II. Amount of the concession
    III. Appointment of the bond counsel
    IV. Establishment of the takedown

    A. I and III
    B. I and IV
    C. II and III
    D. II and IV

14. New Housing Authority (NHA) bonds are a relatively safe investment because

    A. rental income provides a hedge against inflation
    B. the U.S. government guarantees a contribution to secure the bonds
    C. they are backed by the full faith and credit of the issuing municipalities
    D. banks buy these bonds

15. Which of the following types of municipal bond issues is (are) associated with a flow of funds?

    A. TANs
    B. General obligation bonds
    C. Revenue bonds
    D. All of the above.

16. New issues of municipal securities are available in

    I. bearer form
    II. book entry form
    III. registered form
    IV. registered as to principal only form

    A. II and III
    B. II, III and IV
    C. III and IV
    D. I, II, III and IV

17. All of the following statements regarding a municipality's debt limit are true EXCEPT that

    A. the purpose of debt restrictions is to protect taxpayers from excessive taxes
    B. revenue bonds are not affected by statutory limitations
    C. the debt limit is the maximum amount a municipality can borrow in any one year
    D. unlimited GO bonds may be issued when a community's taxing power is not restricted by statutory provisions

18. The proceeds from a new municipal bond issue sold for the purpose of advance refunding may be invested in all of the following EXCEPT

    A. agency issues
    B. AAA municipal bonds
    C. government bonds
    D. bank CDs

19. An issuer's proportionate share of the debt of other local governmental units in the area in which the issuer is located is defined as

    A. net direct debt
    B. overlapping debt
    C. bonded debt
    D. reversionary working interest

20. Nonmembers of a syndicate buy the bonds at a discount called

    A. a takedown
    B. a net designated price
    C. a concession
    D. the basis price

21. The Bond Buyer Revenue Bond Index

    I. includes 30-year bonds
    II. includes 20 bonds
    III. is compiled weekly

    A. I and II
    B. I and III
    C. II and III
    D. I, II and III

22. Special tax bonds are

    A. general obligation bonds
    B. self-supporting bonds
    C. backed by property taxes
    D. backed by sales and/or excise taxes

23. In a municipal underwriting, total takedown can be described as

    A. additional takedown + concession
    B. underwriting fee + additional takedown
    C. underwriting fee + manager's fee
    D. additional takedown + underwriting fee

24. Which of the following is a double-barrelled bond?

    A. New Housing Authority bond
    B. Project note
    C. Hospital bond backed by revenues and taxes
    D. GO bond to construct a new grade school

25. Which of the following statements regarding callable municipal bonds is TRUE?

    A. Noncallable bonds usually yield more than callable bonds.
    B. Bonds are typically called when interest rates are rising.
    C. Bond call premiums generally compensate the bondholder for interest payments lost if the bond is called.
    D. As interest rates rise, callable bonds trading at a premium will generally rise in value.

26. Seventy-five basis points is equal to

    I. 7.5%
    II. .75%
    III. $7.50
    IV. $75.00

    A. I and III
    B. I and IV
    C. II and III
    D. II and IV

27. An unqualified legal opinion means that the
    A. issue is legal, but certain contingencies may limit the flow of funds in the future
    B. interest is not exempt from state or local taxes
    C. bond counsel has rendered an opinion without any qualifying limitations
    D. underwriter has failed to disclose sufficient information to qualify the issue

28. Which of the following should a registered representative consider before recommending a municipal security?
    A. Customer's state of residence
    B. Customer's tax status
    C. Municipal security's rating
    D. All of the above.

29. All of the following statements regarding municipal bond official statements are true EXCEPT
    A. all purchasers of a new municipal bond issue must receive a final official statement
    B. a customer must receive an official statement no later than the settlement date
    C. an official statement must be delivered only upon customer request
    D. the MSRB does not require the preparation of a final official statement for new municipal bond issues

30. In the context of municipal bond underwritings, what distinguishes the true interest cost from the net interest cost?
    A. TIC reflects the time value of money.
    B. TIC reflects the credit risk.
    C. TIC is the method required by the IRS.
    D. TIC produces a lower cost of borrowing for the issuer.

31. Which of the following governmental bodies receive the least amount of their revenues from property taxes?
    A. State governments
    B. County governments
    C. Municipalities
    D. School districts

32. TANs, RANs, and BANs are issued by municipalities seeking
    A. short-term financing
    B. special tax assessments for GO bonds
    C. bond insurance
    D. financing for low-cost housing

33. A municipal securities representative intends to give $50 crystal vases to 10 of his favorite clients. According to MSRB rules, this is
    A. not permitted because the representative is not allowed to give gifts to customers
    B. not permitted because the aggregate amount exceeds the permissible annual limit
    C. permitted
    D. only permitted with written permission from the MSRB

34. An abstract of an official statement for a municipal securities issue must be maintained on file for
    A. 12 months
    B. three years
    C. five years
    D. There is no requirement to file abstracts of official statements.

35. Which of the following would be considered in analyzing the credit of a revenue bond issue?

    I. Per capita debt
    II. Debt service coverage
    III. Management
    IV. Debt to assessed valuation

    A. I and II
    B. I and IV
    C. II and III
    D. II, III and IV

36. A legal opinion evaluates which of the following features of a municipal issue?

    I. Marketability
    II. Legality
    III. Tax-exempt status
    IV. Economic feasibility

    A. I and II
    B. II and III
    C. III and IV
    D. I, II, III and IV

37. The interest from which of the following bonds would be included in the alternative minimum tax calculation?

    A. General obligation bonds
    B. Industrial development revenue bonds
    C. TANs
    D. Special Assessment bonds

Series 7 Unit Test 3 Answers & Rationale

1. **C.** The call premium represents the difference between the call price and par. The further away a call date and price, the lower the call premium. QID: 36435

2. **A.** Municipal bonds are exempt from federal income tax. Direct federal debt, such as Treasury bonds, is subject to federal income tax but is exempt from state tax. GNMA bonds are subject to federal, state, and local taxes. QID: 30546

3. **A.** Real property tax is based on the assessed value assigned to the property by the municipality's tax assessor (in this case, $40,000). Property tax rates use the mill (or mil) as a base unit. One mill = $1 of tax per year for each $1,000 of assessed value. Five mills would equal $5 for each $1,000 of assessed value. Because there are 40 thousands, 40 × $5 = $200 in annual tax. A short-cut method is: take the assessed value, remove the last three 0s and multiply by the number of mills of tax ($40 × 5 mills = $200). QID: 29636

4. **C.** The agreement amount underwriters (the syndicate agreement) spells out the rights and obligations of each syndicate member. It also details how the responsibility for unsold bonds will be handled. In a Western account, liability is divided, which means each syndicate member is responsible only for its participation. In an Eastern account, each syndicate member assumes pro-rata responsibility for unsold bonds. QID: 36511

5. **C.** A notice of sale is published to provide syndicates with information on proposed new (primary market) issues. QID: 35081

6. **C.** The MSRB does not regulate issuers. Rather, it regulates the underwriting of municipal securities and the subsequent secondary market trading. Disclosure requirements for issuers are mandated by the SEC. QID: 29960

7. **D.** The Comptroller of the Currency, the FRB, and the FDIC regulate banks. The NASD enforces MSRB rules for broker/dealers that trade municipals. The MSRB has no enforcement authority. QID: 29479

8. **C.** As the term suggests, a municipal broker's broker deals with other dealers and institutions, not with the general public. QID: 36492

9. **C.** Hospitals, airports, and golf courses all generate revenue and can be financed with revenue bond issues. Schools are financed through GO bond sales. QID: 32160

10. **C.** IDBs are issued by a municipality and the proceeds are used to construct facilities or purchase equipment for a private corporation. The corporation leases the facilities/equipment; funds from the lease are used to repay investors. In addition to a first mortgage on the property, IDBs are backed by the full faith and credit of the corporation (not the municipality). QID: 29940

11. **A.** A good faith deposit is required when the syndicate places a bid on a competitive offering. It is generally 1% to 2% of the par value of the bonds offered for sale. If the bid is unsuccessful, the deposit is returned by the issuer to the syndicate manager. QID: 36528

12. **C.** Condemnation is considered a catastrophe and only applies to revenue bonds. QID: 35144

13. **D.** The agreement among underwriters describes the rights, duties and commitments of the syndicate members with respect to the securities being underwritten. It appoints the syndicate manager to act on behalf of the syndicate, and includes provisions dealing with underwriting

compensation (takedown and concession). The legal opinion is a document prepared by the bond counsel, and the appointment of the bond counsel is the responsibility of the issuer. QID: 29971

14. B. NHAs are considered to have high safety because, in addition to the backing of rental income, they are secured by an annual contribution from the U.S. government. Thus, they are rated AAA. QID: 29521

15. C. The flow of funds only relates to municipal revenue bonds. It describes the priority of disbursing revenues from the project. TANs (tax anticipation notes) are backed by taxes to be collected while GO bonds are backed by the taxing authority of the issuer. QID: 36509

16. A. Although municipal bonds used to be issued in bearer form, this is no longer permitted. The same is true of bonds registered as to principal only. Newly-issued bonds can either be fully registered or book entry, which is a "certificate-less" form of ownership. QID: 34866

17. C. The debt limit is the maximum amount of debt a municipality can have outstanding. QID: 29942

18. B. Proceeds from a prerefunding are deposited in an escrow account which in turn invests the proceeds in securities issued by the U.S. government or bank CDs which are insured. QID: 36659

19. B. Overlapping, or coterminous, is an issuer's proportionate share of debt. This debt is used in calculating a municipality's net overall debt. QID: 35204

20. C. Members of the syndicate buy the bonds at the offering price less the takedown, nonmembers less a concession. The basis price is the yield to maturity. QID: 29981

21. B. The Bond Buyer Revenue Bond Index (Revdex) is computed weekly just like the Bond Buyer's GO index. It consists of 25 revenue bonds with 30-year maturities. The Bond Buyer GO index includes 20 bonds each with approximately 20 years to maturity. The Revdex measures yields of revenue bonds in the secondary market while the GO index measures yields of GO bonds in the secondary market. QID: 29611

22. D. A special tax bond is one backed by one or more designated taxes (sales, cigarette, fuel, alcohol, etc.) other than ad valorum taxes. The designated tax does not have to be directly related to the project purpose. These bonds are not considered "self-supporting" debt. QID: 36510

23. A. The total takedown has two components. Concession plus additional takedown. QID: 34876

24. C. A double-barrelled bond is backed by a defined source of revenue, other than property taxes, plus the full faith and credit of an issuer with taxing authority. NHA bonds are not double-barrelled. If rental income from the housing is insufficient to meet servicing costs, the shortfall is covered by the federal government (HUD). To be double-barrelled, the issue must be backed by more than one municipal source. QID: 29941

25. C. As callable bonds represent more risk to the investor, they generally trade at higher yields than comparable noncallable bonds. Bonds are called when rates are falling or have fallen, allowing the issuer to replace the called issue with one with a lower coupon. As rates rise, bond prices fall. The call premium on a callable bond, which represents the difference between the call price and par, compensates bondholders for lost interest if the bond is called. QID: 36658

26. C. There are 100 basis points in each point. As one point represents 1% of the value of a bond, 75 basis points represents .75%. Also, each point is worth $10. Therefore, 75 basis points represents $7.50. QID: 36434

27. C. An unqualified legal opinion means that the bond counsel found no problems with the issue. A qualified opinion means that the issue is legal, but certain contingencies exist. For example, the bond counsel might render a qualified opinion because competing facilities may restrict the flow of funds in the future. If the issuer does not have clear title to the property, the legal opinion may be qualified. QID: 29980

28. D. The customer's state of residence and tax status are essential when determining suitability of a municipal security. The security's rating is also important because it measures the safety and quality of the bond. QID: 29560

29. C. A final official statement must be delivered to buyers of a new issue on or prior to settlement date. The MSRB does not regulate issuers. QID: 36503

30. A. The true interest cost method uses present value calculations which take into consideration the time value of money (as opposed to net interest cost, which does not consider the timing of interest payments). It is a more complicated calculation than net interest cost. The IRS does not stipulate which should be used. QID: 32164

31. A. State governments generally do not assess property (ad valorem) taxes. These are assessed by local governments. Generally, state governments receive most of their income from sales and income taxes. QID: 29944

32. A. Municipal short-term notes (tax anticipation notes, revenue anticipation notes, and bond anticipation notes) are used as interim financing until a permanent long-term issue is floated. QID: 29939

33. C. Provided each gift meets the $100 annual gift limitation, the gifts are permitted. QID: 36468

34. B. The MSRB requires firms to retain copies of abstracts of official statements, like all other municipal advertising, for three years. QID: 30610

35. C. Revenue bonds are paid out of revenues from a particular project or facility, not from tax revenue. Therefore, debt service coverage and the personnel in charge of managing the facility are important. Overall debt of the issuer would be important in analyzing a general obligation bond backed by the issuer's full faith and credit. QID: 35115

36. B. A legal opinion, rendered by bond counsel, deals with the tax exempt status of the proposed issue and the legality of the issue. The marketability of the new issue of bonds is dealt with by the syndicate. Economic feasibility relates to revenue bond issues and is performed by independent consultants. QID: 36519

37. B. Industrial revenue bonds (IRBs), sometimes called industrial development bonds (IDBs), are nonpublic purpose bonds, and the proceeds are used to benefit private corporations. As such, the interest income from these bonds is a tax-preference item in the AMT calculation. QID: 36664

4

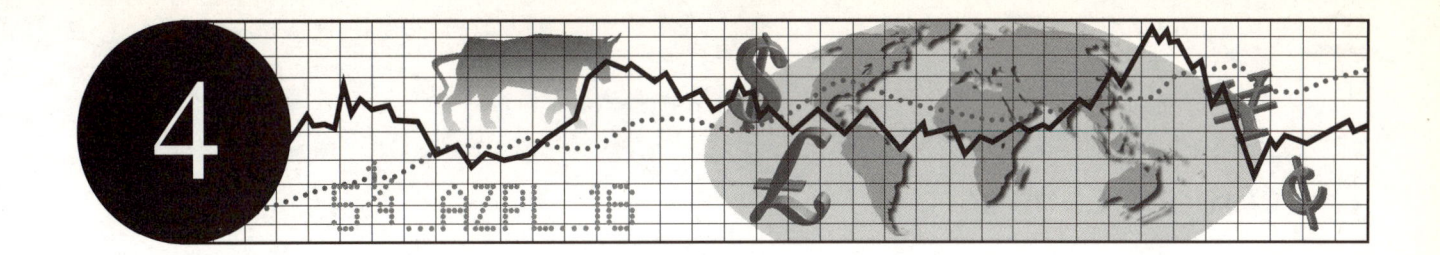

Options

INTRODUCTION For many Series 7 candidates, this is one of the more challenging sections. Be sure to review each section of the unit thoroughly.

Options account for approximately 40–45 questions on the Series 7 exam. The majority of questions will be on equity options (options on stock), but approximately 8–10 will involve nonequity options (index, interest rate, foreign currency). As you review the unit, concentrate on the basic concepts. If you are well grounded in the basics, proficiency with the more complex concepts and strategies will follow.

UNIT OBJECTIVES When you have completed this unit, you should be able to:

- list the basic features of option contracts;
- name the components of an options premium and calculate intrinsic value;
- calculate breakeven, maximum gain, and maximum loss for single options, hedging strategies, spreads, and straddles;
- determine profit and loss on options transactions involving exercise, expiration, or closing a position;
- identify investor strategies for single options, hedges, and multiple option positions;
- describe the functions of the Options Clearing Corporation (OCC);
- describe the process of opening an options account;
- describe the unique features and usage of nonequity options; and
- identify tax consequences of exercise, expiration, or closing a position.

The Options Contract

An **option** is a two-party contract that conveys a right to the buyer and an obligation to the seller. The **terms** of option contracts are standardized by the OCC, which allows them to be traded easily on an exchange such as the CBOE. The underlying security for which an option contract is created may be a stock, stock market index, foreign currency, interest rate, or government bond.

Type The two types of options are calls and puts.

Class All calls of one issuer, or all puts of one issuer are classes of options.

Series All options of one issuer with the same class, exercise price, and expiration month are in the same series (e.g., all XYZ Jan 40 calls).

Style Call or put buyers can exercise a contract anytime before expiration if the contract is an **American-style** option. **European-style** options can only be exercised on the day preceding expiration. Nearly all equity options are American style. Foreign currency options may be either American style or European style.

The Option Contract The most common type of option contracts are **equity options**. Each contract includes **100 shares** when issued.

Two Parties are Involved in an Options Contract

Buyer = Long = Holder = Owner	Seller = Short = Writer
Pays premium (the cost of the contract) to seller. There is a debit (DR) to the account of the buyer when the premium is paid. The buyer *opens his position* with a debit to his account. Has *rights* to exercise (buy or sell stock)	*Receives premium* from buyer. There is a credit (CR) to the account of the seller when the premium is received. The seller *opens his position* with a credit to his account. Has *obligations* at exercise (must buy or sell as required by contract)

Every Option Contract Has Three Specifications

- **Underlying Instrument**—Anything with fluctuating value can be the underlying instrument of an option contract.
- **Price**—The contract specifies a **strike** or **exercise** price at which purchase or sale of the underlying security will occur.

- **Expiration**—All contracts expire on a specified date (the Saturday following the third Friday of the month, 11:59 pm ET). New contracts are issued with **9-month** expirations. A special type of option contract called a **LEAP (Long-term Equity AnticiPation Securities)** is also available. A 39-month expiration has been authorized, but LEAPS that are currently traded expire in 30 months. Options can be bought or sold any time during their life cycle.

Options are called **derivative securities** because their value is derived from the value of the underlying instrument, such as stock, an index, or a foreign currency.

Calls and Puts

There are two types of option contracts: the **call** and the **put**.

Calls An investor may buy calls (go long) or sell calls (go short). The features of each side of a call contract are noted below.

- **Long call**—Call buyer owns the **right to buy** 100 shares of a specific stock at the strike price before the expiration if he chooses to exercise.
- **Short call**—Call writer (seller) has the **obligation to sell** 100 shares of a specific stock at the strike price if the buyer exercises the contract.

Puts An investor may buy puts (go long) or sell puts (go short). The features of each side of a put contract are noted below.

- **Long put**—Put buyer owns the **right to sell** 100 shares of a specific stock at the strike price before the expiration if he chooses to exercise.
- **Short put**—Put writer (seller) has the **obligation to buy** 100 shares of a specific stock at the strike price if the buyer exercises the contract.

✓ *Take Note:* Buyers of options call the shots; they choose to exercise or not to exercise. That's why buyers pay premiums. The writer is at the mercy of the buyer's decision. Writers are only exercised against; they do not have the opportunity to choose to exercise.

- The buyer wants the contract to be **exercised**. He wins, the seller loses at exercise.
- The seller wants the contract to **expire**. The seller wins at expiration because he gets to keep the premium. No purchase or sale of stock is required.

A significant number of test questions can be answered by knowing that: buyers have **rights** and sellers have **obligations.**

Single Option Strategies

There are four basic strategies available to options investors.

- Buying calls
- Writing calls
- Buying puts
- Writing puts

The Four Basic Option Transactions

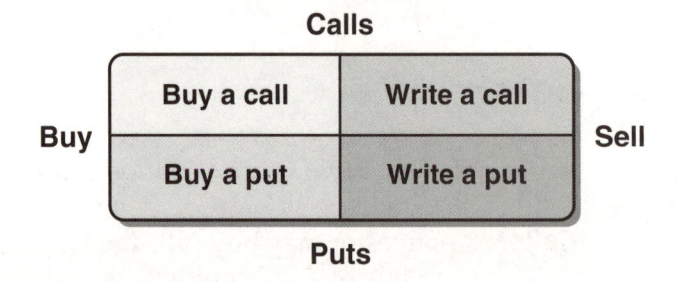

	Calls	
Buy	Buy a call	Write a call	Sell
	Buy a put	Write a put	
	Puts	

Calls Identified below are the key features of call contracts.

Long XYZ Jan 60 call at 3

Long Investor has bought the call and has the right to exercise the contract.

XYZ The contract includes 100 shares of XYZ stock.

Jan The contract expires on the Saturday following the third Friday of January at 11:59 pm ET.

60 The strike price of the contract is 60.

Call The **type** of option is a call, and the investor has the right to buy the stock at 60 since he is long the call.

3 The premium of the contract is $3 per share. Contracts are issued with 100 shares, so the total premium is $300. The investor paid the premium to buy the call.

Buyers of calls want the market price of the underlying stock to rise. The investor that owns this call hopes that the market price will rise above 60. He then has the right to buy the stock at the strike price of 60, even if the market price is higher (80, for example).

Short XYZ Jan 60 call at 3

- **Short** — Investor has sold the call and has obligations to perform if the contract is exercised.
- **XYZ** — The contract includes 100 shares of XYZ stock.
- **Jan** — The contract expires on the Saturday following the third Friday of January at 11:59 pm ET. If expiration occurs, the writer keeps the premium without any obligation.
- **60** — The strike price of the contract is 60.
- **Call** — The **type** of option is a call, and the investor is obligated to sell the stock at 60, if exercised, because he is short the call.
- **3** — The premium of the contract is $3 per share. Option contracts are issued with 100 shares, so the total premium is $300.

Writers of calls want the market price of the underlying stock to fall or stay the same. The investor that owns this call hopes that the market price will rise or go above 60. The contract will not be exercised if the market price is at or below 60 at expiration, and the writer keeps the premium of $300 with no obligation.

Market Attitude

A call **buyer** is a bullish investor because he wants the market to rise. The call is exercised only if the market price rises.

A call **writer** is a bearish investor because he wants the market to fall. The contract is not exercised if the market price falls below the strike price.

Quick Quiz 4.1

Consider the following contract:

Long XYZ Jan 60 call at 3
At expiration, the market price of XYZ is 70.

1. Which of the following will occur?

   A. Exercised by the buyer
   B. Expires worthless

2. Which of the following will the seller do if exercised?

   A. Buy 100 shares of XYZ at 60.
   B. Sell 100 shares of XYZ at 60.
   C. Buy 100 shares of XYZ at 70.
   D. Sell 100 shares of XYZ at 70.

3. Which of the following will the buyer do if he elects to exercise?

   A. Buy 100 shares of XYZ at 60.
   B. Sell 100 shares of XYZ at 60.
   C. Buy 100 shares of XYZ at 70.
   D. Sell 100 shares of XYZ at 70.

Answers

1. **A.** A call is exercised when the market price is greater than the strike price.

2. **B.** The seller of a call is required to sell 100 shares of stock at the strike price when the call is exercised. Exercise occurs in this situation because the market price of the stock is greater than the strike price.

3. **A.** The buyer of the call has the right to buy 100 shares of stock at the strike price if he elects to exercise.

Quick Quiz 4.2

Consider the following contract:

Short XYZ Oct 25 call at 4.50
At expiration the market price of XYZ is 20.

1. Which of the following will occur?

   A. Exercised by the buyer
   B. Expires worthless

2. Which of the following will the seller do at expiration?

   A. Buy 100 shares of XYZ at 25.
   B. Sell 100 shares of XYZ at 25.
   C. Pay $450 to the buyer.
   D. Keep the $450 premium, no further obligation.

3. Which of the following will the buyer do at expiration?

   A. Buy 100 shares of XYZ at 25.
   B. Sell 100 shares of XYZ at 25.
   C. Neither buy nor sell, but lose the $450 premium paid for the option.
   D. Receive $450 premium from the seller.

Answers

1. **B.** Expiration occurs in this situation because the market price of the stock is less than the strike price. There is no value for the holder in exercising a call with a strike price that is more than the market price.

2. **D.** *The seller has no obligation to perform at expiration because the market price of the stock is less than the strike price. The option will expire and the seller will keep the premium received without obligation.*

3. **C.** *Because the market price of the stock is less than the strike price, the buyer will not exercise the call. The buyer will lose the premium of $450 paid.*

Puts Identified below are the key features of put contracts.

Long XYZ Jan 60 put at 3

Long	Investor has bought the put and has the right to exercise the contract.
XYZ	The contract includes 100 shares of XYZ stock.
Jan	The contract expires on the Saturday following the third Friday of January at 11:59 pm ET.
60	The strike price of the contract is 60.
Put	The **type** of option is a put, and the investor has the right to sell the stock at 60 since he is long the put.
3	The premium of the contract is $3 per share. Contracts are issued with 100 shares, so the total premium is $300. The investor paid the premium to buy the put.

Buyers of puts want the market price of the underlying stock to fall. The investor that owns this put hopes that the market price will fall below 60. He then has the right to sell the stock at the strike price of 60, even if the market price is lower (40, for example).

Short XYZ Jan 60 put at 3

Short	Investor has sold the put and has obligations to perform if the contract is exercised.
XYZ	The contract includes 100 shares of XYZ stock.
Jan	The contract expires on the Saturday following the third Friday of January at 11:59 pm ET. If expiration occurs, the writer keeps the premium without any obligation.
60	The strike price of the contract is 60.
Put	The **type** of option is a put, and the investor is obligated to buy the stock at 60, if exercised, because he is short the put.
3	The premium of the contract is $3 per share. Option contracts are issued with 100 shares, so the total premium is $300.

Writers of puts want the market price of the underlying stock to rise or stay the same. If the market price is at or above 60, the investor keeps the premium of $300 with no obligation because the contract will not be exercised.

Market Attitude

A put **buyer** is a bearish investor because he wants the market to fall. The put is exercised only if the market price falls below the strike price. A put **writer** is a bullish investor because he wants the market to rise or remain unchanged. The contract is not exercised if the market price rises above the strike price.

Quick Quiz 4.3   Consider the following contract:

Long XYZ Jan 60 put at 3
At expiration, the market price of XYZ is 70.

1. Which of the following will occur?

    A. Exercised by the buyer
    B. Expires worthless

2. Which of the following will the seller do at expiration?

    A. Buy 100 shares of XYZ at 60.
    B. Sell 100 shares of XYZ at 60.
    C. Do nothing; keep the premium of $300 already received.
    D. Pay the premium of $300 to the buyer.

3. Which of the following will the buyer do at expiration?

    A. Buy 100 shares of XYZ at 60.
    B. Sell 100 shares of XYZ at 60.
    C. Do nothing; the put expires and the buyer loses the $300 premium.
    D. Pay the premium of $300 to the buyer.

Answers

1. **B.** *A put is exercised when the market price is less than the strike price. In this situation, the put is not exercised. The buyer will lose the premium; the seller will keep the premium with no obligation.*

2. **C.** *The put will expire because the market price is greater than the strike price. The seller has no obligation to perform and keeps the premium received.*

3. **C.** *The buyer of the put will not exercise this put because the market price is greater than the strike price. The buyer will lose the premium of $300.*

Quick Quiz 4.4

Consider the following contract:

Short XYZ Oct 25 put at 4.50
At expiration the market price of XYZ is 20.

1. Which of the following will occur?

   A. Exercised by the buyer
   B. Expires worthless

2. Which of the following will the seller do at expiration of the option?

   A. Buy 100 shares of XYZ at 25.
   B. Sell 100 shares of XYZ at 25.
   C. Pay $450 to the buyer.
   D. Keep the $450 premium, no further obligation.

3. Which of the following will the buyer do at expiration?

   A. Buy 100 shares of XYZ at 25.
   B. Sell 100 shares of XYZ at 25.
   C. Neither buy nor sell, but lose the $450 premium paid for the option.
   D. Receive $450 premium from the seller.

Answers

1. **A.** A put is exercised when the market price is less than the strike price. The investor is obligated to buy 100 shares of XYZ at $25 per share.

2. **A.** The put will be exercised because the market price is less than the strike price. The seller of the put is obligated to buy 100 shares of XYZ at a price of $25.

3. **B.** Because the market price of the stock is less than the strike price of the put, the buyer will exercise the put. The buyer of the put has the right to sell 100 shares of XYZ at the strike price of $25. The buyer of the put can buy the stock in the market place at 20 and exercise his right to sell the stock at 25.

Basic Options Definitions

Options contracts are described with various terms unique to the options marketplace. Basic terms in the discussion of options contracts are:

- in-the-money;
- at-the-money;
- out-of-the-money;
- intrinsic value; and
- breakeven.

These terms are defined differently for calls and puts.

Calls

For both long and short calls, the definitions are as follows.

In-the-Money Call A call is **in-the-money** when the market price exceeds the strike price. A buyer will exercise calls that are in-the-money at expiration. Buyers want options to be in-the-money; sellers do not.

At-the-Money Call A call is **at-the-money** when the market price equals the strike price. A buyer will not exercise contracts that are at-the-money at expiration. Sellers want at-the-money contracts at expiration; buyers do not. Sellers then keep the premium without obligations to perform.

Out-of-the-Money Call A call is **out-of-the-money** when the market price is less than the strike price. A buyer will not exercise calls that are out-of-the-money at expiration. Sellers want contracts to be out-of-the-money; buyers do not. Sellers then keep the premium without obligations to perform.

Intrinsic Value: Calls **Intrinsic value** is the in-the-money amount. A call has intrinsic value when the market price is above the strike price. The amount of intrinsic value is found by subtracting the strike price from the market price. Options never have negative intrinsic value; intrinsic value is always a positive amount or 0. Options that are at-the-money or out-of-the-money have an intrinsic value of 0. Buyers like calls to have intrinsic value; sellers do not. A call that has intrinsic value at expiration will be exercised.

During the lifetime of an option contract, buyers want the contract to move in-the-money; sellers want the contract to move out-of-the-money.

Parity: Calls An option is at **parity** when the premium equals intrinsic value.

✓ *For Example:* An ABC June 60 call trading at 2 when ABC is at 62 is at parity.

Breakeven: Calls The **breakeven point** is the point at which the investor neither makes nor loses money. For calls, the breakeven is found by adding the strike price and the premium. For the call buyer, the contract is profitable above the breakeven; for the call seller the contract is profitable below the breakeven.

✓ *Take Note:* Note that the definitions are the same whether the contract is long or short. An easy way to remember the call definitions is CALL UP. A call has intrinsic value (or is in the money) when the market price is up above the strike price, whether it is long or short. Also, the call breakeven is up above the strike price (strike price + premium).

Quick Quiz 4.5

Consider the following contracts (CMV = current market value):

Long XYZ Jan 65 call at 7, CMV of XYZ is 70

___ 1. Is this contract in-, at-, or out-of-the-money?

___ 2. What is the breakeven point?

___ 3. How much intrinsic value does the contract have?

Short XYZ Jan 65 call at 7, CMV of XYZ is 70

___ 4. Is this contract in-, at-, or out-of-the-money?

___ 5. What is the breakeven point?

___ 6. How much intrinsic value does the contract have?

Short XYZ Sep 45 call at 4, CMV of XYZ is 39

___ 7. Is this contract in-, at-, or out-of-the-money?

___ 8. What is the breakeven point?

___ 9. How much intrinsic value does the contract have?

Short XYZ Sep 70 call at 5, CMV of XYZ is 73

___ 10. Is this contract in-, at-, or out-of-the-money?

___ 11. What is the breakeven point?

___ 12. How much intrinsic value does the contract have?

Answers

1. In   Market price is greater than the strike price.

2. 72   Strike price + premium.

3. 500 Market price is greater than strike price by $5; $5 × 100=$500.

4. In   Market price is greater than the strike price.

5. 72   Strike price + premium.

6. 500 With the stock price at 70, a Jan 65 call with a market value of 70 has 5 points of intrinsic value.

7. Out Market price is less than the strike price.

8. 49   Strike price + premium.

9. 0   *Intrinsic value is never negative.*

10. In   *Market price is greater than the strike price.*

11. 75   *Strike price + premium.*

12. 300 *Market price is greater than the strike price by $3; $3 × 100 shares=$300.*

✓ **Take Note:** An option that is in-the-money is not necessarily at breakeven. Options that are in-the-money are not always profitable. Review these terms carefully, as it is very easy to confuse them.

Puts

The basic definitions for **puts** are listed below. For puts, the definitions are the opposite of what they are for calls.

In-the-Money Put A put is **in-the-money** when the market price is less than the strike price. A buyer will exercise puts that are in-the-money at expiration. Buyers want in-the-money contracts; sellers do not.

At-the-Money Put A put is **at-the-money** when the market price equals the strike price. A buyer will not exercise contracts that are at-the-money at expiration. Sellers want at-the-money contracts; buyers do not.

Out-of-the-Money Put A put is **out-of-the-money** when the market price is greater than the strike price. A buyer will not exercise puts that are out-of-the-money at expiration. Sellers want out-of-the-money contracts; buyers do not.

Intrinsic Value: Puts **Intrinsic value** is the in-the-money amount. A put has intrinsic value when the market price is below the strike price. The amount of intrinsic value is found by subtracting the market price from the strike price. Options never have negative intrinsic value; it is always a positive number or 0. Buyers like options to have intrinsic value; sellers do not. An option (call or put) that has intrinsic value at expiration will be exercised.

Breakeven: Puts The **breakeven point** is the point at which the investor neither makes nor loses money. For puts, the breakeven is found by subtracting the premium from the strike price. For the put buyer, the contract is profitable below the breakeven at expiration; for the put seller the contract is profitable above the breakeven at expiration.

Comparison of In-, At-, and Out-of-the-Money Options

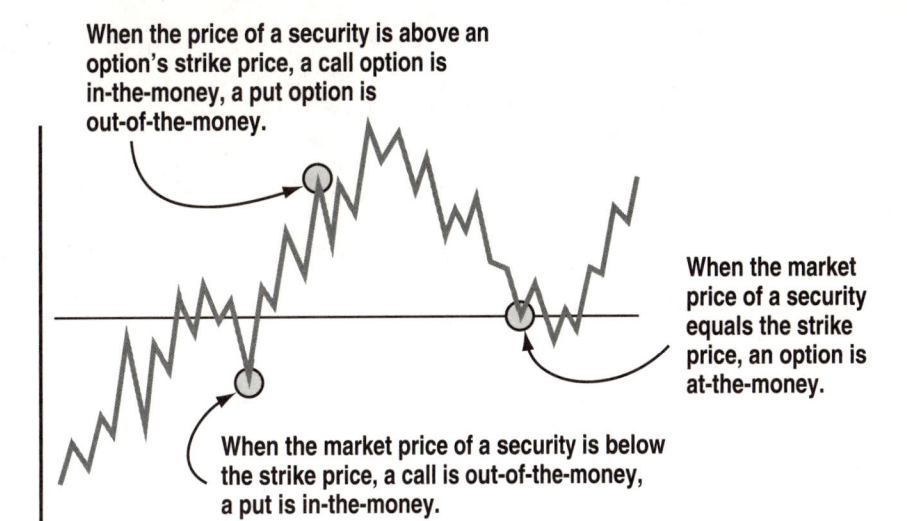

When the price of a security is above an option's strike price, a call option is in-the-money, a put option is out-of-the-money.

When the market price of a security equals the strike price, an option is at-the-money.

When the market price of a security is below the strike price, a call is out-of-the-money, a put is in-the-money.

✓ **Take Note:** An easy way to remember the put definitions is PUT DOWN. A *put* has intrinsic value (or is in the money) when the market price is down below the strike price, whether it is long or short. Also, the put breakeven is down below the strike price (strike price – premium). Think: "Call up your friends to put them down" and you will remember the concept. These put definitions are the opposite as they were for calls; options are a game of opposites. Calls are opposites of puts, and buyers are opposite of sellers.

Quick Quiz 4.6 Consider the following contracts:

Long XYZ Sep 65 put at 2, CMV of XYZ is 70.

___ 1. Is this contract in-, at-, or out-of-the-money?

___ 2. What is the breakeven point?

___ 3. How much intrinsic value does the contract have?

Short XYZ Jan 65 put at 2, CMV of XYZ is 70.

___ 4. Is this contract in-, at-, or out-of-the-money?

___ 5. What is the breakeven point?

___ 6. How much intrinsic value does the contract have?

202 Options

Short XYZ Sep 45 put at 8, CMV of XYZ is 39.

___ 7. Is this contract in-, at-, or out-of-the-money?

___ 8. What is the breakeven point?

___ 9. How much intrinsic value does the contract have?

Long XYZ Sep 70 put at 5, CMV of XYZ is 70.

___ 10. Is this contract in-, at-, or out-of-the-money?

___ 11. What is the breakeven point?

___ 12. How much intrinsic value does the contract have?

Answers
1. Out Market price is greater than the strike price.
2. 63   Strike price – premium.
3. 0   Intrinsic value is never negative.
4. Out Market price is greater than the strike price.
5. 63   Strike price – premium.
6. 0   Intrinsic value is never negative.
7. In   Market price is less than the strike price.
8. 37   Strike price – premium.
9. 6   Market price is below the strike price by $6; $6 x 100 shares = $600.
10. At Market price is equal to the strike price.
11. 65 Strike price – premium.
12. 0   Market price is equal to the strike price.

Quick Summary of Basic Definitions The following table summarizes the basic definitions for calls and puts.

(CMV = Current market value, SP = Strike price)

The Options Contract

Basic Definitions for Calls and Puts

Calls		Puts
CMV > SP	In-the-Money	CMV < SP
CMV = SP	At-the-Money	CMV = SP
CMV < SP	Out-of-the-Money	CMV > SP
"Call up"	Intrinsic Value	"Put down"
SP + Premium	Breakeven	SP – Premium

✓ ***Take Note:*** The following chart will help you remember the basics of options. When you take the exam, consider drawing and referring to it when you encounter options questions. Each quadrant represents one of the four basic options positions.

- Buyers are on the left side, sellers on the right.
- The arrow identifies the investor's market attitude. Up arrows represent bullish investors; down arrows represent bearish investors.
- The information in the parentheses identifies what occurs at the exercise of the option.
- The solid horizontal line represents the strike price. The dashed horizontal lines represent the breakevens. For calls, the breakeven is strike price + premium, long or short, and for puts the breakeven is strike price – premium, long or short.
- Calls are above the horizontal line because they are in-the-money when the market price is above the strike price, long or short (CALL UP).
- Puts are below the horizontal line because they are in-the-money when the market price is below the strike price, long or short (PUT DOWN).

Basic Options Chart

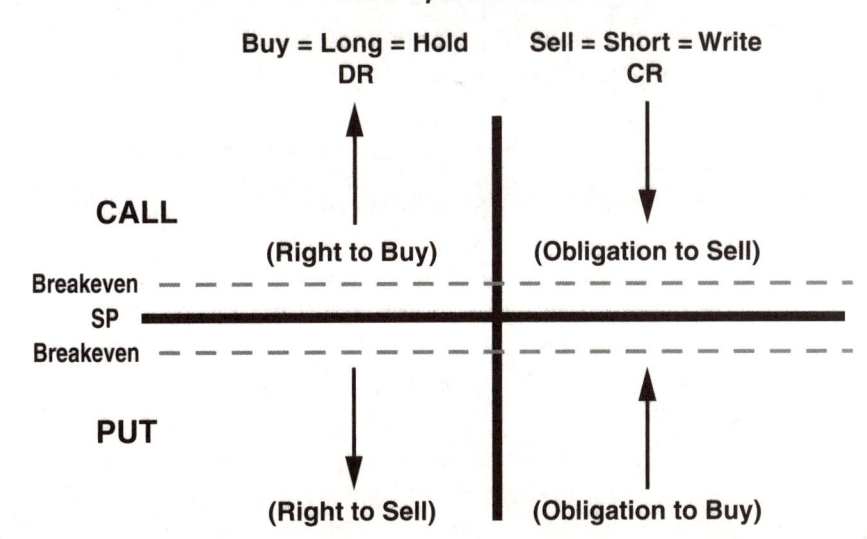

```
                 Buy = Long = Hold    Sell = Short = Write
                        DR                    CR
                        ↑                     ↓
   CALL
                   (Right to Buy)       (Obligation to Sell)
Breakeven  ─ ─ ─ ─ ─ ─ ─ ─ ─ ─ ─ ─ ┼ ─ ─ ─ ─ ─ ─ ─ ─ ─ ─ ─ ─
       SP ─────────────────────────┼──────────────────────────
Breakeven  ─ ─ ─ ─ ─ ─ ─ ─ ─ ─ ─ ─ ┼ ─ ─ ─ ─ ─ ─ ─ ─ ─ ─ ─ ─

   PUT              ↓                     ↑
                (Right to Sell)      (Obligation to Buy)
```

204   Options

- Buy = Long = Hold = Open the position with a DR to the account
- Sell = Short = Write = Open the position with a CR to the account

Quick Quiz 4.7

Using only the options chart on page 207, answer the following questions:

1. An investor is short a call. What is the BE?

2. An investor is the holder of a put. What is the BE?

3. An investor is the buyer of a call. What is the BE?

4. An investor is the writer of a put. What is the BE?

Answers   1. SP + Premium   2. SP − Premium   3. SP + Premium   4. SP − Premium

Quick Quiz 4.8   Multiple Choice

1. Under which of the following circumstances is an investor in a position to acquire stock?

   I. He is a buyer of a call.
   II. He is a buyer of a put.
   III. He is a seller of a call.
   IV. He is a seller of a put.

   A. I and III
   B. I and IV
   C. II and III
   D. II and IV

2. An investor is in the position to sell stock if he is a

   I. buyer of a call
   II. buyer of a put
   III. seller of a call
   IV. seller of a put

   A. I and III
   B. I and IV
   C. II and III
   D. II and IV

For questions 3–13, write **A** if the position is bullish and **B** if bearish.

___ 3. Long 1 XYZ Jul 60 put

___ 4. Short 1 XYZ Oct 60 put

___ 5. Sell 10 ABC Jan calls

___ 6. Write 1 ABC call

___ 7. Buy 1 JKL call

___ 8. Write 10 KLM puts

___ 9. Sell 10 ABC Jan calls

___ 10. Write 1 ABC call

___ 11. Buy 1 JKL call

___ 12. Write 10 KLM puts

___ 13. Buy 10 MNO Jul 35 puts

Answers

1. **B.** The holder of a call has the right to buy stock at the strike price; the seller of a put is obligated to buy stock at the strike price if exercised.

2. **C.** The holder of a put has the right to sell stock at the strike price; the seller of a call is obligated to sell stock at the strike price if exercised.

3. **B.** Bear. Put owners have the right to sell stock by exercising their options. The lower the market price of the underlying stock, the more one profits from the right to sell stock at a price fixed by the option.

4. **A.** Bull. When the market price goes up, put owners will sell stock in the market rather than exercise their options. Put writers, therefore, will not have to take delivery of stock. The options will expire, and the writers will keep the premium received.

5. **B.** Bear. The seller of a call receives a premium and is obligated to sell the underlying stock if a call buyer exercises the option. When the market price of the stock falls, call owners will be more likely to buy at the market price than to exercise their options to purchase stock at the strike price.

6. **B.** Bear. Writing means the same as selling. Writers of calls are bears.

7. **A.** Bull. Call buyers have the right to buy stock from call writers. The more the market price of the stock rises, the more attractive is the fixed strike price of the option.

8. **A.** Bull. Writing a put is the same as shorting a put. Writers of puts are bulls.

9. **B.** Bear. The seller of a call receives a premium and is obligated to sell the underlying stock if a call buyer exercises the option. When the market price of the stock falls, call owners will be more likely to buy at the market price than to exercise their options to purchase stock at the strike price.

10. **B.** Bear. Writing means the same as selling. Writers of calls are bears.

11. **A.** Bull. Call buyers have the right to buy stock from call writers. The more the market price of the stock rises, the more attractive is the fixed strike price of the option.

12. **A.** Bull. Writing a put is the same as shorting a put. Writers of puts are bulls.

13. **B.** Bear. Put buyers are bearish because the right to sell at the strike price is attractive only if the market price of the stock falls below the strike price.

Options Premiums

As stated earlier, the price of an option contract is known as the **premium**. Both bid and ask prices are quoted in cents, with a minimum price interval of five cents ($0.05). An option buyer will pay the **ask**, or **offer** price, and the option seller will receive the **bid** price. An option's premium reflects two types of values: **intrinsic value**—the amount by which the option is in-the-money; and **time value**—the market's perceived worth of the time remaining to expiration.

Options Quotes Options premiums are quoted on a **per share** basis. Option contracts are issued to include 100 shares of stock, so the total premium is calculated by multiplying by 100. However, some contracts may be subject to stock splits and stock dividends and may include more than 100 shares. This is discussed later in this unit.

Factors Affecting Premium The premium of an option is affected by many factors, including:

- volatility;
- amount of intrinsic value;
- time remaining until expiration; and
- interest rates.

The factor with the greatest influence is the **volatility** of the underlying stock. A stock that is highly volatile has the potential to experience greater price movement; it has the possibility of greater profit because of high volatility.

Premiums for options fluctuate constantly, just like stock prices. If the underlying stock price falls from one day to the next, a call premium would fall and a put premium would rise. The amount of intrinsic value is affected by any change in the stock's price.

The Options Contract 207

For AOL, note that the closing price on the previous day was $49.00. The strike prices range from $42.50 to $60.00. The next column shows the expiration month followed by volume and premium on the AOL calls and by volume and premium on the AOL puts.

From the chart below, find the premium for the AOL July 45 call. The premium of $7.40 is made up of two components: intrinsic value and time value. Once you know intrinsic value, it is easy to back into time value.

Intrinsic value + Time value = the premium

OPTION/STRIKE		EXP.	-CALL- VOL.	LAST	-PUT- VOL.	LAST
AmOnline	4250	Apr	2431	650	49	010
49	4250	May	902	760	409	090
49	45	Apr	5790	420	3298	020
49	45	May	1376	530	1573	150
49	45	Jul	1371	740	94	150
49	4750	Apr	3169	205	1229	055
49	4750	May	3333	340	530	230
49	4750	Oct	294	820	2696	570
49	50	Apr	7618	050	1031	165
49	50	May	5307	220	1017	320
49	50	Jul	2436	450	197	520
49	55	May	3548	050	57	660
49	55	Jul	2574	230	18	8
49	55	Oct	86010	420	251	970
49	60	Jul	2869	110	22	12
ASM Litho	25	Apr	1060	165	...	...
ATT Wris	20	May	1752	130	3360	180
AT&T	20	Apr	1885	2	11	005
22	2250	Apr	1396	020	445	065

A call option has intrinsic value if the market price of the underlying stock is greater than the strike price. In the case of the July 45 call, the intrinsic value (in the money amount) is $4.00 ($49.00 – $45.00). The intrinsic value of $4.00 when added to the time value must equal $7.40. The time value of the July 45 call is $3.40 ($7.40 – $4.00).

✓ **Take Note:** If an option is at-the-money or out-of-the-money, the intrinsic value is zero. There is no such thing as negative intrinsic value. Therefore, the premium on any out-of-the-money option is composed entirely of time value.

From the chart, compare the premium of the May 45 call ($5.30) to the premium of the July 45 call ($7.40). Both contracts are in the money by the same amount ($4.00) but the July contract has a higher premium due to a greater time value. The further to expiration, the greater the time value.

The May 50 call is at 2.20 while the premium on the July 50 call is 4.50. Both of these contracts are out-of-the-money by $1. Again, the further to expiration, the greater the time value.

Options

The May 50 put is trading at 3.20 while the July 50 put is at 5.20. Both of these contracts are in-the-money by $1. The time value of these options is $2.20 and $4.20 respectively. Again, the further to expiration, the greater the time value.

Test Topic Alert!

You are likely to see a question or two on option premiums. Be prepared to calculate the time value of an option premium and recognize the features that affect premiums. In calculating the premium, remember to determine intrinsic value by thinking Call Up or Put Down. What's left of the premium is the time value.

A likely test question might be: An XYZ Jan 50 put is trading for a premium of 5. The current market value of XYZ stock is 55. What are the time value and intrinsic value of the premium?

Think Put Down. A put has intrinsic value when the market price of the stock is down below the strike price. In this example that market price is up, so this option has no intrinsic value. The premium of 5 is all time value.

The solution is: intrinsic value = 0, time value = 5.

Quick Quiz 4.9

RST is trading for $54.

What are the intrinsic values and time values of the following options?

1. RST September 50 call for 6
2. RST October 55 call for 2.25
3. RST September 60 put for 7.25
4. RST October 50 put for 1.15

Answers

1. $4 intrinsic; $2 time
2. No intrinsic; $2.25 time
3. $6 intrinsic; $1.25 time
4. No intrinsic; $1.15 time

Test Topic Alert!

1. Your customer buys 1 MCS Jul 70 call at 2.50 when the market is at 71. As time passes, the market price of MCS remains stable at 71. The premium, therefore, will probably

    A. stay the same
    B. go up
    C. go down
    D. exhibit extreme volatility

Answer

1. **C.** *Remember that options are wasting assets. As the expiration date approaches, the option's time value diminishes. Time, therefore, is against the option owner. In this case, the intrinsic value stays the same because the stock price remains stable at 71. Intrinsic value for a call is the difference between the strike price and the market price—if the strike price is lower.*

Basic Option Transactions

Four basic options positions are available to the options investor. Investors use these strategies to accomplish a variety of objectives. An overview of these strategies and their potential risks and rewards follows.

Buying Calls

Call buyers are **bullish** on the underlying stock. By purchasing calls an investor can profit from an increase in a stock's price while investing a relatively small amount of money. There are many reasons why investors purchase calls.

Speculation Speculation is the most common reason for buying calls. Investors can speculate on the upward price movement of the stock by paying only the premium. Buying the actual stock would require a far greater investment.

Deferring a Decision An investor can buy a call on a stock and lock in a purchase price until the option expires. This allows him to postpone making a financial commitment other than the premium until the expiration date of the option.

Diversifying Holdings With limited funds, an investor can buy calls on a variety of stocks and possibly profit from any rise in the options premium.

Protection of a Short Stock Position Investors can use calls to protect a short stock position. The option acts as an insurance policy against the stock rising in price.

Options

Maximum Gain Theoretically, the potential gains available to call owners are unlimited because there is no limit on the rise in a stock's price.

Maximum Loss The most the call buyer can lose is the premium paid; this happens if the market price is at or below the strike price at the option's expiration.

Writing Calls

Call writers are **bearish** or **neutral** on the price of the underlying stock. An investor who believes a stock's price will decline or stay the same can write calls for any of the following reasons.

Speculation By writing calls, an investor can profit if the stock's price falls below or stays at the strike price. The investor can earn the amount of the premium.

Increasing Returns Additional income can be earned for a portfolio by writing calls. Investors hope for expiration of the calls so they can keep the premiums.

Locking in a Sale Price If an investor has an unrealized profit in a stock and is interested in selling it, a call can be written at a strike price that will attempt to lock in that profit.

Protection of a Long Stock Position The premium collected from writing a call provides limited downside protection to the extent of the premium received.

Maximum Gain An uncovered call (or naked call) writer's maximum gain is the premium received. If a call is uncovered, the investor does not own the underlying stock. The maximum gain is earned when the stock price is at or below the exercise price at expiration.

Maximum Loss An uncovered call (or naked call) writer's maximum loss is unlimited, because the writer could be forced to buy the stock at a potentially unlimited price, if the option is exercised against him, for delivery at the strike price.

Long Call/Short Call

Position	Maximum Gain	Maximum Loss
Long Call	Unlimited	Premium
Short Call	Premium	Unlimited

Basic Option Transactions

Quick Quiz 4.10 Multiple Choice

1. An investor buys 1 DWQ May 60 call at 3.50. The investor's maximum potential gain is

   A. $350
   B. $5,650
   C. $6,350
   D. unlimited

2. An investor buys 1 DWQ May 60 call at 3.50. What is the investor's maximum potential loss?

   A. $350
   B. $5,650
   C. $6,350
   D. Unlimited

3. An investor sells 1 KLP Dec 45 call at 3. What is the investor's maximum potential gain?

   A. $300
   B. $4,200
   C. $4,800
   D. Unlimited

4. An investor sells 1 KLP Dec 45 call at 3. What is the investor's maximum potential loss?

   A. $300
   B. $4,200
   C. $4,800
   D. Unlimited

5. An investor buys 1 ALF Jun 55 call at 4. What is the investor's maximum potential gain?

   A. $400
   B. $5,100
   C. $5,500
   D. Unlimited

6. An investor buys 1 ALF Jun 55 call at 4. What is the investor's maximum potential loss?

   A. $400
   B. $5,100
   C. $5,500
   D. Unlimited

7. An investor sells 1 COD Jun 50 call at 3.50. What is the investor's maximum potential gain?

   A. $350
   B. $4,650
   C. $5,350
   D. Unlimited

8. An investor sells 1 COD Jun 50 call at 3.50. What is the investor's maximum potential loss?

   A. $350
   B. $4,650
   C. $5,350
   D. Unlimited

9. All of the following will usually result in a profit to a naked call writer EXCEPT when the

   A. option contract expires without being exercised
   B. price of the underlying security falls below and remains below the exercise price of the option
   C. call is exercised and the price of the underlying security is greater than the exercise price plus the premium received
   D. price of the option contract declines

10. In buying listed call options as compared to buying the underlying stock, which of the following is not an advantage?

    A. Buying a call would require a smaller capital commitment.
    B. Buying a call has a lower dollar loss potential than buying the stock.
    C. The call has a time value beyond an intrinsic value that gradually dissipates.
    D. Buying a call allows greater leverage than buying the underlying stock.

11. All of the following are objectives of call buyers EXCEPT

    A. speculating for profit on the rise in price of stock
    B. delaying a decision to buy stock
    C. hedging a long stock position against falling prices
    D. diversifying holdings

Answers

1. **D.** The maximum gain on a long call is unlimited because theoretically there is no limit on a rise in stock price.

2. **A.** The maximum loss on a long call is equal to the premium paid for the option. One contract represents 100 shares and the buyer paid a $3.50 per share premium, which equals $350.

3. **A.** The maximum gain on a short call is equal to the premium received by the seller. One contract represents 100 shares and the seller received a $3 per share premium, which equals $300.

4. **D.** The maximum loss on a short call is unlimited because theoretically there is no limit on a rise in stock price.

5. **D.** The maximum gain on a long call is unlimited because theoretically there is no limit on a rise in stock price.

6. **A.** The maximum loss on a long call is equal to the premium paid for the option. One contract represents 100 shares and the buyer paid a $4 per share premium, which equals $400.

7. **A.** The maximum gain on a short call is equal to the premium received by the seller. One contract represents 100 shares and the seller received a $3.50 per share premium, which equals $350.

8. **D.** The maximum loss on a short call is unlimited because theoretically there is no limit on a rise in stock price.

9. **C.** If the option expires out-of-the-money, the naked call writer keeps the premium. This occurs when the market price stays below the strike price. Breakeven is the strike price plus the premium. If the price rises above this, the naked call writer, when exercised, will lose.

10. **C.** Call options allow greater leverage than buying the underlying stock, and the capital requirements are smaller, allowing for a smaller loss potential. The fact that options expire (i.e., have a time value that erodes as the option nears expiration) is a disadvantage of options. Stock purchases have no time value component—there is no expiration and therefore no value erosion due to this factor.

11. **C.** The right to purchase more shares of stock does not provide a hedge against falling prices.

Buying Puts

Put buyers are **bearish** on the underlying stock. By purchasing puts, an investor can profit from a decrease in a stock's price while investing a relatively small amount of money. Reasons that investors purchase puts are listed below.

Speculation Investors can speculate on the downward price movement of the stock that is not owned by paying only the premium.

Deferring a Decision — An investor can buy a put on a stock and lock in a sale price until the option expires. This allows him to postpone a selling decision until the expiration date of the option. With this strategy, an investor can lock in an acceptable sales price for stock that is owned, but also protect its appreciation potential until the expiration date.

Protection of a Long Stock Position — Investors can use puts to protect a long stock position. The option acts as an insurance policy against the stock declining in price.

Maximum Gain — The maximum potential gain available to put owners is the option's strike price less the amount of the premium paid (same as the breakeven). A stock's price can fall no lower than zero.

Maximum Loss — The most the put buyer can lose is the premium paid. This happens if the market price is at or above the strike price at the option's expiration.

Writing Puts

Put writers are **bullish** or neutral on the price of the underlying stock. An investor who believes a stock's price will increase or stay the same can write puts for the following reasons.

Speculation — By writing puts, an investor can profit if the stock's price rises above or stays at the strike price. The investor can earn the amount of the premium.

Increasing Returns — Additional income can be earned for a portfolio by writing puts. Investors hope for expiration of the puts so that they can keep the premium.

Buying Stock Below Its Current Price — The premium received from writing puts can be used to offset the cost of stock when the put is exercised against the writer. The writer buys his stock at a price that is reduced by the premium received.

Maximum Gain — An uncovered put writer's maximum gain is the premium received. The maximum gain is earned when the stock price is at or above the exercise price at expiration.

Maximum Loss — An uncovered put writer's maximum loss is the put's strike price less the premium received (the same as the breakeven); it occurs when the stock price drops to zero. The investor is forced to buy the worthless stock at the option's strike price. The investor's loss is reduced by the premium received.

Position	Maximum Gain	Maximum Loss
Long Put	Strike price – Premium	Premium
Short Put	Premium	Strike price – Premium

Quick Quiz 4.11 Multiple Choice

1. An investor buys 1 ABC Jan 50 put at 2. What is the investor's maximum potential gain?

   A. $200
   B. $4,800
   C. $5,200
   D. Unlimited

2. An investor buys 1 ABC Jan 50 put at 2. What is the investor's maximum potential loss?

   A. $100
   B. $200
   C. $4,800
   D. $5,200

3. An investor sells 1 DWQ Feb 30 put at 4.50. What is the investor's maximum potential gain?

   A. $450
   B. $2,550
   C. $3,450
   D. Unlimited

4. An investor sells 1 DWQ Feb 30 put at 4.50. What is the investor's maximum potential loss?

   A. $450
   B. $2,550
   C. $3,450
   D. Unlimited

5. An investor buys 1 KLP Oct 95 put at 6.50. What is the investor's maximum potential gain?

   A. $8,850
   B. $9,500
   C. $9,650
   D. $10,150

6. An investor buys 1 KLP Oct 95 put at 6.50. What is the investor's maximum potential loss?

   A. $300
   B. $650
   C. $8,850
   D. $9,650

7. An investor sells 1 ALF Dec 65 put at 2.50. What is the investor's maximum potential gain?

   A. $250
   B. $6,500
   C. $6,750
   D. Unlimited

8. The holder of a long put will realize a profit upon exercise of the option if the price of the underlying stock

   A. exceeds the exercise price
   B. exceeds the exercise price plus the premium paid
   C. falls below the exercise price
   D. falls below the exercise price minus the premium paid

Answers

1. **B.** The maximum gain on a long put is calculated by subtracting the premium from the strike price. Subtract the premium paid of 2 from the strike price of 50 and multiply by the number of shares to determine the maximum potential gain. One contract represents 100 shares, so the buyer's maximum gain is $4,800.

2. **B.** The maximum loss on a long put is equal to the premium paid for the option. One contract represents 100 shares and the buyer paid a $2 per share premium, which equals $200.

3. **A.** The maximum gain on a short put is equal to the premium received by the seller. One contract represents 100 shares and the seller received a $4.50 per share premium, which equals $450.

4. **B.** The maximum loss on a short put occurs when the stock drops to $0 and is calculated by subtracting the premium from the strike price. Subtract the premium received by the seller of 4.50 from the strike price of 30 to determine the maximum loss of 25.50 per share. One contract represents 100 shares, so the seller's maximum loss is $2,550.

5. **A.** The maximum gain on a long put is calculated by subtracting the premium from the strike price. Subtract the premium paid of 6.50 from the strike price of 95 to determine the maximum potential gain of 88.50 per share. One contract represents 100 shares, so the buyer's maximum gain is $8,850.

6. **B.** The maximum loss on a long put is equal to the premium paid for the option. One contract represents 100 shares and the buyer paid a $6.50 per share premium, which equals $650.

7. **A.** The maximum gain for an option writer is the premium received.

8. **D.** Breakeven for the buyer of a put is the strike price of the option minus the premium paid for the option.

Test Topic Alert!

Options offer investors a great deal of flexibility. You will typically see several test questions that require you to know the strategies just reviewed. Maximum gain and loss are concepts that are normally heavily tested. When learning them, focus on the long positions. If you know the long position definitions, you can always remember the short position definitions because they are the opposite. The following chart summarizes this relationship.

Position	Maximum Gain	Maximum Loss
Long Call	Unlimited	Premium
Short Call	Premium	Unlimited
Long Put	Strike price – Premium	Premium
Short Put	Premium	Strike price – Premium

Choices at Expiration

The owner of a put or call option contract has three choices prior to the expiration of the contract. The investor can exercise the option, let the option expire, or sell the option contract before the expiration date.

Exercise the Option
- The holder of a call will buy the stock at the strike price
- The holder of a put will sell the stock at the strike price

Let the Option Expire
- The holder of a call will allow the option to expire if the market price of the stock is equal to or less than the strike price.
- The holder of a put will allow the option to expire if the market price of the stock is equal to or greater than the strike price.

Sell the Option Contract Before the Expiration Date
- The holder can sell the option for its current premium; there is no purchase or sale of underlying stock in this situation. The investor has profit or loss based on the increase or decrease of the option's premium from the time the option was purchased (**closing the position**).

Test Topic Alert!

A significant number of your options questions will require determining the amount of profit or loss in an options transaction. Consider using the following T-chart to compare money paid out to money received in a transaction. Money paid out is identified as a **debit (DR)** to the investor's account. Money received is a **credit (CR)** to the investor's account.

```
   DR  |  CR
       |
       |
```

If an investor pays a premium to buy an option, he opens his position with a debit to the account in the amount of the premium.

✓ **For Example:** An investor buys one XYZ January 50 call for 3. The T-chart is filled out like this:

DR	CR
3	

If the investor had instead sold the XYZ January 50 call for 3, the T-chart would reflect that:

DR	CR
	3

Try using the T-chart on any option question that requires a calculation. It will keep your accounting organized, making it easy to determine profit and loss.

Option Exercise

Option contracts are **exercised** if they are in-the-money. Writers are required to fulfill their obligations as required. Exercises of listed equity options settle regular way: three business days from the exercise date.

Option Expiration

Option contracts **expire** worthless if they are at-the-money or out-of-the-money at expiration. At expiration, the buyer of the option loses the premium paid; the seller of the option profits in the amount of the premium received.

💡 **Test Topic Alert!** Do this question using the master options chart and T-chart:

An investor with no other positions buys 1 DWQ May 75 call at 6.50. The investor exercises the call when the stock is trading at 77 and immediately sells the stock in the market. What is the investor's profit or loss?

The solution is a calculation, so draw a T-chart.

DR	CR
6.50	
75	77
81.50	77
4.50	

Basic Option Transactions   219

The position is opened by buying: a debit of the premium is made. The call is exercised. Exercise of a long call requires the investor to buy the stock at the strike price. A debit of 75 must be made to the account.

When the stock is trading at 77, the investor sells. A credit of 77 must be made to the account. The resulting loss is $450 (4.50 × 100), because the investor paid out 81.50 and only received 77.

Quick Quiz 4.12   Multiple Choice

1. An investor with no other positions sells 1 KLP Jul 40 call at 3.50. The call is exercised when the stock is trading at 47. What is the investor's profit or loss?

   A. $350 profit
   B. $350 loss
   C. $450 profit
   D. $450 loss

2. An investor with no other positions buys 1 COD May 65 put at 3.50. The investor buys the stock in the market and exercises the put when the stock is trading at 63.50. What is the investor's profit or loss?

   A. $200 profit
   B. $200 loss
   C. $350 profit
   D. $350 loss

3. An investor with no other positions sells 1 ALF 95 Jan put at 5.50. The put is immediately exercised when the stock is trading at 79 and the investor immediately sells the stock in the market. What is the investor's profit or loss?

   A. $550 profit
   B. $550 loss
   C. $1,050 profit
   D. $1,050 loss

Answers   1. **B.**   The solution is a calculation, so draw a T-chart.

DR	CR
	3.50
	40
47	
47	43.50
3.50	

1. The position is opened by selling; a credit of the premium is made.
2. The call is exercised. Refer to the chart. Exercise of a short call requires the investor to sell the stock at the strike price. A credit of 40 must be made to the account.
3. The investor must buy the stock at the current price to have it to sell. A debit of 47 must be made.

2. **B**. The solution is a calculation, so draw a T-chart.

DR	CR
3.50	
63.50	
	65
67	65
2	

1. The position is opened by buying; a debit of the premium of 3.50 is made.
2. The investor buys the stock at the current price; a debit of 63.50 must be made.
3. The put is exercised. Exercise of a long put enables the investor to sell the stock at the strike price. A credit of 65 must be made to the account.

3. **D**. The position is a calculation, so draw a T-chart.

DR	CR
	5.50
95	79
95	84.50
10.50	

1. The position is opened by selling; a credit of the premium is made.
2. The put is exercised. Exercise of a short put requires the investor to buy the stock at the strike price. A debit of 95 must be made to the account.
3. The investor sells the stock at the current price. A credit of 79 must be made.

Quick Quiz 4.13   Multiple Choice

1. An investor with no other positions buys 1 DWQ Jun 70 call at 4.50. The option expires when the stock is trading at 68. What is the investor's profit or loss?

    A. $200 profit
    B. $200 loss
    C. $450 profit
    D. $450 loss

2. An investor with no other positions sells 1 KLP Jan 45 call at 2.50. The option expires when the stock is trading at 44.50. What is the investor's profit or loss?

   A. $50 profit
   B. $50 loss
   C. $250 profit
   D. $250 loss

3. An investor with no other positions buys 1 COD Jun 30 put at 5. The option expires when the stock is trading at 31. What is the investor's profit or loss?

   A. $100 profit
   B. $100 loss
   C. $500 profit
   D. $500 loss

Answers

1. **D.** *The option was out-of-the-money so the investor would let the option expire. When the investor lets the long call expire the loss is the premium paid for the option, which is 4.50. [4.50 × 100 = $450]*

2. **C.** *The option was allowed to expire because it was out-of-the-money. When the option expires, the investor profits by the amount of the premium received, which is 2.50. [2.50 × 100 = $250]*

3. **D.** *The option was out-of-the-money so the investor would let the option expire. When the investor lets the long put expire his loss is the premium paid for the option, which is 5. [5 × 100 = $500]*

Closing Transactions

If an investor has purchased an option, prior to expiration the investor can sell the option. A profit is made if the premium is greater than originally paid. In this situation, the sale of the option is known as the **closing transaction**.

If an investor initially sold an option, the investor can close the position by buying the option. This closing transaction is profitable if the investor is able to buy the option for a premium less than was received for its sale. Trading options accounts for a very large portion of activity in the options market.

Test Topic Alert! If an investor opens an option position by buying, he must close it by selling; if the position is opened by selling, he must close it by buying. Opening and closing transactions are always opposites of each other.

Opening and Closing Transactions

	Open	Close
Long	Buy Contract ⟶	Sell Contract
Short	Sell Contract ⟶	Buy contract

The test may ask you to close transactions for their intrinsic value.

Normally, a transaction is closed for its premium amount, but if an option is about to expire, it has no time value—intrinsic value is all that is left. Use a T-chart on questions that require you to close out options positions.

Quick Quiz 4.14 Multiple Choice

1. A customer with no other positions sells 1 MTN Jul 80 call for 10 and buys 100 shares of MTN stock for $85 per share. If the customer enters into a closing purchase for $10 for the MTN Jul call and sells 100 shares of MTN stock for $88 per share, he would realize a

   A. $300 loss
   B. $300 profit
   C. $800 loss
   D. $800 profit

2. In April, a customer buys 1 MTN Oct 50 call for 9 and sells 1 MTN Jul 50 call for 4. What will the customer's pretax profit or loss be if he buys back the July call for $1 and sells the October call for $12?

   A. $100 loss
   B. $100 profit
   C. $600 loss
   D. $600 profit

3. In April, a customer purchases 1 TCB Jul 85 call for 5 and purchases 1 TCB Jul 90 put for 8. TCB stock is trading at 87. If TCB stays at 87 and both options are sold for their intrinsic value, the customer would realize a(n)

   A. $500 profit
   B. $800 loss
   C. $1,000 profit
   D. $1,100 profit

Answers

1. **B.** The customer bought and sold the call for 10, experiencing no gain or loss. Because the stock purchased for $85 was sold for $88, the gain is $300.

DR	CR
	10
85	88
10	
95	98
	3

2. **D.** $600 profit.

DR	CR
9	4
1	
	12
10	16
	6

3. **B.** The opening purchase of the Jul 85 call was made at 5, and the closing sale of that call was made at 2; the difference of 3 represents a $300 loss. The opening purchase of the Jul 90 put was made at 8, and the closing sale of that put was made at 3; the difference of 5 represents a $500 loss. The total loss for the account was $800.

DR	CR
5	
8	
	2 (87 − 85)
	3 (90 − 87)
13	5
8	

With the stock at 87, the intrinsic value of the 85 call is 2 and the intrinsic value of the 90 put is 3.

Test Topic Alert! Use a T-chart to simplify all questions that ask the investor's profit or loss.

If you feel comfortable with what you've done so far, advance to a different use of options—hedging. If not, go back and review before proceeding. With hedging, options can be used to protect a stock position. Expect up to 10 questions on this concept. Even though hedging appears to be a short part of this unit, learn it well—it's a heavily-tested portion of the options unit.

Using Options to Protect a Position

An investor with an established stock position can use options to help protect against the risk of the position. The option helps "insure" the investor against some of the possible loss from the stock position.

The investor who has a long stock position hopes for the market price of the stock to increase. The risk of the position, a market price decline, can be offset by the purchase of a put or, to a limited degree, the sale of a call.

The investor who has a short stock position hopes for the market price of the stock to decline. The risk of the position, a market price increase, can be offset by the purchase of a call or, to a limited degree, the sale of a put.

✓ **Take Note:** Here's an easy way to think about hedging strategy using the master options chart.

An investor has a long stock position that he wishes to protect. What is the risk of the long stock position?

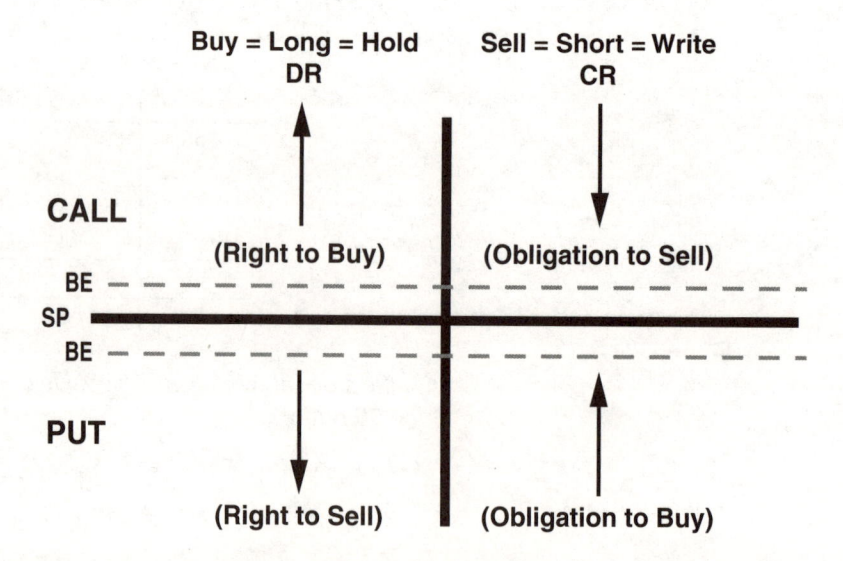

```
                Buy = Long = Hold      Sell = Short = Write
                       DR                      CR
                        ↑                       │
                        │                       ↓
        CALL
                   (Right to Buy)        (Obligation to Sell)
         BE  ─ ─ ─ ─ ─ ─ ─ ─ ─ ─ ─ │ ─ ─ ─ ─ ─ ─ ─ ─ ─ ─ ─
         SP ─────────────────────────────────────────────
         BE  ─ ─ ─ ─ ─ ─ ─ ─ ─ ─ ─ │ ─ ─ ─ ─ ─ ─ ─ ─ ─ ─ ─
                        │                       ↑
                        ↓                       │
         PUT
                   (Right to Sell)       (Obligation to Buy)
```

The risk is that the market price will fall (a downward arrow). To hedge the position, select an option position with a downward (bearish) arrow. The investor can protect a long stock position with a long put or short call.

Let's try this with a short stock position. If an investor has a short stock position, it is profitable when the market price declines. (Remember, in a short stock position, the investor has borrowed stock from the broker/dealer. He needs to buy back the shares to return to the broker/dealer. If he can buy them back at a lower price than the price at which he sold them, he makes a profit.) What is the risk of the short stock position?

Using Options to Protect a Position

The risk is that the market price will rise (an upward arrow). To hedge the position, select an option position with an upward (bullish) arrow. The investor can protect a short stock position with a long call or short put.

Sometimes the hedging strategy questions on the exam will ask you to determine which option will "best" or "fully" protect a stock position. The best protection is to buy an option (remember "Best Buy").

If the question asks for partial protection, or how the investor could improve his rate of return, select a short option position. The sale of the option generates premium income to improve the investor's rate of return. The risk of the stock position is reduced by the amount of the premium received, which is partial protection only.

The Use of Option Positions to Protect Stock Positions

Stock Position	Full Protection	Partial Protection
Long stock position	Long put	Short call
Short stock position	Long call	Short put

If an investor holds a long stock position, buying puts provides nearly total downside protection. The upside potential of the stock is only reduced by the amount of premiums paid. Selling calls when holding a long stock position, also known as **covered call writing**, is partial protection that generates income and reduces the stock's upside potential.

The following examples explain the use of options to protect a long stock position.

An investor buys 100 shares of RST at 53 and buys an RST 50 put for 2. The maximum gain is unlimited. Should the stock price fall below the strike price of 50, the investor will exercise the put to sell the stock for 50. The investor loses $3 per share on the stock and has spent $2 per share for the put. The total loss equals $500. The breakeven point is reached when the stock rises by the amount paid for the put; in this case, 53 + 2 = 55.

✓ **Take Note:** In the above example, no matter how far the stock falls, the investor can get out at 50 by exercising the put. Therefore, the most the investor can lose on the stock position is $3 per share. The cost of this protection is $2 per share. Therefore, maximum potential loss is $5 per share or $500. On the other hand, maximum gain is unlimited because the stock price could rise infinitely. To breakeven, the stock must rise by the cost of the put option purchased. The breakeven point for long stock—long put is cost of stock purchased plus premium.

An investor buys 100 shares of RST at 53 and writes 1 RST 55 call for 2. The maximum gain equals $400: if the stock price rises above 55, the call will be exercised; thus, the investor will sell the stock for a gain of $200, in addition to the $200 premium received. The maximum loss is $5,100. Should the stock become worthless, the $200 premium reduces the loss on the stock. The breakeven point is reached when the stock falls by the amount of the premium received. Therefore, 53 − 2 = 51.

✓ **Take Note:** In the above example, the customer is only protected on the downside by the amount of the premium received for writing the call. Thus, the stock could fall to $51, at which point the customer breaks even; the $2 loss on the stock is exactly offset by the premium received. Below $51, losses begin. If the stock becomes worthless, the customer could lose $5,100 which is maximum loss. If the stock rises above $55, the customer will be exercised, forced to sell stock at $55 for a $2 per share gain. Combined with the $2 per share premium received, maximum potential gain is $400. One of the drawbacks of writing calls against a long stock position is that it limits upside potential. Therefore, covered call writing is normally done in a stable market. The breakeven point for long stock—short call is cost of stock purchased minus premium.

An investor who is short stock is selling borrowed stock and expecting a price decline. The short seller must repay the stock loan and hopes to do so at a lower price. A short seller can buy calls to eliminate the risk of a rise in the stock's price. The investor may also sell puts for partial protection. This strategy, known as **writing a covered put**, limits the investor's potential profit and may subject the investor to unlimited loss.

The following examples explain the use of options to protect a short stock position.

An investor sells short 100 shares of RST at 58 and buys an RST 60 call for 3. The investor's maximum gain is $5,500: if the stock becomes worthless, the investor gains $5,800 from the short sale minus the $300 paid for the call. The maximum loss is $500: if the stock price rises above $60, the investor will exercise the call to buy the stock for 60, incurring a $200 loss on the short sale, in addition to the $300 paid for the call. The breakeven point is the stock's sale price minus the premium paid in this case, 58 − 3, or 55.

✓ **Take Note:** In the above example, no matter how high the stock rises, the investor can buy back his short position at 60 by exercising the call. Therefore, the most the investor can lose on the short stock position is $2 per share. The cost of this protection is $3 per share. Therefore, maximum potential loss is $5 per share or $500. On the other hand, maximum gain will occur if the stock becomes worthless. If the stock falls to zero, the customer will make $5,800 on the short stock position less the $300 paid to buy the call. Overall, maximum potential gain is $5,500. The breakeven point for short stock—long call is short sale price minus premium

A customer sells short 100 RST at 55 and writes an RST 55 put for 2.50 for partial protection. The maximum gain is $250. If the stock declines to zero and the put is exercised against him, the customer is obligated to pay $5,500 to buy the stock, losing $5,500. However, he receives a $5,500 gain from the short sale. Because he received the $250 premium, the stock can increase to 57.50, the breakeven point, before the short stock position generates a loss, which is potentially unlimited.

✓ *Take Note:* In the above example, the customer is only protected on the upside by the amount of the premium received for writing the put. Thus, the stock could rise to $57.50, at which point the customer breaks even; the $2.50 per share loss on the short position is exactly offset by the premium received. Potentially unlimited losses could result if the stock rises above the breakeven point. If the stock falls below $55, the put will be in the money at which point the customer will be exercised and forced to buy stock at $55 to close out his short position. Therefore, there is no gain or loss on the short stock position. The customer's gain is limited to $250, the premium received. The breakeven point for short stock—short put is the short sale price plus premium.

Collar Occasionally, an investor may hedge his downside risk on a long position of stock for no out-of-pocket cash.

✓ *For Example:* An investor is long 100 shares of XYZ at 50 and buys a 45 put at 3 and sells a 55 call for 3. The net cost is zero. In return, if the stock should fall to a very low price, the investor can put the stock to someone at 45. He knows that he can never lose more than $500. The downside is that he sacrifices any upside potential beyond $55. This is also known as a **cashless collar**.

Ratio Call Writing **Ratio call writing** involves selling more calls than the long stock position covers. This strategy generates additional premium income for the investor, but also entails unlimited risk due to the short uncovered calls.

Test Topic Alert! The following Quick Quiz questions require you to compute the breakeven, maximum gain, and maximum loss of hedged positions. To find breakeven, draw a T-chart and identify the debit/credit for both the stock position and the option position. The result is the breakeven point. To find maximum gain and maximum loss, focus on the stock position. What happens if the market goes up or down? Will the option be exercised?

Quick Quiz 4.15 Multiple Choice

1. A customer holds the following positions:
   Long 100 XYZ shares at 62
   Long 1 XYZ 60 put at 3
   The customer breaks even if XYZ trades at

   A. 57
   B. 59
   C. 63
   D. 65

2. **Long 100 XYZ shares at 62**
   Long 1 XYZ 60 put at 3
   What is the maximum gain the customer can realize on these positions?

   A. $5,700
   B. $6,500
   C. $11,900
   D. Unlimited

3. **Long 100 XYZ shares at 62**
   Long 1 XYZ 60 put at 3
   What is the most the customer can lose on these positions?

   A. $300
   B. $500
   C. $1,000
   D. Unlimited

4. **Long 100 shares at 38**
   Long 1 XYZ 35 put at 1
   The customer breaks even if XYZ trades at

   A. 34
   B. 36
   C. 37
   D. 39

5. **Long 100 shares at 38**
   Long 1 XYZ 35 put at 1
   What is the maximum gain the customer can realize on these positions?

   A. $3,400
   B. $3,900
   C. $7,200
   D. Unlimited

6. **Long 100 shares at 38**
   Long 1 XYZ 35 put at 1
   What is the most the customer can lose on these positions?

   A. $400
   B. $3,400
   C. $3,700
   D. $7,200

7. **Short 100 shares of XYZ at 26**
   Long XYZ 30 call at 1
   The customer breaks even if XYZ trades at

   A. 25
   B. 27
   C. 29
   D. 31

8. **Short 100 shares of XYZ at 26**
   Long XYZ 30 call at 1
   What is the maximum potential gain for the customer?

   A. $2,500
   B. $2,700
   C. $2,900
   D. $3,100

9. **Short 100 shares of XYZ at 26**
   Long XYZ 30 call at 1
   What is the maximum potential loss on the positions?

   A. $400
   B. $500
   C. $2,500
   D. Unlimited

10. **Short 100 shares of XYZ at 54**
    Long XYZ 55 call at 2
    The customer breaks even if XYZ trades at

    A. 52
    B. 53
    C. 56
    D. 57

11. **Short 100 shares of XYZ at 54**
    Long XYZ 55 call at 2
    What is the maximum potential gain?

    A. $300
    B. $5,200
    C. $5,300
    D. Unlimited

12. **Short 100 shares of XYZ at 54**
    Long XYZ 55 call at 2
    What is the maximum potential loss to the customer?

    A. $100
    B. $200
    C. $300
    D. Unlimited

13. **Long 100 XYZ shares at 62**
    Short 1 XYZ 65 call at 3
    The customer breaks even if XYZ trades at

    A. 57
    B. 59
    C. 63
    D. 65

14. **Long 100 XYZ shares at 62**
    Short 1 XYZ 65 call at 3
    What is the maximum gain the customer can realize on these positions?

    A. $300
    B. $600
    C. $5,900
    D. Unlimited

15. **Long 100 XYZ shares at 62**
    Short 1 XYZ 65 call at 3
    What is the most the customer can lose on these positions?

    A. $300
    B. $600
    C. $5,900
    D. Unlimited

Using Options to Protect a Position 231

16. **Short 100 shares of XYZ at 54**
    Short XYZ 50 put at 2
    What is the maximum potential loss to the customer?

    A. $200
    B. $60
    C. $5,200
    D. Unlimited

17. A customer is long 200 shares of XYZ at 90 and simultaneously writes 3 XYZ July 90 calls at 3. What is the maximum loss?

    A. $900
    B. $18,000
    C. $1,800
    D. Unlimited

Answers

1. **D.** The customer must recover the cost of the premium paid to be at the breakeven. Since this is a long stock position, the market must advance 3 points for this to occur. Therefore, the breakeven of this hedged position is found by adding the premium of the option to the price of the stock (62 + 3 = 65).

DR	CR
62	
3	
65	

2. **D.** The customer has protected his stock position from downside loss by purchasing the put. If the market rises, the put is not exercised and the unlimited upside potential of the stock is not affected. If the market falls the put would be exercised, allowing the customer to sell his stock at the option strike price.

3. **B.** The customer has protected his stock position from downside loss by purchasing the put. If the market falls the put would be exercised, allowing the customer to sell his stock at the option strike price of 60. Therefore, the most the customer can lose is $200 on the stock position (62 – 60), plus the premium paid for the option. ($200 + $300 = $500).

DR	CR
62	60
3	
65	60
5	

4. **D.** The customer must recover the cost of the premium paid to be at the breakeven. Because this is a long stock position, the market must advance one

point for this to occur. Therefore, the breakeven of this hedged position is found by adding the premium of the option to the price of the stock (38 + 1 = 39).

DR	CR
38	
1	
39	

5. **D.** The customer has protected his stock position from downside loss by purchasing the put. If the market rises, the put is not exercised and the unlimited upside potential of the stock is not affected. If the market falls the put would be exercised, allowing the customer to sell his stock at the option strike price.

6. **A.** The customer has protected his stock position from downside loss by purchasing the put. If the market falls the put would be exercised, allowing the customer to sell his stock at the option strike price of 35. Therefore, the most the customer can lose is $300 on the stock position (38 − 35), plus the premium paid for the option. ($300 + $100 = $400).

DR	CR
38	35
1	
39	35
4	

7. **A.** The customer must recover the cost of the premium paid to be at the breakeven. Because this is a short stock position, the price of the stock must decline 1 point for this to occur. Therefore, the breakeven of this hedged position is found by subtracting the premium of the option from the price of the stock (26 − 1 = 25).

DR	CR
	26
1	
	25

8. **A.** The customer has protected his short stock position from a market advance by buying the call. If the market rises the call would be exercised, allowing the customer to buy the stock and cover his short position at the option strike price. But because a premium was paid to buy the option, the premium reduces the gain. The max gain is the stock price minus the option premium (26 − 1 = 25). On 100 shares, this translates into a $2,500 maximum potential gain, which occurs if the stock becomes worthless.

9. **B.** The customer has protected his short stock position from loss by purchasing a call. If the market rises, the call would be exercised, allowing the customer to buy the stock at the option strike price of 30 to cover the short position. Therefore, the most the customer can lose is $400 on the stock position (the differ-

Using Options to Protect a Position 233

ence between the option strike price and the short sale price), plus the premium paid for the option. ($400 +$100 = $500).

DR	CR
	26
30	
1	
31	26
5	

10. **A.** The customer must recover the cost of the premium paid to be at the breakeven. Because this is a short position, the price of the stock must decline 2 points for this to occur. Therefore, the breakeven of this hedged position is found by subtracting the premium of the option from the price of the stock (54 − 2 = 52).

DR	CR
	54
2	
	52

11. **B.** The customer has protected his short stock position from a market advance by purchasing the call. If the market falls, the call is not exercised and the investor can make a maximum of $54 per share if the price falls to zero. However, because a premium was paid to buy the option, the premium reduces the gain. Therefore, the maximum gain is the stock price minus the option premium (54 − 2 = 52). If the market rises the call would be exercised, allowing the customer to buy the stock and cover his short position at the option strike price.

12. **C.** The customer has protected his short stock position from loss by purchasing a call. If the market rises, the call would be exercised, allowing the customer to buy the stock at the option strike price of 55 to cover the short position. Therefore, the most the customer can lose is $100 on the stock position (the difference between the option strike price and the short sale price), plus the premium paid for the option. ($100 + $200 = $300).

DR	CR
	54
2	
55	
57	54
3	

13. **B.** Even if the market falls by 3, the investor has not lost money on his overall position. Therefore, the breakeven of this hedged position is found by subtracting the premium of the option from the price of the stock (62 − 3 = 59).

DR	CR
62	
	3
59	

14. **B.** *The customer makes money on the long stock position if the market price of the stock increases. If the stock rises above the strike price of the call, the call will be exercised, requiring the customer to sell his stock at the option strike price, and capping the upside potential of the stock position. The premium received adds to the amount of investor profit.*

DR	CR
62	
	3
	65
62	68
	6

15. **C.** *The customer has protected his stock position from downside loss only by the amount of the premium received from the short call. The investor can lose $5,900 (62 − 3 = 59).*

16. **D.** *The customer has protected his short stock position from loss by the amount of the premium received from writing the put. The premium does little to offset the unlimited risk of the short stock position. The maximum loss is unlimited in this situation.*

17. **D.** *This is a ratio write. There are three short calls to only 200 shares. Two of the calls are covered; one is uncovered (naked). This is an inappropriate recommendation for a risk-averse customer.*

Multiple Option Transactions

Investors can simultaneously buy or sell more than one option contract on opposite sides of the market. These positions, known as **spreads, straddles,** and **combinations,** can be used to speculate on a security's price movement and limit position costs and risks.

Spreads

A **spread** is the simultaneous purchase of one option and sale of another option of the same class.

- A call spread is a long call and a short call.
- A put spread is a long put and a short put.

Multiple Option Transactions

💡 **Test Topic Alert!**   You may see questions on the exam that ask you to identify what position the investor has established. Again, the master options chart will give you the answer. The horizontal ovals shown in the following chart identify the two types of spreads: call spreads and put spreads.

As you solve questions, point at the investor's options positions on your chart. You will easily identify what type of position has been created.

Master Options Chart

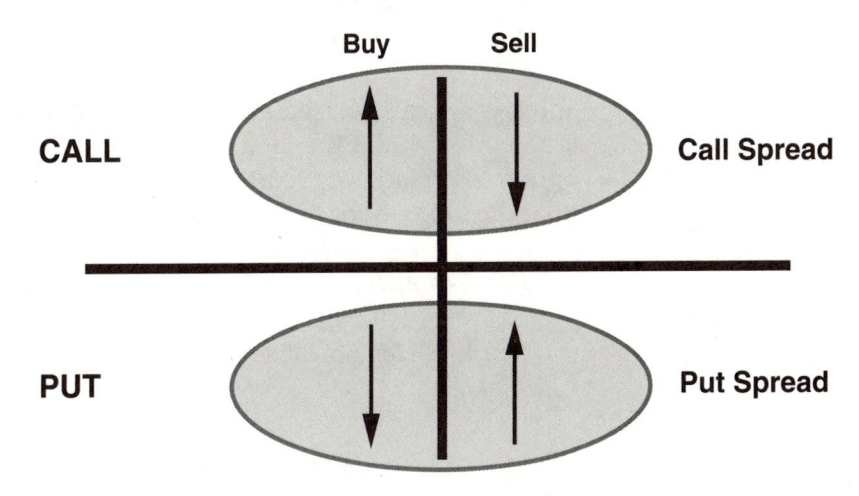

	Buy	Sell	
CALL	↑	↓	Call Spread
PUT	↓	↑	Put Spread

Types of Spreads   Investors can buy or sell three types of spreads: a price or vertical spread, a time or calendar spread, or a diagonal spread.

A **price spread** or **vertical spread** is one that has different strike prices but the same expiration date. It is called a vertical spread because strike prices on options reports are reported vertically.

✓ *For Example:*
Long RST Nov **50** call for 7
Short RST Nov **60** call for 3

✓ *Take Note:* The most common spread, and the one most likely to occur on the Series 7 exam, is the price spread (vertical spread), in which the two options have the same expiration date but different exercise prices.

A **time spread** or **calendar spread,** also known as a **horizontal spread,** includes option contracts with different expiration dates but the same strike prices. Investors who establish these do not expect great stock price volatility; instead they hope to profit from the different rates at which the time values of the two option premiums erode. Time spreads are called horizontal spreads because expiration months are arranged horizontally on options reports.

✓ *For Example:*
Long RST **Nov** 60 call for 3
Short RST **Jan** 60 call for 5

A **diagonal** spread is one in which the options differ in both time and price. On an options report, a line connecting these two positions would appear diagonal.

✓ *For Example:*
Long RST **Jan 55** call for 6
Short RST **Nov 60** call for 3

Spreads are categorized as either **debit spreads** or **credit spreads**. A spread is a debit spread if the long option has a higher premium than the short option; a spread is a credit spread if the short option has a higher premium than the long option.

✓ *For Example:*
Long RST Jan 55 call for 6
Short RST Jan 65 call for 2

DR	CR
6	
	2
4	

This spread is a debit spread because more premium was paid than received.

✓ *For Example:*
Long RST Jan 55 call for 2
Short RST Jan 45 call for 6

DR	CR
2	
	6
	4

This spread is a credit spread because more premium was received than paid.

Debit Call Spread   **Debit call spreads** are used by investors to reduce the cost of a long option position. There is, however, a trade-off, as the potential reward of the investor is also reduced. The investor who establishes a debit call spread is bullish.

✓ **For Example:**
   Buy 1 RST Nov 55 call for 6
   Sell 1 RST Nov 60 call for 3

DR	CR
6	
	3
3	

Instead of paying $600 to buy the call, the investor reduced its cost to $300 by also selling a call. If the market price of the stock rises above 60, both calls will be exercised. The investor has the right to buy the stock for 55, but must then sell the stock for 60: The $500 profit on the stock is reduced by the $300 net premium paid, for a net profit of $200. This is the investor's maximum gain on the position.

If the stock price remains below 55, both options will expire, and the investor will lose the net premium paid. The investor's maximum loss is the $300 net premium.

The investor's breakeven point is always between the two strike prices in a spread. For call spreads, breakeven is found by adding the net premium to the lower strike price. Adding the net premium of 3 to the lower strike price of 55 results in a breakeven point of 58.

Because this is a debit spread, the investor profits if exercise occurs. The difference in premiums on the two options widens as exercise becomes likely. Investors always want net debit spreads to widen.

💡 **Test Topic Alert!**

The following tips may be helpful with spread questions:

Debit = widen = exercise (When you begin to widen, you need to exercise.)

This reminds you that debit spreads are profitable if widening of premiums or exercise occurs. The test may ask you in which type of spread the investor wants the premiums to widen. Look for the debit spread.

Credit = narrow = expire (When you become too narrow, you may expire.)

This reminds you that credit spreads are profitable if premiums narrow and expiration occurs. This is logical because sellers want expiration, and option premiums decline as expiration approaches. In which type of spread does the investor want premiums to narrow? Look for the credit spread.

In finding breakeven points on spreads, remember CAL and PSH:
For **C**all spreads: **A**dd the net premium to the **L**ower strike price.
For **P**ut spreads: **S**ubtract the net premium from the **H**igher strike price.

Here's a last tip on finding maximum gain and maximum loss. Start by completing a T-chart. If the result is a net debit, the net debit = maximum loss. Find the maximum gain by subtracting the net debit from the difference in the two strike prices of the spread.

✓ **For Example:**
Long XYZ 50 call at 9
Short XYZ 60 call at 5

DR	CR
9	
	5
4	

The maximum loss is 4, because buyers of options lose premiums paid. The difference in strike prices is 10 (60 – 50). 10 – 4 leaves 6 for the max gain.

Remember, the maximum loss + the maximum gain must always total the difference in the strike prices.

Breakeven for the investor is found by CAL: 50 + 4 = 54.

If this had been a credit spread, the net premium would represent the maximum gain. The maximum loss would be found by subtracting the maximum gain from the difference in strike prices.

Credit Call Spread Credit call spreads are created by investors to reduce the risk of a short option position. Again, there is a trade-off; the potential reward of the investor is reduced. The investor who establishes a credit call spread is bearish.

✓ **For Example:**
Buy 1 RST Nov 55 call for 2
Sell 1 RST Nov 45 call for 9

DR	CR
2	
	9
	7

The investor reduced the unlimited risk of the short naked call by also purchasing a call. The long call gives the investor the right to purchase the stock at 55 if forced to sell at 45. The investor in this situation is bearish; if the stock price declines below the lower strike price of 45, both options will expire worthless and the investor keeps the net premium. The net premium (in this case $700) is the maximum gain for a credit spread.

If the market price of the stock rises above 45, the investor's loss is limited. The investor's long call can be exercised to buy the stock at 55. The loss on the stock is limited to 10, less the net premium of 7 collected. The maximum loss to the investor in a credit spread is the difference in the strike prices minus the net premium (in this case $300).

The investor's breakeven point is always between the two strike prices in a spread. For call spreads, breakeven is found by adding the net premium to the lower strike price. Adding the net premium of 7 to the lower strike price of 45 results in a breakeven point of 52.

Because this is a credit spread, the investor profits when the options expire. The difference in premiums on the two options narrows as the options are about to expire. Investors always want net credit spreads to narrow.

Quick Quiz 4.16 Multiple Choice

1. Buy 1 QRS Jan 40 call at 2.35; write 1 QRS Jan 45 call at .85. What is the breakeven point?

   A. 3.25
   B. 39.50
   C. 41.50
   D. 95

2. Write 1 MCS Dec 50 call at 5.25; buy 1 MCS Dec 55 call at 2. What is the breakeven point?

   A. 7.25
   B. 53.25
   C. 57
   D. 50

3. Write 1 ABC Oct 30 call at 3.25; buy 1 ABC Oct 40 call at .25. What is the maximum gain and the maximum loss?

   I. Max. gain, $300
   II. Max. gain, $325
   III. Max. loss, $700
   IV. Max. loss, $7,025

   A. I and III
   B. I and IV
   C. II and III
   D. II and IV

4. Buy 1 LMN Oct 80 call at 8; write 1 LMN Oct 90 call at 2.75. What is the maximum gain and the maximum loss?

   I. Max. gain, $475
   II. Max. gain, $525
   III. Max. loss, $475
   IV. Max. loss, $525

   A. I and III
   B. I and IV
   C. II and III
   D. II and IV

5. Write 1 XYZ Jan 130 call at 26.75; buy 1 XYZ Jan 140 call at 19.50. What is the maximum gain and the maximum loss?

   I. Max. gain, $275
   II. Max. gain, $725
   III. Max. loss, $725
   IV. Max. loss, $275

   A. I and III
   B. I and IV
   C. II and III
   D. II and IV

Answers

1. **C.** This is a call spread, so the breakeven point is found by adding the net debit of 1.50 to the lower strike price: 40 + 1.50 = 41.50.

2. **B.** To find the breakeven point on this call credit spread, add the net credit of 3.25 to the lower strike price of 50.

3. **A.** Max gain: $300. The maximum potential gain on a credit spread is the net credit. Max loss: $700. The maximum potential loss on a credit spread is the difference between the strike prices minus the net credit: 10 − 3 = 7; 7 × 100 shares = $700.

4. **B.** Max loss: $525. In a debit spread, the net debit represents maximum loss. To find maximum gain, subtract max loss from the difference between the strike prices.

5. **D.** Max gain: $725. The maximum gain on a credit spread is the net credit received. Max loss: $275. The maximum loss on a credit spread is the difference between the strike price minus the net credit: 10 − 7.25 = 2.75; 2.75 × 100 shares = $275.

Debit Put Spread

Debit put spreads are used by investors to reduce the cost of a long put position. The investor who establishes a debit put spread is bearish.

✓ *For Example:*
Buy 1 RST Nov 55 put for 6
Sell 1 RST Nov 50 put for 3

DR	CR
6	
	3
3	

Instead of paying $600 to buy the put, the investor reduced its cost to $300 by also selling a put. If the market price of the stock falls below 50, both puts will be exercised. The investor will sell the stock for 55, but buy the stock for 50. The $500 profit on the stock is reduced by the $300 net premium paid, for a net profit of $200. This is the investor's maximum gain on the position.

If the stock price remains above 55, both options will expire and the investor will lose the net premium paid. The investor's maximum loss is the $300 net premium.

The investor's breakeven point is always between the two strike prices in a spread. For put spreads, breakeven is found by subtracting the net premium from the higher strike price. Subtracting the net premium of 3 from 55 results in a breakeven point of 52.

This is a debit spread, so the investor profits if exercise occurs. The difference in premiums on the two options widens as exercise becomes likely. Investors always want net debit spreads to widen.

Credit Put Spread

Credit put spreads are created by investors to reduce the risk of a short put position. Again, there is a trade-off: the potential reward of the investor is reduced. The investor who establishes a credit put spread is bullish.

✓ *For Example:*
Buy 1 RST Nov 55 put for 2
Sell 1 RST Nov 65 put for 9

DR	CR
2	
	9
	7

The investor reduced the substantial risk of the short naked put by also purchasing a put. The long put gives the investor the right to sell stock if necessary to provide cash the investor needs to buy stock when the short put is exercised. The investor in this situation is bullish; if the stock price rises above the upper strike price of 65, both options will expire worthless and the investor keeps the net premium. The net premium is the maximum gain for a credit spread.

If the market price of the stock falls below 55, the investor's loss is limited. The exercise of the investor's short put will require purchase of the stock at 65. The loss is limited to 10, less the net premium of 7 collected. The maximum loss to the investor in a credit spread is the difference in the strike prices minus the net premium.

The investor's breakeven point is always between the two strike prices in a spread. For put spreads, breakeven is found by subtracting the net premium from the higher strike price. Subtracting the net premium of 7 from 65 results in a breakeven point of 58.

This is a credit spread, so the investor profits when the options expire. The difference in premiums on the two options narrows as the options are about to expire. Investors always want net credit spreads to narrow.

Maximum Gain and Maximum Loss for Debit and Credit Spreads

Calculation	Credit Spread	Debit Spread
Maximum gain	The net credit	The difference between the strike prices – the net debit
Maximum loss	The difference between the strike prices – the net credit	The net debit

Quick Quiz 4.17 Multiple Choice

1. Which of the following are spreads?

   I. Long 1 ABC May 40 call; short 1 ABC May 50 call
   II. Long 1 ABC May 40 call; long 1 ABC May 50 call
   III. Long 1 ABC Aug 40 call; short 1 ABC May 40 call
   IV. Long 1 ABC Aug 40 call; short 1 ABC Aug 50 put

   A. I and II
   B. I and III
   C. II and III
   D. II and IV

Multiple Option Transactions

2. Buy 1 XYZ Apr 30 put at 3.30; write 1 XYZ Apr 35 put at 5.80. What is the breakeven point?

   A. 21
   B. 26
   C. 27.50
   D. 32.50

3. Buy 1 LMN Jan 40 put at 6.50; write 1 LMN Jan 30 put at 2.25. What is the maximum gain and the maximum loss?

   I. Max gain, $425
   II. Max gain, $575
   III. Max loss, $425
   IV. Max loss, $575

   A. I and III
   B. I and IV
   C. II and III
   D. II and IV

4. An investor who has entered into a debit spread will profit if

   A. the spread widens
   B. the spread narrows
   C. the spread remains unchanged
   D. both contracts expire unexercised

5. In March, a customer sells 1 CW Oct 50 put for 3 and buys 1 CW Oct 60 put for 11. The customer will experience a pretax profit from these positions if

   I. the difference between the premiums narrows to less than $8 per share
   II. the difference between the premiums widens to more than $8 per share
   III. both puts are exercised at the same time
   IV. both puts expire unexercised

   A. I and III
   B. I and IV
   C. II and III
   D. II and IV

Answers

1. **B.** Choices (I) and (III) fit the definition of a call spread because each includes one long and one short option of the same type with either different strike prices (I) or different expiration dates (III). II involves options of the same type but both are long. Choice (IV) involves options of different types.

2. **D.** This is a put spread established at a credit of 2.50. To find the breakeven point on a put spread, subtract the net credit or debit from the higher strike price. (PSH: Puts Subtract from Higher). In this case, subtract the credit of 2.50 from the higher strike price of 35.

3. **C.** *The maximum loss on a debit spread is the net debit. The maximum gain on a debit spread is the difference between the strike price minus the net debit: 10 − 4.25= 5.75; 5.75 × 100 shares = $575. Max. loss: $425.*

4. **A.** *Debit spreads are profitable if the spread between the premiums widens.*

5. **C.** *This is a debit spread that would be profitable if the spread between the premiums widens. If both puts are exercised, the spread is profitable. If the short 50 put is exercised, the customer buys the stock that is then sold for 60 by exercising the long 60 put. The $1,000 profit less $800 paid in premiums equals a net $200 profit.*

Determining a Spread Investor's Market Attitude

The **market attitude** of a spread investor is determined by the option that is the more costly of the two. For calls, the lower strike price commands the higher premium. A call is an option to buy, so investors want to buy at the lower strike price.

For put options, the higher strike price is more valuable. A put is an option to sell, so investors want to sell at the higher strike price.

If an investor buys 1 XYZ Jan 50 call and sells 1 XYZ Jan 60 call, the investor has created a **bull spread**. The 50 call has the higher premium of the two, and because the investor has purchased the 50 call the spread is bullish: buying calls is bullish.

If an investor buys 1 XYZ Jan 50 put and sells 1 XYZ Jan 60 put, the investor has again established a **bull spread**. The 60 put has the higher premium of the two, and because the investor has sold the put the spread is bullish: selling puts is bullish.

An investor who buys 1 XYZ Jan 50 put and sells 1 XYZ Jan 40 put has established a **bear spread**. The 50 put has the higher premium of the two, and because the investor has bought the put the spread is bearish: buying puts is bearish.

An investor who buys a 60 call and sells a 50 call has established a **bear spread**. The 50 call has the higher premium of the two, and because the investor has sold the call, the spread is bearish: selling calls is bearish.

Test Topic Alert!

You may be asked to determine if a spread is bullish or bearish. With premiums shown, use a T-chart to determine debit or credit. If no premiums are shown, it's up to you to determine which of the options is more valuable.

A quick way to determine if a spread is bullish or bearish is the following: in any spread, put or call, if you are buying the lower strike price, you are a bull.

Buy XYZ Jan 20 call at 7; Sell XYZ Jan 30 call at 3: bull call spread – debit spread

Buy ABC Aug 35 call at 1; Sell ABC Aug 25 call at 8; bear call spread – credit spread

Buy DEF Mar 70 put at 6; Sell DEF Mar 90 put at 17; bull put spread – credit spread

Buy LRK Sep 30 put at 9; Sell LRK Sep 20 put at 3; bear put spread – debit spread

Expect to see 1 or 2 questions on this concept.

Quick Quiz 4.18   Multiple Choice

1. A customer buys 1 DOH Nov 70 put and sells 1 DOH Nov 60 put when DOH is selling for 65. This position is a

    A. bull spread
    B. bear spread
    C. combination
    D. straddle

2. All of the following are credit spreads EXCEPT

    A. write 1 Nov 35 put and buy 1 Nov 30 put
    B. buy 1 Apr 40 call and write 1 Apr 30 call
    C. buy 1 Jul 50 call and write 1 Jul 60 call
    D. buy 1 Jan 50 put and write 1 Jan 60 put

In questions 3–10, answer A to identify a bear spread and B for a bull spread.

___ 3. Write 1 Nov 35 put; buy 1 Nov 30 put

___ 4. Buy 1 Jan 70 call; write 1 Jan 75 call

___ 5. Write 1 Apr 30 call; buy 1 Apr 40 call

___ 6. Write 1 Dec 45 put; buy 1 Dec 60 put

___ 7. Buy 1 Jul 50 call; write 1 Jul 60 call

___ 8. Buy 1 Dec 45 put; write 1 Dec 40 put

___ 9. Write 1 Jan 60 put; buy 1 Jan 50 put

___ 10. Buy 1 May 25 put; write 1 May 20 put

11. In which of the following cases would the investor want the spread to widen?

   I. Write 1 May 25 put; buy 1 May 30 put
   II. Write 1 Apr 45 put; buy 1 Apr 55 put
   III. Buy 1 Nov 65 put; write 1 Nov 75 put
   IV. Write 1 Jan 30 call; buy 1 Jan 40 call

   A. I and II
   B. I and IV
   C. II and III
   D. II and IV

Answers

1. **B.** This put spread is established at a debit, because the investor pays more for the 70 put than he receives for the 60 put. Bears buy puts and put spreads. Another easy way to think of this: Long the lower strike price is bullish so the investor is short the lower strike price, the position is bearish.

2. **C.** The lower the strike price, the more expensive the call option. The higher the strike price, the more expensive the put option. The investor has bought the more expensive option with the lower strike price, so this is a debit spread.

3. **B.** This is a credit put spread. The investor receives more for the Nov 35 put than paid for the Nov 30 put. Bulls sell put spreads. The put with the higher strike price is more likely to be in-the-money as the market falls.

4. **B.** This is a debit call spread. Bulls buy calls. A lower strike price call is more likely to be in-the-money as the market rises.

5. **A.** This is a credit call spread. Bears sell calls.

6. **A.** This is a debit put spread. Bears buy puts. The 60 put is worth more because it has a higher strike price.

7. **B.** This is a debit call spread. Bulls buy calls.

8. **A.** Bear spread. This a debit put spread. Bears buy puts.

9. **B.** Bull spread. This is a credit put spread. Bulls sell puts.

10. **A.** Bear spread. This is a debit put spread. Bears buy puts.

11. **A.** Choices (I) and (II) are debit spreads: an investor wants a debit spread to widen. As the distance between the premiums increases, the investor's potential profit also increases.

Straddles

A **straddle** is composed of a call and a put with the same strike price and expiration month. Straddles can be long or short and are used by investors to speculate on the price movement of stock.

✓ **Take Note:** Like spreads, straddles can also easily be identified with the master options chart. Straddles are identified by vertical ovals rather than horizontal ovals on the chart.

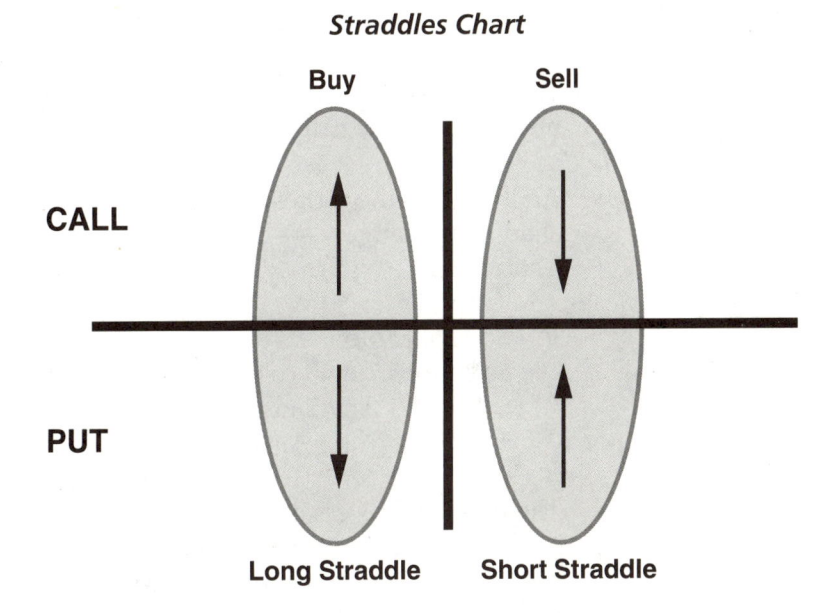

Straddles Chart

CALL

PUT

Buy — Long Straddle

Sell — Short Straddle

The chart also provides a tip about the strategy behind straddles. Notice the market attitude arrows pushing away from each other on the long straddle. This reminds you that the investor who buys a straddle expects a large amount of movement in the price of the stock.

The arrows on the short side are pointing toward each other and signify little or no market price movement: the objective of the seller of the straddle.

Long Straddles

An investor who uses a **long straddle** expects substantial volatility in the stock's price, but is uncertain of the direction the price will move. To be ready for either occurrence, the investor purchases both a call and a put.

✓ **For Example:**
Buy 1 ABC Jan 50 call at 3
Buy 1 ABC Jan 50 put at 4

Maximum gain = unlimited, Maximum loss = $700, Breakevens = 57, 43

The investor has created a long straddle by purchasing a call and a put with the same strike and expiration. If the market price of the stock rises sufficiently, the call will be profitable and the put will expire. The investor's gain on the call will be reduced by the premiums paid on both the call and the put.

If the market price of the stock falls substantially instead, the put will be profitable and the call will expire. The investor's gain on the put will be reduced by the premiums paid on both the call and the put.

The maximum gain of the long straddle is unlimited because the potential gain on a long call is unlimited. The maximum loss of the long straddle is both premiums paid. There are two breakeven points because there are two options. The breakeven for the call is the strike price plus both premiums paid; the breakeven for the put is the strike price minus both premiums paid. The investor does not experience profit unless the market price is above the breakeven of the call or below the breakeven of the put.

Short Straddles

An investor who writes a short straddle expects that the stock's price will not change or change very little. The investor collects two premiums for selling a straddle.

✓ *For Example:*
Sell 1 ABC Jan 45 call at 4
Sell 1 ABC Jan 45 put at 5
Maximum gain = $900, maximum loss = unlimited, breakevens = 54, 36

The investor has created a short straddle by selling a call and a put with the same strike and expiration. If the market price of the stock changes little or not at all, the call and put will expire. The investor's maximum profit is the two premiums collected.

If the market price of the stock rises or falls substantially, either the put or call will be exercised against the investor. The investor's maximum loss in this position is unlimited because of the short naked call.

The breakeven points for the short straddle are found the same way as for the long straddle. The call breakeven is the strike price plus both premiums paid; the breakeven for the put is the strike price minus both premiums paid. The investor does not experience profit unless the market price stays within the breakeven points at expiration.

Straddle Calculations

Calculation	Long Straddle	Short Straddle
Maximum Gain	Unlimited	Total premiums received
Maximum Loss	Total premiums paid	Unlimited
Breakevens	Call: strike + both premiums Put: strike − both premiums	Call: strike + both premiums Put: strike − both premiums

Combinations A **combination** is composed of a call and a put with different strike prices and/or expiration months. Combinations are similar to straddles in strategy. Investors typically use combinations because they are cheaper to establish than long straddles if both options are out-of-the-money.

✓ *For Example:* An investor could establish a long combination by buying an XYZ Jan 40 call and buying an XYZ Jan 45 put. If the investor were to write both options, a short combination would result. Breakeven points are computed in the same manner as straddles. Add the combined premiums to the strike price of the call and subtract combined premiums from the strike price of the put. As with straddles, the holder of a long combination makes money if the underlying stock trades outside the breakeven points. The writer of a short combination makes money if the stock stays inside the breakeven points.

✓ *For Example:* With XYZ trading at 25, a customer writes 1 XYZ Jan 20 call at 6 and writes 1 XYZ Jan 30 put at 7. This is an example of a short combination where both contracts are in-the-money. Both the call and the put are in the money by 5 points. Series 7 could ask you the following question. Just prior to expiration, with XYZ now trading at 27, the customer closes his positions at intrinsic value. How much did the customer make or lose?

In this example, closing means buying back the two options that were originally sold. What will be the cost of buying back both options? The answer is their intrinsic value. With XYZ now at 27, the call is in-the-money by 7 points and the put is in-the-money by 3 points. Now it's just a simple computation. The call was sold for 6 and bought back for 7, a loss of $100. The put was sold for 7 and bought back for 3, a gain of $400. Overall, the gain is $300.

Quick Quiz 4.19 Multiple Choice

1. Your customer sells a DOH Mar 35 call. To establish a straddle, he would

   A. sell a DOH Mar 40 call
   B. buy a DOH Mar 35 put
   C. sell a DOH Mar 35 put
   D. buy a DOH Mar 40 call

2. ACM issues a news release that your customer believes will strongly affect the market price of ACM stock. However, your customer is not sure if the effect will be positive or negative. In this situation, which of the following strategies would be best?

   A. Buy a call
   B. Write a call
   C. Write a straddle
   D. Buy a straddle

3. Your customer buys 2 QRS Jul 30 calls at 2 and 2 QRS Jul 30 puts at 2.50. The customer will break even when the price of the underlying stock is

   I. 25.50
   II. 27.50
   III. 32
   IV. 34.50

   A. I and IV only
   B. II and III only
   C. III only
   D. IV only

   Identify the positions described by indicating one of the following terms.

   A. Price spread
   B. Long straddle
   C. Time spread
   D. Short straddle
   E. Diagonal spread
   F. Combination

   ___ 4. Buy 1 QRS May 40 call; sell 1 QRS May 50 call.

   ___ 5. Buy 1 QRS May 40 call; buy 1 QRS May 40 put.

   ___ 6. Buy 1 QRS Aug 40 call; sell 1 QRS Dec 40 call.

___ 7. Buy 1 DOH May 30 call; buy 1 DOH Jul 40 put.

___ 8. Write 1 DOH Jan 30 call; write 1 DOH Jan 40 put.

___ 9. Buy 1 DOH Mar 35 call; write 1 DOH Jun 45 call.

Answers

1. **C.** *Straddles involve options of different types, but both options must be long or both must be short. They must have the same expiration date and strike price.*

2. **D.** *Investors who are unsure of market attitude but expect substantial volatility may profit from buying straddles.*

3. **A.** *The customer buys calls and puts with the same strike price and expiration date, so the position is a straddle. Straddles have two breakeven points—the strike price plus and minus the sum of the two premiums.*

4. **A.** *The most common spread, and the one most likely to occur on the Series 7 exam, is the price spread (vertical spread), in which the two options have the same expiration date but different exercise prices.*

5. **B.** *The investor is long a call and long a put with the same strike price and expiration date; this is a long straddle.*

6. **C.** *Also called a horizontal or calendar spread, a time spread involves two options with different expiration dates.*

7. **F.** *A combination is similar to a straddle in that the investor buys or sells a call and a put. With a combination, however, the strike prices, expiration dates or both are different. This is a long combination.*

8. **F.** *The investor is selling a call and a put with different strike prices. This is a short combination.*

9. **E.** *A diagonal spread involves the purchase and sale of two options of the same type with different expiration dates and strike prices.*

Nonequity Options

Nonequity options function nearly the same as equity options. However, because the underlying instruments are not shares of stock, nonequity options have different contract sizes and delivery and exercise standards.

Index Options

Options on indexes allow investors to profit from the movements of markets or market segments and hedge against these market swings. They may be based on broad-based or narrow-based indexes.

Broad-based indexes reflect movement of the entire market, and include the S&P 100 (OEX), S&P 500, and the AMEX Major Market Index (XMI).

Narrow-based indexes track the movement of market segments in a specific industry, such as technology or pharmaceuticals.

Index Option Features

Multiplier

Index options typically use a multiplier of $100. The premium amount is multiplied by $100 to calculate the option's cost and the strike price is multiplied by $100 to determine the total dollar value of the index.

Trading

Purchases and sales of index options, like equity options, settle next business day. Index options stop trading at 4:15 ET.

Exercise

The exercise of an index option settles in cash rather than in delivery of a security, and the cash must be delivered on the next business day. If the option is exercised, the writer of the option delivers cash equal to the intrinsic value of the option to the buyer.

Settlement Price

When index options are exercised, their settlement price is based on the closing value of the index on the day of exercise, not the value at the time of exercise.

Expiration Dates

Index options expire on the Saturday following the third Friday of the expiration month.

✓ **Take Note:** With regard to settlement, there is one major difference between index options and equity options. The exercise of an index option settles next business day while the exercise of an equity option settles regular way (three business days). With regard to trading (i.e., buying or selling), settlement is next business day for both.

Index Option Exercise

✓ **For Example:** A customer buys 1 OEX Jan 460 call at 3.20 when the OEX index is trading at 461.

What is the premium?	$320 (3.20 × $100)
What is the breakeven point?	463.20 (strike price + premium)
What is the intrinsic value?	$100 (461 − 460)
What is the time value?	$220 ($320 − $100)

One month later, with the index at 472 and the Jan 460 call trading at 13.70, the customer elects to exercise.

How much cash will the customer receive from the writer?	$1,200, the intrinsic value of the option (472 − 460)
How much profit did the customer make?	$880 which is the cash received from the writer less the premium paid ($1,200 − $320)

Now, instead of exercising, assume the customer closes the position.

How much profit would the customer make?	$1,050, which is the difference between the premium received on selling ($1,370) and the premium paid to open the position ($320)

Note that instead of making $880 by exercising, the customer would have made $1,050 by closing the position. Why the $170 difference? As long as there is time value in the option, the customer will always make more by closing an index option rather than by exercising. The time value of the 460 call trading at 13.70 when the index is at 472 is $170.

Capped Index Options

Capped index options are a unique type of index option automatically exercised when the cap price is reached. The cap interval is normally set at 30 points above the strike price for calls and 30 points below the strike price for puts. A buyer can make no more than the cap amount less the premium paid while a writer can lose no more than the cap amount less the premium received.

✓ **For Example:**
Long OEX capped Jan 410 call at 8.50.
If the OEX is now trading at 445, what is the holder's profit?

This call is capped at 440. The 30 points of intrinsic value must be reduced by the premium to determine the holder's profit. $3,000 − $850 = $2,150 profit.

Index Options Strategy

Index options may be used to speculate on movement of the market overall. If an investor believes the market will rise, he can purchase index calls or write index puts. If an investor believes the market will fall, he can purchase index puts or write index calls.

Hedging a portfolio is an important use of index options. If a portfolio manager holds a diverse portfolio of equity, he can buy a put on the index to offset loss if the market value of the stocks fall. This usage of index puts is known as **portfolio insurance**. Index options protect against the risk of a decline in the overall market, which is **systematic** or **systemic risk**.

✓ *For Example:* Assume a customer has a broad-based stock portfolio worth $920,000 and is concerned about a possible market downturn. In order to hedge, the customer could buy broad-based index puts (e.g., the OEX). If the market does turn downward, the loss on the portfolio would be offset by a gain on the puts. Remember, a put increases in value as the underlying security or portfolio goes down in value. If the OEX is trading at 460, each contract has a value of $46,000 (460 × $100). Therefore, to hedge a $920,000 stock portfolio, the customer would buy 20 OEX 460 puts (20 × $46,000).

Beta

Beta is a measure of the volatility of a stock or a portfolio related to the volatility of the market in general. If a portfolio has a beta of 1.0, it has the same volatility characteristics as the market in general. In other words, if the market were to rise 5%, the portfolio should rise by the same amount. If a portfolio has a beta of 1.2, it is 20% more volatile than the market in general. For example, if the market were to rise by 10%, a portfolio with a beta of 1.2 should rise 20% more, or 12%. Conversely, should the market decline, a portfolio with a beta of more than 1.0 will fall more than the overall market.

Back to our original example: if the $920,000 portfolio has a beta of 1.2, instead of purchasing 20 OEX 460 puts to hedge, the customer must purchase 24 OEX 460 puts. As the portfolio is 20% more volatile, the customer needs 20% more protection (1.2 × 20 puts = 24).

Portfolio managers may also choose to write index options to generate income.

Quick Quiz 4.20 Multiple Choice

1. Your customer is bullish on the market. If he buys 1 Jul 490 call on the XMI, which of the following options might he write to create a debit spread?

    I. Jul 485 call
    II. Jul 480 call
    III. Jul 500 call
    IV. Jul 505 call

    A. I only
    B. I and II only
    C. II, III and IV only
    D. III and IV only

2. Your client owns a portfolio of blue-chip stocks. He tells you that he believes that the securities will provide good, long-term appreciation but also believes that the market will decline over the short term. Which index options strategy should you recommend that will protect against the expected decline and still allow for long-term capital appreciation?

    A. Buy puts
    B. Buy calls
    C. Sell covered puts
    D. Sell covered calls

3. When an investor exercises an OEX option, he receives

    A. common stock
    B. cash equal to the strike price
    C. cash equal to the intrinsic value
    D. It cannot be exercised.

4. Which of the following statements regarding stock index options are TRUE?

    I. Trades are settled the next business day.
    II. Trades are settled on the third business day.
    III. Exercise settlement involves the delivery of stock.
    IV. Exercise settlement involves the delivery of cash.

    A. I and III
    B. I and IV
    C. II and III
    D. II and IV

256   Options

5. Which of the following are considered features of a capped index option?

   I. Automatic exercise as soon as the option is out-of-the-money by the amount of the cap interval
   II. Automatic exercise as soon as the option is in-the-money by the amount of the cap interval
   III. The cap price is set by the Exchange at the time of listing
   IV. Automatic exercise when the underlying index hits or goes through the cap price

   A. I, III and IV only
   B. I and IV only
   C. II and III only
   D. II, III and IV only

6. Your customer buys a capped index call option for a premium of $1,400. The strike price is $360. The option is automatically exercised at the cap price of $390. What is the customer's gain or loss?

   A. $1,400 loss
   B. $1,600 gain
   C. $3,000 gain
   D. $4,400 loss

Answers

1. **D.** If the customer sold either a 500 call or a 505 call, he would have a debit spread because he has purchased the more expensive call—the one with a lower strike price. The customer would create a credit spread by selling the 480 call or the 485 call. Because they have lower strike prices, they would be more expensive than the 490 call.

2. **A.** Because your client is long stock, his position would be hurt by a drop in the market. To hedge against that risk, he must take an option position that appreciates in value as the market declines: long puts or short calls. Because your client also wishes to benefit from any appreciation, the long put is the better hedging vehicle. If the market averages increase, the put position would lose only the premium, and your client could still gain on the portfolio.

3. **C.** Exercise settlement on index option is in cash, not stock. When the owner of an option exercises, the person who has a short position must deliver cash equal to the intrinsic value (the in-the-money amount). This is computed based upon the closing value of the index on the day the option is exercised.

4. **B.** Index option trades settle the next business day, and cash is delivered upon exercise of the option. Exercise of index options is also next business day

5. **D.** Cap prices are set at a certain in-the-money interval by the exchange. These options are exercised automatically when the underlying index hits or goes through the cap price.

6. **B.** When the index call option is exercised, the customer receives, in cash, the difference between the option's strike price and the cap price—in this case,

> *$3,000. To calculate his gain, the customer subtracts the $1,400 premium he paid for the option from the cap interval.*

Interest Rate Options

Interest rate options are yield-based (i.e., they have a direct relationship to movements in interest rates). These options are based on yields of T-bills, T-notes, and T-bonds. A yield-based option with a strike price of 35 reflects a yield of 3.5%. Assume an investor believes that rates on T-notes, currently at 3.5%, will rise in the near term. The investor could purchase a call option with a 35 strike price (at the money). If rates rise to 4.5%, the investor could exercise and receive cash equal to the intrinsic value of the option.

As rates have gone up by 10 points—35 to 45—the investor would receive $1,000 as each point is worth $100. Profit would be the $1,000 received on exercise less the premium paid. On the other hand, the investor could have closed his position, profiting from the difference between the premium paid and the premium received on closing.

The strategy is straightforward. If a portfolio manager believes rates will fall, the manager will buy puts or write calls. If the manager believes rates will rise, buying calls and writing puts would be appropriate.

Foreign Currency Options (FCOs)

FCOs allow investors to speculate on the performance of currencies other than the US dollar, or to protect against fluctuating currency exchange rates. Currency options are available on British pounds, Canadian and Australian dollars, Swiss francs, and Japanese yen, among others. Importers and exporters frequently use them.

Features of Foreign Currency Options

Strike Prices

Strike prices of most foreign currency options are quoted in US cents. A strike price of 167 on the British pound means the pounds must be bought or sold for 167 US cents ($1.67) if the contract is exercised.

Premiums

Most foreign currency options are quoted in cents per unit. The exception to this rule is Japanese yen, quoted in hundredths of a cent.

The total premium of the contract is found by multiplying the premium by the number of units. If a Swiss franc contract (62,500 units) is quoted with a premium of .5, the cost of the contract is 62,500 × .005, or $312.50.

Contract Sizes

Foreign currency options contracts are large because they are designed primarily for institutional trading. A British pound contract, for instance, covers 31,250 pounds. Each currency has its own contract size.

Trading

FCOs are primarily traded on the **Philadelphia Stock Exchange (PHLX)**.

Expiration Date

Foreign currency options expire on the Saturday preceding the third Wednesday of the month.

Settlement

The trading of foreign currency options settles, like other options, on the next business day. If, however, a foreign currency option is exercised, settlement occurs in four business days with the currency delivered to an OCC designated bank.

Styles

Foreign currency options are available either European or American style.

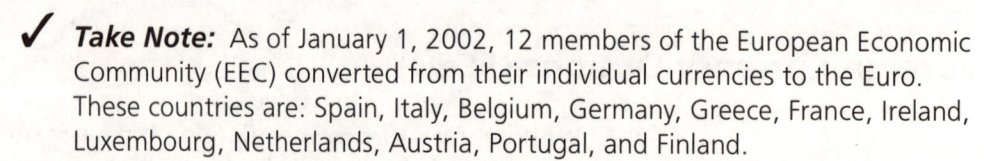

✓ **Take Note:** As of January 1, 2002, 12 members of the European Economic Community (EEC) converted from their individual currencies to the Euro. These countries are: Spain, Italy, Belgium, Germany, Greece, France, Ireland, Luxembourg, Netherlands, Austria, Portugal, and Finland.

Each Euro contract covers 62,500 Euros and is quoted in US cents.

Strategies

If an investor believes the value of a currency is going to rise, he will buy calls or sell puts on the currency. If an investor expects the value of currency will fall, he will buy puts or sell calls on the currency. Currency options are measured relative to the US dollar, and an inverse relationship exists between their exchange rates.

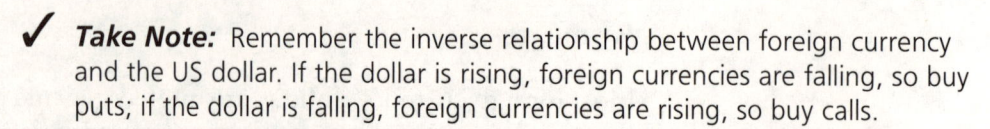

✓ **Take Note:** Remember the inverse relationship between foreign currency and the US dollar. If the dollar is rising, foreign currencies are falling, so buy puts; if the dollar is falling, foreign currencies are rising, so buy calls.

✓ **For Example:** A US importer must pay for Swiss chocolates in Swiss francs within three months. The importer is fearful that the value of the dollar will fall. Using foreign currency options, what should this investor do?

If the importer believes the US dollar will fall, then foreign currency values will rise. The investor should buy calls on the Swiss franc to lock in the purchase price for the francs needed in three months.

💡 **Test Topic Alert!**   Expect to see a question on the calculation of the premium of a foreign currency contract and a question on the strategies of using them.

✓ ***Take Note:*** As a general rule, importers buy calls on the foreign currency to hedge; exporters buy puts to hedge. However, keep in mind that there are no options available on the US dollar. As an example, consider a Japanese company which exports stereos to the US The company will be paid in dollars upon delivery. The risk to the Japanese company is that the dollar will decline between now and the delivery, which means one dollar will be worth less yen. How should this company hedge this risk?

The rule of thumb is that exporters should buy puts on the foreign currency. However, as there are no options on the US dollar, the Japanese company should buy calls on its own currency, the yen.

✓ ***For Example:*** A British company is exporting sweaters to the US. How should the company hedge its foreign exchange risk?

A. Buy BP calls
B. Sell BP calls
C. Buy BP puts
D. Sell BP puts

A: As options on the US dollar are not available, exporters to the US should buy calls on their own currency.

✏ Quick Quiz 4.21   Multiple Choice

1. Which of the following currency options is not traded?

   A. British pound
   B. Japanese yen
   C. Canadian dollar
   D. US dollar

2. An investor is long 5 PHLX Dec puts on the Canadian dollar. These options will expire in December on the

   A. third Friday of the month
   B. Saturday after the third Friday
   C. Wednesday after the third Saturday
   D. Saturday preceding the third Wednesday

3. A US company expects to receive 60,000 British pounds upon delivery of manufactured goods to a British distributor. How can the company best hedge against the risk of a strengthened US dollar?

   A. Buy 2 puts on the pound.
   B. Buy 2 calls on the pound.
   C. Sell 2 puts on the pound.
   D. Sell 2 calls on the pound.

4. An investor who believes the US dollar will soon strengthen in relation to the Canadian dollar might profit from which of the following strategies?

   I. Buying puts on the Canadian dollar
   II. Writing puts on the Canadian dollar
   III. Writing a straddle on the Canadian dollar
   IV. Establishing a call credit spread on the Canadian dollar

   A. I and III only
   B. I and IV only
   C. II and IV only
   D. I, II, III, and IV

5. An investor purchases 2 Dec 56 Swiss franc calls at 2.5. One SF contract includes 62,500 units. How much does the investor pay for this position?

   A. $1,562.50
   B. $3,125
   C. $15,625
   D. $31,250

6. A customer opens a spread on Canadian dollars (50,000 units) by purchasing 1 Dec 74 call for 1.30 and selling 1 Dec. 77 call for .50. What is the total cost of this debit spread?

   A. $400
   B. $1,250
   C. $1,350
   D. $4,000

Answers

1. **D.** Option contracts exist on foreign currencies, not on the US dollar.

2. **D.** Foreign currency options expire on the Saturday preceding the third Wednesday of the month.

3. **A.** The long puts guarantee that the British pounds, when received, can be exercised for a number of US dollars at the strike price. At 31,250 units per contract, two puts will cover the 60,000 pounds.

4. **B.** The investor is bearish on the Canadian dollar. Bears buy puts and write calls and call spreads. Short straddles pay off when the market does not move either way.

5. **B.** Swiss franc options are quoted in cents per unit. One call at 2.5 cents × 62,500 units (.025 × 62,500) = $1,562.50. The investor has purchased two contracts, so the total premium is $3,125.

6. **A.** The customer pays a premium of 1.30 and receives a premium of .50, for a net payment of .80. Multiply the net premium by the number of units in the contract for the answer: 50,000 × .008 (.8 cents) = $400.

How the Options Market Functions

Options trade on the major US exchanges and OTC.

Exchange traded options are known as **listed options** and have standardized strike prices and expiration dates. OTC options are not standardized; as a result, little secondary market activity exists. Contract terms are individually negotiated between buyer and seller.

Standard Features of Options Trading and Settlement

Trading Times Listed stock options trade from 9:30 am to 4:02 pm ET. Note that index options trade until 4:15 pm ET.

Expiration Listed stock options expire on the Saturday following the third Friday of the month at 11:59 pm. Final trades may be made until 4:02 pm on the day preceding expiration. Exercise may take place until 5:30 pm on the day preceding expiration, the last day of trading.

Settlement Listed options transactions settle on the next business day. Stock delivered as a result of exercise is settled on a **regular way basis** (three business days).

Automatic Exercise Customer contracts that are in-the-money by at least .75 at expiration are automatically exercised as a service to the customer, unless other instructions have been given. Automatic exercise for member firms takes place for contracts in the money by at least .25.

EXERCISE OR TRADING OF OPTIONS DIAGRAM

```
         Customer contacts broker to trade
            or exercise options position.
                        |
    ┌───────────────────┼───────────────────┐
    │                                        │
Option is traded                     Option is exercised

Investor sells option to close long   a) OCC uses random assignment
position.                      OR        against a short broker-dealer to fulfill
         OR                              contract obligations.
Investor buys option to close short   b) Short broker-dealer assigns against a
position.                                short customer (random, FIFO, or other
                                         fair method).
                                      c) If call, stock is delivered within three
                                         business days.
                                              OR
                                         If put, cash is delivered within three
                                         business days to buy the stock.
                        |
            Contract reaches expiration date

            Option expires worthless on expiration.
                          OR
            Option contract is automatically exercised
            if in the money by .75.
```

Position Limits For the most heavily traded equity options contracts, position limits are 75,000 contracts on the same side of the market. This limit is subject to frequent adjustment. No more than 75,000 contracts on the same side of the market may be exercised within a five-business-day period.

Position limits apply to individuals, registered representatives acting for discretionary accounts and individuals acting in concert (acting together as one person). LEAPS are added to traditional options to determine if a violation of the position limit rules has occurred.

Position limits are measured by the number of contracts on the same side of the market. There are two sides: the bull side and the bear side. Long calls and short puts represent the former; long puts and short calls, the latter. Take a company subject to a 75,000 contract limit. If a customer were long 40,000 calls and 40,000 puts, there would be no violation. However, if the same customer were long 40,000 calls and short 40,000 puts, the customer would have

80,000 contracts on the bull side of the marker, a violation. In determining whether a violation has occurred, long calls are aggregated with short puts and long puts are aggregated with short calls.

Options Trading Personnel

Options are traded most heavily on the **Chicago Board of Options Exchange** (**CBOE**) in a double-auction market. Following are the key trading roles.

Order Book Official (OBO)   The OBO, also known as the **board broker**, is an employee of the exchange. OBOs keep limit order books and ensure that the auction process runs smoothly. They cannot trade for their own accounts.

Market Makers   Options market makers are registered with the exchange to trade for their own accounts. They must stand ready to buy or sell options in which they make markets to maintain an orderly market.

Floor Brokers   Floor brokers are a firm's representatives on the floor of the exchange. They execute orders on behalf of the firm and its customers.

Order Routing Systems   Computerized order routing systems are often used to route customer orders directly to the trading post and back to the firm. Notice of execution is sent directly to the broker/dealer. The system used on the CBOE is called **OSS (order support system)**.

Options Clearing Corporation (OCC)

The **OCC** is the clearing agent for listed options contracts and is owned by the exchanges that trade options. Its primary functions are to standardize, guarantee the performance of, and issue option contracts. The OCC determines when new option contracts should be offered to the market. It designates the strike prices and expiration months for new contracts within market standards to maintain uniformity and liquidity. The market determines the premium for the contracts.

The exercise of options contracts is guaranteed by the OCC. If a holder of an option wishes to exercise, his broker/dealer notifies the OCC. The OCC then assigns exercise notice against a short broker/dealer, who assigns to a short customer.

The OCC assigns exercise notices on a **random** basis. Broker/dealers may then assign exercise notices to customers on a random basis, on a FIFO (first in, first out) or any other method which is fair and reasonable.

Options contracts are traded without a certificate. An investor's proof of ownership is the trade confirmation.

Documentation of Customer Accounts

The OCC requires that certain documents be provided to customers that open options accounts. The **OCC Options Disclosure Document** must be provided at or prior to the account approval. This document explains options strategies, risks, and rewards and is designed to provide full and fair disclosure to customers before they commence options trading.

Before any trading can take place, an options account must be approved by the branch manager. Then, not later than 15 days after the account approval, the customer must return the signed **Options Agreement**. This document states that the customer has read the disclosure document, understands risks of options trading, and will honor position limit rules. By signing, the customer also agrees to advise the firm if any changes occur in his financial situation, investment objectives, etc.

If the signed options agreement is not returned within 15 days of account approval, the investor can open no new options positions. Only closing transactions are allowed if the options agreement is not returned as required.

All firms must inform the NASD of the identity of their **Senior Registered Options Principal (SROP)** and their **Compliance Registered Options Principal (CROP)**.

The SROP is responsible for developing and enforcing programs providing for sales supervision and review of all customer accounts approved to trade options, including transactions in these accounts. The CROP is responsible for reviewing the firm's compliance with all rules and regulations relating to options. The CROP generally has no sales responsibility.

Any options advertising, sales literature or educational material must be approved by the CROP before distribution to the public. Options worksheets, which identify risks, rewards, and costs of various option strategies, are considered sales literature.

✓ **For Example:** No material relating to options may be sent to a customer unless that person has previously received, or contemporaneously receives, the latest OCC Disclosure Document. Also note that recommendations, past performance, and projected performance are not permitted in options advertising. They are, however, permitted in sales literature.

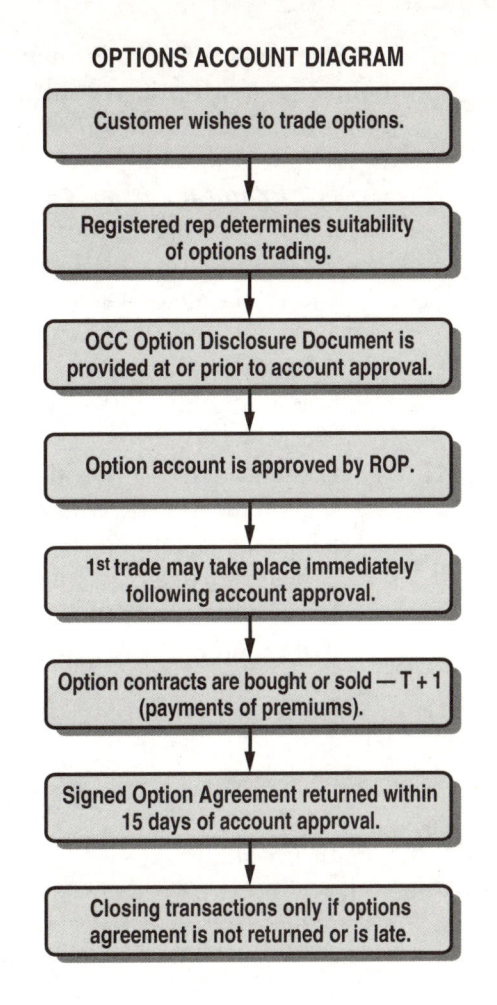

OPTIONS ACCOUNT DIAGRAM

```
Customer wishes to trade options.
          ↓
Registered rep determines suitability
         of options trading.
          ↓
OCC Option Disclosure Document is
provided at or prior to account approval.
          ↓
Option account is approved by ROP.
          ↓
1st trade may take place immediately
    following account approval.
          ↓
Option contracts are bought or sold — T + 1
        (payments of premiums).
          ↓
Signed Option Agreement returned within
    15 days of account approval.
          ↓
Closing transactions only if options
agreement is not returned or is late.
```

Options Contract Adjustments

Options contracts are adjusted for stock splits, reverse stock splits, stock dividends, and rights offerings. They are not adjusted for ordinary cash dividends. When adjustments are made to the strike price, rounding is to the nearest cent (.01). Adjustments to the number of shares are rounded down to the next whole share.

When **even** stock splits occur, new options contracts are created. An even split ends in "1"—such as a 2:1, 3:1, or 4:1 split.

✓ **For Example:** After a 2:1 split, 1 ALF 60 call at 6 becomes 2 ALF 30 calls at 3. A 2:1 creates 200 shares instead of 100, so the owner has twice as many contracts as before, at half the exercise price and premium per share.

The total exercise value and total premium remain the same:

Original Contract: 100 × 60 = $6,000, 100 × 6 = $600
New Contracts: 200 × 30 = $6,000, 200 × 3 = $600

An **uneven split** (also known as a **fractional split**), such as a 3:2 or 5:4 does not create new options contracts. Contracts simply include a larger number of shares.

✓ **For Example:** After a 3:2 split, 1 ALF 60 call at 6 becomes 1 ALF 40 call at 4, with 150 shares in the contract.

The total exercise value and total premium remain the same as before:

Original Contract: 100 × 60 = $6,000, 100 × 6 = $600
New Contracts: 150 × 40 = $6,000, 150 × 4 = $600

Test Topic Alert!

Expect to see 5–7 questions on the information presented in the previous section. Be familiar with documentation of options accounts, the contract adjustments, and know the times and dates discussed. Note that stock dividends are treated as uneven splits; the number of contracts remains the same, the strike price is adjusted downward, and the contract now covers more shares.

Quick Quiz 4.22   Multiple Choice

1. An investor buys 1 DWQ Apr 70 call at 5, giving him the right to buy 100 shares of DWQ at $70 per share. Which aspect of the transaction is not set or standardized by the OCC?

   A. Contract size of 100 shares
   B. Premium of 5
   C. Exercise price of 70
   D. Expiration date in April

2. A customer first discusses options trading with a registered rep on July 3. On July 7, the customer is approved for trading listed options and on July 12, he enters the first trade. The investor must receive an options disclosure document no later than

   A. July 3
   B. July 7
   C. July 12
   D. July 13

3. When applying the exercise limit rules, which of the following could be considered as acting in concert?

   A. Registered representative who has discretionary control over 10 customer accounts
   B. Many options customers of the same brokerage firm acting independently on a recent recommendation published by the firm
   C. Registered representatives making recommendations to nondiscretionary customers
   D. All of the above

4. Which of the following positions violate the rules governing position limits? (SSS is a less actively traded stock subject to a 13,500 options position limit.)

   I. Long 9,600 SSS Aug 40 calls; short 6,000 SSS Aug 40 puts
   II. Long 9,600 SSS Aug 40 calls; short 6,000 SSS Jan 40 puts
   III. Long 9,600 SSS Aug 40 calls; short 6,000 SSS Aug 40 calls

   A. I and II
   B. I and III
   C. II and III
   D. I, II and III

5. If a 50% stock dividend is declared, the owner of 1 XYZ Jul 30 call now owns

   A. 1 contract for 100 shares with an exercise price of 20
   B. 1 contract price for 150 shares with an exercise price of 20
   C. 2 contracts for 100 shares with an exercise price of 20
   D. 2 contracts for 150 shares with an exercise price of 20

6. When must a new options customer who has not yet traded options receive the Options Clearing Corporation's current disclosure document?

   A. At or before the time the registered representative signs the customer approval form
   B. Within 15 days after the CROP has approved the customer's account for options trading
   C. At or before the time the account has received the ROP's final approval for options trading
   D. No later than 15 days after the ROP signs the options customer approval form

7. Equity options cease trading at

   A. 11:00 am ET on the business day before the expiration date
   B. 4:02 pm ET on the business day before the expiration date
   C. 1:00 am ET on the expiration date
   D. 4:10 pm ET on the expiration date

268 Options

8. The Options Clearing Corporation uses which of the following methods in assigning exercise notices?

   I. Random selection
   II. First in, first out
   III. To the member firm holding a long position that first requests an exercise
   IV. On the basis of the largest position

   A. I only
   B. I, II and III only
   C. I and III only
   D. II and IV only

Answers

1. **B.** The OCC sets standard exercise prices and expiration dates for all listed options, but the premiums that buyers pay for options are determined by the market.

2. **B.** The OCC disclosure document must be given to the customer no later than at the time the account is approved for options trading.

3. **A.** Acting in concert rules apply to position limits and exercise limits. Acting in concert means acting together with knowledge of each other's activities or having one person control a number of accounts. Answers B and C would not be considered individuals acting in concert.

4. **A.** The expiration dates and strike prices may be different or the same. However, the total number of contracts on the same side of the market on a less actively traded stock is limited to 13,500. The Options Clearing Corporation (OCC) considers long calls and short puts to be on the same side of the market.

5. **B.** When a company pays a stock dividend or effects a fractional stock split, the underlying option is adjusted by increasing the number of shares the contract covers and reducing the strike price proportionately. The number of contracts remains the same.

6. **C.** Customers must be furnished with options disclosure documents before or at the time their accounts receive a ROP's approval.

7. **B.** Equity options cease trading at 4:02 pm ET on the business day before expiration.

8. **A.** The OCC assigns exercise notices to member firms on a random basis. The members may choose the customers to be exercised on either a random or FIFO basis.

Tax Rules for Options

There are three possible consequences of options strategies, each with unique tax consequences. Because options are capital assets, capital gains tax rules apply to these outcomes.

Expiration At the expiration of an options contract, the buyer loses the premium; the seller profits from the premium. The buyer reports a capital loss equal to the premium amount; the seller reports a capital gain equal to the premium amount.

The tax treatment for LEAP writers at expiration is unique. Although investors may have held the contract for more than 12 months, LEAP writers must report **short-term capital gains** at expiration. LEAP buyers may report long-term losses.

Closing Out Closing sales or purchases generate a capital gain or loss equal to any price difference. This gain or loss must be reported based on the date of the closing transaction.

Exercise The exercise of options does not generate a capital gain or loss until a subsequent purchase or sale of the stock occurs. If a long call is exercised, the option holder buys the stock. Because the investor paid a premium for the stock, the total cost basis for the stock includes the premium and strike price. The chart identifies the tax consequences of these options strategies.

Possible Tax Consequences of Option Strategies

Strategy	Option Expires	Option Exercised	Position Closed at Intrinsic Value
Buy a call	Capital loss	Strike price + Premium = Cost basis	Capital gain or loss
Sell a call	Capital gain	Strike price + Premium = Sale proceeds	Capital gain or loss
Buy a put	Capital loss	Strike price - Premium = Sale proceeds	Capital gain or loss
Sell a put	Capital gain	Strike price - Premium = Cost basis	Capital gain or loss

Options

Stock Holding Periods

The IRS does not allow the use of options to postpone the sale of stock for the purpose of generating long-term capital gains treatment. Options that allow an investor to lock in a sale price are long puts. If stock has been held 12 months or less prior to the purchase of a put, the gain will be classified as short term.

✓ **For Example:** An investor bought XYZ 11 months ago at 50. It now trades for 70. If the investor were to sell it now, the gain would be classified as short term.

Assume the investor buys a 70 put that will expire in nine months. Even though the sale of the stock is postponed until up to 20 months have elapsed, the IRS still requires the holding period to be classified as short term for tax purposes. If the stock had already been held for more than 12 months, its holding period would not be affected by the purchase of a put.

Married Put If, on the same day, a customer buys stock and buys a put option on that stock as a hedge, the put is said to be "married" to the stock. For tax purposes, irrespective of what happens to the put, the cost basis of the stock must be adjusted upwards by the premium paid. Even if the put expires worthless, there is no capital loss on the put. Rather, the premium paid is reflected in the cost basis of the stock which is the breakeven point for long stock/long put (cost of stock purchased plus premium).

✓ **For Example:** If, on the same day, a customer buys 100 XYZ at 52 and buys 1 XYZ Jan 50 put at 2, the customer's cost basis in the stock is 54.

Test Topic Alert! Expect to see about 5–7 questions on options taxation. Many of these questions are a matter of finding the profit or loss, so use a T-chart. Remember that option exercise alone does not create a taxable event.

Quick Quiz 4.23 Multiple Choice

1. In September, an investor sells 2 AMF Jan 60 puts at 3. If the investor buys the 2 puts back at 4.50, the result for tax purposes is a

    A. $150 capital gain
    B. $150 capital loss
    C. $300 capital gain
    D. $300 capital loss

2. In September, an investor sells 2 AMF Jan 60 puts at 3. If the 2 AMF Jan 60 puts expire in January, what are the tax consequences for the seller?

   A. $600 gain realized in September
   B. $600 loss realized in September
   C. $600 gain realized in January
   D. $600 loss realized in January

3. Your customer buys 1 FLB Oct 50 call at 3. He exercises the option to buy 100 shares when the market is at 60. What is the cost basis of the 100 shares?

   A. $5,000
   B. $5,300
   C. $6,000
   D. $6,300

4. A customer writes 1 Jul 50 put at 7. The put is exercised when the market price is 40. For tax purposes, what is the effective cost basis of the stock put to the seller?

   A. 40
   B. 43
   C. 50
   D. 57

5. Your customer buys 100 shares of TIP stock at 59 and sells a TIP 60 call at 4. The stock's price rises to 70 and the option is exercised. For tax purposes, the customer must report sales proceeds of

   A. $6,400 and cost basis of $5,900
   B. $6,000 and cost basis of $5,500
   C. $7,000 and cost basis of $5,900
   D. $7,000 and cost basis of $6,500

6. An investor buys a LEAPS contract at issuance and allows it to expire unexercised. What is the investor's tax consequence at expiration?

   A. Short-term capital gain
   B. Short-term capital loss
   C. Long-term capital gain
   D. Long-term capital loss

Options

7. A customer buys 100 shares of stock at 67 and sells a 70 call for 4. The stock rises to 75 and the option is exercised. For tax purposes, this investor reports sales proceeds of

   A. $7,000, cost basis of $6,300
   B. $7,400, cost basis of $6,700
   C. $7,500, cost basis of $6,700
   D. $7,500, cost basis of $7,400

Answers

1. **D.** The closing cost of $900 minus $600 opening sale proceeds equals a $300 loss.

2. **C.** Expiration of a short option generates a gain at the time the option expires.

3. **B.** The cost basis of the 100 shares is the total amount the investor spent to acquire them. He paid $300 to buy the call option. When he exercised the call, he purchased 100 shares of FLB at $50 per share, for a total price of $5,000. The cost basis therefore is $5,300.

4. **B.** The cost basis is 50 (the price at which the writer must buy) minus 7 (the premium the writer was paid), or $43 per share.

5. **A.** When a call option is exercised, the writer's sale proceeds are equal to the sum of the strike price plus the call premium ($6,000 + $400 = $6,400). The cost basis of the stock is the original purchase price, which equals $5,900. The investor's total gain is $500.

6. **D.** A LEAPS contract has an expiration of more than one year. Upon expiration, the buyer incurs a long-term capital loss equal to the amount of the premium paid.

7. **B.** When the call is exercised the investor must sell the stock at $70 per share. The investor reports sales proceeds of $7,400 ($7,000 from the sale of stock + $400 premium) and cost basis of $6,700 (the original cost to purchase the stock).

Options HotSheet

Options Chart:

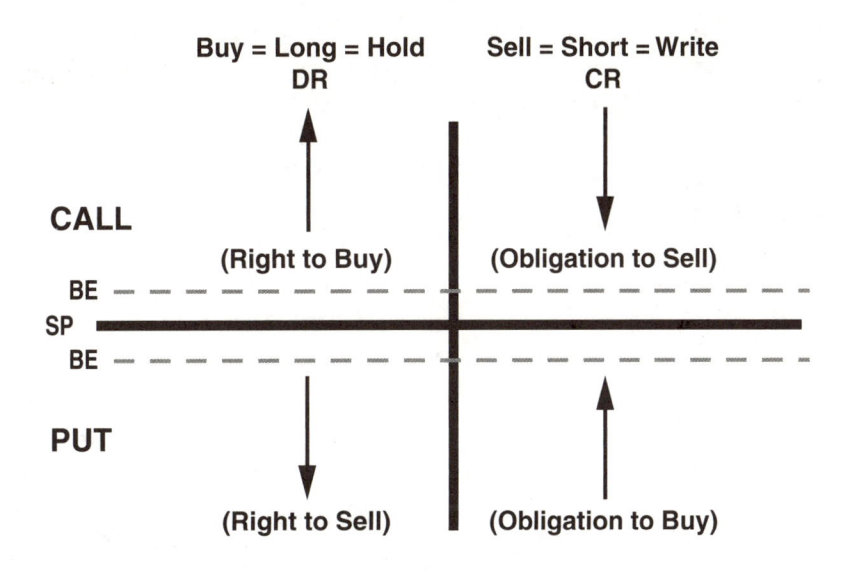

```
                    Buy = Long = Hold        Sell = Short = Write
                           DR                        CR
                            ↑                         │
                            │                         ↓
        CALL
                    (Right to Buy)          (Obligation to Sell)
          BE  - - - - - - - - - - - - │ - - - - - - - - - - - -
          SP ═══════════════════════════╪═══════════════════════
          BE  - - - - - - - - - - - - │ - - - - - - - - - - - -
                                        │                ↑
        PUT                             ↓                │
                    (Right to Sell)         (Obligation to Buy)
```

Single Options:

Position	Maximum Gain	Maximum Loss
Long Call	Unlimited	Premium
Short Call	Premium	Unlimited
Long Put	Strike price − Premium	Premium
Short Put	Premium	Strike price − Premium

Breakevens:
- Calls: SP + Premium
- Puts: SP − Premium

Intrinsic Value:
- Calls: Market price − SP (Call Up)
- Puts: SP − Market price (Put Down)

Hedging:
- Best or full protection = Buy an option
- Partial protection, improve rate of return, earn income: sell an option
- Long stock position: Risk is down: buy puts
- Short stock position: Risk is up: buy calls

Long Stock, Long Put:
- BE: Do T-chart: Stock price + Premium
- Max gain: Unlimited
- Max loss: (Stock price − Strike price) + Premium

Long Stock, Short Call:	• BE: Do T-chart: Stock Price − Premium • Max gain: (Strike price − Stock price) + Premium • Max loss: Stock price − Premium
Short Stock, Short Put:	• BE: Do T-chart: Stock price + premium • Max gain: (Stock price − Strike price) + Premium • Max loss: Unlimited
Short Stock, Long Call:	• BE: Do T-chart: Stock price − Premium • Max gain: Stock price − Premium • Max loss: (Strike price − Stock price) + Premium
Spreads:	• Debits = Widen = Exercise • Credits = Narrow = Expire

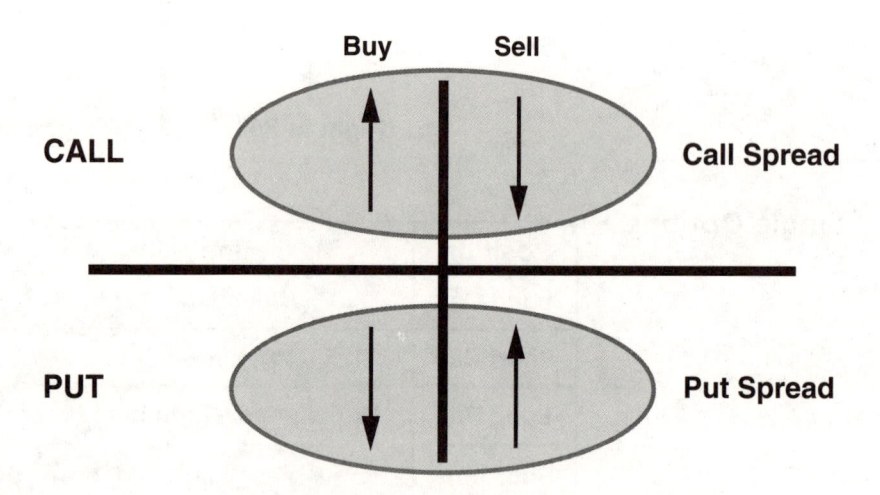

```
                    Buy    Sell
                     ↑      ↓
   CALL           (      |      )         Call Spread
   ─────────────────────────────────
   PUT            (      |      )         Put Spread
                     ↓      ↑
```

Do T-chart to determine net position

Credit Spreads:	• Max gain = Initial net credit • Max loss = Difference in strike prices minus the net credit
Debit Spreads:	• Max gain = Difference in strike prices minus the net debit • Max loss = Initial net debit
Spread Breakevens:	• CAL: For call spreads add net premium to lower strike price • PSH: For put spreads subtract net premium from higher strike price
Market Attitude for Spreads:	• Investor is bullish if long the lower strike price
Straddles:	• Long straddles—expect sharp move in price but uncertain of direction • Short straddles—expect little or no movement in stock price

- Same SP and expiration

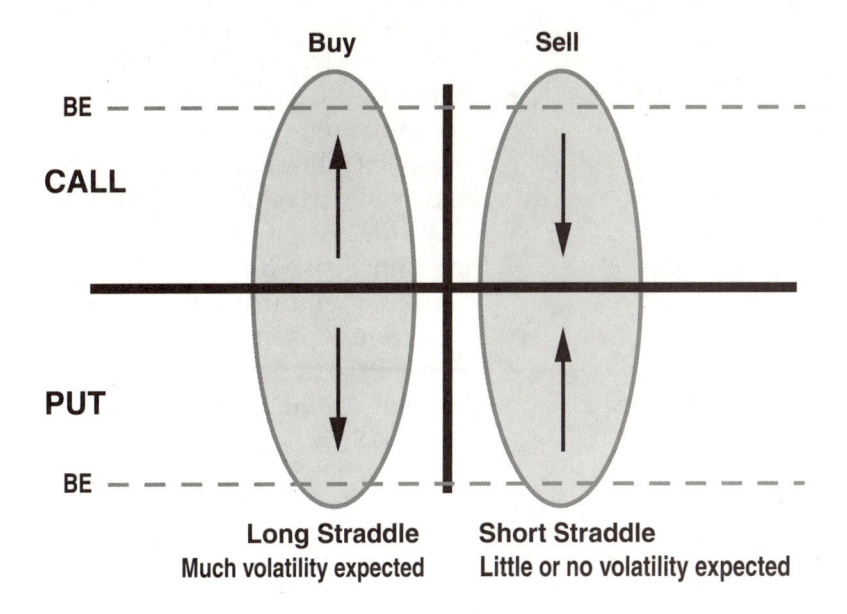

```
                    Buy        Sell
BE  - - - - - - - - ↑  - - - - ↓ - - -
CALL                ↑          ↓
────────────────────┼──────────────────
PUT                 ↓          ↑
BE  - - - - - - - - ↓  - - - - ↑ - - -
                Long Straddle  Short Straddle
            Much volatility    Little or no volatility
                expected       expected
```

Breakevens:
- Call: SP + Both premiums
- Put: SP − Both premiums

Options Concepts:
- A **call option buyer** has the right to purchase the underlying security for a specified price within a specified time frame.
- A **call option seller** is obligated to sell the underlying security for a specified price within a specified time frame if exercised.
- A **put option buyer** has the right to sell the underlying security for a specified price within a specified time frame.
- A **put option seller** is obligated to purchase the underlying security for a specified price within a specified time frame if exercised.
- Because of the **leverage** option contracts offer investors, they may be used to protect investment portfolio positions or to speculate on the direction of the underlying security.
- An **option contract** has a relatively short life span. Time remaining to expiration is important in determining the option's value. The amount by which the contract is in-the-money is also critical. Initial transactions in options are opening purchases or sales. Once a position is established, a closing sale or purchase (offsetting transaction), or the expiration or exercise of the contract, ends the position.
- Option transactions may be straightforward, such as the opening purchase or sale of a call or put. They may be coupled with other portfolio securities or other option contracts in order to use more complicated investment strategies.

The Four Basic Option Transactions:

- LONG CALL
  Max gain: unlimited
  Max loss: premium paid
  Breakeven: strike price + premium
- SHORT CALL
  Max gain: Premium received
  Max loss: Unlimited
  Breakeven: Strike price + Premium
- LONG PUT
  Max gain: Strike price – Premium paid
  Max loss: Premium paid
  Breakeven: Strike price – Premium
- SHORT PUT
  Max gain: Premium received
  Max loss: Strike price – Premium received
  Breakeven: Strike price – Premium

Series 7 Unit Test 4

1. A customer sells an FLB Mar 35 call. To establish a straddle, he would

   A. sell an FLB Mar 40 call
   B. buy an FLB Mar 35 put
   C. sell an FLB Mar 35 put
   D. buy an FLB Mar 40 call

2. Which of the following procedures are required when opening an options account?

   I. The registered representative must document that the client has received a current OCC disclosure document.
   II. The background and financial information provided by the client must be verified by the client and returned in 15 days.
   III. If there is a material change in the client's financial status, amendment of the options agreement is required.
   IV. Any recommendations made must consider the financial needs and financial situation of the client.

   A. I only
   B. II only
   C. I, III and IV only
   D. I, II, III and IV

3. An investor with no other positions sells 1 ABC Jan 45 call at 2.50. If the option expires when the stock is trading at 44.50, what is the investor's profit or loss?

   A. $50 profit
   B. $50 loss
   C. $250 profit
   D. $250 loss

4. An investor buys 1 ABC Jun 55 call at 4. What is the investor's breakeven point?

   A. 51
   B. 55
   C. 59
   D. 60

5. If an investor maintaining a short equity option is assigned an exercise notice, which of the following statements is TRUE?

   A. He may refuse exercise under certain circumstances.
   B. He must accept the exercise notice.
   C. He may offset his obligation with a closing transaction up to the end of trading on the same.
   D. He may offset his obligation with a closing transaction within three days.

6. A customer buys 1 ABC Jan 60 put at 6 and writes 1 ABC Jan 75 put at 13. The maximum loss is

   A. $700
   B. $800
   C. $900
   D. $1,500

7. A customer is short 100 XYZ shares at 26 and long 1 XYZ 30 call at 1. The customer breaks even if XYZ trades at

   A. 25
   B. 27
   C. 29
   D. 31

8. In which of the following strategies would the investor want the spread to widen?

   I. Buy 1 RST May 30 put; write 1 RST May 25 put
   II. Write 1 RST Apr 45 put; buy 1 RST Apr 55 put
   III. Buy 1 RST Nov 65 put; write 1 RST Nov 75 put
   IV. Buy 1 RST Jan 40 call; write 1 RST Jan 30 call

   A. I and II
   B. I and IV
   C. II and III
   D. III and IV

9. The market attitude of a customer who sells a call spread is

   A. bullish
   B. bearish
   C. speculative
   D. neutral

10. After selling short ABC at 70, a customer holds the position as ABC gradually falls to $53 per share. Which of the following strategies would best protect his gain?

    A. Write 55 calls
    B. Buy 55 calls
    C. Write 55 puts
    D. Buy 55 puts

11. An investor buys 1 LMN Jan 50 put at 2. What is the investor's maximum potential loss?

    A. $100
    B. $200
    C. $4,800
    D. $5,200

12. An investor wants to purchase TCB stock (currently trading at 38) and he expects the price of TCB stock to decline in the short term before rising. If he wants to purchase the stock below its current market value and generate additional income, he should

    A. write a call at 35
    B. buy a put and exercise the option
    C. write a put at 35
    D. buy a 40 call and exercise the option

13. A customer sells 3 ABC Feb 25 puts at 4 when ABC is at 24. If the contracts are closed out at intrinsic value when ABC is at 19, the customer has a

    A. $600 loss
    B. $600 gain
    C. $200 loss
    D. $200 gain

14. Options are available on all of the following currencies EXCEPT

    A. Euro
    B. Japanese yen
    C. Canadian dollar
    D. US dollar

15. All of the following would affect option premiums EXCEPT the

    A. volatility of the stock
    B. stock price
    C. time to expiration
    D. account position

16. If a customer writes 1 ABC April 60 put at 5 when ABC is trading at 58, which of the following statements are TRUE?

    I. The time value of the option is two points.
    II. The time value of the option is three points.
    III. Breakeven is 65.
    IV. Breakeven is 55.

    A. I and III
    B. I and IV
    C. II and III
    D. II and IV

17. A customer buys 100 XYZ at 49 and writes 1 XYZ Nov 50 call, receiving $350 in premiums. The breakeven point is

    A. 45.50
    B. 46.50
    C. 52.50
    D. 53.50

18. In a volatile market, which of the following option strategies carries the most risk?

    A. Long straddle
    B. Short straddle
    C. Debit spread
    D. Credit spread

19. Which of the following strategies is considered most risky in a strong bull market?

    A. Buying calls
    B. Writing naked calls
    C. Writing naked puts
    D. Either B or C

20. A customer purchases OEX puts to protect his stock portfolio from an expected downturn. This use of index options to hedge reduces

    A. systematic risk
    B. nonsystematic risk
    C. rate risk
    D. credit risk

21. A customer should receive a current option disclosure document before or at the date of

    A. the first trade
    B. settlement
    C. final account approval
    D. the first monthly statement

22. When an index option is exercised, cash settlement must take place how many business days after exercise?

    A. 1
    B. 2
    C. 3
    D. 5

23. When comparing a short call to a short call spread, all of the following are true EXCEPT

    A. maximum gain is limited
    B. maximum loss is limited
    C. both positions are bearish
    D. both positions generate premium income

24. A Japanese exporter wants to hedge a recent sale of stereo equipment to a US buyer. The exporter will be paid in US dollars upon delivery of the goods. The best hedge would be

    A. sell Japanese yen calls
    B. sell Japanese yen puts
    C. buy Japanese yen calls
    D. buy Japanese yen puts

25. An investor sells 1 DWQ Feb 30 put at 4.50. What is the investor's breakeven point?

    A. 25.50
    B. 27.50
    C. 30.50
    D. 34.50

26. Which of the following has unlimited risk if it is the only position in an account?

    A. Long put
    B. Long call
    C. Short put
    D. Short call

27. Which of the following statements is true regarding a March 80 Canadian dollar call option trading at 6 if the Canadian dollar is at 85 cents?

    A. The contract is out-of-the-money.
    B. The contract has intrinsic value.
    C. The contract is at parity.
    D. The contract has no time value.

28. What is the following position?

    Buy 1 QRS May 40 call
    Sell 1 QRS May 50 call

    A. Price spread
    B. Time spread
    C. Diagonal spread
    D. Combination

29. If a customer wishes to take an option position on a company and does not anticipate that the price of the stock will change, he would most likely

   A. buy a call
   B. buy a put
   C. buy a straddle
   D. sell a straddle

30. A customer buys 1 XYZ Nov 70 put and sells 1 XYZ Nov 60 put when XYZ is selling for 65. This position is a

   A. bull spread
   B. bear spread
   C. combination
   D. straddle

31. If a customer writes 10 DEF Aug 50 calls at 1 when DEF is trading at 44, what is the maximum gain?

   A. $100
   B. $500
   C. $1,000
   D. Unlimited

32. Which of the following investors are bearish?

   I. Buyer of a call
   II. Writer of a call
   III. Buyer of a put
   IV. Writer of a put

   A. I and II
   B. I and IV
   C. II and III
   D. III and IV

33. Which of the following statements regarding stock index options are TRUE?

   I. Trades are settled the next business day.
   II. Trades are settled on the third business day.
   III. Exercise settlement involves the delivery of stock.
   IV. Exercise settlement involves the delivery of cash.

   A. I and III
   B. I and IV
   C. II and III
   D. II and IV

34. The holder of a yield-based call option will profit if

   I. rates rise
   II. rates fall
   III. debt prices rise
   IV. debt prices fall

   A. I and III
   B. I and IV
   C. II and III
   D. II and IV

35. A customer who was recently approved to trade options writes an OEX put which is the initial transaction in the account. The customer fails to return the signed option agreement within 15 days of account approval. Which of the following transactions would the customer be permitted to make?

   A. Opening sale
   B. Closing sale
   C. Opening purchase
   D. Closing purchase

Series 7 Unit Test 4 Answers & Rationale

1. **C.** Straddles involve options of different types, but both options must be long or both must be short. They must have the same expiration date and strike price. QID: 28507

2. **D.** The client must have a current OCC disclosure document. An understanding of the client's financial situation is required in order to make any recommendations. Changes in the client's status must be updated as soon as possible. Also, the option agreement form must be returned within 15 days of account approval. QID: 35162

3. **C.** The option expired because it was out-of-the-money. When the option expires the writer profits by the amount of the premium received, which is 2.50. 2.50 × 100 = $250. QID: 32176

4. **C.** The breakeven point on a call is calculated by adding the premium to the strike price. Add the premium of 4 to the strike price of 55 to determine the breakeven point of 59. The breakeven point of 59 applies to both buyers and writers of calls. QID: 30010

5. **B.** Once exercised, a contract can no longer be traded to another individual. The exercised party must either deliver the stock in three business days (call) or buy the stock in 3 business days (put). QID: 28482

6. **B.** This is a credit spread (more premium was received than was paid). The maximum gain to a seller is the premium received, which is the net credit of 7. In a spread, the maximum gain and the maximum loss added together equal the difference in strike prices (75 − 60 = 15). 15 − maximum gain of 7 = maximum loss of 8 × $100, or $800. In a credit spread, the net credit always represents maximum gain. In a debit spread, the net debit always represents maximum loss. QID: 35009

7. **A.** The customer must recover the cost of the premium paid to be at the breakeven. Since this is a short position, the price of the stock must decline 1 point for this to occur. Therefore, the breakeven on this hedged position is found by subtracting the premium of the option from the short sale price of the stock (26 − 1 = 25). QID: 30939

8. **A.** Choices I and II are debit spreads. An investor wants a debit spread to widen. As the distance between premiums increases, the investor's potential profit also increases. This is because the investor intends to sell the option with the higher premium and buy back the option with the lower premium. With credit spreads, investors profit if the spread between the premiums narrows. QID: 28518

9. **B.** In a call spread, a customer is buying a call and selling a call with different strike prices and/or expirations. In any spread, one of the options is dominant. In a short call spread, it is the short call position that is dominant because it has the higher premium; writing calls is bearish. QID: 36471

10. **B.** If the investor buys the 55 calls, he has the right to purchase the stock at $55 per share. If exercised, the investor has a 15 point gain less the premium paid. QID: 34885

11. **B.** The maximum loss on a long put is equal to the premium paid for the option. One contract represents 100 shares and the buyer paid a $2 per share premium, which equals $200. QID: 30024

12. **C.** If the investor writes a put he collects a premium. If the stock price rises, the put expires worthless and the investor keeps the premium. However, if the stock price declines, as the customer anticipates, the put will be exercised forcing the customer to buy stock at 35. His effective cost of the stock is the breakeven point which is strike price minus premium. QID: 28492

13. A. Because the investor sold the puts for a total of $1,200 to open his position, he must buy the options to close out his position. If he buys when ABC is at 19, the intrinsic value at that time is 6 because puts are in-the-money when the market price is below the strike price (25 – 19 = 6). He pays a total of $1,800 to close out his three contracts. Because he paid more than he received, he has a loss of $600 on the transaction. QID: 35038

14. D. Option contracts exist on foreign currencies, not on the US dollar. QID: 30973

15. D. The number of contracts a client is long or short would not affect option premiums. The volatility of the stock, the price of the stock, and the time to expiration are all factors that would affect option premiums. QID: 29849

16. D. Puts (long or short) are in-the-money if the market price is below the strike price. In this case, the put is in-the-money by two points. As the total premium is five points, the time value is three points. Remember, option premiums consist of two components: intrinsic value and time value. Once the in-the-money amount is determined, it is easy to back into time value. Breakeven for puts (long or short) is SP minus premium. QID: 36638

17. A. This is a covered call. The investor has protection in the event the stock drops to the extent of the premium received and the breakeven is 45.50 (49 – 3.50). QID: 34915

18. B. To establish a short straddle, the investor sells a call and sells a put. The short call exposes the investor to unlimited loss potential. QID: 30078

19. B. Writing naked calls gives unlimited risk and writing naked puts results in the puts expiring if the market rises. In the latter case, the writer profits by the premiums received. QID: 28502

20. A. Systematic risk is market risk and the S&P 100 Index (OEX) is a widely used measure of stock market performance. QID: 35105

21. C. The customer must receive a current disclosure document either before or at the time that the account receives final approval for option trading. QID: 30975

22. A. Exercised stock index options settle on the next business day. QID: 28524

23. B. In any spread, both maximum gain and maximum loss are limited. In a short call, gain is limited to the premium received, but loss is unlimited. Short calls and short call spreads are bearish, and both generate premium income. The investor who writes a call spread receives premium income (a short call spread is a credit spread). QID: 36472

24. C. The Japanese exporter will be paid in US dollars upon delivery of the equipment. He would be adversely affected if the dollar dropped in value in relation to the yen. Therefore, to protect his position in the dollar from falling against the yen, he should buy calls on his own currency, the yen. Then, if the yen appreciates, his loss on the dollar would be offset by his gain on the calls. Remember, exporters buy puts on the foreign currency to hedge but there are no options on the US dollar, so the next best strategy is to buy calls on the "home" currency. QID: 34943

25. A. The breakeven point on a put (long or short) is calculated by subtracting the premium from the strike price. Subtract the premium of 4.50 from the strike price of 30 to determine the breakeven point of 25.50. QID: 30028

26. D. Uncovered short calls entail unlimited risk. QID: 28495

27. B. A call is in-the-money whenever the market value of the underlying instrument is above the strike price. The Canadian dollar is currently at 85 cents which is above the strike price of 80 cents, so this call is in-the-money. The contract does have time value (1 cent). Also, the contract is not at parity. Parity means the premium equals the in-the-money amount. QID: 35034

28. **A.** A price spread is composed of a long and short option of the same type with the same expiration, but different strike prices. A price spread is also termed a vertical spread.
QID: 30945

29. **D.** When selling a straddle (sale of a call and put with same terms) the customer earns combined premiums. He hopes that the market price will not move and both positions will expire unexercised, thus keeping the premiums.
QID: 29927

30. **B.** This put spread is established at a debit because the customer pays more for the 70 put than he receives for the 60 put; bears buy puts. A debit spread is a "net buy" while a credit spread is a "net sale". Therefore, a debit put spread is like buying a put which is bearish. QID: 28515

31. **C.** When writing options, the maximum gain is equal to the premium received. Because there are 10 calls with a premium of $100 each, the maximum gain is 10 × $100 or $1,000. QID: 34982

32. **C.** Buyers of puts and writers of calls are bearish investors. Buyers of calls and writers of puts are bulls. QID: 30929

33. **B.** Index option trades settle the next business day and cash is delivered upon exercise of the option. Note that exercises of index options also settle next business day. QID: 32178

34. **B.** Holders of yield-based call options profit if rates rise. If rates rise, prices of debt securities fall. QID: 36457

35. **D.** If a customer fails to return the signed option agreement within 15 days of the account approval, the customer is permitted closing transactions only. No opening transactions are allowed. As the customer opened a position by selling, the only transaction permitted would be a closing purchase. QID: 36655

5

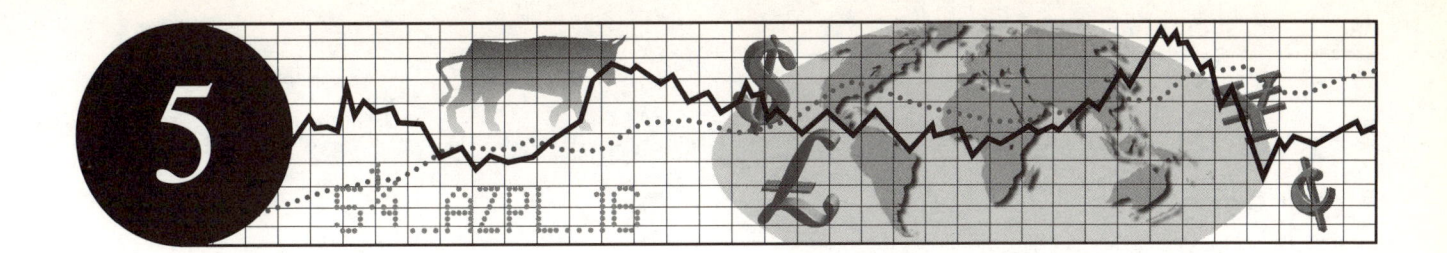

Customer Accounts

INTRODUCTION Customer accounts are the foundation of a brokerage business. The customer account is the record of all customer investment activity, and strict record-keeping requirements apply to all accounts that have been opened.

The customer account serves as the repository for the customer's cash and securities and as a record of the customer's investment objectives and activity. There are many types of accounts, each requiring its own documentation and, in some instances, authorization. All new accounts must be accepted on behalf of the firm by a principal.

Account information is also to be kept in strict confidence. In addition, no one except specifically authorized individuals may make investment decisions for an account.

You can expect to see approximately 10–20 questions on customer accounts on the Series 7 exam.

UNIT OBJECTIVES When you have completed this unit, you should be able to:

- list and describe the steps in opening new accounts;
- describe required brokerage account documentation;
- identify specific account recordkeeping requirements;
- define special procedures for opening accounts for employees of other broker/dealers;
- list discretionary account requirements;
- describe procedures at death or incompetence of an account holder; and
- identify unique features of UGMA accounts.

New Accounts

The following procedures must be followed and taken into consideration by a broker/dealer when opening a new account.

New Account Form

An account opened by a broker/dealer requires a completed new account form or new account card.

A registered representative must fill out certain information on all new account forms.

- Full name of each customer who will have access to the account
- Date of birth
- Address and telephone number (business and residence)
- Social Security number if individual, or tax identification number if other legal entity
- Occupation, employer, and type of business
- Citizenship
- If the customer is of legal age
- Annual income and net worth (excluding value of primary residence)
- Investment objectives
- Bank and brokerage references
- Whether the customer is an employee of another broker/dealer
- How the account was acquired
- Name and occupation of the person(s) with authority to make transactions in the account
- Signatures of the representative opening the account and a principal of the firm

✓ *Take Note:* The customer's signature is not required on the new account form.

All of the items listed are required by NASD and NYSE rules. The **Municipal Securities Rulemaking Board (MSRB)** also requires the customer's tax status.

New Account Form

Greenback Securities, Inc.

Staking Your Financial Future
12654 Futurity Blvd.
Belmont, CA 99462

NEW ACCOUNT FORM

TAXPAYER ID NUMBER	☐ SSN ☐ TAX ID	AGE	BRANCH#	RR#	ACCOUNT#	DATE

LEGAL NAME(S) AND MAILING ADDRESS ☐ HOME ☐ BUS

ACCOUNT TYPE ☐ CASH ☐ OPTION
☐ MARGIN ☐ COMMODITY

MARITAL STATUS ☐ MARRIED ☐ SINGLE
☐ DIVORCED ☐ WIDOWED

ACCOUNT REGIS. ☐ SINGLE ☐ JTWROS
☐ JTIC ☐ INV CLUB
☐ CORP ☐ PARTNER
☐ RETIRE ☐ OTHER

TELEPHONE NO. ☐ HOME ☐ BUS
TELEPHONE NO. ☐ HOME ☐ BUS

DIVIDENDS ☐ HOLD ☐ MAIL
U.S. CITIZEN? ☐ YES ☐ NO _____

IS THE CUSTOMER OR SPOUSE EMPLOYED BY, OR RELATED TO AN EMPLOYEE OF, ANY FINANCIAL INSTITUTION? ☐ YES ☐ NO
DUPLICATE CONFIRMS? ☐ YES ☐ NO
ATTACH SPECIAL INSTRUCTIONS

EMPLOYMENT

EMPLOYER'S NAME   YEARS EMPLOYED
ADDRESS
TYPE OF BUSINESS   CLIENT'S OCCUPATION

DOCUMENTATION   OTHER (DESCRIBE)
MARGIN AGR ☐ PEND ☐ RCVD _____
JOINT ACCT ☐ PEND ☐ RCVD _____
TRADING AUTH ☐ PEND ☐ RCVD _____
CORP/PART AGR ☐ PEND ☐ RCVD _____
RETIRE ACCT ☐ PEND ☐ RCVD _____
SIG CARD ☐ PEND ☐ RCVD _____

REFERENCE

BANK NAME AND ADDRESS   ☐ CHECKING ☐ VERIFIED
☐ SAVINGS ☐ NOT VERIFIED

DOES CLIENT HAVE AN ACCOUNT WITH ANOTHER BROKERAGE FIRM? ☐ YES ☐ NO   IF YES, WITH WHAT FIRM?

SPOUSE

NAME   OCCUPATION   AGE
EMPLOYER   ADDRESS   ANNUAL INCOME

INVESTMENT EXPERIENCE

INVESTMENT OBJECTIVES
☐ GROWTH ☐ SPECULATION
☐ INCOME ☐ RETIREMENT
☐ GRO/INC ☐ TAX

HOME ☐ OWN ☐ RENT
NO. OF DEPENDENTS _____
ANNUAL INC _____
NET WORTH _____

DOES CLIENT OR SPOUSE HAVE ANOTHER ACCOUNT WITH US?
☐ YES ☐ NO
IF YES, LIST: _____

IS CLIENT NOW OR HAS CLIENT EVER BEEN A CORPORATE OFFICER OR OWNER OF 10% OF ANY CORPORATION'S SECURITIES?
☐ YES ☐ NO
IF YES, NAME:

HOW WAS ACCOUNT ACQUIRED?
☐ WALK IN ☐ REFERRAL
☐ PHONE IN ☐ PROSPECT
☐ OTHER ☐ ACQUAINTANCE
INITIAL TRANSACTION
☐ BUY DESCRIBE:
☐ SELL
☐ OTHER
INITIAL DEPOSIT

DISCRETIONARY AUTHORIZATION
☐ FULL ☐ LIMITED ☐ NONE

OPTION TRADES ANTICIPATED
☐ BUY ONLY ☐ STRADDLES
☐ COV CALLS ☐ SPREADS
☐ COV PUTS ☐ COMBINS
☐ UNC OPTS ☐ OTHER
IS CLIENT FAMILIAR WITH OPTIONS?
☐ YES ☐ NO
HAS CLIENT RECEIVED OCC PROSPECTUS?
☐ YES DATE _____
HAS CLIENT PREVIOUSLY TRADED OPTIONS?
☐ YES ☐ NO
ARE OPTIONS SUITABLE?
☐ YES ☐ NO

RR SIGNATURE   AGENT'S NAME AND ADDRESS
BRANCH MGR APPROVAL   DATE   ROP SIGNATURE (OPTIONS APPROVAL)

Customer Information and Suitability

Accounts may be opened by any legally competent person above the age of majority. Legally incompetent individuals may not open accounts.

✓ **Take Note:** NYSE rules also require the new account form to identify whether the customer is a director, officer, or a shareholder of 10% of more of a publicly traded company (this helps monitor potentially unusual trading activity associated with insiders).

When opening an account, NYSE **Rule 405** (**Know Your Customer**) requires that reps should know all essential facts about a customer's current financial situation, his present holdings, risk tolerance, needs, and objectives. Such information should be updated periodically as situations change.

If a customer refuses to provide all information requested, the account may still be opened if the firm believes the customer has the financial resources necessary to support the account. The registered representative can make recommendations only if sufficient information has been given to determine **suitability**. Customers may place transactions that the registered representative considers unsuitable or has not recommended. In this case, the registered representative should mark the order ticket *Unsolicited*. Unmarked order tickets are assumed to be solicited transactions.

A partner or principal of the firm must approve every new account in writing on the new account form before or promptly after the completion of the first transaction in the account.

Patriot Act

Under provisions of the Patriot Act, broker/dealers are required to:

- verify the identity of any new customer;
- maintain records of the information used to verify identity; and
- determine whether the person appears on any list of known or suspected terrorists or terrorist organizations.

These rules are designed to prevent, detect, and prosecute money laundering and the financing of terrorism.

As part of its customer identification program, a broker/dealer must, prior to opening an account, obtain the following information at a minimum:

- Customer name
- Date of birth
- Address
- Social Security number

An exception is granted to persons who do not currently have, but who have applied for, a Social Security number. The firm, in this instance, must obtain the number within a reasonable period of time.

The firm must also verify the identity of each new customer. This can be done by obtaining a copy of the person's unexpired driver's license or a copy of a valid passport. Further, the firm must determine if the customer's name appears on any list of known or suspected terrorists. This is done by contacting the US Treasury.

Lastly, new customers must be advised, before the account is opened, that the firm is requesting information to verify their identities. This notification may be placed on the firm's website, may be delivered verbally, or may be placed on the new account form.

Updating Customer Information

In order to ensure that the information obtained from each new customer is accurate, firms must furnish to each customer, within 30 days of opening the account, a copy of the account record. The firm must include a statement that the customer should mark any corrections on the record and return it along with a statement that the customer should notify the firm of any future changes to information in the account record. If the customer indicates any changes, the firm must furnish the customer with an updated account record within 30 days of receipt of the notice of change. Further, this account updating must occur at least every 36 months thereafter.

Account Ownership and Authority

Accounts can be opened with various types of ownership. The principal types of ownership are **individual**, **joint**, **corporate**, and **partnership**.

Accounts may be opened with someone other than the owner having the authority to buy and sell securities on behalf of the owner. This is known as **trading authorization** or **power of attorney**. The primary types of trading authorization are the following:

- **Discretionary**—a registered representative or other person who has been given written authorization from a customer to make trading decisions for the customer
- **Custodial**—an adult who has been designated to act on behalf of child, who is the beneficial owner of the account
- **Fiduciary**—a third party who has been legally appointed to prudently manage the account on behalf of another person or entity

Opening New Accounts

Generally, any competent person of age may open an account. Any person declared legally incompetent may not. Fiduciary or custodial accounts may be opened for minors or legally incompetent individuals.

Payment and Delivery Instructions

After opening an account, the customer and the registered representative establish payment and delivery instructions. Although these instructions may be changed for individual transactions, the customer selects any of the following.

- **Transfer & Ship**. Securities are registered in the customer's name and shipped to them.
- **Transfer & Hold in Safekeeping**. Securities are registered in the customer's name, and the broker/dealer holds them in safekeeping.
- **Hold in Street Name**. Securities are registered in the broker/dealer's name and held by the broker/dealer. Although the broker/dealer is the securities' nominal owner, the customer is the beneficial owner.
- **Delivery vs. Payment (DVP)**. DVP securities are delivered to a bank or depository against payment. Normally used for institutional accounts, this is a **cash-on-delivery (COD) settlement**. The broker/dealer must verify the arrangement between the customer and the bank or depository, and the customer must notify the bank or depository of each purchase or sale. In addition, the customer designates whether the broker/dealer should hold or forward any cash balance.

Approval and Acceptance of an Account

A partner or a principal of the firm must approve every new account in writing on the account form before or promptly after the completion of the first transaction in the account.

Mailing Instructions

A customer gives specific mailing instructions when opening a new account. Statements and confirms may be sent to someone who holds power of attorney for the customer if the customer requests it in writing and if duplicate confirms are also sent to the customer. A member firm may hold a customer's mail for up to two months if the customer is traveling in the United States and for up to three months if the customer is abroad.

A customer can open either a cash account or a margin account, depending on how he chooses to pay for securities.

Types of Accounts

Cash Accounts

A **cash account** is the basic investment account. Anyone eligible to open an investment account can open a cash account. In a cash account, a customer pays in full for any securities purchased.

Certain accounts may be opened only as cash accounts, such as personal retirement accounts (individual retirement accounts—IRAs, Keoghs, and tax-sheltered annuities/TSAs), corporate retirement accounts, and custodial accounts (Uniform Gifts to Minors Act accounts/UGMAs).

Margin Accounts

A **margin account** allows a customer to borrow money for investing. The term **margin** refers to the minimum amount of cash or marginable securities a customer must deposit to buy securities. Margin accounts will be discussed in detail in an upcoming unit.

Retirement Accounts   Each type of personal and corporate retirement account has its own forms and applications. The most important are those that establish the firm's custodial relationship with the retirement account owner, necessary for **Internal Revenue Service (IRS)** reporting purposes.

Corporate Accounts   A registered representative who opens a corporate account must establish:

- the business's legal right to open an investment account;
- an indication of any limitations that the owners, the stockholders, a court, or any other entity has placed on the securities in which the business can invest; and
- who will represent the business in transactions involving the account.

When opening an account for a corporation, a firm must obtain a copy of the corporate charter as well as a corporate resolution. The charter is proof that the corporation does exist and the resolution authorizes both the opening of the account and the officers designated to enter orders.

Special Account Situations

Sometimes, account owners request that their accounts be handled in a special manner. The most commonly requested situations are numbered accounts, multiple accounts, and account transfers.

Numbered Accounts   At a customer's request, his account may be identified by only a number or symbol. The customer must sign a form certifying that he owns the account(s) identified by the number or symbol and must supply other information identifying himself as the owner.

✓ *For Example:* Celebrities sometimes use numbered accounts to preserve anonymity.

Multiple Accounts   A customer who has both a cash and a margin account is considered to have only one account. If a customer wishes to open more than one individual account with a broker/dealer, the representative must get a statement from the customer attesting that no one else has any interest in the second and subsequent accounts and that each account unreservedly guarantees the others. These are sometimes called **guaranteed accounts**.

Account Transfers   To transfer a customer's account from one broker/dealer to another, a customer submits transfer instructions to the new broker/dealer. The transfer instructions are then sent to the firm currently carrying the account. The firm has three business days to **validate** or to **take exception** to the transfer instructions. The firm may take exception to the transfer instructions if the account number is invalid, the Social Security number on the instruction does not match, the account title does not match or the customer's signature is improper. The firm may not take exception solely because of a dispute about the value of the cash or securities in the account.

Transfer instructions are validated when the current firm returns them to the new firm with an attachment detailing the customer's securities positions. The account is then **frozen**, except for options expiring within seven business days. Account transfers must be completed within three business days of validation.

✓ *Take Note:* Once the transfer instructions are validated by the current firm, any orders to buy or sell must be placed with the new firm, even though the positions, securities, and cash may still be in the possession of the current firm.

Account Records

A registered representative is responsible for maintaining **records** for each customer's account, including each securities holding. All customer transactions are posted daily and maintained at the branch and main offices. The required information includes the following.

- Customer's name, address, and phone number
- Type of account and account number
- Investment objective
- List of all securities deposited with the firm
- List of all transactions

Opening Accounts for Other Brokers' Employees

The **National Association of Securities Dealers (NASD)**, the **New York Stock Exchange (NYSE)**, and **MSRB** require broker/dealers to give permission or written notification to other broker/dealers regarding the establishment of accounts for certain individuals, including:

- employees of broker/dealers; and
- spouses or minor children of broker/dealer employees.

NYSE Requirements NYSE requires prior written approval from the employer broker/dealer before an employee of a member firm can open a cash or margin account with another firm. If the account is approved, the transacting firm must send duplicate statements and confirmations to the employer broker/dealer.

NASD Requirements NASD rules do not require an employee of one NASD member firm to get their employer's permission to open an account with another NASD member, but do require the firm opening the account to notify the customer's employer. The employee is responsible for disclosing that he is an associated person of an NASD member when opening the account. Duplicate confirmations and statements must be sent to the employer broker/dealer if the employer requests them.

MSRB Requirements

Like the NASD, the MSRB does not require an employee of a member firm to obtain prior permission from the employer to open an account with another firm. However, the broker/dealer must notify the employer in writing that the account is being opened and must supply the employer with duplicate confirmations.

SRO Notification and Confirmation Requirements

Employed by:	Margin Account	Cash Account	Duplicate Confirm
NASD member	Notification (not permission)	Notification (not permission)	Upon request
NYSE member	Prior permission	Prior permission	Yes
MSRB member	Notification (not permission)	Notification (not permission)	Yes

Test Topic Alert!

Testable points include the following.

- A principal must approve every new account opened for the firm.
- Account approval does not have to take place prior to the first trade; it can be done promptly after the completion of the first transaction.
- In account transfers, the firm has three days to validate positions and three more days to complete the transfer. (Assume business days any time the number is under 30.)
- NYSE rules are most strict for employee accounts at other firms; NASD rules are most lenient; MSRB rules are in the middle.
- Cash accounts are sometimes called "special cash accounts." Before the crash of 1929, margin accounts were the normal type of account opened. Because cash accounts were unusual, they were referred to as "special."

Quick Quiz 5.1   Multiple Choice

1. A customer wishes her account to be designated by a number, not by her name. The registered representative can

   A. open the account with a written statement of ownership from the customer
   B. open the account with a written statement of approval from an authorized delegate of the customer
   C. open the account without additional documentation
   D. not open the account in this manner

2. An employee of another NASD member broker/dealer would like to open an account with your firm. All of the following statements regarding the employee and the account are true EXCEPT the

   A. employer must receive duplicate copies of all transactions made in the account if requested
   B. employer must be notified of the opening of the account
   C. opening member must notify the employee in writing that the employer will be notified of the employee's intent to open the account
   D. broker/dealer holding the account must approve each transaction made by the person before entry of the order

3. A registered rep is permitted to open all of the following customer accounts EXCEPT a(n)

   A. individual account opened by the individual's spouse
   B. minor's account opened by a custodian
   C. corporate account opened by the designated officer
   D. partnership account opened by the designated partner

4. A registered representative who receives instructions from a customer to "transfer and ship" will instruct the margin department to transfer ownership into the

   A. customer's name and deliver the securities to the customer
   B. brokerage firm's name and deliver the securities to the customer
   C. brokerage firm's name and deliver the securities to the brokerage firm's commercial bank for safekeeping
   D. customer's name and deliver the securities to the customer's bank for safekeeping

5. Which of the following must sign a new account form?

   I. Principal
   II. Registered representative
   III. Customer
   IV. Spouse of the customer

   A. I and II only
   B. I, II, and III only
   C. II and III only
   D. I, II, III, and IV

Answers

1. **A.** The customer can have her account listed in any manner she wishes as long as she has filed a written statement of ownership.

2. **D.** The broker/dealer has no obligation to approve every transaction prior to entry.

3. **A.** A representative is not permitted to open an individual account in the name of another individual, even in the name of a spouse.

4. **A.** Transfer and ship means to transfer the securities into the name of the customer and ship (deliver) the securities to the customer. Hold in street name would require the securities to be transferred into the name of the broker/dealer and held for safekeeping.

5. **A.** To open a cash account, only the signatures of the registered rep introducing the account and the principal accepting the account are required. For margin accounts, the signature of the customer is required on the margin agreement. The signature of the spouse is required only for a joint account.

Types of Accounts

When an account is opened, it is **registered** in the name(s) of one or more persons. They are the account owners and the only individuals allowed access to and control of the investments in the account.

Account Registration

Single Accounts A **single account** has one beneficial owner. The account holder is the only person who can control the investments within the account and request distributions of cash or securities from the account.

Transfer on Death (TOD)

This is a relatively new type of individual account that allows the registered owner of the account to pass all or a portion of it, upon death, to a named beneficiary. This account avoids probate because the estate is bypassed.

Joint Accounts

In a **joint account**, two or more adults are named on the account as co-owners, with each allowed some form of control over the account.

In addition to the appropriate new account form, a **joint account agreement** must be signed, and the account must be designated as either **tenants in common** (TIC) or j**oint tenants with right of survivorship (JTWROS)**.

The account forms for joint accounts require the signatures of all owners. Both types of joint account agreements provide that any or all tenants may transact business in the account. Checks must be made payable to the names in which the account is registered and endorsed for deposit by all tenants, although mail need be sent to only a single address. To be in **good delivery form**, securities sold from a joint account must be signed by all tenants.

Tenants in Common (TIC)

TIC ownership provides that a deceased tenant's fractional interest in the account is retained by that tenant's estate and is not passed to the surviving tenant(s).

Joint Tenants with Right of Survivorship

JTWROS ownership stipulates that a deceased tenant's interest in the account passes to the surviving tenant(s).

Test Topic Alert!

- JTWROS—all parties have an undivided interest in the account
- TIC—each party must specify a percent interest in the account

Checks or distributions must be made payable to all parties and endorsed by all parties.

Partnership Accounts

A **partnership** is an unincorporated association of two or more individuals. Partnerships frequently open cash, margin, retirement, and other types of accounts necessary for business purposes.

The partnership must complete a **partnership agreement** stating which of the partners can make transactions for the account. If the partnership opens a margin account, the partnership must disclose any investment limitations.

An amended partnership agreement must be obtained each year if changes have been made. A partnership agreement is similar to a corporate resolution.

Forms Needed to Open an Account

Form	Individual Cash	Individual Margin	Joint Cash	Joint Margin	Partnership Cash	Partnership Margin	Corporate Cash	Corporate Margin
New account form	✓	✓	✓	✓	✓	✓	✓	✓
Margin agreement		✓		✓		✓		✓
Joint account agreement			✓	✓				
Corporate charter and bylaws								✓
Partnership agreement					✓	✓		
Corporate/partnership resolution					✓	✓	✓	✓
Discretionary authorization	As needed							
Power of attorney	As needed							
Options agreement	As needed							

Fiduciary and Custodial Accounts

When securities are placed in a **fiduciary**, or **custodial**, **account**, a person other than the owner initiates trades. The most familiar example of a fiduciary account is a **trust account**. Money or securities are placed in trust for one person, often a minor, but someone else manages the account. The manager or trustee is a fiduciary.

In a fiduciary account, the investments exist for the owner's beneficial interest, yet the owner has little or no legal control over them. The fiduciary makes all of the investment, management, and distribution decisions and must manage the account in the owner's best interests. The fiduciary may not use the account for his own benefit, although he may be reimbursed for reasonable expenses incurred in managing the account.

Securities bought in a custodial account must be registered in such a way that the custodial relationship is evident.

✓ **For Example:** Marilyn Johnson (the donor) has appointed her daughter's aunt, Barbara Wood, as custodian for the account of her minor daughter, Alexis. The account and the certificates would read "Barbara Wood as custodian for Alexis Johnson."

The beneficial owner's Social Security number is used on the account.

A **fiduciary** is any person legally appointed and authorized to represent another person, act on his behalf, and make whatever decisions are necessary to the prudent management of his account. Fiduciaries include:

- trustee designated to administer a trust;
- executor designated in a decedent's will to manage the affairs of the estate;
- administrator appointed by the courts to liquidate the estate of a person who died intestate (without a will);
- guardian designated by the courts to handle a minor's affairs until the minor reaches the age of majority or to handle an incompetent's affairs;

- custodian of an UGMA account;
- receiver in a bankruptcy; and
- conservator for an incompetent.

Any trades the fiduciary enters must be compatible with the investment objectives of the underlying entity.

Opening a Fiduciary Account

Opening a fiduciary account may require a court certification of the individual's appointment and authority. An account for a trustee must include a **trust agreement** detailing the limitations placed on the fiduciary. No documentation of custodial rights or court certification is required for an individual acting as the custodian for an UGMA.

The registered representative for a fiduciary account must be aware of the following rules:

- Proper authorization must be given (the necessary court documents must be filed with and verified by the broker/dealer).
- Speculative transactions are generally not permitted.
- Margin accounts are only permitted if authorized by the legal documents establishing the fiduciary accounts.
- The **prudent man** rule requires fiduciaries to make wise and safe investments.
- Many states publish a **legal list** of securities approved for fiduciary accounts.
- No authority may be delegated (a power of attorney cannot be accepted for a fiduciary account).
- A fiduciary may not share in an account's profits, but may charge a reasonable fee for services.

Power of Attorney

If a person not named on an account will have trading authority, the customer must file written authorization with the broker/dealer giving that person access to the account. This trading authorization usually takes the form of a power of attorney. Two basic types of trading authorizations are full and limited powers of attorney.

Full Power of Attorney

A **full power of attorney** allows someone who is not the owner of an account to:

- deposit or withdraw cash or securities; and
- make investment decisions for the account owner.

Custodians, trustees, guardians, and other people filling similar legal duties are often given full powers of attorney.

Limited Power of Attorney

A **limited power of attorney** allows an individual to have some, but not total, control over an account. The document specifies the level of access the person may exercise.

Test Topic Alert! Limited power of attorney, also called **limited trading authorization**, allows the entering of buy and sell orders, but no withdrawal of funds. Entry of orders and withdrawal of funds is allowed if full power of attorney is granted.

Discretionary Accounts

An account set up with preapproved authority for a registered rep to make transactions without having to ask for specific approval is a discretionary account. **Discretion** is defined as the authority to decide:

- what security;
- the number of shares or units; and
- whether to buy or sell.

Discretion does not apply to decisions regarding the timing of an investment or the price at which it is acquired.

✓ **For Example:** An order from a customer worded "Buy 100 shares of ABC for my account whenever you think the price is right" is not a discretionary order.

Discretionary Authority A customer can only give discretionary power over his account(s) by filing a **trading authorization** or a limited power of attorney with the broker/dealer. No transactions of a discretionary nature can take place without this document on file. Once authorization has been given, the customer is legally bound to accept the decision made by the person holding discretionary authority, although the customer may continue to enter orders on his own.

Regulation of Discretionary Accounts In addition to requiring the proper documentation, discretionary accounts are subject to the following rules.

- Each discretionary order must be identified as such at the time it is entered for execution.
- An officer or a partner of the brokerage house must approve each order promptly and in writing, not necessarily before order entry.
- A record must be kept of all transactions.
- No excessive trading (**churning**) may occur in the account, relative to the size of the account and the customer's investment objectives.
- To safeguard against the possibility of churning, a designated supervisor or manager must review all trading activity frequently and systematically.

Test Topic Alert! If you are having difficulty identifying a discretionary order, try this method: An order is discretionary if any one of the **3 As** is missing. The 3 As are:

- Activity (buy or sell)
- Amount (number of shares)
- Asset (the security)

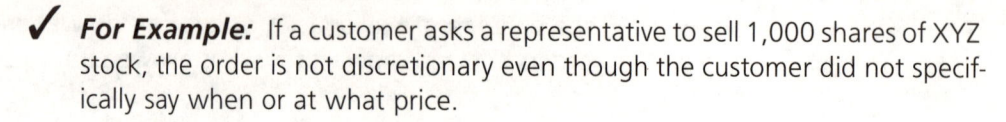

✓ **For Example:** If a customer asks a representative to sell 1,000 shares of XYZ stock, the order is not discretionary even though the customer did not specifically say when or at what price.

Activity = sell
Amount = 1,000 shares
Asset = XYZ stock

All 3 As were defined.

However, if a customer asks a representative to buy 1,000 shares of the best computer company stock available, the order is discretionary. The *Asset* is missing, because the company was not defined.

✓ **For Example:** A customer wishes to buy 1,000 shares of XYZ whenever you think he can get the best price. The order is nondiscretionary. The 3 As were all defined. Omitting the time or price does not make an order discretionary.

Death of an Account Holder

With regard to individual accounts, once a member becomes aware of the death of the account owner, the member must cancel all open orders, mark the account *Deceased*, and freeze the assets in the account until receiving instructions and the necessary documentation from the executor of the decedent's estate. If the account has a third-party power of attorney, the authorization is revoked.

✓ **Take Note:** Discretionary authority also ends at the death of the account owner.

The documents necessary in order to release the assets of a decedent are:

- certified copy of the death certificate;
- inheritance tax waivers; and
- letters testamentary

If one party in a JTWROS account dies, the account can not be transferred into the name of the new owner (the other party) until the documents noted above are presented to the member firm.

If one party in a JTIC account dies, the decedent's interest in the account goes to his estate. The executor for the decedent must present the proper documents before the assets belonging to the decedent can be released. In some states, the death of a tenant in a JTIC account requires that the executor present an affidavit of domicile to the member which shows the decedent's estate will be handled under the laws of that state.

Also note that in JTIC accounts, the death of a tenant requires that the member firm freeze the account and acceptance of orders until the required documents are presented. Compare this with a JTWROS account where the death of one tenant does not preclude the remaining tenant from entering orders.

With regard to partnership accounts, if one partner dies, the member needs written authority from the remaining partners before executing any further orders. This written authorization generally takes the form of an amended partnership agreement.

Test Topic Alert! Three basic steps apply at the death of a customer:

- Freeze the account (mark it deceased).
- Cancel open orders.
- Await instructions from the executor of the estate.

Uniform Gifts to Minors Act (UGMA) Accounts

Uniform Gifts to Minors Act (UGMA) and **Uniform Transfers to Minors Act (UTMA)** accounts require an adult to act as custodian for a minor (the beneficial owner). Any kind of security or cash may be given to the account without limitation.

Characteristics of UGMA Accounts

Donating Securities When a person makes a gift of securities to a minor under the UGMA laws, that person is the **donor** of the securities. A gift under UGMA conveys an **indefeasible title**; that is, the donor may not take back the gift, nor may the minor return the gift. Once the gift is donated, the donor gives up all rights to the property.

When the minor reaches the age of majority the property in the account is transferred into the name of the new adult.

Custodian Any securities given to a minor through an UGMA account are managed by a **custodian** until the minor reaches the age of majority. The custodian has full control over the minor's account and can:

- buy or sell securities;
- exercise rights or warrants; or
- liquidate, trade, or hold securities.

The custodian may also use the property in the account in any way deemed proper for the minor's support, education, maintenance, general use, or benefit. However, the account is not normally used to pay expenses associated with raising a child because the parents can incur negative tax consequences.

Registered representatives must know the following rules of UGMA custodial accounts:

- An account may have only one custodian and one minor or beneficial owner.
- A minor can be the beneficiary of more than one account and a person may serve as custodian for more than one UGMA as long as each account benefits only one minor.
- The donor of securities can act as custodian or can appoint someone else to do so.
- Unless acting as custodians, parents have no legal control over an UGMA account or the securities in it.

Opening an UGMA Account When opening an UGMA account, a representative must ensure that the account application contains the custodian's name, the minor's name and Social Security number, and the state in which the UGMA is registered.

Registration of UGMA Securities Any securities in an UGMA account are registered in the custodian's name for the benefit of the minor; they cannot be registered in street name. Typically, the securities are registered to "Joan Smith as custodian for Brenda Smith," for example, or a variation of this form.

Fiduciary Responsibility An UGMA custodian is charged with **fiduciary responsibilities** in managing the minor's account. Certain restrictions have been placed on what is deemed to be proper handling of the investments in an UGMA. The most important limitations follow.

- UGMAs may be opened and managed as cash accounts only.
- A custodian may not purchase securities in an account on margin or pledge them as collateral for a loan.
- A custodian must reinvest all cash proceeds, dividends, and interest within a reasonable time. Cash proceeds from sales or dividends may be held in a noninterest-bearing custodial account for a reasonable period, but should not remain idle for long.

- Investment decisions must take into account a minor's age and the custodial relationship. Commodities futures, naked options, and other high-risk securities are examples of inappropriate investments. Options may not be bought in a custodial account because no evidence of ownership is issued to an options buyer. Covered call writing is normally allowed.
- Stock subscription rights or warrants must be either exercised or sold.
- A custodian for an UGMA account cannot grant trading authority to a third party.
- A custodian may loan money to an account, but cannot borrow from it.

A custodian may be reimbursed for any reasonable expenses incurred in managing the account unless the custodian is also the donor.

Taxation The minor's Social Security number appears on an UGMA account, and the minor must file an annual income tax return and pay taxes on any investment income produced by the UGMA at the parent's tax rate until the minor reaches the age of 14. Exclusions are available, and they are indexed for inflation.

✓ ***Take Note:*** When the minor reaches age 14, the account will be taxed at the minor's tax rate.

Although the minor is the account's beneficiary and is responsible for any and all taxes on the account, in most states it is the custodian's responsibility to see that the taxes are paid.

Death of the Minor If the beneficiary of an UGMA dies, the securities in the account pass to the minor's estate, not to the parents' or custodian's estate.

Death of the Custodian In the event of the custodian's death or resignation, either a court of law or the donor must appoint a new custodian.

✓ ***Take Note:*** The information just covered also pertains to UTMA accounts with one exception: the transfer to the minor can be delayed up to age 25 (21 in certain states).

Quick Quiz 5.2 Multiple Choice

1. Which of the following persons are considered fiduciaries?

    I. Executor of an estate
    II. Administrator of a trust
    III. Custodian of an UGMA/UTMA account
    IV. Conservator for a legally incompetent person

    A. I and II only
    B. I, II, and III only
    C. III and IV only
    D. I, II, III, and IV

2. If a customer would like to open a custodial UGMA or UTMA account for his nephew, a minor, the uncle

    A. can open the account provided the proper trust arrangements are filed first
    B. can open the account and name himself custodian
    C. needs a legal document evidencing the nephew's parents' approval of the account
    D. can be custodian for the account only if he is also the minor's legal guardian

3. All of the following statements regarding customer accounts are true EXCEPT

    A. stock held in a custodial account may not be held in street name
    B. the customer who opens a numbered account must sign a statement attesting to ownership
    C. stock held under JTWROS goes to the survivor(s) in the event of the death of one of the tenants
    D. margin trading in a fiduciary account does not require any special consideration

4. An investor wishes to provide for his three nephews after his brother dies. Under the Uniform Gifts to Minors Act, which of the following actions may the investor take?

    A. Open 1 account for all 3 nephews
    B. Open 3 separate accounts and deposit cash and securities
    C. Open 3 separate margin accounts and deposit insurance policies
    D. Open 3 separate accounts with authority to short securities

5. An incompetent person wishes to open an account. Which of the following actions must the registered representative take?

   A. Obtain a power of attorney
   B. Obtain a copy of a guardianship document
   C. Open the account as a cash account
   D. Request to talk to a relative

6. Which of the following individuals may not open a joint account?

   A. Two spouses
   B. Three sisters
   C. Two strangers
   D. Parent and a minor

7. Securities owned by a donor and given to a minor under the Uniform Gifts to Minors Act become the property of the minor

   A. when the securities are paid for by the minor
   B. on the settlement date
   C. when the securities are registered in the custodian's name for the benefit of the minor
   D. when the donor decides to give the securities to the minor

Answers

1. **D.** All of the persons listed have fiduciary responsibilities because of the authority with which they are entrusted.

2. **B.** The donor may name himself the custodian of an UGMA or UTMA account. No documentation of custodial status is required to open an UGMA account and the custodian is not required to be the minor's legal guardian.

3. **D.** Trading on margin is prohibited in fiduciary accounts except with the appropriate documentation.

4. **B.** UGMA rules require that any UGMA account have only one beneficial owner and one custodian. Only cash and securities may be donated into the account.

5. **B.** Court papers appointing a guardian must be on file before an account can be opened for a person declared legally incompetent. The guardian will be the nominal owner of the account.

6. **D.** A minor may not be a party in a joint account because a minor cannot legally exercise control over the account. A custodial account should be set up for the minor.

7. **C.** Transfer of securities into the custodial account completes the gift. At that time the minor becomes the owner of the securities.

Customer Accounts HotSheet

New Account Forms:
- Required for all accounts
- Birthdate required
- Customer signature not required for cash accounts; is required for margin accounts
- Signed by representative and approving principal
- Identity verification required

Account Approval:
- By principal, either prior to or promptly after the first transaction

Trading Authorization:
- Limited—third party can trade only
- Full—third party can trade and withdraw cash and securities

Fiduciary Accounts:
- Subject to prudent man rule or legal list
- All require written legal document, except UGMA/UTMA
- Margin accounts permitted only if authorized in document
- No short sales, naked options

Account Transfers:
- Verify positions within three business days; then freeze the account; three more business days to transfer

Accounts for Other Broker/Dealer Employees:
- NYSE—permission first, prior written notification, duplicate statements and confirms
- MSRB—prior written notification, duplicate confirms
- NASD—prior written notification, duplicate confirms request only

Joint Accounts:
- All signatures required to open
- Any party can trade
- Distributions payable to all
- Each owns undivided interest

JTWROS:
- Equal ownership interest
- Passes to remaining tenant at death; no probate

TIC:
- Unequal interests OK
- Passes by will to heirs, not to remaining tenant(s)

Discretionary:
- Authority from customer must be in writing
- Account must be approved before the first trade
- Principal must review discretionary accounts frequently for churning
- Time and price not discretionary

UGMA:
- Cash accounts only
- Minor is beneficial owner; minor's Social Security number on account
- One minor, one custodian
- No short sales, no uncovered options, no margin

Series 7 Unit Test 5

1. A customer opens a margin account with a broker/dealer and signs a loan consent agreement. The loan consent agreement allows the firm to

    A. hypothecate securities in the account
    B. loan out the customer's margin securities
    C. commingle the customer's securities with securities owned by the firm
    D. lend the customer money

2. If a customer wishes to open a numbered account, you should inform him that

    A. it may only be opened with prior permission from the SEC
    B. numbered accounts are restricted to cash accounts
    C. he will have to supply a written statement attesting to his ownership of the account
    D. he will have to supply proof of US citizenship and reside permanently in the US

3. Which of the following occurs in a partnership account if one partner dies?

    A. The surviving partners receive the deceased partner's share.
    B. The account is frozen until an amended partnership agreement is received.
    C. The surviving partners are considered joint tenants.
    D. The surviving partners are considered joint tenants and receive the deceased partner's share.

4. Three individuals have a tenants in common account with your firm. If one individual dies, which of the following statements is TRUE?

    A. The account must be liquidated and the proceeds split evenly among the two survivors and the decedent's estate.
    B. Two survivors continue as co-tenants with the decedent's estate.
    C. Trading is discontinued until the executor names a replacement for the deceased.
    D. The account is converted to Joint Tenants With Rights of Survivorship (JTWROS).

5. Who must sign a new account form for a cash account?

    I. Principal
    II. Registered representative
    III. Customer
    IV. Spouse of the customer

    A. I and II only
    B. I, II and III only
    C. II and III only
    D. I, II, III and IV

6. Which of the following accounts is(are) prohibited from using margin?

    I. Joint account for a husband and wife
    II. Discretionary account
    III. Corporation account
    IV. Custodian account under the Uniform Gifts to Minors Act

    A. I and II only
    B. I, II and III only
    C. II and IV only
    D. IV only

7. A dealer must use special procedures whenever it opens a municipal securities account for

   A. a clerical employee of another dealer
   B. the spouse of a trader employed by another dealer
   C. the minor child of an operations supervisor employed by another dealer
   D. all of the above

8. Which of the following would be considered discretionary?

   A. Order that specifies the size of the trade and name of the security but leaves the choice of price and time up to the registered representative
   B. Account in which the broker has the power to decide when and what to trade, without specific customer authorization for those trades
   C. Joint account with right of survivorship
   D. Joint tenants in common account

9. One of your clients dies. Upon notification of the death, you should immediately

   I. mark the account *Deceased* until proper documents are received
   II. cancel all GTC orders for the account
   III. obtain a letter from the attorney representing the estate with instructions for transfer
   IV. obtain the names and addresses of the beneficiaries of the estate

   A. I only
   B. I and II only
   C. II and III only
   D. I, II, III and IV

10. Under which of the following circumstances may a gift given to a minor under UGMA be revoked?

    A. At any time before the minor reaches the age of majority
    B. If the minor dies before reaching the age of majority
    C. If the custodian dies before the minor reaches the age of majority
    D. Under no circumstances.

11. The documents required to open a cash account for a customer and give a sibling trading authorization include a

    I. new account card
    II. loan consent agreement
    III. customer agreement
    IV. limited power of attorney

    A. I only
    B. I, II and IV only
    C. I and IV only
    D. II, III and IV only

12. Which of the following are fiduciaries?

    I. Executor of an estate
    II. Administrator of a trust
    III. Custodian of an UGMA account
    IV. Registered representative granted the authority to choose the security, quantity, and action in a customer's account

    A. I and II only
    B. I, II and III only
    C. II, III and IV only
    D. I, II, III and IV

13. Under the Uniform Gifts to Minors Act, all of the following statements are true EXCEPT

    A. a UGMA account may have only one custodian for only one minor
    B. only an adult can make a gift to a minor
    C. the maximum amount of money an adult can give to a minor in any one year is $11,000
    D. once a gift is given to a minor, it cannot be reclaimed

14. An employee of another broker/dealer would like to open an account with your firm. Under NASD rules, all of the following statements regarding the employee and the account are true EXCEPT that the

   A. employer must receive duplicate copies of all transactions made in the account if requested
   B. employer must be notified of the opening of the account
   C. opening member must notify the employee, in writing, that the employer will be notified of the employee's intent to open the account
   D. broker/dealer holding the account must approve each transaction made by the person before entry of the order

15. A new account is opened joint tenants with rights of survivorship. All of the following statements are true EXCEPT that

   A. orders may be given by either party
   B. mail can be sent to either party with the permission of the other party
   C. checks can be drawn in the name of either party
   D. in the event of death, the decedent's interest in the account goes to the other party

16. All of the following information must be obtained from new customers EXCEPT

   A. employer name and address
   B. date of birth
   C. educational background
   D. citizenship

Series 7 Unit Test 5 Answers & Rationale

1. **B.** A signed loan consent agreement permits the firm to loan out the customer's margin securities. Loaning out customer margin securities is another way to finance the customer's debit balance. A broker/dealer would loan out customer margin securities for another customer's short sale. QID: 32189

2. **C.** Numbered or symbol accounts require a signed, written statement from the client to be kept on file. This type of account is opened for anonymity, not tax evasion. QID: 30649

3. **B.** Upon a partner's death, a partnership account is automatically frozen until an amended partnership agreement is received. The deceased partner's share usually goes to an estate; the other partners do not receive it. QID: 28098

4. **B.** The decedent's estate becomes a tenant in common with the survivors. QID: 35087

5. **A.** To open a cash account, only the signatures of the registered representative introducing the account and the principal accepting the account are required. For margin accounts, the signature of the customer is required on the margin agreement. The signature of the spouse is required only for a joint account. QID: 32184

6. **D.** Although no legal papers are required to open a custodial account, the account must be kept in accordance with state law under the UGMA. This act prohibits securities in a custodial account from being purchased on margin. QID: 28129

7. **D.** The firm must follow special procedures whenever it opens an account for the employee of another broker/dealer. The firm must give the employing broker/dealer written notice that it is opening the account. Also, the firm must send copies of all confirmations to the employer. QID: 28056

8. **B.** An order is discretionary when it is placed by the member firm or its representative for a customer's account without the customer's express authorization for that order. Also, for the order to be considered discretionary, the firm must choose more than just the price or time of execution; that is, the size of the trade, whether to buy or sell, or the security must be chosen by the firm. QID: 32188

9. **B.** The account registered representative should cancel all open orders and mark the account *Deceased*. The firm should not permit any trades until proper documents are received from the estate representative. It is not the responsibility of the firm to contact the decedent's attorney or the beneficiaries. QID: 29632

10. **D.** The Uniform Gifts to Minors Act states that all gifts to minors are irrevocable. QID: 28127

11. **C.** If one party wants to give discretionary privileges to a third party in a cash account, a member firm requires a new account form and a limited power of attorney. A limited power of attorney gives the third party trading authority, but prohibits that party from withdrawing securities from the account. QID: 28091

12. **D.** Each of these has a fiduciary relationship to the customer and is required to act prudently in the customer's best interest. QID: 32186

13. C. Any adult can give a gift to a minor in a custodial account and there is no limitation on the size of the gift. Gift tax applies on gifts given in excess of $11,000 (2004). QID: 28131

14. D. The NASD does not require prior approval of individual transactions by the broker/dealer at which the account has been opened. QID: 32182

15. C. While either party may enter an order, any money or securities delivered out of the account must be in the names of both owners. QID: 35075

16. C. A customer's educational background need not be ascertained when opening an account. QID: 35131

6

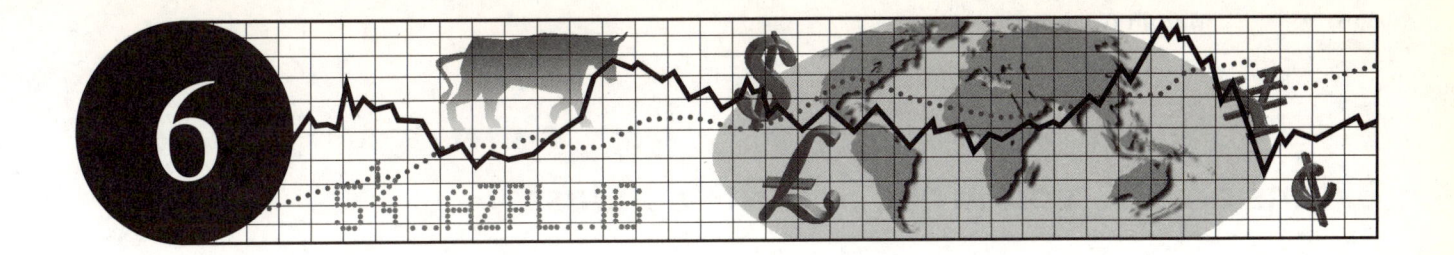

Margin Accounts

INTRODUCTION Margin accounts allow investors to leverage their investment dollars. Through margin accounts, investors can borrow money from brokerage firms by pledging collateral. The Federal Reserve Board regulates margin transactions.

Broker/dealers are required to impose initial and maintenance requirements on all margin accounts. They must mark to the market daily to assure that account equity meets the minimum requirements.

Although this margin accounts unit involves substantial calculation and accounting scenarios, only about one-third to one-half of your margin test questions will involve computations. The others will test your mastery of definitions and regulations associated with margin accounts. Series 7 margin questions are likely to ask about the initial and maintenance requirements for long and short margin transactions. The margin accounting charts presented in this unit will assist you in any calculation questions you encounter.

The information on margin accounts in this unit will account for approximately 8–12 questions on the Series 7 exam.

UNIT OBJECTIVES When you have completed this unit, you should be able to:

- determine initial and maintenance requirements for long and short margin accounts;
- identify regulations and regulatory bodies that impact margin account transactions;
- define Regulation T and its importance to margin accounts;
- compute and describe uses of SMA; and
- calculate equity in long, short, and combined margin accounts.

Extension of Credit in the Securities Industry

Buying **on margin** is a common practice in the securities industry. It allows customers to increase their trading capital by borrowing from broker/dealers.

Types of Margin Accounts

There are two types of margin accounts: **long** and **short**. In a **long margin account**, customers purchase securities and pay interest on the money borrowed until the loan is repaid. In a **short margin account**, stock is borrowed and then sold short, enabling the customer to profit if its value declines. All short sales must be executed through and accounted for in a margin account.

✓ *Take Note:* In long margin accounts, customers borrow money; in short margin accounts, customers borrow securities.

Advantages of margin accounts for customers are that the customer can:

- purchase more securities with a lower initial cash outlay; and
- **leverage** the investment by borrowing a portion of the purchase price.

Leveraging magnifies the customer's rate of return, or rate of loss in adverse market conditions.

Cash/Margin Purchase

	Cash Purchase	Margin Purchase
Purchase of 1,000 shares of ABC for $20	Customer pays $20,000 for purchase	Customer borrows 50% ($10,000) from broker-dealer, deposits equity of $10,000
Return after increase from $20 to $30 per share	Customer experiences 50% return (Gain/Initial investment: $10,000 ÷ $20,000 = 50%)	Customer experiences 100% return (Gain/Initial Investment: $10,000 ÷ $10,000 = 100%)
Return after decrease from $20 to $15 per share	Customer experiences 25% loss (Loss/Initial investment: −$5,000 ÷ $20,000 = −25%)	Customer experiences 50% loss (Loss/Initial investment: −$5,000 ÷ $10,000 = −50%)

The advantages of margin accounts for broker/dealers are:

- margin account loans generate interest income for the firm; and
- margin customers typically trade larger positions because of increased trading capital, generating higher commissions for the firm.

Margin Agreement

Customers who open margin accounts must sign a **margin agreement** before trading can commence. The agreement consists of three parts: the credit agreement, the hypothecation agreement, and the loan consent form.

Credit Agreement The **credit agreement** discloses the terms of the credit extended by the broker/dealer, including the method of interest computation and situations under which interest rates may change.

Hypothecation Agreement The **hypothecation agreement** gives permission to the broker/dealer to pledge customer margin securities as collateral. The firm hypothecates customer securities to the bank, and the bank loans money to the broker/dealer based on the loan value of these securities. All customer securities must be held in **street name** (registered in the name of the firm) to facilitate this process. When customer securities are held in street name, the broker/dealer is known as the **nominal**, or **named, owner**. The customer is the **beneficial owner**, because he retains all rights of ownership.

Loan Consent Form If signed, the loan consent form gives permission to the firm to loan customer margin securities to other customers or broker/dealers, usually for short sales.

✓ *Take Note:* It is mandatory that the customer signs the credit agreement and hypothecation agreement. The loan consent form is optional.

Test Topic Alert! The interest paid by margin customers on money borrowed is a variable rate based on the **broker call rate**.

Regulation T (Reg T)

Reg T, from the Securities Act of 1934, regulates the extension of credit in the securities industry. For margin accounts, Reg T states that customers must deposit a minimum of 50% of the market value of the transaction within five business days. Fifty percent is the minimum required; a customer can choose to pay a larger percentage of the purchase price. The **Federal Reserve Board (FRB)** has been authorized to amend the Reg T requirement as necessary.

Margin Accounts

✓ **Take Note:** Reg T applies to both cash and margin accounts; customers have 5 business days to pay for the purchase regardless of the account type. Firms, however, expect payment regular way: within 3 business days of trade date.

Marginable Securities

Reg T also identifies which securities are eligible for purchase on margin and which may be used as collateral for loans for other purchases.

✓ **Take Note:** Differentiate between use of the terms *margin* and *marginable*.

- **Margin** is the amount of equity that must be deposited to buy securities in a margin account.
- **Marginable** refers to securities that can be used as collateral in a margin account.

May be purchased on margin and used as collateral:
- Exchange listed stocks, bonds
- Nasdaq stocks
- Non-Nasdaq OTC issues approved by the FRB

Cannot be purchased on margin and *cannot* be used as collateral:
- Put and call options
- Rights
- Non-Nasdaq OTC issues *not* approved by the FRB
- Insurance contracts

Cannot be bought on margin but *can* be used as collateral after 30 days:
- Mutual funds
- New issues

💡 **Test Topic Alert!**

With the exception of LEAP options, options cannot be purchased on margin. When buying options, customers must deposit 100% of the premium. When writing a covered call, there is no Reg T requirement for writing the call. All the customer must do is have in the account 50% of the purchase price of the stock. If you see a margin question on covered call writing, be sure to focus on what is being asked: Is it the Reg T requirement or is it the margin deposit? Consider the following examples.

Question: A customer purchases 100 ABC at $62 per share and simultaneously buys 1 ABC 60 put at $3. What is the margin deposit?

Answer: The margin deposit is $3,400. The 50% requirement on the stock is $3,100. Because options cannot be purchased on margin, the customer must pay the entire premium of $300 for a total margin deposit of $3,400.

If a customer buys stock and receives a premium by writing a call, the premium received reduces the margin requirement.

Question: A customer purchases 100 ABC at 62 and also writes an ABC 65 call at 3. What is the margin deposit?

Answer: The Reg T requirement for establishing both positions is $3,100 (50% × $6,200). The margin deposit is $2,800, which is the Reg T requirement reduced by the premium received.

✓ **Take Note:** LEAP options with more than 9 months to expiration can be purchased on margin. The initial (and maintenance) requirement is 75%.

✓ **For Example:** A customer buys 10 XYZ LEAPs at 4.50 each. The LEAPs expire in 24 months. What must the customer deposit?

The customer must deposit $3,375, which is 75% of the total cost of $4,500. When the time remaining to expiration reaches 9 months, the maintenance requirement is 100% of the current market value.

Exempt Securities Certain securities are exempt from Reg T margin requirements. If they are bought or sold in a margin account, they are subject to the firm's determination of an initial requirement, and firms must follow maintenance requirements established by the NYSE and NASD.

Securities exempt from Reg T include:

- US Treasury bills, notes, and bonds;
- government agency issues;
- municipal securities; and
- corporate straight debt (nonconvertible) securities.

✓ **Take Note:** The FRB can change Reg T, but the current requirement has been in place for more than 20 years. Assume Reg T = 50% in test questions.

Summary of Initial Requirements and Loan Values

Securities	Reg T Initial Requirement	Loan Value
Listed equity securities, OTC margin securities, listed warrants	50% of the purchase cost	50%
U.S. government obligations	Exempt (no Reg T requirement)	Set by NASD/NYSE
Municipal bonds	Exempt (no Reg T requirement)	Set by NASD/NYSE
Nonconvertible bonds	Treated as exempt from the Reg T requirement	Set by NASD/NYSE
Listed convertible bonds with and without warrants	50% of the purchase cost	50%

Initial Requirements

Customers are required to deposit a minimum amount of equity for their **first purchase** in a margin account. Although Reg T states that a deposit of 50% of the market value of the purchase is required, the NASD/NYSE insists that this initial deposit cannot generally be less than $2,000.

Initial Requirements Example

Customer Purchase	Reg T Requirement	NASD/NYSE Minimum	Customer Deposit Required
100 shares at $50/sh	$2,500	$2,000	$2,500
100 shares at $30/sh	$1,500	$2,000	$2,000
100 shares at $15/sh	$750	$1,500	$1,500

The customer is required to deposit the greater of the Reg T requirement or the NASD/NYSE minimum. The exception occurs when the customer's initial purchase is less than $2,000; the customer is not required to deposit $2,000, only the full purchase price.

There is another way to look at this: if the customer's first purchase in a margin account is less than $2,000, deposit 100% of the purchase price. If the first purchase is between $2,000 and $4,000, deposit $2,000. If the first purchase is greater than $4,000, deposit 50%.

✓ *Take Note:* The NASD/NYSE minimum rule also applies to short margin accounts. However, because short transactions are more speculative, the minimum of $2,000 is never waived. If a short sale margin requirement is less than $2,000, the customer required deposit is still $2,000.

Deadlines for Meeting Margin Calls

As previously discussed, Reg T requires margin account customers to meet initial margin deposit requirements not more than five business days after the trade date. The deposit may be made in cash or in fully-paid marginable securities valued at twice the amount of the Reg T cash call.

If payment is late, the broker/dealer may apply to its designated examining authority for an extension, as it may do on behalf of cash account customers. For an amount of less than $1,000, the broker/dealer can choose to take no action.

If no extension is applied for, the firm, on the morning of the sixth business day, must sell out the securities purchased and freeze the account for 90 days. If the customer wants to purchase securities in a frozen account, the customer must have good funds in the account prior to order entry.

Quick Quiz 6.1   Match each of the following items with the appropriate description below.

A. Must be signed; allows firm to pledge customer securities as collateral
B. Set by NASD and NYSE
C. May not be purchased on margin
D. Optional part of margin agreement

___ 1. Maintenance requirements

___ 2. Loan consent form

___ 3. Hypothecation agreement

___ 4. Mutual funds

Answers   1. **B.**   2. **D.**   3. **A.**   4. **C.**

✏️ **Quick Quiz 6.2** Match the following descriptions with the appropriate terms below.

A. Time that must pass before new issues can be used for margin account collateral
B. Retains all rights, such as receipt of dividends
C. Subject to NYSE/NASD requirements, not Reg T
D. The firm, when securities are held in street name

___ 1. Beneficial owner

___ 2. Nominal owner

___ 3. 30 days

___ 4. Municipal bonds

Answers   1. **B.**   2. **D.**   3. **A.**   4. **C.**

Margin Accounting

After margin accounts have been opened, broker/dealers must verify that equity in the account meets minimum requirements following fluctuations in market value.

The practice of recalculation to check the status of the equity in the account is called **marking to the market**. It is typically done every business day based on the closing price of the stock. This concept applies to both long and short margin accounts, which will be discussed separately.

Long Margin Accounting

The Series 7 examination uses the following terms to describe activity in long margin accounts.

- **Long market value (LMV)**—the current market value of the stock position the investor purchased
- **Debit register (DR)**—the amount of money borrowed by the customer
- **Equity (EQ)**—the customer's net worth in the margin account; it represents the portion of the securities the customer fully owns

The amount of equity in the account is determined by this equation:

$$LMV - DR = EQ$$

To simplify long margin accounts, think of them like a house with a mortgage. If the market value of a house goes up or down, the mortgage amount does not change, but the equity goes up or down. The same is true in a margin account; when market value of securities goes up, the debit balance (what the customer owes the BD) stays the same, while the equity increases. When market value of securities goes down, the debit balance stays the same and the equity decreases.

Continuing the analogy, consider a house payment. The payment does not affect the market value of the house, but reduces the debit balance and consequently increases the equity. When money is paid into a margin account, the debit balance is decreased and the equity is increased.

Analyzing Long Margin Accounts

To analyze long margin account activity, a simplified balance sheet will be used, as shown:

LMV	DR
	EQ

✓ **Take Note:** Draw a chart whenever asked to compute equity in a margin account. Remember the master margin account equation: **LMV − DR = EQ**. Be sure that your account is balanced before going to the next step.

✓ **For Example:** A customer purchases 1,000 shares of XYZ at 60 on margin and borrows the maximum 50% from the broker/dealer.

The margin chart is set up as follows:

LMV	DR
60,000	30,000
	EQ
	30,000

In this instance, the customer must deposit $30,000. The customer may deposit cash or fully paid securities. To meet the margin requirement in securities requires *double* the necessary cash margin when Reg T is 50%. For a margin requirement of $30,000, the customer may pay $30,000 in cash or deposit $60,000 of fully paid securities to meet the Reg T requirement.

When the market value of securities changes, the broker/dealer must **mark to the market** to assure that enough equity remains in the account. The customer's account must always meet the **maintenance requirement** of the NASD/NYSE. In a long margin account, minimum maintenance is 25% of the long market value.

Marking to the market identifies the status of the customer's account. The determination of the status requires the computation of two **benchmarks**:

- **Reg T** (50% of LMV); and
- **minimum maintenance** (25% of LMV).

If XYZ declines to 50, both of these benchmarks are computed based on the new market value of the account, as shown below:

	LMV	DR
		30,000
	~~60,000~~	
	50,000	
Reg T = 25,000		EQ
Min. Mntc.= 12,500		~~30,000~~
		20,000

✓ *Take Note:* Here are several helpful tips in long margin accounting:

- When the market value of securities goes up or down, the DR doesn't change.
- When marking to the market, the calculation of Reg T and minimum maintenance is based on the new long market value.

Restricted Accounts If the equity in the account is less than the Reg T amount, but greater than or equal to the minimum maintenance requirement, the account is **restricted**.

✓ *Take Note:* If an account becomes restricted, there is no requirement for the customer to take any action to "unrestrict" the account. A maintenance call will only be sent if the account falls below minimum.

Maintenance Requirements When the equity in the account falls below the minimum maintenance requirement, the customer receives a **maintenance margin call**. Maintenance calls are a demand that the customer make a payment to bring the account back to minimum. If payment is not made, the broker/dealer will liquidate enough of the securities in the account to bring the account back to minimum. The customer can meet a maintenance call by depositing cash or fully paid marginable securities.

✓ **Take Note:** A firm can impose a maintenance level higher than the NASD/NYSE minimum maintenance level. This is a **house minimum**. Many firms today impose 30–35% minimum maintenance requirements.

Consider the previous example. By evaluating the amount of equity in the account relative to the Reg T and minimum maintenance benchmarks, it can be determined that the account is in **restricted status**.

The new equity of $20,000 is less than the Reg T requirement of $25,000, but more than the minimum maintenance of $12,500.

	LMV	DR
		30,000
	~~60,000~~	
	50,000	
Reg T = 25,000		EQ
Min. Mntc. = 12,500		~~30,000~~
		20,000

✓ **Take Note:** When calculating equity in the margin account using a T-chart, be sure to follow these steps:

- Calculate the equity after a market value change: LMV − DR = EQ
- Calculate the new Reg T: 50% of the new LMV
- Calculate the new minimum maintenance: 25% of the LMV

Maintenance Call Assume that the market value of the securities falls from $50,000 to $36,000. To find the status of the account, the chart would be adjusted as follows:

	LMV	DR
	~~50,000~~	30,000
	36,000	
Reg T = 18,000		EQ
Min. Mntc. = 9,000		~~20,000~~
		6,000

Note the adjustment to the LMV. The LMV has fallen to $36,000, so the EQ must be changed to $6,000 ($36,000 − $30,000 = $6,000). After adjusting EQ in the account, the new Reg T and minimum maintenance levels are calculated. (Reg T = 50% of $36,000, or $18,000; Min. Mntc. = 25% of $36,000, or $9,000).

This account is subject to a **maintenance call** because the equity is below the minimum requirement by $3,000. If the call is not met promptly, the broker/dealer will liquidate the customer's securities as needed.

A formula can be applied to calculate the market value to which securities can fall before there is a maintenance call. This formula is known as the **market value at maintenance formula**, and is calculated as follows:

$$DR / .75$$

✓ **For Example:** A customer buys $90,000 worth of stock on margin and meets the initial Reg T requirement by depositing $45,000. The debit balance is $45,000. To what level would the market value have to fall in order for the account to be at minimum maintenance?

Divide the debit balance of $45,000 by .75 to result in a maintenance market value of $60,000. If the market value does fall to $60,000, the account would look like this: LMV $60,000; DR $45,000; EQ $15,000. At this point, the account is exactly at 25% equity.

✓ **Take Note:** If an account falls below minimum, a maintenance call will be sent in an amount sufficient to bring the account back up to minimum.

✓ **For Example:** A customer has a long margin account with a market value of $12,000 and a debit balance of $10,000. The equity in the account is $2,000, which is approximately 16% of the market value. To bring the account back to minimum, which is $3,000 (25% × $12,000) the customer will receive a maintenance call for $1,000. Once the call is met, the account will look like this: LMV $12,000; DR $9,000; EQ $3,000.

Excess Equity and SMA

Excess equity in a margin account is the amount of equity exceeding the Reg T requirement.

To illustrate, return to the example account:

LMV	DR
60,000	30,000
	EQ
	30,000

Assume the market value of the securities increases to $80,000. After marking to the market, the account appears as shown below:

	LMV	DR	
		30,000	(2) SMA = 10,000
	~~60,000~~		
	80,000		
Reg T = 40,000		EQ	
Min. Mntc. = 20,000		~~30,000~~	(1) EE = 10,000
		50,000	

The increase in market value creates equity of $50,000 because the DR does not change. The new Reg T requirement is $40,000 (50% of $80,000) and the new minimum maintenance is $20,000 (25% of $80,000). Because the equity exceeds Reg T, this account has **excess equity** of $10,000 ($50,000 − $40,000 = $10,000).

✓ **Take Note:** A rule of thumb to determine SMA is as follows: for every one dollar increase in market value, 50 cents of SMA is created. In the previous example, market value increased by $20,000 which created SMA of $10,000.

Excess equity creates SMA, or **buying power**, in the account.

Item (1) above shows the excess equity. Item (2) above shows the SMA.

SMA stands for **special memorandum account**, a line of credit that a customer can borrow from or use to purchase securities.

SMA is perhaps the most complicated margin concept. The house analogy can also help simplify SMA. Assume a house has increased substantially in value. Homeowners with large amounts of equity sometimes borrow against their equity through home equity loans. When they take a loan, the amount they owe on their house is more than before, and the equity falls. SMA is like a home equity loan. It is created because of increased equity in the account and is an additional line of credit. When the SMA line of credit is used, the debit balance in the customer's account is increased and the equity falls.

✓ **Take Note:** The amount of SMA in the account is equal to the greater of the excess equity or the amount already in SMA.

Until this transaction, our example account had no excess equity. The excess equity of $10,000 generated SMA of $10,000.

Margin Accounts

What happens to SMA if the market value of the securities falls? The example below depicts the market value falling to $70,000:

	LMV	DR	
	~~80,000~~	30,000	(2) SMA = 10,000
	70,000		
Reg T = 35,000		EQ	
Min. Mntc. = 17,500		~~50,000~~	(1) EE = 5,000
		40,000	~~10,000~~

The decrease in market value creates equity of $40,000. The new Reg T requirement is $35,000 (50% of $70,000) and the new minimum maintenance is $17,500 (25% of $70,000). Because the equity exceeds Reg T, this account has **excess equity** of $5,000 ($40,000 − $35,000 = $5,000).

What is the new SMA amount? The rule explains that the SMA amount is equal to the greater of the excess equity or the SMA already in the account. Because the SMA of $10,000 is greater than the excess equity of $5,000, the SMA remains at $10,000. In summary, remember that although SMA increases when market value in the account increases, it does not decrease as a result of a market value decline.

Item (1) in the example shows the excess equity. Item (2) shows the SMA.

✓ **Take Note:** SMA may be more than excess equity and may exist even if there is no excess equity in the account.

✓ **Take Note:** Although the SMA isn't reduced from a decline in market value, its use may be restricted under certain conditions.

SMA can always be used, even in a restricted account, as long as its use does not bring the account below minimum.

One last example in calculating the SMA balance. Assuming the market value of securities rises to $100,000, what is the new SMA balance?

	LMV	DR	
	~~70,000~~	30,000	(2) SMA = ~~10,000~~
	100,000		20,000
Reg T = 50,000		EQ	
Min. Mntc. = 25,000		~~40,000~~	(1) EE = ~~5,000~~
		70,000	20,000

The increase in market value creates equity of $70,000. The new Reg T requirement is $50,000 (50% of $100,000) and the new minimum maintenance is $25,000 (25% of $100,000). Because the equity exceeds Reg T, this account has excess equity of $20,000 ($70,000 − $50,000 = $20,000). What is the new SMA amount? The SMA rule explains that the SMA amount is equal to the greater of the excess equity or the SMA already in the account. Because the excess equity of $20,000 is greater than the existing SMA of $10,000, the SMA balance becomes $20,000.

We have illustrated that SMA is increased by excess equity from market value increases. Any of the following also generate SMA.

- **Nonrequired cash deposits**—if a customer deposits cash that is not required to meet a margin call, the full amount reduces the debit and is also credited to SMA.
- **Dividends**—dividends received on securities in the margin account are added to SMA. The customer can withdraw these income distributions, even if the account is restricted.

✓ **Take Note:** If a customer wants to remove cash dividends coming into his margin account, he must do so within 30 days of receipt. Otherwise, the cash dividend will be applied against the debit balance, thereby increasing the equity in the account.

- **Loan value**—if a customer makes a nonrequired deposit of marginable stock, the stock's loan value is credited to SMA. The credit is equal to half the value of a cash deposit.
- **Sale of stock**—when stock is sold, 50% of the sales proceeds is credited to SMA.

Using SMA SMA is a line of credit, therefore, the investor can use it to withdraw cash or meet the margin requirement on stock purchases.

✓ **For Example:** Assume a margin account as follows:

	LMV	DR	
	70,000	30,000	SMA = 20,000
Reg T = 35,000		EQ	
Min. Mntc. = 17,500		40,000	

The customer can withdraw cash by borrowing against the credit line of $20,000, which will increase the debit balance by $20,000. If the full $20,000 is withdrawn, the account will appear as follows:

	LMV	DR	
	70,000	~~30,000~~	SMA = ~~20,000~~
		50,000	0
Reg T = 35,000		EQ	
Min. Mntc. = 17,500		~~40,000~~	
		20,000	

The use of $20,000 of SMA reduces the SMA balance to 0. The debit balance is increased to $50,000, because SMA is a loan. The equity balance falls to $20,000, and the account is in restricted status. The customer can use SMA as long as it does not cause a maintenance call.

SMA can be used when the account has excess equity or is in restricted status. SMA can also be used to meet the initial margin requirements on stock purchases. SMA gives the investor buying power. Assume a margin account as follows:

	LMV	DR	
	70,000	30,000	SMA = 20,000
Reg T = 35,000		EQ	
Min. Mntc. = 17,500		40,000	

The SMA of $20,000, when used as the margin requirement, allows the customer to purchase $40,000 of stock. In other words, for every $1 of SMA, the customer can purchase $2 of stock. SMA has buying power of 2 to 1. After the purchase of $40,000, the account appears as follows:

	LMV	DR	
	~~70,000~~	~~30,000~~	SMA = ~~20,000~~
	110,000	70,000	0
Reg T = 55,000		EQ	
Min. Mntc. = 27,500		40,000	

The $40,000 purchase was "paid for" by a debit balance increase of $40,000. Any time SMA is used to buy stock, the debit balance increases by the full amount of the purchase.

The use of SMA to meet the purchase price is like borrowing on a credit card. The customer owes more money. This account is in restricted status after the purchase of $40,000 of stock.

SMA Example

Activity	MV−	DR=	Eq−	Reg T=	Ex Eq	SMA	Buy Power
Buy 1,000 shares at 40	40,000 −	20,000 =	20,000	20,000	0	0	0
MV to 50 (UP)	50,000 −	20,000 =	30,000	25,000	5,000	5,000	10,000
MV to 40 (DOWN)	40,000 −	20,000 =	20,000	20,000	0	5,000	10,000
Borrow $5,000	40,000 −	25,000 =	15,000	20,000	0	0	0
Buy $10,000 stock	50,000 −	30,000 =	20,000	25,000	0	0	0

Test Topic Alert! Here is a quick review of critical long margin account concepts:

- The first transaction in a margin account requires a deposit of the greater of 50% of the LMV or $2,000. The $2,000 minimum is waived if 100% of the transaction is less than $2,000.
- The basic margin equation is: LMV − DR = EQ.
- Reg T = 50% of the LMV.
- Minimum maintenance = 25% of the LMV (50% of Reg T requirement).
- SMA can be borrowed from the account, dollar for dollar.
- Utilizing SMA increases the debit balance.
- The buying power of SMA is 2 to 1.
- Excess equity and SMA are not necessarily equal.
- SMA cannot be used to meet a maintenance margin call.
- The market value at maintenance equation for long margin accounts is DR / .75. This calculates what the market value can fall to before a maintenance call is imposed.
- Exempt securities are not subject to Reg T, but are subject to maintenance.

Restricted Accounts Revisited If an account is restricted, the following rules apply:

- To purchase additional securities, put up 50%.
- To withdraw securities from the account, the customer must deposit cash equal to 50% of the value of the securities to be withdrawn.
- If securities are sold in a restricted account, at least half the proceeds must be retained in the account to reduce the debit balance. This is

called the **retention requirement**. Also, 50% of the proceeds are credited to SMA.

The sale of securities in a restricted account can be complicated.

✓ **For Example:** LMV $50,000; DR $30,000; EQ $20,000

This account is restricted by $5,000 (if the equity were $5,000 higher, the account would be at 50% and therefore not restricted). The customer wants to sell $10,000 worth of stock.

Initially, all of the proceeds are applied against the debit balance and a credit of $5,000 is made to SMA. The account now looks as follows:

LMV $40,000; DR $20,000; EQ $20,000; SMA $5,000

If the customer wants to withdraw half the proceeds (remember at least 50% must be retained in the account to reduce the debit balance and the customer can remove the other half) he does so by using SMA and borrowing from the account. After the customer withdraws $5,000, the account looks like this:

LMV $40,000; DR $25,000; EQ $15,000; SMA 0

The reason all of the proceeds of the sale are initially applied against the debit balance is this: what if the customer doesn't want any of the proceeds to be sent to him? In this case, the firm has the obligation to reduce the debit and thus his interest charges. If, however, the customer changes his mind and wants half the proceeds, he can always take out the $5,000 by using SMA.

Test Topic Alert! For the Series 7 exam, watch for the following: if securities are sold in a restricted account, which of the following are affected? LMV, DR, EQ, SMA?

All but equity are affected: LMV, DR, and SMA. Equity is only affected if the customer elects to remove half the proceeds.

Quick Quiz 6.3 Multiple Choice

1. An investor opens a new margin account and buys 200 shares of DWQ at 50, with Reg T at 50%. What is the investor's initial margin requirement?

   A. $2,500
   B. $3,000
   C. $5,000
   D. $10,000

2. An investor has an established margin account with a current market value of $4,000 and a debit balance of $2,250, with Reg T at 50%. How much equity does the investor have in the account?

   A. $1,750
   B. $2,000
   C. $2,250
   D. $4,000

3. An investor has an established margin account with a current market value of $6,000 and a debit balance of $2,500. With Reg T at 50%, how much excess equity does the investor have in the account?

   A. $500
   B. $2,500
   C. $3,500
   D. $6,000

4. In a new margin account, a customer buys 100 shares of GGG, Inc., at 30 and meets the initial margin requirement. If the stock falls to 25, the equity in the account is equal to

   A. $1,000
   B. $1,500
   C. $2,000
   D. $2,500

5. A margin account has long market value of $6,000 and a debit of $5,000. How much money must the investor deposit to satisfy the maintenance requirement?

   A. $500
   B. $1,000
   C. $2,000
   D. $5,000

6. A margin account is restricted by $2,000. Which of the following actions may the customer take to bring the account to the Reg T requirement?

   I. Cancel $2,000 of SMA
   II. Deposit $2,000 cash
   III. Deposit $4,000 of fully paid marginable stock

   A. I only
   B. I and II only
   C. II and III only
   D. I, II, and III

7. When stock held in a long margin account appreciates, which of the following increase(s)?

   I. Current market value
   II. Debit balance
   III. Equity

   A. I only
   B. I and III only
   C. II only
   D. I, II, and III

8. A client has a margin account with $23,000 in securities and a debit of $12,000. If Reg T is 50%, the

   I. account is restricted
   II. client will receive a margin call for $500
   III. client may withdraw securities if he deposits 50% of the securities' value
   IV. account has excess equity of $5,250

   A. I and II only
   B. I and III only
   C. II, III, and IV only
   D. I, II, III, and IV

9. A client has a margin account with $23,000 in securities and a debit of $12,000. The stock increases in value to $26,000. How much money may the client withdraw from the account?

   A. $1,000
   B. $2,000
   C. $3,000
   D. $4,000

10. A customer's margin account contains securities with a market value of $50,000, a debit balance of $30,000, and no SMA balance. After the value of the securities increases to $70,000, the customer sells $20,000 worth of securities. What is SMA after the sale? (Reg T is 50%.)

    A. $0
    B. $5,000
    C. $10,000
    D. $15,000

11. Which of the following can change the SMA balance in a long account?

   I. Sale of securities in the account
   II. Market appreciation of securities in the account
   III. Interest and cash dividends deposited in the account
   IV. Decrease in value of securities in the account

   A. I only
   B. I and II only
   C. I, II, and III only
   D. I, II, III, and IV

Answers

1. **C.** The initial margin requirement is calculated by multiplying the market value of $10,000 by the Reg T requirement of 50%, which equals $5,000.

2. **A.** Equity is calculated by subtracting the debit balance of $2,250 from the current market value of $4,000, which equals $1,750.

3. **A.** The Reg T requirement is 50% of the current market value of $6,000, which equals $3,000. Equity is equal to the current market value of $6,000 minus the debit balance of $2,500, which equals $3,500. Excess equity is then calculated by subtracting the Reg T requirement of $3,000 from the equity of $3,500, which equals $500.

4. **B.** NYSE/NASD rules require a minimum equity deposit of $2,000 on the first transaction in a new margin account. After the customer sends in the required deposit, the equity is $2,000 (LMV of $3,000 − DR of $1,000 = EQ of $2,000). When the market value falls to $2,500 (a decrease of $500) the equity also declines by $500, leaving $1,500 of equity in the account.

5. **A.** The maintenance requirement in a long margin account is 25% of the market value of the stock. The equity in the account is $1,000 and the required maintenance margin is $1,500 (25% of the $6,000 long market value). Therefore, the account will receive a margin call for $500.

6. **C.** Equity may be increased by depositing cash. Depositing fully paid securities increases equity because the loan value of marginable stock is equal to 50% of its market value. SMA represents a line of credit, but there is no such thing as "cancellation" of an SMA balance.

7. **B.** The debit balance changes only when money is borrowed or deposited. A withdrawal of cash is borrowing against the loan value of the securities in the account and increases the debit balance. A deposit of cash into the account reduces the debit balance.

8. **B.** The account is restricted by $500. The client will not, however, receive a margin call for the $500 because Reg T applies only to the initial purchase. Because the account is restricted, withdrawal of securities requires a cash deposit of 50% or a deposit of securities with a loan value of 50% of the value of the securities withdrawn. The account is $5,250 above the required minimum, but this amount is not considered excess equity.

9. **A.** The account now has equity of $14,000. The Reg T requirement is $13,000. This leaves $1,000 in excess equity that may be withdrawn.

$26,000 CMV
−12,000 DR
$14,000 EQ
−13,000 Reg T
$ 1,000 EE

10. **D.** After the value of the securities in the account increased to $70,000, the customer had equity of $40,000. Because Reg T requires equity of $35,000, the customer had $5,000 in excess equity after the increase in market value. The new excess equity was credited to SMA. When the customer sold $20,000 worth of securities, half of the sale proceeds were automatically released to SMA, as prescribed by retention requirements. The $10,000 in sale proceeds released to SMA increased SMA to $15,000.

11. **C.** The sale of securities in the account (I) results in an automatic release of funds to SMA. Nonrequired cash deposits, such as interest and dividends (III), are also automatically credited to SMA. An increase in the value of the securities (II) will increase SMA if the excess equity becomes greater than existing SMA. A decrease in the market value of the securities (IV) will not increase or decrease SMA.

Pattern Day Traders

A **day trader** is one who buys and sells the same security on the same day to try to take advantage of intra-day price movements. A **pattern day trader** is one who executes four or more day trades in a five-business day period.

Under NASD/NYSE rules, the minimum equity requirement for pattern day traders is $25,000 (pattern day traders must have on deposit in the account equity of at least $25,000 on any day on which day trading occurs). The minimum maintenance margin requirement for pattern day traders is 25%, the same as for regular customers.

Pattern day traders are also treated differently when it comes to **buying power**. Buying power for day traders is four times the maintenance margin excess. **Maintenance margin excess** is defined as the equity in the account above the 25% minimum requirement. For regular customers, buying power is two times SMA.

Margin rules also prohibit day trading accounts from using **account guarantees** which are otherwise permitted. A **cross guarantee** is one where another customer, in writing, agrees to the use of money or securities in his account to carry the guaranteed accounts (i.e., to meet any margin calls).

Approval for Day Trading Accounts Member firms who promote day trading strategies must now implement procedures to approve day trading accounts.

Before opening an account, the member must:

- provide the customer with a **Risk Disclosure** statement which outlines all of the risks associated with day trading (the statement can be furnished in writing or electronically); and
- approve the account for a day trading strategy or receive from the customer a written statement that the customer does not intend to engage in day trading.

Short Sales and Margin Requirements

Selling short is a strategy an investor uses to profit from a decline in a stock's price. Selling short must always be done through a margin account because the investor borrows stock from a broker/dealer. The investor then sells the borrowed stock at the market price, with the hope of buying back the shares at a lower price. The short seller profits when the loan of stock can be repaid with shares purchased at a lower price.

In a short sale, there is a **short seller**, a **stock lender** (from whom the shares are borrowed) and a **buyer** who purchases the shares being sold short. One of the basic requirements of short selling is this: the short seller, on the dividend payment date, must make good to the stock lender for the dividends the lender is no longer receiving from the issuer. The buyer of the shares is receiving the dividends directly from the issuer. Therefore, on the dividend payment date, the short seller's account is debited the amount of the cash dividend for remittance to the stock lender.

Margin Deposits To borrow shares for short sales, an investor must make **margin deposits**. Reg T specifies that the initial margin for short sales can be met either with cash or marginable securities, just as in long margin transactions.

Terminology The Series 7 examination uses the following terms to describe activity in short margin accounts:

- **Short Market Value (SMV)**—the current market value of the stock position the investor sells short
- **Credit Register (CR)**—the amount of money in the customer's account; equal to the sales proceeds plus the margin deposit requirement
- **Equity (EQ)**—the customer's net worth in the margin account; the amount by which the credit balance exceeds the current short market value of the securities in the account

The amount of equity in the account is determined by this equation:

$$CR - SMV = EQ$$

Analyzing Short Margin Account Activity

To analyze short margin account activity, a simplified balance sheet will be used, as shown here:

CR	SMV
	EQ

When establishing a short margin account, there is a deposit minimum of $2,000. This minimum must be met even if the customer sells short less than $2,000 worth of securities. The Reg T requirement for short sales is the same as it is for long purchases: 50%.

Customer Sells Short

Customer Sells Short	Reg T Requirement	NASD/NYSE Minimum	Customer Deposit Required
100 shares at $50/sh	$2,500	$2,000	$2,500
100 shares at $30/sh	$1,500	$2,000	$2,000
100 shares at $15/sh	$750	$2,000	$2,000

Minimum Maintenance

The NASD/NYSE **minimum maintenance requirement** on short positions is 30%, compared to 25% on long positions. As with long margin accounts, the firm may impose a higher house minimum.

Test Topic Alert!

Before you go on, answer these questions:

- What is the minimum initial dollar requirement in a short margin account?
- What is the Reg T requirement in a short margin account?
- What is the minimum maintenance requirement in a short margin account?

The answers are:

1. $2,000
2. 50%
3. 30%

Short Margin Account

To illustrate how a short margin account works, assume the following:

A client sells short 1,000 shares of ABC at 70 and meets the Reg T requirement. The market value of securities falls to 60. What is the new equity in the account? The accounting in the short margin chart should appear as follows:

CR	SMV
105,000 (3)	70,000 (1)
	EQ
	35,000 (2)

- The market value of the securities sold short is entered as the SMV
- The Reg T requirement of 50% of the short market value is entered as equity
- The credit balance (CR) is the stock sales proceeds plus the equity deposited (SMV + EQ)

The **credit balance (CR)** provides security to the broker/dealer that there will be cash available for the customer to purchase the securities if the market value of the securities rises. The risk of a short account is a stock price increase; a short seller profits only if the market value of the securities declines.

Test Topic Alert!

For short margin accounting questions: once you get the credit balance by adding the SMV and EQ together, don't change it. Just use it to compute equity after a market value change with the basic equation: CR − SMV = EQ.

The following illustrates the accounting for the market value decline and the resulting new equity:

CR	SMV
105,000	~~70,000~~
	60,000 (1)
	EQ
	~~35,000~~
	45,000 (2)

- The market value of the securities sold short declines to $60,000.
- The equity increases to $45,000 as a result of the decline. This is determined as follows: CR − SMV = EQ ($105,000 − $60,000 = $45,000)

Margin Accounts

What is the status of this investor's account? Just as in long margin accounts, the short margin account statuses are:

- **Excess equity**—equity in excess of Reg T (50% of the current SMV)
- **Restricted**—equity less than Reg T, or greater than or equal to minimum maintenance
- **Maintenance call**—equity less than minimum maintenance (30% of the SMV)

By calculating the Reg T benchmark, we can see that this account has excess equity and has created SMA of $15,000, as shown:

CR	SMV	
105,000	~~70,000~~	Sma = 15,000
	60,000	
	(1)	
Reg T = 30,000	**Eq**	
Min. Mntc. = 18,000	~~35,000~~	Ee = 15,000
	45,000	
	(2)	

The excess equity and SMA of $15,000 are available because the equity in the account ($45,000) exceeds the Reg T requirement ($30,000) by $15,000. Assume now that the market value of the securities in this account rises to $80,000. How much cash must the customer deposit?

CR	SMV	
	~~60,000~~	The increase of short market
	80,000	value to $80,000 causes the equity to fall to $25,000 (CR – SMV = EQ)
		The new Reg T requirement is $40,000 (50% of $80,000); the new min. maintenance is
Reg T = 40,000 105,000	EQ	$24,000 (30% of $80,000).
Min. Mntc. = 24,000	~~45,000~~	Because the equity of $25,000
	25,000	exceeds the minimum maintenance of $24,000, there is no cash deposit required.

To find the maximum market value to which a short sale position can increase before a maintenance call is issued, apply the following formula:

Total credit balance / 130% (1.3)

This is known as the **short market value at maintenance**.

Minimum Maintenance in a Short Account

The minimum maintenance margin requirement for short accounts is 30%. However, there are exceptions based on price per share, as indicated below.

- For stock trading under $5 per share, a customer must maintain 100% of SMV or $2.50 per share, whichever is greater.

✓ **For Example:** A customer sells short 1,000 shares of stock at $4 per share. The margin deposit would be $4,000, not $2,000.

A customer sells short 1,000 shares at $2 per share. The margin deposit would be $2,500.

In both cases, the minimum maintenance margin requirement exceeds the initial requirement. Therefore, each customer must deposit the higher amount.

- For stock trading at $5 per share and above, the minimum requirement is $5 per share or 30%, whichever is greater.

✓ **For Example:** A customer has a short margin account. In it, there is one stock currently trading at $10 per share. Under NYSE rules, the minimum maintenance requirement for this account is

A. 100%
B. 30%
C. $5/share
D. $2.50/share

Answer: **C**. With the stock at $10, $5 per share is greater than 30%.

Quick Quiz 6.4   Multiple Choice

1. An investor opens a new margin account and sells short 100 shares of KLP at 45 and meets the Reg T requirement of 50%. How much equity does the investor have in the account?

    A. $2,000
    B. $2,250
    C. $4,500
    D. $6,750

Margin Accounts

2. An investor opens a new margin account and sells short 100 shares of KLP at 42, with Reg T at 50%. What is the investor's required deposit?

   A. $1,050
   B. $2,000
   C. $2,100
   D. $4,200

3. An investor has an established margin account with a short market value of $6,450 and a credit balance of $9,750, with Reg T at 50%. How much equity does the investor have in the account?

   A. $3,300
   B. $4,775
   C. $6,450
   D. $9,750

4. An investor has an established margin account with a short market value of $4,000 and a credit balance of $6,750, with Reg T at 50%. How much excess equity does the investor have in the account?

   A. $750
   B. $1,500
   C. $2,000
   D. $2,750

5. An investor opens a new margin account and sells short 100 shares of COD at 32.50, with Reg T at 50%. What is the investor's required deposit?

   A. $812.50
   B. $1,625
   C. $2,000
   D. $3,250

6. A customer sells short 100 shares of ABC at $80 per share and meets the minimum Reg T requirement. Two months later, he covers the short position by buying ABC at $70 per share. This was the only transaction in the account. What is the maximum amount he can withdraw from the account after closing the short position? (Reg T is 50%.)

   A. $1,000
   B. $4,000
   C. $5,000
   D. $12,000

Margin Accounting 343

7. An investor opens a new margin account and sells short 100 shares of ALF at 10, with Reg T at 50%. What is the investor's required deposit?

   A. $250
   B. $500
   C. $1,000
   D. $2,000

Answers

1. **B.** *Equity in a short margin account is calculated by subtracting the short market value of $4,500 from the credit balance of $6,750 ($4,500 stock sales proceeds + $2,250 initial margin deposit of 50% = $2,250).*

2. **C.** *The required deposit is calculated by multiplying the market value of $4,200 by the Reg T requirement of 50%, which equals $2,100.*

3. **A.** *Equity in a short margin account is calculated by subtracting the short market value of $6,450 from the credit balance of $9,750, which equals $3,300.*

4. **A.** *The Reg T requirement and equity must be calculated before excess equity can be determined. The Reg T requirement is 50% of the short market value of $4,000, which equals $2,000. Equity is calculated by subtracting the short market value of $4,000 from the credit balance of $6,750, which equals $2,750. Excess equity is then calculated by subtracting the Reg T requirement of $2,000 from the equity of $2,750, which equals $750.*

5. **C.** *When selling stock short in a new account, an investor must meet the NASD/NYSE initial minimum requirement of $2,000. This is required although the Reg T requirement is $1,625 ($3,250 × 50%).*

6. **C.** *The customer originally sold the stock at $80 per share and deposited $4,000 per the Reg T requirement ($8,000 × 50%). He now has an SMV of $8,000 and a credit balance of $12,000 ($8,000 sale proceeds + $4,000 deposit). The market value of the stock is now down to $7,000. The customer may withdraw the equity of $5,000 when the position is closed.*

7. **D.** *The Reg T requirement is $500 ($1,000 × 50%). When selling stock short in a new account, an investor must meet the NASD/NYSE initial minimum requirement of $2,000.*

Combined Accounts

A client who has a margin account with both long and short positions in different securities has a **combined account**. In combined accounts, equity and margin requirements are determined by calculating the long and short positions separately and combining the results.

The following example shows the use of the long and short margin charts in calculating combined equity.

An investor has the following margin account positions:

LMV = $50,000; SMV = $40,000; CR = $60,000; DR = $20,000
SMA = $5,000 (The combined equity in this example is $50,000)

	LMV	DR		CR	SMV
		20,000			40,000
Reg T = 25,000	50,000	EQ	Reg T = 20,000	60,000	EQ
Min. Mntc. = 12,500		30,000	Min. Mntc. = 12,000		20,000

The basic equation for the calculation of combined equity is:

$$LMV + CR - DR - SMV = EQ$$

Test Topic Alert! Besides asking about the calculation of combined equity, questions may ask for combined Reg T requirement or combined minimum maintenance requirements. As with combined equity questions, first calculate the long, then the short, and add the two together.

Quick Quiz 6.5   Multiple Choice

1. A customer's account contains the following balances:

   LMV = $20,000
   CR = $48,000
   DR = $7,000
   SMV = $30,000

   What is the amount of SMA in the account?

   A. $0
   B. $2,000
   C. $3,000
   D. $6,000

2. The formula for computing equity in a combined margin account is

   A. Long market value − short market value + credit balance + debit balance
   B. Long market value − short market value + debit balance − credit balance
   C. Long market value + credit balance − short market value − debit balance
   D. Long market value + short market value − debit balance + credit balance

3. An investor's margin account has the following positions:

   LMV = $50,000
   SMV = $27,000
   DR = $12,000
   CR = $22,000

   What is the total equity in the account?

   A. $43,000
   B. $39,000
   C. $37,000
   D. $33,000

Answers

1. **D.** On the long side, the customer has long market value of $20,000 minus a debit of $7,000, leaving him with equity of $13,000. To find excess equity, subtract 50% of the long market value from the equity in the account: $13,000 – $10,000 = $3,000 excess equity. On the short side, the customer's credit balance is $48,000 minus the short market value of $30,000, which leaves $18,000 of equity. To find excess equity, subtract 50% of the short market value ($15,000) from the equity in the account ($18,000), leaving $3,000 in excess equity.

2. **C.** The formula for equity in a long account is the long market value minus the debit balance. The formula for equity in a short account is the credit balance minus the short market value. Together, they equal answer C.

3. **D.** The equity in a long account is LMV minus DR ($50,000 – $12,000 = $38,000). The equity in a short account is CR minus SMV ($22,000 – $27,000 = -$5,000). The net equity position is $33,000. Note that there is negative equity in the short account.

Special Memorandum Account

As discussed in both the long and short margin accounting sections, SMA is generated from excess equity in margin accounts. The following table reviews the effects on SMA of various account activities in a long margin account.

Activity	Effect on SMA	Remarks
Rise in market value	Increase	Only if the new excess equity is higher than the old SMA.
Sale of securities	Increase	The client is entitled to excess equity in the account after the sale, or to 50% of the sale proceeds, whichever is greater.
Deposit of cash	Increase	The full amount of the deposit is credited to SMA.
Deposit of marginable securities	Increase	Increased by the loan value of the securities deposited, as prescribed by Reg T at the time of the deposit. (50%)
Dividends or interest	Increase	100% of a cash dividend or interest (a non-required deposit) is credited to SMA.
Purchase of securities	Decrease	The margin requirement on new purchases is deducted from SMA. If SMA is insufficient to meet the charge, a Reg T call is issued for the balance.
Withdrawal of cash	Decrease	The full amount of the cash withdrawal is deducted from SMA. Remaining equity may not fall below the NASD/NYSE or house equity requirement.
Fall in long account market value	No effect	After the SMA balance is established, it is not affected by a fall in market value in a long account.
Interest charges to account	No effect	SMA remains the same.
Stock dividend or split	No effect	SMA remains the same.

Pledging Customer Securities for Loans

Hypothecation is the pledging of customer securities as collateral for margin loans.

When customers sign margin agreements, permission is given for this process to occur. After customers pledge their securities to the broker/dealer, the broker/dealer **rehypothecates** (re-pledges) them as collateral for a loan from the bank. Reg U oversees the process of banks lending money based on customer securities as collateral.

Although they may borrow 100% of the customer's debit balance, broker/dealers are limited to **pledging** 140% of a customer's debit balance as collateral. Any customer securities in excess of this amount must be physically segregated. The firm cannot commingle customer securities with securities owned by the firm.

Firms can only commingle one customer's securities with another customer's securities for hypothecation if customers have given specific permission by signing the hypothecation agreement.

Rehypothecation of Customer Securities

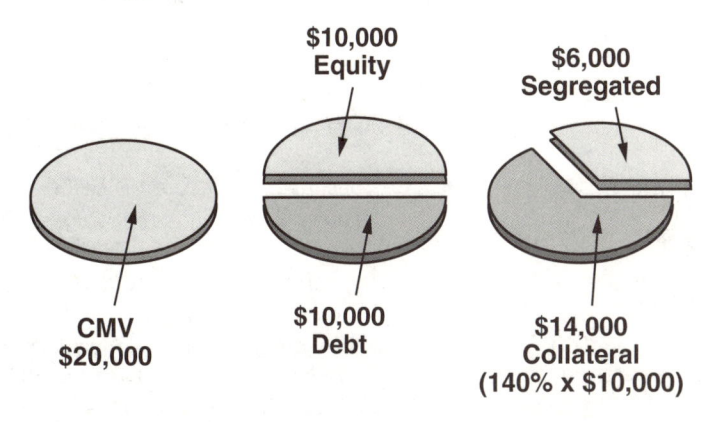

CMV $20,000

$10,000 Equity
$10,000 Debt

$6,000 Segregated
$14,000 Collateral (140% x $10,000)

Quick Quiz 6.6 Multiple Choice

1. If a customer's long margin account has a market value of $50,000 and a debit balance of $12,000, what is the SMA (Reg T 50%)?

   A. $4,800
   B. $8,000
   C. $13,000
   D. $38,000

2. Which of the following increases SMA?

   A. Receipt of a cash dividend
   B. Decline in market value of long positions
   C. Withdrawal of margin securities
   D. Purchase of margin securities

3. A customer is long 200 shares of MTN at 30 and 400 shares of DWQ at 20 in a margin account. The debit balance in the account is $8,000. The customer sells 200 of the DWQ shares for $4,000. The credit to SMA is

A. $0
B. $1,000
C. $2,000
D. $4,000

Answers

1. **C.** The account status is as follows:

    $50,000   LMV
    −12,000   DR
    $38,000   EQ
    −25,000   Reg T 50%
    $13,000   SMA

2. **A.** Cash dividends are automatically credited to SMA.

3. **C.** Because this account is below 50% margin, the account is restricted ($6,000 equity/$14,000 market value = 42.8% equity).

    When securities are sold in a restricted account, 50% of the proceeds must be retained in the account, with the other 50% available to the customer. Thus, the 50% proceeds are credited to SMA. This means that the amount of the line of credit can be borrowed from the account or can be applied toward future purchases. Because $4,000 worth of securities were sold, $2,000 (50%) is credited to SMA.

Margin Accounts HotSheet

Long and Short T-Charts:

LMV	DR		CR	SMV
	EQ			EQ

Margin Accounts HotSheet

Account Status:

Excess Equity	Creates SMA	

━━━━━━━━━━━━━━━━━━━━━━━━━━━━━━━ Reg T

Restricted Status
Buy—Pay 50%
Sell—50% retention
Withdraw securities—Deposit 50%

━━━━━━━━━━━━━━━━━━━━━━━━━━━━━━━ Min. Maintenance

Maintenance Call
Deposit Cash
Deposit Securities
Sell Securities in an Account

Market Value at Maintenance:
- Long account: DR / .75
- Short account: CR / 1.30

Margin Agreement:
- Credit agreement: required; investor pays variable rate interest on money borrowed
- Hypothecation agreement: required; investor pledges securities to broker/dealer
- Loan consent form: optional; if signed, broker/dealer may loan customer margin securities for short sales

Reg T Exemptions:
- Government securities, municipals, corporate debt are subject to SRO requirements only

SMA in Long Account:
- Increased by:
  – increase in market value of securities in account
  – nonrequired cash deposit ($1 for $1)
  – sale of securities (50% of sales proceeds to SMA)
- Decreased by:
  – purchase of securities or withdrawal of cash, not market value decline

SMA Buying Power:
- $1 of SMA buys $2 of stock (2 to 1)

Maintenance Call:
- Must be met promptly; $1,000 exemption

Initial Requirement:
- Reg T or $2,000, whichever is greater (exception for long account: 100% of purchase price if less than $2,000)

Series 7 Unit Test 6

1. An investor opens a new margin account and sells short 200 shares of ALF at 56, with Reg T at 50%. The investor deposits the initial margin requirement. What is the investor's credit balance?

    A. $2,000
    B. $5,600
    C. $11,200
    D. $16,800

2. According to Reg T and the NASD/NYSE, initial and maintenance margin requirements for a short account are

    A. 50% initial; 25% maintenance
    B. 50% initial; 30% maintenance
    C. 50% initial; 50% maintenance
    D. 70% initial; 50% maintenance

3. A customer purchases 200 shares of ABC Health Care at $60 per share and meets the initial margin requirement. If ABC announces an acquisition and its stock appreciates on the news to $75, how much cash can the customer withdraw after this market move?

    A. $0
    B. $1,000
    C. $1,500
    D. $3,000

4. SMA in a long account will be affected by the

    I. sale of securities in the account
    II. decline in market value of securities
    III. cash deposited by the customers
    IV. interest charged on debit balances

    A. I, II and III only
    B. I and III only
    C. I and IV only
    D. II, III and IV only

5. A member firm may commingle the securities of 2 or more customers

    A. with the customers' written permission
    B. with the SEC's written permission
    C. with the NASD's written permission
    D. under no circumstances

6. An investor sells stock short to

    A. profit if prices decline
    B. establish a permanent tax loss
    C. defer taxes
    D. liquidate a long stock position

7. The formula for computing equity in a combined margin account is

    A. long market value – short market value + credit balance + debit balance
    B. long market value – short market value + debit balance – credit balance
    C. long market value + credit balance – short market value – debit balance
    D. long market value + short market value – debit balance + credit balance

8. A customer's margin account contains the following securities:

    100 shares of DEF, CMV $40 per share
    100 shares of AMF, CMV $50 per share
    100 shares of KLP, CMV $80 per share

    The account has a debit balance of $10,800. How much equity is in the account?

    A. $4,030
    B. $6,200
    C. $11,050
    D. $17,000

9. A customer is long 200 shares of MTN at 30 and 400 shares of DWQ at 20 in a margin account. The debit balance in the account is $8,000. The customer sells 200 of the DWQ shares for $4,000. The credit to SMA is

    A. $0
    B. $1,000
    C. $2,000
    D. $4,000

10. An investor opens a new margin account and sells short 200 shares of DWQ at 65, with Reg T at 50%. What is the investor's required deposit?

    A. $2,775
    B. $3,250
    C. $6,500
    D. $13,000

11. In a new margin account, a customer buys 300 XYZ at 48 and simultaneously writes 3 XYZ Jan 50 calls at 1. The Reg T margin requirement is

    A. $6,900
    B. $7,200
    C. $7,350
    D. $7,500

12. A customer has a restricted margin account with SMA of $2,500. If the customer wishes to purchase $10,000 worth of stock, the customer must deposit

    A. $0
    B. $2,500
    C. $5,000
    D. $10,000

Series 7 Unit Test 6 Answers & Rationale

1. **D.** The investor's credit balance is calculated by adding the short sale price of $11,200 to the initial margin deposit of $5,600 ($16,800).
QID: 30051

2. **B.** Initial Reg T margin is 50% and the maintenance margin is 30% for short accounts.
QID: 28223

3. **C.** The customer could withdraw cash equal to the SMA. A purchase of 200 shares at $60 per share would require an initial deposit of $6,000 on a market value of $12,000. The customer would have $6,000 in equity and a $6,000 debit. After a rise to $75 a share, the stock's market value would be $15,000. The customer's debit balance would remain unchanged at $6,000, but the equity would increase to $9,000 ($15,000 CMV − $6,000 DR). For every $1 increase in market value, 50 cents of SMA is created.
QID: 28212

4. **B.** Whenever stock is sold, half of the sales proceeds are credited to SMA. Nonrequired cash deposits are credited to SMA in full. SMA only goes down when a customer uses it to borrow from the account or purchase securities; it is not affected by declines in market value or by interest charges.
QID: 34896

5. **A.** A member may commingle a customer's securities with those of other customers only if all of the customers involved have given their written consent. This occurs in margin accounts where the margin securities of multiple customers are commingled at a bank for debit balance financing purposes.
QID: 28236

6. **A.** Short sales are used to profit if prices fall.
QID: 28215

7. **C.** The formula for equity in a long account is the long market value minus the debit balance. The formula for equity in a short account is the credit balance minus the short market value.
QID: 28213

8. **B.** The total market value in the account is $17,000: CMV − DR = EQ; $17,000 CMV − $10,800 DR = $6,200.
QID: 32193

9. **C.** Because this account is below 50% margin, the account is restricted ($6,000 equity divided by $14,000 market value = 42.8% equity). When securities are sold in a restricted account, 50% of the proceeds are released to SMA. Because $4,000 worth of securities were sold, $2,000 (50%) is credited to SMA.
QID: 28230

10. **C.** The required deposit is calculated by multiplying the short market value of $13,000 by the Reg T requirement of 50%, which equals $6,500.
QID: 30050

11. **B.** The Reg T requirement for purchasing $14,400 of stock (300 × 48) is $7,200. The Reg T requirement for writing covered calls is zero. Therefore, the Reg T requirement for establishing both these positions is $7,200. The margin call (deposit) would be $6,900. The requirement can be reduced by the $300 premiums received. By depositing the $6,900, the customer will have $7,200 in the account.
QID: 36403

12. **B.** With SMA of $2,500, the customer can purchase $5,000 of stock without having to make a deposit. Buying power is twice SMA. This leaves $5,000 to purchase which requires a deposit of $2,500. Or, alternatively, the purchase of $10,000 requires a $5,000 deposit, which can be reduced dollar for dollar by the existing SMA.
QID: 36445

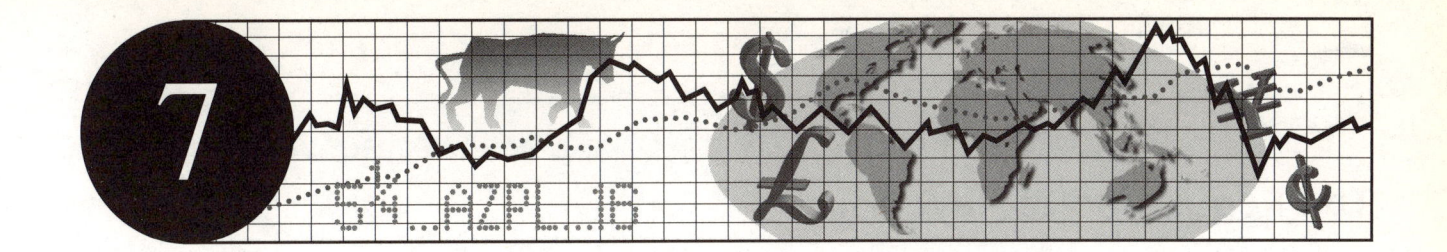

Issuing Securities

INTRODUCTION

This unit describes the process of bringing new issues to the marketplace. It focuses on registering securities, regulations that affect investment bankers, and special exemptions from the normal registration process.

New securities are sold in the primary market. The new issue market is regulated primarily by the Securities Act of 1933, which requires issuers of securities to provide sufficient information to the investing public in a prospectus so that investors may make informed investment decisions. The information must be filed with the SEC before an issue can be offered to the public. The Act of 1933 strictly prohibits fraudulent information or activity in connection with the underwriting and distribution of new issues.

This unit accounts for about 10–15 questions on the Series 7 exam.

UNIT OBJECTIVES

When you have completed this unit, you should be able to:

- describe the scope of the Securities Act of 1933 and the role of the SEC;
- identify the steps in the registration process of nonexempt securities;
- describe the role of investment bankers and syndicates in primary offerings;
- compare and contrast firm commitment and best efforts underwriting agreements;
- list and describe transactions that are exempt from the registration and prospectus requirements of the Securities Act of 1933; and
- define hot issue securities and identify the rules that apply to their sale.

The Regulation of New Issues

After the stock market crash of 1929, Congress examined the causes of the debacle and passed several laws designed to prevent its recurrence. This legislation included the **Securities Act of 1933** and the **Securities Exchange Act of 1934**, among others.

The Legislative Framework

The Securities Act of 1933 The Securities Act of 1933 regulates new issues of corporate securities sold to the public and requires securities issuers to provide enough information for investors to make fully informed buying decisions. This information must be filed with the SEC and published in a prospectus. The act prohibits any fraudulent activity in connection with the underwriting and issuing of all securities.

The Securities Exchange Act of 1934 The Securities Exchange Act of 1934 addresses secondary trading of securities, personnel involved in secondary trading, and fraudulent trading practices. It also created the **Securities and Exchange Commission** (SEC) to oversee the industry.

In 1938, the act was amended by the **Maloney Act**, which provides for the establishment of self-regulatory bodies to help police the industry. Under Maloney Act provisions, the **National Association of Securities Dealers** (NASD) regulates **over-the-counter** (OTC) trading in much the same way as the exchanges regulate their members.

The Trust Indenture Act of 1939 The Trust Indenture Act of 1939 was created to provide the same sort of protection to the purchasers of debt securities as is afforded to investors in equities. The act prohibits the sale of any corporate debt security exceeding $5 million with a maturity of more than nine months unless it is issued under a trust indenture.

The **trust indenture** is a contract that gives a trustee the powers necessary to enforce the issuer's obligations and the debt holder's rights. In addition to providing full disclosure about the nature of the debt issue and the issuer, the trust indenture identifies the trustee's rights and responsibilities.

The Three Phases of an Underwriting

Registration of Securities

The Securities Act of 1933 is also referred to as the **Paper Act**, **Full Disclosure Act**, **New Issues Act**, **Truth in Securities Act**, and **Prospectus Act**. The act's main purpose is to ensure that the investing public is fully informed about a security and its issuing company when the security is first sold in the primary market. The 1933 act protects investors who buy new issues by:

- requiring registration of new issues that are to be distributed interstate;
- requiring an issuer to provide full and fair disclosure about itself and the offering;
- requiring an issuer to make available all material information necessary for an investor to judge the issue's merit;
- regulating the underwriting and distribution of primary and secondary issues; and
- providing criminal penalties for fraud in the issuance of new securities.

The Registration Statement

An issuer must file with the SEC a **registration statement** disclosing material information about the issue. Part of the registration statement is a **prospectus**, which must be provided to all purchasers of the new issue.

The registration statement must contain:

- a description of the issuer's business;
- the names and addresses of company officers and directors, their salaries, and a five-year business history of each;
- the amount of corporate securities company officers and directors own, and identification of investors who own 10% or more of the company;
- the company's capitalization, including its equity and debt;
- a description of how the proceeds will be used; and
- whether the company is involved in any legal proceedings.

The underwriter may assist the issuer in preparing and filing the registration statement and prospectus. However, the accuracy and adequacy of these documents is the responsibility of the issuer.

The registration statement must be signed by the issuer's chief executive officer, chief financial officer, and chief accounting officer, as well as a majority of the issuer's board of directors.

State Registration State securities laws, also called **blue-sky laws**, require state registration of securities, broker/dealers, and registered reps. According to the Uniform Securities Act, an issuer or investment banker may blue-sky an issue by using one of the following three methods.

- **Qualification:** typically used for intrastate offerings, the issue is registered with the state independent of federal registration and it must meet all state requirements.
- **Coordination:** typically used for IPOs, the issuer registers simultaneously with the state and the SEC. Both registrations become effective on the same date.
- **Filing (Notification):** certain states allow some issues to be **blue-skied** by having the issuer notify the state of the issue's SEC registration (the state requires no registration statement, although certain other information must be filed and specific financial criteria must be met).

Most states exempt securities from individual registration if they meet one or more other requirements—typically, listing on a regional or national stock exchange or qualifying as a **National Association of Securities Dealers Automated Quotation system (Nasdaq)** or **Nasdaq National Market (NNM) stock**. This is sometimes known as the **blue chip exemption**. Bonds of investment grade may also be exempt. This is called a **manual exemption**.

Each state has its own registration requirements not only for securities, but also for the registration of broker/dealers, investment advisers, and registered reps. A person or broker/dealer must usually be registered in any state in which it sells or attempts to sell securities.

Test Topic Alert! It is critical that you are able to define the scope of the Act of 1933 for several exam questions. Associate these key phrases with the Securities Act of 1933.

Act of 1933 =

- new issues
- primary market
- investment banking
- full and fair disclosure
- *The Paper Act* because of registrations and disclosure documents

The Cooling-Off Period

Following the issuer's filing of a registration statement with the SEC, a 20-day **cooling-off period** begins. After the issuer (with the underwriter's assistance) files with the SEC for registration of the securities, the cooling-off period ensues before the registration becomes effective.

The registration can become effective as early as 20 calendar days after the date the SEC has received it. In practice, however, the cooling-off period is seldom the minimum 20 days; the SEC usually takes longer to clear registration statements.

The Three Phases of an Underwriting

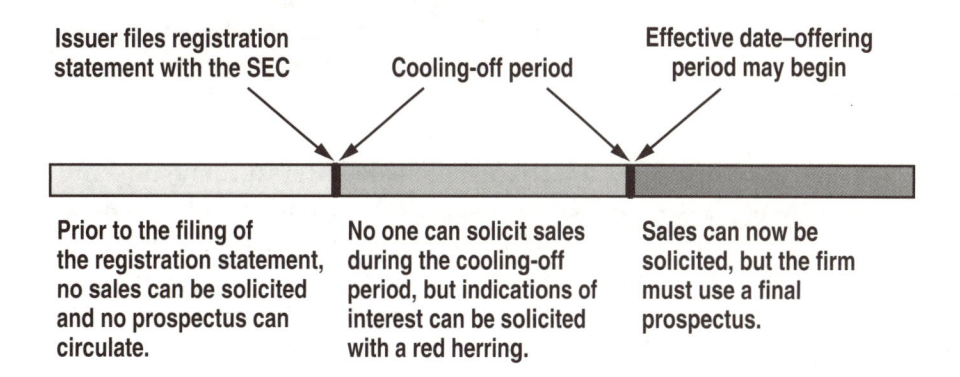

Issuer files registration statement with the SEC → **Cooling-off period** → **Effective date–offering period may begin**

Prior to the filing of the registration statement, no sales can be solicited and no prospectus can circulate.

No one can solicit sales during the cooling-off period, but indications of interest can be solicited with a red herring.

Sales can now be solicited, but the firm must use a final prospectus.

If it finds that the registration statement needs revision or expansion, the SEC may suspend the review and issue a **deficiency letter**. The 20-day cooling-off period resumes when the issuer submits a corrected registration statement.

The cooling-off period can last several months due to the time it takes to make additions and corrections. The SEC sometimes issues a **stop order**, which demands that all underwriting activities cease. This may be done if requirements of the 1933 Act have not been met or if fraud is suspected.

Preliminary Prospectus

The **preliminary prospectus (red herring)** can be used as a prospecting tool, allowing underwriters and selling group members to gauge investor interest and gather indications of interest. There is no final price included in the preliminary prospectus. The preliminary prospectus must be made available to any customer who expresses interest in the securities between the SEC registration filing date and the effective date.

An indication of interest is an investor's declaration that he might be interested in purchasing some of the issue from the underwriter after the security comes out of registration. An investor's indication of interest is not a commitment to buy because sales are prohibited until after the registration becomes effective (the **effective date**).

Test Topic Alert!

During the cooling-off period, underwriters cannot:

- make offers to sell the securities;
- take orders; or
- distribute sales literature or advertising material.

However, they can:

- take indications of interest;
- distribute preliminary prospectuses; or
- publish tombstone ads to provide information about the potential availability of the securities.

✓ **Take Note:** A tombstone ad will show the anticipated gross proceeds of the issue. A final prospectus will show both the gross and net proceeds to the issuer.

Advertising a New Issue

Advertising and **sales literature** include any notice, circular, advertisement, letter, or other communication published or transmitted to any person. The only advertising allowed during the cooling-off period is a **tombstone ad**, a simple statement of facts regarding the issue. The tombstone ad announces a new issue, but does not offer the securities for sale. The tombstone may appear before or after the effective date. Issuers or underwriters are not required to publish tombstone ads.

Due Diligence

Near the end of the cooling-off period, the underwriter holds a **due diligence** meeting. The preliminary studies, investigations, research, meetings, and compilation of information about a corporation and a proposed new issue that go on during an underwriting are known collectively as due diligence.

The underwriter must conduct a formal due diligence meeting to provide information about the issue, the issuer's financial background, and the intended use of the proceeds. Representatives of the issuer and the underwriter attend these meetings and answer questions from brokers, securities analysts, and institutions.

As part of the due diligence process, investment bankers must:

- examine the use of the proceeds;
- perform financial analysis and feasibility studies;
- determine the company's stability; and
- determine whether the risk is reasonable.

The Final Prospectus

When the registration statement becomes effective, the issuer amends the preliminary prospectus and adds information, including the final offering price and the underwriting spread for the **final prospectus**. Registered representatives may then take orders from those customers who indicated interest in buying during the cooling-off period.

A copy of the final prospectus must precede or accompany all sales confirmations. The prospectus must include the following:

- description of the offering;
- offering price;

- selling discounts;
- offering date;
- use of the proceeds;
- description of the underwriting, but not the actual contract;
- statement of the possibility that the issue's price may be stabilized;
- history of the business;
- risks to the purchasers;
- description of management;
- material financial information;
- legal opinion concerning the formation of the corporation; and
- SEC disclaimer.

SEC Review   The SEC examines the prospectus for completeness. It does not guarantee the disclosure's accuracy nor do they approve the security; rather they clear it for distribution. Implying that the SEC has approved the issue violates federal law. The front of every prospectus must contain a clearly printed SEC disclaimer specifying the limits of the SEC's review procedures. A typical SEC disclaimer clause reads as follows:

These securities have not been approved or disapproved by the Securities and Exchange Commission or by any State Securities Commission nor has the Securities and Exchange Commission or any State Securities Commission passed upon the accuracy or adequacy of this prospectus. Any representation to the contrary is a criminal offense.

The information supplied to the SEC becomes public once a registration statement is filed.

Aftermarket Sales by Prospectus

In certain offerings, a final prospectus must be delivered by all members to buyers in the secondary market for a specified time following the effective date. This is termed the **prospectus delivery requirement period**.

For initial public offerings (IPOs):

- 90 days if the security is to be quoted in the *Pink Sheets* or over the OTCBB (non-Nasdaq)
- 25 days if the security is to be listed on an exchange or quoted over Nasdaq

For additional issue offerings:

- If the security is listed or quoted over Nasdaq, a prospectus must be delivered only in connection with purchases at the public offering price. Once the distribution is complete, there is no obligation to deliver a prospectus in secondary market transactions
- If the security is non-Nasdaq, the prospectus delivery requirement period is 40 days

362 Issuing Securities

✓ *Take Note:* If a prospectus delivery requirement period exists in the secondary market, a prospectus must be delivered by all dealers including those that did not participate in the distribution.

✓ *Take Note:* An associated person may never mark (or use a highlighter) a prospectus, whether preliminary or final. Doing so violates federal securities law.

Quick Quiz 7.1

Answer **Y** if the activity is permitted during the cooling-off period, **N** if not.

___ 1. Indications of interest are gathered.

___ 2. Tombstone ads are published.

___ 3. Sales literature is sent to future clients.

___ 4. Post-dated checks are accepted.

___ 5. Red herrings are provided to potential customers.

___ 6. Orders are taken.

___ 7. A due diligence meeting is held.

___ 8. An offer to sell the new stock when available is published in a newspaper.

Answers 1. **Y.**   2. **Y.**   3. **N.**   4. **N.**   5. **Y.**   6. **N.**
7. **Y.**   8. **N.**

Quick Quiz 7.2

Match each of the following numbers with the appropriate description below.

A. 10
B. 20
C. 25
D. 40
E. 90

___ 1. Number of days of prospectus delivery required for a first time offering of securities to be listed on an exchange.

___ 2. Number of days of prospectus delivery required for a non-Nasdaq IPO.

___ 3. Minimum number of days in the SEC cooling-off period.

___ 4. Number of days of prospectus delivery required for an additional issue that is included in the *Pink Sheets*.

___ 5. The prospectus must list the names of all persons who own more than this percentage of a company's outstanding stock.

Answers   1. **C.**   2. **E.**   3. **B.**   4. **D.**   5. **A.**

Quick Quiz 7.3 Multiple Choice

1. Which of the following is not required in a preliminary prospectus?

   A. Written statement in red that the prospectus may be subject to change and amendment and that a final prospectus will be issued
   B. Purpose for which the funds being raised will be used
   C. Final offering price
   D. Financial status and history of the company

2. Which of the following statements about a red herring is NOT true?

   A. A red herring is used to obtain indications of interest from investors.
   B. The final offering price does not appear in a red herring.
   C. Additional information may be added to a red herring at a later date.
   D. A registered rep may send a copy of a company's research report with it.

3. As a registered representative, you can use a preliminary prospectus to

   A. obtain indications of interest from investors
   B. solicit orders from investors for the purchase of a new issue
   C. solicit an approval of the offering from SEC
   D. obtain the NASD's authorization to sell the issue

4. If the SEC has cleared an issue, which of the following statements is TRUE?

   A. The SEC has guaranteed the issue.
   B. The underwriter has filed a standard registration statement.
   C. The SEC has endorsed the issue.
   D. The SEC has guaranteed the accuracy of the information in the prospectus.

Answers

1. **C.** *A preliminary prospectus is issued before the price is established, and it does not include the eventual offering date or the spread.*

2. **D.** *A registered rep is prohibited from sending a research report with either a preliminary or final prospectus.*

3. **A.** *A preliminary prospectus is used to obtain indications of interest from investors.*

4. **B.** *The SEC does not approve, endorse, or guarantee the accuracy of a registration statement.*

The Underwriting Process

The issuer will enlist the help of an **underwriter**, a broker/dealer that specializes in investment banking and the distribution of new issues. The underwriter will often advise the issuer regarding the best financing mechanism (equity or debt) in light of current market conditions and tax considerations.

The underwriter will also normally form an **underwriting syndicate**, a group of other broker-dealers, to assist in the distribution of the new issue. An underwriter may commit to distribute a new issue in several different ways, each involving a different degree of risk to the underwriter. The degree of risk the underwriter assumes in the distribution of a new issue also affects the level of compensation they receive for the underwriting.

Investment Banking

A business or municipal government that plans to issue securities usually works with an **investment bank**, a securities broker/dealer that underwrites new issues. An investment bank's functions may include the following.

- Advising corporations on the best ways to raise long-term capital
- Raising capital for issuers by distributing new securities
- Buying securities from issuers and reselling them to the public
- Distributing large blocks of stock to the public and to institutions
- Helping issuers comply with securities laws

Participants in a Corporate New Issue

The main participants in a new issue are the company selling the securities and the broker/dealer acting as the underwriter.

The Issuer The **issuer** (the party selling the securities to raise money) is responsible for:
- filing the registration statement with the SEC;
- filing a registration statement with the states in which it intends to sell securities (also known as **blue-skying** the issue); and
- negotiating the securities' price and the amount of the spread with the underwriter.

The Underwriter The **underwriter** assists with registration and distribution of the new security and may advise the corporate issuer on the best way to raise capital. The underwriter's considerations include the following.

- **Stocks or bonds?** Although debt financing comprises the bulk of corporate financing, if bonds are currently selling with high coupon rates, the company may choose to issue stock. Determining the cheapest cost of capital is a very important role of the investment bank.
- **Tax consequences of the offering.** The interest a corporation pays on its bonds is tax deductible; cash dividends to stockholders are paid out of after-tax profits.
- **Money-market financing.** Money-market instruments are a short-term financing mechanism, typically one year or less.
- **Capital market financing.** The capital markets represent long-term financing for secured bonds, debentures, and preferred or common stock. These securities require registration and sale by prospectus.

Test Topic Alert! Underwriters of nonexempt corporate securities are required to be NASD member firms. US nonmember firms, like banks, cannot participate as investment bankers in corporate issues. Banks may participate in municipal underwritings.

Types of Offerings

An **offering** is identified by who is selling the securities and whether or not the company is already publicly traded.

New Issues The **new issue market** is composed of companies going public by selling common stock to the public for the first time in an **initial public offering (IPO)**.

Additional Issues The **additional issue** market is made up of new securities issued by companies that are already publicly owned. For instance, these companies may increase their equity capitalization by issuing more stock and having an underwriter either distribute the stock in a public offering or arrange for the shares to be sold in a private placement. In addition to being classified as new or additional issues of stock, offerings can be classified by the final distribution of their proceeds.

Primary Offering — A **primary offering** is one in which the proceeds of the underwriting go to the issuing corporation. It may do this at any time and in any amount, provided the total stock outstanding does not exceed the amount authorized in the corporation's bylaws.

Secondary Offering — A **secondary offering** is one in which one or more major stockholders in the corporation are selling all or a major portion of their holdings. The underwriting proceeds are paid to the stockholders rather than to the corporation.

Split Offering (Combined Distribution) — A **split offering** is a combination of a primary and a secondary offering. The corporation issues a portion of the stock offered and existing shareholders offer the balance.

Shelf Offering (Rule 415) — Through a **shelf offering**, an issuer can register new securities without selling the entire issue at once. The issuer can sell portions of a registered shelf offering over a two-year period without having to reregister the security, but a supplemental prospectus must be filed before each sale. Shelf registrations can be used for both equity and debt offerings.

Offerings and Markets

	New Issue (IPO) Market	Additional Issue Market
Primary Offering	Company is going public; underwriting proceeds go to the company	Company is already public; underwriting proceeds go to the company
Secondary Offering	Company is going public; underwriting proceeds go to the selling stockholders	Company is already public; underwriting proceeds go to the selling stockholders

Public Offerings and Private Placements

Corporate securities are sold to investors through either public offerings or private placements.

Public Offering — In a **public offering**, securities are sold to the investing public through one or more broker/dealers.

Private Placement — A **private placement** occurs when the issuing company, usually with the assistance of its investment bank, sells securities to private investors as opposed to the general investing public. Although private placement buyers tend to be institutional investors, securities may be sold to small groups of wealthy individuals. When an issuer privately places securities with investors, there can be no solicitation of the general public. Private placements are generally exempt from the registration requirements of the Securities Act of 1933.

Underwriting Sequence

Forming the Syndicate The syndicate and selling group may be assembled either before or after the issue is awarded to the underwriter. In **competitive bidding**, the syndicate is assembled first and syndicate members work together to arrive at the bid. In **negotiated underwriting**, the syndicate may be formed after the issuer and underwriting manager have negotiated the terms of the offering.

Pricing the New Issue of Publicly Traded Securities The underwriter advises the issuing corporation on the best price at which to offer securities to the public. The following variables may be considered when pricing new issues.

- Indications of interest from the underwriter's book
- Prevailing market conditions, including recent offerings, and the prices of similar new issues
- Price the syndicate members will accept
- **Price/earnings (P/E) ratios** of similar companies and the company's most recent earnings report (at what price the shares must be offered so that the P/E ratio is in line with the P/Es of other similar publicly traded stocks)
- The company's dividend payment record (if any) and financial health
- The company's debt ratio

An issue's price or yield must be determined by the **effective date** of the registration. The effective date is when the security begins to trade.

Stabilizing Price In the case of a stock offering, when demand is considerably less than supply for a new issue, the price in the **aftermarket** is likely to fall. Under these circumstances, the underwriter can **stabilize** the security by bidding for shares in the open market. The managing underwriter can enter or can appoint a syndicate member to enter stabilizing bids for the security until the end of the offering period.

Test Topic Alert! Stabilizing bids must not be made at a price higher than the public offering price (POP). Stabilization is not illegal; however, if the stabilization bid is made at a price higher than the public offering price, it is called **pegging**, or **fixing**, and is strictly prohibited. If public buying interest does not increase, the managing underwriter may have no choice but to abandon the POP, pull the stabilizing bid, and let the stock find its own price level.

Quick Quiz 7.4   Multiple Choice

1. ALFA Enterprises has filed an offering of 425,000 shares of common stock. One-third of the shares are being sold by existing stockholders, and the balance are new shares. Which of the following statements are TRUE?

    I. ALFA will receive the proceeds from the entire sale.
    II. This offering is a combined distribution.
    III. The selling stockholders will receive some of the proceeds.
    IV. This offering is an exchange distribution.

    A. I and II
    B. I and IV
    C. II and III
    D. II, III and IV

2. The principal functions of an investment banker are to

    I. distribute securities to the public
    II. provide a secondary market
    III. provide financing for an individual
    IV. advise the issuer about alternatives in raising capital

    A. I and II
    B. I and IV
    C. II and III
    D. III and IV

3. Which are considered by an underwriter when establishing an offering price?

    I. Projected earnings for the company
    II. Likely dividends to be paid over the coming years
    III. Demand for the security by the investing public
    IV. Earnings multiples for other companies in the market in the same industry

    A. I and II
    B. I, II, and III
    C. I, II, and IV
    D. I, II, III and IV

Answers 1. **C.** *This is a combined primary and secondary distribution. The corporation receives the proceeds from the shares it sells and the selling stockholders receive the proceeds from the remainder.*

2. **B.** *The principal functions of the underwriter are to advise the issuer about the financing alternatives, the timing of the issue, and to sell securities to the public.*

3. **D.** *The underwriter would consider all the factors listed when pricing a new issue.*

The Underwriting Syndicate

Corporate underwriting normally takes the form of a **negotiated agreement** between the issuer and investment banker. This negotiated agreement, known as the **underwriting agreement**, is signed before the effective date.

Syndicate Formation

Depending on the offering size, the underwriter may want to form a **syndicate**, or a joint account for the purposes of the underwriting. The underwriting syndicate includes a syndicate manager and an association of underwriters.

Underwriting Manager The investment banker that negotiates with the issuer is known as the **underwriting manager** or **syndicate manager**. The underwriting manager directs the entire underwriting process, including signing the underwriting agreement with the issuer and directing the due diligence meeting and distribution process. A syndicate may have more than one manager.

Syndicate Members Underwriting syndicate members make a financial commitment to help bring the securities public. In a firm commitment offering, all syndicate members commit to purchase from the issuer and then distribute an agreed-on amount of the issue (their **participation** or **bracket**). Syndicate members sign a **syndicate agreement**, or **syndicate letter**, that describes the participants' responsibilities and allocation of syndicate profits, if any.

The **agreement among underwriters** details each underwriter's commitment and liability—particularly for any shares that remain unsold at the underwriting syndicate's termination.

Selling Group Formation Although the members of an underwriting syndicate agree to underwrite an entire offering, they frequently enlist other firms to help distribute the securities as members of the **selling group**. Selling group members act as agents with no commitment to buy securities.

The managing underwriter is normally responsible for determining whether to use a selling group and, if so, which firms to include. If the securities to be issued are attractive, broker/dealers will want to participate. If the securities are not attractive, the manager may have to persuade broker/dealers to join.

Selling group members sign a **selling group agreement** with the underwriters, which typically contains the following terms:

- statement that the manager acts for all of the underwriters;
- amount of securities each selling group member will be allotted and the tentative public offering price at which the securities will be sold (this price is firmed up just before the offering date);
- provisions as to how and when payment for shares is to be made to the managing underwriter; and
- legal provisions limiting each selling group member's liability in conjunction with the underwriting.

Test Topic Alert! Syndicate members take on financial liability and act in a principal capacity. Selling group members have no financial liability and act as agents because they have no commitment to buy securities from the issuer.

Negotiated Underwriting In a **negotiated underwriting**, the issuer and the investment banker negotiate the offering terms (including the amount of securities to be offered), offering price or yield, and underwriting fees.

Negotiated underwritings are standard in underwriting corporate securities because of close business relationships between issuing corporations and investment banking firms.

Competitive Bid Competitive bid arrangements are the standard for underwriting most municipal securities and are often required by state law. In a competitive bid, a state or municipal government invites investment bankers to bid for a new issue of bonds. The issuer awards the securities to the underwriter(s) whose bid results in the lowest net interest cost to the issuer.

Types of Underwriting Commitments

Different types of underwriting agreements require different levels of commitment from underwriters. This results in different levels of risk.

Firm Commitment

The **firm commitment** is a widely used type of underwriting contract. Under its terms, the underwriter contracts with the issuer, selling investors, or both to buy the securities described in the contract at a specified price and quantity range, on or about a given date. The terms are detailed in a **letter of intent** (**LOI**) signed by the underwriter and the issuer during the early stages of negotiation.

Although this LOI is conditional for all practical purposes, the underwriter is committing to buy securities from the issuer and paying the underwriting proceeds to the company. Under a firm commitment contract, any losses incurred due to unsold securities are prorated among the underwriting firms according to their participation.

Market-Out Clause In a firm commitment underwriting, the underwriter assumes substantial financial risk for the underwriting. To limit its risks, a **market-out clause** in the underwriting agreement specifies conditions under which the offering may be cancelled.

Risks Beyond the Underwriter's Control Underwriters may suspend or abort an offering if a material, adverse event occurs that affects the issuing corporation and impairs the investment quality of the securities being offered. An example of such an event would be the sudden death of the company president.

Risks that the Underwriter Must Assume Underwriters may not exercise market-out provisions if a nonmaterial, adverse event occurs that affects the issuing company, but does not impair the securities' investment quality. A nonmaterial, adverse event could be a Federal Reserve policy shift that leads to a general market decline before the offering. This would not qualify as a material event for this purpose.

Standby

When a company's current stockholders do not exercise their preemptive rights in an additional offering, a corporation has an underwriter **standing by** to purchase whatever shares remain unsold as a result of rights expiring.

Because the standby underwriter unconditionally agrees to buy all shares, current stockholders do not subscribe to at the subscription price, the offering is a firm commitment.

✓ *Take Note:* By engaging a standby underwriter, an issuer is assured of selling all of the shares being offered.

Best Efforts

A **best efforts underwriting** calls for the broker to buy securities from the issuer as agent, not as principal. This means that the underwriter is not committed and is therefore not at risk. The underwriter acts as agent contingent on the underwriter's ability to sell shares in either a public offering or a private placement.

All or None

In an **all or none (AON) underwriting**, the issuing corporation has determined that it wants an agreement outlining that the underwriter must either sell all of the shares or cancel the underwriting. Because of the uncertainty over the outcome of an AON offering, any funds collected from investors during the offering period must be held in escrow pending final disposition of the underwriting.

Brokers engaged in an AON distribution are prohibited from deceiving investors by stating that all of the securities in the underwriting have been sold if it is not the case.

Mini-Max

A **mini-max offering** is a best efforts underwriting with a floor and a ceiling on the dollar amount of securities the issuer is willing to sell. The underwriter must locate enough interested buyers to support the minimum (floor) issuance requirement. Once the minimum is met, the underwriter can expand the offering up to the maximum (ceiling) amount of shares the issuer specified. Mini-max underwriting terms are most frequently found in limited partnership program offerings and funds collected from investors during the offering period must be held in escrow pending final disposition of the underwriting.

Test Topic Alert!

Be prepared for a question that requires an understanding of underwriter risk in firm commitment and best efforts underwriting.

In a firm commitment underwriting, the underwriter takes on the financial risk because the securities are purchased from the issuer. Because of this risk, the underwriter is acting in a principal capacity.

In a best efforts underwriting, the underwriter sells as much as possible, without liability for what cannot be sold. The underwriter is acting in an agent capacity with no financial risk.

For example, if a corporation plans to sell 100,000 shares of common stock, but after exerting "best efforts," the underwriter can only sell 80,000 shares, the underwriter has no liability for the remaining 20,000 shares.

- Firm commitment = principal capacity, underwriter has risk
- Best efforts = agency capacity, underwriter has no risk

Remember that a standby offering is a firm commitment offering involving unexercised preemptive rights.

Underwriting Compensation

The price at which underwriters buy stock from issuers always differs from the price at which they offer the shares to the public. The price the issuer receives is known as the **underwriting proceeds**, and the price investors pay is the **public offering price (POP)**. The **underwriting spread**, the difference between the two prices, consists of the:

- **manager's fee**, for negotiating the deal and managing the underwriting and distribution process;
- **underwriting fee**, for assuming the risk of buying securities from the issuer without assurance that the securities can be resold; and
- **selling concession**, for placing the securities with investors.

Industry Standard Practices The industry norm for allocating the spread for corporate equity issues is as follows.

Spread Allocation

Underwriting Component	Fee Range
Syndicate manager's fee	10% to 20%
Underwriting syndicate fee	20% to 30%
Selling concession	50% to 60%

The NASD's **Corporate Financing Department** relies on these guidelines when evaluating underwriting spreads for fairness and reasonableness.

✓ *For Example:* Assume a 1 million share initial public offering of common stock. Shares will be sold to the public for $10.00, and the underwriting spread is $.65 per share. The following illustration depicts the distribution of the spread and proceeds of the underwriting. The $.65 spread is allocated as follows:

- Syndicate manager's fee: compensation for the manager's role in the underwriting—in this case, $.12 per share, or $120,000 for 1 million shares. The manager's fee is typically the smallest portion of the spread.
- Underwriting fee: this portion of the spread compensates syndicate members for the risk they assume in the underwriting. The underwriting fee—in this case, $.13 per share—is allocated to syndicate members based on their participation.

Issuing Securities

- Selling concession: the largest portion of the spread is the selling concession, the amount received by any member that sells the shares. In this case, the concession is $.40 per share.

The amount of the spread varies by issue and can be influenced by any of the following.

- Type of commitment: a firm commitment earns a larger spread than a best efforts agreement due to the risks the underwriter assumes.
- Security's marketability: a triple-A (AAA) bond has a smaller spread than a speculative stock.
- Issuer's business: a stable utility stock usually has a smaller spread than a more volatile stock.
- Offering size: in a very large offering, the underwriter can spread costs over a larger number of shares; thus, the per-share cost may be lower.

Who Gets What in an Underwriting

New Issue Incorporated Common Stock
1,000,000 Shares
Price $10

$10,000,000 gross from the sale of the issue to the public.

$9,350,000 of the proceeds goes to the issuer.

New Issue Incorporated Common Stock
1,000,000 Shares
Price $10

$650,000 of the proceeds goes to the underwriters. This fee is known as the gross spread.

$400,000 selling concession paid to syndicate members and selling group members based on the number of shares sold by each firm.

$120,000 management fee paid to the managing underwriter.

$130,000 underwriting fee paid to all syndicate members based on their pro rata underwriting participation.

Quick Quiz 7.5

Match the items below with the best definition or description.

A. Cooling-off period
B. Securities Act of 1933
C. Red herring
D. Split (combined) offering
E. Indication of interest

___ 1. Has aspects of both a primary and secondary offering

___ 2. An investor's expression of a conditional wish to purchase a new security after that investor has read a preliminary prospectus

___ 3. Interval between the filing date of a registration statement and the date on which the security becomes effective

___ 4. Abbreviated prospectus distributed while an issuer's registration statement is reviewed by the SEC

___ 5. Federal securities legislation mandating full and fair disclosure about new issues

Answers 1. **D.**   2. **E.**   3. **A.**   4. **C.**   5. **B.**

Quick Quiz 7.6

Match the items below with the best definition or description.

A. Private placement
B. Mini-max offering
C. Stabilization
D. Best efforts
E. Tombstone

___ 1. Printed ad placed by syndicate manager during a cooling-off period

___ 2. Underwriter acts as an agent for the issuer and attempts to sell as many shares as possible

___ 3. Used when supply exceeds demand for a new issue

___ 4. Type of best-efforts underwriting in which the issuer sets both a floor and ceiling on the amount of securities to be sold

___ 5. An offering not offered to the general investing public

Answers   1. *E.*   2. *D.*   3. *C.*   4. *B.*   5. *A.*

Exemptions from the Securities Act of 1933

Exempt Issuers and Securities

Certain securities are exempt from the registration statement and prospectus requirements of the 1933 act, either because of the issuer's level of creditworthiness or because another government regulatory agency has jurisdiction over the issuer.

These exempt securities include:

- US government securities;
- municipal bonds;
- commercial paper and bankers' acceptances that have maturities of less than 270 days;
- insurance policies and fixed annuity contracts (but not variable annuities);
- national and state bank (not bank holding company) securities;
- building and loan (S&L) securities; and
- charitable, religious, educational, and nonprofit association issues.

Banks are exempted from SEC registration of their securities because they file information on new issues with bank regulators and make it available to investors.

✓ **Take Note:** This exemption applies only to the securities of banks, not to the securities of bank-holding companies.

Insurance policies are not included in the definition of *security*; however, variable annuities, variable life insurance, and variable universal life insurance are funded by separate accounts and must be registered as securities with the SEC.

Exempt Transactions

Securities offered by industrial, financial, and other corporations may qualify for exemption from the registration statement and prospectus requirements of the 1933 Act under one of the following exclusionary provisions:

- Regulation A: corporate offerings of less than $5 million;

- Regulation D: private placements;
- Rule 147: securities offered and sold exclusively intrastate; or
- other exempt transactions, including Rule 144, Rule 144a, Rule 145.

Regulation A: Small Offerings

Regulation A (Reg A) permits issuers to raise up to $5 million in a 12-month period without full registration. This allows a small company access to the capital market to raise a small amount of money without incurring prohibitive costs.

In a Reg A offering, the issuer files an abbreviated **notice of sale**, or **offering circular**, with the regional SEC office. Investors are provided with this offering circular rather than a full prospectus.

The cooling-off period is 20 days between the filing date and effective date, and the issuer need not provide audited financial information. Individuals buying securities in a Reg A offering must receive a final offering circular at least 48 hours prior to confirmation of sale.

Regulation D: Private Placements

The SEC does not require registration of an offering if it is privately placed with any of the following:

- officers or directors of the issuer;
- financial institutions or accredited investors that do not need SEC protection; or
- a maximum of 35 individual (nonaccredited) investors. This is detailed according to Rule 506 of Regulation D.

An **accredited investor** is defined as one who:

- has a net worth of $1 million or more; or
- has had an annual income of $200,000 or more in each of the two most recent years (or $300,000 jointly with a spouse) and who has a reasonable expectation of reaching the same income level in the current year.

Purchasers must have access to the same type of information they would receive if the securities were being sold under prospectus in a registered offering. The amount of capital that can be raised under Rule 506 is not limited.

A private placement investor must sign a letter stating that he intends to hold the stock for investment purposes only. Private placement stock is referred to as **lettered stock** due to this investment letter. The certificate may bear a legend indicating that it cannot be transferred without registration or exemption; therefore, private placement stock is also referred to as **legend stock**.

Test Topic Alert! Sometimes it is difficult to identify private placement stock in a question because of the many terms that can be used to describe it. Recognize all of the following terms as synonymous with private placement stock:

- *Restricted* (because it must be held for a one-year period)
- *Unregistered* (no registration statement on file with the SEC)
- *Letter stock* (investor agreed to terms by signing an investment letter)
- *Legend stock* (a special inscription on the stock certificate indicates restricted transfer)

Rule 147: Intrastate Offerings

Under **Rule 147**, offerings that take place entirely in one state are exempt from registration when:

- the issuer has its principal office and receives at least 80% of its income in the state;
- at least 80% of the issuer's assets are located within the state;
- at least 80% of the offering proceeds are used within the state;
- the broker/dealer acting as underwriter is a resident of the state and has an office in the state; and
- all purchasers are residents of the state.

Purchasers of an intrastate issue may not resell the stock to any resident of another state for at least nine months after the last sale.

Rule 144

Rule 144 regulates the sale of control and restricted securities, stipulating the holding period, quantity limitations, manner of sale, and filing procedures.

Control securities are those owned by directors, officers, or persons who own or control 10% or more of the issuer's voting stock.

✓ **Take Note:** If an unaffiliated individual owns 7% of the voting stock of XYZ, that person is not a control person. However, if that person's spouse owns 4% of the voting stock, then both would be considered control persons. In other words, if there is a 10% or more interest held by immediate family members, then all those family members owning voting stock are control persons.

Restricted securities are those acquired through some means other than a registered public offering. A security purchased in a private placement is a restricted security. Restricted securities may not be sold until they have been held fully paid for one year. According to Rule 144, after holding restricted stock, fully paid, for one year, an investor may begin selling shares but is subject to the volume restriction rules as enumerated below. In any 90-day period, an investor may sell the greater of:

- 1% of the total outstanding shares of the same class at the time of sale; or
- the average weekly trading volume in the stock over the past four weeks on all exchanges or as reported through Nasdaq.

After holding stock fully paid for two years, the volume restriction rules no longer apply to unaffiliated investors (i.e., they can sell all they want). For

Exemptions from the Securities Act of 1933

unaffiliated investors, the volume restriction rules only apply during the one year period following a one-year hold (during the second year).

Selling shares under Rule 144 effectively registers the shares. In other words, buyers of 144 stock are not subject to any restrictions.

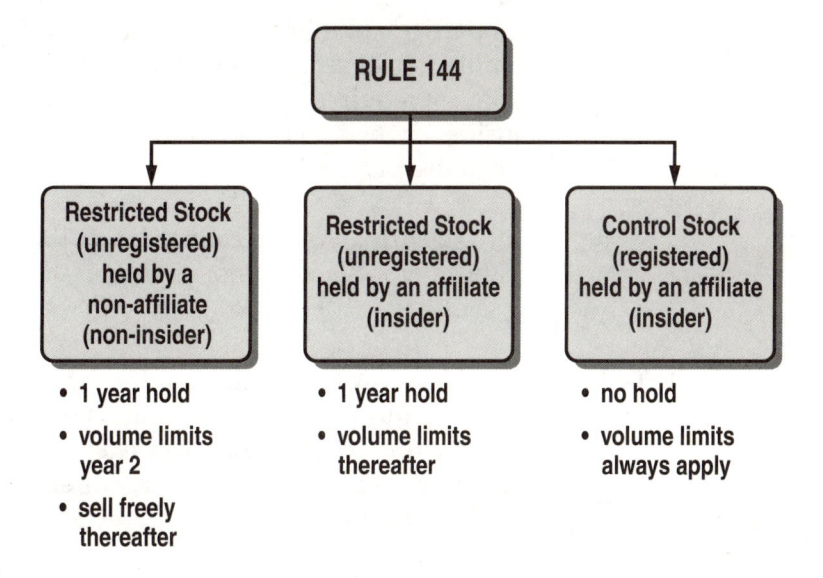

```
                              RULE 144
                                 │
          ┌──────────────────────┼──────────────────────┐
          ▼                      ▼                      ▼
   Restricted Stock       Restricted Stock        Control Stock
    (unregistered)         (unregistered)          (registered)
       held by a          held by an affiliate   held by an affiliate
     non-affiliate             (insider)              (insider)
     (non-insider)
```

- 1 year hold
- volume limits year 2
- sell freely thereafter

- 1 year hold
- volume limits thereafter

- no hold
- volume limits always apply

Test Topic Alert!

When you encounter a Rule 144 question always look for two things:

What kind of stock is being sold? (Restricted or control)
Who is selling it? (Insider or noninsider)

Only *restricted* stock has a holding period. Control stock, unless it is restricted, can be sold immediately, but volume limits **always** apply.

Which of the following is subject to the holding period provisions of Rule 144?

A. A corporate insider who has held restricted stock for two years
B. A nonaffiliate who has held registered stock for three years
C. A corporate affiliate who has held control stock for six months
D. A nonaffiliate who has held restricted stock for nine months

Answer: **D**. Only restricted stock is subject to a holding period. That means you could immediately exclude choices B and C. The insider in choice A has held the stock for the one year required, so a holding period does not apply. Restricted stock must be held for a minimum of one year, whether the owner is an affiliate or a nonaffiliate.

✓ **Take Note:** Sales in amounts not exceeding 500 shares and $10,000 in sale proceeds are permitted without the filing of Form 144. If required, Form 144 must be filed no later than concurrently with the sale of the stock. The filing is good for 90 days.

Current information about the company must be made available to the buyer. This can be accomplished by verifying that the company is a reporting company that regularly files 10K and 10Q reports with the SEC.

Insiders defined under Rule 144 are not allowed to enter short sales in the securities of companies in which they are insiders. They are also restricted from participating in speculative options transactions. If an insider profits from the sale of securities held for less than six months, these **short-swing** profits are required to be disgorged (returned) to the company. Any trading of insider-owned securities must be reported to the SEC within two business days of the transaction.

✓ *Take Note: Insiders cannot short!* They are prohibited from taking short-swing profits and cannot engage in short naked options positions or short sales.

Rule 144a Rule 144a allows nonregistered foreign and domestic securities to be sold to certain institutional investors in the United States without holding period requirements. To qualify for this exemption, the buyer must be a **qualified institutional buyer** (**QIB**). One requirement of a QIB is a minimum of $100 million in assets.

Rule 145 Rule 145 of the 1933 act is intended to protect stockholders of any company that proposes to reorganize its ownership structure, acquire another company, or merge with another company. Any such proposition requires stockholder approval. Rule 145 requires that stockholders be sent a full disclosure document (a proxy statement) to inform them of the proposition.

Transactions Covered by Rule 145

Transactions that Rule 145 covers are reclassifications, mergers or consolidations, and transfers of assets:

- **Reclassification**—when one class of securities is to be exchanged internally for another class in a way that shifts ownership control.
- **Merger or consolidation**—when stockholders in a target company are offered securities in another company in exchange for the surrender of their stock.
- **Transfer of assets**—when all or some of one company's business assets are exchanged for another company's securities. Stockholders thus solicited are being asked to approve their company's dissolution.

✓ *Take Note:* Rule 145 specifically excludes shares resulting from a stock split or a stock dividend from having to be registered with the SEC.

Antifraud Regulations of the Acts of 1933 and 1934

Although a security may be exempt from the registration and prospectus requirements, no offering is exempt from the antifraud provisions of the Securities Act of 1933 or any other securities act, including the Securities Exchange Act of 1934. The antifraud provisions of the Act of 1933 apply to all new securities offerings, whether exempt from registration or not. Issuers must provide accurate information regarding any securities offered to the public.

Quick Quiz 7.7   Multiple Choice

1. SEC Rule 147 provides exemption from registration for

   A. small issues
   B. securities issued by banks
   C. intrastate issues
   D. private placements

2. An investor files the necessary forms to sell stock under Rule 144. The filing is effective for a maximum of how many days?

   A. 30
   B. 60
   C. 90
   D. 120

3. Stock is issued under a Rule 144a exemption. Before reselling the stock, the buyer is subject to a minimum holding period of how many days?

   A. 30
   B. 90
   C. 150
   D. There is no required holding period.

Answers

1. **C.** Rule 147 exempts intrastate issues from registration with the SEC. To qualify, the issuer must have its principal office and at least 80% of its assets in the state; at least 80% of the proceeds must be used within the state; the under-

writer must be a state resident; all purchasers must be state residents; and purchasers may not resell the securities to a resident of another state for at least nine months after the offering.

2. **C.** Investors who wish to sell stock under Rule 144 must file a form with the SEC. The filing is effective for 90 days.

3. **D.** SEC Rule 144a does not require the buyer to hold the stock for a minimum time before reselling.

Hot Issues

Hot issues are public offering securities that sell at an immediate premium over the POP in the secondary market.

Freeriding and Withholding

A member's failure to make a bona fide offering at the POP is considered **freeriding and withholding** under the NASD Conduct Rules.

Any NASD member firm engaged in distributing a stock that proves to be a hot issue must:

- make a **bona fide** public offering of the securities at the announced POP (a member firm must not withhold stock in its investment or trading accounts—or in any other account—for the purpose of selling it later at a higher price in the open market); and
- not sell the stock to any employee or officer of the member firm under any circumstances.

Prohibited Accounts

It violates NASD rules for any of the following persons to purchase hot issues at the POP:

- the underwriters;
- any NASD member broker/dealer;
- any person associated with an NASD member;
- immediate family members of a person associated with an NASD member; or
- any person financially dependent on a person associated with an NASD member.

Broker/dealers engaged solely in the sale of investment company securities or direct partnership programs are excluded from this prohibition.

✓ *Take Note:* Immediate family members are defined as spouses, parents, children, siblings and in-laws. Aunts and uncles as well as grandparents are excluded.

Exceptions

Under certain circumstances, limited amounts of a hot issue may be purchased by the following people.

Nonsecurities Persons Associated with the Underwriting This category includes any person who acts in a business or professional capacity in connection with a public offering. This includes finders, accountants, attorneys, financial consultants, or persons performing a fiduciary service for the managing underwriter, and any person financially supported by a person in this category. A person in this category should not be allowed to buy a hot issue unless it can be proved that it is the person's normal investment practice.

Officers and Certain Employees of Financial Institutions This category includes senior officers of banks, savings and loans, insurance companies, investment companies, investment advisers, and other types of institutional investors, as well as any person supported financially by a person in this category.

Immediate Family Members A family member may buy a hot issue if the:

- family member has a history of purchasing similar securities;
- purchase size is consistent with his normal investment practice;
- sale is of an insubstantial amount compared to the total amount available; and
- total of all sales of the security to all classified accounts is not disproportionate to the amount the dealer has available for sale.

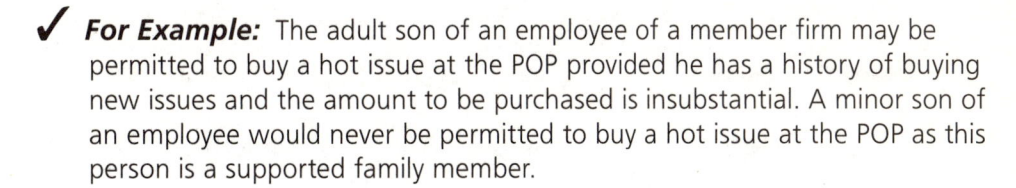

✓ *For Example:* The adult son of an employee of a member firm may be permitted to buy a hot issue at the POP provided he has a history of buying new issues and the amount to be purchased is insubstantial. A minor son of an employee would never be permitted to buy a hot issue at the POP as this person is a supported family member.

Normal Investment Practice This refers to an account's investment history, usually over the previous year, but sometimes longer. Specifically, a hot issue can be sold to a restricted individual if that type of security is consistent with the individual's investment patterns.

Issuing Securities

✏ Quick Quiz 7.8   Multiple Choice

1. The NASD freeriding and withholding policy always prohibits which of the following persons from buying a hot issue at the public offering price?

   I. Officer of an underwriter in the syndicate
   II. Employee of a firm in the syndicate offering the new issue
   III. Bank officer with a long-standing relationship with the underwriter
   IV. Finder of the issue being underwritten

   A. I and II
   B. I and IV
   C. II, III, and IV
   D. III and IV

Answer

1. **A.** *The freeriding and withholding policy categorically prohibits NASD member firms, their officers, and their employees from buying a hot issue at the public offering price. However, officers of institutions and finders (persons who introduce a corporation that wants to be underwritten to the underwriter) may be sold shares of a hot issue at the public offering price if they buy insubstantial amounts and have demonstrated histories of similar purchases.*

Issuing Securities HotSheet

Act of 1933:	• Requires registration of all nonexempt issues • Requires full and fair disclosure of new issues • The "Paper Act"
Exempt Securities:	• Commercial paper, banker's acceptances with maturities of less than 270 days
Exempt Issuers:	• US govt., municipalities, nonprofits/charities/churches, banks
Reg A:	• $5 million or less in 12 months; offering circular for disclosure
Rule 147:	• Home office in state; 80% of business and assets in state • Only state residents can buy, no resale to non-residents for 9 months
Reg D (Private Placements):	• No more than 35 non-accredited investors • Unlimited accredited investors

- Institutions, broker/dealers, individuals with income of more than $200,000 single, $300,000 married in last two years, officers and directors of the issuer
- Sign investment letter, hold for one year
- Private placement memorandum for disclosure

Rule 144:
- One-year hold on restricted securities, insiders or non-insiders
- Volume limitations apply to all control stock sales
- Limits for 90 days are greater of 1% of outstanding voting stock or average of preceding 4 weeks trading volume
- Must file Form 144 with SEC no later than sale date
- Insiders can't sell short; short-swing profits must be disgorged
- Form 144 good for 90 days

Rule 144a:
- No holding period on unregistered securities sold to institutional investors

Rule 145:
- Proxy statement required to inform shareholders of mergers, acquisitions, reclassifications

Prospectus Delivery:
- Final prospectus no later than confirmation of sale
- 40 days for non-Nasdaq subsequent primary; no extended delivery requirement for listed or Nasdaq subsequent primary
- 25 days for listed IPOs and Nasdaq
- 90 days for Pink Sheet, OTCBB IPOs

Cooling-Off Period:
- Minimum of 20 days
- No advertising, sales literature, orders, offers
- Tombstones, red herrings, indications of interest are OK

Underwriting:
- Must be NASD members to underwrite corporate securities
- Firm commitment = principal capacity; underwriters have risk
- Best efforts = agent capacity; issuer has risk
- Syndicate members have liability; selling group members do not

Stabilizing:
- One bid, at or below public offering price, only in underwriting period
- Must be stated in prospectus

Freeriding/Withholding:
- Firms/reps, financially supported persons cannot buy hot issues
- Nonsupported family and officers of financial institutions may if prior history and insubstantial amount

Series 7 Unit Test 7

1. ABC is preparing a registration statement for a new issue consisting of 300,000 new shares and 200,000 existing shares held by officers. The offering price is $30 per share and the spread taken by the underwriters is $2 per share. After the offering is complete, ABC will receive

    A. $8,400,000
    B. $9,000,000
    C. $14,000,000
    D. $15,000,000

2. An offering of securities in compliance with Rule 144A is sold primarily to

    A. American individual investors
    B. qualified institutional buyers
    C. foreign individual investors
    D. all of the above

3. An underwriting spread is the

    A. amount a managing underwriter receives
    B. amount a selling group receives
    C. amount a syndicate receives
    D. difference between an offering price and the proceeds to an issuer

4. A company has filed a registration statement for an initial public offering of its common stock with the SEC. As a registered representative, you can

    I. send out a research report on the company to your customers
    II. take indications of interest from your customers
    III. send a preliminary prospectus to each of your customers
    IV. take orders for the stock from customers in cash accounts only

    A. I only
    B. I, II and III only
    C. II and III only
    D. I, II, III and IV

5. The principal functions of an investment banker are to

    I. distribute securities to the public
    II. provide a secondary market
    III. provide financing for an individual
    IV. advise the issuer about alternatives in raising capital

    A. I and II
    B. I and IV
    C. II and III
    D. III and IV

6. A Regulation A exemption covers a(n)
   A. offering of $5 million or less in 12 months
   B. offering of letter stock
   C. private offering
   D. offering of $5 million or more in 12 months

7. Which of the following are characteristics of the Securities Act of 1933?
   I. Requires registration of exchanges
   II. Called the Truth in Securities Act
   III. Requires full and fair disclosure of material facts
   IV. Requires that debt securities be issued with a trust indenture

   A. I and II only
   B. I, II and IV only
   C. I and III only
   D. II and III only

8. A final prospectus must include
   I. the effective date of the registration
   II. whether the underwriter intends to stabilize the issue
   III. a statement indicating that the SEC has not approved the issue
   IV. disclosure of material information concerning the issuer's financial condition

   A. I, II and IV only
   B. I and IV only
   C. II and III only
   D. I, II, III and IV

9. Which of the following are considered to be nonexempt offerings according to the Securities Act of 1933?
   I. Government securities
   II. Private placements
   III. Public offering of $6,000,000 by a brokerage firm
   IV. Sales of corporate bonds of $10,000,000

   A. I and II only
   B. I and III only
   C. II, III and IV only
   D. III and IV only

10. The largest portion of an underwriting spread is the
    A. manager's fee
    B. underwriting fee
    C. concession
    D. stabilizing bid

11. Under the intrastate offering rule (Rule 147), when may a resident purchaser of securities resell them to a nonresident?
    A. 3 months after the first sale made in that state
    B. 6 months after the last sale made in that state
    C. At least 9 months from the end of the distribution
    D. None of the above

12. Which of the following statements regarding a Rule 144 sale of restricted stock are TRUE?

    I. Stock sold through a 144 sale is considered registered stock after the sale.
    II. After holding the stock for 2 years, there are no volume restrictions for nonaffiliates.
    III. After holding the stock for 2 years, there are no volume restrictions for affiliates.
    IV. Form 144 must be filed with the SEC at least 10 business days prior to a 144 sale.

    A. I and II only
    B. I, III and IV only
    C. II and III only
    D. I, II, III and IV

13. A customer holding restricted stock wishes to sell under Rule 144. The customer has held the shares, fully paid, for one year. The issuer has outstanding 2,400,000 shares. Form 144 is filed on Monday, April 10 and the weekly trading volume for the stock is shown below:

Week Ending	Trading Volume
April 7	23,000
March 31	25,000
March 24	26,000
March 17	24,000
March 10	22,000

    The maximum number of shares the customer can sell with this filing is

    A. 23,000
    B. 24,000
    C. 24,250
    D. 24,500

Series 7 Unit Test 7 Answers & Rationale

1. A. ABC Corporation will receive $28 per share for each of the 300,000 new shares being issued ($30/share price less $2 spread). The proceeds from the 200,000 shares sold by the officers will benefit the officers themselves, not ABC Corporation. QID: 35008

2. B. Rule 144A allows securities to be sold to institutional buyers (qualified institutional buyers) without having to meet the holding period or volume requirements of Rule 144. QID: 30115

3. D. A spread is the difference between the public offering price and the price an underwriter pays an issuer. QID: 27892

4. C. New issues can only be sold by prospectus and indications of interest can be taken when the issue is in registration. During the registration period, only the preliminary prospectus may be sent to clients. Sales literature, such as research reports, may not be distributed while the IPO is in registration, nor may orders be taken. QID: 27847

5. B. The principal functions of the underwriter are to advise the issuer about the financial alternatives and to sell securities to the public. QID: 32202

6. A. A Regulation A filing under the Securities Act of 1933 exempts the security from registration and limits offerings to $5 million or less within a 12-month period. QID: 27920

7. D. The Securities Act of 1933 regulates new issues of corporate securities sold to the public. The act is also referred to as the Full Disclosure Act, the Paper Act, the Truth in Securities Act, and the Prospectus Act. The purpose of the act is to require full, written disclosure about a new issue. The Securities Exchange Act of 1934 requires exchanges to register with the SEC, and the Trust Indenture Act of 1939 requires corporations issuing more than $5 million in bonds to have a trust indenture. QID: 27867

8. D. If the underwriter intends to engage in activities designed to stabilize the security's market price, disclosure in the prospectus is required. The SEC disclaimer must appear on every prospectus and state that the SEC has neither approved nor disapproved the issue. The effective date must be printed on the final prospectus. Its purpose is full disclosure about the issuer and security being issued. QID: 27854

9. D. The Securities Act of 1933 exempts U.S. government bonds and private placements from registration. Public offerings of less than $5 million are also exempt (under Reg A), so an offering of $6 million and sales of corporate bonds are not exempt; they must be registered with the SEC. QID: 32201

10. C. The largest portion of the spread is the concession. QID: 27895

11. **C.** In an intrastate offering, a purchaser of the issue may not sell the securities to a resident of another state for at least nine months from the end of the distribution. QID: 27929

12. **A.** After stock is sold by an affiliate or a nonaffiliate, it is considered registered stock and affiliates are always subject to volume restrictions. Form 144 must be filed with the SEC on or prior to date of sale. After holding the stock, fully paid, for a period totaling two years, nonaffiliates are no longer subject to the volume restriction rules of Rule 144. QID: 34863

13. **D.** Under Rule 144, after holding the fully paid restricted shares for a period of one year, the customer can begin selling. Between the first and second year of ownership, the customer is subject to volume restrictions (i.e., how many shares can be sold with each Form 144 filing). The customer can sell the greater of 1% of the total shares outstanding or the weekly average of the prior four weeks' trading volume (the four weeks preceding the Form 144 filing). In this case, 1% of the total shares outstanding is 24,000 (1% × 2.4 million). The weekly average of the prior four weeks' trading volume is 24,500. Therefore, the most the customer can sell during the 90 days following the Form filing is 24,500 shares. After holding the shares, fully paid, for a period totaling two years, there are no volume restrictions. QID: 36463

8

Trading Securities

INTRODUCTION This unit will examine trading activities both on the exchanges and OTC. It presents many terms and rules that are used by the industry and are critical for exam success.

The trading of securities in the secondary market is regulated by the Securities Exchange Act of 1934. The Act of 1934 created the Securities and Exchange Commission and gave it the authority to regulate securities exchanges and the OTC market.

Exchanges, such as the NYSE, operate as double-auction markets where stocks listed on the exchange are traded. The OTC market is an inter-dealer computer and telephone network where market makers in stocks show the bid and ask price for stocks in which they make a market.

The Series 7 exam is likely to include approximately 15–20 trading questions on the information covered in this unit.

UNIT OBJECTIVES When you have completed this unit, you should be able to:

- explain the impact of the Securities Exchange Act of 1934 on trading activities;
- list and describe the four markets of the secondary marketplace;
- identify the four types of NYSE members and explain their roles;
- compare and contrast the types of orders available to customers;
- describe and interpret reports from several electronic reporting systems used in the secondary marketplace;
- identify unique concepts of OTC trading and the securities included; and
- explain the NASD's 5% markup policy and identify the transactions subject to it.

The Regulation of Trading

The Securities Act of 1933 regulates primary issues of securities, and the Securities Exchange Act of 1934 regulates secondary trading.

The Securities Exchange Act of 1934

The 1934 act, known as the **Exchange Act**, established the **Securities and Exchange Commission (SEC)** and gave it the authority to regulate, in part, broker/dealers, the securities exchanges, and the over-the-counter (OTC) markets to maintain a fair and orderly market for the investing public.

The Securities Exchange Act of 1934 requires exchange members, broker/dealers that trade securities OTC and/or on exchanges, and individuals who make securities trades for the public to be registered with the SEC.

The Securities Exchange Act of 1934 provides for the:

- creation of the SEC;
- regulation of exchanges;
- regulation of the OTC market;
- regulation of credit by the Federal Reserve Board (FRB);
- registration of broker/dealers;
- net capital rules;
- regulation of insider transactions, short sales, and proxies;
- regulation of trading activities;
- regulation of client accounts;
- customer protection rule;
- filing of 10-Qs, 10-Ks, and other financial statements by companies that are required to report; and
- the regulation of officers, directors, and principal shareholders.

The Securities and Exchange Commission (SEC) Composed of five commissioners appointed by the President of the United States and approved by the Senate, the SEC enforces the 1934 Act by regulating the securities markets and the behavior of market participants.

Registration of Exchanges and Firms The 1934 Act requires national securities exchanges to file **registration statements** with the SEC. By registering, exchanges agree to comply with and help enforce the rules of this act. Each exchange gives the SEC copies of its bylaws, constitution, and articles of incorporation. An exchange must disclose to the SEC any amendment to exchange rules as soon as it is adopted.

The Act of 1934 also requires companies that list their securities on the exchanges and certain firms traded OTC to register with the SEC. An SEC-registered company must file both quarterly and annual reports (Form 10-Q and 10-K, respectively) informing the SEC of its financial status and providing other information.

Financial Statements Sent to Customers

Every broker/dealer must provide its customers with copies of its financial statements. A customer is any person for whom the broker/dealer holds funds or securities or anyone who has made a securities transaction at any time up to one month before the date of a financial statement. Other broker/dealers, partners or officers of broker/dealers, and subordinated lenders are not considered customers.

✓ *Take Note:* Customers are entitled to the firm's most recent balance sheet upon written request.

Regulation of Credit The Exchange Act authorized the Federal Reserve Board (**FRB**) to regulate margin accounts, the credit extended for the purchase of securities. Within FRB jurisdiction are:

- **Regulation T**—regulates the extension of credit by broker/dealers; and
- **Regulation U**—deals with the extension of credit by banks and other financial institutions.

✓ *Take Note:* It's important to remember the key features of the Act of 1934. You might think of it as the People Act because it regulates all the people involved in the securities industry, including all broker/dealers and representatives. Associate secondary market activity with this act. The Act of 1933 deals with the primary market and new issues, while the Act of 1934 deals with the secondary marketplace and outstanding issues.

Securities Markets and Broker/Dealers

Securities Markets

The market in which securities are bought and sold is also known as the **secondary market**, as opposed to the primary market for new issues. All securities transactions take place in one of four trading markets.

Exchange Market (Auction Market) The **exchange market** is composed of the NYSE and other exchanges on which listed securities are traded. This market is also known as an **auction market**. The term **listed security** refers to any security listed for trading on an exchange.

Over-the-Counter (OTC) Market (Second Market) The **OTC market** is an interdealer market in which **unlisted** securities—that is, securities not listed on any exchange—trade. It is also known as the **second market**. In the OTC market, securities dealers across the country are connected by computer and telephone. Thousands of securities are traded OTC, including stocks, bonds, and all municipal and US government securities.

As far as equities are concerned, the OTC market is divided into Nasdaq (National Market Stocks and small-cap stocks) and non-Nasdaq (stock in **Pink Sheets** or on the OTC Bulletin Board).

Third Market (OTC-Listed) The **third market**, or **Nasdaq Intermarket,** is a trading market in which exchange-listed securities are traded in the OTC market. Broker/dealers registered as OTC **market makers** in listed securities can affect third market transactions. All securities listed on the NYSE and AMEX and most securities listed on the regional exchanges are eligible for OTC trading as long as the trades are reported on the **Consolidated Tape** within 90 seconds of execution.

Fourth Market The **fourth market** is a market for institutional investors in which large blocks of stock, both listed and unlisted, trade in transactions unassisted by broker/dealers. These transactions take place through **Electronic Communications Networks (ECNs)** such as INSTINET and Archipelago.

Trading Hours Both the NYSE and AMEX trade between 9:30 am and 4:00 pm ET each business day. Normal hours for retail OTC trading are the same as those of the NYSE although many market makers remain open until 6:30 pm in extended hours trading.

Comparison of Listed and OTC Markets

Listed Markets Each stock exchange requires companies to meet certain criteria before it will allow their stock to be listed for trading on the exchange.

Location. Listed markets, such as the NYSE and AMEX, have central marketplaces and trading floor facilities.

Pricing System. Listed markets operate as **double-auction** markets. Floor brokers compete among themselves to execute trades at prices most favorable to the public.

Price Dynamics. When a floor broker representing a buyer executes a trade by taking stock at a current offer price higher than the last sale, a **plus tick**

occurs (**market up**); when a selling broker accepts a current bid price below the last sale price, a **minus tick** occurs (**market down**).

Major Force in the Market. The specialist maintains an orderly market and provides price continuity. He fills limit and market orders for the public and trades for his own account to either stabilize or facilitate trading when imbalances in supply and demand occur.

OTC Markets Historically, the criteria a company was required to meet to have its stock traded in the OTC market were rather loose. In recent years, however, the quality of companies that trade OTC has improved substantially.

Location. No central marketplace facilitates OTC trading. Trading takes place over the phone, over computer networks, and in trading rooms across the country.

Pricing System. The OTC market works through an **interdealer network**. Registered market makers compete among themselves to post the best bid and ask prices. The OTC market is a negotiated market.

Price Dynamics. When a market maker raises its bid price to attract sellers, the stock price rises; when a market maker lowers its ask price to attract buyers, the stock price declines.

Major Force in the Market. Market makers post the current bid and ask prices. The lowest price at which the public can buy (**best ask**) and the highest price at which the public can sell (**best bid**) is called the **inside market**.

Trading Halts If a **trading halt** is called for a security, all trading in the security stops in the market where the halt was declared. During the halt, however, open orders may be cancelled and options may be exercised. If the NASD initiates an OTC trading halt in a security, members may not trade the security until the NASD removes the trading halt.

Quick Quiz 8.1

True or False?

___ 1. During a trading halt, open orders can be cancelled.

___ 2. Unlisted securities trade on regional exchanges.

___ 3. Trades in the third market may take place after 4:00 pm

___ 4. A third market trade is an auction market trade.

___ 5. Municipal bonds and government securities trade OTC.

Trading Securities

___ 6. Reg T deals with the extension of credit by banks.

___ 7. Third market trades must be reported to INSTINET within 90 seconds of execution.

___ 8. The OTC market does not have a centralized marketplace.

___ 9. The Act of 1934 created the SEC.

___ 10. The fourth market is a market for institutional investors.

Answers

1. **T.**
2. **F.** *Unlisted securities trade OTC.*
3. **T.**
4. **F.** *Third market trades are negotiated.*
5. **T.**
6. **F.** *Reg U deals with extension of credit by banks; Reg T deals with extension of credit by broker/dealers.*
7. **F.** *Third market trades must be reported to the Consolidated Tape within 90 seconds. INSTINET is a trading service for the fourth market.*
8. **T.**   9. **T.**   10. **T.**

Role of the Broker/Dealer

Firms engaged in buying and selling securities for the public must register as **broker/dealers**. Most firms act both as brokers and dealers, but not in the same transaction.

Brokers   Brokers are agents that arrange trades for clients and charge commissions. Brokers do not buy shares as principal, but arrange trades between buyers and sellers.

Dealers   Dealers, or **principals**, buy and sell securities for their own accounts, often called **position trading**. When selling from their inventories, dealers charge their clients markups rather than commissions. A markup is the difference between the current interdealer offering price and the actual price charged the client. When a price to a client includes a dealer's markup, it is called a **net price**.

✓ *Take Note:* To clarify the role of dealers in the securities market place, try thinking of them like a car dealer. If you were a car dealer, you would maintain an inventory, or lot, of cars. If someone bought a car from you, you wouldn't sell it at the wholesale price. Instead, you mark up the price to make a profit.

If someone wanted to sell you his used car, you wouldn't offer him top dollar. Instead, you would mark down the price to make a profit. Securities dealers hold inventories of securities and buy and sell from inventory. They profit on transactions by charging markups and markdowns.

Filling an Order A broker/dealer may fill a customer's order to buy securities in any of the following ways:

- The **broker** may act as the client's agent by finding a seller of the securities and arranging a trade.
- The **dealer** may buy the securities from a market maker, mark up the price and resell them to the client.
- If it has the securities in its own inventory, the **dealer** may sell the shares to the client from that inventory.

Broker/Dealer Role in Transactions A firm cannot act as both a broker and a dealer in the same transaction.

Broker	*Dealer*
– Acts as an agent, transacting orders on the client's behalf	– Acts as a principal, dealing in securities for its own account and at its own risk
– Charges a commission	– Charges a markup or markdown
– Is not a market maker	– May make markets and take positions (long or short) in securities
– Must disclose its role to the client and the amount of its commission	– Must disclose its role to the client, and the markup or markdown if a Nasdaq security

An easy way to remember these relationships is to memorize the letters BAC/DPP, which stand for "**B**rokers act as **A**gents for **C**ommissions/**D**ealers act as **P**rincipals for **P**rofits."

The New York Stock Exchange (NYSE)

The **NYSE** is the most widely known stock exchange. Although exchanges are called stock markets, other securities may trade there as well. Often called the **Big Board**, the NYSE handles roughly three-quarters of all exchange transactions. Stocks listed on the NYSE can also be listed on regional exchanges, such as the Chicago Stock Exchange.

Securities traded on the NYSE, known as **listed securities**, must satisfy the Exchange's listing requirements. The Exchange does not influence or determine prices.

Exchange Listing Requirements

Any corporation that wants its stock listed on the NYSE must have:

- at least 1.1 million shares publicly held; and
- two thousand stockholders each holding 100 shares or more (2,000 round-lot owners).

Test Topic Alert! Don't bother memorizing these numbers—they won't be tested. It's more important that you recognize that only companies of significant size and public ownership qualify for listing on the NYSE.

Delisting The NYSE reserves the right to **delist** issuers for a number of reasons including failure to meet the minimum maintenance criteria. In addition, bankruptcy, abnormally low share price or share volume, as well as corporate actions not deemed to be in the public interest will result in delisting.

If an issuer wants to voluntarily delist from the NYSE:

- the board of directors must approve the action;
- the audit committee of the board must approve the action; and
- notification must be made to the issuer's 35 largest shareholders.

Trading on the Floor of the Exchange

Only NYSE members (individual seat owners) can trade on the floor. There are four types of traders.

Commission House Broker (CHB) Also called **floor brokers, commission house brokers (CHBs)** execute orders for clients and for their firms' accounts.

Two-Dollar Broker When commission brokers are too busy to execute all of their firms' orders, they call on **two-dollar brokers** to execute orders for them. Two-dollar brokers charge commissions for their services.

Registered Trader **Registered traders** are members of the Exchange who trade primarily for their own accounts. If they accept a public customer's order from a floor broker, they must give that order priority. They may not execute their own trades while holding an unfilled public order.

Specialist **Specialists** facilitate trading in specific stocks and their chief function is to maintain a fair and orderly market in those stocks. In fulfilling this function, they act as both brokers and dealers; they act as dealers when they execute trades for their own accounts and as brokers when they execute orders other members leave with them. The specialist acts as an auctioneer.

Auction Market

Exchange securities are bought and sold in an **auction market.** Exchange markets are also sometimes referred to as **double auction markets** because both buyers and sellers call out their best bids and offers in an attempt to transact business at the best possible price.

To establish the best bid, a buying broker/dealer must initiate a bid at least a cent higher than the current best bid. The best offer by a selling broker/dealer must be at least a cent lower than the current best offer.

✓ *For Example:* A quote might look like this:

Last	Bid	Ask	Size
$46.71	$46.66	$46.74	30 × 14

Several bids at the same price and several offers at the same price may occur. To provide for the orderly transaction of business on the floor, the highest bids and lowest offers always receive first consideration.

Priority, Precedence, and Parity When more than one broker enters the same bid or offer, the specialist awards the trade in the following order.

1. **Priority**—first order in
2. **Precedence**—largest order of those submitted
3. **Parity**—random drawing

Volatile Market Conditions

The NYSE has adopted **Rules 80A** and **80B** intended to protect against rapid, uncontrolled drops in the market. The specific point change in the **Dow Jones Industrial Average** (**DJIA**) required to initiate market restrictions is subject to change over time.

Currently, **program trading** and **index arbitrage** transactions are curbed if the DJIA increases or decreases by 2% in one day; the collar is removed if it moves back to within 1% (Rule 80A). The circuit breaker rule, Rule 80B, deals solely with declines in the DJIA. If there is a market decline of 10%, a one-hour halt is imposed. A market decline of 20% results in a two-hour halt, and a 30% decline results in a halt for the remainder of the day.

Test Topic Alert! The trading halt (circuit breaker) rules are more complex in reality. The time of the day when the halt takes place also impacts its length. However, the information reviewed here is sufficient for your exam knowledge.

Arbitrage

Arbitrage is a trading strategy specialized traders (called **arbitrageurs**) use to profit from temporary price differences between markets or securities. In general, arbitrageurs look for ways to profit from temporary price disparities in the same or equivalent securities.

Market Arbitrage Some securities trade in more than one market—on two exchanges, for instance—creating the possibility that one security may sell for two different prices at the same time. When that happens, arbitrageurs buy at the lower price in one market and sell at the higher price in the other.

Convertible Security Arbitrage Arbitrage trades are also possible in equivalent securities—convertible bonds and the underlying stock, for instance. If conditions are right, an arbitrageur may be able to convert bonds to stock and sell the stock for a profit.

Risk Arbitrage Risk arbitrage becomes possible in proposed corporate takeovers. Arbitrageurs buy the stock in the company being acquired and sell short the acquiring company's stock, believing that the merger will raise the acquisition's stock price and lower the acquirer's stock price.

The Specialist

The chief function of the **specialist** is to maintain a fair and orderly market in the stocks for which he is responsible.

Role of the Specialist on the Exchange

In addition to maintaining an orderly market, a secondary function of the specialist is to minimize price disparities that may occur at the opening of daily trading. He does this by buying or selling (as a dealer) stock from his own inventory only when a need for such intervention exists. Otherwise, the specialist lets public supply and demand set the market's course.

Market Maker Maintaining a market in a stock requires considerable financial resources, therefore the specialist must have enough capital to maintain a substantial position in the security.

Agent and Principal The specialist is both agent and principal. On the Exchange floor, specialists can act in the following ways.

As **agents** (or brokers' brokers) specialists execute all orders other brokers leave with them. Specialists accept certain kinds of orders from members, such as limit and stop orders, and execute these as conditions permit.

As **principals** (or dealers) specialists buy and sell in their own accounts to make markets in assigned stocks. They are expected to maintain continuous, fair, and orderly markets—that is, markets with reasonable price variations. A specialist, however, may not buy stock for his own account at a price that would compete with the current market. In other words, a specialist cannot buy, as principal, at a price that would satisfy a customer order to buy.

Responsibilities of the Specialist A specialist must abide by certain NYSE floor rules in the daily conduct of his business. The specialist:

- must work to maintain a fair and orderly market;
- must stand ready to buy and sell for his own account, if necessary, to maintain a fair and orderly market;
- is expected to transact business for his own account in such a way as to maintain price continuity and minimize temporary price disparities attributable to supply and demand differences;
- must avoid transacting business for his own account at the opening or reopening of trading in a stock if this would upset the public balance of supply and demand;
- must file the reports and keep the books and records the Exchange requires; and
- may trade for his own account in between the current bid and ask quotes in his book.

Trading Posts Each stock listed with the Exchange is traded at a particular horseshoe-shaped **trading post** surrounded by computer terminals. The specialist positioned at this post has been assigned responsibility for a certain number of issues. The specialist does not participate in every transaction in the stocks in which he specializes, but any transactions in a stock must take place in front of the specialist assigned to it.

✓ *Take Note:* A brief overview of activity around the trading post: When a firm sends a buy or sell order to the floor, its commission house broker (floor broker) takes the order to the post designated for that security. The order may instead be sent to the post electronically through an order routing system.

Order Book A specialist's **order book** records limit and stop orders the specialist holds for execution. The specialist enters buy orders on the left, sell orders on the right.

Quote

A current quote could be "51.13 to .50," meaning market orders to buy can be executed immediately at 51.50 and market orders to sell can be executed immediately at 51.13. The current quote on a stock includes the highest bid limit order and the lowest offer limit order. Market orders are executed immediately at those prices.

Test Topic Alert! There are three question possibilities that arise from the specialist's book.

1. What is the best available quote?
2. What is the market size available?
3. Where can the specialist trade for his own account?

To solve the first question, you need to determine the highest bid and lowest ask currently on the book. Think of the **Buy** side of the book as the bid side, and the **Sell** side of the book as the ask side. Because stop orders are not included in determining the quote, the highest bid currently available is 51.13. The lowest asked is 51.50. Since there are other orders other than the stop, we can use the 51.50 as the asked price.

✓ **Take Note:** The specialist will accept any size market order. However, on the book, round lots only.

To find the market size, add together the number of shares available at the quote just determined. There are 500 shares at the bid and 900 shares at the ask (the 200 shares subject to the stop order are not included). The market size is quoted as 5 × 9, representing 5 round lots at the bid and 9 round lots at the ask.

The answer to the third question is "inside the quote." The specialist can trade between the inside bid and ask when trading for his own account.

Specialist Quotations

Excerpt from a Specialist's Book

BUY	ALF	SELL
1 ML 1 PW	51	
1 AGE 4 Pru	.13	
3 Ray James STOP	.25	
	.38	
	.50	2 Smith Barn STOP 4 Oppen 2 Tucker Anth 3 Piper
	.63	
	.75	2 DWR
	.88	5 Bear Stearns

Around the post, there is a crowd interested in trading the security. The "crowd" may be as small as one specialist or as large as two specialists and any number of interested traders or brokers representing customers. The commission house broker may execute the order in the crowd at the best available price, leave the order with the specialist to execute when the price is right, or hand the order to a two-dollar broker to trade.

Size

The specialist must reveal the number of shares available in a current quote. Upon request, the specialist provides a quote and size:

- The quote "51.13 to .50, 5 by 9" means 500 shares bid for at 51.13, 900 shares offered at 51.50.
- The quote and size are good only for the moment they are given; however, they provide some indication of supply and demand.

Stopping Stock To guarantee that a market order will be filled at the current bid or offer, a specialist **stops stock**. This allows the commission house broker who originated the order time to go into the crowd and try to find a better price. The commission house broker is thus assured of not missing the market while trying to find a better bid or offer for the client.

A specialist may stop stock only for the benefit of a public order and does not require the Exchange's permission to do so. If the price in the crowd moves beyond the stopped price, the specialist automatically executes the order.

Crossing Orders If a member receives two market orders for the same stock—one an order to buy 1,000 shares, the other to sell 1,000 shares—the member may **cross** the two orders and use one order to fill the other.

Before crossing the orders, however, the member must offer the stock in the trading crowd surrounding the specialist's post at a price higher than the bid by the minimum variation. If there are no takers, the order may be crossed.

Quick Quiz 8.2   Multiple Choice

1. The over-the-counter market is a(n)

    A. negotiated market
    B. auction market
    C. transfer market
    D. double-auction market

2. Which of the following would be allowed to trade on the floor of the NYSE?

    I.   Registered representative
    II. Specialist
    III. Registered trader
    IV. Commission broker

    A. I and II only
    B. II and III only
    C. II, III and IV only
    D. I, II, III and IV

3. A company's stock is listed on the NYSE. Which of the following could result in the company's being delisted?

   I. The company files for bankruptcy under Chapter 11.
   II. The company issues preferred stock.
   III. Public interest in the stock declines considerably.
   IV. The company does not mail out proxy statements.

   A. I and III only
   B. I and IV only
   C. II and IV only
   D. I, III and IV

4. Stopping stock is permitted only if the specialist

   A. receives the permission of an NYSE floor governor
   B. is executing an order for another member
   C. has not guaranteed the price
   D. is executing a public order

Answers

1. **A.** The OTC is a negotiated market. The exchanges are auction markets. The new issue market is the primary market. There is no such thing as a "transfer market."

2. **C.** Only members can trade on the floor of the Exchange. Registered representatives may not.

3. **D.** The NYSE takes many factors into consideration when determining if a company should be delisted. Among the factors are all the choices given: the company files for bankruptcy; public interest in the company declines considerably; or the company does not mail out proxy statements.

4. **D.** A specialist may not stop stock for his own account or for the account of another member of the Exchange. The privilege of stopping stock is limited to public orders.

Types of Orders

Price-Restricted Orders

Many types of orders are available to customers. Some orders (limit and stop limit) restrict the price of the transaction. Typical orders include the following.

- **Market**—executed immediately at the market price
- **Limit**—limits the amount paid or received for securities
- **Stop**—becomes a market order if the stock reaches or goes through the stop (trigger or election) price
- **Stop Limit**—entered as a stop order and changed to a limit order if the stock hits or goes through the stop (trigger or election) price

Market Orders

A **market order** is sent immediately to the floor for execution without restrictions or limits. It is executed immediately at the current market price and has priority over all other types of orders. A market order to buy is executed at the lowest offering price available; a market order to sell is executed at the highest bid price available. As long as the security is trading, a market order guarantees execution.

Limit Orders

In a **limit order**, a customer limits the acceptable purchase or selling price. A limit order can be executed only at the specified price or better. If the order cannot be executed at the market, it is placed on the book and executed if and when the market price meets the order limit price.

Risks of Limit Orders

A customer who enters a limit order risks missing the chance to buy or sell, especially if the market moves away from the limit price. The market may never go as low as the buy limit price or as high as the sell limit price. Sometimes limit orders are not executed, even if the stock trades at the limit price.

Stock Ahead. Limit orders on the specialist's book for the same price are arranged according to when they were received. If a limit order at a specific price was not filled, chances are another order at the same price took precedence; that is, there was stock ahead.

✓ **Take Note:** Limit orders stand in time priority. There may be multiple orders to buy stock at a particular price. Once the stock begins trading at that price, those limit orders that were entered first will be filled first.

Limit Order Protection Rule

This SEC rule requires that firms holding customer limit orders cannot trade ahead of these orders. For example, if a firm accepts a customer limit order to buy 500 shares at 31.60, and in its market making capacity buys 200 shares at that price, it must fill that customer's order for 200 shares at 31.60 and protect the remaining 300 shares. The firm cannot, as principal, buy or sell stock at a price that would satisfy a customer limit order without filling that order.

In the above example, the firm could, as principal, buy stock at 31.61 without creating an obligation to fill the customer limit order.

Stop Orders

A **stop order**, also known as a **stop loss order**, is designed to protect a profit or prevent a loss if the stock begins to move in the wrong direction.

The stop order becomes a market order once the stock trades at or moves through a certain price, known as the stop price. Stop orders are left with and executed by the specialist. No guarantee exists that the executed price will be the stop price, unlike the price on a limit order.

A trade at the stop price triggers the order, which then becomes a market order. A stop order takes two trades to execute:

1. **Trigger**. The trigger transaction at or through the stop price activates the trade.
2. **Execution**. The stop order becomes a market order and is executed at the market price, completing the trade.

Buy Stop Order

A buy stop order protects a profit or limits a loss in a short stock position. The buy stop is entered at a price above the current offering price, and is triggered when the market price touches or goes through the buy stop price.

An investor would also place a stop order to "buy 100 COD at 42.25 stop" when the market is at 40 if he believes 42 represents a technical resistance point, above which the stock price will continue to rise.

Buy Stop Order

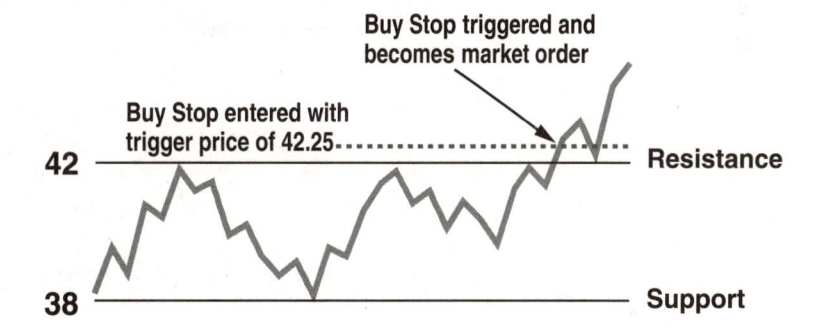

Sell Stop Order

A **sell stop order** protects a profit or limits a loss in a long stock position. (A sell stop is also called a stop loss.) A buy stop order is placed above the market and a sell stop is placed below the market.

Sell Stop Order

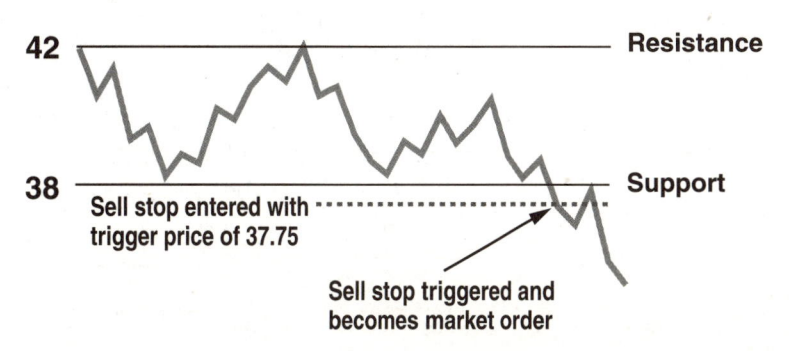

If the market is at 40, a customer who bought the stock at a lower price might place an order to "sell 100 COD at 37.75 stop" if he believes 38 represents a technical support level, below which the stock price will continue to fall.

If a large number of stop orders are triggered at the same price, a flurry of trading activity takes place as they become market orders. This activity may accelerate the advance or decline of the stock price, which can subvert the stop order's intent to curtail a loss or protect a profit.

Stop Limit Order

A stop limit order is a stop order that, once triggered, becomes a limit order instead of a market order.

Stop and Limit Orders

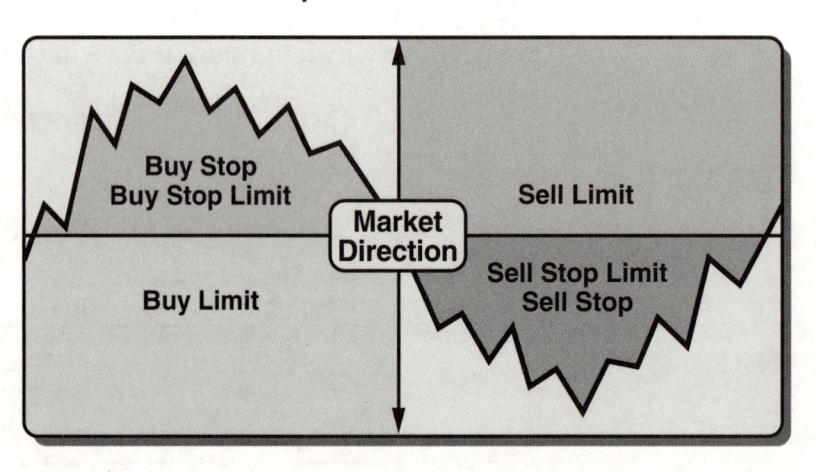

	Market Direction	
Buy Stop / Buy Stop Limit		Sell Limit
Buy Limit		Sell Stop Limit / Sell Stop

Test Topic Alert!

Be prepared for 2–4 questions regarding limit and stop orders. Use the chart to solve some problems, starting with limit orders.

XYZ is currently trading at 52. Where would a customer enter a buy limit order?

Refer to the chart. Think of the horizontal middle line as the current price. The buy limit would be entered somewhere below 52. The investor wants to buy at a better price—a lower price for a buyer. The order would be filled at or below the order price.

A sell limit order for XYZ would be entered above the market price. The seller is waiting for a price that is better than 52. The order would be filled at a price equal to or higher (better for a seller) than the order price.

Stop orders are a little more tricky because they have two parts: trigger (election) and execution. Consider a buy stop at 52 entered when the market is 51. Based on the ticks below, at what price would this order be executed?

51.88   51.99   52.13   52.13   51.88

Look at the chart. The chart shows you that a buy stop is entered above the market price. This reminds you that it is only elected or triggered at the first price where the market is at or above the order price. Stops become market orders when triggered, so it executes at the price immediately following the trigger. Based on this example, this buy stop triggers at 52.13 and could execute at 52.13.

If this had been a buy stop limit at 52, the trigger would still be 52.13. Just as before, it triggers at or above the order price. When a stop limit is triggered it becomes a limit order, which means it will execute only at a price at or below the stated price (lower is better for a buyer).

Based on this example, this buy stop limit triggers at 52.13 and could execute at 51.88.

Consider a sell stop at 52 entered when the market is 53. Based on the ticks shown below, at what price could this order be executed?

52.50   51.88   51.50   51.75   52.25

The chart shows you that a sell stop is entered below the market price. This reminds you that it is only elected or triggered when the market is at or below the order price. Stops become market orders when triggered, so it executes at the next available price immediately following the trigger. Based on this example, this sell stop triggers at 51.88 and executes at 51.50.

If this had been a sell stop limit at 52, the trigger would still be 51.88. Just as before, it triggers at or below the order price. When a stop limit is triggered it becomes a limit order, which means it will execute only at a price at or above the stated price (higher is better for a seller). This sell stop limit triggers at 51.88 and could execute at 52.25.

When drawing your order reference chart, think of the word BLISS. It stands for Buy Limits and Sell Stops. These are the orders that are placed below the market price. ("B" in BLISS reminds you of "B" in below.)

Why use stop orders?

Buy Stop orders:

- protect against loss in a short stock position;
- protect a gain from a short stock position; and
- establish a long position when a breakout occurs above the line of resistance.

Sell Stop orders:

- protect against loss in a long stock position;
- protect a gain from a long stock position; and
- establish a short position when a breakout occurs below the line of support.

✓ **Take Note:** There is no guarantee that if a stop order is elected, the investor will pay or receive the stop price.

Quick Quiz 8.3   Multiple Choice

1. An order to sell at 38.63 Stop, 38.63 Limit is entered before the opening. The subsequent trades are 38.88, 38.50, 38.38. The order

   A. was executed at 38.50
   B. was executed at 38.63
   C. was executed at 38.88
   D. has not yet been executed

2. A sell stop order is entered

   A. above the current market price
   B. below the current market price
   C. either above or below the current market price
   D. at the current market price

3. Stop orders

   I. can limit a loss in a declining stock
   II. become market orders when there is a trade at, or the market passes through, a specific price
   III. are the same as limit orders
   IV. can affect the price of the stock when the specific stop price is reached

   A. I and II only
   B. I, II and IV only
   C. I, III and IV only
   D. II and III only

4. A client bought 100 shares of MCS at 20. The stock rose to 30, and he wants to protect his gain. Which of the following orders should be entered?

   A. Sell stop at 29
   B. Sell limit at 30
   C. Sell limit at 30.13
   D. Sell stop at 30.13

5. A customer sold 100 shares of QRS short when the stock was trading at 19. QRS is now trading at 14, and he wants to protect his gain. Which of the following orders should he place?

   A. Sell stop at 13.88
   B. Sell limit at 14
   C. Buy limit at 14
   D. Buy stop at 14.38

6. ZOO is trading at 50.63. Your customer, who owns 100 shares of the stock, places an order to sell ZOO at 50.25 stop limit. The Tape subsequently reports the following trades:

   ZOO 50.63 50.75 50.13 50.13 50.25
   Your customer's order could first be executed at

   A. 50.13
   B. 50.25
   C. 50.63
   D. 50.75

Answers

1. **D.** A stop limit order is a stop order that becomes a limit order once the stop price has been triggered. When the limit price is the same as the stop price on a stop limit order, the order can be executed only at or better than the limit price. In this case, the order has not yet been executed because no transaction has occurred at or above 38.63 since the stop was triggered at 38.50.

2. **B.** Sell stop orders are always entered below the market price. A sell stop order is triggered when a transaction occurs at or below the price specified on the order. A buy stop order is always entered at a price above the current offering price. Once elected, stop orders become market orders.

3. **B.** A stop order becomes a market order once the market price reaches or passes the specific stop price. An investor in a long position can use the sell stop order for protection against a market decline. When a large number of stop orders are triggered at a particular price, the advance or decline of the market at that point can be magnified. Stop orders are not the same as limit orders because there is no guarantee of a specific execution price or better for a stop order.

4. **A.** A sell limit order is used to sell out a long position at a higher price (when the market moves up). A sell stop order is used to sell out a long position at a lower price (when the market moves down). To protect against a loss of the gain, a sell stop order would be placed just below where the stock is currently trading.

5. **D**. *A buy limit order is used to buy in a short position at a lower price (when the market moves down). A buy stop order is used to buy in a short position at a higher price (when the market moves up). To protect against a loss of the gain, a buy stop order would be placed just above where the stock is currently trading.*

6. **B**. *The sell stop limit order is elected (triggered) at the first trade of 50.13, when the stock trades at or below the stop price of 50.25. The order becomes a sell limit order at 50.25. The order can be executed at that price or higher (the limit placed by the customer). The next trade reported after the trigger is reached is below the limit price. The order will be executed at the next trade of 50.25.*

Comparison of Order Characteristics

Order Type	Description	Exchange Orders	OTC Orders
Market	Buy or sell at the best available market price	Most common order type on all exchanges	Most common OTC order type
Limit	Minimum price for sell orders; maximum price for buy orders	Handled by a specialist as a day or GTC order	Acceptable on either a day or GTC basis
Stop	Buy orders entered above the market; sell orders entered below the market	Acceptable on all exchanges as day or GTC orders	Acceptable by some dealers
Stop Limit	Stop order that becomes a limit order once the stop price has been reached or exceeded	Acceptable on all exchanges as day or GTC orders	Acceptable by some dealers

Reducing Orders Certain orders on the specialist's book are **reduced** when a stock goes ex-dividend. All orders entered below the market are reduced on the **ex-dividend date** (or **ex-date**), the first date on which the new owner of stock does not qualify for the current dividend. On the ex-date, the stock price drops by the amount of the distribution. Orders reduced include buy limits, sell stops and sell stop limits. These orders are reduced by the dividend amount rounded to the next highest .01. Without this reduction, trading at the lower price on the ex-dividend date could cause execution.

✓ **For Example:** ABC closes at 35.00. The following day is the ex-date for a .31 cent cash dividend. ABC stock should open at 34.69.

Do Not Reduce (DNR)

A DNR order is not reduced by an ordinary cash dividend. In this case, the customer does not care if there is an execution due solely to the ex-date reduction.

Test Topic Alert! You are likely to be asked which orders are reduced for cash dividends. Only those placed below the market price are automatically reduced. Remember that BLiSS (buy limits and sell stops) orders are placed below the market price and are reduced for cash dividend distributions. All orders are reduced for stock dividends and stock splits, whether placed above or below the market.

Quick Quiz 8.4   Multiple Choice

1. An order that instructs the specialist not to adjust the limit (or stop) price when a stock goes ex-dividend is designated

   A. DNA
   B. DNR
   C. FOK
   D. EX

2. Which of the following orders would be reduced by the specialist on the ex-dividend date?

   I.   Buy limit order
   II. Sell stop order
   III. Buy stop order
   IV. Sell limit order

   A. I and II only
   B. I and IV only
   C. II, III and IV only
   D. III and IV only

3. A company is about to pay a dividend of $.70. On the ex-dividend date, an open order to sell at 46 stop would

   A. be automatically adjusted to 45.30 Stop
   B. be automatically adjusted to 45.38 Stop
   C. be automatically adjusted to 45.50 Stop
   D. remain 46 Stop

Answers

1. **B.** The qualifying price on a do not reduce (DNR) order will not be reduced by ordinary cash dividends on the ex-dividend date.

2. **A.** When a stock goes ex-dividend, the specialist will reduce open buy limit orders and open sell stop orders because they are placed below the market price and could be triggered when the market price is reduced for the loss of dividend. The specialist will not reduce open sell limit orders and open buy stop orders.

3. **A.** When a stock goes ex-dividend, the price of the stock falls by the amount of the dividend. A dividend of $.70 would reduce the stock price by that amount.

Reductions for Stock Splits (Proportional Reductions)

To calculate an open order's price reduction after a stock split, divide the market price by the fraction that represents the split.

Calculating Order Adjustments for Stock Splits

Order price: $100
Stock split: 5 for 4
5 / 4 = 1.25
$100 / 1.25 = $80
Adjusted order price = $80

Order price: $100
Stock split: 2 for 1
2 / 1 = 2.00
$100 / 2.00 = $50
Adjusted order price = $50

Order price: $100
Stock split: 3 for 2
3 / 2 = 1.50
$100 / 1.50 = $66.67
Adjusted order price = $66.67

Time-Sensitive Orders

Orders based on time considerations include the following.

- Day
- Good till cancelled

- At-the-open and Market-on-close
- Not held
- Fill or kill
- Immediate or cancel
- All or none
- Alternative—provides two alternatives, such as sell a stock at a limit or sell it on stop

Day Orders — Unless marked to the contrary, an open order (stop or limit) is assumed to be a day order, valid only until the close of trading on the day it is entered. If the order has not been filled, it is cancelled at the close of the day's trading.

Good-Till-Cancelled (GTC) Orders — GTC orders are valid until executed or cancelled. An order could be entered as "good for the week" or "good for the month." However, on the book, the order will appear as GTC. It would be up to the firm entering the order to cancel it at the appropriate time, if unexecuted.

At-the-Open and Market-on-Close Orders — At-the-open orders are executed at the opening of the market. Partial executions are allowable. They must reach the post by the open of trading in that security or else they are canceled. Market-on-close orders are executed at or as near as possible to the closing price in the OTC market. On the NYSE, however, a market on close order must be entered before 3:40 pm and will be executed at the closing price.

Not-Held (NH) Orders — A market order coded **NH** indicates that the customer agrees not to hold the floor broker or broker/dealer to a particular time and price of execution. This provides the floor broker with authority to decide the best time and price at which to execute the trade. Market not held orders may not be placed with the specialist.

Fill-or-Kill (FOK) Orders — The commission house broker is instructed to fill an entire FOK order immediately at the limit price or better. A broker that cannot fill the entire order immediately cancels it and notifies the originating branch office.

Immediate-or-Cancel (IOC) Orders — IOC orders are like FOK orders except that a partial execution is acceptable. The portion not executed is cancelled.

All-or-None (AON) Orders — AON orders must be executed in their entirety or not at all. AON orders can be day or GTC orders. They differ from the FOKs in that they do not have to be filled immediately.

Alternative Orders (OCO) — Assume a customer is long stock at $50 which was purchased six months earlier at $30. To protect his unrealized gain, the customer might enter a sell stop at $48. Alternatively, if the stock continues to rise, he wants out at $53. What he might do is enter both orders with the notation "one cancels the other" (OCO). If one of the orders is executed, the other is immediately cancelled.

Quick Quiz 8.5

Match each of the following items with the appropriate description below.

A. Fill or kill
B. All or none
C. Immediate or cancel
D. Not held

___ 1. Executed by the floor broker, who is given authority to select time and price

___ 2. Execute immediately, in its entirety, or cancel

___ 3. Execute in its entirety but not necessarily immediately

___ 4. Execute as much as possible immediately, cancel the rest

Answers   1. **D.**   2. **A.**   3. **B.**   4. **C.**

Long and Short Sale Rules

A purchase order is normally a straight-forward transaction. Certain rules apply to short sales, however.

Long Sale When an investor buys shares of a stock he is **long** the position. When he sells share of stock owned, it is a long sale (the sale of stock held long in the account).

Short Sale Selling **short** is a technique to profit from the decline in a stock's price. The short seller initially borrows stock from a broker/dealer to sell at the market. The investor expects the stock price to decline enough to allow him to buy shares at a lower price and replace the borrowed stock at a later date.

Short sales are risky because if the stock price rises instead of falls, the investor still must buy the shares to replace the borrowed stock. In addition, a stock's price can rise without limit. Therefore, the position has unlimited risk.

Comparison of Long and Short Sales Every investment involves the purchase and eventual sale of the investment.

A Comparison of Long and Short Sales

	Long Position	Short Position
First Transaction	Buy low	Sell high (borrow securities and sell them)
Second Transaction	Sell high	Buy low (buy back securities to replace those borrowed)

✓ *Take Note:* Short sales:

- are always executed and accounted for in a customer's margin account and are subject to Reg T 50% initial margin requirements
- always entail the delivery of borrowed stock to the buy side of the trade
- are subject to higher NASD/NYSE minimum margin maintenance requirements than long purchases in a margin account

Exchange Short Sale Rules

SEC and exchange plus tick rules are designed to block a short seller from feeding orders into a declining market to drive a stock's price lower. An order to sell a listed security short must be executed on either a **plus tick** or a **zero-plus tick**.

A plus tick is a price higher than the last different price—for instance, from 30 to 30.13. A zero-plus tick occurs when the last trade for the security was made at the same price as the trade before, but that trade was higher than the previous trade. The plus or minus tick carries over from the previous day's trading.

Look at the sequence of prices in the chart that follows. According to the **up tick rule**, an order to sell short could be executed on the third, fourth, and fifth trades.

Up, Down, and Zero Ticks

			30.13	30.13		
30		30			30	30
	29.88					
Opening Sale.	Down tick. Short sales not permitted.	Plus tick. Short sales permitted.	Plus tick. Short sales permitted.	Zero plus tick. Short sales permitted.	Down tick. Short sales not permitted.	Zero down tick. Short sales not permitted.

OTC Short Sale Rules Nasdaq's short sale rule prohibits entering a short sale in a **Nasdaq National Market** (**NNM**) security at or below the current inside bid whenever that bid is lower than the previous inside bid. In the OTC market, the inside bid is the best (highest) bid price at which the customer can sell the stock.

A short sale, when the inside bid is a down bid, is permitted if the sale is at least one cent above the current inside bid. An opening bid is a down bid if it is lower than the previous day's closing bid or the same as the previous day's closing bid if that closing bid was a down bid.

Exemptions from the Nasdaq short sale rule include sales by any:

- member in which a sell order is marked long and the member has no reason to know that the sale is actually short;
- member to offset odd lot customer orders;
- member to liquidate a long position that is less than a round lot; and
- person in a special arbitrage or special international arbitrage account.

Short Sale Regulations The Securities Exchange Act of 1934 prohibits directors, officers, and principal stockholders (insiders) from selling short stock in their own companies.

Sell Order Tickets A person is long a security if he:

- has title to it;
- has purchased the security or has entered into an unconditional contract to purchase the security, but has not yet received it;
- owns a security convertible into or exchangeable for the security and has tendered such security for conversion or exchange; or
- has an option to purchase the security and has exercised that option.

Unless one or more of these conditions are met, the SEC considers any sale of securities a short sale.

Sell Orders Must Be Identified

The SEC requires that all sell orders be identified as either **long** or **short**. No sale can be marked long unless the security to be delivered is in the customer's account or is owned by the customer and will be delivered to the broker by the settlement date. If a security the customer owns will not be delivered to complete the sale, the customer goes short against the box.

Shorting Bonds Securities, such as listed stocks, have many equivalent securities trading at any time. For instance, it is easy to short 100 shares of GM because an equivalent 100 shares of GM can be purchased on the NYSE at any time. It is not easy to cover shorts for most municipal bonds because the limited number of bonds available in each issue could make it difficult to buy in the short position.

Quick Quiz 8.6   Multiple Choice

1. An appropriate justification for selling a stock short is to

   A. cut losses on a long position
   B. benefit from a decline in the price of the stock
   C. benefit from a rise in the price of the stock
   D. seek a modest potential reward with limited risk

2. ALFA Enterprises stock was traded as shown:

Open	25	25.25	25.13	25.25	25.25
25.25					
	I	II	III	IV	V

   On which transactions can short sales be made?

   A. I, II, IV and V only
   B. I, III, IV and V only
   C. II, IV and V only
   D. II and V only

Answers

1. **B.** Selling short does not reduce the risk of a long position: the investor is selling borrowed, not owned, stock. The appropriate time to sell short is when one suspects that the stock price is about to drop. The investor wants to sell at a high price, buy later at a lower price. The reward and risk potential of selling short is high; if the stock price moves down dramatically, the investor can reap a large gain. If it moves up dramatically, the investor can lose a lot of money.

2. **C.** Short sales can be made only on up ticks or zero-plus ticks. An up tick occurs when the stock is traded at a price higher than the last different price. A zero-plus tick occurs when there is no change in price but the last time the price changed it was an up tick. Choices II and IV are up ticks. Choice V is a zero-plus tick.

Other Domestic and International Exchanges

American Stock Exchange (AMEX)

The **American Stock Exchange (AMEX)**, a private, not-for-profit corporation located in New York City, handles about one-fifth of all of the listed securities trades in the United States.

The AMEX, also known as the **curb**, is organized and operates in much the same manner as the NYSE. To execute trades on the exchange floor, brokerage firms must be members of the exchange.

Specialists operate as market makers on the AMEX much the same way as they operate on the NYSE and on other exchanges that employ the specialist system.

Regional Exchanges

In addition to the national stock exchanges, other stock exchanges serve the financial communities in different regions of the country. Regional exchanges include the Boston Stock Exchange, Chicago Stock Exchange, Cincinnati Stock Exchange, Pacific Stock Exchange, and the Philadelphia Stock Exchange.

Regional exchanges tend to focus on the securities of companies within their regions, although they also offer trading in many securities listed on the NYSE or AMEX. Listing requirements on regional exchanges are often less stringent than those of the national exchanges, and the companies they list are usually among the smallest and newest in their industries.

International Markets

Foreign companies' stocks trade on the major stock exchanges in the financial centers of Europe and Asia. As a result of increasing global economic interdependence and the instant access to information available through telecommunications, events in London or Tokyo can have a dramatic effect on US markets, and vice versa. Traders in the United States monitor foreign markets closely to detect trends and events that will affect the prices of securities around the world.

Computerized Order Routing

In addition to the electronic systems each exchange develops, automated **order routing systems** link the specialists from each exchange through the **Intermarket Trading System (ITS)**.

New York Stock Exchange SuperDot Nearly 75% of the orders the NYSE receives each day are processed through a computerized trading and execution system called **SuperDot** (Super Designated Order Turnaround). Broker/dealers use this computerized order routing system to route an order directly to the appropriate specialist. Once the specialist receives the order, it is presented in the auction market.

Orders can be sent through the system either preopening or postopening. The computer automatically pairs preopening orders received before the opening of trading with other orders and executes them at the opening price. Any order that cannot be matched before the opening is given to the specialist to handle. If an order is received postopening, it is sent directly to the specialist post and presented to the crowd. All NYSE-listed stocks are eligible for trading on SuperDot.

Nasdaq SuperMontage The quotation and execution for Nasdaq is called SuperMontage. This system will display the total amount of trading interest at the inside market, as well as four price levels away, for a total of five price levels on the bid and offer sides of the market.

The Consolidated Tape

The **Consolidated Tape system** is an NYSE service designed to deliver real-time reports of securities transactions to subscribers as they occur on the various exchanges. Subscribers to the Tape can choose to receive transaction reports through their quote terminals or their ticker lines.

How the Tape Works The Tape reports are distributed over two networks. **Network A** reports transactions in NYSE-listed securities wherever they are traded. As an example, a trade involving NYSE-listed IBM on the Pacific Stock Exchange would be reported on Network A. **Network B** limits its coverage to AMEX-listed and regional exchange transactions. Each network reports transactions within 90 seconds of the trades.

How to Read the Consolidated Tape The Tape prints volumes and prices of securities transactions within seconds of their execution. On the high-speed line, the transactions are reported with market identifiers, letters identifying the security traded, its price, and the number of shares.

Number of Shares

The Tape reports a sale of a single round lot (100 shares) of stock by listing the trading symbol and the price at which the transaction occurred, but with no quantity. A report of "T 25.15" means that 100 shares of AT&T traded at 25.15. Sales of multiples of a round lot are indicated by printing the number of round lots followed by the letter "s" and the price. A report of "AEP6s39.75" indicates that 600 shares of American Electric Power traded at 39.75.

Ticker Tape

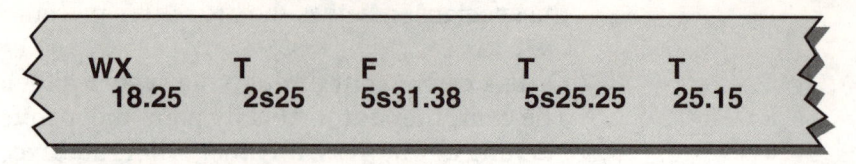

```
WX        T        F          T          T
18.25     2s25     5s31.38    5s25.25    25.15
```

If a transaction is executed for 10,000 shares or more, the entire amount is printed ("T 14,000s25" indicates 14,000 shares of AT&T traded at 25).

Stocks sold in 10-share units have their numbers abbreviated, like round lots, and are followed by the symbol "ṣ" (a trade of 50 shares of XYZ at 24 would appear as "XYZ 5ṣ 24").

The first three transactions listed in the sample Tape, reading from left to right, show trades of 100 shares of WX (Westinghouse Electric) at 18.25, 200 shares of T (AT&T) at 25, followed by 500 shares of F (Ford) at 31.38.

If two similar trades for the same security occur consecutively, the report prints them under the same trading symbol and separates them with a dot. The transaction "T5s25.25" on the Tape above indicates trades of 500 shares of AT&T at 25 followed by 100 shares at 25.

Active Markets   At times, the market and exchanges can be so active that trade information can be inaccurate or out of sequence. Several delete information modes have been established to abbreviate reports and keep the Tape from running late. These notations indicate information will be **omitted**:

- **DIGITS & VOL DELETED**. When this message appears, both the first digit of the price and the volume will be dropped. A trade for 200 shares of IBM at 92.50 will appear as "IBM2.50." DIGITS & VOL RESUMED appears when trading activity slows.
- **REPEAT PRICES OMITTED**. Indicates that the Tape will show only transactions that differ in price from the previous reports.

Other Messages

Other messages might appear on the Tape.

- **SLD** indicates that the exchange did not report a sale on time, so it is out of sequence on the Tape. For example, a customer who sees "AEP25" on the Tape followed by "AEP.SLD2s25.13" might believe that AEP's price is going up. In reality, the price may be going down: the 25.13 is out of sequence and should have appeared before the 25.
- **OPD** announces the initial transaction in a security for which the opening has been delayed. As an example, the delayed opening of 1,200 shares of DWQ at 42 would appear as "DWQ.OPD12s42."
- **HALT** means that trading in a security has been halted.

✓ **Take Note:** If a trade is being reported late (SLD), it is not considered part of the "tick" sequence. Consider the following trades in ABC:

24.00   24.03   23.99   24.13   SLD   24.10

It might appear that the trade at 24.10 is a minus tick. However it must be measured against the prior trade of 23.99.

Quick Quiz 8.7   Multiple Choice

1. A registered rep places an order for a client to buy 1,600 shares of RCA at 36.75 and sees the following trades on the Tape. Assuming he was the only bidder, how many shares did he buy and at what price(s)?

	GE	RCA	TX	RCA
	52.50	5s36.50	2s23.50	10s36.50.75

   A. 500 at 36.50
   B. 1,000 at 36.50
   C. 100 at 36.75
   D. 500 at 36.50, 1,000 at 36.50, 100 at 36.75

Answer   1. **D.** Two separate entries for RCA appear on the Tape. The first indicates that the registered rep was able to partially fill the order by picking up 500 shares at 36.50; he then filled the remainder of the order by buying 1,000 shares at 36.50 plus the final 100 shares at 36.75.

The Over-the-Counter Market

The largest securities market (in terms of number of issues) is the **over-the-counter market (OTC)** in which broker/dealers negotiate trades directly with one another. The OTC market is a highly sophisticated telecommunications and computer network connecting broker/dealers across the country.

✓ **Take Note:** OTC trading is regulated by both the SEC and the NASD, the **self-regulatory organization (SRO)** for the OTC market.

Nasdaq

The computerized information system that tracks OTC trading is called **Nasdaq**—the **National Association of Securities Dealers Automated Quotation** service. Securities that can be traded in the OTC market include, but are not limited to, the following:

- American depositary receipts (ADRs);
- common stocks, especially of banks and insurance and technology companies;
- most corporate bonds;
- municipal bonds;
- US government securities;
- preferred stock;
- equipment trust certificates; and
- closed-end investment companies.

OTC vs. NYSE Markets

OTC	NYSE
Securities' prices determined through negotiation	Securities' prices determined through auction bidding
Regulated by the NASD	Regulated by the NYSE
Market Makers must register with both the SEC and NASD	Specialists must be registered with the SEC and must be Exchange members
Traded at many locations across the country	Traded only on the NYSE floor

Negotiated Market The OTC market is a **negotiated market** in which market makers may bargain during a trade. A negotiated market is competitive: a firm competes against other brokerage firms, each trading for its own inventory.

OTC Market Makers

Specialists on an exchange act as market makers and stand ready to trade in specified securities. The OTC market has no specialists. Rather, firms wishing to make a market in a particular security must register with, and receive approval from, NASD. They buy and sell for their own inventories, for their own profit and at their own risk. A broker/dealer acting as a market maker, buying and selling for its own account rather than arranging trades, acts as a **principal**, not an agent.

✓ *Take Note:* Unlisted securities trade OTC, while listed securities trade on exchanges. Besides unlisted stocks and bonds, other securities traded OTC are municipals and governments.

Quotations

Bids, Offers, and Quotes

A **quote** is a dealer's current bid and offer on a security. The **current bid** is the highest price at which the dealer will buy, and the **current offer** is the lowest price at which the dealer will sell. The difference between the bid and ask is known as the **spread**.

A typical quote might be expressed as "bid 63–offered 63.07." The highest price the dealer will pay is 63, and the lowest price the dealer will accept is 63.07. The spread is .07 of a point between the bid and ask. The broker could also say "63 bid–63.07 ask" or "63 to .07."

The Customer's and the Market Maker's Relationship to the Quote

	Bid-63	Ask/Offer-63.07
Quoting dealer	Buys	Sells
Customer	Sells	Buys

When a customer buys a stock from a firm acting as principal, the broker marks up the ask price to reach the net price to the customer. Likewise, when a customer sells stock to a firm acting as principal, the dealer marks down from the bid price to reach the net proceeds to the customer.

✓ *For Example:* If WXYZ is quoted as "43.25 to .50," for instance, and the dealer wants a half-point for the trade, a customer buying would pay 44 net and a customer selling would receive 42.75 net.

Firm Quote A **firm quotation** is the price at which a market maker stands ready to buy or sell at least one trading unit—100 shares of stock or five bonds—at the quoted price with other NASD member firms. When an OTC firm makes a market in a security, the broker/dealer must be willing to buy or sell at least one trading unit of the security at its firm quote. All quotes are firm quotes unless otherwise indicated.

As is true of market order executions on an exchange floor, an OTC trader may attempt to negotiate a better price with a market maker by making a **counter offer** or a **counter bid**—especially if the spread between the market maker's bid and ask is fairly wide. However, the only way to guarantee an immediate execution is to buy stock at the market maker's ask price or sell at the bid price.

In a typical bond transaction, a trader at one broker/dealer calls a trader at another broker/dealer (a market maker) to buy a specific bond. A market maker might give another broker/dealer a quote that is firm for an hour with five-minute recall. This is a firm quote that remains good for an hour. If, within that hour, the market maker receives another order for the same security, the trader calls the broker/dealer back and gives it five minutes to confirm its order or lose its right to buy that security at the price quoted.

Backing Away

A market maker can revise a firm quote in response to market conditions and trading activity, but a market maker that refuses to do business at the price(s) quoted **backs away** from the quote. Backing away is a violation of NASD trading rules.

Recognized Quotation A recognized quotation under NASD/NYSE rules is any public bid or offer for one or more round lots or other normal trading units. Any bid for less than a round lot must state the amount of the security for which it is good. If the bid or offer is made for multiple round lots, it must also be good for a smaller number of units.

✓ **For Example:** If the bid is for 1,000 shares of stock, the bidder must buy any round lots offered of 100 or more at the same price.

Subject Quote A **subject quote** is one in which the price is tentative, subject to reconfirmation by the market maker. When a market maker knows the transaction size, the broker/dealer firms up the subject quote or gives a replacement quote. Some typical expressions used to denote subject and firm quotes are shown below. Firm quotes are absolute statements but subject quotes are hedged.

Qualified Quotes A quote will often be given with **qualifiers** intended to allow the broker/dealer to back away if market conditions change.

Workout Quote

This term is usually reserved for situations in which a market maker knows that special handling will be required to accommodate a particular trade. Either the order size is too big for the market to absorb without disruption, or the market might be too thin or temporarily unstable.

Quotations

A **workout quote** is an approximate figure used to provide the buyer or seller with an indication of price, not a firm quote. Block positioners use workout quotes frequently.

Subject or Workout Market	Firm Market
"It is around 40-41."	"The market is 40–41."
"Last I saw, it was 40–41."	"It is currently 40–41."
"It is 40–41 subject."	
"40 to 42.50 workout."	

Nominal Quote

A **nominal quote** is someone's assessment of where a stock might trade in an active market. Nominal quotes may be used to give customers an idea of the market value of an inactively traded security, but they are not firm quotes. Nominal quotes in print must be clearly labeled as such.

Quotation Spread and Size

Spread The difference between a security's bid and asked prices is known as the **spread**. Many factors influence a spread's size, including the:

- issue's size;
- issuer's financial condition;
- amount of market activity in the issue; and
- market conditions.

Size Unless otherwise specified, a firm quote is always good for one round lot (100 shares).

✓ **For Example** A firm quote of 8.25–.50 means the market maker stands ready to buy 100 shares of stock from another broker/dealer at the 8.25 bid price or sell 100 shares at the 8.50 ask price.

Non-Nasdaq For securities quoted on either *Pink Sheets* or the **over-the-counter bulletin board** (**OTCBB**), the **three-quote rule** often applies. Unless there are at least two market makers displaying firm quotes, broker/dealers receiving orders to buy or sell non-Nasdaq securities must contact a minimum of three dealers to determine the prevailing price.

Manipulative and Deceptive Practices The Conduct Rules mandate that any quote given must represent a real bid or offer. No fictitious quotes are allowed.

Test Topic Alert!

Following is a list of important test points about OTC quotes.

- Markups and markdowns are charged when a market maker is acting as a principal (dealing from inventory with financial risk).
- Firm quotes are good for a round lot only, unless otherwise stated. A quote of 11–11.50, 3 × 5 is firm between dealers for 300 shares at the bid of 11 and 500 shares at the asked of 11.50.
- Nominal quotes can be given for informational purposes, and can be printed only if clearly labeled as such.
- A relatively wide spread indicates a thin trading market for the security.

NASD 5% Markup Policy

The NASD adopted the **5% markup policy** to ensure that the investing public receives fair treatment and pays reasonable rates for brokerage services in the OTC markets. It is considered a guideline only and is not a firm rule for markups and markdowns. A firm charging a customer more or less than a 5% markup may or may not be in violation of fair and equitable trade practices. The markup may be considered excessive once all of the relevant factors are taken into account.

A broker/dealer can fill a customer order in the OTC market in three ways:

- If the broker/dealer is a market maker in the security, it will (as principal) buy from or sell to the customer, charging a markup or markdown.
- If the firm is not a market maker in the security, it can fill the order as agent, without taking a position in the security, and charge a commission for its execution services.
- Riskless and simultaneous transaction.

Markup Based on Representative Market Prices

In OTC principal transactions, the 5% markup is based on the price representative of prevailing (inside) market prices at the time of a customer transaction. The NASD 5% markup policy applies to all transactions in nonexempt listed or unlisted securities traded OTC regardless of whether the transactions are executed as agency or principal trades.

✓ **Take Note:** The NASD's 5% policy applies to markups, markdowns, and commissions.

Fixed Public Offering Price Securities

The 5% markup policy does not apply to mutual funds, variable annuity contracts, or securities sold in public offerings—all of which are sold by a prospectus. It also does not apply to exempt securities.

Dealer's Inventory Costs

If a customer's buy order is filled from a broker/dealer's inventory, the net price to the customer is based on the prevailing market price. This is regardless of whether or not the broker/dealer selling to the customer is also making a market in the stock and regardless of what the firm's quote might be.

The price at which the broker/dealer acquired the stock being sold to the customer has no bearing on the net price to the customer; the price to the customer must be reasonably related to the current market.

Riskless and Simultaneous Transactions

A **riskless and simultaneous transaction** is an order to buy or sell stock in which the firm receiving the order is not a market maker. The dealer has two options for filling the order.

- As agent for the customer, it could buy or sell on the customer's behalf and charge a commission, subject to the 5% policy.
- It could buy or sell for its riskless principal account, then buy or sell to the customer as principal, charging a markup or markdown subject to the 5% policy.

When the order is filled as a principal transaction, the broker/dealer must disclose the markup to the customer.

Proceeds Transactions

When a customer sells securities and uses the proceeds to purchase other securities in a proceeds transaction, the broker/dealer's combined commissions and markups must be consistent with the NASD's 5% markup policy. In other words, member firms must treat proceeds transactions as one transaction for markup and markdown purposes.

Markup Policy Considerations

In assessing the fairness of a broker/dealer's commission and markup practices, the NASD considers the following factors.

Type of Security. In general, more market risk is associated with making markets and trading common stocks than is associated with dealing in bonds. The more risk a broker/dealer assumes, the greater the justification for higher markups.

Inactively Traded Stocks. The thinner the market for a security, the more volatile the stock and the greater the market risk to anyone dealing in the stock. Thus, a broker/dealer is justified in charging higher markups on inactively traded stocks.

Selling Price of Security. Commission and markup rates should decrease as a stock's price increases.

Dollar Amount of Transaction. Transactions of relatively small dollar amounts generally warrant higher percentage markups than large-dollar transactions.

Nature of the Broker/Dealer's Business. This standard pertains to full-service brokers versus discount brokers. In most cases, the NASD accepts that a general securities firm has higher operating costs than a discount broker and, thus, may justify higher commissions and markups.

Pattern of Markups. Although the NASD is concerned primarily with detecting cases where broker/dealers have established patterns of excessive markups, a single incident could still be considered an unfair markup.

Markups on Inactive Stocks (Contemporaneous Cost). For inactive stocks and situations where no prevailing market quotes are available, a broker/dealer may base a markup on its cost in the stock.

Test Topic Alert!

The NASD 5% markup policy is peculiarly named for two reasons:

1. It applies to markups, markdowns, and commissions, meaning it is applicable to principal and agency transactions.
2. 5% is not the limit. A transaction charge of more than 5% might be fine, if it is reasonable based on the circumstances of the trade.

This policy applies to nonexempt, OTC transactions. Examples of subject transactions are REITS, closed-end company shares, ADRs, third market trades, and unlisted stocks.

Municipal securities and government securities are not subject to this policy.

Remember that all computations must be based on the inside quote (the best available from all the market makers), not the firm's quote.

Expect 2–3 questions on this concept.

Quick Quiz 8.8 Multiple Choice

1. An NASD member firm is selling stock to a customer from inventory. The broker/dealer has held the shares sold for several months. What price should the dealer use as a basis for a markup?

    A. Price at which it purchased the securities
    B. Offer price shown in the *Pink Sheets* on the day of the current sale
    C. Broker/dealer's own current offer price
    D. Best offering price quoted in the interdealer market

2. The NASD's 5% policy applies to

    I. commissions charged when executing customer agency (broker) transactions
    II. markups and markdowns on principal (dealer) transactions filled for customers from a firm's trading inventory
    III. markups on stock bought for inventory, then immediately resold to customers
    IV. markdowns on stocks bought from customers for inventory, then immediately resold to another broker/dealer

    A. I and II only
    B. II only
    C. III and IV only
    D. I, II, III and IV

3. Which of the following transactions are not subject to the NASD's 5% policy on markups and markdowns?

    I. New issue corporate equity securities sold in a public offering
    II. Mutual fund shares sold to the public
    III. Transactions on the NYSE or other national exchanges
    IV. NYSE-listed stock traded in the third market

    A. I and II only
    B. I, II, and III only
    C. III and IV only
    D. I, II, III and IV

4. The NASD's 5% policy

    A. allows a member to determine fair markups based on the firm's actual acquisition costs
    B. is a guide to fairness, not a rule
    C. automatically judges any markup or markdown exceeding 5% to be unfair
    D. applies only to common stock transactions

5. Which of the following is not relevant in applying the 5% policy?

    A. Amount of money involved
    B. Type of security
    C. Current price of the security
    D. Type of account

Answers

1. **D.** *NASD rules require that a dealer's markup to a customer be based on the current market rather than the dealer's cost. The dealer's potential loss on inventory is considered to be the risk of making a market.*

2. **D**. The 5% policy applies both to commission charges on agency transactions and to markups and markdowns on principal transactions with customers.

3. **B**. The NASD's 5% policy applies to all OTC transactions except public offering stocks (including mutual fund shares) and exempt securities. Because the 5% policy applies to all OTC trading, it includes third market transactions in listed stocks, but not listed securities traded on an exchange.

4. **B**. The 5% policy is only a guide to fair markups and commissions; it is not a strict rule. Markups or markdowns that amount to more than 5% may very well be justified; and by the same token, a markup of only 1% or 2% could be excessive, depending on the transaction size and the dollar amount of the markup or commission charge.

5. **D**. The type of account is not relevant in deciding 5% policy because the NASD markup policy is used as a guide in all types of accounts.

NASD Automated Quotation System

Nasdaq Quotation Service

Nasdaq provides a computer link between broker/dealers that trade OTC. The system provides three levels of stock quotation service to the securities industry.

- **Nasdaq Level 1**: available to registered reps through a variety of public vendors. Level 1 displays the inside market only; the highest bids and the lowest asks for securities included in the system. Normal market price fluctuations prevent a registered representative from guaranteeing a Level 1 price to a client.
- **Nasdaq Level 2**: available to NASD-approved subscribers only. Level 2 provides the current quote and quote size available from each market maker in a security in the system. To list a quote on Level 2, a market maker must guarantee that the quote is firm for at least 100 shares.
- **Nasdaq Level 3**: provides subscribers with all of the services of Levels 1 and 2 and allows registered market makers to input and update their quotes on any securities in which they make a market.

Levels of Nasdaq Service

Level 1: The inside quote.

Level 2: The inside quote plus quotes from all market makers.

Level 3: The inside quote, all other quotes, plus ability to enter or change your own quote.

```
DWAQ   35 – 35.13
DWAQ      Bid        Ask

Serendip   35        35.25
Tippec     34.88     35.13
Cheath     35        35.13

Enter      BID:      ASK:
```

Nasdaq Market Maker Requirements

Market Maker Reports Registered market makers must transmit reports of last sales made during designated transaction-reporting hours. These reports must include a security's Nasdaq symbol; the number of shares; the transaction price; and whether the trade was a buy, sell, or cross.

90-Second Reporting. Market maker transactions must be reported within 90 seconds after a trade's execution.

Volume Reports. Registered market makers must make daily reports to Nasdaq of their total daily volume in all securities for which they are registered market makers.

The following table summarizes the Nasdaq system: those who interact with the system at each level and information the participants need and produce.

Features of the Nasdaq System

Level 1	Level 2	Level 3
Registered reps and the investing public	OTC trading room staff and institutional accounts	Registered market makers
Quote monitoring only	Quote monitoring only	Quote monitoring and input
Representative bid and ask prices currently quoted	Full display of all market makers' quotes and size	Full display of all market makers' quotes and size. Update, change, or delete quotes and size of quotes

The Inside Market The **inside market** is the best bid (highest) price at which stock can be sold in the interdealer market and the best ask (lowest) price at which the same stock can be bought.

✓ *For Example:* Four OTC dealers making a market in ABCD may quote the stock as follows:

Market Maker	Bid	Ask
MM #1	10	11
MM #2	10.13	10.75
MM #3	10.25	11
MM #4	10.13	10.88

The inside bid, in this case, belongs to MM #3; its 10.25 bid is the highest of the four. The inside ask belongs to MM #2; its 10.75 ask is the lowest of the four. The inside market of 10.25–10.75 will be released to the quotation vending services as the market in ABCD.

OTC traders across the country will look first to MM #2 and MM #3 as the lead markets, the firms to contact if they want to buy or sell ABCD. If the other market makers merely adjust their quotes to match the current inside market, the stock's price level does not change. If one of them quotes a better market price and a trade occurs at the better price, the price level changes.

Whichever market maker makes the inside market will account for most of the trading in the interdealer market until competing market makers adjust their market quotes. NASD rules require that customer transactions be based on the inside market quotation, even when no business is transacted with the firm(s) making the inside market.

Quote Machines

To provide registered representatives and market makers with as much information as possible, the information provided is condensed into a series of symbols and numbers when it appears on a quote machine.

✓ *For Example:* Current market and trading data for DWAQ might appear as follows.

Current Market/Trading Data for DWAQ

```
DWAQ  25 – 25.50

L 25.38   O 25.38   C 24.88

B 25      H 25.38   NC + .50

A 25.50   L 24.88   V  424

                    T 9:50
```

Abbreviations that appear on the previous screen translate to the following.

Abbreviations

```
DWAQ  25 – 25.50
                         Previous Day's
Last 25.38   Open 25.38  Close 24.88
                         Net
Bid 25       High 25.38  Change + .50

Ask 25.50    Low 24.88   Volume  42,400

                         Time  9:50 ET
```

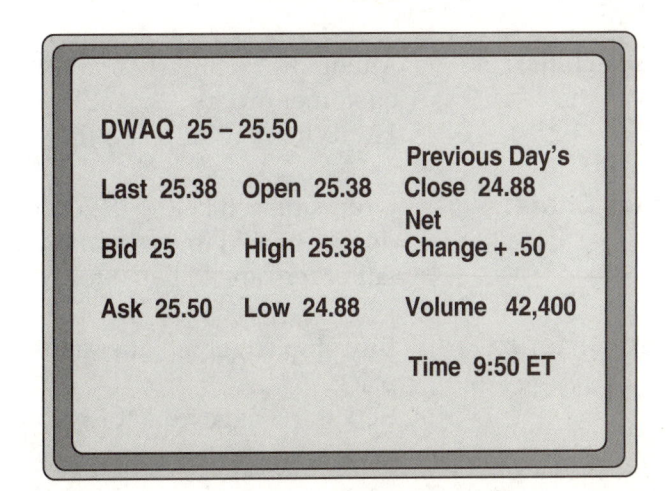

Quick Quiz 8.9

Match the Nasdaq level with the appropriate description by indicating **1**, **2**, or **3** for each statement. There might be more than one answer per description.

___ 1. Viewed by registered reps and the investing public

___ 2. The interactive level

___ 3. Used by trading rooms and institutions

___ 4. Shows only the inside quote

___ 5. Displays all market makers' quotes and sizes

___ 6. All market makers must have this level

Answers   1. **1.**   2. **3.**   3. **2.**   4. **1.**   5. **2. & 3.**   6. **3.**

Trading Securities HotSheet

Act of 1934:
- **People Act;** regulates exchanges and OTC trading activity

Securities Markets:
- **Exchanges**: listed securities, auction market
- **OTC**: unlisted securities, negotiated transactions
- **Third market**: listed securities traded OTC, negotiated trades, trades reported in 90 seconds
- **Fourth market**: institutions trading direct through Instinet service

NYSE Trade Rule:
- Priority, precedence, and parity: determines which order executed first

Specialist:
- Maintains an orderly market; acts as agent and principal, priority to customer orders
- Holds book of stop and limit orders; sets opening quote

Order Chart:
- Orders placed below the current market are adjusted for cash dividends (BLISS) unless marked DNR (do not reduce)
- All orders are adjusted for stock splits and stock dividends

Stop Orders:
- **Buy stop** triggered at or above order price, executed at next available price.
- **Sell stop** triggered at or below order price, executed at next price.

Stop Limit:	• Once stock trades at or through stop price, becomes a limit order to buy or sell
Time-Sensitive Orders:	• FOK: execute all immediately or cancel entire order • AON: execute all, immediacy is not important; hold as GTC on book until filled • IOC: execute whatever is available now, remainder is cancelled
Short Sale Rules:	• Must be executed on plus tick or zero-plus tick for exchanges, OTC has down bid rule • Inside bid = down bid • A legal short sale must be executed at least $.01 above bid if bid is a down bid • Short sale order tickets must be marked
Order Routing:	• SuperDot for NYSE
Non-Nasdaq:	• Quotes not firm unless priced • Three-quote rule generally applies • Corporate bonds on Yellow Sheets
5% Policy:	• Guide for OTC nonexempt (not munis or govs) • For markups, markdowns, commission
Nasdaq Levels:	• Level 1: Inside quote (basis for markup/markdown) • Level 2: Displays quotes of all market makers • Level 3: Market makers enter quotes (interactive level)
SuperMontage:	• Order display and execution system for Nasdaq • Shows trading interest at 5 levels on each side of the market

Series 7 Unit Test 8

1. The Securities Exchange Act of 1934 regulates or mandates

    I. full and fair disclosure on new offerings
    II. creation of the SEC
    III. manipulation of the market
    IV. margin requirements on securities

    A. I only
    B. I, II and III only
    C. II only
    D. II, III and IV only

2. All of the following statements regarding the short sale of a listed security are true EXCEPT that the

    A. sale can only be effected on a plus tick or zero-plus tick
    B. short sales may take place at the opening
    C. buyer must be advised that he is purchasing borrowed shares
    D. short sales may take place at the closing

3. The Nasdaq short-sale rule applies to all

    A. over-the-counter securities
    B. Nasdaq-listed securities
    C. Nasdaq National Market securities
    D. securities traded by NASD firms

4. Each of the following types of orders remains open on the NYSE until certain conditions are met EXCEPT

    A. stop orders
    B. good-till-cancelled orders
    C. all-or-none orders
    D. market orders

5. The SEC regulates the trading of all of the following EXCEPT

    A. commodity futures
    B. options
    C. preferred stock
    D. corporate bonds

6. Which of the following statements regarding the Third Market is(are) TRUE?

    I. It is composed of listed securities traded OTC.
    II. It is composed only of unlisted securities.
    III. The services of a brokerage firm are NOT used.
    IV. It refers to the block trading of unlisted securities.

    A. I only
    B. II and III
    C. III and IV
    D. IV only

7. Which of the following statements describes Nasdaq Level 3 service?

    A. Quotations from all registered market makers entering quotes into the system.
    B. Allows market maker to enter quotations into the system for a security in which it is registered.
    C. Representative bid and ask quotations on a security in which a minimum of two market makers exist.
    D. Representative bid and ask quotations on a security in which a minimum of three market makers exist.

8. During a trading halt, an investor can

    A. cancel an order that was placed before the halt
    B. execute a market order
    C. execute a limit order
    D. close an existing position

9. Which of the following orders are entered above the current market?

   I. Buy stop
   II. Sell stop
   III. Buy limit
   IV. Sell limit

   A. I and II
   B. I and IV
   C. II and III
   D. II and IV

10. If a floor broker asks a specialist to have his order stopped and the specialist replies, "you're stopped at 41," the floor broker

   A. will have a stop limit at 41 or higher
   B. must place a buy stop at or above the market
   C. cannot have his order executed
   D. is guaranteed a fill at 41 and may get a better execution for his customer

11. Which of the following activities is not a function of a specialist on the NYSE?

   A. Setting strike prices for options on the securities he works
   B. Keeping a book of public orders
   C. Guaranteeing an execution price for a trader who requests that the specialist stop stock for him
   D. Buying and selling stock for his own account

12. An immediate-or-cancel order (IOC)

   I. must be executed in its entirety
   II. may be executed in part or in full
   III. must be executed in one attempt
   IV. may be executed after several attempts

   A. I and III
   B. I and IV
   C. II and III
   D. II and IV

13. The over-the-counter market could be characterized as what type of market?

   A. Auction
   B. First
   C. Negotiated
   D. Primary

14. The NASD's 5% policy applies to

   I. commissions charged when executing customer agency (broker) transactions
   II. riskless and simultaneous transactions
   III. markups on stock sold from inventory
   IV. markdowns on stocks bought for inventory

   A. I and II
   B. II only
   C. III and IV
   D. I, II, III and IV

15. An open-end investment company bought preferred stock from a bank through an ECN. This trade took place in which of the following markets?

   A. Primary
   B. Secondary
   C. Third
   D. Fourth

16. A customer has an order to buy 400 at ABC 60 Stop. ABC declares a 20% stock dividend. On the ex-date, the order in the specialist's book will read buy

   A. 400 shares at 60 stop
   B. 480 shares at 50 stop
   C. 400 shares at 50 stop
   D. 480 shares at 60 stop

17. A market maker buys 100 shares of LMN at $14 per share for inventory. Two weeks later, the stock is being quoted at 14.50–15, and the firm sells 100 shares of LMN to a customer. Which of the following is the price that is the basis for the firm's markup?

    A. 14
    B. 14.50
    C. 14.75
    D. 15

18. Your client, who has sold 100 shares of GGZ short, places a buy stop order at 80. The order is activated when the price of GGZ

    A. falls to 80 or below
    B. falls below 80
    C. rises to 80 or above
    D. rises above 80

19. All of the following statements about NYSE listed securities are true EXCEPT that

    A. securities must qualify for listing on the NYSE
    B. securities can be listed on several exchanges at the same time and may sell at different prices
    C. all listed securities are marginable
    D. securities can be delisted any time a company's executive committee requests it

20. A customer places an order to sell short 100 DEF 52.25 STOP. After placing the order, DEF trades as follows: 53, 52.60, 52.20, 52.10, 53 SLD, 52.25. Which trade elects the order?

    A. 52.10
    B. 52.25
    C. 52.20
    D. 52.60

21. An NASD member that is qualified and registered to transact business in listed securities in over-the-counter transactions must report this type of transaction to ACT within how many seconds of execution?

    A. 30
    B. 60
    C. 90
    D. 120

22. Which of the following would be the usual use of a stop order?

    I. To protect the profit on a long position
    II. To prevent loss on a short position
    III. To buy at a specific price only
    IV. To guarantee execution at or near the close

    A. I and II
    B. I and III
    C. II and III
    D. II and IV

23. A fill-or-kill order (FOK)

    I. must be executed in its entirety
    II. may be executed in part or in full
    III. must be executed in one attempt
    IV. may be executed after several attempts

    A. I and III
    B. I and IV
    C. II and III
    D. II and IV

24. Which of the following orders would be executed in a rising market?

    I. Buy stops
    II. Buy limits
    III. Sell limits
    IV. Sell stops

    A. I and III
    B. I and IV
    C. II and III
    D. II and IV

Series 7 Unit Test 8 Answers & Rationale

1. **D.** The Securities Exchange Act of 1934 set up the SEC and regulates the secondary market. The Securities Exchange Act of 1934 does not address full and fair disclosure issues; the Act of 1933 addresses such issues. This act gave the Federal Reserve Board the authority to determine margin requirements. QID: 27953

2. **C.** On an exchange floor, short sales must be effected on a plus tick or a zero-plus tick. In addition, short sales may be effected at either the opening or closing. The buyer is never informed that shares being purchased represent borrowed shares. It makes no difference to the buyer that shares being purchased are being sold long by the seller or short by the seller. However, the order ticket prepared by the brokerage firm representing the seller must indicate that the sale is short and that an affirmative determination has been made. QID: 36477

3. **C.** The Nasdaq short-sale rule applies only to Nasdaq National Market securities. QID: 29609

4. **D.** A market order is executed immediately at the prevailing market price. A stop order is not triggered until a set price is hit or passed through. A good-till-cancelled order remains open until executed or cancelled. An all-or-none order is not filled until the total number of shares specified is bought or sold. QID: 27985

5. **A.** The SEC regulates the trading of all non-exempt securities. Commodity futures, which are not considered securities, are regulated by the Commodities Futures Trading Commission (CFTC). QID: 36582

6. **A.** The third market refers to the trading of listed securities in the over-the-counter market. QID: 29852

7. **B.** Nasdaq Level 3 service allows market makers to enter and update quotations on securities in which the market makers are registered with the NASD. QID: 28049

8. **A.** If trading is halted in a security, investors cannot buy or sell the security. An open order can be cancelled during a trading halt. QID: 27969

9. **B.** A limit order is an order to buy or sell at a specific price or better. Therefore, buy limits are entered below the current market and sell limits are entered above the current market. Stop orders have several uses. The most common of these is to protect gains on both long and short positions. For example, if a customer were to buy stock at $30 a share, and the stock is now trading at $50, the customer could enter a sell stop order below the current market to protect the unrealized gain. If the market should fall, the stop order will be elected once the stock trades at or through the stop price. Similarly, a customer with an unrealized gain on a short stock position could enter a buy stop above the prevailing market in order to protect the gain. QID: 36486

10. **D.** When a specialist agrees to stop stock, he is permitting the floor broker to try to find a better price on the floor than the stopped price. If the floor broker finds a better price, he can take it, but in the event that a better offer doesn't materialize, the broker has been guaranteed an execution by the specialist at the stopped price. QID: 29622

11. **A.** A specialist may keep a book of public orders, guarantee an execution price, and buy or sell stock for his own account. He may not set option strike prices. That is the prerogative of the Options Clearing Corporation (OCC). QID: 27978

12. **C.** An immediate-or-cancel order is one in which the firm handling the order has one attempt to fill the order but a partial execution is binding on the customer. QID: 36565

13. C. The New York Stock Exchange is an auction market and the OTC market is a negotiated market. QID: 30551

14. D. The 5% policy applies both to commission charges on agency transactions and to markups and markdowns on principal transactions, including riskless principal trades. QID: 28025

15. D. The fourth market consists of direct trades between institutions, pension funds, broker/dealers and others. In theory, there are no brokers involved in these transactions. The fourth market is the ECN market. QID: 27958

16. C. Only orders entered below the market (buy limits and sell stops) are automatically reduced on the ex-date for cash dividends. For stock dividends, all orders on the book are adjusted. As the specialist's book contains only round lots, the number of shares in the order will not be adjusted upward. The stop price, however, will be adjusted (60 divided by 120%). The customer is long 480 shares as the result of the stock dividend. However, only 400 can be reflected on the book (round lots only). QID: 34913

17. D. The basis for the markup is the current interdealer offering price, which is, in this case, $15 per share. QID: 29481

18. C. A buy stop order is always entered at a price above the current offering price. A buy stop order at 80 means that if the market price rises to 80 or above, the order becomes a market order to buy and is filled immediately. QID: 27991

19. D. To be listed on the NYSE, a corporation must satisfy stringent Exchange requirements in terms of the market price of its stock, number of stockholders, and earnings. Securities can be listed on several exchanges at once. Because each exchange is independent of all others, what happens on one exchange does not necessarily affect another exchange. All listed securities are marginable under Federal Reserve Board rules. Once a company is listed on the NYSE, voluntary delisting can occur if the board of directors of the issuer approves, the audit committee of the board approves, and notification is made to the issuer's 35 largest stockholders. QID: 27973

20. C. Sell stop orders are elected as soon as the stock trades at or through the stop price. The trade at 52.20 represents the first such transaction after the order is placed. The order cannot be executed until there is a plus tick, which occurs at 52.25. The 53 SLD trade is a late trade report and is not part of the tick sequence. QID: 34880

21. C. Registered third market makers must report transactions of listed securities traded over the counter to ACT within 90 seconds of execution. QID: 28054

22. A. A buy stop could be used to protect an investor who is short and a sell stop could be used to protect an investor who is long. Stop orders never guarantee execution price. QID: 29672

23. A. A fill-or-kill order is one where the firm handling the order can make one attempt to fill the order in its entirety. If unable to do so, the order is cancelled. QID: 36564

24. A. Buy limits and sell stops are entered below the current market and would be executed if the market is falling. On the other hand, sell limits and buy stops are entered above the current market and would be executed if the market is rising. QID: 36633

9

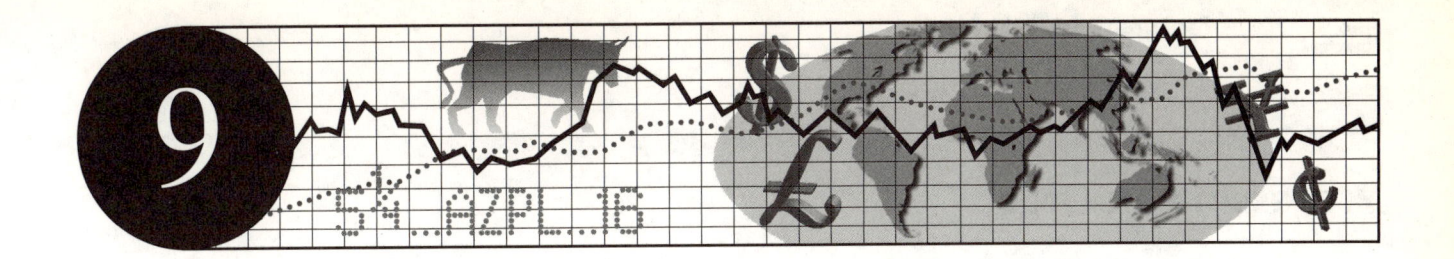

Brokerage Support Services

INTRODUCTION Brokerage firms are required to follow strict procedures for maintaining accurate and thorough client information. This unit discusses the NASD Uniform Practice Code and the standardized procedures that apply to member firms.

It is important to know the general roles of the various departments involved in processing customer orders.

Most records must be maintained for three years, and it is the principal's responsibility to ensure that records are accurate. The Reg T settlement date and regular way settlement dates are different. Unless specified otherwise, always assume regular way settlement.

The Series 7 exam will have approximately 10–15 questions on the material presented in this unit.

UNIT OBJECTIVES After you have completed this unit, you should be able to:

- list the steps and departments involved in processing an order;
- identify the required documentation of customer transactions;
- identify the standard transaction settlement dates; and
- identify critical elements for good delivery of securities.

Processing an Order

Several steps are involved in processing a securities transaction. The process begins when a client places an order with a registered representative. The registered representative enters the transaction on his computer or writes an order ticket. The order is routed through the following departments.

- **Order Department (Wire Room, Order Room)**—transmits orders to the proper markets for execution. Completed trade tickets are sent to the registered representatives who initiated the trades and to the Purchase & Sales department.
- **Purchase & Sales Department (P&S)**—records all transactions in a client's account and handles all billing. It mails trade confirmations, which specify commission and total cost.
- **Margin or Credit Department**—handles activities involving credit for cash and margin accounts. It computes the dates on which clients must deposit money and the deposit amount.
- **Cashiering Department**—is responsible for receiving and delivering securities and money. It issues payment only if the margin department instructs it to do so. It sends certificates to transfer agents to be transferred and registered, then forwards the certificates to clients.

A clearing corporation, such as the **National Securities Clearing Corporation (NSCC)**, can simplify this process by providing specialized comparison clearance and settlement services.

Other departments involved in customer transactions follow.

- **Reorganization Department**—handles any transaction that represents a change in the securities outstanding. This includes exchanging or transmitting customer securities involved in tender offers, bond calls, redemptions of preferred stock, mergers, and acquisitions.
- **Dividend Department**—credits customer accounts with dividends and interest payments for securities held in the firm's name.
- **Proxy Department**—sends proxy statements to customers whose securities are held in the firm's name. It also sends out financial reports and other publications received from the issuer for its stockholders.
- **Stock Record Department**—maintains the ledger that lists each stock owner and the certificate's location.

Test Topic Alert!

Be ready for a question that asks you to identify the flow of an order through a brokerage firm: an easy way to remember is **O**ther **P**eople **M**ight **C**are.

OPMC reminds you that an order starts with the **O**rder department, then goes to the **P**&S department, the **M**argin department and finally the **C**ashiering department. Sometimes the order department is referred to as the wire room, so you might see **WPMC** instead.

Route of an Order

① Customer places order with registered representative.

② Registered representative sends order to order department (wire room).

③ Order department sends order to appropriate market for execution.

④ Market sends wire report of execution back to order department.

⑤ Order department sends report of execution to registered representative.

⑥ Registered representative calls customer to report execution of order.

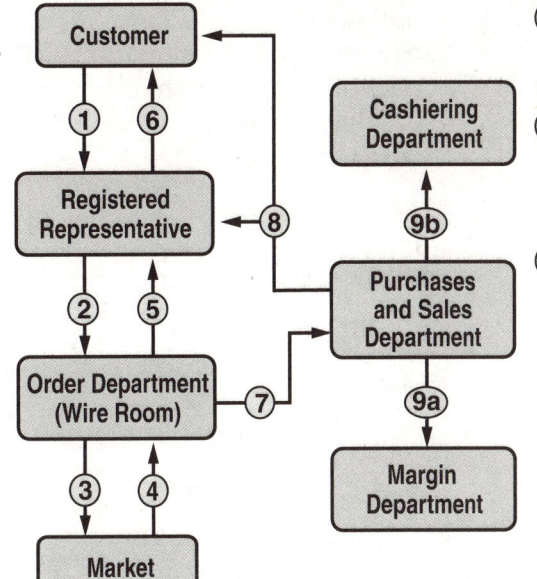

⑦ Order department sends report of trade to P&S department.

⑧ P&S department sends confirmation to customer and a copy to registered representative.

⑨ P&S department processes trade for settlement through the:
   a. Margin department, customer credit area;
   b. Cashiering department, which delivers or receives securities from buyer or seller and exchanges monies.

Transactions and Trade Settlement

Receipt and Delivery of Securities

When a representative accepts a buy or sell order from a customer, the rep must be assured that the customer can pay for or deliver the securities. If the customer claims the securities are being held in street name at another firm, the rep must verify this before executing a sale for the customer.

Order Memorandum

To enter a customer order, the registered rep traditionally has filled out an **order ticket**. Increasingly, representatives are entering orders electronically.

Orders are sent to the wire room and the wire room transmits each order to the proper market for execution. A registered representative must prepare the order ticket, and a principal must approve it on the day of the trade.

A customer order is most susceptible to error at two points: communication of the order between customer and broker, and transmission of the order from broker to wire operator. Breakdowns in communication in the ordering process most often occur because of inaccurate information on a ticket.

The following information is required on the order ticket:

- customer account number;
- registered representative identification number;
- whether the order is solicited or unsolicited;
- whether the order is subject to discretionary authority;
- description of the security (symbol);

- number of shares or bonds to be traded;
- action (buy, sell long, sell short);
- options (buy, write, covered, uncovered, opening, closing);
- price qualifications (market, GTC, day order, etc.);
- type of account (cash, margin);
- the time the order was received, the time of entry and the price at which it was executed.

Order Ticket

1	NEX ☐ BND ☐ OTC ☐ PBW ☐ ASE ☐			NYSE Spec. Handling	Other	Seq. No. & Off.
2	BUY	SELL	SS	OTHER		Dupe. or Orig. Seq. No.
3	Quantity	Symbol or Description		Suffix	Price/MKT	Other than LMT/MKT
4	Add'l info. - GTC - AON - NH - DNR - Cash - etc.				Account Name	
4a	CXL - OR - BUY - SL - SHORT			Price Chg.		
4b	Quantity	Symbol or Description		Suffix	Mgr/VP OK _____	
4c	Add'l former order info., if any			Sol. Unsol. ☐ ☐	☐ Phone ☐ Letter ☐ Person ☐ Power ☐ Other	☐ Long ☐ Deliver ☐ Convert ☐ Borrow ☐ COD/DVP
5	Office	Account No.		AE No.		
ALFA Financial Services, Inc.				Entered by:		Date:

Unless the securities being sold are held by the firm, a representative must make an affirmative determination: in other words, the representative must inquire of the customer as to the location of the securities, whether they are in good deliverable form and whether they will be delivered by settlement date. This information must be noted on the order ticket. Also, if the order is a short sale, the representative must make a determination that the stock can be borrowed to affect delivery.

Test Topic Alert! You are likely to see a question asking when an order ticket must be approved. Order tickets must be approved by a principal not later than the end of the trade date, but orders are not required to be approved before they are entered.

Report of Execution The registered representative receives a report after a trade is executed. He first checks the execution report against the order ticket to make sure that everything was done as the customer requested. If everything is in order, he reports the execution to the customer. If an error exists, the rep must report it to a supervisor or manager immediately.

Erroneous Reports

Sometimes the details of a trade are reported to a customer incorrectly. Despite the mistaken report, the actual trade is binding on the customer. However, if an order is executed outside the customer's limit, the trade is not binding.

Trade Confirmations

A **trade confirmation** is a printed document that confirms a trade, its settlement date, and the amount of money due from or owed to the customer. For each transaction, a customer must be sent or given a written confirmation of the trade at or before the completion of the transaction, the **settlement date**.

The trade confirmation includes the following information.

- **Trade Date**—day on which the transaction is executed (the settlement date is usually the third business day after the trade date)
- **Account No.**—branch office number followed by an account number
- **Registered Representative Internal ID No.** (or **AE No.**)—account executive's identification number
- **BOT** (bought) or **SLD** (sold)—indicates a customer's role in a trade
- **No.** (or **Quantity**)—number of shares of stock or the par value of bonds bought or sold for the customer
- **Description**—specific security bought or sold for the customer
- **Yield**—indicates that the yield for callable bonds may be affected by the exercise of a call provision
- **CUSIP Number**—applicable Committee on Uniform Securities Identification Procedures (CUSIP) number, if any
- **Price**—price per share for stock or bonds before a charge or deduction
- **Amount**—price paid or received before commissions and other charges, also referred to as **extended principal** for municipal securities transactions
- **Commission**—added to buy transactions; subtracted from sell transactions completed on an agency basis. A commission will not appear on the confirmation if a markup has been charged in a principal transaction
- **Net Amount**—obtained on purchases by adding expenses (commissions and postage) to the principal amount (whether the transaction is a purchase or sale, interest is always added whenever bonds are traded with accrued interest)

Disclosure of Capacity

The confirmation must also show the capacity in which the broker/dealer acts (agency or principal) and the commission in cases where the broker/dealer acts as agent. Markups or markdowns are disclosed for Nasdaq Securities.

Confirmation of your order:

Order	No.	Description	Price	Amount	Inter. or Tax	Reg. Fee	Commission
BOT	100	G. Heileman	28 7/8	2887.50	.00	.10	87.20

Trade Date	5/13/99	Account No.	AE No.	AE Name	Odd-lot Diff.
					00.00
Settlement	5/16/99	453-01243-1	27	Walker	Net Amount
					2974.80

Customer Name/Address:
Ms. Jaxson Pollac
5047 W. Kenneth Ave.
Chicago, IL 60699-3287

PLEASE NOTE: On odd-lot orders (orders for other than 100-share lots) on all exchanges purchases are executed at the round-lot price plus a premium (odd-lot differential). Sales are executed at the round-lot price less a discount.

Payment for securities bought and delivery of securities sold are due promptly and in any event on or before the end of payment period in order to comply with federal Regulation T and to avoid interest or premium charges.

ALFA Financial Services, Inc.   **Please keep a copy of this confirmation for your records.**

✓ ***Take Note:*** All firms can act in one of two capacities in a customer transaction. If the firm acts as agent, it is the broker between the buying and selling parties. Agents receive commissions for transactions they perform, and commissions must be disclosed on confirmations.

If the firm acts as a dealer and transacts business for/from its inventory, it acts in a principal capacity and it is compensated by a markup or markdown.

Additionally, confirmations must disclose markups or markdowns for Nasdaq securities and a firm can never act as both agent and principal in a single transaction.

Acting as Agent and Principal

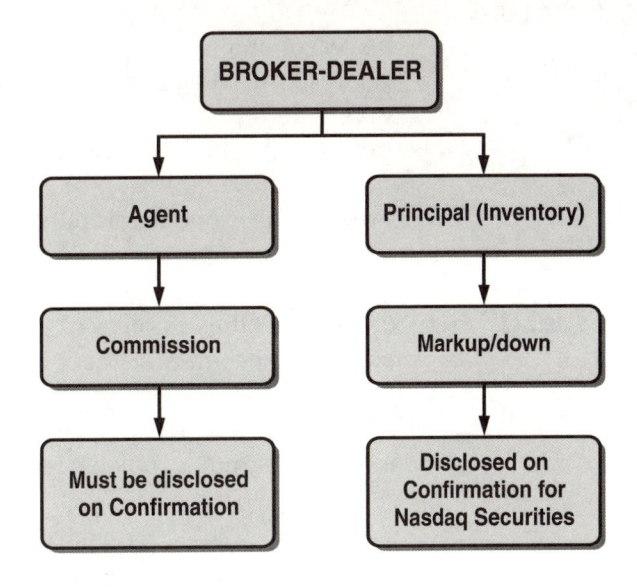

```
                    BROKER-DEALER
                   /            \
               Agent         Principal (Inventory)
                 |                   |
            Commission          Markup/down
                 |                   |
          Must be disclosed    Disclosed on
           on Confirmation    Confirmation for
                              Nasdaq Securities
```

Remember A-B-C-D: Agents = Brokers = Commissions = Disclosure

Timely Mailing of Confirmations

Customer confirmations must be sent no later than at or before the completion of the transaction.

Customer Account Statements

At a minimum, firms must send each customer a quarterly statement, but most firms send customers monthly statements. A statement shows:

- all activity in the account since the previous statement;
- securities positions, long or short; and
- account balances, debit or credit.

If a customer's account has a cash balance, the firm may hold it in the account. However, the statement must advise the customer that these funds are available on request.

✓ **Take Note:** If there is activity in an account, statements are sent monthly. If there is no activity, statements are sent quarterly.

Disclosure of Financial Condition

Upon written request, a member firm must deliver a copy of its most recently prepared balance sheet to:

- any customer with securities or cash held by the member; or
- a member firm with cash or securities on deposit or transacting business with the member.

Charges for Services Performed

A member broker/dealer's fees and charges must:

- be reasonable;
- relate to the work performed, transaction entered, or advisory services given; and
- not be unfairly discriminatory among customers.

A **reasonable fee** is one that is not excessive when compared to the fees other broker/dealers or investment advisers charge for similar services.

Test Topic Alert!

True or False? If a customer of a broker/dealer requests a copy of the firm's most recent income statement in writing, the broker/dealer must comply.

The answer is false. Upon request, the customer is entitled to the most recent balance sheet, not income statement.

ORDER PROCESS DIAGRAM

Customer places order with a Broker-Dealer.
↓
Order is entered, and order ticket is generated.
↓
Order is transmitted to NYSE floor
a) market orders, not-held orders directed to floor brokers
b) limit orders, stop orders to specialist

OR

Order is executed OTC
a) firm acts as agent and acquired security on customer's behalf
b) firm fills order as principal (from inventory)
↓
Execution report is generated.
↓
Trade is reported to Consolidated Tape or Nasdaq.
↓
Customer confirmation is sent and copied to registered rep.
↓
Trade settlement is processed through margin department/cashiering department.

Quick Quiz 9.1 — Multiple Choice

1. Which department in a brokerage firm would handle all credit transactions for a customer?

    A. Margin
    B. Cashiering
    C. Purchases & Sales
    D. Reorganization

2. Once orders are received, in which sequence do they flow through a brokerage firm?

    I. Wire room
    II. Purchases & sales department
    III. Margin department
    IV. Cashiering department

    A. I, II, III, IV
    B. I, IV, II, III
    C. II, I, IV, III
    D. III, IV, II, I

3. According to regulations, a statement for an inactive account should be sent to each customer

    A. weekly
    B. monthly
    C. quarterly
    D. immediately after each trade

Answers

1. **A.** The credit that a broker/dealer extends to its customers is handled by its Margin department.

2. **A.** Orders are received by the wire room and then are sent to the appropriate market. When the wire room receives back the transaction report, it sends it to the Purchases & Sales department. The P&S department sends a confirmation to the customer, and then sends notice of the trade to the Margin department. Margin then notifies the cashier of any balance due to or from the customer.

3. **C.** Broker/dealers must send quarterly statements to customers with inactive accounts.

Transaction Settlement Dates and Terms

Settlement date is the date on which ownership changes between buyer and seller. It is the date on which broker/dealers are required to exchange the securities and funds involved in a transaction and the date on which customers are requested to pay for securities bought and to deliver securities sold.

The **Uniform Practice Code** (**UPC**) standardizes the dates and times for each type of settlement.

Regular Way Settlement

Regular way settlement for most securities transactions is the third business day following the trade date, known as T+3.

✓ **For Example:** If a trade occurs on a Tuesday (trade date), it would settle regular way on Friday. If a trade takes place on a Thursday, it would settle the following Tuesday.

In trades between dealers, if the seller delivers before the settlement date, the buyer may either accept the security or refuse it without prejudice.

US government T-bills, T-notes, and T-bonds settle regular way, the next business day (T+1). Money market securities transactions settle the same day. Government agency securities, however, settle T+3.

Cash Settlement

Cash settlement, or **same day settlement**, requires delivery of securities from the seller and payment from the buyer on the same day a trade is executed. Stocks or bonds sold for cash settlement must be available on the spot for delivery to the buyer.

Cash trade settlement occurs no later than 2:30 pm ET if the trade is executed before 2:00 pm. If the trade occurs after 2:00 pm, settlement is due within 30 minutes.

Seller's Option Contracts

This form of settlement is available to customers who want to sell securities but cannot deliver the physical securities in time for regular way settlement. A **seller's option contract** lets a customer lock in a selling price for securities without having to make delivery on the third business day. Instead, the seller can settle the trade as specified in the contract. Or, if the seller elects to settle earlier than originally specified, the trade can be settled on any date from the fourth business day through the contract date, provided the buyer is given a one-day written notice.

A buyer's option contract works the same way, with the buyer specifying when settlement will take place.

When-, As-, and If-Issued Contracts (When-Issued Trades)

When-issued trades occur through corporate stock splits and new issue municipal bonds. After a stock split is announced and before it is distributed, an investor who owns shares and wants to sell can either sell the old stock with a **due bill**—that is, a promise to deliver the split stock when it is distributed—or sell the stock from the split on a when-issued basis. The NASD's Uniform Practice Committee determines the final settlement date of when-issued trades.

Typically, new municipal bond issues are sold to investors before the bonds are issued. An investor receives a when-issued confirmation describing the bonds. The confirmation does not include a total dollar amount or settlement date because until the settlement date is known, the accrued interest can't be calculated to determine the total dollar amount. Once the bonds are issued, the investor receives a new confirmation stating the purchase price and settlement date.

A when-issued transaction confirmation must include:

- a description of the security, with the contract price (yield); and
- trade date

Because the delivery date is unknown, a when-issued confirm for municipal bonds cannot include accrued interest computed up to the settlement date due to the syndicate.

Reg T Payment

Reg T specifies the date customers are required to pay for purchase transactions. The **settlement date**, however, is the date customers are requested to deliver cash or securities involved in transactions. Under Reg T, payment is due two business days after regular way settlement.

Extensions

If a buyer cannot pay for a trade within five business days from the trade date, the broker/dealer may request an extension from its **designated examining authority (DEA)** before the fifth business day. The broker/dealer has the option of ignoring amounts of less than $1,000 without violating Reg T requirements.

If the customer cannot pay by the end of the extension, the broker/dealer sells the securities in a close-out transaction. After the close-out, the account is frozen for 90 days. A **frozen account** must have sufficient cash before a buy transaction may be executed.

✓ **Take Note:** Reg T deals with the extension of credit for regular security trades. If a broker/dealer must close out a transaction and freeze the account, the customer may not be extended credit.

Frozen Accounts

If a customer buys securities in a cash account and sells them before paying for the buy side by the fifth business day, the account is frozen. Any additional buy transactions require full payment in the account, and sell transactions need securities on deposit. Frozen account status continues for 90 calendar days. Frozen account status is lifted if the customer pays by the fifth business day.

Test Topic Alert! The following table gives a good summary of the highly testable types of settlements and delivery times.

Summary of Settlement Rules

Equity	3 business days
Corporate and Municipal Bonds	3 business days
Equity Options	Next business day
Index Options	Next business day
T-bills, T-notes, and T-bonds	Next business day
US Government Agency	3 business days
Seller's Option	No sooner than T+4
Cash Settlement	Same day
Reg T	T+5

Assume a question is asking about the normal customer settlement terms, regular way, unless the question specifically mentions Reg T.

Also, here's a hint on municipal when-issued settlements. A probable question will ask either what is not included or what is included on a when-issued confirmation. To discern the correct answer, remember **SAT**, which identifies what is not included:

- **S**ettlement date
- **A**ccrued interest
- **T**otal dollar amount due at settlement

If a question asks when customer confirmations must be sent, the answer is no later than the settlement date. But if the question asks when broker-to-broker confirms must be sent, the answer is no later than the business day following the trade date (T+1).

Quick Quiz 9.2

Match each of the following items with the appropriate description below.

A. $1,000
B. Fourth business day after the trade
C. T+5
D. 90 days

___ 1. Earliest possible settlement under seller's option

___ 2. Amount that can be ignored by a broker/dealer without violating Reg T settlement

___ 3. The length of time for which frozen account status is imposed

___ 4. Reg T settlement

Answers 1. **B.** 2. **A.** 3. **D.** 4. **C.**

Quick Quiz 9.3

Match each of the following terms with the appropriate description below.

A. Same day
B. As specified in the contract
C. Settlement date

___ 1. Last possible date for a broker/dealer to send a customer a confirmation

___ 2. Latest possible settlement for seller's option trades

___ 3. Cash settlement terms for municipal securities

Answers 1. **C.** 2. **B.** 3. **A.**

Proxy Department

The Proxy   A corporation's stockholders usually vote by means of a **proxy**, like an absentee ballot. A proxy is a limited power of attorney that a stockholder gives to another person, transferring the right to vote on the stockholder's behalf. A proxy is automatically revoked if the stockholder attends the shareholder meeting, or if the proxy is replaced by another proxy the stockholder executes at a later date.

Proxy Solicitation Stockholders can receive multiple **proxy solicitations** for controversial company proposals. If proxies are solicited, the SEC requires a company to give stockholders information about the items to be voted on and the company must allow the SEC to review this information before it sends the proxies to stockholders. In a proxy contest, everyone who participates must register with the SEC. Also, anyone who is not a direct participant but who provides stockholders with unsolicited advice must register as a participant.

Forwarding Proxies and Other Materials Member firms must cooperate with issuers by seeing to it that customers whose stock is held in street name are alerted to all financial matters concerning issuers (such as quarterly reports, proxy statements). To do so, members act as forwarding agents for all proxies and other corporate materials received from an issuer for street name stock.

Member firms that are owners of record must vote street name stock in accordance with the wishes of the beneficial owners. If a customer signs and returns a proxy statement and fails to indicate how the shares are to be voted, the member must vote the shares as recommended by management.

If a customer does not return the proxy by the tenth day before the annual shareholders meeting, the member may vote the shares as it sees fit as long as the matters to be voted on are of minor importance. If the matters to be voted on are of major importance (e.g., merger, issuance of additional securities) the member may never vote the shares as it sees fit. In this case, if the proxy is not returned, the shares are not voted.

Member firms are reimbursed by issuers for all costs relating to the forwarding of proxy materials. Such costs include postage and related clerical expenses.

Don't Know (DK) Procedures

When one broker/dealer confirms a transaction, the contra broker/dealer must also confirm the transaction within four business days of the trade date. After the fourth business day, the confirming party can demand that the contra party either confirm or **don't know** (**DK**) the trade in question within the next four business days. If the confirming broker/dealer receives no response from the contra party within that time limit, the confirming party may assume that the contra party has "DK'ed" the transaction. At that point, the confirming party is free to disown the trade as well.

Quick Quiz 9.4

Match each of the following terms with the appropriate description below.

A. Trade date
B. Settlement date
C. Ex-date
D. Frozen account

___ 1. Account requiring cash in advance before a buy order is executed because the account holder has violated Regulation T

___ 2. The day that obligates the parties to the terms of the trade

___ 3. First date on which a security trades without entitling the buyer to receive a previously declared distribution

___ 4. Date on which ownership changes between buyer and seller

Answers   1. **D.**   2. **A.**   3. **C.**   4. **B.**

Quick Quiz 9.5

Match each of the following terms with the appropriate description below.

A. Regular way
B. Due bill
C. 1 business day

___ 1. Used when the wrong party receives a dividend from the issuer

___ 2. Regular way settlement on government securities

___ 3. Settlement within a standardized period from the trade date

Answers   1. **B.**   2. **C.**   3. **A.**

Rules of Good Delivery

A security must be in **good delivery form** before it can be delivered to a buyer. It is the registered rep's responsibility to ensure that a security is in good deliverable form when a customer sells it.

Physical Requirements

Good delivery describes the physical condition of, signatures on, attachments to, and denomination of the certificates involved in a securities transaction. Good delivery is normally a back-office consideration between buying and selling brokers. In any broker-to-broker transaction, the delivered securities must be accompanied by a properly executed uniform delivery ticket. The transfer agent is the final arbiter of whether a security meets the requirements of good delivery.

Overdelivery and Underdelivery

In settling customer sell transactions in which the securities delivery matches the exact number of shares or bonds sold, the first rule of good delivery is met. But if the customer overdelivers or underdelivers, the transaction is not good delivery.

✓ *For Example:*
Overdelivery:
A customer sells 300 shares and brings in one certificate for 325 shares.

Underdelivery:
A customer sells 100 shares and brings in one certificate for 80 shares.

Partial Delivery

A broker-to-broker **partial delivery** must be accepted if the remainder of the delivery constitutes a round lot or multiple thereof.

Good Delivery Clearing Rule (100-Share Uniform Units)

When one broker/dealer delivers stock to another broker/dealer, single round lots and odd lots are cleared separately. However, odd-lot certificates can be used to clear round-lot trades provided the odd lot certificates add up to single round lots (100 shares).

✓ *For Example:* For a 300-share sale, the seller could deliver:

- one 300-share certificate; or
- three 100-share certificates; or
- six 50-share certificates; or
- two 100-share certificates, one 60 share certificate, and one 40 share certificate; or
- three 60-share certificates; and three 40 share certificates.

Each of the above deliveries meets the requirements of the rule. However, delivering four 75-share certificates would not be good delivery. Think of it this way: can you take the certificates and make piles of 100 shares? If the answer is *yes*, it is good delivery.

Missing Coupons

If coupons are missing from a bond, the general practice is to deduct the missing coupons' cash value from the sale proceeds to the customer. If an issuer is in default on a coupon bond, all of the unpaid coupons must be attached for it to be good delivery.

Certificate Negotiability

Assignment — Each stock and bond certificate must be **assigned** (endorsed by signature) by the owner(s) whose name is registered on the certificate's face. Certificates registered in joint name require all owners' signatures.

Endorsement by a customer may be made on the back of a certificate on the signature line or on a separate **stock or bond power**. One stock or bond power can be used with any number of certificates for one security, but a separate power is required for each security.

Alteration

If an **alteration** or a correction has been made to an assignment, a full explanation of the change signed by the person or firm who executed the correction must be attached.

Signature Guarantee — All customer signatures must be **guaranteed** by a party acceptable to the transfer agent (e.g., NYSE member, national bank).

Signature Requirements — A customer's signature must match exactly the name registered on the face of a security.

Legal Transfer Items — Any form of registration other than individual or joint ownership may require supporting guarantees or documentation to render a certificate negotiable.

For business registrations involving sole proprietorships or partnerships, a simple guarantee by a broker/dealer is usually sufficient. For corporate registrations and certificates in the names of fiduciaries, a transfer agent may require a corporate resolution naming the person signing a certificate as authorized to do so. Fiduciaries must supply either a certified copy of a trust agreement or a copy of a court appointment, depending on the type of fiduciary involved.

Invalid Signatures — If a broker/dealer guarantees a forged signature, such as of a deceased person, the firm becomes liable. The executor or administrator of the estate must endorse the certificate or furnish a stock power and transfer the securities to the name of the estate before they can be sold.

Minors' signatures are invalid for securities registration purposes.

Good Condition of Security — If a certificate is mutilated or appears to be counterfeit, appropriate authentication must be obtained before a transfer agent can accept the security for replacement. If the damage is so extensive that the transfer agent doubts the certificate's authenticity, it will require a surety bond.

NASD CUSIP Regulations

CUSIP numbers are used in all trade confirmations and correspondence regarding specific securities. A separate CUSIP number is assigned to each issue of securities; if an issue is subdivided into classes with differing characteristics, each class is assigned a separate CUSIP number.

Legal Opinion: Municipal Securities

Unless a municipal bond is traded and stamped *ex-legal* (without a legal opinion), the legal opinion must be printed on or attached to the bond as evidence of the bond's validity. Securities traded ex-legal are in good delivery condition without the legal opinion.

Fail to Deliver

A **fail to deliver** situation occurs when the broker/dealer on the sell side of a contract does not deliver the securities in good delivery form to the broker/dealer on the buy side on settlement. As long as a fail to deliver exists, the seller will not receive payment.

In a fail to deliver situation, the buying broker/dealer may buy in the securities to close the contract and may charge the seller for any loss caused by changes in the market. If a customer fails to deliver securities to satisfy a sale, the firm representing the seller must buy-in the securities after 10 business days from settlement date.

Irrevocable Power on Back of Certificate

ALFA Enterprises, Incorporated

The Company will furnish without charge to each stockholder who so requests the powers, designations, preferences and relative, participating optional or other special rights of each class of stock or series thereof of the Company, and the qualifications, limitations or restrictions of such preferences and/or rights. Such request may be made to the Office of the Secretary of the Company or to the Transfer Agent.

The following abbreviations, when used in the inscription on the face of this certificate, shall be construed as though they were written out in full according to the applicable laws or regulations:

TEN COM	– as tenants in common	UNIFORM GIFT MIN ACT
TEN ENT	– as tenants by entireties	_____ Custodian _____
JT TEN	– as joint tenants with right of survivorship	(Cust) (Minor)
		under Uniform Gifts to Minors Act of
		(State) _____

For value received _____ *hereby sell, assign and transfer unto*

PLEASE INSERT SOCIAL SECURITY NUMBER OR OTHER IDENTIFYING NUMBER OF ASSIGNEE

_____
_____
_____

Please type or print name of assignee

Shares of the capital stock represented by the within Certificate and do hereby irrevocably constitute and appoint _____

Attorney to transfer the said stock on the books of the within-named Company with full power of substitution in the premises.

Dated: _____ X _____
Sign here

X _____
If joint account, both parties must sign

Separate Irrevocable Power

IRREVOCABLE STOCK OR BOND POWER

FOR VALUE RECEIVED, the undersigned do(es) hereby sell, assign and transfer to

_____

_____

                                                    Social Security Number
                                                  or Tax Identification Number

IF STOCK, COMPLETE THIS PORTION ____ shares of the _____ stock of _____ _____ represented by certificate(s) No.(s)_____ inclusive standing in the name of the undersigned on the books of said company.

IF BONDS, COMPLETE THIS PORTION ____ bonds of _____ in the principal amount of $ _____ No.(s) _____ inclusive standing in the name of the undersigned on the books of said company.

The undersigned do(es) hereby irrevocably constitute and appoint

_____

_____

_____

Attorney to transfer said stock or bonds as the case may be on the books of said Company with full power of substitution in the premises.

Dated: _____

X _____

X _____

(Person[s] executing this Power sign[s] here)

IMPORTANT NOTICE – READ CAREFULLY

The signature(s) to this Power must correspond with the name(s) as written upon the face of the certificate(s) or bond(s) in every particular without alteration or enlargement or any change whatever. Signature guarantee should be made by a member or a member organization of the New York Stock Exchange, members of other Exchanges having signatures on file with transfer agents or by a commercial bank or trust company having its principal office or correspondent in the City of New York.

Quick Quiz 9.7   Multiple Choice

1. To be considered in good delivery form, certificates must be

   A. accompanied by a preliminary prospectus
   B. called for redemption by the issuing body
   C. accompanied by an assignment or a stock power
   D. in the name of the deceased person, if they died after the trade date

2. Which of the following would be considered good delivery for a sale of 600 shares of MCS?

   A. 3 certificates for 100 shares each and 8 certificates for 25 shares each
   B. 2 certificates for 100 shares each and 4 certificates for 50 shares each
   C. 6 certificates for 75 shares each and 6 certificates for 25 shares each
   D. 8 certificates for 75 shares each

3. As long as a fail-to-deliver situation exists, the seller

   A. will have all accounts frozen
   B. must conduct all transactions on a cash basis
   C. will not receive payment
   D. will not receive accrued interest on bonds

Answers

1. **C.** To be considered in good delivery form, certificates must be accompanied by an assignment or a stock power.

2. **C.** Each certificate for 25 shares can be matched to a certificate for 75 shares to make a round lot; with 6 round lots, these certificates would be considered good delivery. Choice A is only 500 shares; choice B includes only 400 shares; and choice D cannot be bunched into round lots.

3. **C.** Until the seller delivers the securities sold, he will not receive payment for them.

Brokerage Support Services HotSheet

OPMC:
- Order routing through broker/dealer is:
  - Order department
  - Purchases & Sales department
  - Margin department
  - Cashier department

Order Tickets:
- Must be approved by principal no later than the end of the trade date

Brokerage Support Services

Errors:	• Report first to principal • Reporting errors binding on customer at executed price • Errors of execution are not binding on customer
Confirmations:	• Customer: No later than settlement date • Broker/dealer-to-broker/dealer: No later than T+1 • Must disclose agent or principal • Commissions must be disclosed; markups/downs are disclosed for Nasdaq trades
Customer Statements:	• Minimum of quarterly; monthly statements for active accounts
Financial Disclosure:	• Customers entitled to most recent balance sheet upon written request
Settlement Dates:	• Regular way: Corps and Munis: T+3; Governments: T+1 • Cash settlement: same day • Reg T settlement: T+5 • Seller's option: no sooner than first day after regular way; no later than the date identified in the contract • When issued: determined by Uniform Practice Committee
Frozen Accounts:	• If no extension granted from SRO, 90 day freeze applies • Amounts of less than $1,000 can be ignored
Bonds Traded Flat:	• No accrued interest • Income (adjustment bonds), defaulted bonds, zeros
Invalid Signatures:	• Deceased persons, minors, persons declared legally incompetent

Series 7 Unit Test 9

1. Which of the following statements regarding trade settlements are TRUE?

    I. Trades in a cash account normally settle the same day.
    II. Trades in a cash account normally settle regular way.
    III. Cash transactions settle the same day.
    IV. Cash transactions settle regular way.

    A. I and II
    B. I and IV
    C. II and III
    D. II and IV

2. Which of the following is not good delivery for 470 shares of stock?

    A. Two 100-share certificates and three 90-share certificates
    B. Four 100-share certificates and one 70-share certificate
    C. Eight 50-share certificates, one 40-share certificate, and one 30-share certificate
    D. Forty-seven 10-share certificates

3. In a seller's option, securities may be delivered before the date specified if the seller

    A. gives one day's written notice to the buyer
    B. gives notice to the buyer on the day of delivery
    C. cannot deliver on the specified date
    D. wishes to be paid earlier

4. NASD rules make it clear that any service charges (other than commissions) have to be

    A. limited to less than 1% a year
    B. based on the size and the amount of activity in a client's account
    C. standardized across the board at 5% a year
    D. reasonable and not unfairly discriminatory among clients

5. All of the following transactions must settle on the third business day after the trade date EXCEPT a

    A. broker/dealer buying a corporate bond from another dealer
    B. customer selling a municipal bond through a broker/dealer
    C. broker/dealer buying a Treasury bond for its own account
    D. customer buying closed-end fund shares through a broker/dealer

6. Customer statements must be sent out at least

    A. daily
    B. weekly
    C. monthly
    D. quarterly

7. When a client's cash account is frozen, the client

    A. must deposit the full purchase price no later than the settlement date for a purchase
    B. must deposit the full purchase price before a purchase order may be executed
    C. may make sales with the firm's permission
    D. may not trade under any circumstances

8. Once received, orders flow through a brokerage firm in which sequence?

    I. Wire room
    II. Purchases and sales department
    III. Margin department
    IV. Cashiering department

    A. I, II, III, IV
    B. I, IV, II, III
    C. II, I, IV, III
    D. III, IV, II, I

9. A confirmation of each customer trade must be given or sent

   A. on the trade date
   B. before the trade date
   C. on or before the settlement date
   D. before the settlement date

10. Which of the following appears on the confirmation statement for a when-issued trade of municipal bonds?

    A. Settlement date
    B. Total contract price
    C. Accrued interest
    D. Principal or agency trade

11. A customer's order to buy 500 shares of QRS at 60 is executed and the registered representative reports the trade execution to the customer. One hour later, the customer notices that QRS is down 2 points and informs the representative that he no longer wants the stock and is NOT planning to pay for it. The representative should tell the customer that

    A. the customer owns the stock and must submit payment
    B. the customer may sell the stock at the purchase price in the open market
    C. the firm will repurchase the securities from the customer for the price paid
    D. he personally will repurchase the securities from the customer for the price paid

12. Your customer owns 100 shares of ABC Corporation, which are being held in street name. What procedure will apply regarding your customer's proxy?

    A. ABC Corporation must send a proxy to your customer.
    B. The brokerage firm holding the shares must vote the proxy.
    C. The customer is required to sign one proxy card for his 100 shares.
    D. The brokerage firm must forward the proxy to your customer.

Series 7 Unit Test 9 Answers & Rationale

1. **C.** Cash settlement transactions may take place in any type of account and settle the same day. Regular way settlement for most securities is T+3, regardless of the type of account in which the order is executed. QID: 30110

2. **A.** Shares must add up to 100 or be in multiples of 100, with the exception of odd lots. QID: 28195

3. **A.** In a seller's option trade, the seller may deliver (at his option) by giving the buyer written notice one day before making delivery. QID: 28141

4. **D.** According to the NASD Conduct Rules, charges for services performed (such as the collection of dividends, safekeeping of securities held in street name, etc.) must be reasonable and not unfairly discriminatory among clients. QID: 32217

5. **C.** Regular way settlement for US government bonds is the business day after the trade date. Corporate bonds and closed-end funds fall under the SEC's settlement rule and MSRB rules require 3-day settlement of municipal bond secondary transactions. QID: 29767

6. **D.** The SEC and the NASD require member firms to send out customer account statements at least once per calendar quarter. QID: 28162

7. **B.** When an account is frozen, the client must deposit the full purchase price prior to any subsequent orders. QID: 28152

8. **A.** Once received, the order flows from the Order department (wire room), to Purchases & Sales, to the Margin department, to the Cashiering department. QID: 32216

9. **C.** A confirmation must be sent to a customer at or before the completion of the transaction (the settlement date). QID: 29763

10. **D.** A when-issued trade establishes the contract price but not the settlement date. Because the settlement date will not be established until the securities become available, the amount of accrued interest and the total amount due cannot be calculated at the time of the trade. Trade date and price (expressed in yield) are included on when-issued confirmations. QID: 29836

11. **A.** The customer has entered into a contract to purchase a security as soon as the buy order is executed, and must pay regardless of any subsequent change in the market price. The firm and the representative are prohibited from offering to repurchase the securities at the original price. QID: 32219

12. **D.** The broker/dealer must forward the proxy to the beneficial owner. QID: 35150

10

Investment Company Products

INTRODUCTION

Investment company products offer a diversified portfolio of securities and reduced transaction costs. Because of these features, they are very popular with investors. Mutual funds (one form of investment company) currently manage trillions of dollars for investors.

The Series 7 exam will ask you approximately 7–10 questions on these products and their features.

UNIT OBJECTIVES

When you have completed this unit, you should be able to:

- list and describe the three types of investment companies defined by the Investment Company Act of 1940;
- contrast characteristics of open- and closed-end management companies;
- describe the registration requirements imposed by the Investment Company Act of 1940;
- list several situations that require a majority vote of the outstanding shares;
- identify and explain five significant functions in the operation of an investment company;
- list and describe the unique characteristics of mutual fund shares;
- calculate the POP and the sales charge percentage;
- compare and contrast three different methods for collecting fees for the sale of shares;
- identify three ways to qualify for sales charge reductions;
- discuss tax consequences of mutual fund distributions to shareholders; and
- assess customer goals and risk tolerance and make suitable recommendations.

Investment Company Purpose

An **investment company** pools investors' money and invests in securities on their behalf. Investment company management attempts to invest funds for people more efficiently than the individual investors could themselves. They operate and invest these pooled funds as a single large account jointly owned by every investor in the company.

Like corporate issuers, investment companies raise capital by selling shares to the public. Investment companies must abide by the same registration and prospectus requirements imposed on every other issuer by the Securities Act of 1933 and are also subject to regulations regarding how their shares are sold to the public. The Investment Company Act of 1940 provides for SEC regulation of investment companies and their activities.

Types of Investment Companies

The Investment Company Act of 1940 classifies investment companies into three broad types: **face-amount certificate companies (FACs)**; **unit investment trusts (UITs)**; and **management investment companies**.

Face-Amount Certificate Companies

A **face-amount certificate** is a contract between an investor and an issuer in which the issuer guarantees payment of a stated (or fixed) sum to the investor at some set date in the future. In return for this future payment, the investor agrees to pay the issuer a set amount of money either as a lump sum or in periodic installments. Issuers of these investments are called **face-amount certificate companies**. If the investor pays for the certificate in a lump sum, the investment is known as a fully paid face-amount certificate. Very few face-amount certificate companies operate today because tax law changes have eliminated their tax advantages.

Unit Investment Trusts (UITs)

A **unit investment trust** is an investment company organized under a trust indenture and identified by several characteristics.

UITs do not have boards of directors, employ investment advisers, or actively manage their own portfolios (or trade securities).

A UIT functions as a holding company for its investors. UITs typically purchase other investment company shares or government and municipal bonds. They then issue redeemable shares, also known as **units** or **shares of beneficial interest**, in its portfolio of securities. Each share is an undivided interest in the entire underlying portfolio. Because UITs are not managed, when any securities in the portfolio are liquidated, the proceeds must be distributed.

A UIT may be **fixed** or **nonfixed**. A fixed UIT typically purchases a portfolio of bonds and terminates when the bonds in the portfolio mature. A nonfixed UIT purchases shares of an underlying mutual fund. Under the Act of 1940, the trustees of both fixed and nonfixed UITs must stand ready to redeem the units, thus providing liquidity to shareholders.

Classification of Investment Companies

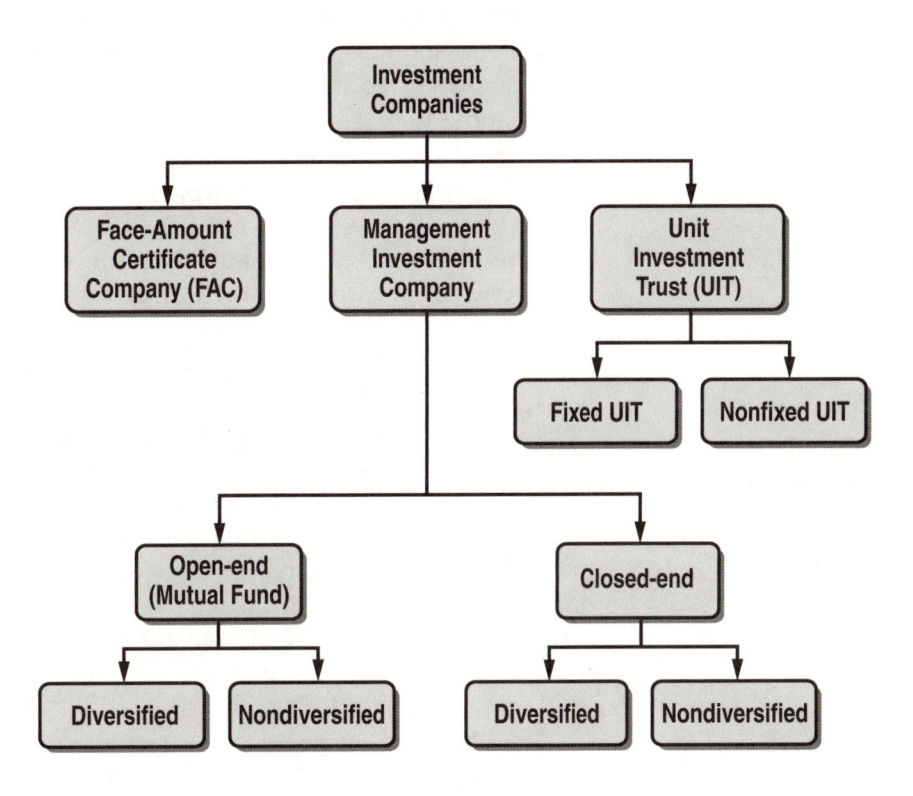

```
                          Investment
                          Companies
              ┌───────────────┼───────────────┐
         Face-Amount      Management         Unit
         Certificate      Investment      Investment
         Company (FAC)    Company         Trust (UIT)
                              │           ┌─────┴─────┐
                              │        Fixed UIT   Nonfixed UIT
                    ┌─────────┴─────────┐
                Open-end             Closed-end
               (Mutual Fund)
              ┌─────┴─────┐         ┌─────┴─────┐
         Diversified  Nondiversified  Diversified  Nondiversified
```

Test Topic Alert! Expect to see no more than one question related to UITs. Know the following:

- UITs are not actively managed; there is no BOD or investment adviser.
- UIT shares (units) are not traded in the secondary market; they must be redeemed by the trust.
- UITs are investment companies as defined under the Investment Company Act of 1940.

Management Investment Companies The most familiar type of investment company is the **management investment company**, which actively manages a securities portfolio to achieve a stated investment objective. A management investment company is either **closed-end** or **open-end**. Initially, both closed- and open-end companies sell shares to the public; the difference between them lies in the type of securities they market, and where investors buy and sell shares.

Test Topic Alert!

Think of a unit investment trust just like a mutual fund—up to a point. Both fixed UITs and mutual funds are comprised of a pool of securities in which investors own a proportionate share.

The major difference is that mutual funds actively trade their portfolios; a portfolio manager gets paid a fee to buy and sell as needed to meet the objectives of the fund. UIT portfolios usually are not traded; they are fixed trusts. The advantage to investors in UITs is that they own a diversified interest but they do not have to pay a management fee—the biggest expense of mutual fund ownership. The downside is that the UIT portfolio cannot be traded in response to market conditions.

Closed-End Investment Companies

When a closed-end investment company wants to raise capital for its portfolio, it conducts a **common stock offering**. For the initial offering, the company registers a fixed number of shares with the SEC and offers them to the public for a limited time through underwriters. The fund's capitalization is fixed unless an additional public offering is made at some future time. Closed-end investment companies can also issue bonds and preferred stock.

Closed-end investment companies are often called **publicly traded funds**. After the stock is distributed, anyone can buy or sell shares in the secondary market, either on an exchange or over-the-counter (OTC). Supply and demand determine the **bid price** (price at which an investor can sell) and the **ask price** (price at which an investor can buy). Closed-end fund shares may trade at a premium or discount to the shares' underlying value.

✓ **Take Note:** Closed-end shares are not redeemed by the issuer. Investors wishing to liquidate their shares must sell them in the secondary market at the prevailing market price, determined by supply and demand.

Test Topic Alert!

An easy way to remember the features of a closed-end company is to think about what would be true for any corporate security.

- Where do shares of closed-end companies trade? Like corporates, in the secondary market.
- What types of securities can closed-ends issue? Like corporates, common, preferred, and bonds.
- Can fractional shares be purchased? Like corporates, only full shares can be purchased.
- When must a prospectus be used? Like corporates, only in the IPO.

No prospectus is given when the shares are purchased in a secondary market transaction.

Open-End Investment Companies

An open-end investment company, or **mutual fund**, does not specify the exact number of shares it intends to issue; it registers an open offering with the SEC. With this registration type, the open-end investment company can raise an unlimited amount of investment capital by continuously issuing new shares. Conversely, when investors liquidate holdings in a mutual fund, the fund's capital shrinks because the fund redeems shares. The offering never "closes" because the number of shares the company can offer is unlimited.

Any person who wants to invest in the company buys shares directly from the company or its underwriters at the **public offering price** (**POP**). A mutual fund's POP is the **net asset value** (**NAV**) per share plus a sales charge.

Comparison of Open-End and Closed-End Investment Companies

	Open-End	Closed-End
Capitalization	Unlimited; continuous offering of shares	Fixed; single offering of shares
Issues	Common stock only; no debt securities; permitted to borrow	May issue: common, preferred, debt securities
Shares	Full or fractional	Full only
Offerings & Trading	Sold & redeemed by fund only Continuous primary offering Must redeem shares	Initial primary offering Secondary trading OTC or on an exchange Does not redeem shares
Pricing	NAV + sales charge Selling price determined by formula in the prospectus	CMV + commission Price determined by supply & demand
Shareholder rights	Dividends (when declared), voting	Dividends (when declared), voting, preemptive
Ex-date	Set by BOD	Set by the exchange or NASD

Diversified and Nondiversified

Diversification provides risk management that makes mutual funds popular with many investors. However, not all investment companies feature diversified portfolios.

Diversified. Under the Investment Company Act of 1940, an investment company qualifies as a **diversified investment company** if it meets the following **75-5-10** test:

- **75%** of total assets must be invested in securities issued by companies other than the investment company or its affiliates. Cash on hand and cash equivalent investments (short-term government and money-market securities) are counted as part of the 75% required investment in outside companies.
- No more than **5%** of total assets can be invested in any one corporation's securities.
- The investment company can own no more than **10%** of an outside corporation's outstanding voting class securities (common stock).

✓ **For Example:** If a mutual fund has $200,000 of assets, no more than $10,000 (5%) can be invested in the securities of a particular company. If a target company has $100,000 of outstanding common stock, the mutual fund could own no more than $10,000 (10%) of the stock.

Nondiversified. A **nondiversified investment company** fails to meet the 75-5-10 test. An investment company that specializes in a single industry is not necessarily a nondiversified company. Some investment companies choose to concentrate their assets in an industry or a geographic area, such as health care, technology stocks, or northeast coast company stocks. These are known as **specialized** or **sector funds**. An investment company that invests in a single industry can still be considered diversified as long as it meets the 75-5-10 test.

✓ **Take Note:** Both open- and closed-end companies can be diversified or nondiversified.

Quick Quiz 10.1   Multiple Choice

1. Which of the following are covered under the Investment Company Act of 1940?

    I. Unit investment trusts
    II. Face-amount companies
    III. Open-end management companies
    IV. Closed-end management companies

    A. I and II
    B. I, III, and IV
    C. III and IV
    D. I, II, III, and IV

Investment Company Purpose

2. What kind of investment company has no provision for redemption of outstanding shares?

    A. Open-end company
    B. Closed-end company
    C. Unit investment trust
    D. Mutual fund

3. Diversified management companies must be invested so that

    I. they own no more than 5% of the voting stock of a single company
    II. no more than 5% of their assets are invested in any one company
    III. they own no more than 10% of the voting stock of any one company
    IV. if they own more than 25% of a target company, they do not vote the stock

    A. I and II
    B. I, II, and IV
    C. II and III
    D. II, III, and IV

4. According to the Investment Company Act of 1940, an investment company with a fixed portfolio, redeemable shares, and no management fee is a

    A. face-amount certificate company
    B. management company
    C. unit investment trust
    D. closed-end investment company

5. Open-end investment companies, but not closed-end investment companies

    I. can make continuous offerings of shares provided the original registration statement and prospectus are periodically updated
    II. can be listed on registered national exchanges
    III. always redeem their shares
    IV. can issue only common stock

    A. I, II, and III
    B. I and III
    C. I, III, and IV
    D. II and IV

Answers

1. **D.** All are covered under the Act of 1940. Unit investment trusts, face-amount companies, and management companies are all mentioned in this act. Both open-end and closed-end management companies are subclassifications of management investment companies.

2. **B.** The closed-end company does not redeem the shares that it issues. The closed-end company has a fixed capitalization and, like regular corporations, outstanding shares trade on the open market.

3. **C.** *A diversified investment company must have at least 75% of its assets invested in cash and/or securities, may have no more than 5% of its total assets invested in one company, and may own no more than 10% of the voting stock of a company.*

4. **C.** *Unlike unit investment trusts, which issue redeemable securities, face-amount certificate companies issue installment certificates with guaranteed principal and interest. A unit investment trust has a diversified portfolio that, once established, does not change. Therefore, it cannot be called a management company. A closed-end investment company is a type of management company.*

5. **C.** *Open-end investment companies, but not closed-end investment companies, can make continuous offerings of shares, redeem their shares, and issue only common stock.*

Investment Company Registration

Registration with the SEC

A company must register with the SEC as an investment company if it:

- is in the business of investing in, reinvesting in, owning, holding, or trading securities; or
- has 40% or more of its assets invested in securities (government securities and securities of majority-owned subsidiaries are not used in calculating the 40% limitation).

A company must meet certain minimum requirements before it may register as an investment company with the SEC. An investment company cannot issue securities to the public unless it has:

- private capitalization (seed money) of at least $100,000 of net assets;
- 100 investors; and
- clearly-defined investment objectives.

If the investment company does not have 100 shareholders and $100,000 in net assets, it can still register a public offering with the SEC if it can meet these requirements within 90 days of registration.

The company must clearly define an **investment objective** under which it plans to operate. Once defined, the objective may be changed only by a majority vote of the company's outstanding shares.

Open-End Companies In addition, the Act of 1940 requires open-end companies, also called mutual funds, to have no more than one class of security issued and a minimum asset-to-debt ratio of 300%. Open-end investment companies may issue only one class of security (common stock) because they are permitted to borrow from banks as long as a company's asset-to-debt ratio is not less than 3-to-1—that is, debt coverage by assets of at least 300%, or no more than one-third of assets from borrowed money.

SEC Registration and Public Offering Requirements

Investment companies must file registration statements with the SEC, provide full disclosure, and generally follow the same public offering procedures required of other corporations when issuing securities. In filing for registration, an investment company must identify:

- the type of investment company it intends to be (i.e., open-end or closed-end);
- plans the company has to raise money by borrowing;
- the company's intention, if any, to concentrate its investments in a single industry;
- plans for investing in real estate or commodities;
- conditions under which investment policies may be changed by a vote of the shares;
- the full name and address of each affiliated person; and
- a description of the business experience of each officer and director during the preceding five years.

In filing for registration, an investment company must identify the overall investment intentions of the fund and background information on affiliated persons, officers, and directors.

Registration Statement and Prospectus

The **registration statement** an investment company must file consists of two parts. **Part 1** is the prospectus that must be furnished to every person to whom the company offers the securities. Part 1 is also called an **N1-A prospectus** or a **summary prospectus**. **Part 2** is the document containing information that need not be furnished to every purchaser, but must be made available for public inspection. Part 2 is called the **statement of additional information (SAI)**.

The prospectus must contain any disclosure that the SEC requires. The fact that all publicly issued securities must be registered with the SEC does not mean that the SEC in any way approves the securities. For that reason, every prospectus must contain a disclaimer similar to the following on its front cover:

These securities have not been approved or disapproved by the Securities and Exchange Commission nor has the Commission passed on the accuracy or adequacy of this prospectus. No state has approved or disapproved this offering. Any representation to the contrary is a criminal offense.

Continuous Public Offering Securities

The SEC treats the sale of open-end investment company shares as a continuous public offering of shares, which means all sales must be accompanied by a prospectus. The financial information (statements) in the prospectus must be dated not more than 16 months prior to the sale. With closed-end funds, only the initial public offering of stock is sold with a prospectus.

Purchasing Mutual Fund Shares on Margin

Because a mutual fund is considered a continuous primary offering, Regulation T of the Federal Reserve Board prohibits the purchase of mutual fund shares on margin. **Margin** is the use of money borrowed from a brokerage firm to buy securities. However mutual fund shares may be used as collateral in a margin account if they have been held fully paid for more than 30 days.

Restrictions on Operations

The SEC prohibits a mutual fund from engaging certain activities unless the fund meets stringent disclosure and financial requirements. The fund must specifically disclose the following activities, and the extent to which it plans to engage in these activities, in its prospectus:

- purchasing securities on margin;
- selling securities short; and
- participating in joint investment or trading accounts or acting as distributor of its own securities, except through an underwriter.

Shareholders Right to Vote

Before any change can be made to a fund's published bylaws or objectives, shareholder approval is mandatory. In voting matters, it is the majority of shares voted for or against a proposition that counts, not the majority of people voting. Thus, one shareholder holding 51% of all the shares outstanding can determine a vote's outcome.

✓ **Take Note:** Among the changes requiring a majority vote of the shares outstanding are:

- changes in borrowing by open-end companies;
- issuing or underwriting other securities;
- purchasing or underwriting real estate;
- making loans;
- changing subclassification (e.g., from open-end to closed-end or diversified to nondiversified);
- changing sales load policy (e.g., from a no-load fund to a load fund);
- changing the nature of the business (e.g., ceasing business as an investment company); and
- changing investment policy (e.g., from income to growth or from bonds to small capitalization stocks).

In addition to the right to vote on these items, shareholders retain all rights that stockholders normally possess.

Management of Investment Companies

Five parties work together to operate an investment company: board of directors, investment adviser, custodian, transfer agent, and underwriter.

Board of Directors

Like publicly owned corporations in general, a management investment company has a chief executive officer (CEO), a team of officers, and a **board of directors (BOD)** to serve the interests of its investors. The officers and directors concern themselves with policy and administrative matters; they do not manage the investment portfolio. As with other types of corporations, the shareholders of an investment company elect the board of directors to make decisions and oversee operations.

A management investment company's board of directors coordinates the different functions of a mutual fund.

The BOD:

- defines the type of fund(s) to offer (e.g., growth, income, or sector);
- defines the fund's objective; and
- approves and hires the transfer agent, custodian, and investment adviser.

The Act of 1940 restricts who may sit on an investment company's board of directors. A majority of the directors must be independent or noninterested persons. **Noninterested** persons are only connected with the investment company in their capacity as director. A noninterested person is not connected with the investment company's investment adviser, transfer agent, or custodian bank. This means that no more than 49% of the board members may be interested persons, including attorneys on retainer, accountants, and any person employed in similar capacities with the company.

Also, no individual who has been convicted of a felony of any type or a misdemeanor involving the securities industry may serve on a BOD, nor may any person who has been temporarily or permanently barred from acting as an underwriter, broker, dealer, or an investment company by any court.

Test Topic Alert! If a question about a mutual fund's Board of Directors asks how many directors can be interested persons, the answer is less than 50%. If it asks about how many must be noninterested, the correct answer would be a minimum of 51%.

Investment Adviser

An investment company's board of directors contracts with an outside **investment adviser** or **portfolio manager** to:

- invest the cash and securities in the fund's portfolio;
- implement investment strategy;
- identify the tax status of distributions made to shareholders; and
- manage the portfolio's day-to-day trading.

Naturally, the adviser must adhere to the objective stated in the fund's prospectus, and cannot transfer the responsibility of portfolio management to anyone else. An investment company cannot contract with an investment adviser who has been convicted of a securities-related felony (unless the SEC has granted an exemption). In addition, an investment company cannot lend money to its investment adviser.

✓ **Take Note:** Because the investment adviser of a mutual fund is paid a fee for investment advice, the adviser must be registered under the Investment Adviser's Act of 1940.

The investment adviser's contract is for a maximum of two years but is subject to annual shareholder approval.

The investment adviser earns a management fee, typically a set annual percentage of the portfolio's value, paid from the fund's net assets. In addition, if the investment adviser consistently outperforms a specified market performance benchmark, he usually earns an incentive bonus.

Custodian

To protect investor assets, the Act of 1940 requires each investment company to place its portfolio securities in the custody of a bank or a stock exchange member broker/dealer. The bank or broker/dealer performs an important safekeeping role as **custodian** of the company's securities and cash. Often, the custodian handles most of the investment company's clerical functions.

The custodian may, with the consent of the investment company, deposit the securities it is entrusted to hold in one of the systems for the central handling of securities established by the NASD or the NYSE. These systems make it easier to transfer or pledge securities. Once securities are placed in the system, most such transfers can be accomplished with a bookkeeping entry rather than physical delivery of the securities.

Once an investment company designates a custodian and transfers its assets into the custodian's safekeeping, the custodian must:

- keep the investment company's assets physically segregated at all times; and
- restrict access to the account to certain officers and employees of the investment company.

The custodian receives a fee for its services.

Transfer Agent (Customer Services Agent)

The **transfer agent's** functions include:

- issuing, redeeming, and canceling fund shares;
- handling name changes for the fund;
- sending customer confirmations and fund distributions; and
- recording outstanding shares so distributions are properly made.

The transfer agent can be the fund custodian or a separate service company. The fund pays the transfer agent a fee for its services.

Underwriter

A mutual fund's **underwriter**, often called the **sponsor** or **distributor**, is appointed by the board of directors and receives a fee for selling and marketing the fund shares to the public. The open-end investment company sells its shares to the underwriter at the current NAV, but only as the underwriter needs the shares to fill customer orders. The underwriter is prohibited from maintaining an inventory of open-end company shares, and is compensated by adding a sales charge to the share's NAV when it makes sales to the public.

In general, a mutual fund may not act as its own distributor or underwriter. An exception exists for no-load and 12b-1 funds.

✓ *Take Note:* A fund is allowed to act as its own underwriter under Section 12b-1 of the Act of 1940. Many funds today follow this section, and 12b-1 distribution fees are very common.

All parties that work together in the operation of a mutual fund are paid from the net assets of the fund except the underwriter. The underwriter's compensation comes from sales charges.

Investment Company Operators and their Functions

Board of Directors	Investment Adviser	Custodian	Transfer Agent	Underwriter
Administrative matters	Makes investment decisions	Holds assets	Issues and redeems shares	Distributes shares
Elected by shareholders	Paid a percentage of assets	Paid a fee by the fund	Paid a fee by the fund	Paid from sales charges
—	—	Clerical duties	Issues and redeems shares	—

Information Distributed to Investors

Investors must be provided with specific information when purchasing and tracking mutual funds.

Prospectus

The **prospectus** must be distributed to an investor before or during any solicitation for sale. The prospectus contains information on the fund's objective, investment policies, sales charges, management expenses, and services offered. It also discloses 1-, 5-, and 10-year performance histories.

The **statement of additional information (SAI)** typically contains the fund's consolidated financial statements, including:

- the balance sheet;
- statement of operations;
- income statement; and
- portfolio list at the time the statement was compiled.

Financial Reports

The Act of 1940 requires that shareholders receive financial reports at least semiannually. One of these must be an audited annual report. The reports must contain:

- the investment company's balance sheet;
- a valuation of all securities in the investment company's portfolio as of the date of the balance sheet (a portfolio list);

- the investment company's income statement;
- a complete statement of all compensation paid to the board of directors and to the advisory board; and
- a statement of the total dollar amount of securities purchased and sold during the period.

In addition, the company must send a copy of its balance sheet to any shareholder who requests one in writing between semiannual reports.

Additional Disclosures

The SEC also requires the fund to include in its prospectus or annual reports the following:

- a discussion of those factors and strategies that materially affected its performance during its most recently completed fiscal year;
- a line graph comparing its performance to that of an appropriate broad-based securities market index; and
- the name(s) and title(s) of the person(s) primarily responsible for the fund portfolio's day-to-day management.

Quick Quiz 10.2 Multiple Choice

1. The custodian of a mutual fund usually

   A. approves changes in investment policy
   B. holds the cash and securities of the fund and performs clerical functions
   C. manages the fund
   D. provides accounting services for companies whose securities are in the fund

2. Investment company financial statements are sent to shareholders

   A. monthly
   B. quarterly
   C. semiannually
   D. annually

3. The role of a mutual fund's underwriter is to

   A. hold the fund's assets and perform clerical responsibilities
   B. administer and supervise the investment portfolio
   C. market shares
   D. provide investment advisory services

4. When a bank is serving as the custodian of a mutual fund, it

   A. manages the portfolio
   B. signs all margin agreements
   C. holds the cash and securities and performs other clerical functions
   D. serves as the distributor of the fund and manages interactions with other underwriters

5. Typically, the largest single expense of a mutual fund is the

   A. custodian fee
   B. registration fee
   C. management fee
   D. brokerage fee

Answers

1. **B.** *The main functions of the custodian, usually a commercial bank, are to hold the fund's cash and assets for safekeeping and to perform related clerical duties. The custodian may also issue and redeem customer shares, send out customer confirmations, and hold customer shares.*

2. **C.** *Investment company financial statements must be sent to shareholders at least semiannually.*

3. **C.** *The underwriter markets the fund's shares. Choice A is the responsibility of the custodian; choice B is the responsibility of the fund; choice D is the manager's responsibility.*

4. **C.** *The primary function of a mutual fund's custodian bank is to safeguard the physical assets of the fund, hold the cash and securities, and perform other purely clerical functions. It does not manage the portfolio or serve in a selling capacity for the fund.*

5. **C.** *Typically, the largest single expense for a mutual fund is the management fee—the fee paid to the management company for buying and selling securities and managing the portfolio. A typical annual fee is ½ of 1% of the portfolio's asset value.*

Characteristics of Mutual Funds and the Mutual Fund Concept

Mutual funds have several unique characteristics. For instance, a mutual fund must redeem shares at the net asset value. Unlike other securities, mutual funds offer guaranteed marketability: there is always a willing buyer for the shares, the fund itself.

Each investor in the mutual fund's portfolio owns an undivided interest in the portfolio and all investors in an open-end fund are mutual participants. No one investor has a preferred status over any other investor because mutual funds issue only one class of common stock. Each investor shares mutually with other investors in gains and distributions derived from the investment company portfolio.

Each investor's interest in the fund's performance is based on the number of shares owned. Mutual fund shares may be purchased in either full or fractional units, unlike corporate stock, which must be purchased in full units.

An investment company portfolio is elastic. Money is constantly being invested or paid out when shares are redeemed. The mutual fund portfolio's value and holdings fluctuate as money is invested or redeemed and as the value of the securities held by the portfolio rises and falls. The investor's account value fluctuates proportionately with the mutual fund portfolio's value.

Test Topic Alert!

- A professional investment adviser manages the portfolio for investors.
- Mutual funds provide diversification by investing in many different companies.
- A custodian holds a mutual fund's shares to ensure safekeeping.
- Most funds allow a minimum investment, often $500 or less, to open an account, and they allow additional investment for as little as $25.
- An investment company may allow investments at reduced sales charges by offering breakpoints, for instance, through larger deposits, a letter of intent, or rights of accumulation.
- An investor retains voting rights similar to those extended to common stockholders, such as the right to vote for changes in the board of directors, approval of the investment adviser, changes in the fund's investment objective, changes in sales charges, and liquidation of the fund.
- Many funds offer automatic reinvestment of capital gains and dividend distributions without a sales charge.
- An investor can liquidate a portion of his holdings without disturbing the portfolios' balance or diversification.
- Tax liabilities for an investor are simplified because each year the fund distributes a 1099 form explaining taxability of distributions.
- A fund may offer various withdrawal plans that allow different payment methods at redemption.
- Funds may offer reinstatement provisions that allow investors that withdraw funds to reinvest up to the amount withdrawn within 30 days with no new sales charge. This provision must be disclosed in the prospectus and is available one time only.

Investment Objectives

Once a mutual fund defines its objective, the portfolio is invested to match it. The objective must be clearly stated in the mutual fund's prospectus and can be changed only by a majority vote of the fund's outstanding shares.

✓ **Take Note:** It's important to know the different types of funds available and the suitability characteristics of each.

Common stock is normally the growth component of any mutual fund that has growth as a primary or secondary objective. Bonds, preferred stock, and blue chip stocks are typically used to provide the income component of any mutual fund that has income as a primary or secondary objective.

Stock Funds

Growth Funds

Growth funds invest in stocks of companies whose businesses are growing rapidly. Growth companies tend to reinvest all or most of their profits for research and development rather than pay dividends. Therefore, growth funds are focused on generating capital gains rather than income.

Income Funds

An income fund stresses current income over growth. The fund's objective may be accomplished by investing in the stocks of companies with long histories of dividend payments, such as utility company stocks, blue chip stocks, and preferred stocks.

Combination Funds

A combination fund, also called a **growth and income fund**, may attempt to combine the objectives of growth and current yield by diversifying its portfolio among companies showing long-term growth potential and companies paying high dividends.

Specialized (Sector) Funds

Many funds attempt to specialize in particular economic sectors or industries. Usually, the funds have a minimum of 25% of their assets invested in their specialties. Examples include gold funds (gold mining stock), technology funds, and low-grade (noninvestment-grade) bond funds, among others. Sector funds offer high appreciation potential but may also pose higher risks to the investor.

Special Situation Funds

Special situation funds buy securities of companies that may benefit from a change within the companies or in the economy. Takeover candidates and turnaround situations are common investments.

Index Funds

Index funds invest in securities to mirror a market index, such as the S&P 500. An index fund buys and sells securities in a manner that mirrors the composition of the selected index. The fund's performance tracks the underlying index's performance. Turnover of securities in an index fund's portfolio is minimal. As a result, an index fund generally has lower management costs than other types of funds.

Foreign Stock Funds

Foreign stock funds invest mostly in the securities of companies that have their principal business activities outside the United States. Long-term capital appreciation is their primary objective, although some funds also seek current income.

Comparison of Common Stock and Mutual Fund Shares

Common Stock	Mutual Fund Shares
Dividends from corporate profits	Dividends from net investment income
Price of stock determined by supply and demand	Price of share determined by forward pricing – the next NAV per share calculated as determined by the fund's pricing policy
Traded on an exchange or the OTC market	Purchased from and redeemed by the investment company; no secondary trading
Sold in full shares only	Can purchase full or fractional shares
First security issued by a public corporation	Only security issued by a mutual fund
Carries voting rights	Carries voting rights
May carry preemptive rights	Does not carry preemptive rights
Ex-dividend: two business days	Ex-dividend: typically the day after record date as set by the BOD

Balanced Funds **Balanced funds** invest in stocks for appreciation and bonds for income. In a balanced fund, different types of securities are purchased according to a formula that the manager may adjust to reflect market conditions.

✓ *For Example:* A balanced fund's portfolio may contain 60% stocks and 40% bonds.

Asset Allocation Funds **Asset allocation funds** split investments between stocks for growth, bonds for income, and money-market instruments or cash for stability. Fund advisers switch the percentage of holdings in each asset category according to the performance, or expected performance, of that group.

✓ **For Example:** A fund may have 60% of its investments in stock, 20% in bonds, and the remaining 20% in cash. If the stock market is expected to do well, the adviser may switch from cash and bonds into stock. The result may be a portfolio of 80% in stock, 10% in bonds, and 10% in cash. Conversely, if the stock market is expected to decline, the fund may invest heavily in cash and sell stocks.

Bond Funds

Bond funds have income as their main investment objective. Some funds invest solely in investment-grade corporate bonds. Others, seeking enhanced safety, invest in government issues only. Still others pursue capital appreciation by investing in lower rated for higher yields.

Tax-Free (Tax-Exempt) Bond Funds

Tax-exempt funds invest in municipal bonds or notes that produce income exempt from federal income tax. Tax-free funds can invest in municipal bonds and tax-exempt money-market instruments.

US Government and Agency Security Funds

US government funds purchase securities issued by the US Treasury or an agency of the US government, such as Ginnie Mae. Investors in these funds seek current income and maximum safety.

Dual-Purpose Funds

Dual-purpose funds are closed-end funds that meet two objectives: investors seeking income purchase income shares and receive all the interest and dividends the fund's portfolio earns, and investors interested in capital gains purchase the gains shares and receive all gains on portfolio holdings. The two types of shares in a dual fund are listed separately in the financial pages of major newspapers.

Money-Market Funds

Money-market funds are usually no-load, open-end mutual funds that serve as temporary holding tanks for investors who are most concerned with liquidity. **No-load** means investors pay no sales or liquidation fees. A fund manager invests the fund's capital in money-market instruments that pay interest and have short maturities.

Interest rates on money-market funds are not fixed or guaranteed and change often. The interest these funds earn is computed daily and credited to customers' accounts monthly. Many funds offer check writing privileges, but checks must normally be written for amounts of $500 or more. The largest expense to investors is the management fee, usually not more than 0.5%.

The NAV of money-market funds is set at $1 per share. Although this price is not guaranteed, a fund is managed in order not to "break the buck" regardless of market changes. Thus, the price of money-market shares does not fluctuate in response to changing market conditions.

Money-market funds and other no-load funds are both purchased and redeemed at their NAV.

Restrictions on Money-Market Funds

SEC rules limit the investments available to money-market funds and require certain disclosures to investors.

Restrictions include the following.

- The front cover of every prospectus must prominently disclose that an investment in a money-market fund is neither insured nor guaranteed by the US government and that an investor has no assurance the fund will be able to maintain a stable NAV. This statement must also appear in all literature used to market the fund.
- No more than 5% of a fund's assets may be invested in any one issuer's securities.
- Investments are limited to securities with remaining maturities of not more than 13 months, with the average portfolio maturity not exceeding 90 days.
- Investments are limited to eligible securities determined to have minimal risk. Eligible securities are defined as those rated by nationally recognized rating organizations in one of the top two categories. (No more than 5% of the portfolio may be in the second tier of ratings.)

Comparing Mutual Funds

When comparing mutual funds, investors should select funds that match their personal objectives. When comparing funds with similar objectives, the investor should review information regarding their:

- performance;
- costs;
- taxation;
- portfolio turnover; and
- services offered.

Performance

Securities law requires that each fund disclose the average annual total returns for one, five, and 10 years, or since inception. Performance must reflect full sales loads with no discounts. The manager's track record in keeping with the fund's objectives as stated in the prospectus is important as well.

Costs

Sales loads, management fees, and operating expenses reduce an investor's returns because they diminish the amount of money invested in a fund.

Sales Loads Historically, mutual funds have charged front-end loads of up to 8.5% of the money invested. This percentage compensates the sales force. Many low-load funds charge between 2% and 5%. Other funds may charge a back-end load when funds are withdrawn. Some funds charge ongoing fees under Section 12b-1 of the Investment Company Act of 1940. These funds deduct annual fees to pay for marketing and distribution costs. Sales loads are covered in detail later in this unit.

Expense Ratio A fund's **expense ratio** compares the management fees and operating expenses to the fund's net assets. All mutual funds, load and no-load, have expense ratios. The expense ratio is calculated by dividing a fund's expenses by its average net assets.

✓ **For Example:** An expense ratio of 1.72% means that the fund charges $1.72 per year for every $100 invested.

Stock funds generally have expense ratios between 1% and 1.5% of a fund's average net assets. Typically, more aggressive funds have higher expense ratios. For bond funds, the ratio is typically between 0.5% and 1%.

Taxation

Mutual fund investors pay taxes on capital gains the fund receives. These taxes are based on how long the fund owned the security it sold. Because tax rates for long-term gains are lower than for short-term gains, it is better for an investor in a high tax bracket to receive a long-term gain than a short-term gain.

Portfolio Turnover

The costs of buying and selling securities, including commissions or markups and markdowns, are reflected in the **portfolio turnover ratio**.

The portfolio turnover rate reflects a fund's holding period. If a fund has a turnover rate of 100%, it holds its securities, on average, for less than one year. Therefore, all gains are likely to be short term and subject to the maximum tax rate. On the other hand, a portfolio with a turnover rate of 25% has an average holding period of four years, and gains are likely taxed at the long-term rate.

It is not uncommon for an aggressive growth fund to reflect an **annual turnover rate** of 100% or more. A 100% turnover rate means the fund replaces its portfolio annually. If the fund achieves superior returns, the strategy is working; if not, the strategy is subjecting investors to undue costs.

Services Offered

The services mutual funds offer may include retirement account custodianship, investment plans, check-writing privileges, telephone transfers, conversion privileges, combination investment privileges, withdrawal plans, and others. However, an investor should always weigh the cost of services provided against the value of the services to the investor.

Quick Quiz 10.3 True or False?

___ 1. Funds are required to show a minimum of five years of sales performance or since inception.

___ 2. Money-market funds have a high volatility (beta) coefficient.

___ 3. A sector fund must have a minimum of 50% of its assets invested in its specialty industry.

___ 4. A liquidation of a portion of an investor's holdings in a mutual fund will disturb diversification within the fund.

___ 5. Mutual funds may be purchased in fractional units.

___ 6. The ex-dividend date for mutual fund share is two business days before the record date.

___ 7. Aggressive growth funds typically have higher expense ratios than index funds.

___ 8. Money-market funds typically charge no load.

___ 9. Balanced funds must invest half of their assets in stock for appreciation and half of their assets in bonds for income.

___ 10. Dual purpose funds are closed-end funds.

Answers   1. *F.*   2. *F.*   3. *F.*   4. *F.*   5. *T.*   6. *F.*

   7. *T.*   8. *T.*   9. *F.*   10. *T.*

Mutual Fund Marketing and Pricing

Mutual fund shares may be marketed in several ways, but mutual fund shares are priced according to a set formula.

Marketing Mutual Fund Shares

A fund can use any number of methods to market its shares to the public. A discussion of some of the marketing methods various firms use follows.

Fund to Underwriter to Dealer to Investor An investor gives an order for fund shares to a dealer. The dealer then places the order with the underwriter. To fill the order, the fund sells shares to the underwriter at the current NAV. The underwriter sells the shares to the dealer at the NAV plus the underwriter's concession (the public offering price less the dealer's reallowance or discount). The dealer sells the shares to the investor at the full POP.

Fund to Underwriter to Investor The underwriter acts as dealer and uses its own sales force to sell shares to the public. An investor gives an order for fund shares to the underwriter. To fill the order, the fund sells shares to the underwriter at the current NAV. The underwriter then adds the sales charge and sells the shares to the investor at the POP. The sales charge is split among the various salespeople.

Fund to Investor Some funds sell directly to the public without using an underwriter or a sales force and without assessing a sales charge. If an open-end investment company distributes shares to the public directly—that is, without the services of a distributor—and the fund offers its shares with no sales charge, the fund is called a no-load fund. The fund pays all sales expenses.

✓ *Take Note:* Funds that offer shares with a 12b-1 fee of less than 0.25% may also be referred to as no-load funds.

Fund to Underwriter to Plan Company to Investor Organizations that sell contractual plans for the periodic purchase of mutual fund shares are called **plan companies**; such a company buys fund shares and holds them in trust for an individual purchasing the shares under a periodic payment plan.

Sales at the POP

Any sale of fund shares to a customer must be made at the public offering price. The NASD defines a **customer** as anyone who is not an NASD member. The route the sale takes is not important—the nonmember customer must be charged the POP. Only an NASD member acting as a dealer or an underwriter may purchase the fund shares at a discount from the issuer.

Determining the Value of Mutual Fund Shares

NAV and Forward Pricing Mutual funds must calculate the NAV of fund shares at least once per business day because purchase and redemption prices are based on the NAV. Most funds wait until after the NYSE closes (4:00 p.m. ET) before making their NAV calculations. The price of purchase or redemption orders for mutual fund shares is determined at the next NAV calculation after an order is entered. This is known as **forward pricing**.

To determine the fund's total NAV, the custodian totals the value of all assets and subtracts all liabilities.

Assets (cash + current value of securities) − liabilities = fund's NAV

The NAV per share is determined by dividing the net asset value by the number of shares outstanding.

$$\frac{\text{Fund's NAV}}{\text{Number of shares outstanding}} = \text{NAV per share}$$

In working with NAV calculations, a fund's total assets include everything of value the fund owns, not just the investment portfolio.

Changes in NAV The NAV can change daily as follows.

- NAV per share increases when portfolio securities increase in value or when the portfolio receives investment income.
- NAV per share decreases when portfolio securities decrease in value or when portfolio income and gains are paid to shareholders.
- NAV per share does not change when shares are sold or redeemed or when portfolio securities are bought or sold. In these circumstances, the fund exchanges securities for cash so that the NAV per share remains unchanged.

Net Asset Value per Share Customers who buy mutual fund shares are charged the **public offering price (POP)**. The POP equals the NAV per share plus the sales charge. When a customer sells, the liquidation price is the current NAV.

Sales Charges

The NASD prohibits its members from assessing sales charges in excess of 8.5% of the POP on customer mutual fund purchases. Mutual funds may charge lower rates if they specify these rates in the prospectus. Typically, mutual fund sales loads today are substantially less than the NASD maximums.

Investment Company Products

Closed-End Funds Closed-end funds do not have sales charges. An investor pays a **brokerage commission** in an agency transaction or pays a **markup** or **markdown** in a principal transaction.

Open-End Funds All **sales commissions** and **expenses** are paid from the sales charges collected. Sales expenses include commissions for the managing underwriter, dealers, brokers, and registered representatives, as well as all advertising and sales literature expenses.

Mutual fund distributors use three different methods to collect the fees for the sale of shares:

1. front-end loads (difference between POP and net NAV);
2. back-end loads (contingent deferred sales loads); and
3. 12b-1 sales charges (asset-based fees).

Front-End Loads **Front-end sales loads** are the charges included in a fund's public offering price. The charges are added to the NAV at the time an investor buys shares. Front-end loads are the most common way of paying for the distribution services a fund's underwriter provides.

✓ *Take Note:* Here's how a front-end load operates. An investor deposits $10,000 with a mutual fund that has a 5% front-end load. The 5% load amounts to $500, deducted from the invested amount. $9,500 would be invested in the fund's portfolio on the investor's behalf.

Back-End Loads A **back-end sales load**, also called a **contingent deferred load**, is charged at the time an investor redeems mutual fund shares. The sales load, a declining percentage charge reduced annually (for instance, 8% the first year, 7% the second, 6% the third, etc.), is applied to the proceeds of any shares sold in that year. The back-end load is usually structured so that it drops to zero after an extended holding period. The sales load schedule is specified in a fund's prospectus.

12b-1 Asset-Based Fees Mutual funds cannot act as distributors for their own fund shares except under **Section 12b-1** of the Investment Company Act of 1940. This section permits a mutual fund to collect a fee for promoting, selling, or undertaking activity in connection with the distribution of its shares. The fee is determined annually as a flat dollar amount or as a percentage of the fund's average total NAV during the year and is charged quarterly. The fee is disclosed in the fund's prospectus. Requirements include the following:

- The maximum annual permissible 12b-1 fee is 0.75% of average annual net assets.
- The fee must reflect the anticipated level of distribution services.

The payments represent fees that would have been paid to an underwriter if sales charges had been negotiated for sales, promotion, and related activities. The following 12b-1 restrictions also exist.

- **Approval**: The 12b-1 plan must be approved initially and reapproved at least annually by a majority of the outstanding shares, the board of directors, and those directors who are noninterested persons.
- **Termination**: The 12b-1 plan may be terminated at any time by a majority vote of the noninterested directors or by a majority vote of outstanding shares.
- **Misuse of No-Load Terminology**: A fund with a deferred sales charge or an asset-based 12b-1 fee of more than 0.25% of average net assets may not be described as a no-load fund. To do so violates the NASDs Conduct Rules; the violation is not alleviated by disclosures in the fund's prospectus.

Computing the Sales Charge Percentage

When the NAV and the POP are known, the sales charge percentage can be determined as shown:

$$POP - NAV = \text{sales charge (\$ amount)}$$

$$\frac{\text{Sales charge (\$ amount)}}{POP} = \text{sales charge \%}$$

If the dollar amounts for the NAV and sales charges are specified, the formula for determining the POP of mutual fund shares is:

$$NAV + \text{sales charge (\$)} = POP\ (\$)$$

A mutual fund prospectus must contain a formula that explains how the fund computes the NAV and how the sales charge is added. The sales charge is always based on the POP, not on the NAV.

To determine the POP, divide the NAV by 100% minus the sales charge. The formula follows:

$$\frac{NAV}{100\% - \text{sales charge \%}} = POP$$

✓ **Take Note:** Because of the possible high front-end sales charge, mutual funds should be recommended for long-term investing.

💡 **Test Topic Alert!** A review of the two calculations just covered:

With NAV of $10 and POP of $10.50, what is the sales charge percentage?

The sales charge percentage is calculated by finding the sales charge amount ($10.50 − $10.00) and dividing by the POP.

Remember, sales charge is a percentage of the *POP*—**not** the NAV.

$.50 ÷ $10.50 = 4.8% (when rounded)

Assume a NAV of $10 and a sales charge of 5%. What is the POP?

The POP is found by dividing the NAV by 100% minus the sales charge percent. In this example, $10 ÷ 0.95 = $10.53.

Reductions in Sales Charges

The maximum permitted sales charge is reduced from 8½% to 6-¼% if an investment company does not offer certain features. To qualify for the maximum 8½% sales charge, the investment company must offer all of the following:

- breakpoints—a scale of declining sales charges based on the amount invested;
- automatic reinvestment of distributions at NAV; and
- rights of accumulation.

Breakpoints The schedule of quantity purchase discounts a mutual fund offers is called the fund's **breakpoints**. Breakpoints are available to any person. For a breakpoint qualification, **person** includes married couples, parents and their minor children, corporations, and certain other entities. Investment clubs or associations formed for the purpose of investing do not qualify for breakpoints. The following table illustrates a breakpoint schedule:

Purchase	Sales Charge
$1 to $9,999	8½%
$10,000 to $24,999	6½%
$25,000 to $49,999	4%
$50,000 +	2%

An investor can qualify for breakpoints in several ways. A large lump-sum investment is one method. Mutual funds offer additional incentives for an investor to continue to invest and qualify for breakpoints through a **letter of intent (LOI)** or **rights of accumulation**.

Letter of Intent (LOI)

A person who plans to invest more money with the same mutual fund company may immediately decrease the overall sales charges by signing a letter of intent. In the LOI, the investor informs the investment company of the intention to invest the additional funds necessary to reach the breakpoint within 13 months.

The LOI is a one-sided contract binding on the fund only. However, the customer must complete the investment to qualify for the reduced sales charge. The fund holds the extra shares purchased from the reduced sales charge in escrow. A customer who deposits the money to complete the LOI receives the escrowed shares. Appreciation and reinvested dividends do not count toward the LOI.

✓ **For Example:** Referring back to the sample breakpoint schedule, a customer investing $9,000 is just short of the $10,000 breakpoint. In this situation, the customer might sign an LOI promising an amount that will qualify for the breakpoint within 13 months from the date of the letter. An additional $1,000 within 13 months qualifies the customer for the reduced sales charge. Each investment is charged the appropriate sales charge at the time of purchase.

If a customer has not completed the investment within 13 months, he will be given the choice of sending a check for the difference in sales charges or cashing in escrowed shares to pay the difference.

Backdating the Letter. A fund often permits a customer to sign a letter of intent as late as the 90th day after an initial purchase. The LOI may be backdated by up to 90 days to include prior purchases, but may not cover more than 13 months in total. This means that if the customer signs the LOI after 60 days, he has 11 months to complete the letter.

Breakpoint Sales

The NASD prohibits registered reps from making or seeking higher commissions by selling investment company shares in a dollar amount just below the point at which the sales charge is reduced. This violation is known as a **breakpoint sale**.

Rights of Accumulation

Rights of accumulation, like breakpoints, allow an investor to qualify for reduced sales charges. The major differences are that rights of accumulation:

- are available for subsequent investments and do not apply to initial transactions;
- allow the investor to use prior share appreciation to qualify for breakpoints; and
- do not impose time limits.

The customer may qualify for reduced charges when the total value of shares previously purchased and shares currently being purchased exceed a certain dollar amount. For the purpose of qualifying customers for rights of accumulation, the mutual fund bases the quantity of securities owned on the higher of current NAV or the total of purchases made to date.

Rights of accumulation allow an investor to combine prior investments in the fund with today's investment in order to determine today's sales charge. Referring back to the sample breakpoint schedule, once an investor accumulates $50,000 in the fund, each additional investment, no matter how small, qualifies for the lowest sales charge; in this case, 2%.

Combination Privilege   A mutual fund sponsor frequently offers more than one fund and refers to these multiple offerings as its **family of funds**. An investor seeking a reduced sales charge may be allowed to combine separate investments in two or more funds within the same family to reach a breakpoint.

Exchanges within a Family of Funds

Many sponsors offer **exchange** or **conversion privileges** within their families of funds. Exchange privileges allow an investor to convert an investment in one fund for an equal investment in another fund in the same family, often without incurring an additional sales charge.

Mutual funds may be purchased at NAV under a no-load exchange privilege. Certain rules apply.

- Purchase may not exceed the proceeds generated by the redemption of the other fund.
- The redemption may not involve a refund of sales charges.
- The exchange must take place within 30 days after the redemption.
- The sales personnel and dealers must receive no compensation of any kind from the reinvestment.

This exchange is considered a taxable event, and there may be tax consequences.

Classes of Shares   Investors can purchase the same underlying mutual fund shares in several ways. Generally, investors can purchase Class A shares, Class B shares, or Class C shares. The differences among these shares is how much, and in what way, investors will pay sales charges and related expenses.

- Class A—front-end load which can be reduced or eliminated by breakpoints
- Class B—back-end load that declines over time combined with 12b-1 fees
- Class C—12b-1 fees which are charged annually

A key point is that Class B and C shares cannot take advantage of breakpoint reductions that are available on large purchases of Class A shares. Therefore, a long term investor contemplating a large investment in a mutual fund should carefully consider the advantages of Class A shares before making a decision.

Redemption of Fund Shares

A mutual fund must redeem shares within seven calendar days of receiving a written request for **redemption**. If the customer holds the fund certificates, the mutual fund must redeem shares within seven days of the date that the certificates and instructions to liquidate arrive at the custodian bank. The customer's signature on the written request must be guaranteed.

The price at which shares are redeemed is the NAV (calculated at least once per business day).

The redemption requirement may be suspended only when:

- the NYSE is closed other than for a customary weekend or holiday closing;
- trading on the NYSE has been restricted; or
- the SEC has ordered the suspension of redemptions for the protection of the company's securities holders.

Otherwise, the fund must redeem shares upon request.

✓ *Take Note:* Some mutual funds charge redemption fees. If redemption fees are charged, all fees and sales loads cannot exceed a maximum of 8.5%. For example, a fund that charges a front-end load of 8% could charge a redemption fee of 0.5%.

Cancellation of Fund Shares

Because an open-end mutual fund makes a continuous public offering, a share is destroyed once a mutual fund share has been redeemed. Unlike other corporate securities, mutual fund shares cannot be sold to other owners. An investor purchasing mutual fund shares receives new shares.

Test Topic Alert!

- The maximum sales charge allowed by the NASD is 8.5% of the POP.
- An investor buys and redeems shares at the price next calculated (forward pricing).
- Only NASD member firms can buy below the POP—not the public or nonmembers.
- The NAV per share does not change when new shares are issued or when shares are redeemed.
- 12b-1 fees are charged quarterly, but must be approved annually.

- Breakpoints are not allowed for investment clubs and a parent and child above the age of majority. They are allowed for corporations, husband and wife, and a parent and child below the age of majority.
- A fund can charge an 8½% sales load only if it offers breakpoints, reinvestment at NAV, and rights of accumulation.
- Mutual fund shares that have been redeemed are cancelled. They are never reissued.

If a customer redeems mutual fund shares within seven business days of purchase, any fees or concessions earned by the firm for selling the shares must be returned to the underwriter. This includes the portion payable to the representative who sold shares to the customer.

Quick Quiz 10.4 Multiple Choice

1. For a company to charge the maximum sales charge of 8½%, it must offer all of the following EXCEPT

   A. automatic reinvestment of dividends and capital gains at NAV
   B. breakpoints
   C. automatic reinvestment at POP
   D. rights of accumulation

2. A mutual fund is quoted at $16.56 NAV and $18.00 POP. The sales charge is

   A. 7%
   B. 7½%
   C. 8%
   D. 8½%

3. Redemption of a no-load fund may be made at the

   A. NAV minus the sales charge
   B. POP minus the sales charge
   C. NAV plus the sales charge
   D. NAV

4. A customer purchased mutual fund shares with a net asset value of $7.82 and an 8% sales charge. The sales charge is

   A. $.68
   B. $.74
   C. $.80
   D. $.87

5. Which of the following statements regarding a letter of intent and breakpoints are TRUE?

   I. The letter of intent can be backdated a maximum of 30 days.
   II. The letter of intent is valid for 13 months.
   III. The investor is legally bound to meet the terms of the agreement.
   IV. The fund holds the additional shares in escrow.

   A. I and II
   B. II and III
   C. II and IV
   D. III and IV

6. Which of the following investors can take advantage of breakpoints?

   I. Individual
   II. Investment club
   III. Trust
   IV. Corporation

   A. I and II
   B. I, III and IV
   C. II, III and IV
   D. III and IV

Answers

1. **C.** The maximum sales load is 8½% only if the company offers rights of accumulation, breakpoints, and automatic reinvestment at NAV, not at POP.

2. **C.** The formula is sales cost divided by public offering price. The sales cost is the difference between NAV and POP, or $1.44 per share ($1.44 ÷ $18 = 8%).

3. **D.** No-load funds are redeemed at net asset value.

4. **A.** To find the dollar amount of the sales charge when the NAV and the sales charge percentage are provided, calculate the complement of the sales charge by subtracting the sales charge from 100% (100% − 8% = 92%). Then divide the NAV by the complement of the sales charge to find the offering price ($7.82 ÷ 0.92 = $8.50, the offering price). The dollar amount of the sales charge is the offering price − the NAV ($8.50 − $7.82 = $.68, the sales charge).

5. **C.** Only II and IV are true. I is false because the letter of intent can be backdated 90 days. III is false because the investor is not required by law to satisfy the letter of intent although, in the case of default, he will pay a higher sales charge.

6. **B.** Breakpoint advantages are available only to individuals. An investment club is not considered an individual, but trusts and corporations are.

Mutual Fund Distributions and Taxation

Distributions from mutual funds are derived from income received from portfolio securities or gains from the sale of portfolio securities. Whether taken in cash or reinvested, distributions are taxable.

Distributions from Mutual Funds

Many mutual fund distributions are taxed according to the **conduit theory**, as described in this section.

Dividend Distributions A mutual fund may pay dividends to each shareholder in the same way corporations pay dividends to stockholders. Dividends are paid from the mutual fund's net investment income.

Net investment income includes gross investment income—dividend and interest income from securities held in the portfolio—minus operating expenses. Advertising and sales expenses are not included in a fund's operating expenses when calculating net investment income. Dividends from net investment income are taxed at a 15% rate.

The Conduit Theory Because an investment company is organized as a corporation or trust, one might assume its earnings are subject to tax. Consider, however, how an additional level of taxation shrinks a dividend distribution's value.

✓ **For Example:** ABC Fund owns shares of XYZ Co. First, XYZ is taxed on its earnings before it pays a dividend; then ABC pays tax on the amount of the dividend it receives; then the investor pays income tax on the distribution from the fund.

Triple taxation of investment income may be avoided if the mutual fund qualifies under **Subchapter M** of the **Internal Revenue Code (IRC)**. If a mutual fund acts as a conduit, or pipeline, for the distribution of net investment income, the fund may qualify as a regulated investment company, subject to tax only on the amount of investment income the fund retains. The investment income distributed to shareholders escapes taxation at the mutual fund level.

Subchapter M requires a fund to distribute at least 90% of its net investment income to shareholders. The fund then pays taxes only on the undistributed 10%. If the fund distributes 89%, it pays taxes on 100% of net investment income.

Capital Gains Distributions The appreciation or depreciation of portfolio securities is an **unrealized capital gain or loss** if the fund does not sell the securities. Therefore,

Mutual Fund Distributions and Taxation

shareholders experience no tax consequences. When the fund sells the securities, the gain or loss is **realized** and affects shareholder taxes.

Capital gains distributions are derived from realized gains. If the fund has held the securities for more than one year, the gain is a **long-term capital gain**, taxed at a 15% rate. A long-term capital gains distribution may not be made more often than once per year.

A **short-term gain** is identified, distributed, and taxed at ordinary income tax rates.

✓ *Take Note:* Only realized gains are taxable to shareholders. Unrealized gains result in an increased NAV only.

Calculating Fund Yield

To calculate fund yield, divide the annual dividend paid from net investment income by the current offering price. Yield quotations must disclose the:

- general direction of the stock market for the period in question;
- fund's NAV at the beginning and the end of the period; and
- percentage change in the fund's price during the period.

Current yield calculations may be based only on income distributions for the preceding 12 months. Gains distributions may not be included in yield calculations. Most mutual funds distribute dividends quarterly. A mutual fund must disclose the source of a dividend payment if it is from other than retained or current income.

Ex-Dividend Date

Unlike the ex-dividend date for other corporate securities, the ex-dividend date for mutual funds is set by the board of directors. Normally, the ex-dividend date for mutual funds is the day after the record date.

Selling Dividends

If an investor purchases fund shares just before the ex-dividend date, the fund shares' market value decreases by the distribution amount. The investor is also taxed on the distribution. A registered representative may not encourage investors to purchase fund shares before a distribution because of this tax liability. Doing so is **selling dividends**, a violation of NASD rules.

Reinvestment of Distributions   Dividends and capital gains are distributed in cash. However, a shareholder may elect to reinvest distributions in additional mutual fund shares. The automatic reinvestment of distributions is similar to compounding interest. The reinvested distributions purchase additional shares, which may earn dividends or gains distributions.

Typically, customers may systematically reinvest dividends and capital gains at less than the POP and can use them to buy full and fractional shares only if:

- shareholders who are not already participants in the reinvestment plan are given a separate opportunity to reinvest each dividend;
- the plan is described in the prospectus;
- the securities issuer bears no additional costs beyond those that it would have incurred in the normal payout of dividends; and
- shareholders are notified of the availability of the dividend reinvestment plan at least once every year.

A mutual fund may apply a reasonable charge against each dividend reinvestment.

If a company wishes to establish a plan through which investors can reinvest their capital gains distributions (as opposed to their dividends) at a discount to the POP, the plan must be described in the prospectus, and all participants must be given a separate opportunity to reinvest capital gains at each distribution and be notified at least once every year of the availability of the distribution reinvestment plan.

Taxation of Reinvested Distributions

Distributions are taxable to shareholders whether the distributions are received in cash or reinvested. The fund must disclose whether each distribution is from income or capital tax transactions. **Form 1099**, sent to shareholders after the close of the year, details tax information related to distributions for the year.

Fund Share Liquidations to the Investor When an investor sells mutual fund shares, he must establish his cost base, or **basis**, in the shares to calculate the tax liability. A simple definition of cost base is the amount of money invested. Upon liquidation, cost base represents a return of capital and is not taxed again.

Valuing Fund Shares

The cost base of mutual fund shares includes the shares' total cost, including sales charges plus any reinvested income and capital gains. For tax purposes, the investor compares cost base to the amount of money received from selling the shares. If the amount received is greater than the cost base, the investor reports a taxable gain. If the amount received is less than the cost base, the investor reports a loss.

Calculate the gain or loss on mutual fund shares as illustrated.

Total value of fund shares − cost base = taxable gain or loss

The investor does not receive a separate tax form from the mutual fund identifying the cost base of the shares sold. Recordkeeping for purchases and sales is the shareholder's responsibility.

Calculating Net Gains and Losses

To calculate tax liability, taxpayers must first total all capital gains for the year. Then, they separately total all capital losses. Finally, they offset the totals to determine the net capital gain or loss for the year. Net capital losses are deductible against earned income up to a maximum of $3,000 per year. Any capital losses not deducted in a year may be carried forward indefinitely to be used in future years.

Accounting Methods

If an investor decides to liquidate shares, he determines the cost base by electing one of three accounting methods: **first in, first out (FIFO)**, **share identification**, or **average basis**. If the investor fails to choose, the IRS assumes the investor liquidates shares on a FIFO basis.

First In, First Out

When FIFO shares are sold, the cost of the shares held the longest is used to calculate the gain or loss. In a rising market, this method normally creates adverse tax consequences.

Share Identification

When using the share identification accounting method, the investor keeps track of the cost of each share purchased and uses this information when deciding which shares to liquidate. He then liquidates the shares that provide the desired tax benefits.

Average Basis

The shareholder may elect to use an average cost basis when redeeming fund shares. The shareholder calculates average basis by dividing the total cost of all shares owned by the total number of shares. The shareholder may not change his decision to use the average basis method without IRS permission.

Other Mutual Fund Tax Considerations

Mutual fund investors must consider many tax factors when buying and selling mutual fund shares.

Withholding Tax

If an investor neglects or fails to include a Social Security number or tax ID number when purchasing mutual fund shares, the fund must withhold 31% of the distributions to the investor as a withholding tax.

Cost Basis of Shares Transferred Upon Death

The cost basis of inherited property is either stepped up or stepped down to its **fair market value (FMV)** at the date of the decedent's death.

Taxation of Investment Returns

The taxation of investment returns can be summarized as follows.

- Dividends are taxed at 15%.
- Long term capital gains distributions are taxed at 15%.
- Short term capital gains distributions are taxed as ordinary income.

Exchanges Within a Family of Funds

Even though exchange within a fund family incurs no sales charge, the IRS considers a sale to have taken place, and if a gain occurs, the customer is taxed. This tax liability can be significant, and shareholders should be aware of this potential conversion cost.

Test Topic Alert!

Below are testable points about mutual fund distributions and taxation:

- Funds that comply with Subchapter M (conduit theory) are known as regulated investment companies.
- Mutual fund yield is calculated by dividing the annual dividend by the POP. Capital gains distributions are not included.
- When is the ex-date of a mutual fund? The best answer is as determined by the BOD, but if that choice is not given, choose the business day after the record date.
- Dividends and capital gains are taxable if reinvested or taken in cash.
- An investor's cost basis in mutual fund shares is what was paid to buy the share plus reinvested dividends and capital gains distributions.
- The IRS always assigns FIFO for share liquidation unless the investor chooses a different method.
- Although an exchange from one fund to another within the same family is not subject to a sales charge, it is a taxable event. Any gain or loss on the shares sold is reportable at the time of the exchange.

Quick Quiz 10.5 Multiple Choice

1. Which of the following decides when a mutual fund goes ex-dividend?

   A. NASD
   B. NYSE
   C. SEC
   D. BOD

2. The conduit theory

   A. is described in the Investment Company Act of 1940
   B. refers to a favorable tax treatment available to investment companies
   C. was developed by the NASD
   D. is stated in the SEC statement of policy

3. Your client owns shares in an open-end investment company. The shares are currently quoted in the newspaper at $10 NAV and $10.80 POP. Within the past 12 months, the investment company has distributed capital gains of $1.20 per share and dividends of $.60 per share. What is the current yield on your client's shares?

   A. 1.8%
   B. 5.0%
   C. 5.6%
   D. 6.0%

Answers

1. **D.** The ex-date for a mutual fund is set by its board of directors.

2. **B.** Regulated companies under Subchapter M of the IRS code may pass through income to beneficial owners without a tax at the fund level on the distributed income. This is known as conduit or flow-through of income and taxation.

3. **C.** In open-end investment companies, current yield is calculated as follows: Annual dividends divided by asked price equals yield. Your client would find the yield of his open-end investment company as follows: $.60 ÷ $10.80 = 0.0555 = 5.55% (5.6% rounded).

Mutual Fund Purchase and Withdrawal Plans

Mutual fund investors may select from among several methods by which to buy mutual fund shares or withdraw money from their mutual fund accounts.

Types of Mutual Fund Accounts

When a customer opens an account with a mutual fund, he makes an initial deposit and specifies whether fund share distributions are to be made in cash or reinvested. If the customer elects to receive distributions in cash rather than reinvesting them, his proportionate interest in the fund is reduced each time a distribution is made. A customer may make additional investments in an open account at any time and in any dollar amount—the law sets no minimum requirement, although each fund may set its own.

Accumulation Plans Mutual funds have established several accumulation plans that allow investors to use the dollar cost averaging strategy.

Voluntary Accumulation Plan

A **voluntary accumulation plan** allows a customer to deposit regular periodic investments on a voluntary basis. The plan is designed to help the customer form regular investment habits while still offering some flexibility.

Voluntary accumulation plans may require a minimum initial purchase and minimum additional purchase amounts. Many funds offer automatic withdrawal from customer checking accounts to simplify contributions. If a customer misses a payment, the fund does not penalize him because the plan is voluntary. The customer may discontinue the plan at any time.

Dollar Cost Averaging. One method of purchasing mutual fund shares is called **dollar cost averaging**, where a person invests identical amounts at regular intervals. This form of investing allows the individual to purchase more shares when prices are low and fewer shares when prices are high. In a fluctuating market and over time, the average cost per share is lower than the average price of the shares. However, dollar cost averaging does not guarantee profits in a declining market because prices may continue to decline for some time. In this case, the investor buys more shares of a sinking investment.

The following example illustrates how average price and average cost may vary with dollar cost averaging.

Month	Amount Invested	Price Per Share	No. of Shares
January	$600	$20	30
February	$600	$24	25
March	$600	$30	20
April	$600	$40	15
Total	$2,400	$114	90

The average cost per share equals $2,400 (the total investment) ÷ 90 (the total number of shares purchased), or $26.67 per share, while the average price per share is $28.50 ($114 ÷ 4).

✓ **Take Note:** Dollar cost averaging is effective if the average cost per share is less than the average price per share.

Withdrawal Plans In addition to **lump-sum withdrawals**, where customers sell all of their shares, mutual funds offer **systematic withdrawal plans**. Withdrawal plans are normally a free service. Not all mutual funds offer withdrawal plans, but those that do may offer the plan alternatives described here.

Fixed Dollar

A customer may request the periodic withdrawal of a **fixed dollar amount**. Thus, the fund liquidates enough shares each period to send that sum. The amount of money liquidated can be more or less than the account earnings during the period.

Fixed Percentage or Fixed Share

Under a **fixed-percentage** or **fixed-share withdrawal plan**, either a fixed number of shares or a fixed percentage of the account is liquidated each period.

Fixed Time

Under a **fixed-time withdrawal plan**, customers liquidate their holdings over a fixed period. Most mutual funds require a customer's account to be worth a minimum amount of money before a withdrawal plan may begin. Additionally, most funds discourage continued investment once withdrawals start.

Withdrawal Plan Disclosures

Withdrawal plans are not guaranteed. With fixed-dollar plans, only the dollar amount to be received each period is fixed. All other factors, including the number of shares liquidated and a plan's length, are variable. For a fixed-time plan, only the time is fixed; the amount of money the investor receives varies each period.

Because withdrawal plans are not guaranteed, the registered rep must:

- never promise an investor a guaranteed rate of return;
- stress to the investor that it is possible to exhaust the account by over-withdrawing;
- state that during a down market it is possible that the account will be exhausted if the investor withdraws even a small amount; and
- never use charts or tables unless the SEC specifically clears their use.

✓ **Take Note:** Mutual fund withdrawal plans are not guaranteed in any way. All charts and tables regarding withdrawal plans must be cleared by the SEC prior to use.

Quick Quiz 10.6 Multiple Choice

1. Under which of the following circumstances will dollar cost averaging result in an average cost per share lower than the average price per share?

   I. The price of the stock fluctuates over time.
   II. A fixed number of shares is purchased regularly.
   III. A fixed dollar amount is invested regularly.
   IV. A constant dollar plan is maintained.

   A. I and II
   B. I and III
   C. I, III and IV
   D. II and III

2. All of the following statements regarding dollar cost averaging are true EXCEPT that

   A. dollar cost averaging results in a lower average cost per share
   B. dollar cost averaging is not available to large investors
   C. more shares are purchased when prices are lower
   D. in sales literature, dollar cost averaging cannot be referred to as averaging the dollar

3. Which of the following is a risk of a withdrawal plan?

   A. The sales charge for the service is high.
   B. The cost basis of the shares is high.
   C. The plan is illegal in many states.
   D. The investor may outlive his income.

4. An investor has requested a withdrawal plan from his mutual fund and currently receives $600 per month. This is an example of what type of plan?

   A. Contractual
   B. Fixed-share periodic withdrawal
   C. Fixed-dollar periodic withdrawal
   D. Fixed-percentage withdrawal

Answers

1. **B.** Dollar cost averaging benefits the investor if the same amount is invested on a regular basis over a substantial period, during which the price of the stock fluctuates. A constant dollar plan (IV) is one in which the investor maintains a constant dollar value of securities in the investment portfolio.

2. **B.** Dollar cost averaging is available to both small and large investors.

3. **D.** Mutual fund withdrawal plans are not guaranteed. Because principal values fluctuate, investors may not have sufficient income for their entire lives.

4. **C.** If the investor receives $600 a month, the dollar amount of the withdrawal is fixed; therefore, this must be a fixed-dollar plan.

Tracking Investment Company Securities

Investment company prices, like those for individual securities, are quoted daily in the financial press. However, because various methods are used to calculate sales charges (as described here), the financial press provides several footnotes to explain the type of sales charge a mutual fund issuer uses. A registered representative must understand the presentation and meaning of the footnotes associated with investment company quotes as to accurately describe the quotes to the investing public.

Most newspapers carry daily quotes of the NAVs and offer prices for major mutual funds. A mutual fund's NAV is its bid price. The offer price, also called the **public offering price** or **POP**, is the ask price; it is the NAV plus the maximum sales charge, applicable to the fund. The *NAV Chg.* column reflects the change in NAV from the previous day's quote.

✓ **For Example:** Look at the family of funds called *ArGood Mutual Funds*. *ArGood Growth Fund* is a part of this group; its net asset value, offering price and the change in its net asset value per share are listed. As stated previously, when a difference exists between the NAV and the offering price, the fund is a load fund. A no-load fund is usually identified by the letters NL in the *Offer Price* column. Look at the *Best Mutual* funds, a family of no-load funds.

Mutual Fund Quotations

Mutual Fund Quotations
Tuesday, September 13, 2002
Price ranges for investment companies, as quoted by the National Association of Securities Dealers. NAV stands for net asset value per share. The offering price includes net asset value plus maximum sales charge, if any.

	NAV	Offer Price	NAV Chg.		NAV	Offer Price	NAV Chg.
ArGood Mutual Funds				**FastTrak Funds**			
CapApp	4.80	5.04	+ .02	App	13.79	14.44	− .01
Grwth	6.87	7.21	+ .02	CapAp	22.13	23.17	+ .15
HiYld	10.28	10.79	+ .01	Grwth	18.33	19.24	− .10
TaxEx	11.62	12.20	− .04	**Z Best Invest**			
Best Mutual				Grth p	14.81	15.59	− .03
Balan	12.32	NL	− .06	HiYld p	9.25	9.74	+ .03
Canada	10.59	NL	− .04	Inco p	7.95	8.37	− .04
US Gov	10.49	NL	− .02	MuniB p	8.11	8.54	− .03

e- Ex-distribution. f- Previous day's quote. s- Stock split or div. x- Ex-dividend. NL- No load. p- Distribution costs apply, 12b-1plan. r- Redemption charge may apply.

The final column shows the change in a share's NAV since the last trading date. A plus (+) indicates an upward move, and a minus (-) indicates a downward turn.

From this information, you can calculate any mutual fund's sales charge. For example, find the *FastTrak* group of funds. The first entry is *App*.

Remember the formula for calculating the sales charge:

Public offering price − NAV = sales charge

Therefore, in this case, the calculation is: $14.44 − $13.79 = $.65

To calculate the sales charge percentage, use the following formula:

Sales charge ÷ public offering price = sales charge %

In this case, the calculation follows: $.65 ÷ $14.44 = 4.5%

You can also watch the movements of the fund's share value.

Index Tracking Funds

Standard & Poor's Depositary Receipts (SPDRs), called **Spiders**, are index funds designed to track the performance of an underlying investment portfolio.

✓ *Take Note:* Index tracking funds are not investment company products, but they do have characteristics similar to both open-end and closed-end funds.

The most popular Spider tracks the price performance of an underlying investment portfolio. The most popular Spiders track the price performance and dividend yield of the S&P 500 companies. This tracking fund, like other Spider funds, is listed for trading on the American Stock Exchange. Spiders pay quarterly cash dividends that represent, after expenses, dividends accumulated on the underlying stock portfolio.

Spiders have characteristics of both open-end and closed-end funds. Like closed-end funds, Spiders trade like stock. Like open-end funds, Spiders can create (issue) additional shares. In addition to the S&P 500 tracking fund, there are also Spiders on various components of the S&P 500. There are nine Select Sector index funds (e.g., consumer services, energy, technology, etc.) and each of the 500 stocks in the S&P index is allocated to only one Select Sector index fund.

Investors use Spiders for:

- asset allocation;
- following industry trends;
- balancing a portfolio;
- speculative trading; and
- hedging.

Spider index funds are different from conventional mutual funds in the following ways.

- **Intraday trading**—Investors don't have to wait until the end of a trading day to purchase or sell shares. Shares trade throughout the day, making it easier for investors to react to market changes.
- **Margin eligibility**—Spider index funds can be bought on margin, subject to the same terms that apply to common stock.
- **Short selling on a downtick**—Spider index funds can be sold short on a downtick (– or 0 –) at anytime during trading hours.

Another popular index, also traded on the Amex, is the **Q's** (symbol QQQ), which tracks the price performance of the Nasdaq 100.

Quick Quiz 10.7 Multiple Choice

1. Spiders

    I. can be purchased on margin
    II. cannot be purchased on margin
    III. are subject to the short sale rule
    IV. are not subject to the short sale rule

    A. I and III
    B. I and IV
    C. II and III
    D. II and IV

2. Spider index funds

    I. are priced throughout the trading day
    II. are priced at the close of trading only
    III. can be sold short
    IV. cannot be sold short

    A. I and III
    B. I and IV
    C. II and III
    D. II and III

Answers

1. **B.** Spider index funds can be purchased on margin and are subject to the same terms and conditions that apply to buying common stock on margin. In addition, Spiders can be sold short and are not subject to the short sale rule.

2. **A.** Unlike conventional open-end management companies, Spider index funds are priced throughout the trading day and can be sold short.

Investment Company Products HotSheet

Investment Company Act of 1940:
- Defines and regulates investment companies
- Three types: face amount certificate, UIT, management company

Open-End Company:
- Mutual fund; continuous primary offering
- Redemption in seven calendar days
- Price by formula in prospectus
- Fractional shares

Closed-End Company:	• Trade in secondary market; issues debt and equity • Fixed number of shares • Sold with prospectus in IPO only
Diversified Status:	• 75% invested in other companies • Max of 5% in any one company • Can own no more than 10% of a target company's voting stock • Status applies to open- and closed-end companies
Registration Requirements:	• Minimum $100,000 capital, 100 investors • Clearly defined investment objective • Asset to debt ratio not less than 3-to-1 (300%)
Prohibited Investing:	• No purchases on margin; no short sales
Shareholder Votes:	• Change investment objective; change sales load policy; change fund classification
Shareholder Reports:	• Annual audited report, semiannual unaudited report (two per year)
Sector Funds:	• Minimum of 25% of assets in area of specialty; more aggressive
Money-Market Funds:	• No load, fixed NAV, check-writing privileges, daily interest
Performance History:	• One, five, 10 years (or fund's life if less than 10 years)
Sales Charge %:	• (POP − NAV) ÷ POP (NASD maximum of 8.5% of POP)
POP Calculation:	• NAV ÷ (100% − SC%)
12b-1 Charges:	• Distribution fee approved annually and charged quarterly; cannot be described as no-load fund if exceeds 0.25%
8½% Sales Charge:	• Only if fund offers reinvestment at NAV; rights of accumulation; breakpoints
Letter of Intent:	• Must be in writing; maximum 13 months; can be backdated 90 days
Conduit Theory:	• IRC subchapter M: fund is regulated investment company if it distributes a minimum of 90% of net investment income • Fund taxed only on retained earnings

Ex-dividend Date: • Determined by BOD; typically business day after record date

Calculating Yield: • Annual dividends ÷ POP; capital gains distributions are not included

Dollar Cost Averaging:
• Effective if average cost per share is lower than average price per share
• No guarantees

Series 7 Unit Test 10

1. According to investment company rules, open-end investment companies may not distribute capital gains to their shareholders more frequently than

    A. monthly
    B. quarterly
    C. semiannually
    D. annually

2. Under the definition of a management company, all of the following would qualify EXCEPT

    I. face-amount certificate companies
    II. unit investment trusts
    III. closed-end investment companies
    IV. open-end investment companies

    A. I only
    B. I and II
    C. I, II and III
    D. III and IV

3. If a customer purchases shares in a municipal bond fund, which of the following statements are TRUE?

    I. Dividends are taxable.
    II. Dividends are not taxable.
    III. Capital gains distributions are taxable.
    IV. Capital gains distributions are not taxable.

    A. I and III
    B. I and IV
    C. II and III
    D. II and IV

4. When a customer transfers the proceeds of a sale from one fund to another within the same family of funds, what are the tax consequences?

    A. No gains or losses are recognized until the final redemption.
    B. Gains are taxed at the time of the transfer, but losses are deferred until the final redemption.
    C. Losses are deducted at the time of the transfer, but gains are deferred until the final redemption.
    D. All gains and losses are recognized on the transfer date.

5. An open-end investment company

    I. can sell new shares in any quantity at any time
    II. must redeem shares in any quantity within 7 days of request
    III. provides for mutual ownership of portfolio assets by shareholders

    A. I and II
    B. II only
    C. III only
    D. I, II and III

6. According to the Investment Company Act of 1940, a diversified mutual fund may hold, at most, what percentage of a corporation's voting securities?

    A. 5%
    B. 10%
    C. 50%
    D. 75%

7. Which of the following statements are TRUE of mutual fund dividend distributions?

    I. The fund pays dividends from net investment income.
    II. A single taxpayer may exclude $100 worth of dividend income from taxes annually.
    III. An investor is liable for taxes on distributions whether a dividend is a cash distribution or is reinvested in the fund.
    IV. An investor is NOT liable for taxes if he automatically reinvests distributions.

    A. I and II
    B. I, II and III
    C. I and III
    D. II and IV

8. A certain mutual fund has a bid price of $9.15 and a sales charge of 8.5%. What is the price an investor will pay (rounded to the nearest cent) for each share of this fund?

    A. $8.37
    B. $9.93
    C. $10.00
    D. $10.76

9. XYZ Technology Fund permits rights of accumulation. A shareholder has invested $9,000 and has signed a letter of intent for a $15,000 investment. His reinvested dividends during the 13 months total $720. How much money must he contribute to fulfill the letter of intent?

    A. $5,280
    B. $6,000
    C. $9,000
    D. $15,000

10. Net asset value per share for a mutual fund can be expected to decrease if the

    A. securities in the portfolio have appreciated in value
    B. issuers of securities in the portfolio have made dividend distributions
    C. fund has experienced net redemption of shares
    D. fund has made dividend distributions to shareholders

11. Which of the following events will affect the NAV per share of a mutual fund?

    I. Changes in the market value of the fund's portfolio of securities
    II. Wholesale redemption of fund shares
    III. The fund receives cash dividends on the securities in its portfolio
    IV. The fund pays dividends to its shareholders

    A. I and II
    B. I and III
    C. I, III and IV
    D. II and IV

Series 7 Unit Test 10 Answers & Rationale

1. **D.** Under the Act of 1940, investment companies cannot distribute capital gains more frequently than once per year. QID: 28667

2. **B.** As defined in the Act of 1940, closed and open-end funds are subclassifications of management companies (actively managed portfolios). Face-amount certificate companies and unit trusts are separate investment company classifications under the act. QID: 28538

3. **C.** Municipal bond funds distribute federally tax-free dividends, but any capital gain distribution is subject to taxation. The tax preferential treatment of munis is limited to the income earned, not the gains. QID: 35010

4. **D.** Although a transfer within a family of funds is generally not subject to a sales charge, there is liability for any taxes due. The IRS considers this transaction as a sale and a purchase. Any losses or gains must be declared on that year's tax form. QID: 29687

5. **D.** An open-end investment company can sell any quantity of new shares, redeem shares within seven days, and provide for mutual ownership of portfolio assets by shareholders. QID: 28554

6. **B.** To be considered a diversified investment company, a mutual fund can own no more than 10% of a target company's voting securities. Additionally, no diversified investment company may invest more than 5% of its portfolio in a single company's securities. QID: 28548

7. **C.** Mutual funds pay dividends from net investment income, and shareholders are liable for taxes on all distributions, whether reinvested or taken in cash. QID: 30574

8. **C.** To calculate the offering price when you know the bid price (the NAV) and the percentage of sales charge, divide the bid price ($9.15) by the complement of the sales charge (.915). This equals $10, the offering price. QID: 29497

9. **B.** The shareholder must put in the full $15,000, so he owes an additional $6,000. Reinvested dividends and changes in the NAV do not affect the amount required to fulfill a letter of intent. QID: 30568

10. **D.** The NAV per share will rise or fall relative to the value of the underlying portfolio. If dividends are distributed to shareholders, the fund's assets decrease and per share value will decline accordingly. Appreciation of the portfolio and dividends received will increase the value. Redemption of shares will have no impact on the NAV per share as the money paid out is offset by a reduced number of shares outstanding. QID: 35028

11. **C.** Dividends paid and received by the fund directly affect NAV. Changes in the portfolio value affect NAV because the securities are marked to market daily. While share redemption will reduce total net asset value, the number of shares outstanding decreases in proportion, so the NAV per share stays the same. QID: 35050

11

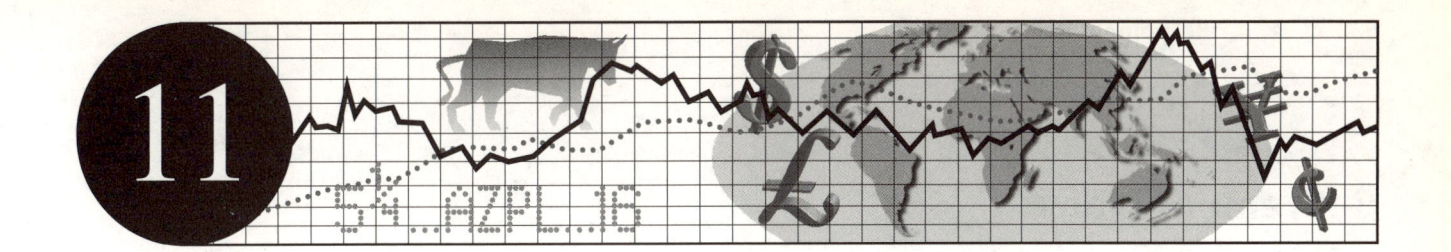

Retirement Plans

INTRODUCTION   Providing income for retirement is one of the most important financial goals for many investors. Many regulations accompany the different retirement plan options. Qualified retirement plans allow employer contributions of tax-deductible dollars to an investment account. Contributions to nonqualified retirement plans are not tax deductible, but the income and gains generated by the investments in the plan are not taxed until funds are withdrawn.

Retirement plans may be established by individuals in an IRA, or by a company on behalf of its employees through 401(k), SEP, or Keogh (HR-10) plans, or through tax-sheltered annuities. Corporate qualified retirement plans are either defined contribution or defined benefit plans. A defined contribution plan provides for a specific contribution amount and may permit employee contributions. A defined benefit plan provides a specific retirement benefit (based on a formula) for the participant, and the plan sponsor assumes the investment risk.

The Series 7 exam will ask approximately 5–10 questions on this topic, and most of these are concerned with fairly basic rules.

UNIT OBJECTIVES   When you have completed this unit, you should be able to:

- compare and contrast the features of qualified and nonqualified plans;
- identify eligibility and contribution rules for IRAs and Keogh plans;
- identify eligibility rules and requirements for tax-sheltered annuities;
- describe basic features of pension and profit-sharing plans;
- list penalties that affect retirement plan investors; and
- specify ERISA guidelines for the regulation of retirement plans.

Retirement Plans

Retirement plans are categorized as **qualified** or **nonqualified**. The primary difference between the two types is whether the contributions are tax deductible. Both plans allow tax-deferred growth on earnings attributable to plan contributions.

Qualified Plans vs. Nonqualified Plans

Qualified Plans	Nonqualified Plans
Contributions tax deductible	Contributions not tax deductible
Plan approved by the IRS	Plan does not need IRS approval
Plan cannot discriminate	Plan can discriminate
Tax on accumulation is deferred	Tax on accumulation is deferred
All withdrawals taxed	Excess over cost base taxed
Plan is a trust	Plan is not a trust

Nonqualified Retirement Plans

Deferred compensation and **payroll deduction plans** are two types of nonqualified retirement plans. Both plans may be used to favor certain employees (typically executives) because nondiscrimination rules are not applicable to nonqualified plans.

Deferred Compensation Plans

A nonqualified deferred compensation plan is a contractual agreement between a company and an employee, in which the employee agrees to defer receipt of current income in favor of payout at retirement. It is assumed that the employee will be in a lower tax bracket at retirement age. Persons affiliated with the company solely as board members are not eligible for these plans because they are not considered employees for retirement planning purposes.

Deferred compensation plans may be somewhat risky because the employee covered by the plan has no right to plan benefits if the business fails. In this situation, the employee becomes a general creditor of the firm. Covered employees may also forfeit benefits if they leave the firm before retirement.

When the benefit is payable at the employee's retirement, it is taxable as ordinary income to the employee. The employer is entitled to the tax deduction at the time the benefit is paid out.

Payroll Deductions Plans Payroll deduction plans allow employees to authorize their employer to deduct a specified amount for retirement savings from their paychecks. The money is deducted after taxes are paid and may be invested in any number of retirement vehicles at the employee's option.

Test Topic Alert! You might think of a 401(k) plan as a payroll deduction plan. For the NASD exams, 401(k) plans are considered salary reduction plans, not payroll deduction plans. In test questions, assume payroll deduction plans are nonqualified.

Quick Quiz 11.1 Multiple Choice

1. Each of the following is an example of a qualified retirement plan EXCEPT

    A. deferred compensation plan
    B. 401(k) plan
    C. pension and profit-sharing plan
    D. defined benefit plan

2. A corporate profit-sharing plan must be in the form of a(n)

    A. trust
    B. conservatorship
    C. administratorship
    D. beneficial ownership

3. Deferred compensation plans

    I. are available to a limited number of select employees
    II. must be nondiscriminatory
    III. cannot include corporate officers
    IV. cannot include outside board members

    A. I only
    B. I and IV only
    C. II only
    D. III and IV only

Answers

1. **A.** A deferred compensation plan is considered a nonqualified plan because no IRS approval is required to initiate such a plan for employees. All qualified retirement plans need IRS approval.

2. **A.** All corporate pension and profit-sharing plans must be set up under a trust agreement. A plan's trustee has fiduciary responsibility for the plan.

3. **B.** Deferred compensation plans can be offered to select employees; however, outside board members are not considered employees.

Individual Retirement Accounts (IRAs)

Individual retirement accounts (IRAs) were created to encourage people to save for retirement in addition to any other retirement plans. Anyone who has earned income may make an annual contribution of up to $3,000 or 100% of earned income, whichever is less.

✓ **Take Note:** New IRA contribution laws state that for 2003 and 2004, the maximum contribution can be $3,000. For those individuals age 50 or older, a $500 catch-up contribution is allowed.

Earned income is defined as income from work, such as wages, salaries, bonuses, commissions, tips, etc. Income from investments is not considered earned income. If the contribution limit is exceeded, a 6% excess contribution penalty applies to the amount over the allowable portion.

Individuals with nonworking spouses are allowed to contribute up to a total of $6,000 split between two accounts. This benefit is known as the **spousal IRA** and is only available to couples filing joint tax returns.

Contributions to IRAs must be made by April 15 of the year following the tax year. Individuals may contribute until age 70½, provided they have earned income.

Distributions

Distributions may begin without penalty after age 59½ and must begin by April 1 of the year after the individual turns 70½. Distributions before age 59½ are subject to a 10% penalty as well as regular income tax, except in the event of the following.

- death
- disability
- first time homebuyer for purchase of a principal residence
- education expenses for the taxpayer, spouse, child, or grandchild
- medical premiums for unemployed individuals
- medical expenses in excess of defined adjusted gross income (AGI) limits

If distributions do not begin by April 1 of the year after the individual turns 70½, a 50% **insufficient distribution penalty** applies. It is applicable to the amount that should have been withdrawn based on IRS life expectancy tables. Ordinary income taxes also apply to the full amount.

Contributions

Contributions to IRAs may or may not be tax deductible. Contributions are fully deductible, regardless of income, if the investor is ineligible to participate in any qualified plan. If eligible to participate in other qualified plans, contributions are deductible (or partially deductible) if the taxpayer's AGI falls within established income guidelines.

In other words, high earning individuals, if covered by another qualified plan, cannot take a tax deduction for an IRA contribution. The contribution may still be made, however.

An eligible individual may make contributions up to a maximum dollar amount that changes from year to year, provided that the contribution does not exceed earned income (normally compensation and income from self-employment) for the year. The dollar cap is increased by a catch-up amount for individuals age 50 and over.

IRA Regular and Catch-Up Amount:

Year	Regular Maximum IRA Contribution	Additional Catch-Up Contributions for Individuals Age 50 and Over
2002	$3,000	$ 500
2003	$3,000	$ 500
2004	$3,000	$ 500
2005	$4,000	$ 500
2006	$4,000	$1,000
2007	$4,000	$1,000
2008 and after	$5,000	$1,000

✓ **For Example:** John Jacobs was born in 1954. His maximum contributions to his IRA are as follows: $3,500 for 2004 (because he turned 50 and can make additional catch-up contributions), $4,500 for 2005, $5,000 for 2006 and 2007, and $6,000 for 2008.

Ineligible Funding and Practices Certain investments are not permitted for funding IRAs. Collectibles, such as antiques, gems, rare coins, works of art, and stamps are not acceptable. Life insurance contracts cannot be purchased within an IRA. Municipal bonds are considered inappropriate because of their low yields and tax-exempt status. Why buy tax-free interest income which will be fully taxable on withdrawal?

Certain investment practices are also considered inappropriate. No short sales of stock, speculative option strategies, or margin account trading are permitted within IRAs or any other retirement plan. However, covered call writing is permissible because it does not increase risk.

Ineligible Investments and Ineligible Investment Practices

Ineligible Investments	Ineligible Investment Practices
Collectibles	Short Sales of Stock
Life Insurance	Speculative Option Strategies
	Margin Account Trading

✓ **Take Note:** Although life insurance is not allowed within IRAs, other life insurance company products (like annuities) are. Annuities are frequently used as funding vehicles for IRAs.

Following is a partial list of investments appropriate for IRAs.

- Stocks
- Bonds
- Mutual funds
- UITs
- Government securities
- US government-issued gold and silver coins
- Annuities

Rollovers and Transfers

Individuals may move their investments from one IRA to another IRA or from a qualified plan to an IRA. These movements are known as **rollovers** or **transfers**.

IRA Rollovers Individuals may take possession of the funds and investments in a qualified plan in order to move them to another qualified plan, but may do so not more than once a year. Such a **rollover** into another account must be completed within 60 calendar days of withdrawal.

✓ **For Example:** If an individual changes employers, the amount in her pension plan may be distributed to her in a lump-sum payment. She may then deposit the distribution in an IRA rollover account, where the amount deposited retains its tax-deferred status.

Effective for distributions made after 1992, if an individual receives a distribution of assets from an employer sponsored qualified plan, the payor of the distribution must retain 20% of the distribution as a **withholding tax**. The option to forgo withholding is not available to the participant. This 20% withholding tax does not apply to rollovers made from individual IRAs. If the individual elects a **direct transfer**, there is no withholding on the amount directly transferred.

Transfers IRA assets may be directly transferred from an IRA or qualified plan. A **transfer** occurs when the account assets are sent directly from one custodian to another, and the account owner never takes possession of the funds. There is no limit on the number of transfers that may be made during a 12-month period.

Roth IRA

Roth IRAs, created in 1997, now allow after-tax contributions of up to $3,000 per individual, $6,000 per couple, per year. Contributions to other IRAs reduce the $3,000 limit.

Earnings are not taxed as they accrue nor when distributed from an account as long as money has been in an account for five taxable years and the IRA owner has reached age 59½.

Required minimum distributions at age 70½ do not apply to Roth IRAs. The 10% penalty for distributions before age 59½ is waived for first-time homebuyers if they use the funds to purchase a principal residence.

✓ **Take Note:** Individuals cannot contribute $3,000 to both a traditional and a Roth IRA. $3,000 is the maximum per individual for all IRA contributions.

Coverdell Education Savings Accounts (Education IRA)

Coverdell Education IRAs allow after-tax contributions of up to $2,000 per student per year for children younger than age 18. Distributions are tax free as long as the funds are used for qualified education expenses. If a student's account is not depleted by the age of 30, the funds must be distributed to the individual subject to income tax and 10% penalty or rolled into an education IRA for another family member beneficiary.

Section 529 Plans

There are two basic types of 529 plans: **prepaid tuition plans** and **college savings plans**. Prepaid plans allow donors to lock in current tuition rates by paying now for future education costs. The more popular option are college savings plans.

Any adult can open a 529 plan for a future college student. The donor does not have to be related to the student. With a 529 plan, the donor can invest a lump sum or make periodic payments. When the student is ready for college, the donor withdraws the amount needed to pay for qualified education expenses (e.g., tuition, room and board, books).

Contributions are made with after-tax dollars. Therefore, only the earnings are taxable on withdrawal. However, beginning January 2002, qualified withdrawals became exempt from federal taxation. Most, but not all states, permit tax-free withdrawals as well.

- Overall contribution levels vary from state to state.
- Assets in the account remain under the donor's control even after the student becomes of legal age.
- There are no income limitations on making contributions to a 529 plan.
- Plans allow for monthly payments if desired by the account owner.
- Account balances may be transferred to a related beneficiary.

Simplified Employee Pensions (SEP-IRAs)

Simplified employee pension plans (SEPs) are qualified individual retirement plans that offer self-employed persons and small businesses easy-to-administer pension plans. SEPs allow an employer to contribute money to SEP-IRAs that its employees set up to receive employer contributions.

Self-employed individuals and corporations may contribute the lesser of 25% of their incomes or $40,000 each year to SEP-IRAs.

Generally, an employer can take an income tax deduction for contributions made each year to each employee's SEP. Also, the amounts contributed to a SEP by an employer on behalf of an employee are excludable from the employee's gross income.

Quick Quiz 11.2 Multiple Choice

1. An individual less than age 70½ may contribute to an IRA

    A. if he has earned income
    B. provided he is not covered by a pension plan through an employer
    C. provided he does not own a Keogh plan
    D. provided his income is between $40,000 and $50,000 if married and $25,000 and $35,000 if single

2. An individual 50 years of age wants to withdraw funds from her IRA. The withdrawal will be taxed as

   A. ordinary income
   B. ordinary income plus a 10% penalty
   C. capital gains
   D. capital gains plus a 10% penalty

3. Premature distribution from an IRA is subject to a

   A. 5% penalty plus tax
   B. 6% penalty plus tax
   C. 10% penalty plus tax
   D. 50% penalty plus tax

4. Who of the following will not incur a penalty on an IRA withdrawal?

   A. Man who has just become totally disabled
   B. Woman who turned 59 a month before the withdrawal
   C. Woman, age 50, who decides on early retirement
   D. Man in his early 40s who uses the money to buy a second home

5. Which of the following statements regarding IRAs is not true?

   A. IRA rollovers must be completed within 60 days of receipt of the distribution.
   B. Cash-value life insurance is a permissible IRA investment, but term insurance is not.
   C. The investor must be under 70½ years of age to open and contribute to an IRA.
   D. Distributions may begin at age 59½ and must begin by the year after the year in which the investor turns 70½.

6. Which of the following statements regarding SEP-IRAs is TRUE?

   A. They are used primarily by large corporations.
   B. They are used primarily by small businesses.
   C. They are set up by employees.
   D. They cannot be set up by self-employed persons.

7. Which of the following statements regarding traditional IRAs and Roth IRAs is TRUE?

   A. Contributions are deductible.
   B. Withdrawals at retirement are tax free.
   C. Earnings on investments are not taxed immediately.
   D. To avoid penalty, distributions must begin the year after the year the owner reaches age 70½.

8. The max amount that may be invested in an education IRA in one year is

   A. $500 per parent
   B. $2,000 per child
   C. $500 per couple
   D. $2,000 per couple

9. All of the following are advantages of Section 529 plans EXCEPT

   A. earnings grow tax-deferred
   B. low investment minimums
   C. money can be withdrawn tax-free at a federal level starting in 2002, if the money is used for qualified college expenses
   D. exempt from state and local taxes

Answers

1. **A.** Any individual under age 70½ with earned income may contribute up to $3,000 to an IRA. The deductibility of those contributions will be determined by that person's coverage under other qualified plans and by his level of income.

2. **B.** All withdrawals from IRAs are taxed at the individual's ordinary income tax rate at the time of withdrawal. Distributions taken before age 59½ will incur an additional 10% penalty.

3. **C.** The penalty for premature withdrawals from an IRA or a Keogh account is 10%.

4. **A.** Early withdrawals, without penalty, are permitted only for death or disability.

5. **B.** Cash-value life insurance, term insurance, and collectibles are not permissible investments in an IRA.

6. **B.** Small businesses and self-employed persons typically establish SEP-IRAs because they are much easier and less expensive than other plans for an employer to set up and administer.

7. **C.** The common factor for both traditional and Roth IRAs is that investment earnings are not taxed when earned. Traditional IRAs offer tax-deductible contributions, but withdrawals are taxed. Roth IRAs do not offer tax-deductible contributions, but qualified withdrawals are tax free. Traditional IRAs require distributions to begin in the year after the year an owner reaches age 70½, but this is not true for Roth IRAs.

8. **B.** Only $2,000 may be invested in each child's education IRA every year. If a couple has three children, they may contribute $6,000 in total, or $2,000 for each child.

9. **D.** Section 529 plans have recently become a popular college savings program, primarily because of favorable federal tax treatment. These long-term investments are usually tied to mutual fund performance.

Keogh (HR-10) Plans

Keogh plans, also known as **HR-10 plans**, are qualified plans intended for self-employed persons and owner-employees of unincorporated businesses, or professional practices filing Schedule C with the IRS.

Contributions The Keogh planholder is permitted to make tax-deductible cash contributions of up to 20% of income (pre-contribution) or $40,000, whichever is less. As with IRAs, a person may make contributions to a Keogh until age 70½.

> ✓ **For Example:** A self-employed writer earns $180,000 and contributes $36,000 (20%) to his Keogh.
>
> | | |
> |---|---|
> | Gross Earnings | $180,000 |
> | Keogh Contribution | $ 36,000 |
> | Post-Contribution Income | $144,000 |

As a percentage of post-contribution income, the maximum Keogh contribution is 25%.

In addition, employers must make contributions into the Keogh plans of eligible employees. The contribution rate for eligible employees is complicated. To simplify, if the employer earns $200,000 or more and makes the maximum contribution to his own Keogh, the contribution rate for eligible employees is 25%.

> ✓ **For Example:** A self-employed writer earns $300,000 per year and makes the maximum contribution into his Keogh ($40,000). If the writer has a full-time editor earning $50,000 per year, the writer would have to contribute $12,500 (25%) to the editor's Keogh. The writer gets a tax deduction for the contribution.

Employees are eligible if they:

- have worked at least 1,000 hours in the year;
- have completed one or more years of continuous employment; and
- are at least 21 years of age.

Differences between Keogh Plans and IRAs

Characteristic	Keogh Plans	IRAs
Source of Contributions	Employer; employee may also make non-deductible contributions	Employee
Permissible Investments	Most equity and debt securities, U.S. government-minted precious metal coins, annuities, cash-value life insurance	Most equity and debt securities, U.S. government-minted precious metal coins, and annuities
Nonpermissible Investments	Term insurance, collectibles	Term insurance, collectibles, cash-value life insurance
Change of Employer	Lump-sum distribution can be rolled over into an IRA within 60 days	Does not apply
Penalty for Excess Contribution	10% penalty	6% penalty
Taxation of Distributions	Taxed as ordinary income	Taxed as ordinary income

Quick Quiz 11.3 Multiple Choice

1. Who among the following may participate in a Keogh plan?

    I. Self-employed doctor
    II. Analyst who makes money giving speeches outside regular working hours
    III. Individual with a full-time job who has income from freelancing
    IV. Corporate executive who receives $5,000 in stock options from his corporation

    A. I only
    B. I and II only
    C. I, II and III only
    D. I, II, III and IV

2. Which two of the following are characteristics of a Keogh plan?

   I. Dividends, interest, and capital gains are tax deferred.
   II. Distributions after age 70½ are tax free.
   III. Contributions are allowed for a nonworking spouse.
   IV. Lump-sum distributions are allowed.

   A. I and II
   B. I and III
   C. I and IV
   D. II and III

3. Which one of the following would disqualify a person from participation in a Keogh plan?

   A. She turned 70 eight months ago.
   B. She has a salaried position in addition to her self-employment.
   C. Her spouse has company-sponsored retirement benefits.
   D. She has an IRA.

4. An individual earned $75,000 in royalties from his writings; $5,000 from interest and dividends; $2,000 from long-term capital gains in the stock market; and $3,000 from rents on two houses. He can contribute to his Keogh plan

   A. $12,570
   B. $12,750
   C. $15,000
   D. $37,500

Answers

1. **C.** A person with self-employment income may deduct contributions to a Keogh plan. The receipt of stock options is not considered self-employment income.

2. **C.** All interest, dividends, and capital gains accumulated in a Keogh are tax deferred until their withdrawal (which must begin between age 59½ and the year after the year in which the account owner turns 70½). The account owner may choose to take distributions in the form of regular income payments or as a single lump sum.

3. **A.** Keogh contributions can only be made prior to the date on which an individual turns 70½.

4. **C.** Only the royalties count as self-employment income (20% of $75,000 = $15,000).

Tax-Sheltered Annuities (403(b) Plans)

Tax-sheltered annuities (TSAs) are available to employees of the following organizations:

- public educational institutions;
- tax-exempt organizations (501(c)(3) organizations); and
- religious organizations.

Unlike a qualified plan, a 403(b) plan does not require a formal plan or IRS approval.

In general, the clergy and employees of charitable institutions, private hospitals, colleges and universities, elementary and secondary schools, and zoos and museums are eligible to participate if they are at least 21 years old and have completed one year of service.

TSAs are funded by elective employee deferrals. The employee may contribute up to $12,000 each year. The deferred amount is excluded from the employee's gross income and earnings accumulate tax free until distribution. A written salary reduction agreement must be executed between the employer and the employee.

For employees over the age of 50, a catch-up contribution of $2,000 is allowed.

As with other qualified plans, a 10% penalty is applied to distributions before age 59½.

Test Topic Alert! You might see a question that asks if a student can be a participant in a TSA. The answer is "no," because the plan is only available to employees.

Corporate Retirement Plans

Corporate pension plans fall into one of two categories: **defined benefit** or **defined contribution**.

Defined Benefit Plan

A **defined benefit plan** promises a specific benefit at retirement determined by a formula involving retirement age, years of service, and compensation.

Corporate Retirement Plans

The amount of the contribution must be determined by actuarial calculation because it involves complex assumptions about investment returns, future interest rates, and other matters. This type of plan may be used by firms who wish to favor older key employees because a much greater amount can be contributed for those with only a short time until retirement.

Defined Contribution Plan

Defined contribution plans are much easier to administer. The current contribution amount is specified by the plan; however, the benefit that will be paid at retirement is unknown. A typical defined contribution formula might be expressed as a percent of income.

Profit Sharing **Profit-sharing plans** are a popular form of defined contribution plan. These plans do not require a fixed contribution formula and allow contributions to be skipped in years of low profits. Their flexibility and ease of administration has made them a popular retirement plan option for employers.

401(k) Plans **401(k) plans**, also known as **thrift plans**, are the most popular form of retirement plan today. This type of defined contribution plan allows the employee to elect to contribute a percentage of salary to his retirement account. Contributions are excluded from the employee's gross income and accumulate tax deferred. Employers are permitted to make matching contributions up to a specified percentage of the employee's contributions. In addition, 401(k) plans permit hardship withdrawals.

Test Topic Alert! All corporate retirement plan administrators have fiduciary responsibility. Risk must be the first consideration in investment of plan assets. Short sales, uncovered options, and margin account transactions are not suitable within corporate retirement plans.

Quick Quiz 11.4 Match each of the following items with the appropriate description below.

   A. Defined benefit plan
   B. Keogh plan
   C. Spousal IRA
   D. Payroll deduction plan

   ___ 1. Nonqualified plan in which an employee authorizes regular reductions from his or her check

   ___ 2. Specifies the total amount an employee will receive at retirement

___ 3. Qualified retirement plan for self-employed individuals and unincorporated businesses

___ 4. Separate individual retirement account established for a nonworking husband or wife

Answers   1. **D.**   2. **A.**   3. **B.**   4. **C.**

Quick Quiz 11.5

Match each of the following items with the appropriate description below.

A. Profit-sharing plan
B. Deferred compensation plan
C. Rollover
D. Defined contribution plan

___ 1. A qualified plan that specifies an employer's annual funding

___ 2. Employees receive a portion of profits from a business

___ 3. Movement of funds from one retirement plan to another, generally within a specified period

___ 4. Nonqualified retirement plan in which an employee delays receipt of current compensation, generally until retirement

Answers   1. **D.**   2. **A.**   3. **C.**   4. **B.**

The Employee Retirement Income Security Act of 1974 (ERISA)

ERISA was established to prevent abuse and misuse of pension funds. ERISA guidelines apply to private sector (corporate) retirement plans and certain union plans—not public plans like those for government workers.

Significant ERISA provisions include the following.

- **Participation**: Identifies eligibility rules for employees. States that all employees must be covered if they are 21 years or older and have performed one year of full-time service (which ERISA defines as 1,000 hours).

- **Funding**: Requires that funds contributed to the plan be segregated from other corporate assets. Plan trustees have the responsibility to administer and invest the assets prudently and in the best interest of all participants. IRS contribution limits must be observed.
- **Vesting**: Employees are entitled to their entire retirement benefit within a certain number of years of service, even if they leave the company.
- **Communication**: The plan document must be in writing, and employees must be given annual statements of account and updates of plan benefits.
- **Nondiscrimination**: All eligible employees must be impartially treated through a uniformly applied formula.
- **Beneficiaries**: Must be named to receive an employee's benefits at his or her death.

Quick Quiz 11.6 Multiple Choice

1. Regulations regarding how contributions are made to tax-qualified plans relate to which of the following ERISA requirements?

    A. Vesting
    B. Funding
    C. Nondiscrimination
    D. Reporting and disclosure

2. Which of the following determines the amount paid into a defined contribution plan?

    A. ERISA-defined contribution requirements
    B. Trust agreement
    C. Employer's age
    D. Employee's retirement age

3. Your customer works as a nurse in a public school. He wants to know more about participating in the school's TSA plan. Which of the following statements are correct?

    I. Contributions are made with before-tax dollars.
    II. He is not eligible to participate.
    III. Distributions before age 59½ are normally subject to penalty tax.
    IV. Mutual funds and CDs are available investment vehicles.

    A. I, II and III only
    B. I and III only
    C. I, III and IV only
    D. II only

4. Which of the following statements is TRUE of a defined benefit plan?

   A. All employees receive the same benefits at retirement.
   B. All participating employees are immediately vested.
   C. High-income employees near retirement may receive much larger contributions than younger employees with the same salary.
   D. The same amount must be contributed for each eligible employee.

5. The requirements of the Employee Retirement Income Security Act apply to pension plans established by which of the following?

   A. US government workers
   B. Only public entities, such as the City of New York
   C. Only private organizations, such as Exxon
   D. Both public and private organizations

6. Plan meeting standards set by the ERISA are a characteristic of which of the following?

   A. Profit-sharing plan
   B. Qualified plan
   C. Deferred compensation plan
   D. Rollover

Answers

1. **B.** Funding covers how an employer contributes to or funds a plan. Vesting describes how quickly rights to a retirement account turn over to the employee. Nondiscrimination refers to broad employee coverage by a plan. All retirement plans must meet ERISA's reporting and disclosure requirements.

2. **B.** The retirement plan's trust agreement contains a section explaining the formula(s) used to determine the contributions to a defined contribution plan.

3. **C.** Because he is employed by a public school system, your customer is eligible to participate in the tax-sheltered annuity plan. Employee contributions to a TSA plan are excluded from gross income in the year in which they are made. As in other retirement plans, a penalty tax is assessed on distributions received before age 59½. Mutual funds, CDs, and annuity contracts are among the investment choices available for TSA plans.

4. **C.** The rules regarding the maximum amount of contributions differ for defined contribution plans and defined benefit plans. Defined benefit plans set the amount of retirement benefits that a retiree receives as a percentage of the previous several years' salaries. For the highly paid individual nearing retirement, the defined benefit plan allows a larger contribution in a shorter time. D describes a defined contribution plan rather than a defined benefit plan.

5. **C.** ERISA was established to protect the retirement funds of employees working in the private sector only. It does not apply to self-employed persons or public organizations.

6. **B.**

Retirement Plans HotSheet

Nonqualified Plans:
- Nondeductible contributions; can be discriminatory
- Examples are payroll deduction; deferred compensation
- Risk of deferred compensation is employer failure

IRAs:
- Maximum contribution is $3,000, or 100% of earned income
- Spousal IRA allows $6,000 between spouses filing joint returns, split between two accounts
- No life insurance or collectibles as investments
- 10% penalty, plus applicable ordinary income tax on withdrawals before age 59½
- 6% excess contribution penalty
- 50% insufficient distribution penalty (insufficient if after 70½)
- One rollover allowed each 12 months to be completed within 60 days
- Unlimited trustee-to-trustee transfers
- Contributions are immediately vested

SEPs:
- Qualified plan; allows employers to contribute money to employee IRAs
- Contribution max = $40,000
- Contributions are immediately vested

Roth IRAs:
- New IRA that allows after-tax contributions, possible tax-free distributions
- Maximum contribution of $3,000 per individual, $6,000 per couple
- Does not require distributions to begin at age 70½

Education IRAs:
- New IRA: allows after-tax contributions for children under age 18
- Maximum contribution is $2,000 per year
- Tax-free distributions if funds are used for education
- Contributions may be made by any adult

Keoghs (HR-10 Plans):
- Available to self-employed persons, owners of unincorporated businesses, and professional practices
- Contribution max is lesser of 20% of gross for employer (25% for employee) or $40,000
- All employees must participate if age 21 or older, employed more than one year, work more than 1,000 hours per year
- Life insurance may be held within the plan

TSAs (403(b) Plans):
- Available to employees of nonprofit organizations
- Typically funded by elective employee salary reductions; usually no cost basis

Pension Plans:	• Require annual contribution • Defined benefit: based on formula factoring age, salary, years of service; calculated by actuary; favor older key employees • Defined contribution: simpler to administer, contribution is typically a percent of salary
Profit-Sharing Plans:	• Annual contribution not required; great investment and contribution flexibility
Withholding Rule:	• 20% withholding applied to distributions from qualified plans made payable to participant
ERISA:	• Protects participants in corporate (private) plans, not public plans • Rules for funding, vesting, nondiscrimination, participation, communication

Series 7 Unit Test 11

1. Distribution from a traditional IRA can begin at age 59½ and must begin no later than

   A. age 65
   B. age 68
   C. age 70½
   D. 15 years from the individual's date of retirement

2. ERISA regulations cover

   I. public sector retirement plans
   II. private sector retirement plans
   III. federal government employee retirement plans

   A. I only
   B. II only
   C. III only
   D. I, II and III

3. Which of the following plans requires an actuary's services?

   A. Profit-sharing
   B. Defined benefit
   C. Defined contribution
   D. 401(k)

4. The amount paid into a defined contribution plan is set by the

   A. ERISA-defined contribution requirements
   B. trust agreement
   C. employer's age
   D. employer's profits

5. Who of the following is not eligible to open a Keogh but is eligible to open an IRA?

   A. College professor who makes $10,000 on the sale of a book and several articles
   B. Corporate officer who earns $40,000 plus an additional $10,000 as a part-time speaker
   C. Doctor who receives $10,000 from a restaurant he owns
   D. Corporate officer who receives a $5,000 bonus

6. A self-employed attorney has income of $110,000 per year. He has no other retirement plans and contributes $3,000 to his IRA. His contribution is

   A. fully tax deductible
   B. partially tax deductible
   C. not tax deductible
   D. not permitted

7. Which of the following securities is the LEAST suitable recommendation for a qualified money-purchase plan account?

   A. Blue-chip common stock
   B. Investment-grade municipal bond
   C. Treasury bill
   D. A rated corporate bond

8. Which of the following statements regarding Roth IRAs are TRUE?

   I. Contributions are made with pre-tax dollars
   II. Earnings accumulate tax free
   III. Distributions are not taxable if a holding period is satisfied

   A. I and II only
   B. I and III only
   C. II and III only
   D. I, II and III

9. Which of the following would be permitted to open an IRA?

    I. An individual whose sole income consists of dividends and capital gains
    II. A divorced mother whose sole income is alimony and child support
    III. A self-employed attorney who has a Keogh plan
    IV. A corporate officer covered by a 401(k) plan

    A. I only
    B. II, III and IV only
    C. III and IV only
    D. I, II, III and IV

10. Payments received by the owner of a 403(b) plan are

    A. 100% taxable
    B. taxable only to extent of earnings
    C. taxable only to extent of the owner's cost basis
    D. not taxable

Series 7 Unit Test 11 Answers & Rationale

1. **C.** As a result of the Tax Reform Act of 1986, the owner of a traditional IRA or a Keogh retirement plan has until April 1 of the year after the year in which he turns 70½ to begin withdrawing from the account. QID: 28696

2. **B.** ERISA regulations pertain only to corporate and certain union sponsored pension plans, which are retirement plans for the private sector. QID: 34957

3. **B.** In a defined benefit plan the payout is established, and employers must contribute annually to assure payment of the benefit amount. An actuary must calculate the annual contribution amount necessary to meet the benefit requirement. QID: 32225

4. **B.** A defined contribution plan's trust agreement contains a section explaining the formula(s) used to determine the contributions to the retirement plan. QID: 28741

5. **D.** Anyone with earned income can open an IRA; the tax deductibility of a person's contributions depends on eligibility to participate in an employer-sponsored qualified retirement plan and on the person's income. Each of the listed individuals had income earned from self-employment, and therefore could open a Keogh plan, except for the corporate officer receiving a bonus. QID: 28726

6. **A.** IRA contributions are fully deductible, regardless of income, if the taxpayer is not covered by any other qualified plans. QID: 34858

7. **B.** Municipal bonds provide tax-exempt interest payments, and consequently offer lower yields. Because earnings in a qualified retirement plan account grow tax deferred, the lower yielding municipal bond is not a suitable investment. In addition, they will be fully taxed on withdrawal. QID: 32224

8. **C.** Contributions to Roth IRAs are made with after-tax dollars and distributions are received tax-free if holding period requirements are met. QID: 32226

9. **B.** An IRA contribution can be made only from earned income. Dividends and interest are investment income, but alimony is considered earned income. Individuals can contribute to an IRA even if they are already covered by a corporate pension plan or Keogh plan. However, although a contribution can be made, it may or may not be deductible depending on the individual's income. QID: 34995

10. **A.** When TSA funds are withdrawn, they are fully taxed at ordinary income rates. Funds were contributed pretax and earnings accumulate tax-deferred. Because no taxes were ever paid, the full withdrawal is taxable. QID: 35000

12

Variable Annuities

INTRODUCTION

Variable annuities have become a very popular retirement planning product. Tax-deferred growth and lifetime payout options are among the factors that make variable annuities very popular with investors.

A variable annuity is a contract with an insurance company, with many similarities to a mutual fund. Annuities and mutual funds are subject to many of the same regulations. Like any retirement account, an annuity is most often used to accumulate funds for retirement. Taxes on income and capital gains are deferred until the funds are withdrawn. Unlike a qualified retirement account, however, an annuity does not restrict the amount of funds that may be invested, and the funds invested are not tax deductible.

The Series 7 exam is likely to ask 5–10 questions on this topic.

UNIT OBJECTIVES

When you have completed this unit, you should be able to:

- list the similarities between variable annuities and mutual funds;
- identify the unique features and guarantees associated with variable annuities;
- describe the phases of the annuity contract;
- determine fluctuations in monthly payouts based on comparison of the assumed interest rate (AIR) and separate account rate of return;
- describe the taxation of withdrawals;
- compare and contrast various payout options; and
- explain the risks associated with ownership of variable annuities.

Types of Annuity Contracts

An **annuity** is a life insurance company product designed to provide supplemental retirement income. The term *annuity* specifically refers to a stream of income payments guaranteed for life. This product is unique from other securities products that have been discussed because of the guarantee it offers.

Life insurance companies offer two basic annuity products: **fixed annuities** and **variable annuities**. Both products require that the purchaser make deposits to the insurance company, either in a lump sum or over time, and then at some point begin to withdraw the funds. Although designed to provide monthly income for the life of the annuitant, withdrawals are frequently taken in lump sums or random withdrawals.

Fixed Annuity

In a **fixed annuity**, investors pay premiums to the insurance company that are invested in the company's general account. The insurance company is then obligated to pay a guaranteed amount of payout (typically monthly) to the annuitant based on how much was paid in.

The insurer guarantees a rate of return, and as such bears the investment risk. Because the insurer is at risk, this product is not a security; an insurance license (but not a securities registration) is required to sell fixed annuities.

A significant risk is associated with fixed annuities: **purchasing power risk**. The fixed payment that the annuitant receives loses buying power over time due to inflation.

✓ **For Example:** To understand the risk of a fixed annuity, consider the following:

An individual who purchased a fixed annuity in 1960 began to receive monthly income of $375 in 1980. Years later, this amount, which seemed a sufficient monthly income in 1960, is no longer enough income to live on.

Types of Annuity Contracts

Fixed Annuity

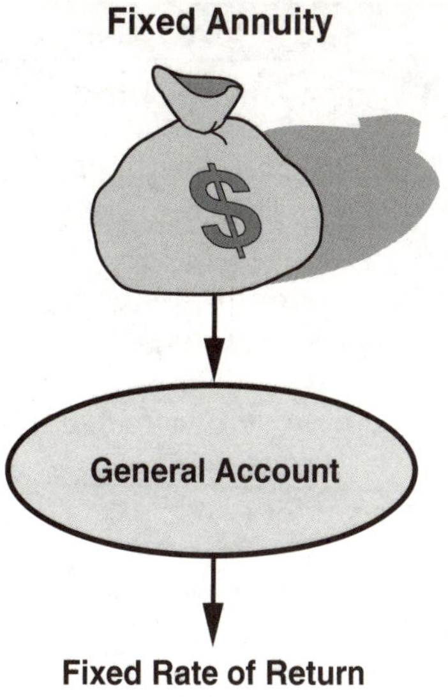

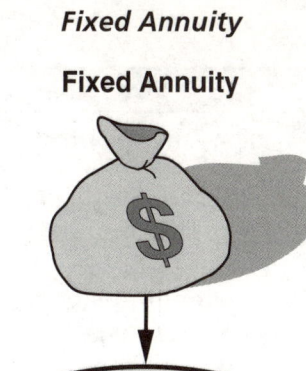

Fixed Annuity

↓

General Account

↓

Fixed Rate of Return

Variable Annuity

Insurance companies introduced the **variable annuity** as an opportunity to keep pace with inflation. For this potential advantage, the investor, rather than the insurance company, assumes the investment risk. Because the investor takes on this risk, the product is considered a security. It must be sold with a prospectus, and by individuals who are both insurance licensed and securities licensed.

Variable Annuity

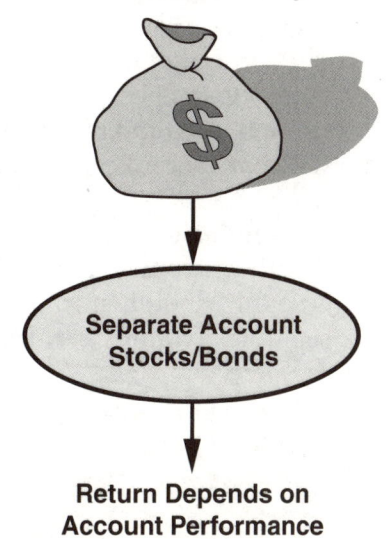

Variable Annuity

↓

Separate Account Stocks/Bonds

↓

Return Depends on Account Performance

Fixed vs. Variable Annuity

Fixed Annuity	Variable Annuity
Payments made with after-tax dollars	Payments made with after-tax dollars
Payments are invested in the general account	Payments are invested in the separate account
Portfolio of fixed-income securities/real estate	Portfolio of equity, debt, or mutual funds
Insurer assumes investment risk	Annuitant assumes investment risk
Not a security	Is a security
Guaranteed rate of return	Return depends on separate account performance
Fixed administrative expenses	Fixed administrative expenses
Income guaranteed for life	Income guaranteed for life
Monthly payment never falls below guaranteed minimum	Monthly payments may fluctuate up or down
Purchasing power risk	Typically protects against purchasing power risk
Subject to insurance regulation	Subject to insurance and securities regulation

Separate Account As with a fixed annuity, the purchaser makes payments to the insurer. However, the premium payments for variable annuities are invested in the **separate account** of the insurer. This account is separated from the general funds of the insurer because it is invested differently. Investments include common stock, bonds, and mutual funds, with the objective of achieving growth that will match or exceed the rate of inflation.

Although annuitants are guaranteed monthly income for life, the amount of monthly income received is dependent on the performance of the separate account. Monthly income either increases or decreases, as determined by the separate account's performance.

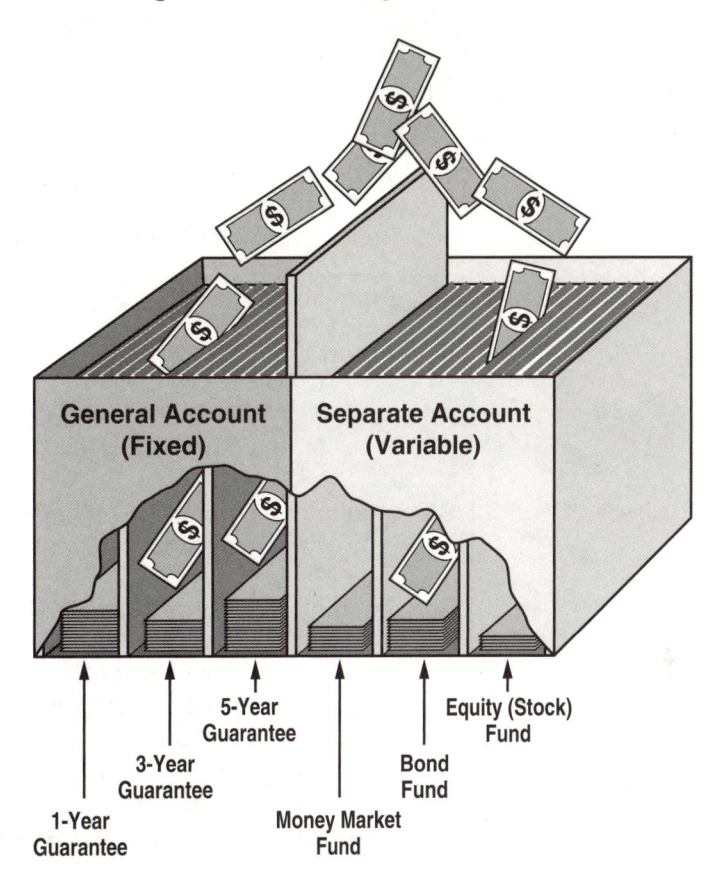

Investing Variable Annuity Premium Dollars

(Diagram: Premium dollars flow into a box divided into "General Account (Fixed)" and "Separate Account (Variable)". The General Account feeds 1-Year Guarantee, 3-Year Guarantee, and 5-Year Guarantee. The Separate Account feeds Money Market Fund, Bond Fund, and Equity (Stock) Fund.)

Combination Annuity

Investors may purchase a **combination annuity** to receive the advantages of both the fixed and variable annuities. In a combination annuity, the investor contributes to both the general and separate accounts, which provides for guaranteed payments as well as inflation protection.

Similarity of Variable Annuities to Mutual Funds

Separate Account

As described previously, the separate account of the variable annuity consists of the purchasers' funds pooled together and invested in a diversified portfolio of stocks, bonds, and mutual funds. Investors own a proportionate share of these securities and the value of their investment rises and falls based on the performance of the securities in the pool. This is precisely how mutual funds perform: the separate account of a variable annuity is operated and regulated just like a mutual fund.

Management and Registration

If the investment manager of an insurance company is responsible for selecting the securities to be held within the separate account, the separate account is **directly managed**, and must be registered under the Investment Company Act of 1940 as an **open-end management investment company**. However, if the investment manager of the insurance company passes the portfolio management responsibility to another party, the separate account is **indirectly managed**, and must be registered as a **unit investment trust (UIT)** under the Act of 1940.

Mutual Fund vs. Variable Annuity

	Mutual Fund	Variable Annuity
Sales Load	8½% max	8½% max
Pricing	NAV calculated once per business day	Unit value calculated once per business day
Share Value	Depends on performance of fund	Depends on performance of separate account
Regulated by	Act of 1933 Act of 1934 Investment Co. Act of 1940 Investment Advisors Act of 1940 (Portfolio manager receives fee)	Act of 1933 Act of 1934 Investment Co. Act of 1940 Investment Advisors Act of 1940 (Separate account manager receives fee)

Although there are many similarities between mutual funds and variable annuities, there are two extremely significant features that differentiate these products.

- **The earnings on dollars invested into a variable annuity accumulate tax deferred.** Mutual funds periodically distribute dividends and capital gains, and all of these distributions are typically taxable upon receipt. Such distributions are never paid directly to owners of annuities; instead, they increase the value of units in the separate account. Tax liability is postponed until withdrawals take place. This feature of tax-deferred growth has established the annuity as a popular product for retirement accumulation. If withdrawals are made prior to age 59½, a 10% penalty is applied to the earnings.
- **Variable annuities offer the advantage of guaranteed lifetime income.** Mutual fund shareholders are offered no guarantees on income provided.

Quick Quiz 12.1 Multiple Choice

1. Which of the following represent rights of an investor who has purchased a variable annuity?

    I. Right to vote on proposed changes in investment policy
    II. Right to approve changes in the plan portfolio
    III. Right to vote for the investment adviser
    IV. Right to make additional purchases at no sales charge

    A. I and III
    B. I and IV
    C. II and III
    D. II and IV

2. Which of the following statements are TRUE for both variable annuities and mutual funds?

    I. They contain managed portfolios.
    II. An owner's account value typically passes to his estate at the time of his death.
    III. They are regulated by the Investment Company Act of 1940.
    IV. All investment income and realized capital gains are taxable to the owner in the year they are generated.

    A. I and III
    B. I and IV
    C. II and III
    D. II and IV

3. Which of the following has the greatest effect on the value of annuity units in a variable annuity?

    A. Changes in the Standard & Poor's index
    B. Changes in cost-of-living index
    C. Fluctuations in the securities held in the separate account
    D. Changes in stock market prices

Variable Annuities

4. Variable annuity salespeople must register with the

   I. SEC
   II. State banking commission
   III. NASD
   IV. State insurance department

   A. I, II and III only
   B. I and III only
   C. I, III and IV only
   D. II and IV only

5. A variable annuity contract guarantees a

   I. rate of return
   II. fixed mortality expense
   III. fixed administrative expense

   A. I and II only
   B. I and III only
   C. II and III only
   D. I, II and III

6. Separate accounts are similar to mutual funds in that both

   I. may have diversified portfolios of common stock
   II. are managed by full-time professionals
   III. give investors voting rights

   A. I and II only
   B. I and III only
   C. II and III only
   D. I, II and III

Answers

1. **A.** Owners of variable annuities, like owners of mutual fund shares, have the right to vote on changes in investment policy and the right to vote for an investment adviser.

2. **A.** The Act of 1940 regulates both mutual funds and variable annuities. Mutual funds owned in a single name typically pass to the owner's estate at death. Variable annuity proceeds, however, usually pass directly to the owner's designated beneficiary at death, like a typical insurance policy. Investment income and capital gains realized generate current income to the owner of mutual funds, but in variable annuities income is deferred until withdrawal begins.

3. **C.** Annuity unit price changes are based on changes of value of securities held in the separate account. This price change is a risk that is passed on to the investor in a variable annuity.

4. **C**. *Variable annuity salespeople must be registered with the NASD and the state insurance commission. Registration with the NASD is de facto registration with the SEC. No registration is required by the state banking commission.*

5. **C**. *A variable annuity does not guarantee an earnings rate but it does guarantee payments for life (mortality) and normally guarantees that expenses will not increase above a specified level.*

6. **D**. *Separate accounts as well as mutual funds may contain diversified portfolios of securities and be managed by professional investment advisers. Voting rights for policy and management elections are available.*

Purchasing Annuities

An investor is offered a number of options when purchasing an annuity. Payments to the insurance company can either be made with a single **lump-sum** investment, or **periodically** on a monthly, quarterly, or annual basis.

- A **single premium deferred annuity** is purchased with a lump sum, but payment of benefits is delayed until a later date selected by the annuitant.
- A **periodic payment deferred annuity** allows investments over time. Payments of benefits on this type of annuity are always deferred until a later date selected by the annuitant.
- An **immediate annuity** is purchased with a lump sum, and the payout of benefits usually commences within 60 days.

Test Topic Alert! There is no such thing as an immediate deferred annuity; deferred annuities have delayed payouts.

The Two Phases of Variable Annuities

The variable annuity has two distinct phases. The growth phase is its **accumulation phase**, while the payout phase is its **annuity phase**. A contract owner's interest in the separate account is known as either **accumulation units** or **annuity units** depending on the contract phase. Both accumulation units and annuity units vary in value based on the separate account's performance.

At some point, the annuitant will begin to take income from the account. This is known as the **annuitization** of the contract. Technically, the value of the accumulation units is converted into a fixed number of annuity units. These annuity units are then liquidated to provide monthly income guaranteed for the life of the annuitant.

Variable Annuities

Annuitization

```
                    Annuitization
                          ↓
   Accumulation Phase  |  Annuity Phase
   Accumulation Units  |  Annuity Units
```

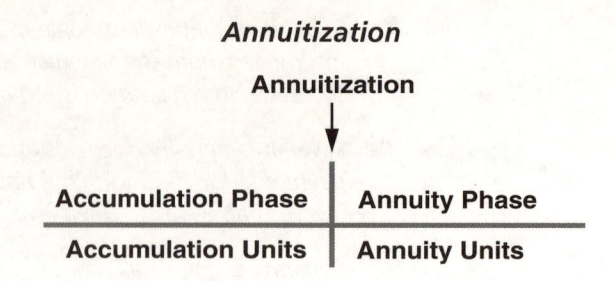

✓ **Take Note:** The value of both accumulation units and annuity units will vary based on the performance of the separate account. The number of accumulation units varies as additional investments purchase additional units. However, once the contract is annuitized, the number of annuity units received is fixed.

Receiving Distribution from Annuities

An annuity offers several payment options for money accumulated in the separate account. The investor can withdraw the funds **randomly**, in a **lump sum**, or **annuitize** the contract (receive monthly income).

Payout and Assumed Interest Rate (AIR)

If annuitization is chosen, the actuarial department of the insurance company determines the initial value for the annuity units and the amount of the first month's annuity payment. At this time an **assumed interest rate** (**AIR**) is established. The AIR is a conservative projection of the performance of the separate account over the estimated life of the contract. It is only relevant in the annuity phase of the contract.

The value of each annuity unit and the annuitant's subsequent monthly income will vary, depending on separate account performance as compared to the AIR. To determine whether the monthly income will increase, decrease, or stay the same as the previous month, the following rules are applied.

- If separate account performance is greater than the AIR, the monthly income is more than the previous month's payment.
- If separate account performance is equal to the AIR, the monthly income stays the same as the previous month's payment.
- If separate account performance is less than the AIR, the monthly income is less than the previous month's payment.

Receiving Distribution from Annuities

✓ **Take Note:** Review the following for mastery of the AIR concept.

Month 1: AIR of 4%. The actuaries have determined the first month's payment to be $1,000.

Month 2: Separate account performance is 8%. Does monthly income go up, go down, or stay the same?

It goes up. Remember, you must compare the 8% rate of the separate account to the AIR. Since 8% is greater than 4%, the payment increases. The amount of the increase is actuarially determined.

Month 3: Separate account performance drops to 6%. Does monthly income go up, go down, or stay the same?

Although you might be tempted to say *goes down*, because the separate account performance fell, the payment still increases. The separate account return is greater than the 4% AIR.

Month 4: Separate account performance is 4%. What happens to monthly income?

According to the rules, when separate account performance equals the AIR, the monthly income does not change. The monthly income amount is the same as the previous month's.

Month 5: Separate account performance is 3%. What happens to monthly income?

It falls. When the separate account return is less than the AIR the monthly income is lower than the previous month.

Month 6: Separate account performance is 3% again. What happens to monthly income?

Because the separate account return is less than the AIR, the monthly income decreases, even though the separate account performance did not change.

AIR/Separate Account Return/Effect on Income

	Month 2	Month 3	Month 4	Month 5	Month 6
AIR	4%	4%	4%	4%	4%
Separate Account Return	8%	6%	4%	3%	3%
Effect on Income	Up	Up	Equal to previous month	Down	Down

Quick Quiz 12.2 Multiple Choice

1. Your customer invests in a variable annuity. At age 65, she chooses to annuitize. Under these circumstances, which two of the following are TRUE?

   I. She will receive the annuity's entire value in a lump-sum payment.
   II. She may choose to receive monthly payments for the rest of her life.
   III. The accumulation unit's value is used to calculate the total number of annuity units.
   IV. The accumulation unit's value is used to calculate the annuity unit's value.

   A. I and III
   B. I and IV
   C. II and III
   D. II and IV

2. An investor is in the annuity period of a variable annuity he purchased 15 years ago. During the present month, the annuitant receives a check for an amount less than the previous month's payment. Which of the following events caused the annuitant to receive the smaller check?

   A. Account performance was less than the previous month's performance.
   B. Account performance was greater than the previous month's performance.
   C. Account performance was less than the assumed interest rate.
   D. Account performance was greater than the assumed interest rate.

3. An insurance company offering a variable annuity makes payments to annuitants on the 15th of each month. The contract has an assumed interest rate of 3%. In July of this year, the contract earned 4%. In August, the account earned 6%. If the contract earns 3% in September, the payments to annuitants will be

   A. greater than the payments in August
   B. less than the payments in August
   C. the same as the payments in August
   D. less than the payments in July

Answers

1. **C.** When a variable contract is annuitized, the number of accumulation units is multiplied by the unit value to arrive at the total annuitization value. An annuity factor has been actuarially determined considering the investor's gender, age, mortality, and payout option selected, for example. This factor is used to establish the dollar amount of the first annuity payment. Future annuity payments will vary according to the separate account's value.

2. **C.** In the annuity period of a variable annuity, the amount received depends on the account performance compared to the assumed interest rate. If actual performance is less than the AIR, the payout's value declines.

3. **C.** *The contract earned 3% in September. The AIR for the contract is 3%. Payment size will not change from the payment made the previous month.*

Payout Options

At the time of annuitization, the annuitant is required to select an annuity payout option. The choices that you must understand for Series 7 are:

- life income (also called life only or straight life);
- life with period certain; and
- joint life with last survivor.

Life Income If an annuitant selects the **life income** option, the insurance company will pay the annuitant for life. When the annuitant dies, there are no continuing payments to a beneficiary.

Life with Period Certain To guarantee that a minimum number of payments are made even if the annuitant dies, the **life with period certain** option can be chosen. The contract will specifically allow the choice of a period of 10 or 20 years, for example. The annuitant is guaranteed monthly income for life with this option, but if death occurs within the period certain, a named beneficiary receives payments for the remainder of the period.

✓ **For Example:** A client selects a life annuity with a 10-year period certain. If the annuitant lives to be 100 years old, annuity payments are still made by the insurer. But, if the annuitant dies after receiving payments for two years, the beneficiary will receive payments for 8 more years.

Joint Life with Last Survivor The **joint life with last survivor** option guarantees payments over two lives. It is often used for husbands and wives. If the husband were to die first, his spouse would continue to receive payments as long as she lives. If the wife were to die first, her spouse would receive payments as long as he lives.

Test Topic Alert! There is a risk-reward trade-off with annuity payout options.

1. Which of the following annuity options typically pays the largest monthly income?

    A. Life only
    B. Joint life with last survivor
    C. Life with 10-year period certain
    D. Contingent deferred option

    The best answer is **A**. Life only. Remember that there is no beneficiary with this option. Greater risk means greater reward.

2. Which of the following annuity options is likely to provide the smallest monthly income?

   A. Life only
   B. Joint life with last survivor
   C. Life with 10-year period certain
   D. Life with 20-year period certain

   The correct answer is **B**. Joint life with last survivor. There is a cost in monthly income amount for the guarantee on two lives.

Quick Quiz 12.3

Match each of the following items with the appropriate description below.

A. Accumulation unit
B. Joint life with last survivor annuity
C. Deferred annuity
D. Variable annuity

___ 1. Delays distributions until the owner elects to receive them

___ 2. Determines an annuitant's interest in the insurer's separate account during accumulation stage of an annuity

___ 3. Performance of a separate account determines value

___ 4. Annuity payments continue as long as one of the annuitants remains alive

Answers   1. **C.**   2. **A.**   3. **D.**   4. **B.**

Quick Quiz 12.4

Match each of the following terms with the appropriate description below.

A. Assumed interest rate
B. Immediate annuity
C. Life income with period certain
D. Separate account

___ 1. Contract starts to pay the annuitant immediately following its purchase

___ 2. Forms the basis for projected annuity payments, but is not guaranteed

___ 3. Holds funds paid by variable annuity contract holders

___ 4. If the annuitant dies before a specified time expires, payments go to the annuitant's named beneficiary

Answers   1. **B**.   2. **A**.   3. **D**.   4. **C**.

Taxation of Annuities

All contributions to annuities are made with after-tax dollars, unless the annuity is part of an employer-sponsored (qualified) retirement plan or held in an IRA.

Test Topic Alert! Assume an annuity is nonqualified unless a question specifically states otherwise.

When contributions are made with after-tax dollars, these already taxed dollars are considered the investor's cost basis and are not taxed when withdrawn. The earnings in excess of the cost basis are taxed as ordinary income when withdrawn.

✓ **For Example:** An investor has contributed $100,000 to a variable annuity. The annuity is now worth $150,000. Two questions: What is the investor's cost basis, and what amount is taxable upon withdrawal?

The cost basis is equal to the contributions, or $100,000. The taxable amount at withdrawal will be the earnings of $50,000.

Because annuities are designed to supplement retirement income and provide tax-deferred growth, withdrawals before age 59½ are subject to the 10% early withdrawal penalty and ordinary income tax on the earnings portion of the withdrawal.

When an investor chooses to annuitize and selects a monthly income payout option, each month's payment is considered partly a return of cost basis and partly earnings. Only the earnings portion is taxable. The amount of each payment considered a return of cost basis (and not taxed) is determined by the **exclusion ratio**.

Many contract owners choose random withdrawals over the annuity option. If this choice is made, **last in, first out** (**LIFO**) taxation applies. The IRS requires that all earnings are withdrawn first and are taxed at ordinary income rates. After earnings are completely withdrawn there is no additional taxation, because the cost basis has already been taxed.

✓ **Take Note:** Assume the following:

$100,000   after-tax contributions (cost basis)
+ 50,000   earnings
$150,000   total account value

If the investor makes a random withdrawal of $60,000, what are the tax consequences?

Remember that LIFO applies—the IRS chooses tax revenue as early as possible. Those earnings that accumulated tax deferred are now fully taxable. The investor must pay ordinary income taxes on the first $50,000 withdrawn, because that is the amount of earnings. And, if the investor is under age 59½, an extra 10% early withdrawal tax applies. The remaining $10,000 is a return of the cost basis and is not taxed.

Any answer choice that mentions capital gains taxation on annuities or retirement plans is wrong. There is only ordinary income tax on distributions from annuities and retirement plans.

Quick Quiz 12.5   Multiple Choice

1. Your customer buys a nonqualified variable annuity at age 60. Before the contract is annuitized, she withdraws some funds. What are the consequences?

    A. 10% penalty plus payment of ordinary income on all funds withdrawn
    B. 10% penalty plus payment of ordinary income on all funds withdrawn in excess of basis
    C. Capital gains tax on earnings in excess of basis
    D. Ordinary income tax on earnings in excess of basis

2. Distributions from both an IRA and a variable annuity are subject to which of the following forms of taxation?

    A. Short-term capital gains
    B. Long-term capital gains
    C. Ordinary income
    D. No tax is due.

3. What is the capital gains tax rate that an individual pays on appreciation in the reserves held for his variable annuity in a separate account while the contract is in the accumulation period?

   A. 0%
   B. 10%
   C. 25%
   D. 50%

4. Your customer invests in a tax-qualified variable annuity. What is the tax treatment of the distributions he receives?

   A. Partially tax free; partially ordinary income
   B. Partially tax free; partially capital gains
   C. All ordinary income
   D. All capital gains

Answers

1. **D.** Contributions to a nonqualified variable annuity are made with after-tax dollars. Distributions from a nonqualified plan represent both a return of the original investment made in the plan with after-tax dollars (a nontaxable return of capital) and the income from that investment. Because the income was deferred from tax over the plan's life, it is taxable as ordinary income once it is distributed.

2. **C.** All retirement account distributions exceeding cost basis are taxed at the owner's then-current ordinary tax rate. The advantage of most retirement accounts is that withdrawals usually begin after an account owner is in a lower tax bracket (i.e., upon retirement).

3. **A.** Gains in a separate account are tax deferred. The annuitant pays ordinary income tax on the earnings portion of the distribution upon receipt.

4. **C.** Because the annuitant has no basis, all payments are considered ordinary income. In a nonqualified annuity, contributions are made with after-tax dollars, which establish the annuitant's basis. Annuity payments from a nonqualified annuity are treated as ordinary income to the extent that they exceed the basis.

Variable Annuities HotSheet

Fixed Annuity:
- Guaranteed rate of return; insurance company has investment risk
- Subject to purchasing power risk
- Fixed income guaranteed for life; not a security

Variable Annuity:
- Rate of return dependent on separate account performance
- Investor has investment risk; sold with prospectus
- Can keep pace with inflation
- Variable income guaranteed for life; principal is not guaranteed

Accumulation Phase:
- Investor pays money to insurer; units vary in number and in value

Annuity Phase:
- Investor receives payments from insurer; fixed number of units; vary in value

Purchase Methods:
- **Periodic deferred**: paid in installments; payouts taken later
- **Single premium immediate**: lump-sum payment; payouts begin immediately, no accumulation period
- **Single premium deferred**: lump-sum payment; payouts taken later

Payout Methods:
- Lump sum or random withdrawals
- Annuitization (monthly income guaranteed for life)
- **Life income**: no beneficiary, largest monthly payment
- **Life with period certain**: minimum guaranteed period
- **Joint life w/last survivor**: annuity on two lives; smallest month

AIR:
- Used to determine monthly income
- Income goes up from previous month if separate account performance is greater than AIR
- Income stays the same as previous month if separate account performance is equal to AIR
- Income falls from the previous month if separate account performance is less than the AIR

Taxation:
- Monthly income: part return of cost basis, part taxable; proportion determined by exclusion ratio
- Lump sum/random withdrawals: LIFO applies; earnings withdrawn first, taxable as ordinary income; no tax on remainder because it is a return of cost basis

Regulated by:
- Act of 1933; Act of 1934, Investment Company Act of 1940; Investment Advisers Act of 1940, State Insurance Departments; Federal insurance law

Max Sales Charge:
- 8½%

Series 7 Unit Test 12

1. Which of the following characteristics are shared by both a mutual fund and a variable annuity's separate account?

    I. The investment portfolio is professionally managed.
    II. The client may vote for the board of directors or board of managers.
    III. The client assumes the investment risk.
    IV. The payout plans guarantee the client income for life.

    A. I, II and III only
    B. II and IV only
    C. III and IV only
    D. I, II, III and IV

2. A joint life with last survivor annuity

    I. covers more than one person
    II. continues payments as long as one annuitant is alive
    III. continues payments as long as all annuitants are alive
    IV. guarantees payments for a certain period of time

    A. I and II
    B. I and III
    C. I and IV
    D. II and IV

3. A customer is about to buy a variable annuity contract. He wants to select an annuity that will give him the largest possible monthly payment. Which of the following payout options would be most suitable?

    A. Life annuity with period certain
    B. Unit refund life option
    C. Life annuity with 10-year period certain
    D. Life-only annuity

4. Your 65-year-old client owns a nonqualified variable annuity. He originally invested $29,000 4 years ago; it now has a value of $39,000. Your client, who is in the 28% tax bracket, makes a lump-sum withdrawal of $15,000. What tax liability results from the withdrawal?

    A. $0
    B. $2,800
    C. $3,800
    D. $4,200

5. A variable annuity's separate account is

    I. used for the investment of monies paid by variable annuity contract holders
    II. separate from the insurance company's general investments
    III. operated in a manner similar to an investment company
    IV. as much a security as it is an insurance product

    A. I only
    B. I and II only
    C. II and III only
    D. I, II, III and IV

6. According to the NASD, the maximum sales charge on a variable annuity contract is generally

    A. 8.5% of the total amount invested
    B. 8.5% of the net amount invested
    C. 9% of the total amount invested
    D. unlimited

7. Variable annuities must be registered with the

    I. state banking commission
    II. state insurance commission
    III. SEC
    IV. NASD

    A. I and III only
    B. II and III only
    C. II and IV only
    D. I, II, III and IV

8. A customer has a nonqualified variable annuity. Once the contract is annuitized, monthly payments to the customer are

   A. 100% taxable
   B. partially a tax free return of capital and partially taxable
   C. 100% tax free
   D. 100% tax deferred

9. An accumulation unit in a variable annuity contract is

   A. an accounting measure used to determine the contract owner's interest in the separate account
   B. an accounting measure used to determine payments to the owner of the variable annuity
   C. exactly the same as a shareholder's ownership interest in a mutual fund
   D. none of the above

Series 7 Unit Test 12 Answers & Rationale

1. **A.** Both a mutual fund and a variable annuity's separate account offer professional management and a board of managers or directors. Additionally, the client assumes the investment risk. Only variable annuities have payout plans that guarantee the client income for life.
QID: 30591

2. **A.** A joint life with last survivor contract covers multiple annuitants and ceases payments at the death of the last surviving annuitant. A period certain contract guarantees payments for a certain amount of time.
QID: 28766

3. **D.** Generally, a life-only contract pays the most per month because payments cease at the annuitant's death.
QID: 28761

4. **B.** This annuity is nonqualified, which means the client has paid for it with after-tax dollars and therefore has a basis equal to the original $29,000 investment. Consequently, the client pays taxes only on the growth portion of the withdrawal ($10,000). The tax on this is $2,800 ($10,000 × 28%). Because the client is older than age 59½, he pays no 10% premature distribution penalty tax. However, had the client been younger than age 59½, he would have paid a $1,000 penalty tax ($10,000 × 10%) in addition to the $2,800 income tax.
QID: 28756

5. **D.** The separate account is used for the monies invested in variable annuities. It is kept separate from the general account and operated very much like an investment company. It is considered both an insurance product and an investment product.
QID: 30590

6. **A.** NASD rules allow a maximum sales charge on a variable annuity contract of 8.5% of the total amount invested.
QID: 28763

7. **B.** A variable annuity is a combination of two products: an insurance contract and a mutual fund. Therefore, variable annuities must be registered with the state insurance commission and the Securities and Exchange Commission.
QID: 29523

8. **B.** The investor has already paid tax on the contributions but the earnings have grown tax-deferred. When the annuitization option is selected, each payment represents both capital and earnings. The money paid in will be returned tax-free but the earnings portion will be taxed as ordinary income.
QID: 35121

9. **A.** When money is being deposited into the annuity it is purchasing "accumulation units."
QID: 35196

13

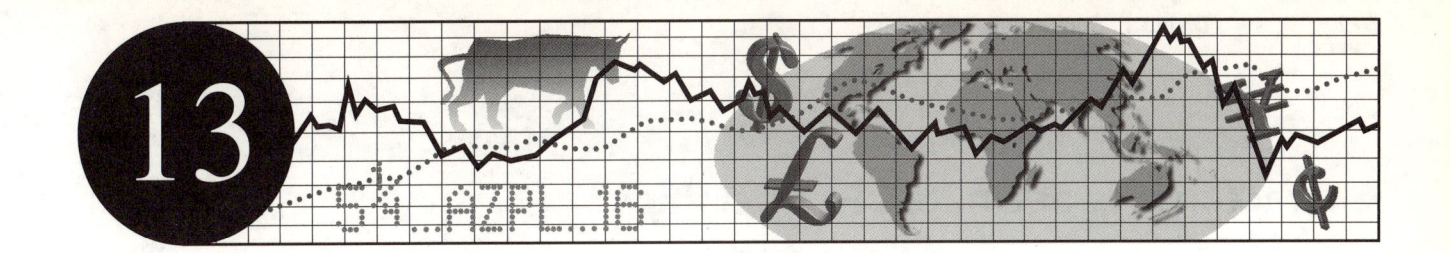

Direct Participation Programs

INTRODUCTION Direct participation programs (DPPs) are illiquid investments that pass income, gains, losses, and tax benefits (such as depreciation, depletion and tax credits) directly to the limited partners. There are some unique tax concepts and suitability issues involving DPPs, also known as limited partnerships (LPs).

A general partner runs the partnership business and assumes certain liabilities with regard to the partnership's commitments. Limited partners are not allowed to be actively involved in business decisions, and have limited liability in the event of a business failure. Most limited partnerships invest in real estate or oil & gas programs.

Limited partnership programs are either private placements (offered to wealthy accredited investors who make substantial investments) or public programs requiring much smaller investments. Under current tax law, limited partnerships generate passive income and losses. Passive losses may be used to shelter passive income only.

DPPs account for about 8–15 questions on the Series 7 exam.

UNIT OBJECTIVES When you have completed this unit, you should be able to:

- outline the structure of DPPs as flow-through vehicles;
- list the rights and responsibilities of DPP participants;
- name and define the critical documents in the administration of Limited Partnerships;
- identify the unique tax concepts related to DPP interests;
- compare and contrast the features of various real estate, and oil & gas programs; and
- describe methods of analysis of DPP performance.

Characteristics of Limited Partnerships

Limited partnerships are unique investment opportunities that permit the economic consequences of a business to flow through to investors. These programs offer investors a share in the income, gains, losses, deductions, and tax credits of the business entity.

Limited partners in DPPs enjoy several advantages:

- an investment managed by others;
- limited liability; and
- flow-through of income and certain expenses.

The greatest disadvantage to limited partners is their lack of liquidity. The secondary market for limited partnership interests is extremely limited; investors who wish to sell their interests frequently cannot locate buyers (i.e., the shareholder's interest is not freely transferable).

✓ **Take Note:** A small number of limited partnership interests are negotiable and trade on the OTC and exchanges. These partnerships are known as **master limited partnerships** (**MLPs**).

Tax Reporting for Partnerships

DPPs are generally structured as **limited partnerships** or **Subchapter S corporations**. These business forms are not tax-paying entities like a corporation; instead, they only report income and losses to the IRS, and then the **partners** (in a limited partnership) or **shareholders** (in a Subchapter S corporation) have the responsibility to report income and losses individually and pay the taxes due.

By contrast, in a typical corporation, taxes must be paid on the earnings of the corporation before a dividend is distributed. Then the shareholder is taxed again on the dividend received.

Since an investment in a DPP is not taxed first at the level of the business, double taxation is avoided. The term *flow-through* (or pass-through) means that all the income and losses and corresponding tax responsibilities go directly to the investors with no taxation to the business entity.

Characteristics of Limited Partnerships

Features of Corporations and DPPs

Corporation	Direct Participation Program
Tax-paying entity	Tax reporting entity (entity does not pay taxes)
Shareholders receive dividend distributions	Investors receive a share of all income and losses of the business reported on Form K-1
Dividend distributions are subject to double taxation	No double taxation on distributions

Test Topic Alert! DPPs (limited partnerships) are the only investment opportunity that you will study that offer a pass-through of losses to the investor. Also, DPP passive losses shelter passive income, not ordinary income.

Profit Motive Any DPP established without a profit motive or with the intention of only generating tax losses for investors may be determined abusive. Investors in abusive DPPs may be subject to any of the following consequences:

- back taxes;
- recapture of tax credits;
- interest penalties; or
- prosecution for fraud.

Organizations Classified as Partnerships An unincorporated organization with two or more members is generally classified as a partnership for federal tax purposes if its members carry on a trade, business, financial operation, or venture and divide its profits. However, a joint undertaking merely to share expenses is not a partnership. For example, co-ownership of property maintained and rented or leased is not a partnership unless the co-owners provide services to the tenants.

The rules used to determine whether an organization is classified as a partnership changed for organizations formed after 1996.

Organizations Formed after 1996

An organization formed after 1996 is classified as a **partnership** for federal tax purposes if it has two or more members and is none of the following.

- An organization formed under a federal or state law that refers to it as incorporated or as a corporation, body corporate, or body politic
- An organization formed under a state law that refers to it as a joint-stock company or joint-stock association
- An insurance company
- Certain banks

- An organization wholly owned by a state or local government
- An organization specifically required to be taxed as a corporation by the Internal Revenue Code (e.g., certain publicly traded partnerships)
- Certain foreign organizations
- A tax-exempt organization
- A real estate investment trust
- An organization classified as a trust under section 301.7701-4 of the regulations or otherwise subject to special treatment under the Internal Revenue Code
- Any other organization that elects to be classified as a corporation by filing Form 8832

Test Topic Alert! For partnerships formed in 1996 and earlier, the definition is as follows: a partnership must avoid most all corporate characteristics. The Series 7 exam focuses on this definition of a partnership.

The easiest of the corporate characteristics to avoid is **continuity of life**. Typically, partnerships have a predetermined date of dissolution when they are established.

Test Topic Alert! Several test questions are possible from the list of corporate characteristics.

1. Which of these characteristics is the most difficult to avoid?

   Centralized management—no business can function without it.

2. Which of these characteristics is the easiest to avoid?

   Continuity of life—there is a predetermined time at which the business interest is sold.

3. Which two corporate characteristics are most likely to be avoided by a DPP?

   Continuity of life and *freely transferable interests*—interests cannot be freely transferred; general partner approval is required to transfer shares.

Other important tax concepts of DPPs include the following.

- DPPs were formerly known as tax shelters because investors used losses to reduce or shelter ordinary income (by writing off passive losses against ordinary income).
- Tax law revisions now classify income and loss from these investments as **passive income and loss**. Current law allows passive losses to shelter only passive income, not all ordinary income as before. Many programs lost their appeal because of this critical change in tax law.
- Investors should not purchase DPPs primarily for tax shelter; they should be economically viable and offer investors the potential of cash distributions and capital gains.

Test Topic Alert!

1. When considering the purchase of a limited partnership interest, an investor should be most concerned with

   A. loss pass-through
   B. potential tax shelter
   C. economic viability
   D. short-term trading opportunities

   ***Answer:* C.** Economic viability is the number one reason for the purchase of an interest in a limited partnership. Tax sheltering and loss pass-through are also considerations, but should not be the primary motive to invest. Short-term trading opportunities do not exist. The investor should expect to hold the interest until the partnership is dissolved or liquidated.

Forming a Limited Partnership

LPs may be sold through private placements or public offerings. If sold privately, investors receive a **private placement memorandum** for disclosure. Generally, such private placements involve a small group of limited partners, each contributing a large sum of money. These investors must be **accredited investors**—they must have substantial investment experience. The general public does not meet this description.

In a public offering, limited partnerships are sold with prospectus to a larger number of limited partners, each making a relatively small capital contribution, such as $1,000 to $5,000.

The **syndicator** oversees the selling and promotion of the partnership. The syndicator is responsible for the preparation of any paperwork necessary for the registration of the partnership. Syndication fees are limited to 10% of the gross dollar amount of securities sold.

Required Documentation

Three important documents are required for a limited partnership to exist:

- the **Certificate of Limited Partnership;**
- the **Partnership Agreement;** and
- the **Subscription Agreement.**

Certificate of Limited Partnership

For legal recognition, this document must be filed in the home state of the partnership. It includes the following:

- partnership's name;
- partnership's business;
- principal place of business;
- amount of time the partnership expects to be in business;
- size of each LP's current and future expected investments;

- contribution return date, if set;
- share of profits or other compensation to each LP;
- conditions for LP assignment of ownership interests;
- whether LPs may admit other LPs; and
- whether business can be continued by remaining general partners (GPs) at death or incapacity of a GP.

If any material information on the certificate has changed, an update must be made within 30 days of the event.

Partnership Agreement

Each partner receives a copy of this agreement. It describes the roles of the general and limited partners and guidelines for the partnership's operation.

✓ **Take Note:** Rights of the general partner as defined in the partnership agreement include the:

- right to charge a management fee for making business decisions for the partnership;
- authority to bind the partnership into contracts;
- right to determine which partners should be included in the partnership; and
- right to determine whether cash distributions will be made.

Subscription Agreement

All investors interested in becoming limited partners must complete a subscription agreement. It appoints the GP to act on behalf of the limited partners, and is only effective when the GP signs it. Along with the subscriber's money, the subscription agreement must include:

- the investor's net worth;
- the investor's annual income;
- statement attesting that the investor understands the risk involved; and
- power of attorney appointing the GP as the agent of the partnership.

In addition to a cash contribution, subscribers may assume responsibility for the repayment of a portion of a loan to the partnership. This type of loan is called a **recourse loan**. Frequently, partnerships borrow money through **nonrecourse loans**; the general partners have responsibility for repayment of nonrecourse loans.

💡 **Test Topic Alert!** Limited partners are liable for a proportionate share of recourse loans assumed by partnerships. Limited partners have no liability for nonrecourse loans, except in real estate partnerships.

Dissolving a Limited Partnership

Generally, limited partnerships are liquidated on the date specified in the partnership agreement. Early shutdown may occur if the partnership sells or disposes of its assets, or if a decision is made to dissolve the partnership by the LPs holding a majority interest. When **dissolution** occurs, the GP must cancel the certificate of limited partnership and settle accounts in the following order.

- Secured lenders
- Other creditors
- Limited partners
  - *first* for their claims to shares of profits
  - *second* for their claims to a return of contributed capital
- General partners
  - *first* for fees and other claims not involving profits
  - *second* for a share of profits
  - *third* for capital return

DPP Life Cycle Diagram

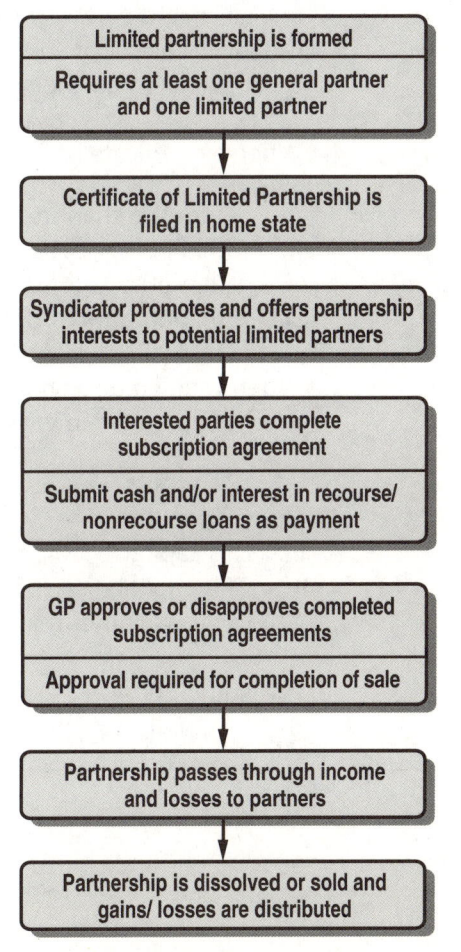

```
┌─────────────────────────────────────────┐
│      Limited partnership is formed      │
├─────────────────────────────────────────┤
│  Requires at least one general partner  │
│         and one limited partner         │
└─────────────────────────────────────────┘
                    ↓
┌─────────────────────────────────────────┐
│   Certificate of Limited Partnership is │
│          filed in home state            │
└─────────────────────────────────────────┘
                    ↓
┌─────────────────────────────────────────┐
│ Syndicator promotes and offers partnership │
│  interests to potential limited partners │
└─────────────────────────────────────────┘
                    ↓
┌─────────────────────────────────────────┐
│       Interested parties complete       │
│          subscription agreement         │
├─────────────────────────────────────────┤
│  Submit cash and/or interest in recourse/│
│     nonrecourse loans as payment        │
└─────────────────────────────────────────┘
                    ↓
┌─────────────────────────────────────────┐
│    GP approves or disapproves completed │
│         subscription agreements         │
├─────────────────────────────────────────┤
│   Approval required for completion of sale │
└─────────────────────────────────────────┘
                    ↓
┌─────────────────────────────────────────┐
│   Partnership passes through income     │
│          and losses to partners         │
└─────────────────────────────────────────┘
                    ↓
┌─────────────────────────────────────────┐
│   Partnership is dissolved or sold and  │
│       gains/losses are distributed      │
└─────────────────────────────────────────┘
```

Quick Quiz 13.1 Multiple Choice

1. DPP stands for

   A. direct placement program
   B. directed profits program
   C. direct participation program
   D. directors' and principals' program

2. The person who organizes and registers a partnership is known as a(n)

   A. syndicator
   B. property manager
   C. program manager
   D. underwriter

3. A limited partnership becomes effective when

   A. the certificate is filed with the proper authorities
   B. all limited partnership interests are sold
   C. all LPs are notified that all units are sold
   D. the limited partnership registration is filed

4. When a certificate of limited partnership must be rerecorded, it must be filed

   A. before the change
   B. within 5 business days of the change
   C. within 30 days of the change
   D. within 60 days of the change

5. When winding up a limited partnership without an agreement, the following accounts are paid in what order?

   I. LP's profits
   II. GP's profits
   III. LP's capital
   IV. GP's capital
   V. Payments other than GP's profits and capital

   A. I, II, III, IV, V
   B. I, III, V, II, IV
   C. III, IV, V, I, II
   D. V, I, III, II, IV

6. The rights and liabilities of general and limited partners are listed in the

    A. certificate of partnership
    B. Uniform Limited Partnership Act
    C. agreement of limited partnership
    D. partnership title

7. Which of the following corporate characteristics do most limited partnerships avoid?

    I. Continuity of life
    II. Limited liability
    III. Centralized management
    IV. Free transferability of interest

    A. I and II
    B. I and IV
    C. II and III
    D. II and IV

8. A subscription for a limited partnership is accepted when the

    A. proposed LP signs the partnership agreement
    B. LP's check is cashed
    C. GP signs the subscription agreement
    D. certificate of limited partnership is filed

9. All of the following statements are true with respect to a limited partnership subscription agreement EXCEPT the

    A. investor's registered representative must verify that the investor has provided accurate information
    B. general partner endorses the subscription agreement, signifying that a limited partner is suitable
    C. investor's signature indicates that he has read the prospectus
    D. general partner's signature grants the limited partners power of attorney to conduct the partnership's affairs

10. The most important element to consider in evaluating a tax-shelter program is the

    A. registration statement's completeness
    B. economics and cash flow
    C. legal protection
    D. salesperson

Answers

1. **C.** DPP stands for direct participation program.

2. **A.** The individual who organizes and registers the partnership is the syndicator.

3. **A.** The certificate creates the partnership's limited nature; until the document is properly filed, the partnership is a general partnership.

4. **C.** Refiling must occur within 30 days.

5. **B.** Without a provision stating otherwise, first profits and then capital are paid to the LPs; next, other payments such as fees and commissions are paid to the GP; and finally, profits and capital contributions are paid to the GPs.

6. **C.** The agreement is the contract between the partners and contains each entity's rights and duties.

7. **B.** The two corporate characteristics that most limited partnerships avoid are continuity of life and free transferability of interest.

8. **C.** Acceptance of an investor as an LP occurs when the GP signs the subscription agreement. The LP receives confirmation of acceptance when the subscription agreement is returned.

9. **D.** The limited partner's signature on the subscription agreement grants the general partner power of attorney to conduct the partnership's affairs. The subscription agreement for a limited partnership is deemed accepted when the general partner signs the subscription agreement.

10. **B.** More important than any other consideration is whether the offering is a viable economic entity. If the offering is nothing more than a tax scam, not only will the IRS disallow the tax benefits, but the money invested most likely will be lost because the program has no economic merit.

Investors in a Limited Partnership

The limited partnership form of DPP involves two types of partners: the **general partner(s)** and the **limited partners**. A limited partnership must have at least one of each.

General Partners vs. Limited Partners

General Partners	Limited Partners
Unlimited Liability: personal liability for all partnership business losses and debts	**Limited Liability:** can lose no more than their investment and proportionate interest in recourse notes
Management Responsibility: assumes responsibility for all aspects of the partnership's operation	**No management responsibility:** provides capital for the business but cannot participate in its management. Known as a passive investor. Attempting to take part in a management role jeopardizes limited liability status.
Fiduciary Responsibility: morally and legally bound to use invested capital in the best interest of the investors	**May Sue the General Partner:** lawsuits may recover damages if the GP does not act in the best interest of the investors or uses assets improperly.

The following tables compare other activities of general and limited partners:

General Partners and Limited Partners can:

General Partners can:	Limited Partners can:
Make decisions that legally bind the partnership	Vote on changes to partnership investment objectives or the admission of a new general partner (GP)
Buy and sell property for the partnership	Vote on sale or refinancing of partnership property
Maintain a financial interest in the partnership (must be a minimum of 1%)	Receive cash distributions, capital gains, and tax deductions from partnership activities
Receive compensation as specified in the partnership agreement	Inspect books and records of the partnership Exercise the partnership democracy (vote under special circumstances, such as permitting the GP to act contrary to the agreement, to contest a judgment against the partnership, or admit a new GP)

Direct Participation Programs

General Partners and Limited Partners cannot:

General Partners cannot:	Limited Partners cannot:
Compete against the partnership for personal gain	Act on behalf of the partnership or participate in its management
Borrow from the partnership	Knowingly sign a certificate containing false information
Commingle partnership funds with personal assets or assets of other partnerships	Have their names appear as part of the partnership's name
Admit new GPs or LPs or continue the partnership after the loss of a GP unless specified in the partnership agreement	

Quick Quiz 13.2 Match each of the following descriptions with the appropriate item below.

A. Provides creditors with information regarding an LP's term and member contributions
B. Allows LPs to vote on major decisions, but not on day-to-day operations
C. Passive investors only
D. Outlines roles of both general and limited partners

___ 1. Partnership Agreement

___ 2. Subscription Agreement

___ 3. Certificate of Limited Partnership

___ 4. Partnership Democracy

Answers 1. **D.**   2. **C.**   3. **A.**   4. **B.**

Quick Quiz 13.3 Match each of the following descriptions with the appropriate item below.

A. Manages the business of the partnership and is personally responsible for its debt
B. Maximum compensation is 10% of gross sold
C. Passive investors only

D. Receive memorandums when purchasing LP interests through private placements

___ 1. Limited Partners

___ 2. General Partners

___ 3. Syndicator

___ 4. Accredited Investors

Answers   1. **C.**   2. **A.**   3. **B.**   4. **D.**

Quick Quiz 13.4 Match each of the following statements with the appropriate description.

A. Limited partners have liability
B. General partners have liability
C. Organized to pass through all income, gains, losses, and tax benefits to its owners

___ 1. Direct Participation

___ 2. Nonrecourse loan

___ 3. Recourse loan

Answers   1. **C.**   2. **B.**   3. **A.**

Types of Limited Partnership Programs

Limited partnerships can be formed to run any type of business. The most common types are real estate, oil & gas, and equipment-leasing businesses.

Real Estate Partnerships

Real estate limited partnerships provide investors with these benefits:

- **Capital growth potential**: achieved through appreciation of property
- **Cash flow (income)**: collected from rents

- **Tax deductions**: from mortgage interest expense and depreciation allowances for "wearing out the building" and capital improvements
- **Tax credits**: for government-assisted housing and historic rehabilitation (reduce tax liability dollar for dollar, but are subject to recapture)

Five types of real estate programs and their features follow.

(1) Raw Land

(1) Raw Land	
Partnership Objective	Purchase undeveloped land for its appreciation potential
Advantages	Appreciation potential of the property
Disadvantages	Offers no income distributions or tax deductions
Tax Features	No income or depreciation deductions Not considered a tax shelter
Degree of Risk	Most speculative real estate partnership

(2) New Construction

(2) New Construction	
Partnership Objective	Build new property for potential appreciation
Advantages	Appreciation potential of the property and structure; minimal maintenance costs in the early years
Disadvantages	Potential cost overruns; no established track record; difficulty of finding permanent financing; inability to deduct current expenses during construction period
Tax Features	Depreciation and expense deductions after construction is completed and income is generated
Degree of Risk	Less risky than new land; more risky than existing property

(3) Existing Property

(3) Existing Property	
Partnership Objective	Generate an income stream from existing structures
Advantages	Immediate cash flow; known history of income and expenses
Disadvantages	Greater maintenance or repair expenses than for new construction; expiring leases that may not be renewed; less than favorable rental arrangements
Tax Features	Deductions for mortgage interest and depreciation
Degree of Risk	Relatively low risk

(4) Government-Assisted Housing Programs

(4) Government-Assisted Housing Programs	
Partnership Objective	Develop low income and retirement housing
Advantages	Tax credits and rent subsidies
Disadvantages	Low appreciation potential; risk of changing government programs; high maintenance costs
Tax Features	Tax credits and losses
Degree of Risk	Relatively low risk

(5) Historic Rehabilitation

(5) Historic Rehabilitation	
Partnership Objective	Develop historic sites for commercial use
Advantages	Tax credits for preserving historic structure
Disadvantages	Potential cost overruns; no established track record; difficulty of finding permanent financing; inability to deduct current expenses during construction period
Tax Features	Tax credit and deductions for expenses and depreciation
Degree of Risk	Similar to risk of new construction

Oil & Gas Partnerships

Oil & gas programs include speculative drilling programs and income programs that invest in producing wells. Unique tax advantages associated with these programs include intangible drilling costs and depletion allowances.

Intangible Drilling Costs (IDCs) Write-offs for the expenses of drilling are usually 100% deductible in the first year of operation. These include costs associated with drilling such as wages, supplies, fuel costs, and insurance. An intangible drilling cost can be defined as any cost that, after being incurred, has no salvage value.

Tangible Drilling Costs (TDCs) Tangible drilling costs are those costs incurred which have salvage value. For example, storage tanks and wellhead equipment. These costs are not immediately deductible; rather, they are deducted (depreciated) over a seven-year period.

Depletion Allowances Tax deductions that compensate the partnership for the decreasing supply of oil or gas (or any other resource or mineral).

✓ *Take Note:* Depletion allowances can only be taken once the oil or gas is sold.

Three types of oil & gas programs and their features are **exploratory**, **developmental**, and **income**.

(1) Exploratory (Wildcatting)

(1) Exploratory ("Wildcatting")

Partnership Objective	Locate undiscovered reserves of oil and gas
Advantages	High rewards for discovery of new reserves
Disadvantages	Few new wells actually produce
Tax Features	High IDCs for immediate tax sheltering
Degree of Risk	High; most risky oil and gas program

(2) Developmental

(2) Developmental

Partnership Objective	Drill near existing fields to discover new reserves (called step out wells)
Advantages	Less risk of discovery than exploratory
Disadvantages	Few new wells actually produce
Tax Features	Medium IDCs, immediate tax sheltering
Degree of Risk	Medium to high risk

(3) Income

(3) Income	
Partnership Objective	Provide immediate income from sale of existing oil
Advantages	Immediate cash flow
Disadvantages	Oil prices; well stops producing
Tax Features	Income sheltering from depletion allowances
Degree of Risk	Low

✓ **Take Note:** There is a fourth type of oil & gas partner: Combination. In this program, the partnership allocates dollars between income and exploratory drilling.

Quick Quiz 13.5 Multiple Choice

1. Raw land is which of the following types of investment?

    A. Speculative
    B. Conservative
    C. Balanced
    D. Income-producing

2. Which of the following would not generate IDCs in an oil-drilling program?

    A. Labor costs
    B. Cost of casing the well
    C. Fuel costs
    D. Geologist's fees

3. An investor should consider which of the following to be a potential source of conflict of interest for the sponsor of an oil & gas program?

   I. Undeveloped adjacent sponsor lease
   II. Loan by the program to the sponsor
   III. Sponsor's compensation rates
   IV. Commingling of program funds

   A. I only
   B. I, II and IV
   C. III only
   D. I, II, III and IV

4. If your objective is capital appreciation only, in which type of DPP should you invest?

   A. Raw land
   B. Oil & gas exploratory drilling
   C. Existing property
   D. Government-assisted housing

5. A GP in a newly formed limited partnership is deciding between two properties for investment purposes: one is a 25-year-old apartment building and the other is a newly constructed, although not occupied, apartment building. Which is a(n) advantage of investing in the 25-year-old building?

   A. Lower maintenance costs
   B. More predictable projection of operating expenses and rental income
   C. Possible higher rent because the building already is occupied
   D. Ability to claim an immediate write-off on any rehabilitation expenses

6. Which of the following statements is(are) TRUE regarding the risk and return potential of oil & gas direct participation programs?

   I. Exploratory drilling programs are less risky than developmental programs.
   II. Income programs provide the lowest return potential.
   III. Developmental programs are speculative investments.
   IV. A successful exploratory program provides a higher rate of return than a successful developmental program.

   A. I and II
   B. II, III and IV
   C. II and IV
   D. IV only

7. An investor in a high tax bracket has considerable passive income from various rental properties. Which of the following limited partnership interests would be most suitable in her situation?

A. Raw land
B. Wildcatting
C. Equipment leasing
D. Oil & gas income

Answers

1. **A.** *Raw land is the most speculative of these investments. The partnership can actually lose money to debt service and taxes because raw land offers neither income nor depreciation deductions.*

2. **B.** *The cost of casing a well is a tangible cost and, therefore, does not qualify for intangible drilling cost (IDC) write-offs. Well casing has an ongoing value.*

3. **D.** *All of the choices listed are potential conflicts of interest for the sponsor in a DPP.*

4. **A.** *Raw land is purchased solely for its appreciation potential. Exploratory drilling, existing property, and government-assisted housing programs all emphasize income more than capital appreciation potential.*

5. **B.** *The greatest benefit of existing property is that it has a track record, which makes projections easier.*

6. **B.** *Income programs generate income from proven oil or gas reserves, making them the safest and lowest yielding type of oil & gas DPP. Both exploratory and developmental drilling programs are speculative. An exploratory program offers the highest level of risk and the highest potential return on investment.*

7. **B.** *An exploratory oil & gas program would be a suitable tax shelter in this situation because of the high IDCs that are generated. These passive losses can offset the passive income the investor received from real estate investments and help in minimizing taxes.*

Sharing Arrangements

The costs and revenues associated with oil & gas programs are shared in a variety of ways. A description of these arrangements follows.

Overriding Royalty Interest. The holder of this interest receives royalties but has no partnership risk. An example of this arrangement is a landowner that sells mineral rights to a partnership.

Reversionary Working Interest. The GP bears no costs of the program and receives no revenue until LPs have recovered their capital. LPs bear all deductible and nondeductible costs.

Net Operating Profits Interest. The GP bears none of the program's costs but is entitled to a percentage of net profits. The LP bears all deductible and nondeductible costs. This arrangement is only available in private placements.

Disproportionate Sharing. The GP bears a relatively small percentage of expenses but receives a relatively large percentage of the revenues.

Carried Interest. The GP shares tangible drilling costs with the LPs but receives no IDCs. The LP receives the immediate deductions, while the GP receives write-offs from depreciation over the life of the property.

Functional Allocation. Under this most common sharing arrangement, the LP receives the IDCs which allow immediate deductions. The GP receives the tangible drilling costs which are depreciated over seven years. Revenues are shared.

Equipment Leasing Programs

Equipment leasing programs are created when DPPs purchase equipment leased to other businesses. Investors receive income from lease payments and also a proportional share of write-offs from operating expenses, interest expense, and depreciation. Tax credits were once available through these programs but were discontinued by tax law changes. The primary investment objective of these programs is tax-sheltered income.

Test Topic Alert!

1. Which of the following limited partnership programs provide potential tax credits to partners?

    I. Rehabilitation of historic properties
    II. Equipment leasing
    III. Developmental oil & gas programs
    IV. Government-assisted housing programs

    A. I only
    B. II and III
    C. III and IV
    D. I and IV

The right answer is **D**–choices (I) and (IV). Historic rehabilitation and government-assisted housing are the programs discussed that offer potential tax credits. Tax credits were formerly available through equipment leasing, but Congress changed the rules. Developmental oil & gas programs offer high IDCs, not ITCs (Investment Tax Credits).

2. Which of the following sharing arrangements is the most common?

   A. Net operating profits interest
   B. Carried interest
   C. Functional allocation
   D. Overriding royalty interest

   The best answer is **C**. Functional allocation is most commonly used because it gives the best benefits to both parties. The LPs receive the immediate tax write-offs from the IDCs, while the GPs receive continued write-offs over seven years from the tangible costs. Both share equally in the revenues.

Analysis of Limited Partnerships

In selecting a limited partnership interest, an investor should first consider that the partnership matches his investment objectives and has economic viability. **Economic viability** means that there is potential for returns from cash distributions and capital gains. Although tax benefits may be attractive, they should not be the first consideration in the purchase of an LP interest.

Measuring Economic Viability

How is economic viability measured? Two methods applied to the analysis of DPPs are cash flow analysis and internal rate of return.

- **Cash flow analysis** compares income (revenues) to expenses.
- **Internal rate of return** determines the present value of estimated future revenues and sales proceeds to allow comparison to other programs.

Tax Features to Consider

As described, limited partnerships distribute income, losses, and gains to limited partners because of their pass-through nature. Limited partners are able to apply certain deductions and/or tax credits to income as described here.

Deductions

Expenses of the partnership, such as salaries, interest payments, and management fees result in deductions in the current year to the LPs. Principal payments on property are not deductible expenses.

Cost recovery systems offer write-offs over a period of years as defined by IRS schedules. **Depreciation** write-offs apply to cost recovery of expenditures for equipment and real estate (land cannot be depreciated). **Depletion** allowances apply to the using up of natural resources, such as oil and gas. Depreciation and depletion allowances may only be claimed when income is being produced by the partnership.

✓ **Take Note:** Depreciation may be written off on a straight line (same amount each year) or accelerated basis, as determined by IRS tables and definitions. Accelerated depreciation is an AMT (alternative minimum tax) preference item.

Tax Credits

These are dollar-for-dollar reductions of taxes due and are the greatest tax benefit available to taxpayers. Currently, there are few available. The limited partnership programs that offer them presently are government-assisted housing programs and historic rehabilitation programs. Formerly, tax credits were available through equipment leasing programs, but tax law changes discontinued this credit. The partnership reports its income and losses to the IRS and then reports to each partner their individual share of income, gains, losses, deductions, and credits.

✓ **Take Note:** The **cross-over point** is the point where the program begins to generate taxable income instead of losses. This generally occurs in later years when income increases and deductions decrease.

Limited partners must keep track of their **tax basis**, or amount at risk, to determine their gain or loss upon the sale of their partnership interest. An investor's basis is subject to adjustment periodically for occurrences such as cash distributions and additional investments.

The tax benefits offered by the partnership should be of secondary importance to the economic viability it offers.

✓ **Take Note:** A limited partner's basis consists of the following:

- cash contributions to the partnership;
- property contributions to the partnership;
- recourse debt of the partnership; and
- nonrecourse debt for real estate partnerships only.

Partners must adjust their basis at year-end. Any distributions of cash or property, and repayments of recourse debt (also nonrecourse debt for real estate only) are reductions to a partner's basis.

Partners are allowed deductions up to the amount of their adjusted cost basis.

✓ **For Example:** If a partner's basis is $25,000 at year-end and the investor has losses of $35,000, only $25,000 of the losses may be used to deduct against passive income. The remaining $10,000 may be carried forward.

Other Features to Analyze   Other important factors that investors should consider in their overall analysis of limited partnerships include the following.

- Management ability and experience of the GP in running other similar programs
- **Blind pool** or specified program—in a blind pool, less than 75% of the assets are specified as to use; in a specified program, more than 75% have been identified
- Time frame of the partnership
- Similarity of start-up costs and revenue projections to those of comparable ventures
- Lack of liquidity of the interest

Limited partnership interests are not for all investors. Careful consideration must be given to the overall safety and lack of liquidity of these programs before investing.

Cash Flow

Cash flow is defined as follows: net income or loss plus noncash changes (such as depreciation).

✓ *For Example:*

Revenue	$300,000
Costs	
Selling	50,000
Interest	70,000
Operating	160,000
Depreciation	50,000
	$330,000
Net Loss	(30,000)

The above shows a loss of $30,000. However, its cash flow is a positive of $20,000.

Net Income or Loss	(30,000)
+ Depreciation	50,000
Cash Flow	+20,000

Basis

In a limited partnership, the term **basis** defines the liability assumed by the limited partners (LP). An LP can lose no more than his basis, and his basis puts a limit on how much he can deduct on his tax return. This ensures that an LP cannot deduct losses in excess of his basis.

Basis is computed using the following formula:

Investment in Partnership + Share of Recourse Debt – Cash Distribution

Test Topic Alert!

1. A customer invests $10,000 in a DPP and signs a recourse note for $40,000. During the first year, the investor receives a cash distribution from the partnership in the amount of $5,000. At year end, he receives a statement showing that his share of partnership losses is $60,000. How much of that $60,000 can he deduct on his tax return?

    Answer: The investor cannot deduct losses in excess of his year-end basis, $45,000, computed as follows:

Investment	$10,000
+ Recourse Debt	$40,000
	$50,000
– Cash Distributions	$ 5,000
Year-End Basis	$45,000

    Therefore, the customer can deduct $45,000 on his tax return. The remaining $15,000 is carried forward.

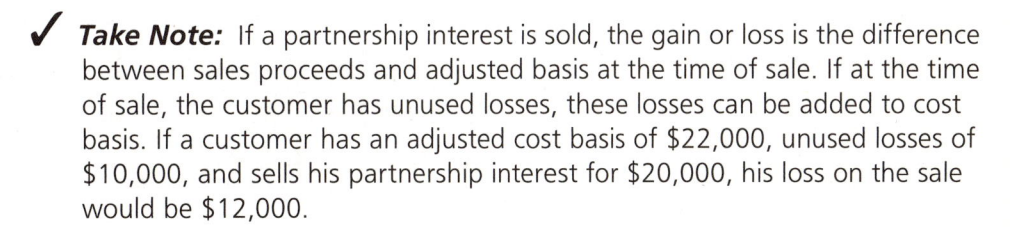

✓ **Take Note:** If a partnership interest is sold, the gain or loss is the difference between sales proceeds and adjusted basis at the time of sale. If at the time of sale, the customer has unused losses, these losses can be added to cost basis. If a customer has an adjusted cost basis of $22,000, unused losses of $10,000, and sells his partnership interest for $20,000, his loss on the sale would be $12,000.

Direct Participation Programs HotSheet

DPPs:
- Not investment companies
- Distribute proportionate share of losses, gains, income

DPP: *Real Estate*
- Raw land
- Existing property, least risky
- Tax credits from government assisted housing programs

Oil & Gas
- Exploratory, most risky (high IDC write-offs)
- Income Programs, least risky (provide depletion allowances)

Sharing Arrangements:	• Most common is functional allocation
Limited Partners:	• No management • Limited liability • Passive investors only • Can sue GP
General Partners:	• Active management • Fiduciary responsibility • Cannot borrow, compete, or commingle
Syndicator:	• Distributes partnership interests • Compensation max is 10%
Documentation:	• Certificate of Limited Partnership: identifies GP and LPs • Partnership Agreement: rules of "the club"; empowers GP to manage • Subscription Agreement: application for membership; effective when signed by GP; discloses income, net worth, understanding of risk
Partnership Democracy:	• Special vote for switching GPs, dissolving partnership
Taxation:	• Passive loss can only be used to shelter passive income • LPs provide pass-through of all income, losses, gains to partners
Reason to Invest:	• Economic viability is first concern
Methods of Analysis:	• Cash flow analysis and internal rate of return computations
Liquidation Priority:	• 1. Secured creditors • 2. Other creditors • 3. Limited partners • 4. GP(s)

Series 7 Unit Test 13

1. Which of the following would NOT be a valid use of the partnership democracy?

    A. Deciding which partnership assets should be liquidated to pay creditors
    B. Removing the general partner
    C. Consenting to an action of a general partner that is contrary to the agreement of limited partnership
    D. Consenting to a legal judgment against the partnership

2. Which two statements are TRUE regarding limited partnerships?

    I. Maximum commission in selling partnership offerings is 5%.
    II. Maximum commission in selling partnership offerings is 10%.
    III. Commissions taken are deducted from the original investment to determine beginning basis.
    IV. Commissions taken are not deducted from the original investment to determine beginning basis.

    A. I and III
    B. I and IV
    C. II and III
    D. II and IV

3. The rights and liabilities of general and limited partners are listed in the

    A. certificate of partnership
    B. Uniform Limited Partnership Act
    C. agreement of limited partnership
    D. partnership title

4. A client invests $100,000 in a tax shelter as a limited partner, giving him a 10% interest in the program. The general partners cannot meet the expenses of the program. There is a mortgage balance remaining of $3 million. The property of the program is then liquidated for $1 million. How much does the investor get back from his original investment?

    A. $0
    B. $10,000
    C. $33,000
    D. $100,000

5. If an investor expects to have a large amount of passive income over the next two years, which of the following programs will most likely lead to the largest amount of shelter?

    A. Equipment-leasing
    B. Undeveloped land purchasing
    C. Oil and gas drilling
    D. Real estate income

6. All of the following would be considered tax advantages relating to a DPP investment EXCEPT

    A. depreciation recapture
    B. depletion
    C. intangible drilling costs
    D. accelerated depreciation

7. Which of the following sequences reflects the priority, from first to last, of payments made when a limited partnership is liquidated?

    I. General partners
    II. Limited partners
    III. General creditors
    IV. Secured creditors

    A. I, II, III, IV
    B. I, IV, III, II
    C. IV, III, II, I
    D. IV, III, I, II

8. A customer has an annual income of $38,000 from a fairly secure job and is in the 28% bracket. She has a balanced portfolio of stocks and fixed-income securities and has $10,000 to invest in a limited partnership. She is willing to accept only a moderate amount of risk. Which of the following types of limited partnerships would be the MOST appropriate recommendation?

   A. Oil and gas income program
   B. Exploratory oil and gas drilling program
   C. New construction real estate limited partnership
   D. Blind pool raw land real estate limited partnership

9. In considering a direct participation program, rank the following in order of priority.

   I. Tax write-offs
   II. Liquidity and marketability
   III. Potential for economic gain

   A. I, II, III
   B. II, III, I
   C. III, I, II
   D. III, II, I

10. An investor in a limited partnership generating passive losses can offset these against

    I. passive income from other partnerships
    II. rental income from direct investments in real estate
    III. dividends received from listed securities
    IV. capital gains from sale of unlisted securities

    A. I only
    B. I and II
    C. I, II and III
    D. III and IV

11. A general partner is considered to have a conflict of interest with the business of a limited partnership if he

    A. manages the business
    B. loans money to the business
    C. borrows money from the business
    D. acts as agent for the business

12. Which of the following statements describes an oil & gas blind pool offering?

    A. The oil exploration occurs in an area that is not adjacent to any known oil reserves.
    B. Money is raised without a specific property being stated and the GP selects the investments.
    C. The income from producing wells is purchased at a discount from the present value of the projected future flows.
    D. An unknown number of representatives participates in the sale of known partnership units.

13. If a limited partnership interest is sold, the gain or loss in the sale is the difference between the sales proceeds and the

    A. original basis
    B. total of the deductible losses taken by the investor
    C. adjusted basis
    D. total of tax preference items allocated to the investor

14. Rank the following oil & gas programs from highest risk to lowest risk.

    I. Income
    II. Exploratory
    III. Developmental

    A. II, I, III
    B. I, II, III
    C. II, III, I
    D. I, III, II

Series 7 Unit Test 13 Answers & Rationale

1. **A.** Deciding which partnership assets should be liquidated to pay creditors involves limited partners in the active management of partnership affairs. This would result in their being treated as general partners with respect to liability, and possible loss of limited partner status.
QID: 29484

2. **D.** Under NASD rules, the maximum compensation that can be taken by sponsors selling DPPs is 10%. Up-front costs, such as commissions taken, accounting costs, etc. do not affect the beginning basis.
QID: 36538

3. **C.** The agreement is the contract between the partners and contains each entity's rights and duties.
QID: 32232

4. **A.** The limited partner will not receive any return of his investment. In a program that has failed, the creditors of the partnership will be paid first out of any sale proceeds before the limited partners receive any money. Because the limited partners had not signed a recourse agreement, even though the partnership still owes $2 million on the mortgage, the limited partners are not liable for any money beyond their original investments.
QID: 29539

5. **C.** Oil & gas drilling programs allocate the majority of investment dollars to drilling. These costs are intangible drilling costs (IDCs), which are 100% deductible when drilling occurs. In equipment-leasing programs, the investment dollars are recovered through depreciation over the lives of the leased assets.
QID: 28782

6. **A.** Depreciation recapture can occur when an investor sells his interest in a real estate program. If, at the time of the sale, the amount of accelerated deprecation taken exceeds the straight line depreciation amount, the difference (called recapture) must be reported by the investor as ordinary income.
QID: 36396

7. **C.** Creditors are paid first in a liquidation, with priority given to the secured lenders. General partners are the last to get paid.
QID: 30105

8. **A.** The customer is not in a high tax bracket and would not be able to take full advantage of the tax benefits produced by an exploratory oil and gas program or by new construction real estate limited partnerships. A raw land real estate partnership is usually speculative. Of the answers listed, the income and moderate risk from an oil and gas income program would probably be of greatest benefit to this investor.
QID: 29517

9. **C.** A program's economic viability is the first priority in the assessment of DPPs. The IRS considers programs designed solely to generate tax benefits abusive. Because there is a very limited secondary market for DPPs, liquidity and marketability should be a low priority.
QID: 28784

10. **B.** Passive losses can be deducted against passive income and income from certain real estate investments. It cannot be deducted against active or portfolio (investment) income.
QID: 34868

11. **C.** The general partner manages the business and acts as agent for the business. The general partner may loan money to the partnership at a reasonable rate of interest, but may not borrow from the partnership.
QID: 30082

12. **B.** A blind pool offering, also known as a nonspecified program, involves an investment in a program without specific prospects or properties being identified.
QID: 30704

13. **C.** The adjusted basis is a limited partner's cost basis at any point in time. Gain or loss on the sale of the partnership is determined by comparing the sales proceeds to the adjusted basis.

QID: 36466

14. **C.** Exploratory drilling programs represent the highest risk as they involve drilling in previously unexplored areas. Developmental drilling involves drilling in areas where oil and gas have already been discovered, so the risk is less. Income programs involve purchasing existing oil and gas wells and selling the production, and the risk is low.

QID: 36539

14

Economics & Analysis

INTRODUCTION The economy has a significant effect on the performance of various industries and corporations. Analysts in firms study economic conditions to make and check predictions about market activity. The Series 7 examination expects you to know fundamental concepts about economic performance and monetary policy.

Analysts also derive information about company performance from the study of financial data in the form of balance sheets and income statements. It is important to have a familiarity with these statements and the type of ratios that analysts compute.

Expect to see 10–15 questions on economics and analysis on the exam. These questions will typically be concept questions, not mathematical calculations.

UNIT OBJECTIVES When you have completed this unit, you should be able to:

- describe the four phases of the business cycle and key characteristics of each;
- provide examples of leading, lagging, and coincident indicators;
- name three economic theorists and describe the theories they originated;
- compare and contrast fiscal and monetary policy;
- list and describe the three monetary policy tools of the FRB;
- contrast basic theories of fundamental and technical analysis and the type of information important for each study;
- list and describe several technical market theories;
- identify the basic components of the balance sheet and key ratios calculated from it; and
- identify the basic components of the income statement and key ratios calculated from it.

Economics

Economics is the study of supply and demand. When people want to buy an item that is in short supply, the item's price rises. When people do not want to buy an item that is in plentiful supply, the price declines. This simple notion, the foundation of all economic study, is true for bread, shoes, cars, clothes, stocks, bonds, and money.

The economic climate has an enormous effect on the conditions of individual companies and therefore, the securities markets. In addition to a company's earnings and business prospects, any changes in business cycles, the money supply, and Federal Reserve Board (FRB) actions affect securities prices and trading.

Business Cycles

Throughout history, periods of economic expansion have been followed by periods of economic contraction in a pattern called the **business cycle**.

Business cycles go through four stages:

- Expansion
- Peak
- Contraction
- Trough

Expansion is characterized by increased business activity—increasing sales, manufacturing, and wages—throughout the economy. For a variety of reasons, an economy can expand for only so long; when it reaches its upper limit, it has reached its peak. When business activity declines from its **peak**, the economy is **contracting**. Economists call mild short-term contractions **recessions**. Longer, more severe contractions are **depressions**. When business activity stops declining and levels off, it is known as a **trough**.

According to the US Commerce Department, the economy is in a recession when a decline in real output of goods and services—the **gross domestic product (GDP)**—lasts for six months or more. It defines a depression as a severe downturn lasting for six quarters (18 months) or more, with unemployment rates greater than 15%.

The Four Stages of the Business Cycle

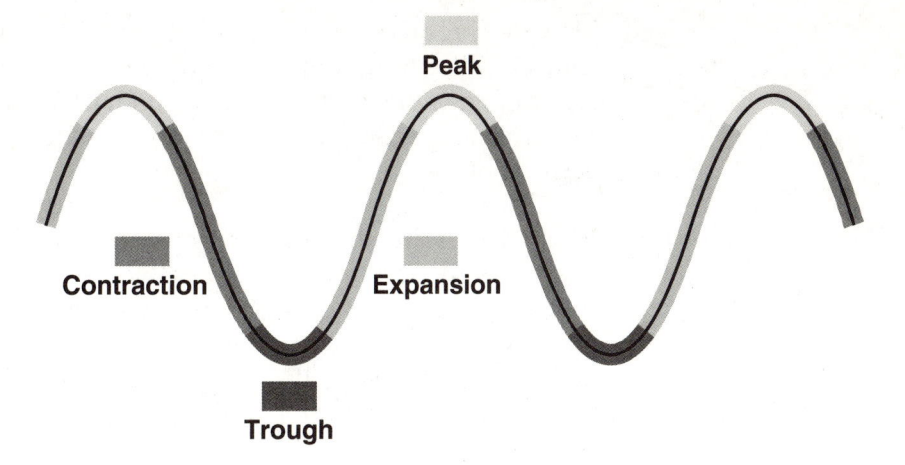

Peak

Contraction **Expansion**

Trough

In the normal course of events, some industries or corporations prosper as others fail. So to determine the economy's overall direction, economists consider many aspects of business activity. **Expansions** are characterized by:

- increased consumer demand for goods and services;
- increases in industrial production;
- rising stock prices;
- rising property values; and
- increasing GDP.

Downturns in the business cycle tend to be characterized by:

- rising numbers of bankruptcies and bond defaults;
- higher consumer debt;
- falling stock prices;
- rising inventories (a sign of slackening consumer demand in hard times); and
- decreasing GDP.

✓ **Take Note:** If asked to put the four components of the business cycle in sequence, always start with expansion.

Gross Domestic Product A nation's annual economic output—all of the goods and services produced within the nation—is known as its **gross domestic product**. The United States' GDP includes personal consumption, government spending, gross private investment, foreign investment, and the total value of exports.

✓ **Take Note:** On the exam, you may see the term **GNP (gross national product)** instead of GDP.

Price Levels *Consumer Price Index*

The most prominent measure of general price changes is the **Consumer Price Index (CPI)**. The CPI measures the rate of increase or decrease in a broad range of consumer prices such as food, housing, transportation, medical care, clothing, electricity, entertainment, and services. The CPI is computed each month.

When comparing the economic output of one period with that of another, analysts must account for changes that have occurred during the intervening time in the relative prices of products. Economists adjust GDP figures to **constant dollars** rather than compare actual dollars. This allows the economists and others who use GDP figures to compare the actual purchasing power of the dollars rather than the dollars themselves.

Inflation

Inflation is a general increase in prices. Mild inflation can encourage economic growth because gradually increasing prices tend to stimulate business investments. High inflation reduces a dollar's buying power, which hurts the economy.

Increased inflation drives up interest rates of fixed-income securities, which drives down bond prices. Decreases in the inflation rate have the opposite effect: as inflation declines, bond yields decline and prices rise.

Inflation is a barometer of the general direction of price levels. As such, it is a measure of the buying power of a dollar. Periods of low inflation have relatively stable prices and low interest rates and, as a result, are positive for business and the stock market. Periods of high inflation have increasing prices and high interest rates, and tend to be bad for business and the stock market. In a growing economy, there is always some amount of inflation.

Deflation

Though rare, **deflation** is a general decline in prices. Deflation usually occurs during severe recessions when unemployment is on the rise.

Test Topic Alert! A constant dollar adjustment is used to account for the impact of inflation.

Economic Indicators Certain aspects of economic activity serve as barometers, or **indicators**, of business cycle phases.

Leading Indicators

Leading indicators are spot-checks of business activity that reliably predict trends in the economy. Positive changes in these indicators predict economic improvement. Negative changes predict economic contraction.

Leading indicators used most often include:

- money supply (M2);
- building permits (housing starts);
- average weekly initial claims for state unemployment compensation;
- average work week in manufacturing;
- new orders for consumer goods;
- changes in inventories of durable goods;
- changes in sensitive materials prices;
- stock prices; and
- changes in business and consumer borrowing.

Not all of the indicators move in tandem. Positive changes in a majority of leading indicators point to increased spending, production, and employment. Negative changes in a majority of indicators can forecast a recession.

Coincident Indicators

Leading indicators reflect where the economy is going; coincident indicators confirm where it is. Coincident indicators are those measurable factors that vary directly and simultaneously with the business cycle. Widely used coincident indicators include:

- number of hours worked (as a proxy for personal income);
- employment levels;
- nonagricultural employment;
- personal income;
- industrial production;
- manufacturing and trade sales; and
- GDP.

Lagging Indicators

Lagging indicators are those factors that change after the economy has begun a new trend, but serve as confirmation of the new trend. Lagging indicators help analysts differentiate long-term trends from short-term reversals that occur in any trend. Lagging indicators include:

- corporate profits;
- average duration of unemployment;
- labor cost per unit of output (manufacturing);
- ratio of inventories to sales;
- commercial and industrial loans outstanding; and
- ratio of consumer installment credit to personal income.

Test Topic Alert! Be able to differentiate between leading, lagging, and coincident indicators.

Quick Quiz 14.1

Choose **LE** for leading, **LA** for lagging, and **C** for coincident.

___ 1. Decrease in number of weekly unemployment claims

___ 2. Increase in personal income

___ 3. Decrease in corporate profits

___ 4. Increase in industrial production

___ 5. Decrease in building permits

___ 6. Increase in the S&P 500 index

___ 7. Decrease in the duration of unemployment

Answers 1. **LE**   2. **C**   3. **LA**   4. **C**   5. **LE**
6. **LE**   7. **LA**

Test Topic Alert! Expect to see two questions on leading, lagging, or coincident indicators.

An indicator is not affected by whether there was an increase or decrease in the type of economic activity. For instance, an increase in inventories is a leading indicator that signifies a weakening economy. A decrease in inventories is still a leading indicator, but it signifies a strengthening economy.

Economic Theories and the Business Cycle

Keynesian Theory The economist **John Maynard Keynes** held that active government involvement in the economy was vital to the health and stability of a nation's economy. Keynesians believe that demand for goods ultimately controls employment and prices. Insufficient demand for goods causes unemployment; too much demand causes inflation. Keynes believed that it was the government's right and responsibility to manipulate overall demand (and therefore artificially manipulate the economy) by changing its own levels of spending and taxation.

The Government's Role in Keynesian Economics

According to Keynes, a government's fiscal policies determine the country's economic health. Fiscal policy involves adjusting the level of taxation and government spending. The government is expected to intervene in the economy as a major force in creating prosperity by engaging in activities that affect aggregate demand.

Government affects individual levels of spending and saving by adjusting taxes. Increasing taxes removes money from the private sector, which reduces private sector demand and spending. Government spending puts money back into the economy. To increase private sector demand for goods, the government reduces taxes, which increases people's disposable income.

Monetarist Theory

Milton Friedman is considered the originator of **monetarist economic theory**. Monetarists believe the quantity of money, the **money supply**, is the major determinant of price levels. Too many dollars chasing too few goods leads to inflation; conversely, too few dollars chasing too many goods leads to deflation.

Monetarists believe a well-controlled, moderately increasing money supply leads to price stability. Price stability allows business managers (considered to be more efficient allocators of resources than the government) to plan and invest, which in turn keeps the economy healthy.

Monetary economic policy is controlled by the Federal Reserve Board. Monetarists believe that the amount of money in the system is the major influence on economic performance. The reserve requirement, discount rate, and open market operations are the tools used by monetarists to regulate the economy.

Supply-Side Economics

Supply-side economics holds that government should allow market forces to determine prices of all goods. Supply-siders believe the federal government should reduce government spending as well as taxes. In this way, sellers of goods will price them at a rate that allows them to meet market demand and still sell them profitably.

The Laffer Curve

Economist **Arthur Laffer** studied government revenues as a function of tax rates to find the tax rate that produces the most revenue for the government. The Laffer Curve shows the relationship between tax rates and tax revenue collected by governments. As tax rates increase from low levels, tax revenue would increase. As tax rates continue to rise, there would come a point where people would not work as hard or as much. This lack of incentive would lead to a fall in income and therefore a fall in tax revenue. The logical endpoint is with tax rates at 100%; no one would work and there would be no tax revenue.

💡 Test Topic Alert!

The Series 7 exam may require that you know the originators of fundamental economic theories. Keynesian economists believe in government intervention, while Laffer and supply-side economists believe the government should step aside and let market forces take over.

Quick Quiz 14.2   Identify each item below with the appropriate theory.

A. Keynes
B. Friedman
C. Laffer/Supply-side

___ 1. Government intervention is necessary to stimulate the economy.

___ 2. Market forces should be allowed to determine prices.

___ 3. The quantity of money is the major determinant of price levels.

___ 4. The federal government should reduce spending and taxes.

___ 5. Aggregate demand controls employment and prices.

Answers   1. **A.**   2. **C.**   3. **B.**   4. **C.**   5. **A.**

Economic Policy

In a nutshell, the difference between Keynesians and monetarists is their perspectives toward the government's role in the economy. Keynesians believe the government, through its fiscal policies, should be a driving force in determining the level and allocation of economic resources. Monetarists, on the other hand, believe the private sector allocates resources much more efficiently, and the government's role is to provide a stable monetary environment within which private sector decisions can be made.

Monetary Policy

Definition of Money   Most people think of money as cash in their pockets. An economist takes a much broader view and includes loans, credit, and other liquid instruments. Economists divide money into three categories, as shown here.

The Parts of the Money Supply

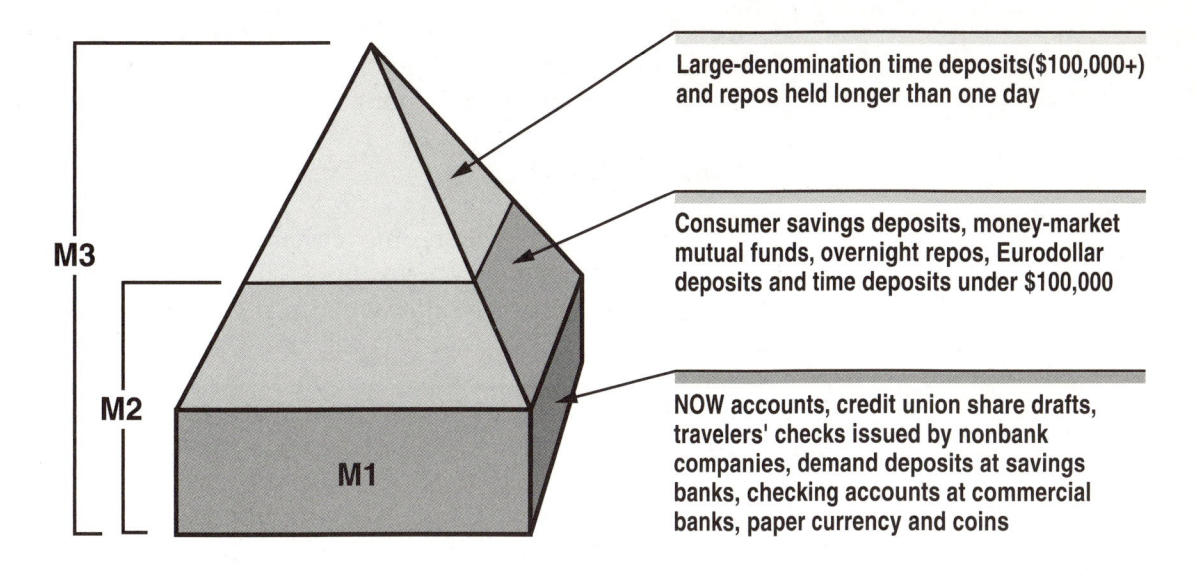

M3 — Large-denomination time deposits ($100,000+) and repos held longer than one day

M2 — Consumer savings deposits, money-market mutual funds, overnight repos, Eurodollar deposits and time deposits under $100,000

M1 — NOW accounts, credit union share drafts, travelers' checks issued by nonbank companies, demand deposits at savings banks, checking accounts at commercial banks, paper currency and coins

M1. The most readily available type of money, M1 consists of currency in circulation and demand deposits (checking accounts) that can be converted to currency immediately. It is the money consumers use for ordinary purchases of goods and services. Most money (M1) is in demand deposits—that is, checking accounts. M1 is the largest and most liquid component of the money supply.

M2. In addition to M1, M2 includes some time deposits (less than $100,000) that are fairly easy to convert into demand deposits. These time deposits include savings accounts, nonnegotiable CDs, money market funds, and overnight repurchase agreements.

M3. In addition to M1 and M2, M3 includes time deposits of more than $100,000 and repurchase agreements with terms longer than one day.

The Federal Reserve Board (FRB)

The **FRB** consists of 12 regional Federal Reserve Banks and hundreds of national and state banks that belong to the system. The FRB determines monetary policy and takes actions to implement its policies, including:

- acting as an agent of the US Treasury;
- regulating the US money supply;
- setting reserve requirements for members;
- supervising the printing of currency;
- clearing fund transfers throughout the system; and
- examining members to ensure compliance with federal regulations.

Because the FRB determines how much money is available for businesses and consumers to spend, its decisions are a critical aspect of the US economy.

The FRB affects the money supply through its use of three policy tools:

- open-market operations (buying/selling government securities);
- changes in the discount rate (on loans to member banks); and
- changes in reserve requirements.

Open-Market Operations

The Fed buys and sells US government securities in the open market to expand and contract the money supply. The **Federal Open Market Committee** (**FOMC**) meets regularly to direct the government's open-market operations.

When the FOMC buys securities, it increases the supply of money in the banking system, and when it sells securities, it decreases the supply.

When the Fed wants to expand (loosen) the money supply, it buys securities from banks. The banks receive direct credit in their reserve accounts. The increase of reserves allows banks to make more loans and effectively lowers interest rates. Thus, by buying securities, the Fed pumps money into the banking system, expanding the money supply and reducing rates.

When the Fed wants to contract (tighten) the money supply, it sells securities to banks. Each sale is charged against a bank's reserve balance. This reduces the bank's ability to lend money, which tightens credit and effectively raises interest rates. By selling securities, the Fed pulls money out of the system, contracting the money supply and increasing rates.

Discount Rate

The Fed can also adjust the money supply by raising or lowering the **discount rate**—the interest rate the Fed charges its members for short-term loans. To compensate for shortfalls in its reserve requirement, a bank may borrow money directly from the Fed at its discount rate or borrow the **excess reserves** (federal funds) from another member bank. The interest rate banks charge each other for such loans is called the **federal funds rate**.

The federal funds rate fluctuates daily and is among the most volatile interest rates. A rising rate usually indicates that member banks are more reluctant to lend their funds and want a higher rate of interest in return. A higher rate usually results from a shortage of funds to lend and probably indicates that deposits in general are shrinking. A falling federal funds rate generally means that the lending banks are competing to loan money and are trying to make their loans more attractive by lowering their rates. A lower rate often results from an excess of deposits.

Lowering the discount rate reduces the cost of money to banks, which increases the demand for loans. Raising the discount rate increases the cost of money and reduces the demand for loans.

Reserve Requirements and Federal Funds

Commercial banks must deposit a certain percentage of their depositors' money with the Federal Reserve. This is known as the **reserve requirement**. All money commercial banks deposit at Federal Reserve Banks, including money exceeding the reserve requirement, is known as **federal funds**.

When the Fed raises the reserve requirement, banks must deposit more funds with the Fed and thus have less money to lend. Reducing the reserve requirement has the opposite effect.

Federal Reserve Policy Tactics

To expand credit during a recession to stimulate a slow economy:	To tighten credit to slow economic expansion and prevent inflation:
• buy U.S. government securities in the open market	• sell U.S. government securities in the open market
• lower the discount rate	• raise the discount rate
• lower reserve requirements	• raise reserve requirements

Fiscal Policy

Fiscal policy refers to governmental budget decisions, which can include increases or decreases in:

- federal spending;
- money raised through taxes; and
- federal budget deficits or surpluses.

Fiscal policy is based on the assumption that the government can control unemployment levels and inflation by adjusting overall demand for goods and services.

The political process determines fiscal policy. Therefore, it takes time for conditions and solutions to be identified and implemented. Because of the time and negotiations involved, fiscal policy is an inefficient means to solve short-term economic problems.

The Stock Market Fiscal and monetary policies have considerable influence on the stock market. If the FRB eases interest rates, the money supply increases, making credit easier to obtain. This increases overall liquidity.

Similarly, lower tax rates can stimulate spending by leaving more spendable dollars in the hands of individuals and businesses. Like easier credit, lower tax rates are bullish for the stock market. Raising taxes has the opposite effect, reducing the amount of money available to businesses and consumers for spending and investment.

Interest Rates A loan's interest rate is the cost of the money. In large measure, the supply and demand of money determine interest rates. When the money available for loans exceeds demand, interest rates fall. When the FRB tightens the money supply, interest rates rise. The Fed influences the money supply in several ways, which directly or indirectly affect interest rate levels.

Disintermediation When people deposit money with a bank, interest is earned on their funds. The bank, in turn, acts as an intermediary by lending the money at a higher interest rate that allows it to pay the depositor and earn a profit.

Disintermediation is the flow of money from traditional, low-yielding savings accounts to higher yielding investments in the marketplace without a bank acting as an intermediary or a middleman. Disintermediation often takes place when the FRB tightens the money supply and interest rates rise.

International Monetary Factors

Balance of Payments The flow of money between the United States and other countries is known as the **balance of payments**. The balance of payments may be a **surplus** (more money flowing into the country than out) or a **deficit** (more money flowing out of the country than in). A deficit may occur when interest rates in another country are high because money flows to where it earns the highest return.

The largest component of the balance of payments is the **balance of trade**—the export and import of merchandise.

On the US credit side are sales of American products to foreign countries. On the debit side are American purchases of foreign goods that cause American dollars to flow out of the country. When debits exceed credits, a deficit in the balance of payments occurs; when credits exceed debits, a surplus exists.

Economic Policy

Balance of Trade

Debit Items	Credit Items
Imports	Exports
U.S. spending abroad	Foreign spending in the U.S.
U.S. investments abroad	Foreign investments in the U.S.
U.S. bank loans abroad	
U.S. foreign aid	

✓ ***Take Note:*** The value of the dollar against foreign currencies impacts the balance of trade. If the dollar is weak, foreign currency buys more US goods so exports increase. When the dollar is strong, foreign currency buys fewer US goods. The dollar buys more foreign goods so imports increase.

Test Topic Alert!

Know the fundamentals of fiscal and monetary policy.

Fiscal Policy:

- Actions of Congress and the president
- Government spending and taxation

Monetary Policy:

- Policy of the Federal Reserve Board (FRB)
- Discount rate
- Reserve requirement (most drastic)
- Open-market operations (most frequently used)

Note the following:

- The FRB sets the discount rate, not the federal funds rate.
- A change in the reserve requirement has a multiplier effect on the money supply; it has the most drastic impact of the FRB's tools.
- Open-market operations are the most frequently used tool of the FRB.

Quick Quiz 14.3 Multiple Choice

1. When the FOMC purchases T-bills in the open market, which of the following scenarios are likely to occur?

    I. Secondary bond prices will rise.
    II. Secondary bond prices will fall.
    III. Interest rates will rise.
    IV. Interest rates will fall.

    A. I and III
    B. I and IV
    C. II and III
    D. II and IV

2. Which of the following situations could cause a fall in the value of the US dollar in relation to the Japanese yen?

    I. Japanese investors buying US Treasury securities
    II. US investors buying Japanese securities
    III. Increase in Japan's trade surplus over that of the United States
    IV. General decrease in US interest rates

    A. I, II and III only
    B. I and IV only
    C. II and III only
    D. II, III and IV only

3. Disintermediation is most likely to occur when

    A. money is tight
    B. interest rates are low
    C. margin requirements are high
    D. the interest ceilings on certificates of deposit have been raised

4. To tighten credit during inflationary periods, the Federal Reserve Board can take any of the following actions EXCEPT

    A. raise reserve requirements
    B. change the amount of US government debt held by major banks
    C. sell securities in the open market
    D. lower taxes

5. Which of the following is not part of M1?

    A. Traveler's checks
    B. Money market mutual funds
    C. Coins
    D. Consumer checking accounts

Answers

1. **B.** When the FOMC buys T-bills in the open market, it pays for the transaction by increasing the reserve accounts of member banks, the net effect of which increases the total money supply and signals a period of relatively easier credit conditions. Easier credit means interest rates will decline and the price for existing bonds will rise.

2. **D.** Increased foreign investment in the United States (I) would raise the US dollar's relative value. A decrease in US interest rates (IV) would chase money out of the United States and increase the foreign currency's relative value. In choice II, the value of the yen should increase, meaning the dollar will fall in comparison. In choice III, US consumers are buying more Japanese goods than the Japanese are buying US goods. Therefore, the value of the dollar should fall relative to the yen.

3. **A.** Disintermediation is the flow of deposits out of banks and savings and loans into alternative, higher paying investments. It occurs when money is tight and interest rates are high because these alternative investments may then offer higher yields than S&Ls and banks. However, when interest rates are low, investors may prefer to keep their money in banks and S&Ls.

4. **D.** To curb inflation, the Fed can sell securities in the open market, thus changing the amount of US government debt institutions hold. It can also raise the reserve requirements, discount rate, or margin requirements. The Fed has no control over taxes, which are changed by Congress.

5. **B.** Although money market funds are highly liquid investments, they are considered time deposits and so are part of M2.

Technical Analysis

Both technical and fundamental analysis attempt to predict the supply and demand of markets and individual stocks. **Technical analysis** attempts to predict the direction of prices based on historic price and trading volume patterns when laid out graphically on charts. **Fundamental analysts** concentrate on broad-based economic trends; current business conditions within an industry; and the quality of a particular corporation's business, finances, and management.

Market Averages and Indexes

Stock prices tend to move, or **trend**, together, although some move in the opposite direction. The average stock, by definition, tends to rise in a bull market and decline in a bear market. Technical analysts chart the daily prices and volume movements of individual stocks and market indexes to discern patterns that allow them to predict the direction of market price movements.

Trading Volume **Market trading volume** substantially above normal signifies or confirms a pattern in the direction of prices. If overall volume has been listless for months and suddenly jumps significantly, a technical analyst views that as the beginning of a trend.

Advances/Declines The number of issues closing up or down on a specific day reflects **market breadth**. The number of advances and declines can be a significant indication of the market's relative strength. When declines outnumber advances by a large amount, the market is bearish even if it closed higher. In bull markets, advances substantially outnumber declines. Technical analysts plot daily advances and declines on a graph to produce an **advance/decline line** that gives them an indication of market breadth trends.

Charting Stocks

In addition to studying the overall market, technical analysts attempt to identify patterns in the prices of individual stocks.

Trendlines While a stock's price may spike up or down daily, over time its price tends to move in one direction. Technical analysts identify patterns in the **trendlines** of individual stocks from graphs as they do patterns in the overall market. They base their buy or sell recommendations on a stock's price trendline. An upward trendline is bullish; a downward one is bearish.

Upward and Downward Trendlines

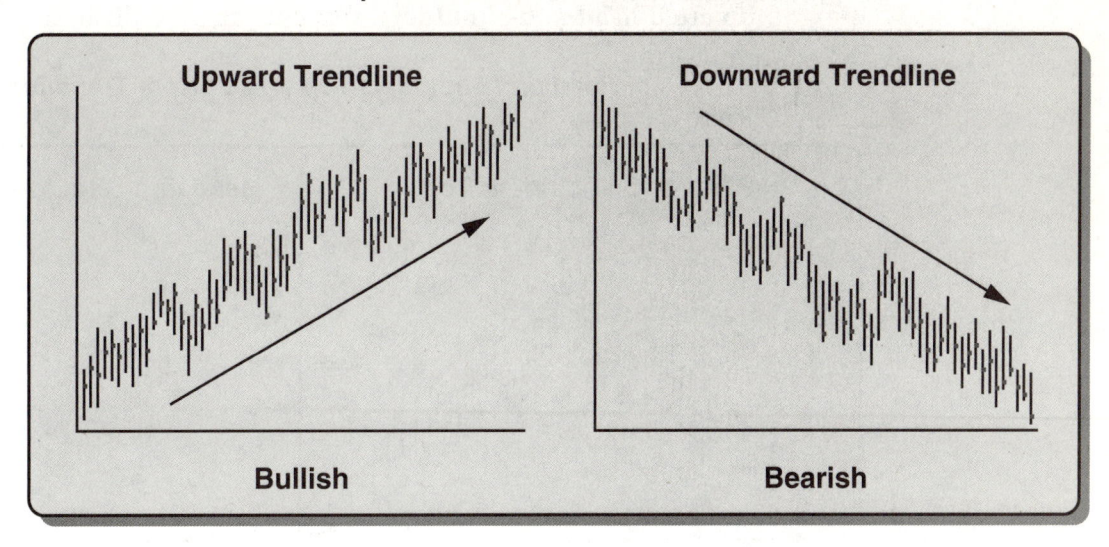

A trendline connects the lows in an uptrend and the highs in a downtrend. Three common patterns in stock price trendlines are **consolidations**, **reversals**, and **support and resistance levels**.

Consolidations

If a stock's price stays within a narrow range, it is said to be **consolidating**. When viewed on a graph, the trendline is horizontal and moves sideways, neither up nor down.

Reversals

A **reversal** indicates that an upward or a downward trendline has halted and the stock's price is moving in the opposite direction. In between the two trendlines, a period of consolidation occurs, and the stock price levels off. A genuine reversal pattern can be difficult to recognize because trends are composed of many rises and declines, which may occur at different rates and for different lengths of time.

Because of its gently curving shape, an easily identifiable reversal pattern is called a **saucer** (reversal of a downtrend) or an **inverted saucer** (reversal of an uptrend). A similar reversal pattern is the **head-and-shoulders** pattern, named for its resemblance to the human body.

The head and shoulders top pattern indicates the beginning of a bearish trend in the stock. First, the stock price rises, then it reaches a plateau at the neckline (left shoulder). A second advance pushes the price higher, but then the price falls back to the neckline (head). Finally, the stock price rises again, but falls back to the neckline (right shoulder) and continues downward, indicating a reversal of the upward trend.

When reversed, this pattern is called a **head-and-shoulders bottom**, or an **inverted head-and-shoulders**, and indicates a bullish reversal.

Head and Shoulders Top and Bottom Trendlines

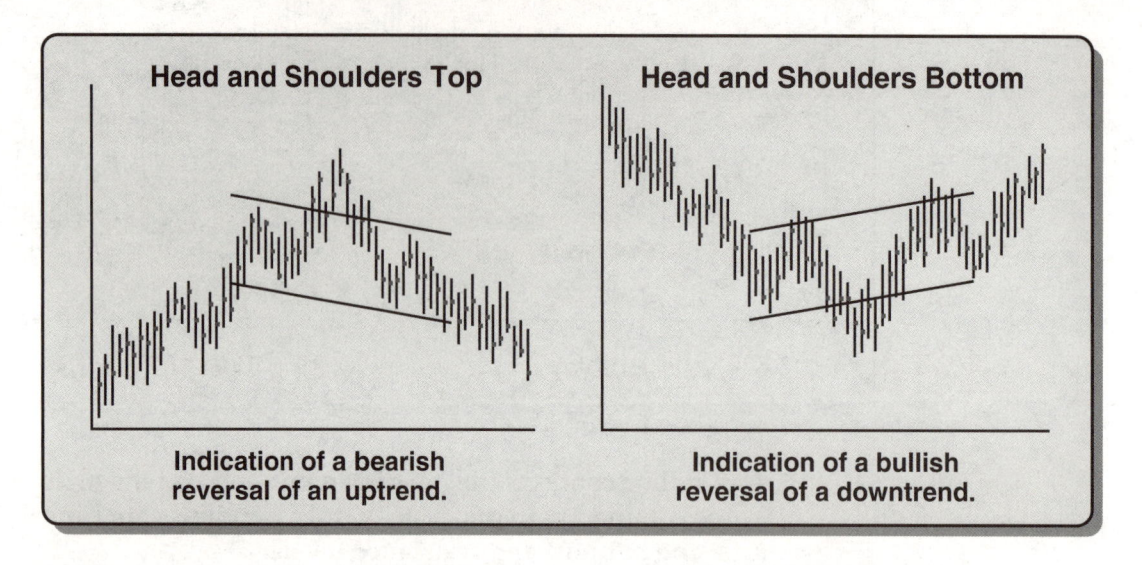

Head and Shoulders Top

Indication of a bearish reversal of an uptrend.

Head and Shoulders Bottom

Indication of a bullish reversal of a downtrend.

Support and Resistance Levels Stock prices may move within a narrow range for months or even years. The bottom of this trading range is known as the **support level**; the top of the trading range is called the **resistance level**.

Support and Resistance Levels

Resistance

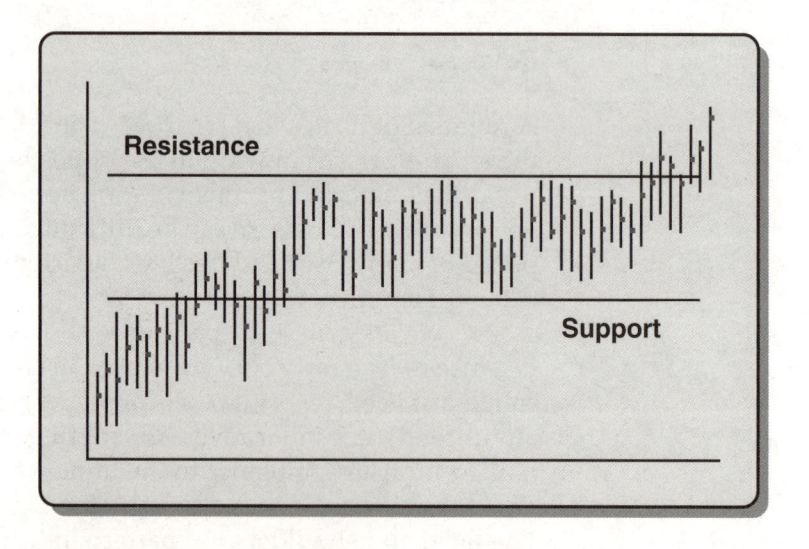

Support

When a stock declines to its support level, the low price attracts buyers, whose buying supports the price and keeps it from declining farther. When a stock increases to its resistance level, the high price attracts sellers, whose selling hinders a further price rise. Stocks may fluctuate in trading ranges for months, testing their support and resistance levels. If a particular stock's price penetrates either the support or the resistance level, the change is considered significant.

A decline through the support level is called a **bearish breakout**; a rise through the resistance level is called a **bullish breakout**. Breakouts usually signal the beginning of a new upward or downward trend.

Technical Market Theories

Technical analysts follow various theories regarding market trends. Some of them are outlined below.

Dow Theory Analysts use the **Dow theory** to confirm the end of a major market trend. According to the theory, the three types of changes in stock prices are **primary trends** (one year or more), **secondary trends** (3–12 weeks), and **short-term fluctuations** (hours or days).

In a bull market, the primary trend is upward. However, stock prices may still drop in a secondary trend within the primary upward trend, even for as long as 12 weeks. The trough of the downward secondary trend should be higher than the trough of the previous downward trend. In a bear market, secondary upward trends may occur, but the highs reached during those secondary upward movements are successively lower.

According to the Dow theory, the primary trend in a bull market is a series of higher highs and higher lows. In a bear market, the primary trend is a series of lower highs and lower lows. Daily fluctuations are considered irrelevant.

A primary upward trend interrupted by secondary downward movements is shown in the following chart. The chart illustrates a series of successively higher highs and lows, conforming to the definition of a primary upward trend.

Any change in direction is considered deceptive unless the Dow Jones Industrial and Transportation Averages reflect the change. However, using this average lacks precision and is sometimes slow in confirming changes in market trends.

Dow Theory of Market Trends

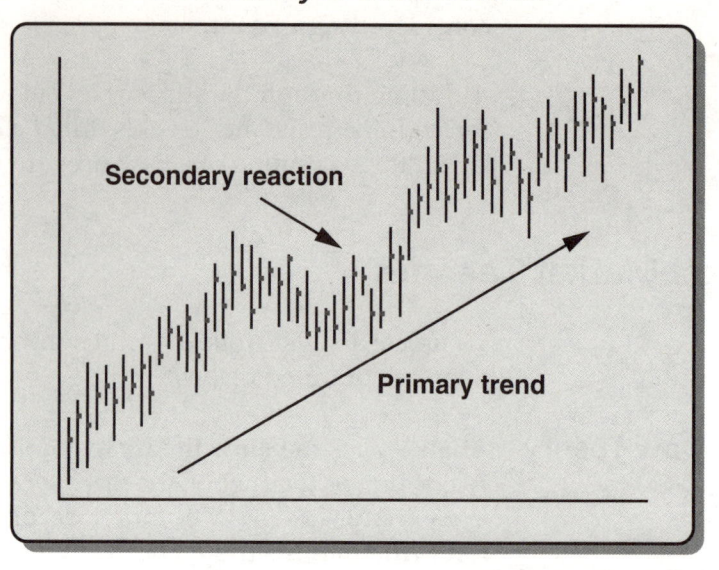

Odd-Lot Theory Typically, small investors engage in **odd-lot trading**. Followers of the **odd-lot theory** believe that these small investors invariably buy and sell at the wrong times. When odd-lot traders buy, odd-lot analysts are bearish. When odd-lot traders sell, odd-lot analysts are bullish.

Short Interest Theory **Short interest** refers to the number of shares that have been sold short. Because short positions must be repurchased eventually, some analysts believe that short interest reflects mandatory demand, which creates a support level for stock prices. High short interest is a bullish indicator, and low short interest is a bearish indicator.

Modern Portfolio Theory Instead of emphasizing particular stocks, **modern portfolio theory** (MPT) focuses on the relationship of all the investments in a portfolio. The theory holds that analysts' ability to predict price movements is of no value. Adherents to MPT believe securities markets are efficient markets, meaning securities prices react so quickly to most investment information that no analyst is likely to outsmart the market as a whole. MPT portfolio managers select a general mix of investments weighted to emphasize economic trends.

Random Walk Theory The **random walk theory** is an academic theory maintaining that the direction of stock or market prices is unpredictable. This hypothesis is based on the **efficient market theory**, which holds that the stock market is perfectly efficient, with prices reflecting all known information at any given time. It is impossible, therefore, to beat the market using fundamental or technical analysis (i.e., throwing darts at the stock listings is as good a method as any for selecting stocks for investment). Many people have become wealthy investing in stocks, but few have done so using the random walk theory.

Test Topic Alert! Technical analysts are sometimes called **market timers**. They determine whether to buy or sell based on trends like market breadth, trading volume, and the market theories you have just read about. Be prepared to identify technical analysis tools versus fundamental analysis tools for test questions.

Be aware of the following about market indices:

- The Dow Jones Industrial Average is the oldest and most widely quoted index.
- The Dow Jones Composite includes 30 industrial, 20 transportation, and 15 utility issues.
- The Value Line Index includes 1,700 NYSE, AMEX, and OTC stocks.
- The Wilshire 5000 Index is the broadest market index and includes all NYSE and AMEX listed stocks as well as all Nasdaq listed stocks.
- S&P 500

Quick Quiz 14.4 Multiple Choice

1. When a technical analyst says that the market is consolidating, the trendline is moving

   A. upward
   B. downward
   C. sideways
   D. unpredictably

2. From a chartist's (technical analyst) viewpoint, which of the following statements is TRUE?

   A. Once a trendline is established, the price movement of a stock usually follows the trendline.
   B. More odd-lot buying than selling is bullish.
   C. Heavy volume in a declining market is bullish.
   D. Light volume in an advancing market is bullish.

3. Proponents of which of the following technical theories assume that small investors are usually wrong?

   A. Breadth-of-market theory
   B. Short-interest theory
   C. Volume of trading theory
   D. Odd-lot theory

4. Which of the following is the narrowest measure of the market?

   A. NYSE Composite Index
   B. Value Line Index
   C. DJIA
   D. Standard & Poor's 500

Answers

1. **C.** *If a market is staying within a narrow price range, it is said to be consolidating.*

2. **A.** *A trendline connects the lows in an uptrend and the highs in a downtrend. Once established, trendlines are not easily halted or reversed.*

3. **D.** *Odd-lot trading typically is done by small investors. Followers of the odd-lot theory act on the belief that small investors invariably buy and sell at the wrong times.*

4. **C.** *The narrowest measure of the market is the Dow Jones Industrial Average, which charts the performance of 30 industrial stocks.*

Fundamental Analysis

Fundamental analysis is the study of the business prospects of an individual company within the context of its industry and the overall economy.

Industry Analysis

Because business cycle phases have different effects on different industries, fundamental analysts look for companies in industries that offer better-than-average opportunities in the context of the business cycle. It is useful to distinguish between the four types of industries and investments: defensive, cyclical, growth, and special situation.

Defensive Industries

Defensive industries are least affected by normal business cycles. Companies in defensive industries generally produce nondurable consumer goods such as food, pharmaceuticals, and tobacco. Public consumption of such goods remains fairly steady throughout the business cycle. During recessions and bear markets, stocks in defensive industries generally decline less than stocks in other industries, but during expansions and bull markets, defensive stocks may advance less. Investments in defensive industries tend to involve less risk and, consequently, lower investment returns.

Cyclical Industries

Cyclical industries are highly sensitive to business cycles and inflation trends. Most cyclical industries produce durable goods such as heavy machinery, and raw materials such as steel and automobiles. During recessions, the demand for such products declines as manufacturers postpone investments in new capital goods and consumers postpone purchases of automobiles. **Counter-cyclical industries,** on the other hand, tend to turn down as the economy heats up and to rise when the economy turns down.

Growth Industries Every industry passes through four phases during its existence: **introduction, growth, maturity,** and **decline.** An industry is considered in its **growth phase** if the industry is growing faster than the economy as a whole because of technological changes, new products, or changing consumer tastes. Computers and bioengineering are current growth industries. Because many growth companies retain nearly all of their earnings to finance their business expansion, growth stocks usually pay little or no dividends.

Special Situation Stocks **Special situation stocks** are stocks of a company with unusual profit potential due to nonrecurring circumstances such as new management, the discovery of a valuable natural resource on corporate property, or the introduction of a new product.

Quick Quiz 14.5

Categorize the following industries or industry characteristics as **D** (Defensive), **C** (Cyclical), or **G** (Growth).

___ 1. Automobile industry

___ 2. Pay little or no dividend

___ 3. Tobacco

___ 4. Decline less in recession, advance less in expansion

___ 5. Computer industry

___ 6. Demand declines during recession

___ 7. Generally produce nondurable consumer goods

___ 8. Generally produce heavy equipment

Answers   1. **C.**   2. **G.**   3. **D.**   4. **D.**   5. **G.**
              6. **C.**   7. **D.**   8. **C.**

Corporate Analysis

After considering the state of the economy and the health of various industries, fundamental analysts study a company's position within its industry, prospects for growth and stability, and financial strength. Fundamental analysts look at a firm's quality of management, its historical earnings trends, compare the level and stability of its projected growth with that of its competitors, and also examine the structure of a corporation's capitalization and use of working capital.

Financial Statements

A corporation's **financial statements** provide a fundamental analyst with the raw material needed to assess that corporation's profitability, financial strength, and operating efficiency. By examining how certain static numbers from the statement relate to one another and how the resulting ratios relate to the company's competitors, the analyst can determine how financially viable the company is.

Companies issue quarterly and annual financial reports to their stockholders that include a company's **balance sheet** and **income statement**.

Balance Sheet — The **balance sheet** provides a snapshot of a company's financial position at a specific time. It identifies the value of the company's assets (what it owns) and its liabilities (what it owes). The difference between these two figures is the corporation's **equity**, or **net worth**.

A corporation can be compared to a homeowner who borrows money to buy a home. The homeowner's equity is the difference between the mortgage balance (liability) and the home's market value (asset value). A corporation can buy assets using borrowed money (liabilities) and equity raised by selling stock. The value of its assets must equal (balance with) the value of its liabilities and equity.

While useful in determining a company's current value, the balance sheet cannot tell the analyst whether the company's business is improving or deteriorating.

The Balance Sheet Equation

Assets
  Current assets
  Fixed assets
  Other assets

Liabilities
  Current liabilities
  Long-term liabilities

Equity (net worth)
  Preferred stock par value
  Common stock par value
  Additional paid-in capital
  Treasury stock
  Retained earnings

Assets = Liabilities + Shareholders' equity

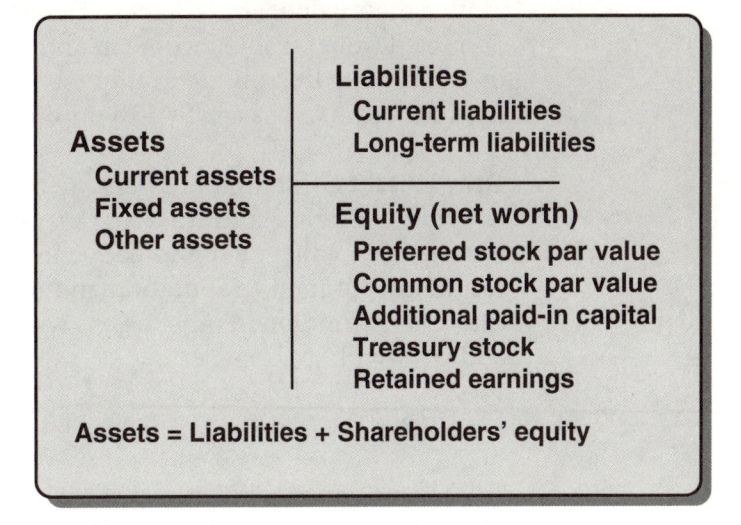

Balance Sheet Components

The balance sheet gets its name from the fact that its two sides must balance. The balance sheet equation mathematically expresses the relationship between the two sides of the balance sheet.

✓ *Take Note:* Assets − liabilities = net worth

Assets

Assets appear on the balance sheet in order of **liquidity** (the ease with which they can be turned into cash). Those most readily convertible into cash are listed first, followed by less liquid assets. Balance sheets commonly identify three types of assets: **current assets** (cash and assets easily convertible into cash); **fixed assets** (physical assets that could eventually be sold); and **other assets** (usually intangible and only of value to the corporation owning them).

Current Assets. Current assets include all cash and other items expected to be converted into cash within the next 12 months and include the following.

- **Cash and equivalents**—Cash and short-term safe investments (such as money-market instruments) that can be sold readily, as well as other marketable securities.
- **Accounts receivable**—Amounts due from customers for goods delivered or services rendered, reduced by the allowance for bad debts.
- **Inventory**—The cost of raw materials, work in process, and finished goods ready for sale.
- **Prepaid expenses**—Items a company has already paid for but has not yet benefited from (e.g., prepaid advertising, rents, taxes, and operating supplies).

Fixed Assets. Fixed assets are typically property, plant, and equipment. Unlike current assets, they are not easily converted into cash. Fixed assets, such as factories, have limited useful lives because wear and tear eventually reduce their value. For this reason, their cost can be **depreciated** over time—deducted from taxable income in annual installments to compensate for loss in value. Note that on the example balance sheet (shown later) depreciation has reduced fixed assets by $10 million.

Other Assets. Intangible assets are nonphysical properties, such as formulas, contract rights, and trademarks. **Goodwill**, also an intangible asset, is a company's value over and above its book value. This extra sum is paid for the corporation's reputation and relationship with its clients. In the example, $5 million in other assets was reported, including intangible assets and goodwill.

Liabilities

Total liabilities on a balance sheet represent all financial claims by creditors against the corporation's assets. Balance sheets usually include two main types of liabilities: **current liabilities** (debts due within 12 months) and **long-term liabilities** (debts or bonds maturing in more than 12 months).

Current Liabilities. Current liabilities are corporate debt obligations due for payment within the next 12 months. In the example, these include:

- **accounts payable**—amounts owed to suppliers of materials and other business costs;
- **accrued wages payable**—unpaid wages, salaries, commissions, and interest; and
- **current long-term debt**—any portion of long-term debt due within 12 months.

A balance sheet might also include the following as current liabilities:

- **notes payable**—the balance due on equipment purchased on credit or cash borrowed; and
- **accrued taxes**—unpaid federal, state, and local taxes.

Long-Term Liabilities. Long-term debts are financial obligations due for payment after 12 months. Examples of long-term debts are mortgages on real property, long-term promissory notes, and outstanding corporate bonds. **Funded debt** is any long-term debt payable in five years or more.

Sample Balance Sheet

Balance Sheet
Amalgamated Widget
as of Dec. 31, 1999

ASSETS

Current assets	Cash and equivalents	$ 5,000,000	
	Accounts receivable	15,000,000	
	Inventory	19,000,000	
	Prepaid expenses	1,000,000	
	Total Current Assets		$ 40,000,000
Fixed assets	Buildings, furniture and fixtures (including $10,000,000 depreciation)	$40,000,000	
	Land	15,000,000	
	Total Fixed Assets		$ 55,000,000
Other (intangibles, goodwill)			$ 5,000,000
Total Assets			$100,000,000

LIABILITIES AND NET WORTH

Current liabilities	Accounts payable	$ 5,000,000	
	Accrued wages payable	4,000,000	
	Current portion of long-term debt	1,000,000	
	Total Current Liabilities		$ 10,000,000
Long-term liabilities	8% 20-year convertible debentures		$ 50,000,000
Total Liabilities			$ 60,000,000
Net worth	Preferred stock $100 par ($5 noncum conv, 200,000 shares issued)	$20,000,000	
	Common stock $1 par (1,000,000 shares)	1,000,000	
	Capital in excess of par	4,000,000	
	Retained earnings	15,000,000	
Total Net Worth			$ 40,000,000
Total Liabilities and Net Worth			$100,000,000

Shareholders' Equity

Shareholders' equity, also called **net worth** or **owners' equity**, is the stockholders' claims on a company's assets after all of its creditors have been paid. Shareholders' equity equals total assets less total liabilities. On a balance sheet, three types of shareholders' equity are identified: **capital stock at par**, **capital in excess of par**, and **retained earnings**.

Capital Stock at Par

Capital stock includes preferred and common stock, listed at par value. **Par value** is the total dollar value assigned to stock certificates when a corporation's owners (the stockholders) first contributed capital. Par value of common stock is an arbitrary value with no relationship to market price.

Capital in Excess of Par

Capital in excess of par, often called **additional paid-in capital** or **paid-in surplus**, is the amount of money over par value that a company received for selling stock.

Retained Earnings

Retained earnings, sometimes called **earned surplus**, are profits that have not been paid out in dividends. Retained earnings represent the total of all earnings held since the corporation was formed, less dividends paid to stockholders. Operating losses in any year reduce the retained earnings from prior years.

Capitalization

A company's **capitalization** is the combined sum of its long-term debt and equity accounts. The **capital structure** is the relative amounts of debt and equity that compose a company's capitalization. Some companies finance their business with a large proportion of borrowed funds; others finance growth with retained earnings from normal operations and little or no debt.

Liquidity

Working capital is the amount of capital or cash a company has available. Working capital is, therefore, a measure of a firm's liquidity—its ability to quickly turn assets into cash to meet its short-term obligations. The formula for working capital is:

$$\text{Current assets} - \text{current liabilities} = \text{working capital}$$

Liquidity is important because it is the measure of a company's ability to pay the expenses associated with running the business.

Changes that Affect the Balance Sheet

Balancing the Balance Sheet

Balance sheets, by definition, must balance. Every financial change in a business requires two offsetting changes on the company books, known as **double-entry bookkeeping**.

Depreciating Assets

Because fixed assets, such as buildings, equipment, and machinery, wear out as they are used, they decline in value over time. This decline in value is called **depreciation**. A company's tax bills are reduced each year the company depreciates fixed assets used in the businesses.

Depreciation affects the balance sheet in two ways: accumulated depreciation reduces the value of fixed assets, and the depreciation deduction reduces taxable income.

✓ **Take Note:** The basic balance sheet equation can be expressed in two ways:

$$\text{Assets} - \text{liabilities} = \text{net worth}$$
$$\text{Assets} = \text{liabilities} + \text{net worth}$$

Capital Structure

A corporation builds its capital structure with four elements:

- long-term debt;
- capital stock (common and preferred);
- capital in excess of par; and
- retained earnings (earned surplus).

✓ **For Example:** (See the graphic for reference and explanation of the following terms.) The total capitalization on the sample balance is $90 million ($50 million in long-term debt, $20 million in preferred stock, and $20 million in common shareholders' equity). Remember, capital stock + capital in excess of par + retained earnings = shareholders' equity (net worth).

Total capitalization	$90 million
LT debt	$50 million
+ Pfd.	$20 million
+ Common	$1 million
+Ret. earnings	$15 million
+ Cap. surplus	$4 million

If a company changes its capitalization by issuing stock or bonds, the effects will show up on the balance sheet.

Sample Income Statement

Income Statement
Amalgamated Widget
Jan 1 – Dec 31, 1999

Net sales		$60,000,000
Cost of goods sold	$10,000,000	
General operating expenses (including $2,000,000 depreciation)	$30,000,000	$40,000,000
Operating income		$20,000,000
Interest expense		$ 4,000,000
Pretax income		$16,000,000
Taxes		$ 6,000,000
Net income after taxes		$10,000,000
Preferred dividends		$ 1,000,000
Earnings available to common		$ 9,000,000

Issuing Securities — The example balance sheet indicates the company issued 1 million shares of $1 par common stock. If it issues another 1 million shares, the net worth (shareholders' equity) will increase by the additional capital raised and the amount of cash on the asset side of the balance sheet will increase.

Convertible Securities — When a stockholder converts a convertible bond into shares of common stock, the amount of liabilities decreases and equity increases. The changes are on the same side of the balance sheet, so the bottom line is unchanged.

Bond Redemption — When bonds are **redeemed**, liabilities on the balance sheet are reduced. The offsetting change would be a decrease in cash on the asset side of the balance sheet. The company would have less debt outstanding, but it would also have less cash. The balance sheet balances.

Dividends — When a cash dividend is declared, retained earnings are lowered and current liabilities are increased. The declaration of a cash dividend establishes a current liability until it is paid. Once paid, it reduces cash in current assets and also reduces current liabilities.

Distribution of stock dividends has no effect on corporate assets or liabilities, nor does it change the stockholders' proportionate equity in the corporation. The number of shares each stockholder owns increases, but each single share represents a smaller slice of ownership in the corporation.

Stock Splits — Like a stock dividend, a **stock split** does not affect shareholders' equity. On the balance sheet, only the par value per share and number of shares outstanding change.

Financial Leverage — **Financial leverage** is a company's ability to use long-term debt to increase its return on equity. A company with a high ratio of long-term debt to common stock is said to be **highly leveraged**.

Stockholders benefit from leverage if the return on borrowed money exceeds the debt service costs. But leverage is risky because excessive increases in debt raise the possibility of default in a business downturn.

In general, industrial companies with debt-to-equity ratios of 100% or higher are considered highly leveraged. However, utilities, with their relatively stable earnings and cash flows, can be more highly leveraged without subjecting stockholders to undue risk. If highly leveraged, the company is also affected more by changes in interest rates.

> **Test Topic Alert!**
>
> The Series 7 exam does not generally ask for calculations with balance sheet or income statement items. Make sure to recognize the main components of each of these financial statements. You may be asked about the impact of a certain transaction on the balance sheet.
>
> 1. Which of the following choices are affected when a corporation purchases a printing press for cash?
>
>   A. Current assets
>   B. Current liabilities
>   C. Working capital
>   D. Total assets
>   E. Total liabilities
>   F. Net worth
>
>   Answer: **A** and **C** (current assets and working capital). A payment of cash reduces current assets. Whenever either current assets or current liabilities change, working capital is also affected. The new printing press increases the value of the fixed assets. Total assets, however, are unchanged because the decrease in current assets is offset by the increase in fixed assets.
>
> 2. Which are affected when a corporation declares a cash dividend?
>
>   Answer: **B, C, E,** and **F** (current liabilities, working capital, total liabilities, and net worth). The declaration (not payment) of a dividend creates a current liability on the books of the corporation. Because current liabilities are affected, working capital and total liabilities also change. The declaration of a dividend reduces the net worth because the dividend will be paid from retained earnings. When the dividend is paid, current assets will decrease and current liabilities will decrease (this also decreases both total assets and total liabilities). Working capital does not change because both current assets and current liabilities decrease by the same amount.
>
>   If a corporation has a stock split, the balance sheet categories above are not affected. A stock split will increase the number of shares and reduce the value of each share, but the total par value as shown in the equity section of the balance sheet is not affected.

Quick Quiz 14.6 Multiple Choice

1. The difference between current assets and current liabilities is called

    A. net worth
    B. working capital
    C. cash flow
    D. quick assets

2. As a result of corporate transactions, a company's assets remain the same and its equity decreases. Which of the following statements is TRUE?

    A. Prepaid expenses decrease
    B. Total liabilities increase
    C. Accrued expenses decrease
    D. Net worth increases

3. Which of the following is not affected by the issuance of a bond?

    A. Assets
    B. Total liabilities
    C. Working capital
    D. Shareholders' equity

4. A company has been experiencing increased earnings but has kept its dividend payments constant. Due solely to this, the company's balance sheet would reflect

    A. decreased net working capital
    B. decreased net worth
    C. decreased retained earnings
    D. increased shareholders' equity

Answers

1. **B.** Working capital (or net working capital) is, by definition, the difference between current assets and current liabilities.

2. **B.** The formula for the balance sheet is: assets = liabilities + shareholders' equity. If assets stay the same and equity (net worth) decreases, liabilities must increase. Choice A is incorrect because prepaid expenses are assets; choice C is incorrect because accrued expenses are liabilities.

3. **D.** On the issuance of a bond, cash is received (thus increasing current assets) and long-term debt increases (increasing total liabilities). Because there is no corresponding increase in current liabilities, working capital will increase; it would have no effect on shareholders' equity.

4. **D.** If earnings increase, retained earnings also increase. If the increased retained earnings are not paid out as dividends, shareholders' equity increases.

Income Statement

The **income statement** summarizes a corporation's revenues and expenses for a fiscal period, usually quarterly, year-to-date, or the full year. It compares revenue against costs and expenses during the period.

Fundamental analysts use the income statement to judge the efficiency of a company's operation, and its profitability.

Income Statement Entries

	Net Sales
minus	Cost of goods sold (COGS)
minus	Operating costs (including depreciation)
equals	Operating profit
plus	Nonoperating income
equals	Operating income (earnings before interest and taxes)
minus	Interest expenses
equals	Taxable income
minus	Taxes
equals	Net income after taxes
minus	Preferred dividends
equals	Earnings available to common
minus	Common dividends
equals	Retained earnings

The various operating and nonoperating expenses on the income statement are discussed here.

Operating Income — Operating income, also called **operating profit, operating margin,** or **earnings before interest and taxes (EBIT)**, is a company's profits from business operations.

Interest Expense — Interest payments on a corporation's debt is not considered an operating expense. Interest payments reduce the corporation's taxable income. Pretax income (the amount of taxable income) is operating income less interest payment expenses.

Net Income After Taxes — If dividends are paid to stockholders, they are paid out of net income after taxes have been paid. After preferred dividends have been paid, the remaining income is available to invest in the business or pay dividends to common stockholders.

Economics & Analysis

Interest payments reduce a corporation's taxable income, while dividend payments to stockholders are paid with after-tax dollars. Because they are taxable as income to stockholders, dividends are taxed twice, but interest payments are taxed once, as income to the recipient.

Earnings Per Share (EPS) Earnings per share is what remains after payment of interest, taxes, and preferred dividends. Dividing net income after taxes, interest, and payment of preferred dividends by the number of common shares outstanding determines earnings per share.

$$\frac{\text{Earnings available to common}}{\text{Number of shares outstanding}}$$

✓ **For Example:** To determine EPS, divide Earnings Available to Common by the number of shares outstanding. Amalgamated Widgets has 4,500,000 shares outstanding. With its earnings available to common of $9,000,000, EPS is $2.00.

Retained Earnings Retained earnings (earned surplus) are earnings not paid out in dividends.

✎ **Quick Quiz 14.7** Indicate **B** (Balance Sheet) or **I** (Income Statement) for each of these items:

___ 1. Net sales

___ 2. Long-term liabilities

___ 3. Current assets

___ 4. Operating income

___ 5. Prepaid expenses

___ 6. Earnings available to common

___ 7. Cost of goods sold

___ 8. Fixed assets

Answers 1. *I.*   2. *B.*   3. *B.*   4. *I.*
            5. *B.*   6. *I.*   7. *I.*   8. *B.*

Financial Ratios and Analyzing Corporate Equity

Figures from the balance sheet or income statement can be expressed as **ratios**. Financial ratios allow an analyst to compare a company's performance to its past performance and to the performances of other companies within its industry. Such comparisons provide a more thorough understanding of a company's financial strengths and weaknesses.

Test Topic Alert! As you review financial ratios, remember that the test asks very few questions on this section, and usually tests concepts rather than math. Understanding what the ratios measure is more important than mastering the calculations.

Capitalization Ratios

Analysts can assess the risk of a company going bankrupt by studying the amount of **leverage** (the proportionate amount of long-term debt) in its overall **capitalization** (long-term debt plus equity).

When assessing a company's capitalization, analysts use ratios that express the percentage of capitalization composed of long-term debt, common stock, and preferred stock. The following four ratios are commonly used to assess the stability of a corporation's capitalization.

Debt-to-equity ratio = total long-term debt / total shareholders' equity

Bond ratio (debt ratio) = long-term liabilities / total capitalization

Common stock ratio = common shareholders' equity / total capitalization

Preferred stock ratio = preferred stock / total capitalization

Leverage Leverage is the use of long-term debt financing to increase earnings. The **debt-to-equity ratio** provides a common measure of leverage.

More debt can lead to greater EPS, but can also increase risk to the common stockholders. A company with a disproportionately high amount of debt may not be able to meet its interest obligations during a business downturn. Low debt-to-equity ratios are considered more conservative than high debt-to-equity ratios. The debt-to-equity ratio is similar to the **bond ratio**, which compares total long-term debt to total capitalization rather than to shareholders' equity.

The **bond ratio**, or **debt ratio**, measures the percentage of total capitalization provided by long-term debt financing. The **common stock ratio** measures the percentage of total capitalization contributed by common stockholders, including the stock's par value, amount paid for the stock in excess of par, and retained earnings. The **preferred stock ratio** measures the percentage of total capitalization from preferred stock.

✓ **Take Note:** The capitalization of a company is calculated from its balance sheet. Add the long-term debt and the equity (net worth) to calculate a company's total capitalization. Highly leveraged companies have greater capital risk.

Liquidity Ratios

Liquidity ratios measure a firm's ability to meet its current financial obligations. **Working capital**, though not a ratio, is the amount of liquid assets available to pay for short-term obligations. It is calculated as follows:

$$\text{Working capital} = \text{current assets} - \text{current liabilities}$$

Because working capital is a dollar amount, it does not, by itself, allow analysts to compare companies. The **current ratio**, on the other hand, compares current assets with a company's current financial obligations, regardless of the company's size or business.

$$\text{Current ratio} = \frac{\text{Current assets}}{\text{Current liabilities}}$$

Another measure of liquidity is **quick assets**, which subtracts **unsold inventory**, a current asset, from other current assets because inventory is not as **liquid** (as quick to convert to cash) as cash or receivables. Analysts use quick assets instead of current assets to calculate the **acid-test ratio**. The acid-test ratio, also called the **quick ratio**, is a more stringent measure of a company's liquidity than its current ratio. The quick assets and acid-test ratio equations are as follows:

$$\text{Quick assets} = \text{current assets} - \text{inventory}$$

$$\text{Acid test ratio} = \frac{\text{Quick assets}}{\text{Current liabilities}}$$

The **cash assets ratio** is the most stringent measure of a company's liquidity.

$$\text{Cash assets ratio} = \frac{\text{Cash and equivalents}}{\text{Current liabilities}}$$

Financial Ratios and Analyzing Corporate Equity

Debt Service Ratio The **debt service ratio** reflects a company's ability to meet the principal and interest payments on its bonds.

$$\text{Debt service ratio} = \frac{\text{EBIT}}{\text{(Annual interest + Principal payments)}}$$

Book Value Per Share In a **liquidation**, a company sells its tangible assets and uses the proceeds to pay creditors and stockholders. Potential investors want to know how the value of **tangible assets**, also known as **net tangible asset value**, compares to the size of the company's debt and equity.

The **book value** of a company's assets (the amount at which they are carried on the books) is determined by deducting all liabilities and preferred stock from the company's total tangible assets. Dividing this figure by the number of shares of common stock shows how much a company's assets are worth (assuming they be sold for their book value) per share.

$$\frac{\text{(Assets − Liabilities − Intangibles − Par value of preferred stock)}}{\text{Shares of common stock outstanding}} = \text{Book value per share}$$

Valuation Ratios

Valuation ratios are used by analysts to compare companies within an industry as well as in different industries.

Earnings Per Share (EPS) Among the most widely used statistics, EPS measures the value of a company's earnings for each common share.

$$\text{EPS} = \frac{\text{Earnings available to common}}{\text{No. of common shares outstanding}}$$

Earnings available to common are the remaining earnings after the preferred dividend has been paid. Earnings per share relates to common stock only. Preferred stockholders have no claims to earnings beyond the stipulated preferred stock dividends.

Earnings Per Share After Dilution If a corporation has rights, warrants, convertible preferred stock, or convertible bonds outstanding, the EPS could be diluted by an increase in the number of shares of common outstanding. That is, if the same amount of earnings available to common stockholders were allocated to more shares of stock, earnings would be less for each share. EPS is sometimes called **primary earnings per share** or **basic earnings per share** to differentiate it from earnings after dilution.

EPS after dilution assumes that all convertible securities have been converted into the common. Because of tax adjustments, the calculations for figuring EPS after dilution can be complicated.

Dividends Per Share The **dividends per share** is simply the dollar amount of cash dividends paid on each common share during the year.

$$\text{Current yield} = \frac{\text{Annual cash dividends}}{\text{No. of common shartes outstanding}}$$

Current Yield (Dividend Yield) A common stock's **current yield**, like the current yield on bonds, expresses the annual dividend payout as a percentage of the current stock price.

$$\text{Current yield} = \frac{\text{Annual dividends per common share}}{\text{Market value per common share}}$$

Dividend Payout Ratio The **dividend payout ratio** measures the proportion of earnings paid to stockholders as dividends.

$$\text{Dividend payout ratio} = \frac{\text{Annual dividends per common share}}{\text{Earnings per share (EPS)}}$$

In general, older companies pay out larger percentages of earnings as dividends. Utilities as a group have an especially high payout ratio. Growth companies normally have the lowest ratios because they reinvest their earnings in the businesses. Companies on the way up hope to reward stockholders with gains in the stock value rather than with high dividend income.

Price/Earnings Ratio The widely used **price/earnings (PE) ratio** provides investors with a rough idea of the relationship between the prices of different common stocks compared to the earnings that accrue to one share of stock.

$$\text{PE / ratio} = \frac{\text{Current market price of common stock}}{\text{Earnings per share (EPS)}}$$

Growth companies usually have higher PE ratios than cyclical companies. Investors are willing to pay more per dollar of current earnings if a company's future earnings are expected to be dramatically higher than earnings for stocks that rise and fall with business cycles. Companies subject to cyclical fluctuations generally sell at lower PEs; declining industries sell at still lower PEs. Investors should beware of extremely high or extremely low PEs. Speculative stocks often sell at one extreme or the other.

If a stock's market price and PE ratio are known, the earnings per share can be calculated as follows:

$$\text{EPS} = \text{Current market price of common stock} / \text{PE ratio}$$

Test Topic Alert!

A quick rundown of the most testable points about ratios follows.

- Low debt-equity ratios are considered more conservative than high debt-equity ratios.
- The acid-test ratio is a more stringent measurement of liquidity than the current ratio.
- Book value is the company's theoretical liquidation value expressed on a per share basis.
- Speculative companies typically have very high or very low PE ratios.
- Growth companies have higher PE ratios than cyclical companies.
- Earnings per share relates only to common stock; it assumes preferred dividends were paid.

Quick Quiz 14.8 Match each of the following terms with the appropriate item.

A. Liquidity
B. Capitalization
C. Valuation

___ 1. Price/earnings ratio

___ 2. Earnings per share

___ 3. Current ratio

___ 4. Bond ratio

Answers 1. **C.**   2. **C.**   3. **A.**   4. **B.**

Quick Quiz 14.9 Choose T (Technical analysis) or F (Fundamental analysis):

___ 1. Concerned with the overall economy

___ 2. Interested in corporate annual reports

___ 3. Concerned with daily trading volumes on the NYSE

___ 4. Studies support and resistance diagrams

___ 5. May follow the odd-lot trading theory

___ 6. Concerned with a company's financial strength within an industry

___ 7. Concerned with structure and use of a company's capital

Answers 1. *F.*   2. *F.*   3. *T.*   4. *T.*   5. *T.*
 6. *F.*   7. *F.*

Economics & Analysis HotSheet

Business Cycle:
- **Expansion**: low unemployment, increased business activities
- **Peak**
- **Contraction**: falling stock markets, rising inventories, decreasing GDP
- **Trough**: (Recession = 6 months of declining GDP; Depression = 6 quarters of declining GDP) accompanied by high unemployment

CPI:
- Measures inflation through comparison of constant dollars

Leading Indicators:
- Money supply; building permits; number of unemployment claims; orders; stock prices

Coincident Indicators:
- Personal income; GDP; industrial production

Lagging Indicators:
- Duration of unemployment; corporate profits; commercial loans outstanding

Economic Theories:
- **Keynes**: aggregate demand; government intervention encouraged
- **Friedman**: monetarist theory; quantity of money determines price levels
- **Laffer**: supply-side economics; government should reduce spending and taxes

Money Supply:
- M1 = currency and demand deposits
- M2 = M1 + money markets, savings accounts, overnight repos
- M3 = M2 + large time deposits, longer repos

Fiscal Policy:
- Taxation; spending by Congress and president

Monetary Policy:
- FRB's tools: discount rate, reserve requirement (greatest impact) and FOMC (most used)

Economics & Analysis HotSheet

Technical Analysis:
- Charting; market timing; price predictions based on trends

Technical Theories:
- **Dow theory**: confirms end of market trends; changes in stock prices reflected by indexes
- **Odd-lot theory**: do the opposite of the small investor
- **Short interest theory**: large amount of short interest is bullish
- **MPT**: focuses on portfolio relationships; efficient markets
- **Random walk**: direction of stock market or prices is unpredictable

Fundamental Analysis:
- Study of a company's prospects based on overall economy, financial statements

Industry Analysis:
- Defensive: food, tobacco, pharmaceuticals, utilities
- Cyclical: heavy machinery
- Growth: technology (low dividend payouts)

Balance Sheet:
- Assets – liabilities = net worth;
- Assets = liabilities + net worth
- Used to compute capitalization and liquidity ratios

Income Statement:
- Summarizes revenues and expenses to determine efficiency and profitability

Ratios:
- Capitalization: debt/equity; bond ratio; common stock ratio
- Liquidity: current ratio; acid-test ratio
- Valuation: PE ratio; current yield; dividend payout ratio
- Working capital: current assets – current liabilities

Series 7 Unit Test 14

1. A fundamental analyst is concerned with all of the following EXCEPT

   A. historical earnings trends
   B. inflation rates
   C. capitalization
   D. trading volumes

2. Which of the following is a lagging economic indicator?

   A. S&P 500
   B. Housing permits issued
   C. Corporate profits
   D. Hours worked

3. Disintermediaton is a movement of funds which results when what occurs?

   I. The money supply tightens.
   II. The FRB increases reserve requirements.
   III. Money market rates are higher than typical savings account rates.
   IV. The discount rate is decreased by FRB.

   A. I, II and III
   B. I and III
   C. II and IV
   D. I, II, III and IV

4. All of the following ratios are measures of the liquidity of a corporation EXCEPT

   A. acid-test ratio
   B. debt-to-equity ratio
   C. current ratio
   D. quick ratio

5. The FOMC purchases T-bills in the open market. Which of the following scenarios are likely to occur?

   I. Secondary bond prices will rise.
   II. Secondary bond prices will fall.
   III. Interest rates will rise.
   IV. Interest rates will fall.

   A. I and III
   B. I and IV
   C. II and III
   D. II and IV

6. Which of the following statements regarding the economics of fixed-income securities are TRUE?

   I. Short-term rates are more volatile than long-term rates.
   II. Long-term rates are more volatile than short-term rates.
   III. Short-term bond prices react more than long-term bond prices given a change in interest rates.
   IV. Long-term bond prices react more than short-term bond prices given a change in interest rates.

   A. I and III
   B. I and IV
   C. II and III
   D. II and IV

7. Which of the following interest rates is considered the most volatile?

   A. Discount rate
   B. Federal funds rate
   C. Prime rate
   D. Broker call loan rate

8. To tighten credit during inflationary periods, the Federal Reserve Board can take any of the following actions EXCEPT to

   A. raise reserve requirements
   B. increase the amount of US government debt held by primary dealers
   C. sell securities in the open market
   D. lower taxes

9. Which of the following is a leading economic indicator?

    A. Stock market index
    B. Gross domestic product
    C. Duration of unemployment claims
    D. Industrial production

10. Which of the following are used by the Federal Reserve to control the money supply?

    I. Open market operations
    II. Setting reserve requirements for member banks
    III. Setting the discount rate
    IV. Setting the fed funds rate

    A. I, II and III only
    B. I and III only
    C. II and IV only
    D. I, II, III and IV

11. If the US dollar depreciates in value, which of the following statements is NOT true?

    A. The same amount of yen would buy more dollars.
    B. The balance of payments deficit probably would be reduced.
    C. Foreign goods would become more expensive in the U.S.
    D. Travel abroad would be less expensive for Americans.

12. Which organization or governmental unit sets fiscal policy?

    A. Federal Reserve Board (FRB)
    B. Government Economic Board
    C. Congress and the President
    D. Secretary of the Treasury

13. Which of the following economists is(was) a supporter of demand-side economics?

    A. Adam Smith
    B. John Maynard Keynes
    C. Arthur Laffer
    D. Milton Friedman

14. ABC, with 3 million shares outstanding, reports after-tax earnings of $7½ million. Annual cash dividends total $1.00 per share. The dividend payout ratio is

    A. 20%
    B. 25%
    C. 33%
    D. 40%

15. Which of the following stocks is regarded as a defensive stock?

    A. Aerospace stock
    B. Stock selling close to its support level
    C. Stock with a strong cash position and a low ratio of debt
    D. Electric utility stock

16. If XYZ Corporation sells an additional 1,000,000 common stock with a par value of $1 for $10 per share, which of the following is TRUE?

    A. Its EPS will increase.
    B. Its paid-in surplus will increase.
    C. Its liquidity ratio will decrease.
    D. Current ratio will decrease.

17. Which of the following four corporations is MOST likely a growth company?

	ABC	DEF	GHI	JKL
EPS	$1.10	$1.25	$1.50	$1.90
Div.	0	.25	.75	1.33

    A. ABC
    B. DEF
    C. GHI
    D. JKL

18. Stock market indices such as the S&P 500 and the DJIA are declining daily but the number of declining stocks relative to advancing stocks is falling. A technical analyst would conclude that the market is

    A. overbought
    B. oversold
    C. becoming volatile
    D. unstable

Series 7 Unit Test 14 Answers & Rationale

1. **D.** A fundamental analyst is concerned with the economic climate, the inflation rate, how an industry is performing, a company's historical earnings trends, how it is capitalized, and its product lines, management, and balance sheet ratios. A technical analyst is concerned with trading volumes or market trends and prices.
QID: 28286

2. **C.** Both the S & P 500 and housing permits are leading indicators. The measure of hours worked also is a leading indicator as it reflects changes in the average work week during the current period of time. Corporate profits are a lagging indicator. QID: 28244

3. **A.** Money flowing from banks and thrifts into money market instruments is known as disintermediation which tends to occur when money is tight and rates are rising, making money funds more attractive than passbook savings rates.
QID: 35186

4. **B.** Liquidity ratios measure a firm's ability to meet its current financial obligations and include the current ratio and acid-test (quick) ratio. However, the debt-to-equity ratio is a capitalization ratio, and measures the amount of leverage compared to equity in a company's overall capital structure. QID: 30562

5. **B.** When the Federal Open Market Committee purchases T-bills in the open market, it pays for the transaction by increasing member banks' reserve accounts, the net effect of which increases the total money supply and signals a period of relatively easier credit conditions. Easier credit means interest rates will decline and therefore the price for existing or secondary bonds will rise. QID: 28259

6. **B.** There are two separate issues in this question: the volatility of rates and volatility of bond prices. Short-term rates are more volatile than long-term rates and will move quicker than long-term rates. The most volatile interest rate in the US economy is the federal funds rate, which is an overnight rate of interest. Given a change in rates, long-term bond prices move more than short-term bond prices due to the compounding effect over a much longer period of time.
QID: 36418

7. **B.** The federal funds rate is the interest rate that banks with excess reserves charge other banks that are associated with the Federal Reserve System and that need overnight loans to meet reserve requirements. Because the federal funds rate tends to fluctuate daily, it is the most sensitive indicator of interest rate direction. QID: 32155

8. **D.** To curb inflation, the Fed can sell securities in the open market, thus changing the amount of US government debt institutions hold. It can also raise the reserve requirements, discount rate, or margin requirements. The Fed has no control over taxes, which are changed by Congress.
QID: 28273

9. **A.** Stock market indices are generally leading indicators. GDP and industrial production are coincident indicators; the duration of unemployment claims is a lagging indicator. QID: 28241

10. **A.** The fed funds rate is a market rate of interest heavily influenced by, but not set by, the Fed. QID: 35122

11. **D.** If the dollar is devalued, travel abroad for Americans will become more expensive. Because the dollar is worth less, it will buy fewer London theater tickets, Swiss watches, and French perfumes. QID: 29515

12. **C.** Congress and the President set fiscal policy, while the FRB sets monetary policy.
QID: 28261

13. B. John Maynard Keynes was the first demand-side economist; he believed that by increasing the income available for spending and saving, a government could increase demand and improve the country's economic wellbeing. Higher taxes and higher government spending are key tenets of this theory. QID: 28248

14. D. First compute earnings per share by dividing $7.5 million by the 3 million shares outstanding to get $2.50. Then divide the $1 dividend by $2.50 to get a 40% dividend payout ratio. The corporation paid out 40% of earnings to its shareholders. QID: 35078

15. D. Analysts regard a defensive stock as one that is in an industry that is least affected by business cycles. Most defensive industries produce nondurable consumer goods (for example, the food industry or the utility industry). QID: 29509

16. B. Paid-in surplus is a balance sheet entry which accounts for money raised from the issuance of stock in excess of par value. When more shares are sold, paid-in surplus will increase. QID: 30571

17. A. A growth company pays out very little in dividends and retains most of its earnings to fund future growth. ABC Corporation has the highest retained earnings ratio and is most likely to be a growth company. QID: 35258

18. B. The momentum of the market decline seems to be easing as the number of decliners to advancers is leveling out. It looks like the advance/decline line is moving in a direction away from decliners. A technical analyst would conclude that the market is oversold and is approaching a bottom. QID: 36589

15

Ethics, Recommendations & Taxation

INTRODUCTION

This unit reviews the importance of strict ethical standards in the securities industry. When registered representatives deal with customers, providing suitable recommendations is a critical aspect of the relationship. To offer suitable investment recommendations, a rep must consider the customer's financial objectives, financial status, investment constraints, and tax situation.

Tax considerations will often be an important consideration in selecting an investment. Income-oriented investors, in particular, must be aware of the after-tax returns of investment alternatives. When securities are sold, the cost basis of the original investment must be calculated.

Expect to see 10–15 questions on ethics, recommendations, and taxation on the Series 7 exam.

UNIT OBJECTIVES

When you have completed this unit, you should be able to:

- describe a registered representative's ethical responsibility to the public;
- list and describe at least 10 prohibited customer account practices;
- identify financial and nonfinancial criteria essential to customer recommendations;
- define the basic types of investment risks;
- compare and contrast various portfolio management strategies;
- describe the tax treatment of investment income and capital gains or losses;
- calculate the adjusted cost basis of bonds purchased at a premium or discount; and
- contrast progressive and regressive taxes and give examples of each.

Ethics in the Securities Industry

Ethical Business Practices

The securities industry is governed by a very strict code of ethics. Unacceptable behavior is subject to sanctions ranging from fines and reprimands to expulsion from the industry and/or jail. Business behavior and practices are measured against clear standards for fairness and equity.

Securities industry regulators work to prevent and detect unethical behavior. Investigators regularly examine activity at all levels—from large firms and investment advisers, to registered reps and individual investors. Even the most junior of broker/dealer employees is expected to adhere to high standards of business ethics and commercial honor in dealing with the public.

Corporate Ethics and Responsibility

The rules that guide relationships between members of the securities industry and all other participants are set by the states, **North American Securities Administrators Association (NASAA)**, NASD, SEC, MSRB, and other regulatory bodies and exchanges throughout the country.

The federal securities acts, state laws, **NASAA's Statement of Policy on Unethical Business Practices of Investment Advisers**, NASD Manual, NYSE Constitution and Rules, and various other legislative acts governing securities all contain guidelines for acceptable behavior. It is the responsibility of broker/dealers, investment advisers, registered representatives, and others in the securities industry to understand and follow these guidelines.

One aspect of corporate responsibility for ethical behavior involves a commitment to **self-regulation**. It is every broker/dealer's duty to supervise all of its associated persons. Each firm must have a **written procedures manual** and must designate one or more supervisors (principals) responsible for enforcing its rules.

The principal must review and approve all correspondence and keep a record of all securities transactions and correspondence. Member firms must regularly review all branch office activities to detect and discipline any individuals who engage in unethical behavior. Member firms' compliance departments generally conduct such reviews.

Customer Ethics and Responsibility

Practices (such as insider trading) that provide an unfair advantage to certain investors over the general public are strictly prohibited. The individual investor must abide by the regulations that guide customer ethics.

It is the customer's responsibility to provide **full and honest disclosure** to his registered rep or investment adviser. The rep or adviser will base recommendations on information the customer provides. A customer's failure to provide information could result in inappropriate recommendations, and is a red flag to compliance departments.

Test Topic Alert! Several points on ethical business practices follow.

- All broker/dealers are required to maintain written supervisory procedures.
- A principal is responsible for enforcing the rules of the broker/dealer.
- A broker/dealer may have its own house rules that can be more stringent than those of the self-regulatory organization (SRO), but these rules can never be less stringent.
- The NASD Conduct Rules deal with ethical treatment of customers.

Prohibited Business Practices

The following practices in customer dealings are prohibited at all times.

Manipulative and Fraudulent Devices NASD member firms are strictly prohibited from using manipulative, deceptive, or other fraudulent tactics or methods to induce a security's sale or purchase. The statute of limitations under the Act of 1934 is three years from the alleged manipulation and within one year of discovering it. No dollar limit is placed on damages in lawsuits based on allegations of manipulation.

Outside Business Activity An associated person cannot work for any business other than his member firm (**independent activity**) without his employing broker/dealer's knowledge. If a registered person wants to be employed by, or accept compensation from, an entity other than the member firm, that person must provide written notice to the member. The firm has the right to reject or restrict any outside affiliation if a conflict of interest exists.

Private Securities Transactions A **passive investment**, such as the purchase of a limited partnership unit, is not considered an outside business activity, even if the purchaser receives money as a result of the investment. An associated person may make a passive investment for his own account without providing written notice to or receiving written approval from the employing broker/dealer.

The NASD's Conduct Rules define a **private securities transaction** as any sale of securities outside an associated person's regular business and his employing member. Private securities transactions are also known as **selling away**.

Notification

If an associated person wishes to enter into a private securities transaction, that person must:

- provide prior written notice to his employer;

- describe in detail the proposed transaction;
- describe in detail his proposed role in the transaction; and
- disclose if he has or may receive compensation for the transaction.

With Compensation. If the transaction involves compensation, the employing member may approve or disapprove the associated person's participation. If the member approves the participation, it must treat the transaction as if it is being done on its own behalf by entering the transaction on its own books and supervising the associated person during the transaction. If the member disapproves the transaction, the associated person may not participate in it.

Without Compensation. If the associated person has not received or will not receive compensation for the private securities transaction, the employing member must acknowledge that it has received written notification and may require the associated person to adhere to specified conditions during his participation.

Transactions that the associated person enters into on behalf of immediate family members and for which the associated person receives no compensation are excluded from the definition of private securities transactions.

Recommendations Investment **recommendations** must be consistent with customer needs, financial capability, objectives, and risk tolerance. Investment recommendations should be in a customer's best interest—not the registered representative's. Each investment (especially its risks) should be explained fully. At no time should customers own an investment that could put them at risk beyond their financial capacity.

Fair Dealing

The NASD's **Conduct Rules** and the laws of most states require broker/dealers, registered representatives, and investment advisers to inquire into a customer's financial situation before making any recommendation to buy, sell, or exchange securities. This includes determining the client's other security holdings, income, net worth, and financial goals and objectives.

The following activities violate the fair dealing rules.

- Recommending any investment that is not suitable for the customer's financial situation and risk tolerance
- Short-term trading of mutual funds
- Setting up fictitious accounts to transact business that otherwise would be prohibited
- Making unauthorized transactions or use of funds
- Recommending purchases inconsistent with customer ability to pay

Ethics in the Securities Industry

- Committing fraudulent acts, such as forgery and the omission or misstatement of material facts

Excessive Trading **Excessive trading** in a customer's account to generate commissions, rather than to help achieve the customer's stated investment objectives, is an abuse of fiduciary responsibility known as **churning**. Churning occurs due to excessive frequency or excessive size of transactions.

To prevent such abuses, self-regulatory organizations require that a principal of the member firm review all accounts, especially those in which a registered rep or an investment adviser has discretionary authority.

Influencing Employees of Other Firms Broker/dealers cannot distribute business-related compensation (cash or noncash gifts or gratuities) to the employees of other member firms. However, a broker/dealer may give other firms' employees some form of compensation without violating the rules providing:

- the compensation is not conditional on sales or promises of sales;
- it has the employing member's prior approval; and
- the compensation's total value does not exceed the annual limit set by the NASD Board of Governors (currently $100 per year) or the MSRB (currently $100 per year).

✓ *Take Note:* These rules permit occasional noncash expenditures that exceed the $100 limit, such as dinners, seminars, tickets to entertainment events, or reminder advertising. Vacations or season tickets are always violations.

Employment Contracts This rule does not apply to legitimate employment contracts in which an employee of one firm supplies or performs services for another firm. The leasing of another firm's employee is acceptable provided a written employment agreement specifies the employment duties and compensation and the person's employer, the temporary employer, and the employee give their written consent.

Selling Dividends It is improper to recommend that an investor buy mutual fund shares just before a dividend distribution. The fund shares' market value will decrease by the distribution amount and the customer will incur a tax liability on the distribution.

A registered rep is forbidden to encourage an investor to purchase shares before a distribution because of this tax liability and doing so is a violation known as **selling dividends**.

Breakpoint Sales In a **breakpoint sale**, a customer unknowingly buys investment company shares in an amount just below an amount that would qualify the investment for a reduction in sales charges. As a result, the customer pays a higher dollar amount in sales charges, which reduces the number of shares purchased and increases the cost basis per share.

Encouraging a customer to purchase in such a manner, or remaining silent when a customer unknowingly requests such a transaction, is unethical and violates the NASD Conduct Rules.

Borrowing and Lending
Firms that permit lending arrangements between representatives and customers must have written procedures in place to monitor such activity. Registered persons who wish to borrow from or lend money to customers are required to provide prior written notice of the proposed arrangement to the firm and the firm must approve the arrangement in writing.

NASD rules permit five types of lending arrangements:

- there is an immediate family relationship between the rep and the customer;
- the customer is in the business of lending money (e.g. a bank);
- the customer and the rep are both registered persons with the same firm;
- the customer and the rep have a personal relationship outside of the broker-customer relationship; and
- the customer and the rep have a business relationship outside of the broker-customer relationship.

✓ *Take Note:* Before borrowing from or lending to a customer, a rep must advise his firm in writing and receive written permission.

Misrepresentations
Registered reps and investment advisers may not misrepresent themselves or their services to clients or potential clients. Included in this prohibition are misrepresentations covering:

- qualifications, experience, education;
- nature of services offered; and
- fees to be charged.

It is a misrepresentation to inaccurately state or fail to state a material fact regarding any of these.

Research Reports
An investment adviser or a broker/dealer is prohibited from presenting to a client research reports, analyses, or recommendations prepared by other persons or firms without disclosing the fact that the adviser did not prepare them. An adviser or a broker/dealer may base a recommendation on reports or analyses prepared by others, as long as these reports are not represented as the adviser's or broker/dealer's own.

Guarantees and Sharing in Customer Accounts
Broker/dealers, investment advisers, and registered representatives cannot guarantee any customer against a loss or guarantee that he will achieve a gain. Members, advisers, and representatives are also prohibited from sharing in any profits or losses in a customer's account. An exception is made if a joint account has received the member firm's prior written approval and

the registered representative shares in the profits and losses only to the extent of his proportionate contribution to the joint account.

If the member firm authorizes such a **shared account**, any such sharing must be **directly proportionate** to the financial contributions each party makes. If a member or an associated person shares an account with a member of that person's immediate family, directly proportionate sharing of profits and losses is not required.

Immediate family members include parents, siblings, spouses, in-laws, and children. It also includes any person who is financially dependent on the employee.

Misuse of Nonpublic Information Every investment adviser must establish, maintain, and enforce written policies and procedures to prevent the use of nonpublic inside information.

Abuse of Fiduciary Information During the normal course of business, employees of member firms will have access to proprietary information regarding individual customers and securities issuers. Such information is to be treated with strict confidentiality.

Confidentiality of Customer Information

Broker/dealer and investment adviser employees may not divulge any personal information about customers without a customer's express permission. This includes security positions, personal and financial details, and trading intentions.

Numbered Accounts

For privacy reasons, a customer may have a designated account identified with a number or a letter rather than a name if the member has a signed statement from the customer claiming ownership of that account.

Confidentiality of Issuer Information

When a member broker/dealer serves an issuer as a paying agent, transfer agent, underwriter, or in another similar capacity, the member has established a fiduciary relationship with that issuer. In this role, the member may obtain confidential information.

The member cannot use information it obtains through its fiduciary role unless the securities issuer specifically asks and authorizes the member to do so.

✓ **Take Note:** NASD rules basically tell reps to never lie, cheat, or steal when dealing with customers.

Criminal Penalties A person convicted of willfully violating federal securities regulation or of knowingly making false or misleading statements in a registration document can be fined up to $1 million, sentenced to prison for not more than 10 years, or both. The maximum fine is $2 million for other than a natural person (broker/dealers or other businesses).

Assistance to Foreign Authorities The SEC is pledged to help foreign regulatory authorities investigate any person who has violated any laws or rules relating to securities matters.

Quick Quiz 15.1

Match each of the following terms with the appropriate description below.

A. Selling away
B. Breakpoint sale
C. Selling dividends
D. Material facts
E. Excessive trading

___ 1. Encouraging a purchase below the amount that would qualify for a reduction in sales load

___ 2. Omitting these in a recommendation violates NASD rules

___ 3. Encouraging a customer purchase just prior to a distribution

___ 4. Also called churning

___ 5. A prohibited practice without the broker/dealer's knowledge and consent

Answers 1. **B.**   2. **D.**   3. **C.**   4. **E.**   5. **A.**

Other Unethical Trading Practices

Transactions intended to portray an artificial market for a stock are prohibited.

Painting the Tape When one party sells stock to another with the understanding that the stock will be repurchased later in the day at virtually the same price, it is known as **painting the Tape**. The intent of such transactions is to make it appear that far more activity in a stock exists than actually does.

Matching   **Matching transactions** in an attempt to create the impression of a hot market for a stock is prohibited. Matching involves two parties working in collusion, where one customer enters an order to buy while a second person enters an order to sell the same stock, at the same time, at virtually the same price, through the same broker/dealer. The broker/dealer crosses the buy and sell orders and reports the trade to the Tape, thus showing a trade where one really did not occur.

Broker/dealers must not enter orders for the purchase or sale of securities with the knowledge that contra orders for the same stock, in the same amount, at approximately the same price have been or will be placed for the same customer or for different parties working in concert.

Participating in Rings or Pools   Broker/dealers cannot participate directly or indirectly in any pool, ring, syndicate, or other joint account venture formed for the purpose of rigging or otherwise influencing market prices.

Payments Designed to Influence Market Prices   NASD member firms are prohibited from attempting to influence the market price of securities by paying for favorable reviews, articles, or other mention in newspapers or other financial publications. This prohibition does not apply to paid advertisements placed in these publications and marked as such.

Spreading False Information   Broker/dealers must not promote or disseminate false or misleading information.

Front Running   If a firm or any associated person has non-public knowledge of an impending block order to buy or sell, that firm or person cannot place an order in front of the block order. For purposes of this rule, a block order is an order for 10,000 shares or more.

> ✓ **For Example:** Assume a representative has non-public knowledge of an impending order to buy 100,000 shares of a Nasdaq stock. If the representative places an order to buy stock for his personal account in front of the order, the representative would likely benefit from a free ride as the stock would rise on the execution of a large block.

Capping   Any attempt to place selling pressure on a stock to keep a price low or move it lower is known as capping and is prohibited.

Ethical behavior in the securities industry can be summarized as follows:

- Do not fabricate information.
- Disclose any conflicts of interest.
- Know which investments are suitable for your customers' needs.

Ethics, Recommendations & Taxation

Quick Quiz 15.2
Match each of the following terms with the appropriate description below.

A. Front running
B. Capping
C. Matching
D. Painting the Tape

___ 1. Placing pressure on a stock's price to keep it low

___ 2. Selling stock to a party with the understanding that repurchase will occur later in the day

___ 3. Trading in front of a pending block order

___ 4. A broker/dealer placing simultaneous buy and sell orders in a stock for the purpose of staging a hot market

Answers   1. **B.**   2. **D.**   3. **A.**   4. **C.**

Quick Quiz 15.3 Multiple Choice

1. Under the Securities Exchange Act of 1934, a lawsuit alleging market manipulation must be filed within

   A. 3 years of the activity and 1 year of discovering it
   B. 1 year of the activity and 3 years of discovering it
   C. 5 years of the activity and 3 years of discovering it
   D. 3 years of the activity and 5 years of discovering it

2. A member firm accepts a limit order from a customer to buy 100 shares of GIZ at 27. Which two of the following can the member do before executing the customer's order?

   I. Buy 100 shares of GIZ for its own trading account at 27.
   II. Buy 100 shares of GIZ for its investment account at 27.
   III. Sell 100 shares of GIZ for another customer at 27.13.
   IV. Buy 100 shares of GIZ for another customer at 27.

   A. I and II
   B. I and III
   C. II and IV
   D. III and IV

3. A registered representative signs an agreement to borrow money from a customer. This is permitted under which of the following circumstances?

   A. With written permission from a firm
   B. With written permission from the NASD
   C. If the customer is a bank
   D. Under no circumstances

4. A registered representative is also an amateur filmmaker. He and his film colleagues decide to form a limited partnership to produce a short film. Before acting as a general partner in this enterprise, the rep must

   I. provide written notice to his employer
   II. provide his employer with a list of the limited partners' names
   III. comply with blue-sky laws
   IV. comply with SEC regulations

   A. I only
   B. I, III and IV only
   C. I and IV only
   D. II, III and IV only

Answers

1. **A.** According to the 1934 act, the statute of limitations extends for three years from an alleged manipulative act and for one year after the manipulative act is discovered.

2. **D.** A member firm may execute for the firm's own account only at prices above a customer's outstanding buy limit. However, the firm can execute trades for other customers at the same price (the trader should use time priority for customer limit orders).

3. **C.** The prohibition against borrowing money from customers does not include customers in the business of lending money. Otherwise, borrowing money or securities from customers is strictly prohibited.

4. **B.** Forming a limited partnership requires compliance with state and federal laws regarding registration or exemption of securities. Also, the NASD considers this activity an outside business activity, so the representative must provide prior written notice to his employing firm. The NASD does not require the representative to provide the investors' names to the employing firm. If the representative will engage in selling limited partnership interests, the rules on selling away apply.

Investment Considerations and Suitability

Know Your Customer (NYSE Rule 405)

The NYSE requires brokers to know their customers. This implies understanding a customer's financial status (net worth and net income), investment objectives, and all facts essential in making suitable recommendations. It is a registered rep's responsibility to perform due diligence to determine the validity of a customer's information.

Nonfinancial Considerations A customer's **nonfinancial considerations** are often as important as his financial concerns. Therefore, a registered representative or an investment adviser should know the following:

- customer's age;
- customer's marital status;
- number and ages of customer's dependents;
- customer's employment status;
- employment of customer's family members; and
- customer's current and future financial needs.

Risk Tolerance and Investment Goals A customer's risk tolerance and investment goals are other important considerations that will shape his portfolio. To understand a customer's attitude about investment alternatives, the representative or adviser should ask the customer the following questions.

- What kind of risks can you afford to take?
- How liquid must your investments be?
- How important are tax considerations?
- Are you seeking long-term or short-term investments?
- What is your investment experience?
- What types of investments do you currently hold?

Customer Investment Outlook

Typical financial objectives that customers often have are outlined here.

Preservation of Capital For many people, the most important investment objective is to preserve their capital. In general, when clients speak of safety, they usually mean preservation of capital.

Current Income Many investors, particularly those on fixed incomes, want to generate current income from their investments.

Corporate bonds, municipal bonds, government and agency securities, income-oriented mutual funds, some stocks (including utilities and real estate investment trusts—REITs), money market funds, annuities, and some direct participation programs (DPPs) are among the investments that can contribute current income through dividend or interest payments.

The Investment Pyramid

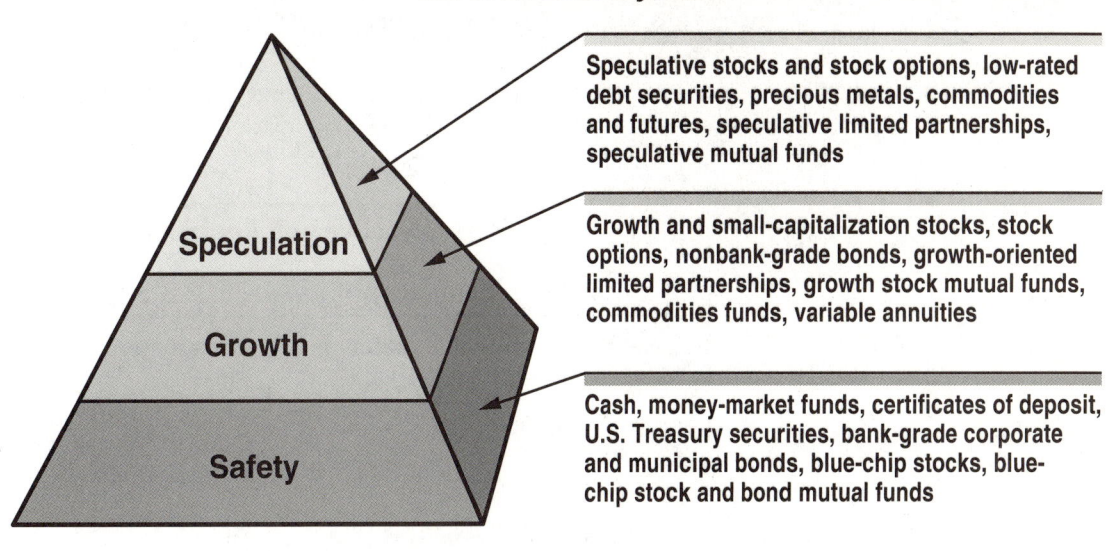

Pyramid levels (top to bottom): **Speculation**, **Growth**, **Safety**

- **Speculation**: Speculative stocks and stock options, low-rated debt securities, precious metals, commodities and futures, speculative limited partnerships, speculative mutual funds
- **Growth**: Growth and small-capitalization stocks, stock options, nonbank-grade bonds, growth-oriented limited partnerships, growth stock mutual funds, commodities funds, variable annuities
- **Safety**: Cash, money-market funds, certificates of deposit, U.S. Treasury securities, bank-grade corporate and municipal bonds, blue-chip stocks, blue-chip stock and bond mutual funds

Capital Growth — **Growth** refers to an increase in an investment's value over time. This can come from increases in the security's value, the reinvestment of distributions, or both. The most common growth-oriented investments are common stock and common stock mutual funds.

Tax Advantages — Investors often seek ways to reduce their taxes. Some vehicles, like **individual retirement accounts (IRAs)** and annuities, allow earnings to accumulate tax deferred (an investor pays no taxes until he withdraws money from his account). Other products, like municipal bonds, offer tax-free interest income.

Portfolio Diversification — Investors with portfolios concentrated in one or just a few securities or investments are exposed to much higher risks and the value of the entire portfolio can be wiped out if one investment or industry performs poorly.

For these investors, **portfolio diversification** can be an important objective. These customers may be retirees with large profit-sharing distributions of one company's stock, or investors with all of their money invested in **certificates of deposit (CDs)** or US government bonds.

Liquidity — Some people want immediate access to their money at all times. A product is **liquid** if a customer can sell it quickly at a fair market price.

Stock, for instance, has varying degrees of liquidity, while DPPs, annuities, and bank CDs generally are considered illiquid. Real estate is the classic example of an illiquid investment because of the time and money it takes to convert it into cash. Money market funds are highly liquid and are often used for this purpose.

Speculation A customer may want to **speculate**—that is, try to earn much higher than average returns in exchange for higher than average risks.

Test Topic Alert! You may see several questions about recommendations based on a customer's investment objectives. The following table is a quick guide of key words to help with these questions.

Investor Objective and Recommendation

Investor Objective	Recommendation
Preservation of capital; safety	Government securities or Ginnie Maes
Growth	Common stock or common stock mutual funds
"Balanced" or "moderate" growth	Blue chip stocks
"Aggressive" growth/speculation	Technology stocks or sector funds
Income	Bonds–but not zero-coupons
Tax-free income	Municipal bonds or muni bond funds
High-yield income	Corporate bonds or corporate bond funds
Form an income-oriented stock portfolio	Preferred stock and utility stocks
Liquidity	Money-market funds (DPPs, real estate, and annuities are not considered liquid)
Keep pace with inflation	Stock portfolio

Quick Quiz 15.4 Multiple Choice

1. Which of the following characteristics best define(s) the term *growth*?

   A. Increase in the value of an investment over time
   B. Increase in principal and accumulating interest and dividends over time
   C. Investments that appreciate tax deferred
   D. All of the above

2. Which of the following investments is least appropriate for a client primarily concerned with liquidity?

   A. Preferred stock
   B. Municipal bond mutual funds
   C. Bank savings accounts
   D. Direct participation programs

3. Which of the following securities generates the greatest current income with moderate risk?

   A. Common stock of a new company
   B. Security convertible into the common stock of a company
   C. Fixed-income security
   D. Income bond

4. Which of the following investments is most suitable for an investor seeking monthly income?

   A. Zero-coupon bond
   B. Growth stock
   C. Mutual fund investing in small-cap issues
   D. GNMA mutual fund

Answers

1. **A.** Growth refers to an increase in the value of an investment over time. This growth can come from increases in the value of the security, the reinvestment of distributions, or both.

2. **D.** Direct participation programs or limited partnerships are illiquid investments because there is no immediate market for them.

3. **C.** Of the answers offered, to generate the greatest return a fixed-income security (a bond) is most suitable. Common stock is not suitable; convertibles (bonds or preferred) generally pay out a lower income rate than nonconvertibles because the investors receive benefit from the conversion feature; income bonds pay interest only if the corporation meets targeted earnings levels.

4. **D.** The GNMA mutual fund is the most suitable investment for an investor seeking monthly income. The other securities offer higher long-term growth potential but they are not designed to provide monthly income.

Suitability: Analyzing Financial Risks and Rewards

Because all investments involve trade-offs, the investment adviser's or registered representative's task is to select securities that provide the right balance between investor constraints and investment capabilities. Registered representatives are expected to make suitable investment recommendations for the customer.

Unsuitable Trades

Occasionally, a customer asks a registered rep to enter a trade that the rep believes is **unsuitable**. It is the representative's responsibility to explain why the trade might not be appropriate for the customer. If the customer insists on entering the transaction, the registered rep should consider having the customer sign a statement acknowledging that the rep advised against the trade, and the rep should mark the order ticket *Unsolicited*.

Investment Risks

In general terms, the greater the risk an investor assumes, the greater the potential for reward. Several types of risk must be considered in determining the suitability of various investment types.

Inflation Risk

Also known as **purchasing power risk**, inflation risk is the effect continually rising prices have on investment returns. If a bond's yield is lower than the inflation rate, the purchasing power of the client's money diminishes over time. A client who buys a bond or a fixed annuity is usually able to purchase far less with money distributed when the investment matures.

Capital Risk

Capital risk is the potential for an investor to lose some or all of his money—his invested capital—under circumstances unrelated to an issuer's financial strength.

Timing Risk

Even an investment in the strongest company with the most profit potential might do poorly simply because the investment was timed incorrectly. The risk to an investor of buying or selling at the wrong time and incurring losses or lower gains is known as **timing risk**.

Interest Rate Risk

Interest rate risk is the sensitivity of an investment's value to fluctuations in interest rates. This risk is generally associated with bonds because bond prices correspond inversely with interest rate changes. Bonds with long-term maturities, low coupons, or deep discounts are most susceptible to interest rate risk.

Reinvestment Risk When interest rates decline, it is difficult to invest proceeds from redemptions, calls, or investment distributions to maintain the same level of income without increasing credit or market risks.

Test Topic Alert! The Series 7 exam expects you to know that mortgage-backed instruments are susceptible to reinvestment risk.

When interest rates fall, mortgage holders typically refinance at lower rates. This means that they pay off their mortgages early, which causes a prepayment of principal to holders of mortgage-backed securities. The early principal payments cannot be reinvested at a comparable return.

Sometimes the test asks which instruments are not subject to reinvestment risk. Of the ones listed, the best answer to choose is typically a zero-coupon bond. Because no interest is paid on a current basis, the investor has no reinvestment risk.

Call Risk Related to reinvestment risk, **call risk** is the risk that a bond might be called before maturity and an investor will be unable to reinvest the principal at a comparable rate of return. When interest rates are falling, bonds with higher coupon rates are most likely to be called. Investors concerned about call risk should look for **call protection**—a period during which a bond cannot be called. Most corporate and municipal issuers generally provide some years of call protection.

Market Risk Both stocks and bonds involve some degree of **market risk**—that is, the risk that investors may lose some of their principal due to price volatility in the overall market (**systematic risk**). Stock market momentum may affect stock prices independently of matters affecting a particular corporation. Bond prices fluctuate with changing interest rates, and an inverse relationship between bond prices and bond yields exists: as bond yields rise, bond prices decline, and vice versa.

✓ **Take Note:** Systematic risk, or the risk of a general market decline, cannot be diversified away. Nonsystematic risk, also known as selection risk, is the risk that a single investment will not perform. Diversifying a portfolio minimizes nonsystematic risk.

Credit Risk **Credit risk**, also called **financial risk** or **default risk**, is the danger of losing one's invested principal through an issuer's failure. Credit risk varies with the investment product. Bonds backed by the federal government or most municipalities have low credit risk. Long-term bonds involve more credit risk than short-term bonds because of the future's uncertainty.

Liquidity (Marketability) Risk The risk that a client might not be able to sell his investment quickly at a fair market price is known as **liquidity** or **marketability risk**. The marketability of the securities a registered representative recommends must be consistent with the client's liquidity needs.

> ✓ **For Example:** Government bonds are sold easily, while DPPs are illiquid and extremely difficult to sell. Municipal securities have regional markets rather than a national market; therefore, they may be less marketable than more widely held securities.

Legislative Risk Congress has the power to change laws affecting securities. The risk that such legal changes might affect an investment adversely is known as **legislative risk** or **political risk**. When recommending suitable investments, a registered representative should warn clients of any pending changes in the law that may affect those investments.

Risk Measurements

In finance, risk is defined as the "uncertainty that an investment will earn its expected rate of return."

Beta A stock's **beta** is a measure of its volatility in relation to the overall market. Stocks with a beta of 1 move in line with the market; stocks with a beta greater than 1 are more volatile than the market; and stocks with a beta less than 1 move less than, or are less volatile than, the overall market.

> ✓ **For Example:** If the S&P 500 rises or falls by 10%, a stock with a beta of 1 rises or falls by about 10%; a stock with a beta of 1.5 rises or falls by about 15%; and a stock with a beta of 0.75 rises or falls by about 7.5%.

Beta measures a security's **systemic** (or **systematic**) **risk**—the risk that can be associated with the market in general. The higher the beta, the more volatile the stock. High betas imply greater capital gains in a rising market and greater potential losses in declining markets. High beta stocks are usually considered aggressive and low beta stocks are considered conservative. Risks specific to a stock, such as from competition, mismanagement, or product deficiencies, are independent of the general market. This is **nonsystematic risk**.

> ✓ **Take Note:** While a systematic risk to a portfolio cannot be diversified away, it can be hedged by purchasing OEX puts.

Correlation and Correlation Coefficient **Correlation** means that securities move in the same direction. A strong or perfect correlation means two securities prices move in a perfect positive linear relationship with each other.

> ✓ **For Example:** Two securities are correlated if one security's price rises by 5% and the other security's price then rises by 5%; or if one declines by 4%, the other will also decline by 4%.

The correlation coefficient is a number that ranges from -1 to +1. Securities that are perfectly correlated have a correlation coefficient of +1. Securities whose price movements are unrelated to each other have a correlation coefficient of 0. If prices move in perfectly opposite directions, they are negatively correlated or have a correlation coefficient of -1.

Standard Deviation

Standard deviation is a measure of the volatility of an investment's projected returns. The larger the standard deviation the larger the security's returns are expected to deviate from its average return, and, hence, the greater the risk.

Standard deviation is expressed in terms of percentage. A standard deviation of 7.5 means the return of a stock for a given period may vary by 7.5% above or below its predicted return.

✓ **For Example:** Security X has an expected return of 12% and a standard deviation of 5%. Investing in a security with an expected 12% return, an investor can expect the market price at any time to be 5% above or below the 12% rate at any point in time.

An investor can use standard deviation as a tool to compare the risk/reward between investments. If an investor has a choice between an investment that returned 12% with a standard deviation of 6% and another investment that also returned 12% but has a standard deviation of 10%, the investor would choose the first one. In effect, he would receive that same return for less risk.

✓ **Take Note:** Beta is a volatility measure of a security compared with the overall market; standard deviation is a volatility measure of a security compared with its expected performance.

Duration

Duration measures the time in years it takes for a bond to pay for itself.

✓ **For Example:** If a bond has a duration of 9, the owner of the bond will receive his investment back in 9 years.

Duration can also be used to measure the percentage change in price of a bond (or bond portfolio) as a result of a small change in interest rates. The formula is:

Percentage change in price = +/− duration × the change in interest rate

✓ **For Example:** If an investor owns a bond with a duration of nine years, the investor could estimate the price change the bond would experience if there were an increase 1% in interest rates.

To calculate the increase in the price of the bond, the investor would apply the formula as follows: − 9 (duration) × 1% increase in interest rates results in a 9% price decline in the bond.

The (–) sign is used before the duration measure because an increase in interest rates results in a decline in price. Had interest rates declined, a (+) sign is used because declining rates mean higher bond prices.

Test Topic Alert! The general properties of duration follow.

- The lower the coupon rate, the greater a bond's duration—likewise the higher the coupon rate, the lower the duration.
- The longer a bond's maturity the greater the bond's duration.
- For coupon bonds, duration is less than the bond's maturity.
- Duration for a zero-coupon bond is equal to its maturity.
- The higher a bond's duration, the more its value will change for a 1% change in interest rates; the lower the duration the less it will change.

✓ *Take Note:* The duration of a bond with coupon payments is always shorter than the maturity of the bond. By the same token, the duration of zero-coupon bonds is equal to its maturity.

✓ *For Example:* A 5-year zero coupon bond has a duration of 5 because it takes five years to get your money back; you get a single payment (par) at maturity five years after purchase.

Test Topic Alert! There are several types of risk measures. Some measures refer to historical or past risk and some to expected or future risk of individual securities or portfolios of securities. Other than the three types of measures listed above (beta, standard deviation, duration), take note of the following measures of risk.

- **Sharpe Measure**: A relative measure of a portfolio's benefit-to-risk ratio. The measure is calculated as the average return that is in excess of the risk-free rate divided by the standard deviation.
- **Treynor Measure**: A relative measure of portfolio benefit-to-risk like the Sharpe measure except that the average excess return is divided by the portfolio's beta as opposed to the standard deviation.
- **Correlation**: A measure of the extent to which securities move together. A correlation of +1 means the securities move in the same direction on a one-for-one basis. A correlation of -1 means the securities move in opposite directions.

Quick Quiz 15.5 Match each of the following items with the appropriate description below.

- A. Market risk
- B. Credit risk
- C. Marketability risk
- D. Purchasing power risk

___ 1. Also known as liquidity risk, or the risk that a security cannot be sold quickly at a fair market price

___ 2. Also known as inflation risk, or the risk of continually rising prices on investments

___ 3. Also known as default risk, or the risk that principal may be lost due to issuer failure

___ 4. Also known as systematic risk, or the risk that principal may be lost due to price volatility

Answers   *1.* **C.**   *2.* **D.**   *3.* **B.**   *4.* **A.**

Portfolio Management

A **portfolio** is an individual's combined investment holdings. A portfolio of securities offers investors **diversification**.

Many things influence a portfolio's makeup, including personal and market factors. A portfolio of securities appropriate for a 25-year-old unmarried man may not be appropriate for a 45-year-old married man with two children in college or a 65-year-old woman facing retirement.

Defensive investment strategies may have growth or income as an objective, but safety of principal tends to be the top priority. Such portfolios often are invested in blue chip stocks with moderate or low volatility and AAA or government bonds.

Examples of defensive stock include food, utility, and drug companies. These stocks tend to hold their value during poor economic times.

Aggressive investment strategies attempt to maximize investment returns by assuming higher risks. Such strategies include:

- selecting highly volatile stocks;
- buying securities on margin; and
- using put and call option strategies.

Most investors adopt a combination of aggressive and defensive strategies when making decisions about the securities in their portfolios. A **balanced**, or mixed, portfolio holds securities of many types.

Modern Portfolio Theory and Risk Management

Modern portfolio theory is an approach that attempts to quantify and control portfolio risk. It differs from traditional securities analysis in that it emphasizes determining the relationship between risk and reward in the total portfolio rather than analyzing specific securities. This is derived from the **Capital Asset Pricing Model (CAPM)**.

Where investments are concerned, **risk** is normally associated with losing money. Investors use many techniques to reduce the potential for portfolio losses. Some of the most common are discussed here.

Diversification

Diversification (buying different types of securities in various economic sectors) is a widely used investment strategy. A portfolio can be diversified in many ways, including:

- type of instrument (equity, debt, packaged, etc.);
- industry;
- companies within an industry;
- length of maturity;
- investment rating; and
- geography.

By mixing industries and types of securities, investors attempt to spread their risk.

✓ *Take Note:* With regard to a domestic bond portfolio, diversification by geography is relevant if the portfolio consists of municipal bonds. However, if the portfolio consists of corporate bonds, geographical diversification is not relevant. For example, it does not matter if IBM is based in New York or Illinois.

Dollar Cost Averaging

Dollar cost averaging involves periodic purchases of a fixed dollar amount in one or more common stocks or mutual funds. In a fluctuating market, the average cost of the stock purchased in this manner is always less than the average market price. Dollar cost averaging does not guarantee against loss (it is fraudulent to imply so), but it does help control the cost of investing.

Constant Ratio Plan

In a **constant ratio plan**, an investor buys or sells securities in a manner that keeps the portfolio balanced between equity and debt securities. The investor initially sets an equity-to-debt ratio, such as 60% equity and 40% debt, and buys or sells stocks and bonds to maintain the ratio.

Constant Dollar Plan

The **constant dollar plan**'s primary goal is to buy and sell securities so that a set dollar amount remains invested at all times.

By using this technique, the client sells as prices rise and buys as prices fall, thus selling when the market rallies and buying when the market declines.

Measuring Stock Price Volatility

Volatility is the speed and degree with which a stock's price will change. The two most common analytical tools for measuring stock volatility are **alpha** and **beta**.

Alpha   A stock's **alpha** is a measure of its projected rate of change in price independent of market-related factors. If all other factors are equal and the market remains at the same level for a year, the price of a stock with an alpha of 1.5 could be expected to increase by 50% based solely on the strength of the company's business prospects.

Beta   A stock's **beta** is a measure of its price volatility compared to the overall market. The S&P 500 index is traditionally used as the benchmark for overall market performance and is assigned a beta of 1. Stocks with a beta of 1 move with the market; stocks with a beta greater than 1 move more than the market; stocks with a beta less than 1 move less than the market. The higher the **beta coefficient**, the more volatile the stock. High betas imply greater profits during rising markets and greater potential losses during declining markets. High beta stocks are usually considered aggressive and low beta stocks are considered defensive. Investors with buy and hold strategies select lower beta stocks.

Beta Coefficient

If the beta coefficient is:	The stock will probably move:
Exactly 1	Exactly with the market
Less than 1	Less than the market moves
Greater than 1	More than the market moves

✓ **Take Note:** Examples of high beta stocks include technology and automobile companies. These stocks are quite volatile because their earnings fluctuate substantially. Low beta stocks include utilities and drug companies. Because their earnings are more consistent from year to year, their prices generally move more slowly than the market overall.

Asset Allocation

Asset allocation refers to the balancing of different asset classes, generally stocks, bonds, and cash, within an investment portfolio. In asset allocation, the mix of assets within a portfolio, rather than individual security selection, is the primary factor underlying portfolio performance.

Strategic Asset Allocation Strategic asset allocation refers to the proportion of various types of investments that should comprise a long-term investment portfolio.

> ✓ **For Example:** A standard asset allocation model suggests subtracting a person's age from 100 to determine the percentage of the portfolio that should be invested in stocks. Under this method, a 30-year-old would be 70% invested in stocks and 30% in bonds and cash; a 70-year-old would be invested 30% in stocks with the remainder in bonds and cash.

Tactical Asset Allocation Tactical asset allocation refers to short-term portfolio adjustments that adjusts the portfolio mix between asset classes in consideration of current market conditions.

> ✓ **For Example:** If the stock market is expected to do well over the near term, a portfolio manager may allocate greater portions of a portfolio to stocks. If the market is expected to decline, the portfolio manager may allocate greater portions of the portfolio to bonds and cash.

Active and Passive Management

An active portfolio manager, using a particular stock selection approach, buys and sells individual stocks. **Active management** relies on the manager's stock picking and market timing ability to outperform market indices.

> ✓ **For Example:** An active portfolio manager may position the portfolio in stocks within a few market sectors, such as drugs and technology, frequently trading in and out of the stocks. An active manager may change his sector focus to capitalize on relative performance of different sectors during different stages of the business cycle.

A **passive portfolio manager** believes that no particular management style will consistently outperform market averages. Therefore, by constructing a portfolio that mirrors a market index, such as the S&P 500; passive portfolio management seeks a low-cost means of generating consistent, long-term returns with minimal turnover.

Growth Growth portfolio managers focus on stocks of companies whose earnings are growing faster than most other stocks and are expected to continue to do so. Because rapid growth in earnings is often priced into the stocks, growth investment managers are likely to buy stocks that are at the high end of their 52-week price range.

> ✓ **For Example:** KLM Co., a 10-year-old company, is the dominant provider of routers used in telecommunications switching systems. Its earnings have grown in excess of 20% annually for the past 7 years; it has $1.2 billion in annual sales and operating profit of 40% of sales; it has no debt; and it pays no dividend. The stock trades at 50 times annual earnings.

Value Value portfolio managers concentrate on undervalued or out-of-favor securities whose price is low relative to the company's earnings or book value, and whose earnings prospects are believed to be unattractive by investors and securities analysts. Value investment managers seek to buy undervalued securities before the company reports positive earnings surprises. Value investment managers are more likely to buy stocks that are at the bottom of their 52-week price range.

✓ **For Example:** ABC Co., established after World War II, is a metal processor for parts used in the automotive industry. The company has grown by 10% per year for the past 15 years but is highly susceptible to downturns in the economy. Twenty percent of its capitalization is in debt used to build a factory and the stock has paid a quarterly dividend that has increased five times in the past 10 years. Conservatively managed, the company owns assets and cash that exceed the market value of its common stock.

Quick Quiz 15.6 Multiple Choice

1. Which of the following constitutes a constant dollar plan?

   A. 60% equities, 40% fixed income
   B. 40% equities, 60% fixed income investments
   C. Fixed amount in the portfolio regardless of market price
   D. Fixed amount in fixed-income investments regardless of market price

2. An investor who makes transactions once a month using dollar cost averaging would

   A. buy the same dollar amount of a stock
   B. buy the same number of shares of a stock
   C. put 70% of the money in a bond fund and buy stocks with the rest
   D. buy equal amounts of speculative and blue chip securities

3. A customer is pursuing an aggressive stock buying strategy. Which of the following is most suitable for the customer's needs?

   A. ABC stock with a beta coefficient of 1.0
   B. DEF stock with a beta coefficient of 0.93
   C. GHI stock with a beta coefficient of 1.20
   D. Convertible bonds of a blue-chip company

4. An investor's portfolio has a beta coefficient of 1.1. If the overall market goes up 10%, the portfolio's value is likely to

   A. increase by 10%
   B. increase by 11%
   C. decrease by 10%
   D. decrease by 11%

Answers

1. **C.** In a constant dollar plan, a fixed dollar amount is invested in the portfolio. If the market value rises, the excess is sold. If the market value falls, securities are purchased to restore the constant dollar position.

2. **A.** Because the dollar amount remains constant, the investor will automatically buy more shares when the price is low, thus reducing the average cost.

3. **C.** Beta coefficients over 1 signify that the stock will fluctuate more than the market as a whole. In general, the higher the beta, the greater the risk. Such risk-taking is appropriate for investors who seek aggressive stock-buying strategies and have both the financial ability and the temperament to withstand downturns in the market.

4. **B.** A beta of 1.1 means the portfolio is considered to be 1.1 times more volatile than the overall market. Therefore, if the market is up 10%, the portfolio with a beta of 1.1 is likely to be up 11% (1.1 × 10%).

Federal and State Taxation

Taxes are labeled as either **regressive** or **progressive**.

Regressive Taxes

Regressive taxes, such as sales, excise, payroll, property, and gasoline taxes, are levied equally regardless of income, thus representing a smaller portion of income for wealthy taxpayers than for taxpayers with lower incomes. Because low-income families spend a larger percentage of their incomes than they save or invest, regressive taxes take a larger fraction of the income of economically disadvantaged people than of wealthy people.

Progressive Taxes

Progressive taxes, such as estate and income taxes, increase the tax rate as income increases. Progressive taxes affect people with high incomes more than people with low incomes.

Types of Income

Earned Income **Earned income** includes salary, bonuses, and income derived from active participation in a trade or business. Earned income is sometimes known as active income.

Passive Income **Passive income and losses** come from rental property, limited partnerships, and enterprises (regardless of business structure) in which an individual is not actively involved. For the general partner, income from a limited partnership is earned income; for the limited partner, such income is passive. Passive income is netted against passive losses to determine net taxable income. Passive losses may be used to offset passive income only.

Portfolio Income **Portfolio income** includes dividends, interest, and net capital gains derived from the sale of securities. No matter what the source of the income, it is taxed in the year in which it is received.

Income Tax Brackets

US income tax tables are structured so that successively higher portions of a person's income are taxed at progressively higher rates. US income tax brackets for the tax year 2003 range from a minimum of 10% to a maximum of 35%.

Taxation and Investment Portfolios

Investments may generate income, capital gains, or capital losses. Income and capital gains are taxed at different rates. Tax law separates capital gains (or losses) into short term and long term. Longer term capital gains are eligible for lower tax rates.

✓ **Take Note:** Short-term capital gains have a holding period of 12 months or less, and are taxed as ordinary income. Long-term capital gains have a holding period of over 12 months with a maximum tax rate of 15%.

Capital losses may offset capital gains, but if capital losses exceed capital gains, a taxpayer may use only $3,000 of net capital losses to offset income. The taxpayer may carry unused capital losses forward indefinitely.

✓ **For Example:** In the current year, an investor has capital losses of $12,000 and capital gains of $5,000. The investor has a net capital loss of $7,000. $3,000 may be deducted from ordinary income on next year's tax return. The remaining $4,000 is unused but may be carried forward to subsequent years.

Interest Income Interest paid on debt securities is income to the bondholder. It may or may not be taxable, depending on the type of security.

Taxable Interest Income

Corporate Bonds. Interest income from corporate bonds is taxable by federal, state, and some local governments.

US Government Securities. Interest income on US Treasury bills, notes, and bonds is exempt from state and local taxes, but is federally taxable.

Agency Issues. The interest income on most federal agency debt, like that on Treasury securities, is taxable by the federal government but is exempt from state and local taxes. However, mortgage-backed securities issued by government agencies are taxable at all levels.

✓ **Take Note:** Fannie Mae and Freddie Mac are corporations and are therefore taxable at all levels.

Accrued Interest. Interest income includes **accrued interest** an investor receives when bonds are sold between interest payment dates. The trade confirmation discloses two amounts: the amount received for the bond and the amount of accrued interest. The accrued interest is taxable income to the seller. For tax reporting, the buyer deducts the amount of accrued interest paid the seller from the total interest received to ensure that the buyer pays tax only on the net amount.

Tax-Exempt Interest Income

Municipal Securities. Interest on municipal bonds is exempt from federal taxes. Furthermore, interest from municipal obligations of US territories (Puerto Rico, Guam, the Virgin Islands) is exempt from federal, state, and local taxes. Interest on a municipal bond or note normally is not taxable for residents of the state in which the bond or note is issued.

States or municipalities issue **private purpose bonds** (a.k.a. Industrial Revenue Bonds) to meet nonessential government functions. Although federally tax exempt for most taxpayers, the interest on such municipal securities is a tax preference item for the **alternative minimum tax** (**AMT**), discussed later. These bonds are issued by local or regional Industrial Development Authorities to provide jobs and to enhance the area's economic base. They are often used to finance shopping centers and manufacturing plants by the private sector.

Dividend Income

Dividend income from stocks is taxed at 15%.

Dividend Income from Mutual Funds

Owners of mutual fund shares receive dividends that represent the pass-through of dividends and interest earned on the underlying portfolio. Tax consequences depend on the types of securities in the underlying portfolio.

Federal and State Taxation

- Municipal bond mutual funds and municipal unit investment trusts (UITs) distribute federally tax-free dividends to shareholders.
- Dividend distributions from corporate bond funds are taxable as ordinary income in the year an investor receives them.
- Dividend distributions from stock funds are taxed at 15%.
- Long-term capital gains distributions are taxed at 15%.
- Short-term capital gains distributions are taxed as ordinary income.

✓ **Take Note:** Whether mutual fund distributions are taken in cash or reinvested into additional shares, they are taxable in the year of distribution.

Foreign Securities The interest and dividend income from a foreign investment, such as stock issued by a foreign corporation or bonds issued by a foreign government, is taxed by the country in which the investor is a citizen. A US citizen who owns bonds or stock issued in another country is liable for state and federal taxes (but not foreign taxes) on interest and dividend income received.

If foreign tax has been withheld on a distribution of dividends or interest from a foreign security, a US citizen is eligible for an income tax credit for the amount withheld.

Taxable Upon Receipt

Interest and dividends are taxable only in the year they are received. Investors do not owe taxes on cash dividends or interest declared or accrued until they receive the money.

✓ **Take Note:** While cash dividends payable to shareholders are taxable, stock dividends or stock splits are not taxable. Instead, the shareholder has an increased number of shares with a reduced cost basis.

Capital Gains and Losses

The sale of securities can result in a capital gain or a capital loss. A **capital gain** occurs when a security is sold for a price higher than the cost basis; if the selling price is lower than the cost basis, a **capital loss** occurs.

Adjusting Cost Basis An investment's **cost basis** is used to determine whether a taxable gain or a tax-deductible loss occurs when an asset is sold. Because many events affect an asset's cost basis, the IRS allows the cost basis to be adjusted for such occurrences as stock splits and stock dividends.

Capital Gains

A **capital gain** occurs when capital assets (securities, real estate, and tangible property) are sold at prices that exceed the adjusted cost basis. Usually, computing the capital gain or loss on an asset involves comparing the purchase price with the selling price.

✓ **For Example:** A customer bought 100 shares of ABC at $90 plus commission of $100. The payment due was $9,100. The customer's cost basis was $91 per share. The customer sold the shares six months later at $96 less commission of $100. The customer's net proceeds were $9,500 ($9,600 − $100).

The customer's capital gain is calculated by comparing the cost basis to the sales proceeds as follows.

Cost basis	$9,100	or	$91 per share
Sales proceeds	$9,500	or	$95 per share
Total	$ 400	or	$4 per share

Because the customer sold the shares after holding them for six months, the customer has a short-term capital gain taxable as ordinary income.

Capital Losses

A **capital loss** occurs when capital assets are sold at prices that are less than the adjusted cost basis.

Net Capital Gains and Losses

To calculate tax liability, a taxpayer must first add all short-term capital gains and losses for the year. Then he separately adds all long-term capital gains and losses. Finally, the taxpayer offsets the totals to determine his **net capital gain or loss** for the year. If the result is a net capital gain, it is included in gross income and taxed.

Net capital losses are deductible against earned income to a maximum of $3,000 per year. Any capital losses not deducted in a taxable year may be carried forward indefinitely to be used in future years.

Determining Which Shares to Sell An investor holding identical securities with different acquisition dates and cost bases may determine which shares to sell by electing one of three accounting methods: **first in, first out (FIFO)**; **share identification**; or **average basis**. If the investor fails to choose, the IRS assumes the investor liquidates shares on a FIFO basis.

Share identification is the most flexible of the three methods. The investor keeps track of the cost of each share purchased and specifies which shares to sell based on his tax needs. The average basis method is commonly used by mutual fund investors because it is the simplest.

Wash Sales An investor may not use capital losses to offset gains or income if the investor sells a security at a loss and purchases the same or a substantially identical security within 30 days before or after the trade date establishing the loss. The sale at a loss and the repurchase within this period is a **wash sale**.

Buying call options, rights, warrants, and convertible bonds of the same issuer is considered buying a substantially identical stock. Writing deep-in-the-money puts on the stock sold, or to be sold, at a loss is also included in this definition.

If a loss is disallowed due to the wash sale rule, investors are permitted to adjust the cost basis of the reacquired position by the amount of the disallowed loss.

✓ *For Example:*
10-21-02 Buy 1000 XYZ at 30
11-17-03 Sell 1000 XYZ at 28
11-24-03 Buy 1000 XYZ at 27

The $2,000 loss on the 11-17-2003 sale is disallowed as the investor bought back the security within 30 days of sale date. However, the investor can adjust the cost basis of the reacquired stock by the amount of the disallowed loss. Therefore, the cost basis of the stock bought on 11-24-2003 is 29 per share (27 + 2). In other words, the investor will eventually be able to take the loss when the reacquired stock is sold.

Similarly, the wash sale rule applies to short sales.

✓ *For Example:*
10-21-03 Sell short 1000 ABC at 72
11-17-03 Buy back 1000 ABC at 75
11-24-03 Sell short 1000 ABC at 76

The $3,000 loss on the 11-17-2003 covering purchase is disallowed, as the investor sold short the security within 30 days of covering date. The sale price of the reacquired position is adjusted by the amount of the disallowed loss (76 − 3 = 73).

The wash sale rule applies only to realized losses; it does not apply to realized gains.

✓ *Take Note:* Municipal tax swaps occur frequently at year-end. As a tax strategy, investors sell depreciated bonds to generate a deductible capital loss for the year. In a year when rates have risen (forcing bond prices down), investors, at year-end, often sell their bond positions for a loss and immediately use the proceeds of the sale to buy other bonds. The bonds purchased will provide a higher yield to the investor than the ones sold as rates have risen.

Ethics, Recommendations & Taxation

To avoid the wash sale rule, investors generally will buy bonds of a different issuer. Tax advisors generally recommend changing two characteristics of the following three to avoid the wash sale rule:

- issuer;
- coupon; or
- maturity.

✓ **For Example:** Changing the maturity and coupon or changing the maturity and issuer are acceptable characteristics to alter to be in compliance with the wash sale rule.

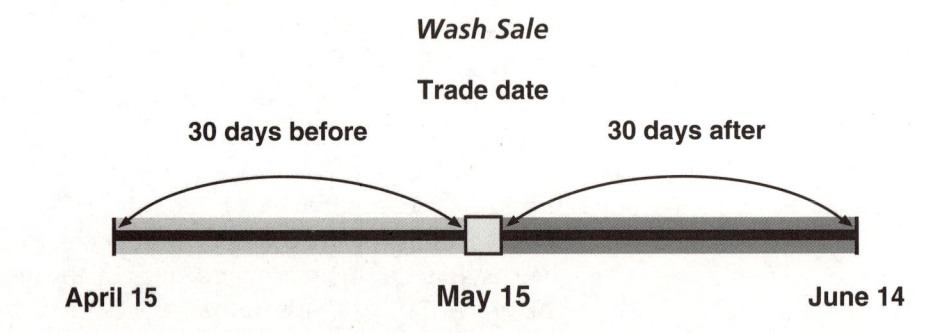

Wash Sale

Trade date

30 days before — 30 days after

April 15   May 15   June 14

✓ **Take Note:** The wash sale rule will apply to an investor who, after selling for a loss, writes deep in-the-money puts on the same issuer.

Quick Quiz 15.7 Multiple Choice

1. A US citizen owns stock in a Canadian company and receives dividends. The Canadian government withholds 15% of the dividends as tax. As a result, the investor reports a

   A. 15% reduction in the investor's ordinary income
   B. 15% tax credit on the investor's US tax return
   C. 15% tax credit on the investor's Canadian tax return
   D. nonrecoverable loss on the investor's US tax return

2. An American citizen purchases a bond issued by the government of Sweden. The interest payments received are taxed at which of the following levels?

   I. Federal
   II. State
   III. Local

   A. I only
   B. II only
   C. II and III only
   D. I, II and III

3. Which of the following bonds pay interest that is totally tax exempt?

   A. Hawaii GO bond
   B. US government bond
   C. Guam GO bond
   D. US Steel bond

4. The income from all of the following securities is fully taxable at the federal, state, and local levels EXCEPT

   A. Ginnie Maes
   B. Treasury bonds
   C. reinvested mutual fund dividends
   D. corporate bonds

5. If each of the bonds under consideration has the same maturity, place the following bonds in order of their pretax yields, from highest to lowest.

   I. US government bonds
   II. AAA municipal bonds
   III. AA corporate bonds

   A. I, II, III
   B. II, I, III
   C. III, I, II
   D. III, II, I

6. Losses from direct participation programs can be used to offset

   A. earned income from salary or commissions
   B. portfolio income
   C. income from limited partnerships
   D. none of the above

Answers

1. **B.** An investor receives a credit for taxes withheld on investments by countries with which the United States has diplomatic relations. The tax credit decreases the investor's US tax liability.

2. **D.** Interest income from foreign securities is fully taxable to US citizens. If foreign tax is withheld in the country of origin (Sweden, in this case), the investor will receive a tax credit to offset the foreign tax liability.

3. **C.** Interest on bonds issued by territories and political subdivisions of the United States (Puerto Rico, Guam, and the US Virgin Islands) are exempt from federal, state, and local taxes.

4. **B.** Dividends (whether reinvested or not), Ginnie Maes, Fannie Maes, and corporate bonds are all fully taxable. US government securities are exempt from state and local taxes.

5. **C.** Normally, the greater the risk, the higher the yield that must be offered to potential investors. Therefore, government securities yield less than corporate securities. In this problem, take into account the difference in taxable bonds (corporate and governments) versus tax-free bonds (municipals); this difference in taxation causes the pretax yield of municipals to be lower than that of corporate and government bonds.

6. **C.** Passive losses can be used only to offset passive income.

Adjusting the Cost Basis of Municipal Bonds

Bonds Purchased at a Premium

The investor who buys a municipal bond at a premium, whether as a new issue or in the secondary market, must **amortize** the premium (**straight line**) over the remaining life of the bond.

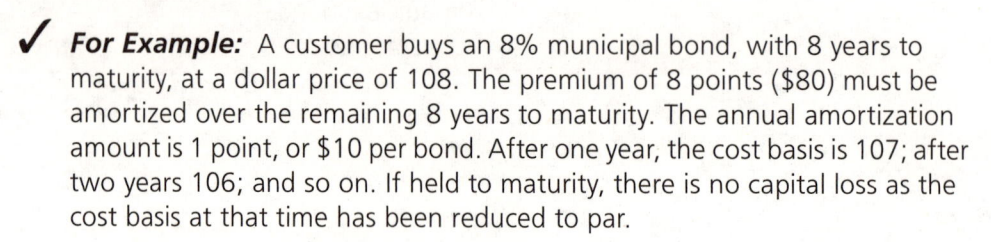

✓ **For Example:** A customer buys an 8% municipal bond, with 8 years to maturity, at a dollar price of 108. The premium of 8 points ($80) must be amortized over the remaining 8 years to maturity. The annual amortization amount is 1 point, or $10 per bond. After one year, the cost basis is 107; after two years 106; and so on. If held to maturity, there is no capital loss as the cost basis at that time has been reduced to par.

Amortization does two things:

- it reduces cost basis; and
- it reduces reported interest income.

In the example, cost basis is reduced each year by $10 per bond. In addition, interest income of $80 per bond is reduced to $70 per bond (the amount of the annual amortization). As interest income on municipal bonds is not taxed, its annual amortization has no tax effect.

Bonds Purchased at a Discount

If a municipal bond is bought at a discount, the discount must be accreted. **Accretion** is the process of adjusting the cost basis back up to par. The actual tax effect of accretion depends on whether the bond was purchased as an **original issue discount (OID)** (i.e., a new issue being offered at a discount or an issue purchased at a discount in the secondary market).

Accretion does two things:

- it increases cost basis; and
- it increases reported interest income.

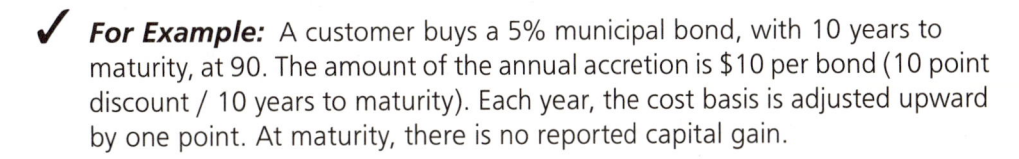

✓ **For Example:** A customer buys a 5% municipal bond, with 10 years to maturity, at 90. The amount of the annual accretion is $10 per bond (10 point discount / 10 years to maturity). Each year, the cost basis is adjusted upward by one point. At maturity, there is no reported capital gain.

If the bond were purchased as an OID, the reported interest income would be $60 per bond ($50 plus the annual accretion of $10). As interest income on municipal bonds is tax free, the accretion has no tax effect. If, however, the bond were purchased at a discount in the secondary market, the annual accretion would be taxed as ordinary income.

With municipal bonds, the yield to maturity is the effective after-tax yield with one exception: discounts bought in the secondary market. In this case, the effective after-tax yield is somewhere between the stated YTM and the coupon on the bond.

Test Topic Alert!

An investor buys a 5% bond at 94. The yield to maturity is 6%. If bought as an OID, the customer's effective after-tax yield is 6%. If bought in the secondary market, the customer's effective tax yield would be somewhere between 5% and 6% as the annual accretion is taxable as ordinary income.

A customer buys a 5% municipal bond, with 10 years to maturity at 110. At that price, the basis (YTM) is 3.95%. After taking taxes into consideration, the customer's effective after-tax yield is

A. less than 3.95%
B. 3.95%
C. between 3.95% and 5%
D. more than 5%

B. In almost all cases, the stated yield to maturity on municipal bonds is the effective after-tax yield. The only exception is for bonds purchased at a discount in the secondary market. There the effective after-tax yield is somewhere between the stated yield to maturity and the coupon on the bond.

Adjusting the Cost Basis of Corporate Bonds

If a corporate bond is bought at a discount, either as an OID or in the secondary market, the annual accretion is taxable as ordinary income.

✓ **Take Note:** Accretion increases reported interest income, which for corporate bonds, is fully taxable.

If, however, a corporate bond is purchased at a premium, either as an OID or in the secondary market, the investor has the option as to whether or not to amortize. If the customer elects not to amortize and holds the bond until maturity, the investor will have a capital loss for tax purposes. If the customer elects to amortize, there will be no capital loss at maturity. However, each year the investor will report lower interest income for tax purposes.

💡 **Test Topic Alert!**
- The discount on all bonds bought in the secondary market is taxed as interest income.
- For corporate bonds bought at a premium, the investor has the option to amortize.

✓ **For Example:** A customer buys a corporate bond at 104, paying $30 of accrued interest per bond. The customer elects not to amortize. What is the customer's cost basis on this bond for tax purposes?

A. 107
B. 101
C. 104
D. 100

C. As the customer elects not to amortize, the cost basis is 104. Accrued interest has no effect on cost basis.

Donated and Inherited Securities

Donations to Charity

When donations of appreciated property are made to charitable organizations, the donor receives a tax deduction equal to the market value on the date of the donation. The recipient's cost basis is equal to the higher current market value. There is no tax liability on the appreciation if the asset was held for more than one year prior to the donation. If the asset was held for one year or less, tax is due on the increase in value.

Donations to Others

When donations or gifts are made to family members or others, no deduction is available. The cost basis to the recipient is the original cost basis of the donor. Such gifts are subject to **gift taxes**.

Inherited Securities

When a person dies and leaves securities to heirs, the cost basis to the recipients is the fair market value on the date of the owner's death.

Estate and Gift Taxes

Donor Taxes

When a person dies, tax is due on the estate. This tax is payable by the estate, not by heirs that inherit the estate (although certain other taxes may apply to heirs). Likewise, if a person gives a gift, tax is due on the gift. Gift tax is payable by the donor, not the recipient. Estate and gift taxes are **progressive taxes** that increase to a maximum rate of 55%. For tax purposes, the valuation of the estate is the date of death; the valuation of a gift is the date it is given.

Gift Tax Exemption

Individuals may give gifts of $11,000 per year to any number of individuals without incurring gift tax. Inter-spousal gifts, no matter what the size, are not subject to tax.

Estate Tax Exclusion

Deceased persons are allowed to exclude the first $1 million of their estate from taxation. The exclusion will be fully phased in by 2006 when the exclusion will be $2 million.

✓ **Take Note:** Estate and gift taxes are progressive taxes that increase with the size of the estate of the gift.

Unlimited Marital Deduction

Married couples are allowed to transfer their entire estate to the surviving spouse at death. This unlimited marital deduction results in taxes being due on the death of the survivor.

Margin Expenses

Margin interest is a tax-deductible expense. The one exception is interest expenses incurred in the purchase of municipal securities. Because municipal interest income is federally tax exempt, the IRS does not allow taxpayers to claim deductions for the margin interest expense on municipal securities. Investors can deduct interest expenses for other securities to the extent that they do not exceed their net investment income, which includes interest income, dividends, and all capital gains.

Shorting Against the Box

Selling **short against the box** is a strategy that has been used to lock in a capital gain that was to be deferred into a later tax period. Instead of selling shares a customer holds long, the customer borrows the same shares and sells them short. Because the borrowed shares were sold, there is no tax event. The customer instead is taxed at the point when the borrowed shares are replaced with the shares the customer owns.

A 5% margin requirement applies on the proceeds from selling short against the box. The firm may release 95% of the sales proceeds to the customer.

✓ **Take Note:** The tax law revisions of 1997 greatly minimized the effectiveness of shorting against the box for tax deferral. The law now allows tax deferral only if the short position is closed within 30 days of year-end and customer stays long in the stock for an additional 60 days. Shorting against the box cannot be used to stretch a short-term gain into a long-term gain.

Alternative Minimum Tax (AMT)

Congress enacted the **alternative minimum tax** to make certain that high-income taxpayers do not escape paying taxes.

Tax Preference Items Certain items receive favorable tax treatment. These items must be added back into taxable income for the AMT. They include:

- accelerated depreciation on property placed in service after 1986;
- certain costs associated with DPPs, such as research and development costs and intangible drilling costs;
- local tax and interest on investments that do not generate income;
- tax-exempt interest on private purpose nonessential government service municipal bonds issued after August 7, 1986; and
- incentive stock options exceeding their fair market value.

✓ **Take Note:** The Internal Revenue Code (IRC) language says that taxpayers are required to add the excess of the alternative minimum tax over the regular tax to their regular tax to determine their total tax liability.

Corporate Taxes

Corporations are major investors in securities. Some IRC provisions affecting corporations as investors include the following.

Dividend Exclusion Rule Dividends paid from one corporation to another are 70% exempt from taxation. A corporation that receives dividends on stocks of other domestic corporations, therefore, pays taxes on only 30% of the dividends received. This provision encourages corporations to invest in common and preferred stock of other US corporations.

Municipal Securities Like individual taxpayers, corporations do not pay federal taxes on income received from municipal bonds.

✓ **Take Note:** There are no dividend exclusions for individual investors.

Quick Quiz 15.8 Multiple Choice

1. A couple who file a joint tax return has $275 in corporate preferred dividends. According to the tax law, this couple can exclude how much of this dividend income?

   A. $0
   B. $100 on a joint return
   C. $200 on a joint return
   D. All of it

2. A high-income customer is subject to AMT. Which of the following preference items must be added to adjusted gross income to calculate his tax liability?

   A. Interest on a private purpose municipal bond issued after September 1987
   B. Interest on a municipal bond issued to finance highway construction
   C. Income from a municipal security issued to finance parking garages
   D. Distributions from a corporate bond mutual fund

3. The cost basis in the stock an heir receives from her mother's estate is the

   A. original cost of the stock to her mother
   B. original cost of the stock to her mother adjusted for any estate taxes paid
   C. market value of the stock on the date of death
   D. market value of the stock on the date of distribution to the customer

Answers

1. **A.** Individual taxpayers must pay taxes on the full amount of their dividend income.

2. **A.** If more than 10% of a bond's proceeds go to private entities, the interest on the bond is a tax preference item for the alternative minimum tax.

3. **C.** The cost basis of inherited stock is adjusted to reflect the fair market value on the date of the decedent's death. The date of distribution to the beneficiary is not considered.

Ethics, Recommendations & Taxation HotSheet

Private Transactions:
- Not allowed without broker/dealer's knowledge and consent; prior written notice and disclosure of compensation required
- Passive investments not subject to this requirement

Gift Limit:
- No more than $100 cash per year to employees of other member firms; both NASD and MSRB rule

Selling Dividends:	• Prohibited practice due to tax liability
Breakpoint Sales:	• Encouraging customer to purchase below the opportunity for a discount; prohibited practice
Research Reports:	• Must disclose if prepared by someone outside firm
Shared Accounts:	• Allowable only if firm grants prior written approval; sharing only in proportion to contribution
Prohibited Trading Practices:	• **Painting the Tape**: party sells with agreement from buyer that repurchase will occur the same day • **Matching**: broker/dealer stages a hot market by simultaneous purchases and sales • **Front running**: broker/dealer order placed ahead of customer order for better price • **Capping**: exerting selling pressure to keep stock prices from rising
Investment Objectives:	• Preservation of capital; safety = government securities or Ginnie Maes • Growth = common stock or common stock mutual fund • Balanced or moderate growth = blue-chip stocks • Aggressive growth = technology stocks or sector funds • Income = bonds (but not zero-coupons); preferred stock and utilities also provide income • Tax-free income = municipal bonds or muni bond funds • High-yield income = corporate bonds or corporate bond funds • Liquidity = money market funds; (DPPs, CDs, real estate, and annuities are illiquid)
Investment Risks:	• **Purchasing power risk**: inflation • **Reinvestment risk**: mortgage-backed securities and callable bonds are susceptible • **Market risk**: also called systematic risk; diversification does not reduce • **Credit risk**: risk of issuer's default causing loss of principal • **Liquidity risk**: also called marketability risk; risk that investor cannot convert to cash quickly and at a fair price
CAPM:	• Determines risk and reward from total portfolio; basis of modern portfolio theory
Beta:	• Overall market has beta of 1; S&P 500 is benchmark; beta higher than 1 is more volatile, aggressive
Foreign Stock:	• Income taxed by country of investor's citizenship; typically 15% withholding on foreign distributions

Wash Sales:	• Loss disallowed if substantially identical security purchased 30 days before or after sale for loss
Bond Cost Basis:	• Amortize all premiums; secondary market discounts are subject to taxation as ordinary income
Gifted/Inherited Stock:	• For gifts, cost basis is giver's original basis; heirs' cost basis is MV on date of death
Dividend Exclusion:	• 70% exclusion on corporate dividends; no dividend exclusion for individuals

Series 7 Lesson Exam 15

1. Income from which of the following investments is passive income?

    I. Real estate DPP
    II. Real estate investments
    III. REITs
    IV. CMOs

    A. I only
    B. I and II
    C. III and IV
    D. I, II, III and IV

2. Which of the following statement(s) regarding gift taxes is(are) TRUE?

    I. Gifts of $11,000 in 2003 per person per year can be given without a tax liability.
    II. Gifts in excess of $11,000 in 2003 per person per year are subject to tax.
    III. The donor, not the recipient, is responsible for any tax liability.
    IV. The tax rate increases with the size of the gift.

    A. I only
    B. II and III
    C. II, III and IV
    D. I, II, III and IV

3. Which of the following statements regarding the alternative minimum tax is TRUE?

    A. The alternative minimum tax is added to the regular tax.
    B. The tax bracket will determine whether the regular tax or the alternative tax is paid.
    C. The excess of the alternative tax over the regular tax is added to the regular tax.
    D. The lesser of the regular tax or the alternative tax is paid.

4. If a customer buys a new issue municipal bond at a discount in the primary market, which of the following statements are TRUE?

    I. The discount must be accreted.
    II. The discount may not be accreted.
    III. At maturity, there is a capital gain.
    IV. At maturity, there is no capital gain.

    A. I and III
    B. I and IV
    C. II and III
    D. II and IV

5. A father makes a gift of securities to his 10-year-old daughter. Gift taxes would be based on the

    A. cost of the securities
    B. market value of the securities at date of gift
    C. market value of the securities as of April 15 of the year in which the gift is made
    D. market value of the securities as of December 31 of the year in which the gift is made

6. Which of the following investments should a representative recommend to a corporate client whose objective is current income with moderate risk?

    A. Preferred stock
    B. Aggressive growth fund
    C. Money-market fund
    D. High-yield bond fund

7. A person's investment decisions should be based primarily on their

    I. risk tolerance
    II. representative's recommendations
    III. investment needs

    A. I only
    B. I and III only
    C. II and III only
    D. I, II and III

8. Income from all of the following is partially exempt to a corporate investor EXCEPT income from

   A. convertible bonds
   B. common stock
   C. preferred stock
   D. preferred stock mutual funds

9. When determining whether a tax swap of municipal bonds will result in a wash sale, which of the following are considered?

   I. Maturity
   II. Principal amount
   III. Issuer
   IV. Coupon

   A. I and II only
   B. I, II and III only
   C. I, III and IV only
   D. II, III and IV only

10. A married couple sets up a JTWROS account with a balance of $1 million. If the wife dies, what is the husband's estate tax liability?

    A. He pays federal and state taxes on the entire balance.
    B. He pays federal and state taxes on $500,000.
    C. He pays federal taxes only on $500,000.
    D. He pays no estate tax.

11. Which of the following taxes are known as progressive taxes?

    I. Sales
    II. Cigarette
    III. Income
    IV. Estate

    A. I and II
    B. II and IV
    C. III and IV
    D. I, II, III and IV

12. A municipal bond is purchased in the secondary market at 102½. The bond has five years to maturity. Two years later, the bond is sold for 102. The tax consequence to the investor is

    A. a capital loss of $5 per bond
    B. a capital gain of $5 per bond
    C. a capital loss of $20 per bond
    D. no capital gain or loss

13. A mother makes a gift of appreciated securities to her 10-year-old son. The son's cost basis in the stock is the

    A. original cost of the securities to the mother
    B. market value of the securities on the date of the gift
    C. market value of the securities on April 15 of the year the gift is made
    D. market value of the securities on December 31 of the year the gift is made

14. A customer bought 100 ABC at 60 in January of 1998. In February 2000, the stock is worth $100 per share and the customer donated it to charity. The consequences are

    I. $6,000 deduction
    II. $10,000 deduction
    III. no tax is due on appreciation
    IV. tax is due on appreciation

    A. I and III
    B. I and IV
    C. II and III
    D. II and IV

15. A customer has $12,000 of capital gains and $15,000 of capital losses. How much unused loss is carried forward to the following tax year?

    A. $0
    B. $3,000
    C. $12,000
    D. $15,000

16. A husband makes a gift of $100,000 to his wife. How much of the gift is subject to gift taxes?

    A. $0
    B. $50,000
    C. $90,000
    D. $100,000

Series 7 Lesson Exam 15 Answers & Rationale

1. **B.** Passive income is income from DPPs and from direct investments in real estate. REITs and CMOs are securities and income from securities is considered portfolio income.
QID: 36548

2. **D.** In accordance with gift tax regulations, an individual may give a gift of up to $11,000 per person in one year with no gift tax liability. If the gift exceeds $11,000, it is the donor who is responsible for any tax. The gift tax is a progressive tax, which means that as the size of the gift increases, the percentage of tax that applies will also increase.
QID: 34965

3. **C.** The excess of the alternative tax over the regular tax is added to the regular tax amount. The taxpayer does not have the option of paying the alternative tax or the regular tax depending on his tax bracket. The purpose of the alternative minimum is to ensure that certain taxpayers pay a tax consistent with their wealth and income.
QID: 28342

4. **B.** If a new issue municipal bond is bought at a discount in the primary market, the discount must be accreted. The accretion is considered interest income and, therefore, is not taxable.
QID: 36605

5. **B.** If a gift tax is due, it is paid by the donor based upon the value of the gift on the date it is given.
QID: 35054

6. **A.** Preferred stock generates current income in the form of dividends. Aggressive growth funds strive for capital appreciation rather than current income. Money market funds have low yields, not the high yields that an income investor wants. While high-yield bonds provide current income they entail a high degree of risk.
QID: 28355

7. **B.** Understanding and acceptance of risk, and investment objectives should determine an individual's investment decisions. Recommendations by a representative may merit possible actions, but the client must make a decision based on whether the investment is suitable.
QID: 28320

8. **A.** 70% of dividend income received from investments in common stock and preferred stock is excluded from taxation for a corporate investor. This exclusion applies to dividends from mutual funds where all of the portfolio securities are preferred or common stock.
QID: 36483

9. **C.** In judging whether bonds purchased are substantially identical to bonds sold for a loss, the tax code considers maturity, issuer, and coupon rate. If at least two of the three are different, a wash sale will generally not result.
QID: 29607

10. **D.** Establishing a joint tenants with right of survivorship account allows for the transfer of assets to the survivor upon death. The surviving spouse is not taxed on assets transferred in this manner.
QID: 28352

11. **C.** With a progressive tax, the tax percentage amount increases as the taxable amount increases. Income and estate taxes are progressive. Sales and cigarette taxes are regressive because all persons pay the same percentage tax regardless of their income.
QID: 28336

12. **B.** Municipal bonds bought at a premium, either in the new issue or secondary market, must be amortized. Each year, the premium must be amortized so that, if held to maturity, there is no reported capital gain or loss. The amount of the premium is 2½ points or $25. As the bond has five years to maturity, the annual amortization amount is $5 per bond. After two years, the bond's basis has been amortized down to 101½. At that point, a sale at 102 generates a capital gain of $5 per bond.
QID: 36465

13. A. When a gift of securities is made while the donor is alive, the original cost of the securities is the cost basis, not the value of the security on the date of the gift. Note that market value at date of gift is used to determine if gift taxes are applicable. QID: 28356

14. C. When an investor donates appreciated securities to charity, the investor will receive a tax deduction based on the value as of the donation date. There will be no tax due on the amount of appreciation as long as the stock was held long-term as of the date of the charitable donation.
QID: 34993

15. A. After netting capital gain and losses, the customer has a net capital loss of $3,000. Since $3,000 of net losses can be deducted in any one tax year, there is no carry forward. QID: 36604

16. A. Inter-spousal gifts, regardless of amount, are not subject to gift taxes.
QID: 36618

16

US Government & State Rules & Regulations

INTRODUCTION

The securities industry is heavily regulated. The stock market crash of 1929 caused significant government response to the functioning of the securities business. The government took an active interest in implementing legislation to protect the public and correct abusive practices by industry practitioners.

This unit presents an overview of the major pieces of federal legislation and state securities law. It is important to know the general boundaries of these rules and regulations for success on the exam and as a representative.

On the Series 7 exam, you will encounter approximately 10–15 questions on these regulations.

UNIT OBJECTIVES

When you have completed this unit, you should be able to describe the scope and boundaries of the following major securities legislation.

- Securities Act of 1933
- Securities Exchange Act of 1934
- Maloney Act
- Trust Indenture Act of 1939
- Investment Company Act of 1940
- Investment Advisers Act of 1940
- Securities Investor Protection Act of 1970
- Insider Trading Act of 1988
- Penny Stock Cold Calling Rule
- Blue-Sky Laws

Overview of Federal and Securities Legislation

This section highlights the Acts of 1933 and 1934 and discusses other legislation that expanded or amended these acts.

The Securities Act of 1933

The Act of 1933 was the federal government's first legislative response to the crash of 1929. After investigating the conditions that led to the crash, it was determined that investors had little protection from fraud in the sale of new issues of securities. To correct this problem, the Act of 1933 required full and fair disclosure of nonexempt issues. The following list encompasses the major aspects of the act.

- Issuers of nonexempt securities must file registration statements with the SEC.
- Prospectuses must be provided to all purchasers of new, nonexempt issues for full and fair disclosure.
- Fraudulent activity in connection with underwriting and issuing of all securities is prohibited.

Test Topic Alert! If a question discusses the new issue market or primary market, or activity associated with the sale of new issues, the regulation involved is the Act of 1933.

Act of 1933 =

- New issues
- Underwriting
- Registration statements
- Prospectus
- Primary market

Consider the Act of 1933 the *Paper Act* because of the full and fair disclosure requirements that must be met through registration statements and prospectus delivery.

The Securities Exchange Act of 1934

The Act of 1934 was a further reaction to the crash of 1929. It picks up where the Act of 1933 finished, addressing fraudulent practices in the secondary marketplace.

The Act of 1934 is responsible for the:

- creation of the SEC;
- registration of all persons and firms that trade securities OTC and on exchanges for the public;
- regulation of exchanges and the OTC market;
- regulation of credit by the Federal Reserve Board;
- regulation of trading activities;
- regulation of insider transactions, short sales, and proxies;
- regulation of client accounts;
- customer protection rule;
- net capital rule and financial responsibility for broker/dealers; and
- reporting requirements for issuers.

Test Topic Alert!

Key words help identify the Act of 1934 in test questions.

Act of 1934 =

- Secondary market
- Outstanding securities
- Trading activities

Consider the Act of 1934 as the *People Act*. It regulates all the persons involved in trading securities on behalf of customers.

Although certain securities are exempt from the registration requirements of the Act of 1933, no security is exempt from the antifraud provisions of the Act of 1934. This means that certain securities are exempt from registration and prospectus requirements, but fraud or market manipulation can't be involved in the trading of any security, exempt or nonexempt.

Quick Quiz 16.1 Determine if each phrase below describes the Act of **1933** or the Act of **1934**:

___ 1. Prohibits fraud in the primary markets

___ 2. Requires registration of broker/dealers

___ 3. Created the SEC

___ 4. Requires nonexempt issuers to file registration statements

___ 5. Prohibits fraudulent trading practices

___ 6. The Paper Act

___ 7. Regulates underwriting activity

___ 8. Regulates extension of credit by brokerage firms

___ 9. Regulates client accounts

___ 10. The People Act

Answers 1. 1933   2. 1934   3. 1934   4. 1933   5. 1934
6. 1933   7. 1933   8. 1934   9. 1934   10. 1934

Maloney Act of 1938   The **Maloney Act** amended the Act of 1934 and enabled the SEC to create SROs or **designated examining authorities (DEAs)** for monitoring brokers and dealers not affiliated with a stock exchange. The National Association of Securities Dealers (NASD) was officially chartered as the SRO of the over-the-counter market.

Trust Indenture Act of 1939

The **Trust Indenture Act of 1939** applies to corporate bonds with the following characteristics:

- issue size of more than $5 million within 12 months; and
- maturity of nine months or more.

This act was passed to protect bondholders and requires that issuers of these bonds appoint a trustee to ensure that promises (covenants) between the issuer and trustee who acts solely for the benefit of the bondholders are carried out. The document is filed at the office of a custodian so that investors may review it if they choose.

Test Topic Alert!   The test might ask about the definition of a trust indenture. The best answer defines the trust indenture as a series of promises between the issuer and the trustee for the benefit of the bondholders.

The Investment Company Act of 1940

The **Investment Company Act of 1940** defines and regulates investment companies, including mutual funds. It requires investment companies to:

- register with the SEC before selling shares publicly;
- clearly state their investment objectives in their registration statement and prospectus;

- have net worth of at least $100,000 before offering shares to the public;
- be owned by a minimum of 100 shareholders; and
- comply with standards on pricing, public sale, and reporting.

✓ **Take Note:** The three classifications of investment companies—face amount certificate companies (FACs), unit investment trusts (UITs), and management companies—are described in the **Investment Company Products** unit.

The Investment Advisers Act of 1940

The purpose of the **Investment Advisers Act of 1940** is to require anyone who, as part of their business, gives investment advice for compensation to register as investment advisers under the act. Broker/dealers who provide advice for a fee (e.g., a **wrap account**) are subject to registration under this act. Agents of investment advisers must register and pass the 65 exam or 66 exam (for reps with a Series 7).

The Securities Investor Protection Act and the SIPC

After many brokerage firm defaults in the 1960s, the **Securities Investor Protection Act** was passed in 1970 to protect customers from broker/dealer failure or insolvency. This act intensified broker/dealer financial requirements and also created the **Securities Investor Protection Corporation (SIPC)**.

Membership and Assessments

SIPC is an independent government-sponsored corporation that collects annual assessments from broker/dealers. These assessments create a general insurance fund for customer claims from broker/dealer failure.

All broker/dealers registered with the SEC must be SIPC members except for those handling only:

- mutual funds or unit trusts; and
- variable annuities or insurance.

However, investment advisers are not broker/dealers and are therefore not SIPC members.

Firms that fail to pay their SIPC assessments cannot engage in the brokerage business.

Violation of Net Capital

If a firm is suspected by the SEC or any SRO of a violation of its minimum net capital requirements, a notification is made to SIPC. If SIPC believes that a violation has occurred or that the firm is insolvent, it will petition a court to appoint a **liquidating trustee**, and the firm ceases doing business.

When a liquidation proceeding takes place, the order of events is as follows:

- securities held in **customer name** are delivered to registered owners;
- cash and street name securities are distributed on a pro-rata basis;
- SIPC funds are distributed to meet remaining claims up to the maximum allowed per customer; and then
- customers with excess claims become general creditors of the broker/dealer.

Test Topic Alert! The valuation date for customer securities claims is generally the day that the customer protection proceedings commence.

SIPC Coverage Under SIPC, customer accounts are covered to a maximum of $500,000, with cash claims not to exceed $100,000 of that total. Each separate customer may enter a claim up to the $500,000 limit for all accounts in the customer's name.

Sample SIPC Customer Coverage Limits

Examples of Customer Coverage Limits	
John Doe — Cash account John Doe — Margin account	1 customer = $500,000 coverage
John and Mary Doe — Joint account	1 customer = $500,000 coverage
John Doe as Custodian for Jane Doe	1 customer = $500,000 coverage

Commodities and commodities futures contracts are not covered by SIPC because they are not considered securities. Customers with claims in excess of SIPC limits become general creditors of the broker/dealer.

Use of SIPC Membership in Advertising Broker/dealers must include their SIPC membership on all advertising, but may not imply that SIPC coverage is more than it actually is, or that its benefits are unique to only that firm. The term *SIPC* may not appear larger than the firm's own name. Also, all member firms must post a sign that indicates SIPC membership.

Fidelity Bonds Firms required to join SIPC must purchase a **blanket fidelity bond**. The purpose of this bond is to protect against employee theft. The minimum coverage amount is $25,000, although firms may require additional coverage based on their scope of operations. A firm must review the sufficiency of its fidelity bond coverage once per year.

Test Topic Alert! Be sure to recognize that SIPC coverage is per customer, not per account. Use the "C" in SIPC to help you remember that each customer is entitled to $500,000 of coverage on all of the customer's accounts combined. Cash and margin accounts are combined for SIPC coverage purposes.

Also, if asked when securities are valued for the purpose of a SIPC liquidation, look for an answer similar to: "the date the court was petitioned to appoint an SIPC trustee." This is just another way of saying the appointment must occur at the time liquidation proceedings begin.

The Securities Acts Amendments of 1975

The **Securities Acts Amendments of 1975** established the **Municipal Securities Rulemaking Board (MSRB)**. The MSRB regulates the issuance and trading of municipal securities.

Insider Trading and Securities Fraud Enforcement Act of 1988

Although the Securities Act of 1934 prohibited the use of insider information in making trades, the Insider Trading and Securities Fraud Enforcement Act of 1988 amends its provisions and specifies penalties for insider trading and securities fraud.

Insiders An **insider** is any person who has access to nonpublic information about a company that would most likely influence the price of the company's stock. Inside information is any information that has not been disseminated to, or is not readily available to, the general public.

Tippers and Tippees The act prohibits insiders trading on or communicating nonpublic information. Both **tippers** (the person who gives the tip) and **tippees** (the person who receives the tip) are liable, as is anyone who trades on information that they know or should know is not public, or has control over the misuse of this information. No trade need be made for a violation to occur; even a personal benefit of a nonfinancial nature could lead to liability under the rules.

The key elements of tipper and tippee liability under insider trading rules are as follows.

- Is the information material and nonpublic?
- Does the tipper owe a fiduciary duty to a company/its stockholders? Has he breached it?
- Does the tipper meet the personal benefits test (even something as simple as enhancing a friendship or reputation)?
- Does the tippee know or should the tippee have known that the information was inside or confidential?

Written Supervisory Procedures

All broker/dealers must establish written supervisory procedures specifically prohibiting the misuse of inside information. Additionally, they must establish policies that restrict the passing of potentially material nonpublic information between a firm's departments. This barrier against the free flow of sensitive information is known as a **Chinese Wall,** a **firewall,** or an **information barrier**.

The SEC can investigate any person suspected of violating any of the provisions of the Insider Trading Act. If the SEC determines that a violation has occurred, civil penalties of up to 300% of profits made or losses avoided may be levied. Violators may also face criminal penalties of up to 10 years in jail.

✓ *Take Note:* If the violator is an employee of the broker/dealer, the firm (which is supposed to have procedures in place to prevent this) could be fined up to treble damages, or $1 million, whichever is greater.

Contemporaneous Traders

Persons who enter trades at or near the same time in the same security as a person who has inside information are known as **contemporaneous traders**. Contemporaneous traders may sue persons that have violated insider trading regulations, and suits may be initiated up to five years after the violation has occurred.

Informer Bounty

The Insider Trading Act allows for payment to informers of up to 10% of the amounts recovered under civil penalties.

✓ *Take Note:* Simply giving someone inside information, while imprudent, is not a violation. When the information is used to trade for profit or to avoid a loss, a violation occurs. In this case, both the tipper and tippee are liable.

Quick Quiz 16.2   Multiple Choice

1. A client not covered by SIPC in a broker/dealer bankruptcy

   A. becomes a secured creditor
   B. becomes a general creditor
   C. becomes a preferred creditor
   D. loses his investment

2. A client has a special cash account with stock valued at $460,000 and $40,000 in cash. The same client also has a joint account with a spouse that has a market value of $320,000 and $180,000 in cash. SIPC coverage is

   A. $460,000 for the special cash account; $320,000 for the joint account
   B. $500,000 for the special cash account; $420,000 for the joint account
   C. $500,000 for the special cash account; $500,000 for the joint account
   D. Total of $1 million for both accounts

3. SIPC uses which of the following to determine the value of customer claims when a broker/dealer becomes insolvent?

   A. Market value on the date the broker/dealer becomes insolvent
   B. Market value on the date a federal court is petitioned to appoint a trustee
   C. Market value on the date the trustee pays the customers their balances
   D. Average market value from the time a trustee is appointed to the payment date

4. Which of the following statements is not true regarding the civil penalties that may be imposed for insider trading violations under the Securities Exchange Act of 1934?

   A. A civil penalty may be imposed only on a person registered under a securities act.
   B. The violation for which the penalty may be imposed is defined as "buying or selling securities while in possession of material, nonpublic information."
   C. The SEC may ask a court to impose a penalty of up to three times the loss avoided or profit gained on an illegal transaction.
   D. Improper supervision may cause a broker/dealer to be liable if one of its reps commits an insider trading violation.

5. Under the Securities Exchange Act of 1934, insiders include the

   I. attorney who writes an offering circular for a company
   II. bookkeeper in a company's accounting department
   III. wife of a company's president
   IV. brother of a company's president

   A. I only
   B. II only
   C. II, III and IV
   D. I, II, III and IV

6. Which of the following acts requires corporations to issue annual reports?

   A. Securities Act of 1933
   B. Securities Exchange Act of 1934
   C. Trust Indenture Act of 1939
   D. Investment Company Act of 1940

7. Under the Securities Exchange Act of 1934, the SEC

   I. regulates the securities exchanges
   II. requires the registration of brokers and dealers
   III. prohibits inequitable and unfair trade practices
   IV. regulates the over-the-counter markets

   A. I and II
   B. I and IV
   C. II, III and IV
   D. I, II, III and IV

Answers

1. **B.** Any customer claims that SIPC does not cover result in the customer becoming a general (unsecured) creditor of the company.

2. **B.** SIPC coverage is $500,000 per separate customer account, with cash not to exceed $100,000. Thus, in the single-name account, SIPC provides full coverage, while in the joint account, SIPC covers the full value of the securities, but only $100,000 of the $180,000 in cash. The remaining $80,000 becomes a general debt of the bankrupt broker/dealer.

3. **B.** Under SIPC rules, customer claims are valued on the day customer protection proceedings commence; this is the day a federal court is petitioned to appoint a trustee.

4. **A.** The penalty may be imposed on anyone who trades on inside information and not just persons registered under the act. The other statements are correct: B defines insider trading; the penalty is up to 3 × profit gained or loss avoided (C); and an advisory firm may face a penalty for the actions of its reps (D).

5. **D.** While the Act of 1934 defines an insider as an officer, a director, or a 10% stockholder of a company, the courts have broadened the definition to include anyone who has inside information.

6. **B.** The Securities Exchange Act of 1934 mandates that companies file annual reports with the SEC.

7. **D.** The Securities Exchange Act of 1934, which has greater breadth than the Act of 1933, addresses the following: creation of the SEC; regulation of exchanges; regulation of credit by the FRB; registration of broker/dealers; regulation of insider transactions; short sales and proxies; regulation of trading activities; regulation of client accounts; the customer protection rule; regulation of the OTC market; and the net capital rule.

Penny Stock Cold Calling Rules

The SEC adopted the **Penny Stock Cold Calling Rule** to prevent certain abusive sales practices involving high-risk securities sold to unsophisticated investors. These rules involve the solicitation of non-Nasdaq equity securities traded in the OTC market for prices of less than $5 per share. These equity securities are frequently referred to as **penny stocks,** and are considered highly speculative.

These rules state that when a broker/dealer's representative contacts a noncustomer to purchase penny stock, the representative must first determine suitability based on information about the buyer's financial situation and objectives. The customer must sign and date this suitability statement before the penny stock trades can be effected.

In addition, the broker/dealer must disclose:

- the name of the penny stock;
- the number of shares to be purchased;
- a current quotation; and
- the amount of commission that the firm and the rep received.

Regardless of activity, if the account holds penny stocks, broker/dealers must provide a monthly statement of account to the customer. This must indicate the market value and number of shares for each penny stock held in the account, as well as the issuer's name.

Established Customers

Established customers are exempt from the cold calling rule, but not from the disclosure requirements.

An **established customer** is someone who has:

- held an account with the broker/dealer for at least one year (and has made a deposit of funds or securities); or
- made at least three penny stock purchases of different issuers on different days.

✓ *Take Note:* The provisions of the penny stock rules apply only to solicited transactions. Transactions not recommended by the broker/dealer are exempt.

USA Patriot Act (2001)

The Patriot Act establishes the US Treasury Department as the lead agency for developing regulation in connection with anti-money laundering programs. It also requires broker/dealers to establish internal compliance procedures to detect abuses. Prior to September 11, money laundering rules were concerned with the origin of the cash.

Under the Patriot Act, regulators are more concerned with where the funds are going. The idea is to prevent "clean" money from being used for "dirty" purposes (such as funding terrorist activities).

Current regulations require that:

- currency transaction deposits of $10,000 or more be reported to the IRS on Form 4789;
- broker/dealers file **Suspicious Activity Reports** on "financial behavior which is commercially illogical and serves no apparent purpose."

✓ **For Example:** If a customer were to pay for a $60,000 securities purchase with 120 $500 postal money orders, a SAR should be filed.

State Securities Regulations

In addition to federal securities regulations, each state has laws that pertain to the issuance and trading of securities. These state securities laws are known as **blue-sky laws** because of a statement made by a Kansas Supreme Court justice, who referred to "speculative schemes that have no more basis than so many feet of blue sky."

The Uniform Securities Act (USA)

The **Uniform Securities Act** provides a legal framework for the state registration of securities. It may be adopted by individual states and adapted to their needs. State registration requirements apply to broker/dealers, investment advisers, investment adviser representatives, and registered representatives. State securities administrators have the power to revoke any of these registrations if a violation of the state's law has occurred.

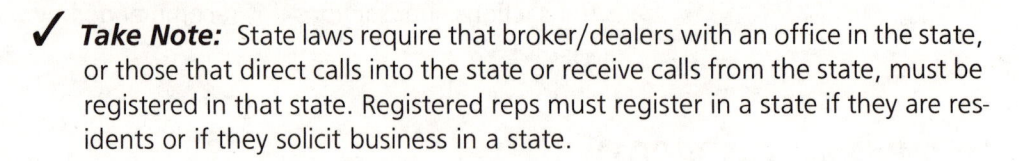

✓ **Take Note:** State laws require that broker/dealers with an office in the state, or those that direct calls into the state or receive calls from the state, must be registered in that state. Registered reps must register in a state if they are residents or if they solicit business in a state.

Registering Securities States have three ways to register (or blue-sky) securities: coordination, filing, and qualification.

Coordination. The issuer files with the state at the same time it files with the SEC. Registration is effective at the time the federal filing becomes effective. Coordination can only be used for IPOs (securities that have not been previously registered with the SEC).

Filing (Notification). If an issuer has met various financial criteria and has filed previously in a state, it can notify the state that it is about to sell securities. If the state does not reply, the registration is effective on the fifth business day after the filing.

Qualification. If registration cannot be accomplished by coordination or filing, it must be registered by qualification. In this situation, the issuer must respond to any requirement the state specifies. This type of registration is effective only when so ordered by the state securities commissioner. It is the most difficult way of registering securities in a state.

Test Topic Alert! Success in this business is dependent upon the ability to work within these rules. Don't worry about memorizing the dates of the acts; it is more important to be able to clearly identify the context of each act and its significance.

Quick Quiz 16.3

Match each of the following terms with the appropriate description below.

A. Blue-sky laws
B. Inside information
C. Investment adviser
D. Penny Stock Cold Calling Rule
E. Investment Company Act of 1940

___ 1. Requires a minimum of $100,000 and 100 shareholders

___ 2. To register a securities offering in a particular state

___ 3. Person who provides investment recommendations for a flat fee or percentage of assets managed

___ 4. New customer signs suitability statement prior to first trade

___ 5. Material information not readily available to the general public

Answers   1. *E.*   2. *A.*   3. *C.*   4. *D.*   5. *B.*

Quick Quiz 16.4

Match each of the following items with the appropriate description below.

A. Maloney Act
B. Trust Indenture Act
C. Insider
D. Securities Act of 1933
E. Securities Exchange Act of 1934

___ 1. Directors, officers, and stockholders who own more than 10% of any class of a corporation's stock

___ 2. Chartered the NASD as the SRO of the over-the-counter market

___ 3. Regulates only senior corporate securities

___ 4. Regulates the issuing process

___ 5. Prohibits trading practices like front running, price fixing, and market manipulation

Answers   1. **C.**   2. **A.**   3. **B.**   4. **D.**   5. **E.**

US Government and State Rules & Regulations HotSheet

Act of 1933:
- The Paper Act
- Nonexempt issuers must file registration statements with the SEC
- Requires use of prospectus when selling new issues
- Requires full and fair disclosure of new issues
- Regulates primary market activity (issuing and underwriting)

Act of 1934:
- The People Act; regulates secondary market activity
- Created the SEC
- Requires registration of all reps and firms that trade securities for the public
- Oversees exchanges and OTC market
- Regulates extension of credit
- Prohibits fraudulent trading activities
- Regulates insider transactions, short sales, proxies, and client accounts
- Prohibits use of inside information
- No security is exempt from antifraud provisions (even if exempt from 1933 registration)

Maloney Act:
- Chartered the NASD as the SRO of the OTC

Trust Indenture Act of 1939:
- Regulates senior corporate securities (bonds)
- Requires trust indenture/trustee for issues of more than $5 million in 12 months
- Trust indenture is covenant between issuer and trustee for protection of bondholders

Investment Advisers Act of 1940:
- Requires registration of persons who receive fees for giving investment advice

Investment Company Act of 1940:
- Regulates and defines investment companies
- Three types of investment companies: face amount certificate companies; unit investment trusts; management companies
- Requires clearly stated investment objectives
- Minimum of $100,000 assets, 100 shareholders

Insider Trading Act of 1988:
- Tippers and tippees are guilty
- Penalties up to greater of $1,000,000 or 3 × profit made/loss avoided
- Broker/dealers must have written supervisory procedures
- Chinese Walls prohibit sensitive information passed between departments of broker/dealers

Penny Stock Cold Calling Rule:
- Persons that buy non-Nasdaq stock of less than $5 must sign suitability statements before transactions
- Firms required to provide monthly statements of penny stock accounts regardless of activity
- Customers receive disclosure of risk and commissions made by rep firm
- Customers who opened account more than 12 months before, or made three different penny stock transactions with the firm

Uniform Securities Act (USA):
- Blue-sky laws—coordination, filing, qualification for registering securities
- Requires registration of securities, broker/dealers, and reps at state level

Series 7 Unit Test 16

1. All of the following refer to blue-sky laws EXCEPT

    A. state laws are designed to protect the public against fraud in securities sales within a state
    B. Securities Act of 1933 and Securities and Exchange Act of 1934
    C. forms requiring issuers selling securities in the state to comply with state securities laws
    D. state securities law which grants state securities Administrators the power to deny or revoke a broker/dealer or a registered rep's registration within its state

2. The Trust Indenture Act of 1939 applies to

    I. Nonexempt debt securities
    II. Interstate offerings
    III. Offerings over $5 million
    IV. Offerings under $5 million

    A. I, II and III
    B. I and III
    C. I and IV
    D. II and III

3. The Securities Exchange Act of 1934 contains sections that deal with

    A. regulation of investment companies
    B. trading activities such as short sales, stabilizing, and registering over-the-counter brokers and dealers
    C. form and content of the prospectus that must be given to all prospective purchasers of a security
    D. registration of persons engaged in the business of advising others about investment company transactions

4. In which of the following situations must a broker/dealer registered with the SEC under the Act of 1934 also be registered as an investment adviser under the Investment Advisers Act of 1940?

    A. Its registered representatives provide investment advice as part of its service.
    B. Its publications make purchase and sale recommendations without charge.
    C. It provides a financial planning service for a separate fee.
    D. No additional registration requirement applies.

5. The determination of a broker/dealer's financial failure is made under the provisions of the

    A. Securities Act of 1933
    B. 1939 Trust Indenture Act
    C. Securities Investor Protection Act of 1970
    D. 1939 Maloney Act

6. Under SEC rules, a penny stock is defined as an unlisted, non-Nasdaq security trading at less than

    A. $1.00/share only
    B. $2.00/share only
    C. $2.50/share only
    D. $5.00/share only

7. Which of the following legislative acts exclusively regulates debt securities?

    A. Securities Act of 1933
    B. Securities Exchange Act of 1934
    C. Trust Indenture Act of 1939
    D. Investment Advisers Act of 1940

8. To which of the following do the antifraud provisions of the Securities Exchange Act of 1934 apply?

    I. Municipal bonds
    II. National exchange-listed securities
    III. Nasdaq-listed securities
    IV. Investment company securities

    A. I, II and III
    B. II, III and IV
    C. III only
    D. I, II, III and IV

9. Which of the following customer accounts is(are) not SIPC-insured?

    I. Customer margin account
    II. JTWROS account with spouse
    III. JTIC commodities account with son
    IV. JTIC account with business partner

    A. I only
    B. II and III
    C. II, III and IV
    D. III only

10. Which of the following statements about SIPC are true?

    I. It is a nonprofit membership corporation.
    II. It is an agency of the US Government.
    III. It is funded by broker/dealers.
    IV. Coverage is limited to $500,000 per customer.

    A. I and III
    B. I, III and IV
    C. I and IV
    D. II, III and IV

11. Which of the following persons require state registration?

    I. In-state salesperson
    II. In-state broker/dealer
    III. Out-of-state salesperson doing business in that state
    IV. Out-of-state broker/dealer doing business in that state

    A. I and II only
    B. II and IV only
    C. III and IV only
    D. I, II, III, and IV

12. Which of the following acts requires full disclosure of all material information about securities offered for the first time to the public?

    A. Securities Act of 1933
    B. Securities Exchange Act of 1934
    C. Trust Indenture Act of 1939
    D. Securities Investor Protection Act of 1970

13. Under terms of the Telephone Consumer Privacy Act, which of the following statements are TRUE?

    I. The firm must maintain a Do Not Call list.
    II. Cold calls can be made only between 8:00 a.m. and 9:00 p.m.
    III. The time period of the call applies to the time zone in which the representative is making the call.
    IV. The time period of the call applies to the time zone where the phone call is received.

    A. I, II and III
    B. I, II and IV
    C. I and III
    D. II and IV

14. The chairman of XYZ Corporation confides to a neighbor that his company will be announcing a major acquisition the following week. As a result of this conversation, the neighbor buys call options on the target company in his personal account. Who violated insider trading rules?

    A. The chairman
    B. The neighbor
    C. Both A and B
    D. Neither A nor B

Series 7 Unit Test 16 Answers & Rationale

1. B. Blue-sky laws are state securities laws. The Securities Act of 1933 and the Securities Exchange Act of 1934 are federal securities laws. QID: 29613

2. A. Corporate debt offerings under $5 million and exempt issues are not subject to the Trust Indenture Act of 1939. QID: 35125

3. B. The Securities Exchange Act of 1934, which has greater breadth than the Securities Act of 1933, addresses the creation of the SEC, the regulation of exchanges, the regulation of credit by the FRB, the registration of broker/dealers, the regulation of insider transactions, short sales and proxies, the regulation of trading activities, the regulation of client accounts, the customer protection rule, the regulation of the OTC market, the net capital rule. The Investment Company Act of 1940 defines and regulates investment companies. The Securities Act of 1933 addresses registration and prospectus requirements. Persons who provide investment advice to others for a fee are subject to the Investment Advisers Act of 1940. QID: 32256

4. C. A broker/dealer that receives special compensation for providing investment advice (separate from any commissions, markups, or markdowns) must register as an investment adviser. QID: 29678

5. C. Determination of financial failure is made under the Securities Investor Protection Act of 1970. QID: 28366

6. D. SEC rules define penny stock as non-Nasdaq stock of less than $5.00 per share. QID: 35041

7. C. The Trust Indenture Act of 1939 protects investors in corporate bonds in the case of the default of the issuing company. While the Acts of 1933 and 1934 both impact debt securities, the Trust Indenture Act of 1939 is the only act that regulates them exclusively. QID: 32253

8. D. All securities are subject to the antifraud provisions of federal securities law. QID: 29651

9. D. SIPC coverage only applies to accounts holding securities; therefore, commodities accounts are not covered. QID: 28368

10. B. SIPC is a membership corporation formed to protect investors as of the Securities Investor Protection Act (SIPA) of 1970. It is not an agency of the US government. Broker/dealers, other than mutual fund and variable annuity dealers, are required to pay membership assessments which provide coverage of up to $500,000 per customer upon broker/dealer default. QID: 35026

11. D. Any broker/dealer or salesperson doing business in the state must be registered in that state. QID: 32251

12. A. The Securities Act of 1933 regulates new issues of corporate securities sold to the public. QID: 32255

13. B. This federal law allows a prospect to request that the firm make no further phone calls. Any solicitation made must occur between 8:00 a.m. and 9:00 p.m. in the recipient's time zone. QID: 35076

14. C. Once inside information is used to trade for profit or to avoid a loss, both the tipper (the chairman) and the tippee (the neighbor) have violated insider trading rules. QID: 36458

17

Other SEC & SRO Rules & Regulations

INTRODUCTION

The securities industry in the United States is among the most heavily regulated in the world. Firms and representatives must comply with SEC rules, the rules of the SROs, and house rules developed by the firm internally. The intent of these rules is to protect the public, and your career depends on your ability to follow the rules and regulations of the industry.

The SEC was created by the Securities Exchange Act of 1934 and is the primary regulatory body over the securities industry. SROs, acting under authority approved by the SEC, regulate the conduct of business. These include the NYSE, NASD, MSRB, and CBOE. The type and location of a security transaction determines which SRO has jurisdiction. A very substantial portion of the exam will be devoted to these and other industry rules.

The SEC and SRO rules presented in this unit will account for approximately 10–15 questions on the Series 7 examination.

UNIT OBJECTIVES

When you have completed this unit, you should be able to:

- define the role of the SEC in the securities industry;
- explain the relationship between the SEC and SROs;
- list and describe the function of the four largest SROs;
- describe the process of NASD registration for broker/dealers and associated persons;
- identify the four sets of rules and codes of the *NASD Manual*;
- compare the Code of Procedure and the Code of Arbitration;
- identify unique rules of the NYSE;
- define advertising and sales literature and describe applicable disclosure and filing rules; and
- outline compliance requirements of the Telephone Consumer Protection Act of 1991.

Registration and Regulation of Broker/Dealers

The Securities and Exchange Commission (SEC)

The SEC is the securities industry's primary regulatory body. Broker/dealers that transact securities business with customers or with other broker/dealers must apply and be approved for registration with the SEC.

Although a broker/dealer must register with the SEC, the broker/dealer may not claim that this registration in any way implies that the Commission has passed upon or approved the broker/dealer's financial standing, business, or conduct. Any such claim or statement is misrepresentation.

Broker/Dealer Registration and Compliance

Broker/dealers must comply with SEC rules and regulations when conducting business. A broker/dealer that does not comply is subject to:

- censure;
- limits on activities, functions, or operations;
- suspension of its registration (or one of its associated person's license to do business);
- revocation of registration; or
- fine.

Associated Persons

An associated person can also be disciplined for violating SEC rules and regulations. If the SEC bars an associated person, no broker/dealer may allow that person to associate with it without the Commission's express permission. If a member firm suspends an associated person, the firm must report the suspension to the exchanges where the firm is a member.

Fingerprinting

Registered broker/dealers must have fingerprint records made for most of their employees, and all directors, officers, and partners must submit those fingerprint cards to the US attorney general for identification and processing.

Exemptions. Certain broker/dealer employees (typically clerical) are exempt from the fingerprinting requirement if they:

- are not involved in securities sales;
- do not handle or have access to cash or securities or to the books and records of original entry relating to money and securities; and
- do not supervise other employees engaged in these activities.

💡 **Test Topic Alert!**

Just as the SEC does not approve the release of new issues of securities, it does not approve the way a firm or rep transacts business.

The SEC was created under the Securities Exchange Act of 1934, requires registration of all broker/dealers, and regulates all exchanges and trading markets.

Persons who must be fingerprinted are those involved in sales and those that handle cash or customer securities. Clerical persons (sometimes called ministerial persons) need not be fingerprinted.

Self-Regulatory Organizations (SROs)

Eight self-regulatory organizations function under the SECs oversight. Each SRO is accountable to the Commission for enforcing federal securities laws as well as supervising securities practices within an assigned jurisdiction. The largest of these SROs and their jurisdictions follow.

National Association of Securities Dealers (NASD) — The **NASD** regulates all matters related to investment banking (securities underwriting) and trading in the OTC market and to the conduct of NASD member firms and associated persons. The NASD also regulates investment companies and limited partnership transactions.

New York Stock Exchange (NYSE) — The **NYSE** regulates all matters related to trading in NYSE-listed securities and to the conduct of NYSE member firms and associated persons.

Municipal Securities Rulemaking Board (MSRB) — The **MSRB** regulates all matters related to the underwriting and trading of state and municipal securities. The MSRB regulates, but does not have enforcement powers—it depends on other SROs for the enforcement of its rules.

Chicago Board Options Exchange (CBOE) — The **CBOE** regulates all matters related to trading standardized options and related contracts listed on that exchange.

The National Association of Securities Dealers (NASD)

The National Association of Securities Dealers is the OTC industry's SRO and **membership corporation**.

The NASD's purposes and objectives are to:

- promote the investment banking and securities business, standardize principles and practices, promote high standards of commercial honor and encourage the observance of federal and state securities laws;
- provide a medium for communication among its members, and between its members, the government, and other agencies;
- adopt, administer, and enforce the NASD's Conduct Rules and rules designed to prevent fraudulent and manipulative practices, as well as to promote just and equitable principles of trade; and
- promote self-discipline among members and investigate and adjust grievances between the public and members and between members.

Characteristics of the NASD

Districts The NASD divides the United States into 11 districts to facilitate its operation. Each district elects a district committee to administer NASD rules.

Dues, Assessments, and Other Charges

Assessments

The NASD is funded by **assessments** of member firms' registered reps and applicants and by annual fees. The annual fee each member pays includes a(n):

- basic membership fee;
- assessment based on gross income;
- fee for each principal and registered representative; and
- charge for each branch office.

Failure to pay dues can result in suspension or revocation of membership.

Use of the NASD Corporate Name NASD members cannot use the NASD name in a manner that would suggest that the NASD has endorsed a member firm. Members may use the phrase *Member of the NASD* as long as the firm places no undue emphasis on it.

The NASD Manual

NASD policies are specified in the *NASD Manual*. The Manual describes four sets of rules and codes by which the OTC market is regulated:

Conduct Rules The **Conduct Rules** set out fair and ethical trade practices that member firms and their reps must follow when dealing with the public.

Uniform Practice Code (UPC) The **UPC** established the Uniform Trade Practices, including settlement, good delivery, ex-dates, confirmations, don't know (DK) procedures, and other guidelines for broker/dealers to follow when they do business with other member firms.

Code of Procedure — The **Code of Procedure** describes how the NASD hears and handles member violations of the Conduct Rules.

Code of Arbitration Procedure — The **Code of Arbitration Procedure** governs the resolution of disagreements and claims between members, registered reps, and the public; it addresses monetary claims.

NASD Membership and Registration

The NASD's **National Adjudicatory Council (NAC)** establishes rules, regulations, and membership eligibility standards. At present, the following membership standards and registration requirements are in place.

Broker/Dealer Registration — Any broker/dealer registered with the SEC is eligible and may apply for membership in the NASD. Any person who effects transactions in securities as a broker, a dealer, or an investment banker also may register with the NASD, as may municipal bond firms. Application for NASD membership carries the applying firm's specific agreement to:

- comply with the Association's rules and regulations;
- comply with federal securities laws; and
- pay dues, assessments, and other charges in the manner and amounts fixed by the Association.

A **membership application** is made to the NASD district office in the district in which the applying firm has its home office. If a district committee passes on the firm's qualifications, the firm can be accepted into NASD membership.

Associated Person Registration — Any person associated with an NASD member firm who intends to engage in the investment banking or securities business must be registered with the NASD as an associated person. Anyone applying for registration with the NASD as an associated person must be sponsored by a member firm.

Qualifications Investigated

Before submitting an application to enroll any person with the NASD as a registered representative, a member firm must ascertain the person's business reputation, character, education, qualifications, and experience. As part of the application process, the member firm must certify that it has made an investigation and that the candidate's credentials are in order.

Failure to Register Personnel

A member firm's failure to register an employee who performs any of the functions of a registered rep may lead to disciplinary action by the NASD.

Postregistration Rules and Regulations

Continuing Education

Registered persons are required to participate in continuing education programs. The CE requirement has two components: a **regulatory element** and a **firm element**.

Regulatory Element

The **regulatory element** requires that all registered persons complete a computer-based training session within 120 days of the person's second registration anniversary and every three years thereafter (i.e., within 120 days of the person's 5th, 8th, 11th registration anniversary and so on). The content of the regulatory element is determined by the NASD and is appropriate to either the registered representative or principal status of the person.

There is a one-time exemption from the regulatory element for persons who, as of July 1, 1998, have been continuously registered for more than 10 years and who have no significant disciplinary history. If a person fails to complete the regulatory element within the prescribed period, the NASD will inactivate that person's registration until the requirements of the program are met.

Firm Element

The **firm element** requires member firms to prepare an annual training plan taking into account such factors as recent regulatory developments, the scope of the member's business activities, the performance of its personnel in the regulatory element and its supervisory needs. This annual in-house training must be given to all registered persons who have direct contact with the public.

Registered Persons Changing Firms

NASD registration is **nontransferable**. A registered person who leaves one member firm to join another firm, must terminate registration at the first firm on a **U-5 form** and reapply for registration with the new employing member firm on a **U-4 form**. If a person terminates his registration with one firm, he must register with another firm within two years or he will be required to requalify for his license.

Continuing Commissions

A registered rep who leaves a member firm—upon retirement, for instance—may continue to receive commissions on business placed while employed. However, the rep must have a contract to this effect before leaving the firm. A deceased representative's heirs also may receive continuing commissions on business the representative placed if a contract exists.

Notification of Disciplinary Action A member firm must notify the NASD if any associated person in the firm's employment is subjected to disciplinary action by one of the following:

- national securities exchange or association;
- clearing corporation;
- commodity futures market regulatory agency; or
- federal or state regulatory commission.

The notification must include the individual's name and the nature of the action. A member firm must notify the NASD of disciplinary action the firm has taken against an associated person and the nature of the action.

Terminations If an associated person voluntarily ends his employment with a member, his NASD registration ceases 30 calendar days from the date the NASD receives written notice from the employing member firm. Whenever any registered person's employment is terminated, the member firm must notify the NASD and the NYSE in writing within 30 calendar days.

Terminating Reps Under Investigation

If a registered rep or another associated person is under investigation for federal securities law violations or has disciplinary action pending against him from the NASD or any other SRO, a member firm may not terminate its business relationship with the person until the investigation or disciplinary action has been resolved.

Exemptions from Registration

Certain people do not have to register with the NASD as associated persons.

Foreign Associates Non-US citizens employed by NASD member firms (usually in Canadian or overseas branch offices) are not subject to licensing with the Association. This does not include US citizens living and working in overseas or Canadian branch offices.

Clerical Personnel and Corporate Officers A member firm's clerical employees need not register with the NASD.

Employees in Other Specific Functions Employees registered with an exchange as floor members who work or trade only on the floor or who transact business only in exempted securities or commodities are exempt from registration.

State Registration In addition to registering with the NASD, registered representatives and broker/dealers must register with the state securities administrator in each state in which they intend to do business.

Qualifications Examinations

To become a registered representative or principal, an individual must pass the appropriate licensing examination(s).

Registered Representatives

All associated persons engaged in the investment banking and securities business are considered **registered representatives**, including any:

- assistant officer who does not function as a principal;
- individual who supervises, solicits, or conducts business in securities; and
- individual who trains people to supervise, solicit, or conduct business in securities.

General Securities Representative License (Series 7)

A Series 7 general securities license allows a registered representative to sell almost all types of securities products. A general securities representative cannot sell commodities futures without a Series 3 license.

Registered Principals

Anyone who manages or supervises any part of a member's investment banking or securities business must be registered as a **principal** with the NASD (including people involved solely in training associated persons). Unless the member firm is a sole proprietorship, it must employ at least two registered principals.

General Securities Principal License (Series 24)

Any person actively engaged in managing a member's securities or investment banking business, including supervising, soliciting, and conducting business, or in training persons associated with the member, must qualify by examination and register with the NASD as a **general securities principal**.

A person registered as a general securities principal is not qualified to function as a municipal securities principal, a **registered options principal (ROP)**, a **financial and operations principal (FinOp)**, or a general securities sales supervisor. A registered general securities principal expecting to function in one or more of these areas also must be registered with the NASD in each separate field of expertise. The Series 7 is a prerequisite for the Series 24.

Limited Principal Licenses

Registered Options Principal (Series 4)

If a member does options business with the public, it must employ at least one ROP (Series 4) in the firm. In addition, the member must notify the Association as to which of the firm's ROPs is to be designated as a **compliance registered options principal (CROP)** and which as a **supervisory registered options principal (SROP)**. No additional qualifications examinations are necessary before designation as a CROP or SROP. The Series 7 is a prerequisite for registration as a ROP.

Series 9 and 10

Each NYSE firm must have a supervisory principal overseeing sales of securities products within the firm. Branch managers and sales managers who report to a ROP may qualify as **options sales supervisors** by passing the General Securities Sales Supervisor exam, the Series 9 and 10 exam. This registration is appropriate for individuals who must register as principals to supervise sales activities in corporate, municipal, and options securities; investment company products; variable contracts; and DPPs. The Series 7 is a prerequisite for registration as a general securities sales supervisor.

Series 27

In addition to having at least one general principal, each member must have at least one **financial and operations principal**. The FinOp is responsible for supervising the firm's financial administration and preparing, maintaining, approving, and filing the reports required of general securities member firms. Currently, no prerequisite exams are necessary to qualify for the Series 27 principal license.

Series 53

A member that conducts municipal securities business with the public must have at least one municipal securities principal (Series 53). This license entitles the principal to manage the member's municipal and government securities business. The Series 52 or the Series 7 is a prerequisite for the Series 53 principal examination.

Ineligibility and Disqualifications

A person may not act as a registered representative or principal unless the NASD's eligibility standards regarding training, experience, and competence are met.

Statutory Disqualification Disciplinary sanctions by the SEC, another SRO, a foreign financial regulator, or a foreign equivalent of an SRO can be cause for statutory disqualification of NASD membership.

An individual applying for registration as an associated person will be rejected if he:

- has been or is expelled or suspended from membership or participation in any other SRO or from the foreign equivalent of an SRO;

- is under an SEC order or an order of a foreign financial regulator denying, suspending, or revoking his registration or barring him from association with a broker/dealer; or
- has been found to be the cause of another broker/dealer or associated person being expelled or suspended by another SRO, the SEC, or a foreign equivalent of an SRO.

The following also can automatically disqualify an applicant for registration:

- misstatements willfully made in an application for membership or registration as an associated person;
- a felony conviction, either domestic or foreign, or a misdemeanor conviction involving securities or money within the past 10 years; and
- court injunctions prohibiting the individual from acting as an investment adviser, an underwriter, or a broker/dealer or in other capacities aligned with the securities and financial services industry.

Quick Quiz 17.1 Match each of the following items with the appropriate description below.

A. NASD
B. Department of Enforcement
C. MSRB
D. Uniform Practice Code (UPC)

___ 1. The SRO that cannot enforce its own rules

___ 2. Handles trade complaints within an NASD district

___ 3. The set of rules that establishes guidelines for business between firms

___ 4. The SRO of the OTC

Answers 1. **C.** 2. **B.** 3. **D.** 4. **A.**

Terms with Specific NASD Meanings

	Terms with Specific NASD Meanings
Associated Person of a Member	An employee, manager, director, officer, or partner of a member broker-dealer or another entity (issuer, bank, etc.) or person controlling, controlled by, or in common control with that member.
Broker	(1) An individual or a firm that charges a fee or commission for executing buy and sell orders submitted by another individual or firm. (2) The role of a brokerage firm when it acts as an agent for a customer and charges the customer a commission for its services. (3) Any person engaged in the business of effecting transactions in securities for the accounts of others who is not a bank.
Completion of the Transaction	The point at which a customer pays any part of the purchase price to the broker-dealer for a security he has purchased or delivers a security he has sold. If the customer makes payment to the broker-dealer before the payment is due, completion of the transaction occurs when the broker-dealer delivers the security.
Customer	Any individual, person, partnership, corporation, or other legal entity who is not a broker, dealer, or municipal securities dealer – that is, the public
Dealer	(1) The role of a brokerage firm when it acts as a principal in a particular trade. A firm acts as a dealer when it buys or sells a security for its own account and at its own risk, then charges the customer a markup or markdown. (2) Any person engaged in the business of buying and selling securities for his own account, either directly or through a broker, who is not a bank.
Member	(1) Of the NYSE: One of the 1,366 individuals owning a seat on the New York Stock Exchange. (2) Of the NASD: Any individual, partnership, corporation, or other legal entity admitted to membership in the NASD.
Security	Under the Act of 1934, any note, stock, bond, investment contract, variable annuity, profit sharing or partnership agreement, certificate of deposit (jumbo CD), option on a security, or other instrument of investment commonly known as a security.

Quick Quiz 17.2

Match each of the following numbers with the appropriate description below.

A. 30
B. 24
C. 10
D. 2

___ 1. The minimum number of principals a firm must have

___ 2. The number of days a broker/dealer has to notify the NASD of a representative's termination

___ 3. A felony conviction within this number of years can disqualify an individual from registration

Answers   1. **D.**   2. **A.**   3. **C.**

Investigation: Code of Procedure & Code of Arbitration Procedure

In connection with any investigation, complaint, or examination by the NASD, the Association can require a member firm or any person associated with a member to:

- provide information, orally, in writing, or electronically;
- give testimony under oath; and
- provide access to or copies of any books, records, or accounts.

If a member or associated person fails to comply, the **National Adjudicatory Council (NAC)**, after providing 20 days' written notice, has the right to **suspend** the member and **revoke the registration** of any associated person.

The NAC is responsible for the development of regulatory and enforcement policy and rule changes relating to the business and sales practices of member firms. It is also responsible for the oversight of the Department of Enforcement, which has the authority to file complaints against member firms and their associated persons.

Code of Procedure

The **Code of Procedure** was created to deal with alleged violations of NASD rules, MSRB rules, and federal securities laws. If after an investigation or audit, the NASD believes a member and/or its associated persons have violated one or more rules or laws, the Department of Enforcement will issue a **formal complaint**. With the filing of a complaint, the Department will name a Hearing Officer to preside over the disciplinary proceeding (Hearing) and will appoint panelists to serve as a jury. All panelists in Code of Procedure hearings are from the industry.

The **respondent** has 25 days after receiving the complaint to file an answer with the Hearing Officer. Answers must specifically admit, deny, or state that the respondent does not have sufficient information to admit or deny. If the respondent does not answer within 25 days, the Department will send a second notice requiring an answer within 14 days of receipt. This notice states that failure to reply allows the Hearing Officer to enter a default decision. At this point, the respondent is essentially considered guilty as charged.

If additional facts come to light that cause the Department to file an amended complaint, the time for filing an answer or amended answer is 14 days after receipt of the amended complaint.

✓ **Take Note:** If a complaint is filed against a registered representative, it is not all that unusual for that person's designated supervisor (e.g., branch manager) to be charged as well for **failure to supervise**.

Offer of Settlement

A respondent has the option of proposing a **settlement**. An **offer to settle** must be in writing and must:

- describe the specific rule or law that the member or associated person is alleged to have violated;
- describe the acts or practices that the member or associated person is alleged to have engaged in or omitted;
- include a statement consenting to findings of fact and violations contained in the complaint; and
- propose sanctions consistent with the Association's sanction guidelines.

Uncontested Offer

By submitting an offer of settlement, the respondent waives the right to a hearing and the right to appeal. If the offer is accepted by the Department of Enforcement, it is then sent to the NAC for review. If uncontested by the NAC, the offer is accepted and final—case closed.

Contested Offer

If the DOE opposes the offer, the offer is contested. At this point the offer and the Department's written opposition are submitted to the Hearing Officer. The Hearing Officer may order a settlement conference between the parties in an attempt to work out a compromise or may forward the offer and the

Department's opposition to the NAC. If the NAC rejects the offer (or compromise offer), the hearings begin. If accepted by the NAC, the offer (or compromise offer) is final. The good news is that if an offer of settlement is ultimately rejected, it may not be introduced as evidence at the hearing.

Acceptance, Waiver and Consent (AWC)

If the respondent does not dispute the allegations, the Department of Enforcement may prepare and request that the respondent sign a letter accepting a finding of violation, consenting to the imposition of sanctions, and waiving the right to a hearing and the right to appeal. If agreed to by the respondent, the letter is then sent to the NAC and becomes final if approved. If opposed by the NAC, next stop is formal hearings. However, it is most likely that if the Department of Enforcement felt there was a chance of opposition from the NAC, it would not have offered AWC in the first place.

Minor Rule Violation (MRV)

If the complaint involves a minor violation and the respondent does not dispute the allegation, the Department of Enforcement may prepare and request that the respondent sign an **MRV letter**, accepting a finding of violation. **Minor rule violations** are failure to:

- have advertising or sales literature approved by a principal prior to use;
- maintain a file for advertising and sales literature;
- file advertising and sales literature with the NASD within the required time frame;
- file timely reports on short positions;
- keep books and records in accordance with SEC rules; or
- submit trading data if requested by the NASD.

Once the respondent signs an MRV letter, the settlement is final. The NAC, as a sanction, may impose a fine not to exceed $2,500.

Prehearing Conference Assuming the respondent does not make an offer of settlement or if made is rejected, and assuming the Department of Enforcement does not offer either AWC or MRV as options, a **prehearing conference** is scheduled. Under Code of Procedure rules, it must be held within 21 days of receipt of the respondent's answer to the complaint. This conference deals with matters such as:

- simplification and clarification of the issues;
- witness lists and exhibit lists;
- criteria for including and excluding certain evidence; and
- the determination of a hearing date.

At the conference, parties to the dispute are warned that contemptuous or frivolous conduct by any person, including attorneys, will result in sanctions being imposed by the NAC.

Hearing At the **hearing**, which resembles a courtroom proceeding, the prosecution (Department of Enforcement) proceeds first. Cross-examination of witnesses is permitted. At the conclusion, panelists convene and within 60 days, render a written decision reflecting the majority view.

Sanctions **Sanctions** against a member or associated person, if found guilty, are included with the **written decision**. Under Code of Procedure, sanctions could include one or more of the following:

- censure;
- fine;
- suspension of the membership of a member or suspension of the registration of an associated person for a definite period;
- expulsion of the member, canceling the membership of the member, or revoking or canceling the registration of an associated person;
- barring a member or associated person from association with all members; and
- imposition of any other fitting sanction.

Suspension

If an associated person is **suspended**, that person cannot remain associated with the member in any capacity, including a clerical or administrative capacity (during the suspension period, that person cannot remain on the member's premises). Also, the member is prohibited from paying a salary, commission, or remuneration that the person might have earned during the suspension period.

✓ *Take Note:* The suspended person could be paid monies earned prior to the suspension period.

Effective Date of Sanctions

Other than a bar or an expulsion, effective as of the decision date, sanctions imposed are effective on a date specified by the Hearing Officer, but no earlier than 30 days after the written decision is handed down.

If the decision includes a fine or other monetary sanction (the member could be charged for a portion of the hearing costs) and the fine is not paid in accordance with the timetable set down in the decision, the NASD will send written notice to the member. The notice will state that if the fine is not paid within seven days, suspension or other sanctions may result.

Appeals If either side is displeased with the decision, an **appeal** can be made to the NAC. Any appeal must be made within 25 days of decision date; otherwise the decision is final. If no satisfaction is received from the NAC, the appealing party may take the case to the SEC. Again, if turned down, the appealing party has the right to continue the appeal process by taking its case to the federal court system. Appealing a decision stays the effective date of any sanctions, other than a bar or expulsion.

Quick Quiz 17.3   Match the numbers with the descriptions below.

A. 7
B. 14
C. 20
D. 21
E. 25
F. 30
G. 60

___ 1. The number of days after a Code of Procedure decision within which an appeal can be made to the NAC.

___ 2. If a fine or monetary sanction is not paid by the date set in a Code of Procedure decision, the NASD will send written notice to the member, which then has this many days to pay.

___ 3. Under Code of Procedure, sanctions other than a bar or expulsion are effective on a date specified by a Hearing Officer, but not earlier than this number of days after the decision is handed down.

___ 4. Number of days after a Code of Procedure Hearing within which panelists will render a written decision

___ 5. Under Code of Procedure rules, the number of days after receipt of a respondent's answer to a complaint, within which a prehearing conference must be held.

___ 6. Number of days respondent has to answer a second notice or an amended complaint from the Department of Enforcement.

___ 7. The number of days a respondent has to file an answer to a formal complaint from the Department of Enforcement.

___ 8. The number of days after giving written notice, that the NAC can suspend a member firm or revoke a registration for failure to comply with an information request related to an NASD investigation.

Answers   1. E.   2. A.   3. F.   4. G.
5. D.   6. B.   7. E.   8. C.

Code of Arbitration

The **Code of Arbitration** of the NASD was originally established to mediate unresolved intra-industry disputes. It was mandatory in controversies involving:

- a member against another member or registered clearing agency;
- a member against an associated person; and
- an associated person against another associated person.

Over time, customer complaints became subject to mandatory arbitration.

✓ *Take Note:* In the absence of a signed arbitration agreement, a customer can still force a member to arbitration but a member cannot force a customer to arbitration.

Today, virtually all new account forms contain a predispute arbitration clause that must be signed by customers prior to account opening. Thus, unresolved customer complaints must be mediated under the Code of Arbitration.

Class action claims are not subject to arbitration. In addition, claims alleging employment discrimination, including sexual harassment claims, are not required to be arbitrated unless the parties agree.

The advantages of arbitration over suits in state or federal courts are savings of time, money, and the fact that all decisions are final and binding; no appeals are allowed. One party may not like the result, but the problem is history.

Initiation of Proceedings Any party to an unresolved dispute can initiate proceedings by filing a claim with the director of arbitration of the NASD. The **statement of claim** must describe in detail the controversy in dispute, include documentation in support of the claim, and state the remedy being sought (dollars). The **claimant** must also include a check for the required claim filing fee. The director will then send a copy of the claim to the other party (respondent).

The respondent then has 45 calendar days to respond to both the director and the claimant. The answer must specify all available defenses and any related counterclaim the respondent may have against the claimant. A respondent who fails to answer within 45 days may, at the sole discretion of the director, be barred from presenting any matter, arguments, or defenses at the hearing.

The claimant, after receiving the respondent's answer, must provide each party (the respondent and the director) with a written reply within 10 calendar days. At this point, the initial discovery is over.

If the dispute involves **irreparable injury** to one of the parties, that party may seek an interim injunction or a permanent injunction. The party seeking relief must make a clear showing that its case is likely to succeed on its merits and that it will suffer permanent harm unless immediate relief is granted.

Mediation If both parties agree, prior to the opening of hearings, a meeting may be held in an attempt to work out a settlement. A mediator is selected to preside over the discussions and to assist the parties in reaching their own solution. If mediation is unsuccessful, then the problem goes on to the hearing.

✓ *Take Note:* A mediator is prohibited from serving on an arbitration panel regarding any matter in which that person served as mediator.

Selection of Arbitrators The NASD maintains a list of arbitrators divided into two categories; **nonpublic** and **public**. A nonpublic arbitrator is one who is, or within the past three years was either associated with a broker/dealer or registered under the Commodity Exchange Act.

In addition, attorneys, accountants, or other professionals who devote at least 20% of their time to work in the securities or commodity business fit this category. A public arbitrator is one who is not engaged directly or indirectly in the securities or commodities business. In intra-industry disputes, all of the arbitrators are generally nonpublic. In disputes involving a customer, the majority of arbitrators will be public.

Simplified Arbitration Any dispute involving a dollar amount of $25,000 or less is eligible for **simplified arbitration**. In this instance, a single arbitrator reviews all of the evidence and renders a binding decision within 30 business days.

✓ *Take Note:* Both parties have to agree to this simplified arbitration, otherwise, a formal hearing is required.

Awards All monetary awards must be paid within 30 days of decision date. Any award not paid within this time frame will begin to accrue interest as of the decision date. In addition, all awards and details on the underlying arbitration claim are made publicly available by the NASD.

Failure to Act It is a violation of NASD rules for a member or an associated person to fail to:

- submit a dispute for arbitration;
- comply with any injunction order;
- appear or produce any document as directed;
- honor an award; or
- comply with an executed collective agreement obtained as the result of mediation.

Action by members requiring associated persons to waive the arbitration of disputes is also a rules violation.

Statute of Limitations No claim is eligible for submission to arbitration if six years or more have elapsed from the time of the event giving rise to the claim.

Test Topic Alert! When distinguishing between Code of Procedure and Code of Arbitration Procedure, remember that the COP handles complaints.

If asked which section of the NASD rule manual addresses complaints, choose the Code of Procedure (COP). Associate disciplinary action with a COP.

If asked which section applies to settling disputes between members, or any problem between parties associated with the securities industry, choose the Code of Arbitration Procedure.

Arbitration is the industry choice over civil court because it is cheaper. There are no appeals, and decisions are binding on all parties.

Finally, the NASD has the authority to impose virtually any disciplinary action, other than a jail sentence, against a guilty rep or firm.

Quick Quiz 17.4 True or False?

___ 1. In the absence of a signed arbitration agreement, customers can still force member firms to arbitration, but member firms cannot force customers to arbitration.

___ 2. Arbitrators, who are attorneys, accountants, or other professionals that devote at least 20% of their time to work in the securities or commodity business, are considered nonpublic arbitrators.

___ 3. In simplified arbitration, a panel of three arbitrators reviews all the evidence and renders a binding decision.

___ 4. The statute of limitations for submission of a claim to arbitration is six years.

___ 5. Monetary awards, if not paid immediately, begin accruing interest as of the decision date.

___ 6. Under the Code of Arbitration, a respondent to a statement of claim must respond to the director of arbitration of the NASD and the claimant within 45 days.

Answers

1. **T.** Customers can force members into arbitration, but without an arbitration agreement, a member cannot force a customer to arbitration. However, virtually all new account forms contain a predispute arbitration clause that must be signed by customers prior to opening an account; this way unresolved customer complaints must be mediated under the Code of Arbitration.

2. **T.**

3. **F.** In simplified arbitration, a single arbitrator reviews the evidence and renders a binding decision within 30 days.

4. **T.**

5. **F.** Monetary awards resulting from arbitration must be paid within 30 days of the decision date. If not paid within 30 days, the award will begin accruing interest as of the decision date.

6. **T.**

Quick Quiz 17.5
Match the numbers with the description. Choices can be used more than once.

A. 25
B. 30
C. 45

___ 1. Number of days to begin an appeal of a DOE decision to the NAC

___ 2. Number of calendar days to respond to a DOE complaint notice

___ 3. Number of days after which a DOE decision becomes final

___ 4. Number of days from the Department of Enforcement's decision the NAC has to call for decision review

___ 5. Number of business days for an arbitration panel to render a decision

Answers 1. **A.** 2. **A.** 3. **C.** 4. **C.** 5. **B.**

Quick Quiz 17.6 Multiple Choice

1. The Code of Arbitration is for

    A. handling violations of the Conduct Rules
    B. ensuring just and equitable practices of fair trade
    C. establishing uniform trade practices
    D. handling disagreements and claims between member firms, registered representatives, and the public

2. Disciplinary decisions of the NASD National Adjudicatory Council and appellate and review procedures are matters covered in the

    A. SEC Bylaws
    B. Conduct Rules
    C. Code of Procedure
    D. Uniform Practice Code

3. If a case has gone to the Board of Arbitration of the NASD or NYSE, the decisions made are

    A. not binding on a client but are binding on the member
    B. binding only if the two parties agree on the decision
    C. not binding if the two parties decide not to accept the decision
    D. always binding on all parties to the arbitration

Answers

1. **D.** The Code of Arbitration provides procedures for settling disputes, claims, and controversies that arise between broker/dealers, registered reps, and the public.

2. **C.** The Code of Procedure outlines the methods for handling trade practice complaints when a violation of the Conduct Rules is involved.

3. **D.** The decisions of the board of arbitration are final and are binding on the parties involved. There is no appeal of these decisions.

SROs: The NYSE Constitution and Rules

The NYSE is a corporation operated by a board of directors consisting of 10 Exchange members, 10 public representatives, and a chairperson. The board is responsible for setting policy, supervising Exchange and member activities, listing securities, overseeing the transfer of members' seats on the Exchange, and judging whether an applicant is qualified to be a specialist.

NYSE Membership

The number of memberships (seats) on the NYSE is fixed at 1,366. Because all of the seats are owned, to become a member one must buy a seat from a member. A seat's price is negotiated between the buyer and seller. Membership can be transferred from one person to another only with the board of directors' approval.

Only individuals can own seats on the Exchange. Many seat ownerships, however, are sponsored and funded by firms, which is where the term *member firms* originates.

Allied Members **Allied members** are executive officers, directors, or holders of more than 5% of a member firm's voting stock. Though allied members are responsible for supervising their organizations, they are not allowed to trade on the Exchange floor. The number of allied memberships is unlimited and they are not transferable.

Member Firm Conduct

A member organization must be open for business every day that the Exchange is open for business. Each office must display its certificate of membership with the NYSE. A member organization may not share its office with another broker/dealer except under special circumstances. The NYSE requires each member firm to undergo an annual audit by an independent accountant to verify the firm's financial health.

Branch Offices A member firm must obtain prior approval from the Exchange to open a branch office. If a registered representative uses his home as an office, this is considered an office of the employing firm. Every branch must be supervised by a principal who has passed the appropriate principal's examination. A very small office may be supervised by a registered representative if a principal in another office supervises the representative.

Although principals in branch offices are responsible for the business in their respective offices, the ultimate responsibility rests with the member firm's general partner or directors. The principal's supervisory duties include:

- approving new accounts;
- reviewing all correspondence, trade blotters and registered representatives' client statements;
- reviewing all transactions with clients and representatives' accounts of clients; and
- initialing all of these items.

Commissions An NYSE member firm must charge a commission for acting as a broker for trades done on the Exchange, but no minimum rate is required.

Registration of Employees

Salespersons of NYSE member firms must be registered with the NYSE through their firms. The Exchange can deny registration to unacceptable applicants. Registered reps must agree to abide by the NYSE constitution and regulations.

Training Program The NYSE imposes a 120-day (four-month) training program, or **apprenticeship period**, on all registered rep candidates. During this time, the Series 7 exam must be passed, but the new hires cannot solicit customer orders or receive commissions. They may be paid salary only.

A registered rep cannot be employed in name only. The rep must have the intention of building a real clientele. Registered reps must, in most cases, work full-time for their firms.

Termination A registered rep may voluntarily terminate his employment. Transfer of registration is not permitted; a rep must resign from one employer and reapply for registration with the new firm. The NYSE jurisdiction over a registered rep continues for one year after a termination.

Employment Other than with the Employing Broker/Dealer Under NYSE rules, a registered representative must have his firm's written permission before taking a second job. Permission is also required for becoming an officer, director, or partner of another entity.

Compensation A representative can receive compensation for securities transactions only from his employer. The registered representative can be paid a salary or a commission.

NYSE Arbitration

The NYSE Board of Arbitration hears and settles disagreements between members, allied members, member organizations, and their employees. Nonmembers and customers may submit voluntarily to arbitration in disputes with members or employees. The arbitrators' decisions are final; no appeal is possible.

Discipline *Disciplinary Hearing*

A grievance or complaint against an employee of a member organization must be made in writing. The employee has 25 days to respond in writing. Then a hearing is held before an NYSE panel. The employee may have an attorney present.

The panel's decision can be appealed to the NYSE Board of Directors, but no appeal beyond that point is possible. The board's decision is final.

Penalties and Review

If a member, an allied member, or an associated person of a member is found guilty in any disciplinary hearing, the hearing panel may impose any of the following penalties:

- censure;
- fine;
- suspension of registration;
- expulsion; or
- barring of the member firm or associated person from association with any other member.

Test Topic Alert! The following list contains the most testable points about NYSE rules.

- Allied members do not trade; they supervise their firms.
- Principals must approve all new accounts and all client transactions.
- Commission must be charged for acting as a broker in an NYSE trade, but there is no minimum amount required.
- Permission from the employer is required for a representative to have another job.
- Transfer of a representative's registration is not permitted; a rep must resign from the old firm and reapply to the new firm.
- Registered representatives associated with NYSE firms must serve a 120-day apprenticeship period.

Communications with the Public: Advertising and Sales Literature

Although the general public often uses the terms interchangeably, the NASD and the NYSE expect principals and representatives to recognize the difference between **advertising** and **sales literature**.

Advertising and Sales Literature

Advertising In advertising, there is no control over the audience or who receives or reads the information.

Advertising includes copy, support graphics, and other support materials intended for:

- publication in newspapers, magazines, or other periodicals;
- radio or television broadcast;
- prerecorded telephone marketing messages and tape recordings;

- videotape displays;
- signs or billboards;
- motion pictures and filmstrips;
- electronic (computer) communication devices;
- telephone directories; or
- any other use of the public media.

Generic Advertising (Rule 135a)

Generic advertising promotes securities as an investment medium, but does not refer to any specific security. Generic advertising often includes information about:

- the securities that investment companies offer;
- the nature of investment companies;
- services offered in connection with the described securities;
- explanations of the various types of investment companies;
- descriptions of exchange and reinvestment privileges; and
- where the public can write or call for further information.

All generic advertisements must contain the name and address of the registered sponsor of the advertisement. A generic advertisement can be placed only by a firm that offers the type of security or service described.

Sales Literature

Sales literature is any written communication distributed to customers, to the public in general, or is available to people upon request, that does not meet the definition of advertising. Sales literature has a targeted audience and the firm distributing the material has control over who receives it. Standardized sales pitches, telephone scripts, and seminar tapes are all classed as sales literature and are subject to the same rules and regulations that apply to sales literature.

Sales literature includes materials such as:

- circulars;
- research reports;
- market letters;
- form letters;
- option worksheets;
- performance reports and summaries;
- text prepared and used for educational seminars;
- telemarketing scripts; and
- reprints and excerpts from any advertisement, sales literature, or published news item or article.

Sales literature can be distributed in written, oral, or electronic form.

Tombstones (Rule 134 Advertisements)

An underwriter is limited in what it can publicly state about a security in registration. Under Rule 134, advertising copy and other sales materials need not be filed with the SEC as part of the registration statement if the body copy is limited to:

- the name of the issuer of the securities being offered;
- a brief description of the business in the offering;
- the date, time, and place of the meeting at which stockholders will vote on or consent to the proposed transaction;
- a brief description of the planned transaction; or
- any legend or disclaimer statement required by state or federal law.

Advertisements that meet these restrictions are more commonly known as **tombstones**, or Rule 134 advertisements. Any advertising copy in a tombstone must include the name and address of the person or firm to contact for a prospectus and also contain the following disclaimers.

- The issuer has filed the registration statement, but it is not yet effective.
- The communication does not represent an offer to sell the securities described—securities are sold by prospectus only.
- A response to this advertisement does not obligate the prospect to a buying commitment of any kind.

Rule 134 also covers advertisements and other promotional materials created in support of open-end investment company securities being sold on a continuous new issue offering basis.

Approval and Filing Requirements

A registered principal of the member firm must **approve** each advertisement and piece of sales literature before use and, if applicable, before filing with the NASD.

For advertisements or sales literature specific to options, the material must be approved by a registered options principal or compliance ROP. A supervisory analyst must approve research reports.

✓ *Take Note:* If a firm is in its first year of operation, all advertising and sales literature must also be filed with the NASD 10 days prior to use.

All advertisements and sales literature must be on file with the member for a period of three years; for the first two years, the file must be kept in an easily accessible place. This file must include the name(s) of the person(s) who prepared the material and approved its use.

If the NASD Department of Enforcement determines that a member's advertising departs from the standards of fair dealing and good faith, it may require the member to file all advertising and sales literature with the Association's advertising department 10 days before use. The Department of Enforcement notifies the member in writing of the types of material to be filed and the length of time the filing requirement is in effect.

Investment Company A member must file its advertisements and sales literature relating to investment company securities with the NASD's advertising department no later than 10 days after first use or publication.

Options or CMOs Options and CMO advertising must be filed with the NASD 10 business days in advance of first use. Any options sales literature a member sends to a customer must be preceded or accompanied by a current **Options Clearing Corporation (OCC) Options Disclosure Document**.

Direct Participation Program A member must file its advertising and sales literature concerning direct participation programs with the NASD within 10 days of first use. The member need not file advertising and sales literature that has been filed by sponsors, the program's general partner or underwriter, or another member.

Spot Checks Members' advertising and sales literature is subject to **spot checks** by the NASD. Upon written notice, a member must submit all material that the NASD advertising department requests. Except for advertisements relating to municipal securities and investment companies, advertisements that have been subject to spot checks by a registered securities exchange or an SRO within the past calendar year are not subject to NASD spot checks.

Exceptions to Filing Requirements Excluded from the filing requirements are prospectuses, preliminary prospectuses, offering circulars, tombstones, and similar documents used in connection with the offering of securities that have been filed with the SEC or any state.

NASD Rules Concerning Public Communications

Securities rules and regulations protect the general public from unscrupulous investment professionals.

The NASD's code of professionalism addresses two main problems in advertising and sales literature. These are **omissions** and **distortions** of material facts. In general, all communications from a member to the public must be based on principles of fair dealing and good faith. A communication should provide sound basis for evaluating the facts in regard to the product, service, or industry promoted. Exaggerated, unwarranted, or misleading statements are strictly prohibited.

Identification of Source

Sales literature—including market letters and research reports—must identify the member firm's name, the person or firm that prepared the material if copy was prepared outside the member firm, and the date the material was first used. If the literature contains information that is not current, that fact should be stated in the material.

Customer Recommendations

A member should have reasonable grounds for believing that a security is a suitable investment for a customer before recommending its purchase.

Disclosure Requirements

Proposals and written presentations that include specific recommendations must have reasonable basis to support the recommendation, and the member firm must provide these in the proposal or other document, or offer to furnish them upon request.

✓ **For Example:** If a recommendation includes a stock purchase, the firm must provide the stock's current price.

References. When, in recommending a security to a customer, a firm uses material referring to the performance of past recommendations, it must reveal certain information, including the following:

- price or price range of the recommended security at the date and time that the recommendation is made;
- market's general direction;
- availability of information supporting the recommendation;
- any recommendations made of similar securities within the past 12 months and the nature of the recommendations (buy, sell, hold); and
- all recommendations (winners and losers) the firm made over the time in question.

Time. The time span covered in the list of recommendations must run through consecutive periods, without skipping periods in an attempt to hide particular recommendations or negative price performance data.

Costs and Member Involvement. All recommendations to customers must disclose:

- all transaction costs;
- whether the firm intends to buy or sell any of the recommended security for its own account;
- whether the firm is a market maker in the recommended security;
- whether the firm or its officers or partners own options, rights, or warrants to buy the recommended security;
- whether officers or employees of the firm are directors of the company being recommended; and

- whether the firm managed or co-managed a public offering of the recommended security or any other of the same issuer's securities during the past 12 months.

A knowledgeable investor uses this type of information to determine if a recommendation is appropriate for his situation.

Prohibitions

In addition to meeting certain information requirements, the firm making the recommendation must not:

- imply that any guarantees accompany the recommendation;
- compare the recommended security to dissimilar products;
- make fraudulent or misleading statements about the recommended security;
- make any predictions about the recommended security's future performance or potential; or
- make statements of advantages without stating risks.

Test Topic Alert! Be careful of questions that ask you to differentiate between advertising and sales literature according to the NASD definition.

- Advertising is nontargeted; there is no control over who will read, see, or hear it.
- Consider sales literature as targeted material; it is given or mailed to a specific recipient.

Quick Quiz 17.7 Choose **A** (Advertising) or **SL** (Sales Literature) to identify the following:

___ 1. Billboard

___ 2. Seminar

___ 3. Radio broadcast

___ 4. Form letter

___ 5. Research report

___ 6. Recruitment ad

___ 7. Circular

___ 8. Options worksheet

___ 9. Telemarketing script

___ 10. Telephone directory

Answers 1. **A**   2. **SL**   3. **A**   4. **SL**   5. **SL**
         6. **A**   7. **SL**   8. **SL**   9. **SL** 10. **A**

Test Topic Alert!   Whether a communication is classified as advertising or sales literature, it must still be approved by a principal before use and kept on file for three years from the date of first use.

The NASD advertising department does not approve advertising. It just collects material so that it can be subject to a spot check. Recruitment ads are the only form of advertising not required to disclose the identity of the member firm.

Be sure that only suitable recommendations are made. Each recommendation must disclose any possible conflicts of interest, like large ownership positions by the firm (however, not the specific number of shares owned), market making in that security, and control relationships with the issuer, among others. Customers have a right to know anything that might influence their investment decision.

Finally, any statement of past performance must remind the reader or listener that past performance does not guarantee future results.

Recommending Investment Company Products

When recommending mutual funds to clients as investments and when using advertisements or sales literature developed for those investments, a broker/dealer should:

- use charts or graphs showing a fund's performance over a period long enough to reflect variations in value under different market conditions, generally at least 10 years;
- reveal the source of the graphics;
- separate dividends from capital gains when making statements about a fund's cash returns;
- not state that a mutual fund is similar to or safer than any other type of security;
- reveal a fund's highest sales charge, even if the client appears to qualify for a breakpoint; and
- not make fraudulent or misleading statements or omissions of facts.

Periodic Payment Plans. Mutual fund plans that make periodic payments (frequently sold in this manner so investors receive the benefits of dollar cost averaging) cannot be described in advertisements or sales literature without the disclosure that:

- a profit is not assured;
- they do not provide protection from losses in a declining market;
- the plans involve continuous investments regardless of market fluctuations; and
- investors should consider their financial ability to continue purchases during periods of declining prices.

Advertising Returns. An investor's total return from a mutual fund investment may include income distributions, gains distributions, and share appreciation, minus any sales charges and fees. However, average annual total return, as defined by the SEC, assumes reinvestment of all dividends and capital gains distributions and does not deduct any sales charges or management fees.

Advertisements that feature total return must also explain how the SEC calculates fund performance. If an advertisement includes any performance figures, the minimum information provided must be 1-, 5- and 10-year or life-of-fund average annual total returns.

Similarly, the SEC requires that **current yield calculations** be based only on income distributions for the past 12 months divided by the current per-share price: annual dividend / current price = current yield.

Test Topic Alert!

A typical question about mutual funds requires calculation of current yield.

NavCo mutual fund has a NAV of $9.50 and POP of $10.00. Over the past 12 months it distributed dividends totaling $1 and capital gains totaling $.75. What is NavCo's current yield?

This question gives you excess information. The first point is that capital gains are not included in calculation of a mutual fund's current yield. You must also remember that the NAV is not involved. The calculation is:

$$\frac{\text{Annual Dividend}}{\text{POP}}$$

NavCo's current yield is $1 ÷ $10 or 10%.

Other Communication Prohibitions

Claims and Opinions Couched as Facts and Conclusions It violates regulations to pass off opinions, projections, and forecasts as guarantees of performance. Any attempt of a representative to make a customer believe a claim or opinion is a fact is prohibited.

Testimonials Testimonials and endorsements by celebrities and public opinion influencers related to specific recommendations or investment results must not mislead or suggest that past performance indicates future performance. If a member firm pays a fee or other compensation to a person for a testimonial or an endorsement, it must disclose this fact.

If a broker/dealer assembles a sales piece about a particular investment company that includes testimonials by one or more customers, the sales piece must state that:

- past performance does not indicate future performance;
- the company compensated the person who made the testimonial, if this is true; and
- the person making the testimonial has the qualifications to do so (these qualifications must be listed) if the testimonial implies that the statement is based on the customer's special experience or knowledge.

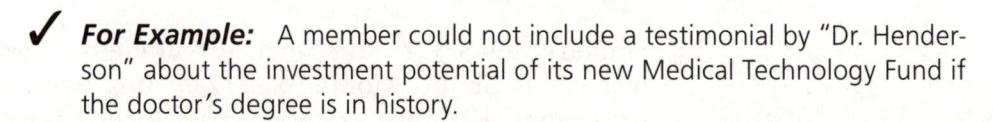

✓ **For Example:** A member could not include a testimonial by "Dr. Henderson" about the investment potential of its new Medical Technology Fund if the doctor's degree is in history.

Offers of Free Service Offers of free service cannot include obligations of any kind. Reports, analyses, or other services offered to the public must be furnished entirely free and without condition or obligation.

✓ **Take Note:** Some additional rules regarding unprofessional practices:

- A communication must not state or imply that research facilities are more extensive than they actually are.
- Hedge clauses, caveats, and disclaimers must not be used if they are misleading or inconsistent with the material's content.

Ambiguous References Ambiguous references to the NASD or other SROs must not be made with the aim of leading people to believe that a broker/dealer acts with the endorsement and approval of the Association or one of the other SROs. If the NASD's name or logo is used in a member's sales literature, it must not appear in a typeface larger or more prominent than the one used for the member's own name.

✓ **For Example:** A registered rep gives you the following business card:

> **John H. Doe**
> (555) 234-5678
> **NASD Registered Representative**
> ABC Securities

Is there anything wrong with this card? Yes—the large, bold print used to identify the NASD affiliation could mislead the recipient of this business card into thinking that John H. Doe is actually associated with the NASD. The NASD cannot be more prominent than the name of the rep's firm. Someone might mistakenly be led to believe that the NASD approves of or endorses this rep.

Use of Members' Names

General Standards

No material fact is to be omitted if the omission causes the advertisement or literature to be misleading. As a result, all advertising and sales literature must:

- clearly and prominently disclose the NASD member's name;
- clearly describe the relationship between the NASD member and the named entities and products when multiple entities and products are being offered;
- clearly disclose the relationship of an individual and an NASD member when an individual is named in the communication;
- not use or refer to nonexistent degrees or designations; and
- not use degrees or designations in a misleading manner.

Fictional Names

A **fictional name** or **DBA (doing business as)** designation is permitted if the name is filed with the NASD and the SEC on Form BD and is the name used to designate the member.

Generic Names

The NASD permits a member to use an altered version of a firm name as an umbrella identification for purposes of promoting name recognition. A **generic**, or an **umbrella**, name can be used as long as:

- it is displayed with the NASD member name also prominently displayed;
- its relationship with the member name is clear (i.e., the information describes the link or separation between the member and the generic name); and

- there is no implication that the generic or umbrella name is the broker/dealer.

Other Designations

A member may designate a portion of its business using terms such as *division of*, *service of*, or *securities offered through* only if a bona fide division exists. The member name must be clearly designated and the division clearly identified as a division of the member.

For use by a nonmember firm, the nonmember must clearly and prominently display the member firm's name and its relationship to the member. Additionally, the securities function must be clearly identified as a function of the member, not as a nonmember function.

Recruitment Advertising Companies that advertise to attract new registered reps are regulated by the same Conduct Rules that cover companies advertising investment products. The advertisements must be truthful, informative, and fair in representing the opportunities in the industry and must not contain exaggerated or unwarranted claims.

The advertisements may not emphasize the salaries of top-paid salespeople without revealing that they are not representative, and they may not contain any other statements that may be misleading or fraudulent.

Broker/dealers are permitted, in this one instance of recruitment advertising, to run blind advertisement (advertisements that do not list a company's name).

Interviews Once a company starts interviewing potential employees, it is the principal's responsibility to see that both the industry and the job opportunity are represented honestly. Any discussions of the business must present both the upside and the downside of the position and should not misrepresent the average employee's compensation.

Review of NASD Advertising and Sales Literature Regulations

The following summarizes NASD regulations regarding advertising and sales literature.

- A principal must approve all advertising and sales literature before use and before filing with the NASD.
- All advertising and sales literature must be kept in a separate file for a minimum of three years.
- All advertising and sales literature concerning registered investment companies must be filed within 10 days of first use by any member act-

ing as a principal underwriter for the securities. With each filing, the member must provide the actual or anticipated date of first use.
- New members must file with the NASD all advertising they produce or distribute during their first year at least 10 days before first use and must provide the actual or anticipated date of first use with each filing.
- The NASD may require any member to resume filing all of its advertising and sales literature before use if the member deviates from acceptable standards.

Research Analyst Conflicts of Interest

In May of 2002, the SEC approved new NASD Rule 2711, which is intended to improve the objectivity of research reports. The SEC also approved similar amendments to NYSE Rule 472.

Members must take steps to ensure that all research reports reflect an analyst's honest view and that any recommendation is not influenced by conflicts of interest such as investment banking business with the issuer.

Contacts between Research Analysts and Investment Banking Personnel

The new rules:

- prohibit investment banking departments from supervising or controlling research analysts;
- bar investment banking personnel from discussing research reports with analysts prior to issuance. Investment bankers cannot review or approve research reports;
- preclude firms from tying analyst compensation to specific investment banking transactions.

Limitations on Contacts between Research Analysts and Issuers

The new rules:

- prevent analysts from showing draft reports with issuers for any reason other than fact checking (further, a firm's legal or compliance department must approve any changes suggested by the issuer);
- prohibit analysts from offering or threatening to withhold favorable ratings as inducement for future investment banking business;
- impose a quiet period of 40 days for IPOs and 10 days for additional issue offerings on firms which act as manager or co-manager (i.e., these firms may not publish a research report on the subject issuer for 40 days following an IPO and 10 days following a secondary offering.

Required Disclosures in Research Reports and Public Appearances

The new rules:

- require firms to clearly explain their rating systems;

- require analysts to disclose if their compensation is tied to the firm's general investment banking revenues;
- require disclosure in their research reports and public appearances if they or any member of their households have a financial interest in the subject security and if their employer firms owned 1% or more of any class of a subject company's equity securities at the close of the previous month;
- require that research reports disclose if, within the last 12 months, they have received fees for investment banking services (they must also disclose if they expect to receive or intend to seek in the three months following publication of a research report, any investment banking fees from any company that is the subject of a report).

Restrictions on Personal Trading by Analysts and Related Persons

The new rules:

- prohibit analysts and members of their households from investing in a company's securities either (1) prior to the company's initial public offering if the company is in the business sector covered by the analyst or (2) for 30 days before and five days after the analyst issues a research report on the company;
- prohibit analysts and household members from trading against the analyst's most recent recommendation.

Quick Quiz 17.8 Multiple Choice

1. A testimonial used by a member firm must state which of the following?

   A. Qualifications of the person giving the testimonial if a specialized or experienced opinion is implied
   B. Fact that past performance does not indicate future performance and that other investors may not obtain comparable results
   C. Fact that compensation was paid to the person giving the testimonial if such is the case
   D. All of the above

2. Which of the following forms of written communication must be approved by a branch officer or manager before its use?

   A. Letter to a customer confirming an annual account review appointment
   B. Letter sent to 50 customers offering advice about a stock
   C. Interoffice memorandum
   D. Preliminary prospectus

3. The recommendation to purchase ABC stock should not contain

   A. the stock's price at the time of the recommendation
   B. the disclosure of market-making activity or ownership of warrants to purchase the stock by the member firm
   C. a statement forecasting a continued decline in the security's price
   D. an offer to provide supporting information on request

4. If AFM uses performance charts and return on investment statistics in its sales literature, which of the following NASD policy statements apply?

   I. Performance charts and similar financial information displays should cover a minimum of 10 years or the life of the fund, if shorter; periods exceeding 10 years can be reported in five-year increments.
   II. All earnings and total return figures should disclose reinvestment of dividends and capital gains.
   III. In computing and reporting historical yields and return on investment, the fund should use the shares' maximum sales charge.
   IV. Current yield figures must be based on the fund's dividend distributions only.

   A. I and III only
   B. II and IV only
   C. III and IV only
   D. I, II, III and IV

5. A research report distributed by a member firm must disclose that the firm

   I. is a market maker in the issue
   II. has a 1% interest in the issuer
   III. was a selling group member in an underwriting of the company's stock within the past 12 months
   IV. was a managing underwriter of the company's stock within the past 12 months

   A. I and III only
   B. II and IV only
   C. III and IV only
   D. I, II and IV only

Answers

1. **D.** *Testimonials must state whether the testimonial giver was paid, that the giver's experience may not indicate other investors' experiences, and the giver's qualifications if a specialized or experienced opinion is implied.*

2. **B.** *Form letters fall into the category of sales literature and must be approved by a principal or manager before use.*

3. **C.** *Because this is a purchase, it would be inappropriate for a firm to recommend a stock if it projects a continued decline in the security's price.*

4. **D.** Performance charts should cover enough years to allow prospective buyers to evaluate a mutual fund's performance during good times as well as bad, which is why the NASD approves of 10-year performance histories. The NASD also believes that prospective buyers should be alerted as to whether a fund's performance is based on reinvestment of capital gains only or on reinvestment of capital gains and dividends. Furthermore, for purposes of both reporting fairness and statistical consistency, yield and total return figures should be based on the maximum sales charge during the period covered.

5. **D.** In its research report on a company, the member firm must disclose whether it has any financial interest in the company (e.g., owning the company's stock, owning call options, or having acted as an underwriter in an offering of the company's stock). However, the member firm need not disclose that it was a selling group member in an underwriting of the company's stock.

Telephone Communications with the Public

The **Telephone Consumer Protection Act of 1991 (TCPA)**, administered by the **Federal Communications Commission (FCC)**, was enacted to protect consumers from unwanted telephone solicitations.

A **telephone solicitation** is defined as a telephone call initiated for the purpose of encouraging the purchase of or investment in property, goods, or services.

The act governs commercial calls, recorded solicitations from autodialers, and solicitations and advertisements to fax machines and modems.

The act requires an organization that does telemarketing (cold calling in particular) to:

- maintain a *Do-Not-Call* list of prospects who do not want to be called and keep a prospect's name on the list for 10 years from the time they make the request;
- institute a written policy on maintenance procedures for the *Do-Not-Call* list;
- train reps on using the list;
- ensure that reps acknowledge and immediately record the names and telephone numbers of prospects who ask not to be called again;
- ensure that anyone making cold calls for the firm informs prospects of the firm's name and telephone number or address;
- ensure that telemarketers do not call a prospect within 10 years of their *Do-Not-Call* request; and
- ensure that solicitation occurs only between the hours of 8:00 am and 9:00 pm of the time zone in which the prospect is located.

Communications with the Public: Advertising and Sales Literature

The act exempts calls:

- made to parties with whom the caller has an established business relationship or where the caller has prior express permission or invitation;
- made on behalf of a tax-exempt nonprofit organization;
- not made for a commercial purpose; and
- made for legitimate debt collection purposes.

Quick Quiz 17.9 Multiple Choice

1. Which of the following parties is covered under the TCPA of 1991?

    A. University survey group
    B. Nonprofit organization
    C. Church group
    D. Registered representative

2. When making cold calls, a rep must

    I. immediately record the names and telephone numbers of customers who ask not to be called again
    II. inform customers of the firm's name and telephone number or address
    III. limit calls to between the hours of 8:00 am and 9:00 pm of the time zone in which customers are located
    IV. not call customers who make a *Do-Not-Call* request

    A. I and II only
    B. I and IV only
    C. II and III only
    D. I, II, III and IV

3. An investor receives a telephone solicitation from a registered rep at your firm. Under which two of the following conditions is this solicitation exempt from the Telephone Consumer Protection Act of 1991?

    I. The investor asked the rep to call him with investment recommendations.
    II. The investor is an active trader with an account at your firm.
    III. The investor is an active trader with an account at another firm.
    IV. The rep received permission from a principal of the firm.

    A. I and II only
    B. I, II, and III only
    C. II and III only
    D. III and IV only

Answers

1. **D.** The Telephone Consumer Protection Act of 1991 covers all registered reps. Each firm must have a Do-Not-Call list that every registered rep is required to check before soliciting any person. The act applies to commercial solicitation and does not include a university survey group or nonprofit organization.

2. **D.** All of the choices are requirements of the TCPA of 1991.

3. **A.** The TCPA of 1991 exempts calls made to established customers and calls made at the invitation of prospective customers. A registered principal does not have the authority to exempt certain calls from the act's provisions.

Legal Recourse of Customers

The Securities Exchange Act of 1934 and the Acts of 1933 and 1940 all contain sections prohibiting the use of any fraudulent or manipulative device in the selling of securities to the public. The rules make it unlawful for any person to use the mails or any facilities of interstate commerce to:

employ, in connection with the purchase or sale of any security, any manipulative or deceptive device in contravention of such rules and regulations as the Commission may prescribe as necessary.

In essence, this passage states that an act is unlawful if the SEC says it is, and the enforcement of the intent of the act is not to be limited by the letter of the law.

Statute of Limitations Any client may sue for damages if he believes that a broker/dealer used any form of manipulative or deceptive practices in the sale of securities. The client must bring the lawsuit within three years of the manipulative act and within one year of his discovery of the manipulation or deception.

Other SEC & SRO Rules & Regulations HotSheet

NASD Manual:
- **Conduct Rules**: fair and ethical dealing with the public
- **Uniform Practice Code**: standardizes practices between broker/dealers (DKs, settlements, ex-dates)
- **Code of Procedure (COP)**: handles complaints, disciplinary action; Department of Enforcement investigates
- **Code of Arbitration**: handles monetary disputes between BDs or within the industry

Other SEC & SRO Rules & Regulations HotSheet

Principals:
- Minimum of two per firm; manage, train, and supervise
- Approve all accounts and client transactions

Felony Conviction:
- May be disqualified for 10 years

Code of Procedure:
- Respond to DOE notice within 25 days
- DOE can administer any penalty other than jail
- Decision final after 45 days

Minor Rule Violation:
- Maximum fine $2,500
- Appeal within 25 days of decision date

Code of Arbitration:
- Between members, with public only with written consent
- Decisions are final and binding on all parties
- Awards after 30 days
- Simplified is $25,000 for public and industry
- 6-year statute of limitations

NYSE Rules:
- Prior permission for outside employment; no transfer of registration

NASD Communications:
- Advertising = nontargeted communications; sales literature = targeted communications
- Both must be approved by principal before use; filed for 3 years, 2 years easily accessible
- Investment company material must be filed with NASD within 10 days of use
- 1st year firms must file with NASD 10 days before first use
- Generic advertising is OK if product or service offered is available
- Name of member required except on recruitment ads
- Testimonials OK with disclosure of compensation

Recommendations:
- Must be suitable; disclose current price; potential conflicts of interest
- "Past performance does not guarantee future results"

Investment Company Recommendations:
- Advertising/sales literature must disclose performance history for a 10-year period unless new fund
- Advertise based on highest charge: no breakpoint
- Yield = Annual dividend/POP

Telephone Consumer Protection Act:
- Must call noncustomers at home between 8 am and 9 pm
- Firms must maintain *Do-Not-Call* list and written procedures
- Not applicable to nonprofit organizations

Series 7 Unit Test 17

1. A registered rep's recommendations to a customer
   A. must be approved in advance by a principal and must be suitable based on the facts the customer discloses regarding other holdings and investment objectives
   B. must be suitable based on the facts the customer discloses regarding other holdings and investment objectives
   C. must be approved in advance by a principal
   D. are not covered by NASD rules

2. Which of the following disputes may be resolved using arbitration under the NASD Code of Arbitration?
   I. Member against a person associated with a member
   II. Member against another member
   III. Member against a public customer with consent of the customer
   IV. Public customer against a member
   A. I only
   B. I, II and IV only
   C. II only
   D. I, II, III and IV

3. A registered rep who does not complete the Regulatory Element of Continuing Education within the prescribed time frame
   A. can continue to function as a representative with the written permission of a principal
   B. cannot perform any of the functions of a representative until the CE requirement is met
   C. is limited to accepting unsolicited orders only until the CE requirement is met
   D. is required to take a 120-day leave of absence

4. Which of the following materials is(are) subject to the NASD's filing requirements?
   I. Sales literature describing the performance ranking of an open-end management investment company
   II. Prospectus for a face amount certificate company
   III. Prospectus for a closed-end management investment company
   IV. Internal memo describing the benefits of an investment in a certain unit investment trust
   A. I only
   B. I and IV only
   C. II and III only
   D. I, II, III and IV

5. All research reports must disclose
   I. any control relationship with the issuer
   II. the price at the time the original recommendation was made
   III. the fact that the member firm has a 1% or more position in the security
   IV. the name of the member firm providing the recommendation
   A. I and III only
   B. II and IV only
   C. III only
   D. I, II, III and IV

6. To which of the following persons may a broker/dealer pay commissions under a continuing commission contract?
   I. Retired employee, for past business
   II. Widow of a former employee, for past business
   III. Retired employee who refers an old neighbor to the broker/dealer
   IV. Retired employee who, in the course of his travels, acquires new business for the broker/dealer
   A. I and II only
   B. II and III only
   C. III and IV only
   D. I, II, III and IV

7. A customer buys 100 shares of RFTQ at $10 per share. Several months later, the stock is trading at 4.60–5, at which time the registered rep offers to buy back the stock from the customer for his own account at $9 per share. This action is

   A. permitted because it allows the customer to sell at a price higher than the current market
   B. prohibited because NASD rules do not allow registered reps to guarantee customers against loss
   C. permitted with the written permission of a principal
   D. prohibited because it violates the Uniform Practice Code of the NASD

8. Which of the following statements regarding recruiting advertising by NASD member firms is(are) TRUE?

   I. It is not subject to NASD filing rules.
   II. It may not contain exaggerated claims about opportunities in the securities business.
   III. It is not permitted.
   IV. During a firm's first year of business, it must be filed with the NASD.

   A. I only
   B. II and III
   C. II and IV
   D. III only

9. Under NYSE rules, before a registered representative may take a second job he must obtain written permission from the

   A. registered rep's employer
   B. NYSE
   C. SEC
   D. NASD

10. The NASD may take which of the following actions against members that violate the Conduct Rules?

    I. Expulsion
    II. Censure
    III. Fine
    IV. Suspension

    A. I, II and IV only
    B. I and IV only
    C. II and III only
    D. I, II, III and IV

11. Rulings under the NASD Code of Arbitration

    A. are binding on members but not on customers
    B. are binding on all parties
    C. may be appealed to the NASD National Adjudicatory Council
    D. may be appealed to the SEC

12. Which of the following must be included in a testimonial made on behalf of a member firm and distributed to potential clients?

    I. Qualifications of the person giving the testimonial if a specialized or an expert opinion is implied
    II. Length of time the testimonial covers
    III. Fact that the returns and investment performance cited in the testimonial may not be easily duplicated
    IV. Whether compensation was paid to the person giving the testimonial

    A. I, III and IV only
    B. I and IV only
    C. II and III only
    D. I, II, III and IV

13. Written recommendations prepared by a registered rep need the prior approval of

    A. the appropriate SRO
    B. a principal of the firm
    C. the SEC
    D. the FCC

14. Which of the following would a principal of a municipal securities firm who has the responsibility of supervising municipal securities representatives perform?

    I. Review a registered rep's correspondence
    II. Approve the opening of a new account
    III. Write all sales material and advertising copy
    IV. Approve each municipal securities transaction

    A. I and II only
    B. I, II and IV only
    C. III and IV only
    D. I, II, III and IV

15. A registered representative leaves the industry to accept a position as a professor. The representative must requalify by examination to return to the industry if he is unaffiliated with a broker/dealer for more than

    A. 2 years
    B. 3 years
    C. 5 years
    D. 10 years

Series 7 Unit Test 17 Answers & Rationale

1. **B.** Recommendations made to a customer must be suitable for that customer. Individual recommendations do not require principal approval.
QID: 28435

2. **D.** The Code of Arbitration is mandatory in member-against-member disputes. In a dispute between a member and a public customer, the member cannot force the customer to arbitrate but arbitration may be used at the customer's request. Arbitration is optional in claims of employment discrimination (including sexual harassment) by associated persons against broker/dealers.
QID: 28404

3. **B.** If a registered person does not complete the regulatory element of CE within the prescribed time frame, the rep's license will be suspended by the NASD. Therefore, until completed, the rep cannot perform any of the functions of a registered representative. The regulatory element must be completed within 120 days of the rep's second registration anniversary and every 3 years thereafter.
QID: 36459

4. **A.** Prospectuses and internal memos need not be filed with the NASD.
QID: 29684

5. **D.** The source of the recommendation, the security's price, any member firm interest in the security of 1% or more, and the fact that the member firm is a market maker in the security must all be disclosed in the research report. In addition, if a control relationship exists between the member and the company being recommended, this fact must also be disclosed.
QID: 28426

6. **A.** A member firm may continue to pay commissions to either a retired employee or to a former employee's widow, provided that a prior written contract exists. Commissions can only be paid on business generated while employed.
QID: 28381

7. **B.** A rep may never guarantee a customer against a loss. This is specified in the NASD Conduct Rules, not the Uniform Practice Code.
QID: 35109

8. **C.** All advertising during a firm's first year of business must be filed with the NASD 10 days before use. Recruiting advertising may not contain exaggerated claims about brokerage business opportunities.
QID: 28432

9. **A.** To take a second job, a registered representative must get prior written permission from his employer.
QID: 28424

10. **D.** Members or employees of members found to have violated the Conduct Rules are subject to any of the penalties listed.
QID: 28401

11. **B.** A customer who chooses to submit a claim or dispute to arbitration under the NASD's Code of Arbitration is bound by the arbitration decision.
QID: 29704

12. **A.** When a member firm uses a testimonial, the testimonial must be accompanied by a statement that this person's experience does not necessarily represent those of other customers; disclosure of any compensation paid, if material; and the testimonial giver's qualifications if an expert opinion is implied.
QID: 28431

13. **B.** Written recommendations are classified as sales literature; therefore, a principal must review and approve the communication before use.
QID: 28448

14. B. A principal must approve all new accounts and approve each transaction and all correspondence. Although a principal must approve advertising, he does not have to write it.
QID: 35199

15. A. All securities licenses become null and void once an individual is unaffiliated for more than 2 years.
QID: 36555

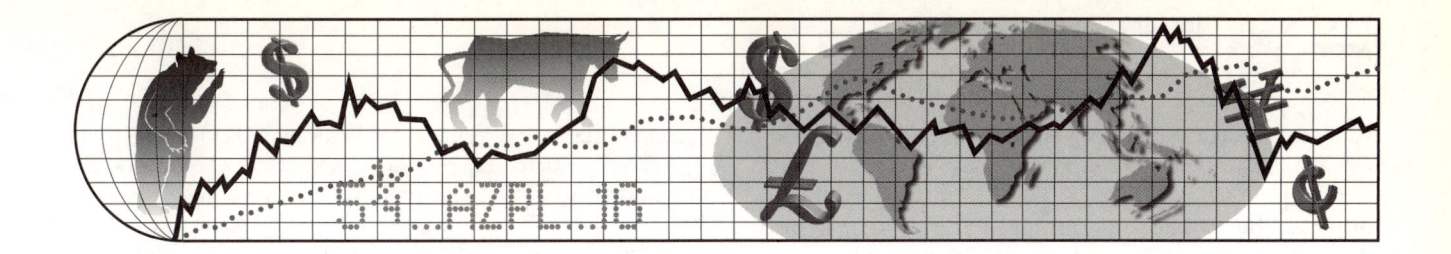

Glossary

A

acceptance, waiver, and consent A process for settling a charge or complaint that is quicker and less formal than the NASD's regular complaint procedure. *Related item(s):* Code of Procedure.

account executive (AE) *See* registered representative.

accredited investor As defined in Rule 502 of Regulation D, any institution or individual meeting minimum net worth requirements for the purchase of securities qualifying under the Regulation D registration exemption.

An accredited investor is generally accepted to be one who:
- has a net worth of $1 million or more; or
- has had an annual income of $200,000 or more in each of the two most recent years (or $300,000 jointly with a spouse) and who has a reasonable expectation of reaching the same income level in the current year.

accretion of bond discount An accounting process whereby the initial cost of a bond purchased at a discount is increased annually to reflect the basis of the bond as it approaches maturity.

accrual accounting A method of reporting income when earned and expenses when incurred, as opposed to reporting income when received and expenses when paid.

accrued interest The interest that has accumulated since the last interest payment up to, but not including, the settlement date and that is added to a bond transaction's contract price.

There are two methods for calculating accrued interest: the 30-day-month (360-day-year) method for corporate and municipal bonds and the actual-calendar-days (365-day-year) method for government bonds. Income bonds, bonds in default and zero-coupon bonds trade without accrued interest (flat). *Related item(s):* flat.

accumulation account An account established to hold securities pending their deposit into a municipal securities unit investment trust.

accumulation stage The period during which contributions are made to an annuity account. *Related item(s):* accumulation unit; distribution stage.

accumulation unit An accounting measure used to determine an annuitant's proportionate interest in the insurer's separate account during an annuity's accumulation (deposit) stage. *Related item(s):* accumulation stage; annuity unit; separate account.

acid-test ratio A measure of a corporation's liquidity, calculated by adding cash, cash equivalents, and accounts and notes receivable, and dividing the result by total current liabilities. It is a more stringent test of liquidity than current ratio. *Syn.* quick ratio. *Related item(s):* cash assets ratio; current ratio.

ACT *See* Automated Confirmation Transaction Service.

act of 1933 *See* Securities Act of 1933.

act of 1934 *See* Securities Exchange Act of 1934.

adjacent acreage Producing or nonproducing oil or gas leases located within the area of an existing well site.

Adjacent acreage may prove valuable for continued development of the original oil or gas prospect.

adjusted basis The value attributed to an asset or security that reflects any deductions taken on, or capital improvements to, the asset or security. Adjusted basis is used to compute the gain or loss on the sale or other disposition of the asset or security.

adjusted gross income (AGI) Earned income plus net passive income, portfolio income and capital gains. *Related item(s):* tax liability.

administrator (1) A person authorized by a court of law to liquidate an intestate decedent's estate. (2) An official or agency that administers a state's securities laws.

ADR *See* American depositary receipt.

ad valorem tax A tax based on the value of real or personal property. Property taxes are the major source of revenues for local governing units. *Related item(s):* assessed value.

advance/decline line A technical analysis tool representing the total of differences between advances and declines of security prices. The advance/decline line is considered the best indicator of market movement as a whole. *Related item(s):* breadth-of-market theory.

advance refunding Refinancing an existing municipal bond issue prior to its maturity or call date by using money from the sale of a new bond issue. The proceeds of the new bond issue are used to purchase government securities, and the municipality puts the principal and interest received from these securities into an escrow account; it then uses these funds to pay off the original bond issue at the first call date. *Syn.* prerefunding. *Related item(s):* defeasance; refunding.

advertisement Any promotional material designed for use by newspapers, magazines, billboards, radio, television, telephone recording or other public media where the firm has little control over the type of individuals exposed to the material. *Related item(s):* sales literature.

advisory board Under the Investment Company Act of 1940, a board that advises an investment company on matters concerning its investments in securities, but does not have the power to make investment decisions or take action itself. An advisory board must be composed of persons who have no other connection with, and serve no other function for, the investment company.

AE *See* registered representative.

affiliate (1) A person who directly or indirectly owns, controls or holds with power to vote 10% or more of the outstanding voting securities of a company. (2) With respect to a direct participation program, any person who controls, is controlled by or is under common control with the program's sponsor and includes any person who beneficially owns 50% or more of the equity interest in the sponsor. (3) Under the Investment Company Act of 1940, a person who has any type of control over an investment company's operations, which includes anyone with 5% or more of the outstanding voting securities of the investment company or any corporation of which the investment company holds 5% or more of outstanding securities. *Related item(s):* control person; insider.

agency basis *See* agency transaction.

agency issue A debt security issued by an authorized agency of the federal government. Such an issue is backed by the issuing agency itself, not by the full faith and credit of the US government (except GNMA and Federal Import Export Bank issues). *Related item(s):* government security.

agency transaction A transaction in which a broker/dealer acts for the accounts of others by buying or selling securities on behalf of customers. *Syn.* agency basis. *Related item(s):* agent; broker; principal transaction.

agent (1) An individual or a firm that effects securities transactions for the accounts of others. (2) A person licensed by a state as a life insurance agent. (3) A securities salesperson who represents a broker/dealer or an issuer when selling or trying to sell securities to the investing public; this individual is considered an agent whether he actually receives or simply solicits orders. *Related item(s):* broker; broker/dealer; dealer; principal.

aggressive investment strategy A method of portfolio allocation and management aimed at achieving maximum return. Aggressive investors place a high percentage of their investable assets in equity securities and a far lower percentage in safer debt securities and cash equivalents, and they pursue aggressive policies including margin trading, arbitrage and option trading. *Related item(s):* balanced investment strategy; defensive investment strategy.

AGI *See* adjusted gross income.

agreement among underwriters The agreement that sets forth the terms under which each member of an underwriting syndicate will participate in a new issue offering and states the duties and responsibilities of the underwriting manager. *Related item(s):* syndicate; underwriting manager.

agreement of limited partnership The contract that establishes guidelines for the operation of a direct participation program, including the roles of the general and limited partners.

AIR *See* assumed interest rate.

allied member A general partner of an NYSE member firm who is not an NYSE member, an owner of 5% or more of the outstanding voting stock of an NYSE member corporation, or a principal executive director or officer of a member corporation. Allied members do not own seats on the NYSE.

all or none order (AON) An order that instructs the firm to execute the entire order. Firm does not have to execute immediately.

all or none underwriting (AON) A form of best efforts underwriting in which the underwriter agrees that if it is unable to sell all the shares (or a prescribed minimum), the issuer will cancel the offering. This type of agreement may be used when the issuer requires a minimum amount of capital to be raised; if the minimum is not reached, the securities sold and the money raised are returned. Commissions are not paid unless the offering is completed. *Related item(s):* underwriting.

alpha coefficient A measure of the projected rate of change in a security's price independent of market-related factors but based instead on such indicators as the strength of the company's earnings and the expected level of sales. *Related item(s):* beta coefficient.

alternative minimum tax (AMT) An alternative tax computation that adds certain tax preference items back into adjusted gross income. If the AMT is higher than the regular tax liability for the year, the regular tax and the amount by which the AMT exceeds the regular tax are paid. *Related item(s):* tax preference item.

alternative order An order to execute either of two transactions—for example, placing a sell limit (above the market) and a sell stop (below the market) on the same stock. *Syn.* either/or order; one cancels other order.

AMBAC Indemnity Corporation (AMBAC) A corporation that offers insurance on the timely payment of interest and principal obligations of municipal securities. Bonds insured by AMBAC usually receive a AAA rating from rating services.

American depositary receipt (ADR) A negotiable certificate representing a given number of shares of stock in a foreign corporation. It is bought and sold in the American securities markets, just as stock is traded. *Syn.* American depositary share.

amortization (1) The paying off of debt in regular installments over a period of time. (2) The ratable deduction of certain capitalized expenditures over a specified period of time.

amortization of bond premium An accounting process whereby the initial cost of a bond purchased at a premium is decreased to reflect the basis of the bond as it approaches maturity. *Related item(s):* accretion of bond discount.

annual compliance review The annual meeting that all registered representatives must attend, the purpose of which is to review compliance issues.

annual ROI The annual return on a bond investment, which equals the annual interest either plus the prorated discount or minus the prorated premium.

annuitant A person who receives an annuity contract's distribution.

annuitize To change an annuity contract from the accumulation (pay-in) stage to the distribution (pay-out) stage.

annuity A contract between an insurance company and an individual, generally guaranteeing lifetime income to the individual on whose life the contract is based in return for either a lump sum or a periodic payment to the insurance company. The contract holder's objective is usually retirement income. *Related item(s):* deferred annuity; fixed annuity; immediate annuity; variable annuity.

annuity unit An accounting measure used to determine the amount of each payment during an annuity's distribution stage. The calculation takes into account the value of each accumulation unit and such other factors as assumed interest rate and mortality risk. *Related item(s):* accumulation unit; annuity; distribution stage.

AON *See* all or none order; all or none underwriting.

AP *See* associated person of a member.

appreciation The increase in an asset's value.

approved plan *See* qualified retirement plan.

arbitrage The simultaneous purchase and sale of the same or related securities to take advantage of a market inefficiency.

arbitrageur One who engages in arbitrage.

arbitration The arrangement whereby the NASD or a designated arbitration association hears and settles disagreements between members, member organizations, their employees, and customers.

ascending triangle On a technical analyst's trading activity chart, a pattern which indicates that the market has started to move back up; considered to be a bullish indicator. *Related item(s):* descending triangle.

ask An indication by a trader or a dealer of a willingness to sell a security or a commodity; the price at which an investor can buy from a broker/dealer. *Syn.* offer. *Related item(s):* bid; public offering price; quotation.

assessed value The value of a property as appraised by a taxing authority for the purpose of levying taxes. Assessed value may equal market value or a stipulated percentage of market value. *Related item(s):* ad valorem tax.

assessment An additional amount of capital that a participant in a direct participation program may be called upon to furnish beyond the subscription amount. Assessments may be mandatory or optional and must be called within 12 months.

asset (1) Anything that an individual or a corporation owns. (2) A balance sheet item expressing what a corporation owns.

asset allocation fund A mutual fund that splits its investment assets among stocks, bonds and other vehicles in an attempt to provide a consistent return for the investor. *Related item(s):* mutual fund.

assignee A person who has acquired a beneficial interest in a limited partnership from a third party but who is neither a substitute limited partner nor an assignee of record.

assignee of record A person who has acquired a beneficial interest in a limited partnership and whose interest has been recorded on the books of the partnership and is the subject of a written instrument of assignment.

assignment (1) A document accompanying or part of a stock certificate that is signed by the person named on the certificate for the purpose of transferring the certificate's title to another person's name. (2) The act of identifying and notifying an account holder that the option owner has exercised an option held short in that account. *Related item(s):* stock power.

associated person of a member (AP) Any employee, manager, director, officer or partner of a member broker/dealer or another entity (issuer, bank, etc.), or any person controlling, controlled by or in common control with that member. *Related item(s):* registered representative.

assumed interest rate (AIR) The net rate of investment return that must be credited to a variable life insurance policy to ensure that at all times the variable death benefit equals the amount of the death benefit. The AIR forms the basis for projecting payments, but it is not guaranteed.

at-the-close order *See* market-on-close order.

at-the-money The term used to describe an option when the underlying stock is trading precisely at the exercise price of the option. *Related item(s):* in-the-money; out-of-the-money.

at-the-opening order An order that specifies it is to be executed at the opening of the market or of trading in that security or else it is to be canceled. The order will be executed at the opening price. *Related item(s):* market-on-close order.

auction market A market in which buyers enter competitive bids and sellers enter competitive offers simultaneously. The NYSE is an auction market. *Syn.* double auction market.

audited financial statement A financial statement of a program, a corporation or an issuer (including the profit and loss statement, cash flow and source and application of revenues statement, and balance sheet) that has been examined and verified by an independent certified public accountant.

authorized stock The number of shares of stock that a corporation can issue. This number of shares is stipulated in the corporation's state-approved charter and may be changed by a vote of the corporation's stockholders.

authorizing resolution The document enabling a municipal or state government to issue securities. The resolution provides for the establishment of a revenue fund in which receipts or income is deposited.

Automated Confirmation Transaction (ACT) Service The post-execution, on-line transaction reporting and comparison system developed by the NASD.

average A price at a midpoint among a number of prices. Technical analysts frequently use averages as market indicators. *Related item(s):* index.

average basis An accounting method used when an investor has made multiple purchases at different prices of the same security; the method averages the purchase prices to calculate an investor's cost basis in shares being liquidated. The difference between the average cost basis and the selling price determines the investor's tax liability. *Related item(s):* first in, first out; last in, first out; share identification.

average price A step in determining a bond's yield to maturity. A bond's average price is calculated by adding its face value to the price paid for it and dividing the result by two.

B

B Consolidated Tape market identifier for the Boston Stock Exchange.

BA *See* banker's acceptance.

back away The failure of an over-the-counter market maker to honor a firm bid and asked price. This violates the NASD Conduct Rules.

back-end load A commission or sales fee that is charged when mutual fund shares or variable annuity contracts are redeemed. It declines annually, decreasing to zero over an extended holding period—up to eight years—as described in the prospectus. *Syn.* contingent-deferred sales load. *Related item(s):* front-end load.

balanced fund A mutual fund whose stated investment policy is to have at all times some portion of its investment assets in bonds and preferred stock as well as in common stock in an attempt to provide both growth and income. *Related item(s):* mutual fund.

balanced investment strategy A method of portfolio allocation and management aimed at balancing risk and return. A balanced portfolio may combine stocks, bonds, packaged products and cash equivalents.

balance of payments (BOP) An international accounting record of all transactions made by one particular country with others during a certain time period; it compares the amount of foreign currency the country has taken in to the amount of its own currency it has paid out. *Related item(s):* balance of trade.

balance of trade The largest component of a country's balance of payments; it concerns the export and import of merchandise (not services). Debit items include imports, foreign aid, domestic spending abroad and domestic investments abroad. Credit items include exports, foreign spending in the domestic economy and foreign investments in the domestic economy. *Related item(s):* balance of payments.

balance sheet A report of a corporation's financial condition at a specific time.

balance sheet equation A formula stating that a corporation's assets equal the sum of its liabilities plus shareholders' equity.

balloon maturity A repayment schedule for an issue of bonds wherein a large number of the bonds come due at a prescribed time (normally at the final maturity date); a type of serial maturity. *Related item(s):* maturity date.

BAN *See* bond anticipation note.

banker's acceptance (BA) A money-market instrument used to finance international and domestic trade. A banker's acceptance is a check drawn on a bank by an importer or exporter of goods and represents the bank's conditional promise to pay the face amount of the note at maturity (normally less than three months).

bank guarantee letter The document supplied by a commercial bank in which the bank certifies that a put writer has sufficient funds on deposit at the bank to equal the aggregate exercise price of the put; this releases the option writer from the option margin requirement.

banking act *See* Glass-Steagall Act of 1933.

bar chart A tool used by technical analysts to track the price movements of a commodity over several consecutive time periods. *Related item(s):* moving average chart; point-and-figure chart.

basis point A measure of a bond's yield, equal to 1/100 of 1 percent of yield. A bond whose yield increases from 5.0 percent to 5.5 percent is said to increase by 50 basis points. *Related item(s):* point.

basis quote The price of a security quoted in terms of the yield that the purchaser can expect to receive.

BD *See* broker/dealer.

bear An investor who acts on the belief that a security or the market is falling or will fall. *Related item(s):* bull.

bearer bond *See* coupon bond.

bear market A market in which prices of a certain group of securities are falling or are expected to fall. *See* bull market.

best efforts underwriting A new issue securities underwriting in which the underwriter acts as an agent for the issuer and puts forth its best efforts to sell as many shares as possible. The underwriter has no liability for unsold shares, unlike in a firm commitment underwriting. *Related item(s):* underwriting.

beta coefficient A means of measuring the volatility of a security or a portfolio of securities in comparison with the market as a whole. A beta of 1 indicates that the security's price will move with the market. A beta greater than 1 indicates that the security's price will be more volatile than the market. A beta less than 1 means that it will be less volatile than the market.

bid An indication by an investor, a trader or a dealer of a willingness to buy a security; the price at which an investor can sell to a broker/dealer. *Related item(s)*: offer; public offering price; quotation.

bid form The form submitted by underwriters in a competitive bid on a new issue of municipal securities. The underwriter states the interest rate, price bid and net interest cost to the issuer.

blind pool A direct participation program that does not state in advance all of the specific properties in which the general partners will invest the partnership's money. At least 25 percent of the proceeds of the offering are kept in reserve for the purchase of nonspecified properties. *Syn.* nonspecified property program.

block trade In general, 10,000 shares of stock would be considered a block trade.

blue chip stock The equity issues of financially stable, well-established companies that have demonstrated their ability to pay dividends in both good and bad times.

blue-sky To register a securities offering in a particular state. *Related item(s)*: blue-sky laws; registration by coordination; registration by filing; registration by qualification.

blue-sky laws The nickname for state regulations governing the securities industry. The term was coined in the early 1900s by a Kansas Supreme Court justice who wanted regulation to protect against "speculative schemes that have no more basis than so many feet of blue sky." *Related item(s)*: Series 63; Uniform Securities Act.

board of directors (1) Individuals elected by stockholders to establish corporate management policies. A board of directors decides, among other issues, if and when dividends will be paid to stockholders. (2) The body that governs the NYSE. It is composed of 20 members elected for a term of two years by the NYSE general membership.

bona fide quote An offer from a broker/dealer to buy or sell securities. It indicates a willingness to execute a trade under the terms and conditions accompanying the quote. *Related item(s)*: firm quote; nominal quote.

bond An issuing company's or government's legal obligation to repay the principal of a loan to bond investors at a specified future date. Bonds are usually issued with par or face values of $1,000, representing the amount of money borrowed. The issuer promises to pay a percentage of the par value as interest on the borrowed funds. The interest payment is stated on the face of the bond at issue.

bond anticipation note (BAN) A short-term municipal debt security to be paid from the proceeds of long-term debt when it is issued.

bond attorney *See* bond counsel.

Bond Buyer indexes Indexes of yield levels of municipal bonds, published daily by *The Bond Buyer*. The indexes are indicators of yields that would be offered on AA- and A-rated general obligation bonds with 20-year maturities and revenue bonds with 30-year maturities.

bond counsel An attorney retained by a municipal issuer to give an opinion concerning the legality and tax-exempt status of a municipal issue. *Syn.* bond attorney. *Related item(s)*: legal opinion of counsel.

bond fund A mutual fund whose investment objective is to provide stable income with minimal capital risk. It invests in income-producing instruments, which may include corporate, government or municipal bonds. *Related item(s)*: mutual fund.

bond interest coverage ratio An indication of the safety of a corporate bond. It measures the number of times by which earnings before interest and taxes exceeds annual interest on outstanding bonds. *Syn.* fixed charge coverage ratio; times fixed charges earned ratio; times interest earned ratio.

bond quote One of a number of quotations listed in the financial press and most daily newspapers that provide representative bid prices from the previous day's bond market. Quotes for corporate and government bonds are percentages of the bonds' face values (usually $1,000). Corporate bonds are quoted in increments of $1/8$, where a quote of $99 1/8$ represents 99.125% of par ($1,000), or $991.25. Government bonds are quoted in $1/32$nds. Municipal bonds may be quoted on a dollar basis or on a yield-to-maturity basis. *Related item(s)*: quotation; stock quote.

bond rating An evaluation of the possibility of a bond issuer's default, based on an analysis of the issuer's financial condition and profit potential. Standard & Poor's, Moody's Investors Service and Fitch Investors Service, among others, provide bond rating services.

bond ratio One of several tools used by bond analysts to assess the degree of safety offered by a corporation's bonds. It measures the percentage of the corporation's capitalization that is provided by long-term debt financing, calculated by dividing the total face value of the outstanding bonds by the total capitalization. *Syn.* debt ratio.

bond swap The sale of a bond and the simultaneous purchase of a different bond in a like amount. The technique is used to control tax liability, extend maturity or update investment objectives. *Syn.* tax swap. *Related item(s):* wash sale.

bond yield The annual rate of return on a bond investment. Types of yield include nominal yield, current yield, yield to maturity and yield to call. Their relationships vary according to whether the bond in question is at a discount, at a premium or at par. *Related item(s):* current yield; nominal yield.

book-entry security A security sold without delivery of a certificate. Evidence of ownership is maintained on records kept by a central agency; for example, the Treasury keeps records of Treasury bill purchasers. Transfer of ownership is recorded by entering the change on the books or electronic files. *Related item(s):* coupon bond; registered; registered as to principal only.

book value per share A measure of the net worth of each share of common stock. It is calculated by subtracting intangible assets and preferred stock from total net worth, then dividing the result by the number of shares of common outstanding. *Syn.* net tangible assets per share.

branch office Any location identified by any means to the public as a place where a registered broker/dealer conducts business.

breadth-of-market theory A technical analysis theory that predicts the strength of the market according to the number of issues that advance or decline in a particular trading day. *Related item(s):* advance/decline line.

breakeven point The point at which gains equal losses.

breakout In technical analysis, the movement of a security's price through an established support or resistance level. *Related item(s):* resistance level; support level.

breakpoint The schedule of sales charge discounts a mutual fund offers for lump-sum or cumulative investments.

breakpoint sale The sale of mutual fund shares in an amount just below the level at which the purchaser would qualify for reduced sales charges. This violates the NASD Conduct Rules.

broad-based index An index designed to reflect the movement of the market as a whole. Examples include the S&P 100, the S&P 500, the AMEX Major Market Index and the *Value Line* Composite Index. *Related item(s):* index.

broker (1) An individual or a firm that charges a fee or commission for executing buy and sell orders submitted by another individual or firm. (2) The role of a firm when it acts as an agent for a customer and charges the customer a commission for its services. *Related item(s):* agent; broker/dealer; dealer.

broker/dealer (BD) A person or firm in the business of buying and selling securities. A firm may act as both broker (agent) and dealer (principal), but not in the same transaction. Broker/dealers normally must register with the SEC, the appropriate SROs and any state in which they do business. *Related item(s):* agent; broker; dealer; principal.

broker fail *See* fail to deliver.

broker's broker (1) A specialist executing orders for a commission house broker or another brokerage firm. (2) A floor broker on an exchange or a broker/dealer in the over-the-counter market executing a trade as an agent for another broker.

broker's loan Money loaned to a brokerage firm by a commercial bank or other lending institution for financing customers' margin account debit balances. *Related item(s):* call loan; rehypothecation.

bucketing Accepting customer orders without executing them immediately.

bull An investor who acts on the belief that a security or the market is rising or will rise. *Related item(s):* bear.

bulletin board *See* OTC Bulletin Board.

bull market A market in which prices of a certain group of securities are rising or will rise. *Related item(s):* bear market.

business cycle A predictable long-term pattern of alternating periods of economic growth and decline. The cycle passes through four stages: expansion, peak, contraction and trough.

business day A day on which financial markets are open for trading. Saturdays, Sundays and legal holidays are not considered business days.

buyer's option A settlement contract that calls for delivery and payment according to a number of days specified by the buyer. *Related item(s):* regular way; seller's option.

buy-in The procedure that the buyer of a security follows when the seller fails to complete the contract by delivering the security. The buyer closes the contract by buying the security in the open market and charging the account of the seller for transaction fees and any loss caused by changes in the markets. *Related item(s):* sell-out.

buying power The amount of fully margined securities that a margin client can purchase using only the cash, securities and special memorandum account balance and without depositing additional equity.

buy stop order An order to buy a security that is entered at a price above the current offering price and that is triggered when the market price touches or goes through the buy stop price.

C

C Consolidated Tape market identifier for the Cincinnati Stock Exchange.

calendar spread *See* horizontal spread.

call (1) An option contract giving the owner the right to buy a specified amount of an underlying security at a specified price within a specified time. (2) The act of exercising a call option. *Related item(s):* put.

callable bond A type of bond issued with a provision allowing the issuer to redeem the bond before maturity at a predetermined price. *Related item(s):* call price.

callable preferred stock A type of preferred stock issued with a provision allowing the corporation to call in the stock at a certain price and retire it. *Related item(s):* call price; preferred stock.

call buyer An investor who pays a premium for an option contract and receives, for a specified time, the right to buy the underlying security at a specified price. *Related item(s):* call writer; put buyer; put writer.

call date The date, specified in the prospectus of every callable security, after which the security's issuer has the option to redeem the issue at par or at par plus a premium.

call feature *See* call provision.

call loan A collateralized loan of a brokerage firm having no maturity date that may be called (terminated) at any time. The loan has a fluctuating interest rate that is recomputed daily. Generally the loan is payable on demand the day after it is contracted. If not called, the loan is automatically renewed for another day. *Related item(s):* broker's loan; time loan.

call loan rate The rate of interest a brokerage firm charges its margin account clients on their debit balances.

call price The price, usually a premium over the issue's par value, at which preferred stocks or bonds can be redeemed before an issue's maturity.

call protection A provision in a bond indenture stating that the issue is noncallable for a certain period of time (5 years, 10 years, etc.) after the original issue date. *Related item(s):* call provision.

call provision The written agreement between an issuing corporation and its bondholders or preferred stockholders giving the corporation the option to redeem its senior securities at a specified price before maturity and under certain conditions. *Syn.* call feature.

call risk The potential for a bond to be called before maturity, leaving the investor without the bond's current income. As this is more likely to occur during times of falling interest rates, the investor may not be able to reinvest his principal at a comparable rate of return.

call spread An option investor's position in which the investor buys a call on a security and writes a call on the same security but with a different expiration date, exercise price, or both.

call writer An investor who receives a premium and takes on, for a specified time, the obligation to sell the underlying security at a specified price at the call buyer's discretion. *Related item(s):* call buyer; put buyer; put writer.

capital Accumulated money or goods available for use in producing more money or goods.

capital appreciation A rise in an asset's market price.

capital asset All tangible property, including securities, real estate and other property, held for the long term.

capital contribution The amount of a participant's investment in a direct participation program, not including units purchased by the sponsors.

capital gain The profit realized when a capital asset is sold for a higher price than the purchase price. *Related item(s):* capital loss; long-term gain.

capitalization The sum of a corporation's long-term debt, stock and surpluses. *Syn.* invested capital. *Related item(s):* capital structure.

capitalization ratio A measure of an issuer's financial status that calculates the value of its bonds, preferred stock or common stock as a percentage of its total capitalization.

capital loss The loss incurred when a capital asset is sold for a lower price than the purchase price. *Related item(s):* capital gain; long-term loss.

capital market The segment of the securities market that deals in instruments with more than one year to maturity—that is, long-term debt and equity securities.

capital risk The potential for an investor to lose all money invested owing to circumstances unrelated to an issuer's financial strength. For example, derivative instruments such as options carry risk independent of the underlying securities' changing value. *Related item(s):* derivative.

capital stock All of a corporation's outstanding preferred stock and common stock, listed at par value.

capital structure The composition of long-term funds (equity and debt) a corporation has as a source for financing. *Related item(s):* capitalization.

capital surplus The money a corporation receives in excess of the stated value of stock at the time of first sale. *Syn.* paid-in capital; paid-in surplus. *Related item(s):* par.

capped index option A type of index option issued with a capped price at a set interval above the strike price (for a call) or below the strike price (for a put). The option is automatically exercised once the underlying index reaches the capped price. *Related item(s):* index option.

capping Placing selling pressure on a stock in an attempt to keep its price low or to move its price lower; this violates the NASD Conduct Rules.

carried interest A sharing arrangement in an oil and gas direct participation program whereby the general partner shares the tangible drilling costs with the limited partners but pays no part of the intangible drilling costs. *Related item(s):* sharing arrangement.

cash account An account in which the customer is required by the SEC's Regulation T to pay in full for securities purchased not later than two days after the standard payment period set by the NASD's Uniform Practice Code. *Syn.* special cash account.

cash assets ratio The most stringent test of liquidity, calculated by dividing the sum of cash and cash equivalents by total current liabilities. *Related item(s):* acid-test ratio; current ratio.

cash dividend Money paid to a corporation's stockholders out of the corporation's current earnings or accumulated profits. The board of directors must declare all dividends.

cash equivalent A security that can be readily converted into cash. Examples include Treasury bills, certificates of deposit and money-market instruments and funds.

cash flow The money received by a business minus the money paid out. Cash flow is also equal to net income plus depreciation or depletion.

cashiering department The department within a brokerage firm that delivers securities and money to and receives securities and money from other firms and clients of the brokerage firm. *Syn.* security cage.

cash market Transactions between buyers and sellers of commodities that entail immediate delivery of and payment for a physical commodity. *Syn.* cash-and-carry market; spot market.

cash trade *See* cash transaction.

cash transaction A settlement contract that calls for delivery and payment on the same day the trade is executed. Payment is due by 2:30 pm ET or within 30 minutes of the trade if it occurs after 2:00 pm ET. *Syn.* cash trade. *Related item(s):* regular way; settlement date.

catastrophe call The redemption of a bond by an issuer owing to disaster (for example, a power plant that has been built with proceeds from an issue burns to the ground).

CATS *See* Certificate of Accrual on Treasury Securities.

CBOE *See* Chicago Board Options Exchange.

CD *See* negotiable certificate of deposit.

Certificate of Accrual on Treasury Securities (CATS) One of several types of zero-coupon bonds issued by brokerage firms and collateralized by Treasury securities. *Related item(s):* Treasury receipt.

certificate of deposit (CD) *See* negotiable certificate of deposit.

change (1) For an index or average, the difference between the current value and the previous day's market close. (2) For a stock or bond quote, the difference between the current price and the last trade of the previous day.

chartist A securities analyst who uses charts and graphs of the past price movements of a security to predict its future movements. *Syn.* technician. *Related item(s):* technical analysis.

CHB *See* commission house broker.

Chicago Board Options Exchange (CBOE) The self-regulatory organization with jurisdiction over all writing and trading of standardized options and related contracts listed on that exchange. Also, the first national securities exchange for the trading of listed options.

Chicago Stock Exchange (CHX) Regional exchange that provides a listed market for smaller businesses and new enterprises. In 1949, the exchange merged with the St. Louis, Cleveland and Minneapolis/St. Paul exchanges to form the Midwest Stock Exchange, but in 1993, the original name was reinstated. *Related item(s):* regional exchange.

Chinese wall A descriptive name for the division within a brokerage firm that prevents insider information from passing from corporate advisers to investment traders, who could make use of the information to reap illicit profits. *Related item(s):* Insider Trading and Securities Fraud Enforcement Act of 1988.

churning Excessive trading in a customer's account by a registered representative who ignores the customer's interests and seeks only to increase commissions. This violates the NASD Conduct Rules. *Syn.* overtrading.

class Options of the same type (that is, all calls or all puts) on the same underlying security. *Related item(s):* series; type.

Class A share A class of mutual fund share issued with a front-end sales load. A mutual fund offers different classes of shares to allow investors to choose the type of sales charge they will pay. *Related item(s):* Class B share; Class C share; Class D share; front-end load.

Class B share A class of mutual fund share issued with a back-end load. A mutual fund offers different classes of shares to allow investors to choose the type of sales charge they will pay. *Related item(s):* back-end load; Class A share; Class C share; Class D share.

Class C share A class of mutual fund share issued with a level load. A mutual fund offers different classes of shares to allow investors to choose the type of sales charge they will pay. *Related item(s):* Class A share; Class B share; Class D share; level load.

Class D share A class of mutual fund share issued with both a level load and a back-end load. A mutual fund offers different classes of shares to allow investors to choose the type of sales charge they will pay. *Related item(s):* back-end load; Class A share; Class B share; Class C share; level load.

classical economics The theory that maximum economic benefit will be achieved if government does not attempt to influence the economy; that is, if businesses are allowed to seek profitable opportunities as they see fit.

clearing agency An intermediary between the buy and sell sides in a securities transaction that receives and delivers payments and securities. Any organization that fills this function, including a securities depository but not including a Federal Reserve Bank, is considered a clearing agency.

clearing broker/dealer A broker/dealer that clears its own trades as well as those of introducing brokers. A clearing broker/dealer can hold customers' securities and cash. *Syn.* carrying broker.

CLN *See* construction loan note.

close The price of the last transaction for a particular security on a particular day.

closed-end covenant A provision of a bond issue's trust indenture stating that any additional bonds secured by the same assets must have a subordinated claim to those assets. *Related item(s):* junior lien debt; open-end covenant.

closed-end investment company An investment company that issues a fixed number of shares in an actively managed portfolio of securities. The shares may be of several classes; they are traded in the secondary marketplace, either on an exchange or over the counter. The market price of the shares is determined by supply and demand and not by net asset value. *Syn.* publicly traded fund. *Related item(s):* dual-purpose fund; mutual fund.

closed-end management company An investment company that issues a fixed number of shares in an actively managed portfolio of securities. The shares may be of several classes; they are traded in the secondary marketplace, either on an exchange or over the counter. The shares' market price is determined by supply and demand, not by net asset value. *Syn.* publicly traded fund. *Related item(s):* dual-purpose fund.

closing date The date designated by the general partners in a direct participation program as the date when sales of units in the program cease; typically the offering period extends for one year.

closing purchase An options transaction in which the seller buys back an option in the same series; the two transactions effectively cancel each other out and the position is liquidated. *Related item(s):* closing sale; opening purchase.

closing range The relatively narrow range of prices at which transactions take place in the final minutes of the trading day. *Related item(s):* close.

closing sale An options transaction in which the buyer sells an option in the same series; the two transactions effectively cancel each other out and the position is liquidated. *Related item(s):* closing purchase; opening sale.

CMO *See* collateralized mortgage obligation.

CMV *See* current market value.

COD *See* delivery vs. payment.

Code of Arbitration Procedure The NASD's formal method of handling securities-related disputes or clearing controversies between members, public customers, clearing corporations or clearing banks. Any claim, dispute or controversy between member firms or associated persons must be submitted to arbitration.

Code of Procedure (COP) The NASD's formal procedure for handling trade practice complaints involving violations of the Conduct Rules. The NASD Department of Enforcement is the first body to hear and judge complaints. The NASD National Adjudicatory Council handles appeals and review of DOE decisions.

coincident indicator A measurable economic factor that varies directly and simultaneously with the business cycle, thus indicating the current state of the economy. Examples include nonagricultural employment, personal income and industrial production. *Related item(s):* lagging indicator; leading indicator.

collateral Certain assets set aside and pledged to a lender for the duration of a loan. If the borrower fails to meet obligations to pay principal or interest, the lender has claim to the assets.

collateralized mortgage obligation (CMO) A mortgage-backed corporate security. Unlike pass-through obligations issued by FNMA and GNMA, its yield is not guaranteed and it does not have the federal government's backing. These issues attempt to return interest and principal at a predetermined rate.

collateral trust bond A secured bond backed by stocks or bonds of another issuer. The collateral is held by a trustee for safekeeping. *Syn.* collateral trust certificate.

collateral trust certificate *See* collateral trust bond.

collection ratio (1) For corporations, a rough measure of the length of time accounts receivable have been outstanding. It is calculated by multiplying the receivables by 360 and dividing the result by net sales. (2) For municipal bonds, a means of detecting deteriorating credit conditions; it is calculated by dividing taxes collected by taxes assessed.

collect on delivery (COD) *See* delivery vs. payment.

combination An option position that represents a put and a call on the same stock at different strike prices, expirations or both.

combination fund An equity mutual fund that attempts to combine the objectives of growth and current yield by dividing its portfolio between companies that show long-term growth potential and companies that pay high dividends. *Related item(s):* mutual fund.

combination privilege A benefit offered by a mutual fund whereby the investor may qualify for a sales charge breakpoint by combining separate investments in two or more mutual funds under the same management.

combined account A customer account that has cash and long and short margin positions in different securities. *Syn.* mixed account.

combined distribution *See* split offering.

commercial bank An institution that is in the business of accepting deposits and making business loans. Commercial banks may not underwrite corporate securities or most municipal bonds. *Related item(s):* investment banker.

commercial paper An unsecured, short-term promissory note issued by a corporation for financing accounts receivable and inventories. It is usually issued at a discount reflecting prevailing market interest rates. Maturities range up to 270 days.

commingling (1) The combining by a brokerage firm of one customer's securities with another customer's securities and pledging them as joint collateral for a bank loan; unless authorized by the customers, this violates SEC Rule 15c2-1. (2) The combining by a brokerage firm of customer securities with firm securities and pledging them as joint collateral for a bank loan; this practice is prohibited.

commission A service charge an agent assesses in return for arranging a security's purchase or sale. A commission must be fair and reasonable, considering all the relevant factors of the transaction. *Syn.* sales charge. *Related item(s):* markup.

commissioner The state official with jurisdiction over insurance transactions.

commission house broker (CHB) A member of an exchange who is eligible to execute orders for customers of a member firm on the floor of the exchange. *Syn.* floor broker.

Committee on Uniform Securities Identification Procedures (CUSIP) A committee that assigns identification numbers and codes to all securities, to be used when recording all buy and sell orders.

common stock A security that represents ownership in a corporation. Holders of common stock exercise control by electing a board of directors and voting on corporate policy. *Related item(s):* equity; preferred stock.

common stock ratio One of several tools used by bond analysts to assess the degree of safety offered by a corporation's bonds. It measures the percentage of the corporation's total capitalization that is contributed by the common stockholders, and is calculated by adding the par value, the capital in excess of par and the retained earnings, and dividing the result by the total capitalization. *Related item(s):* bond ratio.

competitive bid underwriting A form of firm commitment underwriting in which rival syndicates submit sealed bids for underwriting the issue. Competitive bidding normally is used to determine the underwriters for issues of general obligation municipal bonds, and is required by law in most states for general obligation bonds of more than $100,000. *Related item(s):* negotiated underwriting.

compliance department The department within a brokerage firm that oversees the firm's trading and market-making activities. It ensures that the firm's employees and officers abide by the rules and regulations of the SEC, exchanges and SROs.

compliance registered options principal (CROP) The principal responsible for compliance with options exchange rules and securities laws; with certain exceptions, a CROP may not have sales functions.

Composite Average *See* Dow Jones Composite Average.

concession The profit per bond or share that an underwriter allows the seller of new issue securities. The selling group broker/dealer purchases the securities from the syndicate member at the public offering price minus the concession. *Syn.* reallowance.

Conduct Rules Regulations designed to ensure that NASD member firms and their representatives follow fair and ethical trade practices when dealing with the public. The rules complement and broaden the Securities Act of 1933, the Securities Exchange Act of 1934 and the Investment Company Act of 1940.

conduit theory A means for an investment company to avoid taxation on net investment income distributed to shareholders. If a mutual fund acts as a conduit for the distribution of net investment income, it may qualify as a regulated investment company and be taxed only on the income the fund retains. *Syn.* pipeline theory.

confidence theory A technical analysis theory that measures the willingness of investors to take risks by comparing the yields on high-grade bonds to the yields on lower rated bonds.

confirmation A printed document that states the trade date, settlement date and money due from or owed to a customer. It is sent or given to the customer on or before the settlement date. *Related item(s):* duplicate confirmation.

congestion A technical analysis term used to indicate that the range within which a commodity's price trades for an extended period of time is narrow.

Consolidated Quotation System (CQS) A quotation and last-sale reporting service for NASD members that are active market makers of listed securities in the third market. It is used by market makers willing to stand ready to buy and sell securities for their own accounts on a continuous basis but that do not wish to do so through an exchange. Quotes are those entered by both third market makers and specialists.

Consolidated Tape (CT) A New York Stock Exchange service that delivers real-time reports of securities transactions to subscribers as they occur on the various exchanges.

The Tape distributes reports to subscribers over two different networks that the subscribers can tap into through either the high-speed electronic lines or the low-speed ticker lines. Network A reports transactions in NYSE–listed securities. Network B reports AMEX–listed securities transactions, as well as reports of transactions in regional exchange issues that substantially meet AMEX listing requirements.

consolidation The technical analysis term for a narrowing of the trading range for a commodity or security, considered an indication that a strong price move is imminent.

constant dollar plan A defensive investment strategy in which the total sum of money invested is kept constant, regardless of any price fluctuation in the portfolio. As a result, the investor sells when the market is high and buys when it is low.

constant ratio plan An investment strategy in which the investor maintains an appropriate ratio of debt to equity securities by making purchases and sales to maintain the desired balance.

construction loan note (CLN) A short-term municipal debt security that provides interim financing for new projects.

constructive receipt The date on which the Internal Revenue Service considers that a taxpayer receives dividends or other income.

Consumer Price Index (CPI) A measure of price changes in consumer goods and services used to identify periods of inflation or deflation.

consumption A term used by Keynesian economists to refer to the purchase by household units of newly produced goods and services.

contemporaneous trader A person who enters a trade at or near the same time and in the same security as a person who has inside information. The contemporaneous trader may bring suit against the inside trader. *Related item(s):* Insider Trading and Securities Fraud Enforcement Act of 1988.

contingent-deferred sales load *See* back-end load.

contingent order An order that is conditional upon the execution of a previous order and that will be executed only after the first order is filled.

contra broker The broker on the buy side of a sell order or on the sell side of a buy order.

contraction A period of general economic decline, one of the business cycle's four stages. *Related item(s):* business cycle.

contractionary policy A monetary policy that decreases the money supply, usually with the intention of raising interest rates and combating inflation.

contractual plan A type of accumulation plan in which an individual agrees to invest a specific amount of money in the mutual fund during a specific time period. *Syn.* penalty plan; prepaid charge plan. *Related item(s):* front-end load; mutual fund; voluntary accumulation plan.

control (controlling, controlled by, under common control with) The power to direct or affect the direction of a company's management and policies, whether through the ownership of voting securities, by contract or otherwise. Control is presumed to exist if a person, directly or indirectly, owns, controls, holds with the power to vote or holds proxies representing more than 10 percent of a company's voting securities.

control person (1) A director, an officer or another affiliate of an issuer. (2) A stockholder who owns at least 10 percent of any class of a corporation's outstanding securities. *Related item(s):* affiliate; insider.

control security Any security owned by a director, an officer or another affiliate of the issuer or by a stockholder who owns at least 10 percent of any class of a corporation's outstanding securities. Who owns a security, not the security itself, determines whether it is a control security.

conversion parity Two securities, one of which can be converted into the other, of equal dollar value. A convertible security holder can calculate parity to help decide whether converting would lead to gain or loss.

conversion price The dollar amount of a convertible security's par value that is exchangeable for one share of common stock.

conversion privilege A feature the issuer adds to a security that allows the holder to change the security into shares of common stock. This makes the security attractive to investors and, therefore, more marketable. *Related item(s):* convertible bond; convertible preferred stock.

conversion rate *See* conversion ratio.

conversion ratio The number of shares of common stock per par value amount that the holder would receive for converting a convertible bond or preferred share. *Syn.* conversion rate.

conversion value The total market value of common stock into which a senior security is convertible.

convertible bond A debt security, usually in the form of a debenture, that can be exchanged for equity securities of the issuing corporation at specified prices or rates. *Related item(s):* debenture.

convertible preferred stock An equity security that can be exchanged for common stock at specified prices or rates. Dividends may be cumulative or noncumulative. *Related item(s):* cumulative preferred stock; noncumulative preferred stock; preferred stock.

cooling-off period The period (a minimum of 20 days) between a registration statement's filing date and the registration's effective date. In practice, the period varies in length.

COP *See* Code of Procedure.

corporate account An account held in a corporation's name. The corporate agreement, signed when the account is opened, specifies which officers are authorized to trade in the account. In addition to standard margin account documents, a corporation must provide a copy of its charter and bylaws authorizing a margin account.

corporate bond A debt security issued by a corporation. A corporate bond typically has a par value of $1,000, is taxable, has a term maturity and is traded on a major exchange.

corporation The most common form of business organization, in which the organization's total worth is divided into shares of stock, each share representing a unit of ownership. A corporation is characterized by a continuous life span and its owners' limited liability.

cost basis The price paid for an asset, including any commissions or fees, used to calculate capital gains or losses when the asset is sold.

cost depletion A method of calculating tax deductions for investments in mineral, oil or gas resources. The cost of the mineral-, oil- or gas-producing property is returned to the investor over the property's life by an annual deduction, which takes into account the number of known recoverable units of mineral, oil or gas to arrive at a cost-per-unit figure. The tax deduction is determined by multiplying the cost-per-unit figure by the number of units sold each year.

coterminous A term used to describe municipal entities that share the same boundaries. For example, a municipality's school district and fire district may issue debt separately although the debt is backed by revenues from the same taxpayers. *Related item(s):* overlapping debt.

coupon bond A debt obligation with attached coupons representing semiannual interest payments. The holder submits the coupons to the trustee to receive the interest payments. The issuer keeps no record of the purchaser, and the purchaser's name is not printed on the certificate. *Syn.* bearer bond. *Related item(s):* book-entry security; registered; registered as to principal only.

coupon yield *See* nominal yield.

covenant A component of a debt issue's trust indenture that identifies bondholders' rights and other provisions. Examples include rate covenants that establish a minimum revenue coverage for a bond; insurance covenants that require insurance on a project; and maintenance covenants that require maintenance on a facility constructed by the proceeds of a bond issue.

coverage ratio A measure of the safety of a bond issue, based on how many times earnings will cover debt service plus operating and maintenance expenses for a specific time period.

covered call writer An investor who sells a call option while owning the underlying security or some other asset that guarantees the ability to deliver if the call is exercised.

covered put writer An investor who sells a put option while owning an asset that guarantees the ability to pay if the put is exercised (e.g., cash in the account).

CPI *See* Consumer Price Index.

CQS *See* Consolidated Quotation System.

CR *See* credit balance.

credit agreement A component of a customer's margin account agreement, outlining the conditions of the credit arrangement between broker and customer.

credit balance (CR) The amount of money remaining in a customer's account after all commitments have been paid in full. *Syn.* credit record; credit register. *Related item(s):* debit balance.

credit department *See* margin department.

creditor Any broker or dealer, member of a national securities exchange, or person associated with a broker/dealer involved in extending credit to customers.

credit risk The degree of probability that a bond's issuer will default in the payment of either principal or interest. *Syn.* default risk; financial risk.

credit spread A position established when the premium received for the option sold exceeds the premium paid for the option bought. *Related item(s):* debit spread.

CROP *See* compliance registered options principal.

crossed market The situation created when one market maker bids for a stock at a higher price than another market maker is asking for the same stock, or when one market maker enters an ask price to sell a stock at a lower price than another market maker's bid price to buy the same stock. This violates the NASD Conduct Rules. *Related item(s):* locked market.

crossover point The point at which a limited partnership begins to show a negative cash flow with a taxable income. *Related item(s):* phantom income.

cum rights A term describing stock trading with rights. *Related item(s):* ex-rights.

cumulative preferred stock An equity security that offers the holder any unpaid dividends in arrears. These dividends accumulate and must be paid to the cumulative preferred stockholder before any dividends can be paid to the common stockholders. *Related item(s):* convertible preferred stock; noncumulative preferred stock; preferred stock.

cumulative voting A voting procedure that permits stockholders either to cast all of their votes for any one candidate or to cast their total number of votes in any proportion they choose. This results in greater representation for minority stockholders. *Related item(s):* statutory voting.

current assets Cash and other assets that are expected to be converted into cash within the next 12 months. Examples include such liquid items as cash and equivalents, accounts receivable, inventory and prepaid expenses.

current liabilities A corporation's debt obligations due for payment within the next 12 months. Examples include accounts payable, accrued wages payable and current long-term debt.

current market value (CMV) The worth of the securities in an account. The market value of listed securities is based on the closing prices on the previous business day. *Syn.* long market value. *Related item(s):* market value.

current price *See* public offering price.

current ratio A measure of a corporation's liquidity; that is, its ability to transfer assets into cash to meet current short-term obligations. It is calculated by dividing total current assets by total current liabilities. *Syn.* working capital ratio.

current yield The annual rate of return on a security, calculated by dividing the interest or dividends paid by the security's current market price. *Related item(s):* bond yield.

CUSIP *See* Committee on Uniform Securities Identification Procedures.

custodial account An account in which a custodian enters trades on behalf of the beneficial owner, often a minor. *Related item(s):* custodian.

custodian An institution or a person responsible for making all investment, management and distribution decisions in an account maintained in the best interests of another. Mutual funds have custodians responsible for safeguarding certificates and performing clerical duties. *Related item(s):* mutual fund custodian.

customer Any person who opens a trading account with a broker/dealer. A customer may be classified in terms of account ownership, trading authorization, payment method or types of securities traded.

customer agreement A document that a customer must sign when opening a margin account with a broker/dealer; it allows the firm to liquidate all or a portion of the account if the customer fails to meet a margin call.

customer ledger The accounting record that lists separately all customer cash and margin accounts carried by a firm.

customer statement A document showing a customer's trading activity, positions and account balance. The SEC requires that customer statements be sent quarterly, but customers generally receive them monthly.

cyclical industry A fundamental analysis term for an industry that is sensitive to the business cycle and price changes. Most cyclical industries produce durable goods such as raw materials and heavy equipment.

D

dated date The date on which interest on a new bond issue begins to accrue.

day order An order that is valid only until the close of trading on the day it is entered; if it is not executed by the close of trading, it is canceled.

day trader A trader in securities who opens all positions after the opening of the market and offsets or closes out all positions before the close of the market on the same day.

dealer (1) An individual or a firm engaged in the business of buying and selling securities for its own account, either directly or through a broker. (2) The role of a firm when it acts as a principal and charges the customer a markup or markdown. *Syn.* principal. *Related item(s):* broker; broker/dealer.

dealer paper Short-term, unsecured promissory notes that the issuer sells through a dealer rather than directly to the public.

debenture A debt obligation backed by the issuing corporation's general credit. *Syn.* unsecured bond.

debit balance (DR) The amount of money a customer owes a brokerage firm. *Syn.* debit record; debit register. *Related item(s):* credit balance.

debit register *See* debit balance.

debit spread A futures hedge position established when the premium paid for the option bought exceeds the premium received for the option sold. *Related item(s):* credit spread.

debt financing Raising money for working capital or for capital expenditures by selling bonds, bills or notes to individual or institutional investors. In return for the money lent, the investors become creditors and receive the issuer's promise to repay principal and interest on the debt. *Related item(s):* equity financing.

debt per capita *See* net debt per capita.

debt ratio *See* bond ratio.

debt security A security representing an investor's loan to an issuer such as a corporation, a municipality, the federal government or a federal agency. In return for the loan, the issuer promises to repay the debt on a specified date and to pay interest. *Related item(s):* equity security.

debt service The schedule for repayment of interest and principal (or the scheduled sinking fund contribution) on an outstanding debt. *Related item(s):* sinking fund.

debt service ratio An indication of the ability of an issuer to meet principal and interest payments on bonds.

debt service reserve fund The account that holds enough money to pay one year's debt service on a municipal revenue bond. *Related item(s):* flow of funds.

debt-to-equity ratio The ratio of total long-term debt to total stockholders' equity; it is used to measure leverage.

declaration date The date on which a corporation announces an upcoming dividend's amount, payment date and record date.

decreasing debt service A schedule for debt repayment whereby the issuer repays principal in installments of equal size over the life of the issue. The amount of interest due therefore decreases and the amount of each payment becomes smaller over time. *Related item(s):* level debt service.

deduction An item or expenditure subtracted from adjusted gross income to reduce the amount of income subject to tax.

default The failure to pay interest or principal promptly when due.

default risk *See* credit risk.

defeasance The termination of a debt obligation. A corporation or municipality removes debt from its balance sheet by issuing a new debt issue or creating a trust that generates enough cash flow to provide for the payment of interest and principal. *Related item(s):* advance refunding.

defensive industry A fundamental analysis term for an industry that is relatively unaffected by the business cycle. Most defensive industries produce nondurable goods for which demand remains steady throughout the business cycle; examples include the food industry and utilities.

defensive investment strategy A method of portfolio allocation and management aimed at minimizing the risk of losing principal. Defensive investors place a high percentage of their investable assets in bonds, cash equivalents and stocks that are less volatile than average.

deferred annuity An annuity contract that delays payment of income, installments or a lump sum until the investor elects to receive it. *Related item(s):* annuity.

deferred compensation plan A nonqualified retirement plan whereby the employee defers receiving current compensation in favor of a larger payout at retirement (or in the case of disability or death).

deficiency letter The SEC's notification of additions or corrections that a prospective issuer must make to a registration statement before the SEC will clear the offering for distribution. *Syn.* bedbug letter.

defined benefit plan A qualified retirement plan that specifies the total amount of money that the employee will receive at retirement.

defined contribution plan A qualified retirement plan that specifies the amount of money that the employer will contribute annually to the plan.

deflation A persistent and measurable fall in the general level of prices. *Related item(s):* inflation.

delivery The change in ownership or in control of a security in exchange for cash. Delivery takes place on the settlement date.

delivery vs. payment (DVP) A transaction settlement procedure in which securities are delivered to the buying institution's bank in exchange for payment of the amount due. *Syn.* collect on delivery (COD).

demand A consumer's desire and willingness to pay for a good or service. *Related item(s):* supply.

demand deposit A sum of money left with a bank (or borrowed from a bank and left on deposit) that the depositing customer has the right to withdraw immediately. *Related item(s):* time deposit.

demand-pull An excessive money supply that increases the demand for a limited supply of goods that is believed to result in inflation.

depletion A tax deduction that compensates a business for the decreasing supply of the natural resource that provides its income (oil, gas, coal, gold or other nonrenewable resource). There are two ways to calculate depletion: cost depletion and percentage depletion. *Related item(s):* cost depletion; percentage depletion.

depreciation (1) A tax deduction that compensates a business for the cost of certain tangible assets. (2) A decrease in the value of a particular currency relative to other currencies.

depreciation expense A bookkeeping entry of a noncash expense charged against earnings to recover the cost of an asset over its useful life.

depression A prolonged period of general economic decline.

derivative An investment vehicle, the value of which is based on another security's value. Futures contracts, forward contracts and options are among the most common types of derivatives. Institutional investors generally use derivatives to increase overall portfolio return or to hedge portfolio risk.

descending triangle On a technical analyst's trading activity chart, a pattern which indicates that the market has started to fall; considered to be a bearish indicator. *Related item(s):* ascending triangle.

designated order In a municipal bond underwriting, a customer order that is submitted by one syndicate member but that specifies more than one member to receive a percentage of the takedown. The size of the order establishes its priority for subscription to an issue. *Related item(s):* group net order; member-at-the-takedown order; presale order.

devaluation A substantial fall in a currency's value as compared to the value of gold or to the value of another country's currency.

developmental drilling program A limited partnership that drills for oil, gas or minerals in areas of proven reserves or near existing fields. *Related item(s):* exploratory drilling program; income program; step-out well.

diagonal spread An option position established by the simultaneous purchase and sale of options of the same class but with different exercise prices and expiration dates. *Related item(s):* spread.

dilution A reduction in earnings per share of common stock. Dilution occurs through the issuance of additional shares of common stock and the conversion of convertible securities.

direct debt The total of a municipality's general obligation bonds, short-term notes and revenue debt.

direct paper Commercial paper sold directly to the public without the use of a dealer.

direct participation program (DPP) A business organized so as to pass all income, gains, losses and tax benefits to its owners, the investors; the business is usually structured as a limited partnership. Examples include oil and gas programs, real estate programs, agricultural programs, cattle programs, condominium securities and Subchapter S corporate offerings. *Syn.* program.

discount The difference between the lower price paid for a security and the security's face amount at issue.

discount bond A bond that sells at a lower price than its face value. *Related item(s):* par.

discount rate The interest rate charged by the 12 Federal Reserve Banks for short-term loans made to member banks.

discretion The authority given to someone other than an account's beneficial owner to make investment decisions for the account concerning the security, the number of shares or units and whether to buy or sell. The authority to decide only timing or price does not constitute discretion. *Related item(s):* limited power of attorney.

discretionary account An account in which the customer has given the registered representative authority to enter transactions at the rep's discretion.

disintermediation The flow of money from low-yielding accounts in traditional savings institutions to higher yielding investments. Typically, this occurs when the Fed tightens the money supply and interest rates rise.

disposable income (DI) The sum that people divide between spending and personal savings. *Related item(s):* personal income.

disproportionate sharing A sharing arrangement whereby the sponsor in an oil and gas direct participation program pays a portion of the program's costs but receives a disproportionately higher percentage of its revenues. *Related item(s):* sharing arrangement.

distribution Any cash or other property distributed to shareholders or general partners that arises from their interests in the business, investment company or partnership.

distribution stage The period during which an individual receives distributions from an annuity account. *Syn.* payout stage. *Related item(s):* accumulation stage; accumulation unit.

diversification A risk management technique that mixes a wide variety of investments within a portfolio, thus minimizing the impact of any one security on overall portfolio performance.

diversified common stock fund A mutual fund that invests its assets in a wide range of common stocks. The fund's objectives may be growth, income or a combination of both. *Related item(s):* growth fund; mutual fund.

diversified investment company As defined by the Investment Company Act of 1940, an investment company that meets certain standards as to the percentage of assets invested. These companies use diversification to manage risk. *Related item(s):* management company; nondiversified investment company; 75-5-10 test.

diversified management company As defined by the Investment Company Act of 1940, a management company that meets certain standards for percentage of assets invested. These companies use diversification to manage risk. *Related item(s):* management company; 75-5-10 test.

divided account *See* Western account.

dividend A distribution of a corporation's earnings. Dividends may be in the form of cash, stock or property. The board of directors must declare all dividends. *Syn.* stock dividend. *Related item(s):* cash dividend; dividend yield; property dividend.

dividend department The department within a brokerage firm that is responsible for crediting client accounts with dividends and interest payments on client securities held in the firm's name.

dividend disbursing agent (DDA) The person responsible for making the required dividend distributions to the broker/dealer's dividend department.

dividend exclusion rule An IRS provision that permits a corporation to exclude from its taxable income 70 percent of dividends received from domestic preferred and common stocks. The Tax Reform Act of 1986 repealed the dividend exclusion for individual investors.

dividend payout ratio A measure of a corporation's policy of paying cash dividends, calculated by dividing the dividends paid on common stock by the net income available for common stockholders. The ratio is the complement of the retained earnings ratio.

dividends per share The dollar amount of cash dividends paid on each common share during one year.

dividend yield The annual rate of return on a common or preferred stock investment. The yield is calculated by dividing the annual dividend by the stock's purchase price. *Related item(s):* current yield; dividend.

DJIA *See* Dow Jones Industrial Average.

DK *See* don't know.

DNR *See* do not reduce order.

doctrine of mutual reciprocity The agreement that established the federal tax exemption for municipal bond interest. States and municipalities do not tax federal securities or properties, and the federal government reciprocates by exempting local government securities and properties from federal taxation. *Syn.* mutual exclusion doctrine; reciprocal immunity.

dollar bonds Municipal revenue bonds that are quoted and traded on a basis of dollars rather than yield to maturity. Term bonds, tax-exempt notes and New Housing Authority bonds are dollar bonds.

dollar cost averaging A system of buying mutual fund shares in fixed dollar amounts at regular fixed intervals, regardless of the share's price. The investor purchases more shares when prices are low and fewer shares when prices are high, thus lowering the average cost per share over time.

donor A person who makes a gift of money or securities to another. Once the gift is donated, the donor gives up all rights to it. Gifts of securities to minors under the Uniform Gifts to Minors Act provide tax advantages to the donor. *Related item(s):* Uniform Gifts to Minors Act.

do not reduce order (DNR) An order that stipulates that the limit or stop price should not be reduced in response to the declaration of a cash dividend.

don't know (DK) A response to a confirmation received from a broker/dealer indicating a lack of information about, or record of, the transaction.

double-barreled bond A municipal security backed by the full faith and credit of the issuing municipality, as well as by pledged revenues. *Related item(s):* general obligation bond; revenue bond.

Dow Jones averages The most widely quoted and oldest measures of change in stock prices. Each of the four averages is based on the prices of a limited number of stocks in a particular category. *Related item(s):* average; Dow Jones Industrial Average.

Dow Jones Composite Average (DJCA) A market indicator composed of the 65 stocks that make up the Dow Jones Industrial, Transportation and Utilities Averages. *Related item(s):* average; Dow Jones Industrial Average; Dow Jones Transportation Average; Dow Jones Utilities Average.

Dow Jones Industrial Average (DJIA) The most widely used market indicator, composed of 30 large, actively traded issues of industrial stocks. *Related item(s):* average.

Dow Jones Transportation Average (DJTA) A market indicator composed of 20 transportation stocks. *Related item(s):* average; Dow Jones Composite Average; Dow Jones Industrial Average; Dow Jones Utilities Average.

Dow Jones Utilities Average (DJUA) A market indicator composed of 15 utilities stocks. *Related item(s):* average; Dow Jones Composite Average; Dow Jones Industrial Average; Dow Jones Transportation Average.

down tick *See* minus tick.

Dow theory A technical market theory that long-term trends in the stock market can be confirmed by analyzing the movements of the Dow Jones Industrial Average and the Dow Jones Transportation Average.

DPP *See* direct participation program.

DR *See* debit balance.

dry hole A well that is plugged and abandoned without being completed or that is abandoned for any reason without having produced commercially for 60 days. *Related item(s):* productive well.

dual-purpose fund A closed-end investment company that offers two classes of stock: income shares and capital shares. Income shares entitle the holder to share in the net dividends and interest paid to the fund. Capital shares entitle the holder to profit from the capital appreciation of all securities the fund holds. *Related item(s):* closed-end management company.

due bill A printed statement showing the obligation of a seller to deliver securities or rights to the purchaser. A due bill is also used as a pledge to deliver dividends when the transaction occurs after the record date.

due diligence The careful investigation by the underwriters that is necessary to ensure that all material information pertinent to an issue has been disclosed to prospective investors.

due diligence meeting A meeting at which an issuing corporation's officials and representatives of the underwriting group present information on and answer questions about a pending issue of securities. The meeting is held for the benefit of brokers, securities analysts and institutional investors.

duplicate confirmation A copy of a customer's confirmation that a brokerage firm sends to an agent or an attorney if the customer requests it in writing. In addition, if the customer is an employee of another broker/dealer, SRO regulations may require a duplicate confirmation to be sent to the employing broker/dealer. *Related item(s):* confirmation.

DVP *See* delivery vs. payment.

E

earned income Income derived from active participation in a trade or business, including wages, salary, tips, commissions and bonuses. *Related item(s):* portfolio income; unearned income.

earned surplus *See* retained earnings.

earnings per share (EPS) A corporation's net income available for common stock divided by its number of shares of common stock outstanding. *Syn.* primary earnings per share.

earnings per share fully diluted A corporation's earnings per share calculated assuming that all convertible securities have been converted. *Related item(s):* earnings per share.

Eastern account A securities underwriting in which the agreement among underwriters states that each syndicate member will be responsible for its own allocation as well as for a proportionate share of any securities remaining unsold. *Syn.* undivided account. *Related item(s):* syndicate; Western account.

economic risk The potential for international developments and domestic events to trigger losses in securities investments.

EE savings bond *See* Series EE bond.

effective date The date the registration of an issue of securities becomes effective, allowing the underwriters to sell the newly issued securities to the public and confirm sales to investors who have given indications of interest.

efficient market theory A theory based on the premise that the stock market processes information efficiently. The theory postulates that, as new information becomes known, it is reflected immediately in the price of stock and therefore stock prices represent fair prices.

Employee Retirement Income Security Act of 1974 (ERISA) The law that governs the operation of most corporate pension and benefit plans. The law eased pension eligibility rules, set up the Pension Benefit Guaranty Corporation and established guidelines for the management of pension funds. Corporate retirement plans established under ERISA qualify for favorable tax treatment for employers and participants. *Syn.* Pension Reform Act.

endorsement The signature on the back of a stock or bond certificate by the person named on the certificate as the owner. An owner must endorse certificates when transferring them to another person. *Related item(s):* assignment.

EPS *See* earnings per share.

EQ *See* equity.

equipment bond *See* equipment trust certificate.

equipment-leasing limited partnership A direct participation program that purchases equipment for leasing to other businesses on a long-term basis. Tax-sheltered income is the primary objective of such a partnership.

equipment trust certificate A debt obligation backed by equipment. The title to the equipment is held by an independent trustee (usually a bank), not the issuing company. Equipment trust certificates are generally issued by transportation companies such as railroads. *Syn.* equipment bond; equipment note.

equity (EQ) Common and preferred stockholders' ownership interests in a corporation. *Related item(s):* common stock; preferred stock.

equity financing Raising money for working capital or for capital expenditures by selling common or preferred stock to individual or institutional investors. In return for the money paid, the investors receive ownership interests in the corporation. *Related item(s):* debt financing.

equity option A security representing the right to buy or sell common stock at a specified price within a specified time. *Related item(s):* option.

equity security A security representing ownership in a corporation or another enterprise. Examples of equity securities include:
- common and preferred stock; and
- put and call options on equity securities.

ERISA *See* Employee Retirement Income Security Act of 1974.

escrow agreement The certificate provided by an approved bank that guarantees that the indicated securities are on deposit at that bank. An investor who writes a call option and can present an escrow agreement is considered covered and does not need to meet margin requirements.

Eurobond A long-term debt instrument of a government or corporation that is denominated in the currency of the issuer's country but is issued and sold in a different country.

Eurodollar US currency held in banks outside the United States.

excess equity (EE) The value of money or securities in a margin account that is in excess of the federal requirement. *Syn.* margin excess; Regulation T excess.

excess margin securities The securities in a margin account that are in excess of 140 percent of the account's debit balance. Such securities are available to the broker/dealer for debit balance financing purposes, but they must be segregated and earmarked as the customer's property.

exchange Any organization, association or group of persons that maintains or provides a marketplace in which securities can be bought and sold. An exchange need not be a physical place, and several strictly electronic exchanges do business around the world.

Exchange Act *See* Securities Exchange Act of 1934.

exchange-listed security A security that has met certain requirements and has been admitted to full trading privileges on an exchange. The NYSE, the AMEX and regional exchanges set listing requirements for volume of shares outstanding, corporate earnings and other characteristics. Exchange-listed securities can also be traded in the third market, the market for institutional investors.

exchange market All of the exchanges on which listed securities are traded.

exchange privilege A feature offered by a mutual fund allowing an individual to transfer an investment in one fund to another fund under the same sponsor without incurring an additional sales charge.

exchange rate *See* foreign exchange rate.

ex-date The first date on which a security is traded that the buyer is not entitled to receive distributions previously declared. *Syn.* ex-dividend date.

ex-dividend date *See* ex-date.

executor A person given fiduciary authorization to manage the affairs of a decedent's estate. An executor's authority is established by the decedent's last will.

exempt security A security exempt from the registration requirements (although not from the antifraud requirements) of the Securities Act of 1933. Examples include US government securities and municipal securities.

exempt transaction A transaction that does not trigger a state's registration and advertising requirements under the Uniform Securities Act. Examples of exempt transactions include:
- nonissuer transactions in outstanding securities (normal market trading);
- transactions with financial institutions;
- unsolicited transactions; and
- private placement transactions.

No transaction is exempt from the Uniform Securities Act's antifraud provisions.

exercise To effect the transaction offered by an option, a right or a warrant. For example, an equity call holder exercises a call by buying 100 shares of the underlying stock at the agreed-upon price within the agreed-upon time period.

exercise price The cost per share at which an option or a warrant holder may buy or sell the underlying security. *Syn.* strike price.

ex-legal A municipal issue that trades without a written legal opinion of counsel from a bond attorney. An ex-legal issue must be designated as such at the time of the trade. *Related item(s):* legal opinion of counsel.

expansion A period of increased business activity throughout an economy; one of the four stages of the business cycle. *Syn.* recovery. *Related item(s):* business cycle.

expansionary policy A monetary policy that increases the money supply, usually with the intention of lowering interest rates and combatting deflation.

expense ratio A ratio for comparing a mutual fund's efficiency by dividing the fund's expenses by its net assets.

expiration cycle A set of four expiration months for a class of listed options. An option may have expiration dates of January, April, July and October (JAJO); February, May, August and November (FMAN); or March, June, September and December (MJSD).

expiration date The specified date on which an option buyer no longer has the rights specified in the option contract.

exploratory drilling program A limited partnership that aims to locate and recover undiscovered reserves of oil, gas or minerals. These programs are considered highly risky investments. *Syn.* wildcatting. *Related item(s):* developmental drilling program; income program.

exploratory well A well drilled either in search of an undiscovered pool of oil or gas or with the hope of substantially extending the limits of an existing pool of oil or gas.

ex-rights Stock trading without rights. *Related item(s):* cum rights.

ex-rights date The date on or after which stocks will be traded without subscription rights previously declared.

F

FAC *See* face-amount certificate company.

face-amount certificate company (FAC) An investment company that issues certificates obligating it to pay an investor a stated amount of money (the face amount) on a specific future date. The investor pays into the certificate in periodic payments or in a lump sum.

face value *See* par.

fail to deliver A situation where the broker/dealer on the sell side of a transaction or contract does not deliver the specified securities to the broker/dealer on the buy side. *Syn.* broker fail; fails; fails to deliver; failure to deliver.

fail to receive A situation where the broker/dealer on the buy side of a transaction or contract does not receive the specified securities from the broker/dealer on the sell side. *Syn.* fails; fails to receive; failure to receive.

Fannie Mae *See* Federal National Mortgage Association.

Farm Credit Administration (FCA) The government agency that coordinates the activities of the banks in the Farm Credit System. *Related item(s):* Farm Credit System.

Farm Credit System (FCS) An organization of 37 privately owned banks that provide credit services to farmers and mortgages on farm property. Included in the system are the Federal Land Banks, Federal Intermediate Credit Banks and Banks for Cooperatives. *Related item(s):* Federal Intermediate Credit Bank.

FCA *See* Farm Credit Administration.

FCO *See* foreign currency option.

FCS *See* Farm Credit System.

FDIC *See* Federal Deposit Insurance Corporation.

Fed *See* Federal Reserve System.

Fed call *See* margin call.

federal call *See* margin call.

Federal Deposit Insurance Corporation (FDIC) The government agency that provides deposit insurance for member banks and prevents bank and thrift failures.

federal funds The reserves of banks and certain other institutions greater than the reserve requirements or excess reserves. These funds are available immediately.

federal funds rate The interest rate charged by one institution lending federal funds to another.

Federal Home Loan Bank (FHLB) A government-regulated organization that operates a credit reserve system for the nation's savings and loan institutions.

Federal Home Loan Mortgage Corporation (FHLMC) A publicly traded corporation that promotes the nationwide secondary market in mortgages by issuing mortgage-backed pass-through debt certificates. *Syn.* Freddie Mac.

Federal Intermediate Credit Bank (FICB) One of 12 banks that provide short-term financing to farmers as part of the Farm Credit System.

Federal National Mortgage Association (FNMA) A publicly held corporation that purchases conventional mortgages and mortgages from government agencies, including the Federal Housing Administration, Department of Veterans Affairs and Farmers Home Administration. *Syn.* Fannie Mae.

Federal Open Market Committee (FOMC) A committee that makes decisions concerning the Fed's operations to control the money supply.

Federal Reserve Board (FRB) A seven-member group that directs the operations of the Federal Reserve System. The President appoints board members, subject to Congressional approval.

Federal Reserve System The central bank system of the United States. Its primary responsibility is to regulate the flow of money and credit.

FHLB *See* Federal Home Loan Bank.

FHLMC *See* Federal Home Loan Mortgage Corporation.

FICB *See* Federal Intermediate Credit Bank.

fictitious quotation A bid or an offer published before being identified by source and verified as legitimate. A fictitious quote may create the appearance of trading activity where none exists; this violates the NASD Conduct Rules.

fidelity bond Insurance coverage required by the self-regulatory organizations for all employees, officers and partners of member firms to protect clients against acts of lost securities, fraudulent trading and check forgery. *Syn.* surety bond.

fiduciary A person legally appointed and authorized to hold assets in trust for another person and manage those assets for that person's benefit.

filing *See* registration by filing.

filing date The day on which an issuer submits to the SEC the registration statement for a new securities issue.

fill or kill order (FOK) An order that instructs the floor broker to fill the entire order immediately; if the entire order cannot be executed immediately, it is canceled.

final prospectus The legal document that states a new issue security's price, delivery date and underwriting spread, as well as other material information. It must be given to every investor who purchases a new issue of registered securities. *Syn.* prospectus.

Financial Guaranty Insurance Corporation (FGIC) An insurance company that offers insurance on the timely payment of interest and principal on municipal issues and unit investment trusts.

financial risk *See* credit risk.

firm commitment underwriting A type of underwriting commitment in which the underwriter agrees to sell an entire new issue of securities. The underwriter acts as a dealer, pays the issuer a lump sum for the securities and assumes all financial responsibility for any unsold shares. *Related item(s):* underwriting.

firm quote The actual price at which a trading unit of a security (such as 100 shares of stock or five bonds) may be bought or sold. All quotes are firm quotes unless otherwise indicated. *Related item(s):* bona fide quote; nominal quote.

first in, first out (FIFO) An accounting method used to assess a company's inventory, in which it is assumed that the first goods acquired are the first to be sold. The same method is used by the IRS to determine cost basis for tax purposes. *Related item(s):* average basis; last in, first out; share identification.

fiscal policy The federal tax and spending policies set by Congress or the President. These policies affect tax rates, interest rates and government spending in an effort to control the economy. *Related item(s):* monetary policy.

5% markup policy The NASD's general guideline for the percentage markups, markdowns and commissions on OTC securities transactions. The policy is intended to ensure fair and reasonable treatment of the investing public.

fixed annuity An insurance contract in which the insurance company makes fixed dollar payments to the annuitant for the term of the contract, usually until the annuitant dies. The insurance company guarantees both earnings and principal. *Syn.* fixed dollar annuity; guaranteed dollar annuity. *Related item(s):* annuity; variable annuity.

fixed asset A tangible, physical property used in the course of a corporation's everyday operations; it includes buildings, equipment and land.

fixed charge coverage ratio *See* bond interest coverage ratio.

fixed dollar annuity *See* fixed annuity.

fixed unit investment trust An investment company that invests in a portfolio of securities in which no changes are permissible. *Related item(s):* nonfixed unit investment trust; unit investment trust.

flat A term used to describe bonds traded without accrued interest. They are traded at the agreed-upon market price only. *Related item(s):* accrued interest.

flat yield curve A chart showing the yields of bonds with short maturities as equal to the yields of bonds with long maturities. *Syn.* even yield curve. *Related item(s):* inverted yield curve; normal yield curve; yield curve.

floor broker *See* commission house broker.

floor trader An exchange member who executes transactions from the floor of the exchange only for his own account. *Syn.* local.

flow of funds The schedule of payments disbursed from the proceeds of a facility financed by a revenue bond. The flow of funds determines the order in which the operating expenses, debt service and other expenses are paid. Typically, the priority is (1) operations and maintenance, (2) debt service, (3) debt service reserve, (4) reserve maintenance, (5) renewal and replacement, (6) surplus. *Related item(s):* debt service reserve fund.

flow-through A term that describes the way income, deductions and credits resulting from the activities of a business are applied to individual taxes and expenses as though each incurred the income and deductions directly. *Related item(s):* limited partnership.

FNMA *See* Federal National Mortgage Association.

FOK *See* fill or kill order.

FOMC *See* Federal Open Market Committee.

forced conversion Market conditions created by a corporation to encourage convertible bondholders to exercise their conversion options. Often conversion is forced by calling the bonds when the market value of the stock is higher than the redemption price offered by the corporation. *Related item(s):* redemption.

forced sell-out The action taken when a customer fails to meet the deadline for paying for securities and no extension has been granted: the broker/dealer must liquidate enough securities to pay for the transaction.

foreign currency Money issued by a country other than the one in which the investor resides. Options and futures contracts on numerous foreign currencies are traded on US exchanges.

foreign currency option (FCO) A security representing the right to buy or sell a specified amount of a foreign currency. *Related item(s):* option.

foreign exchange rate The price of one country's currency in terms of another currency. *Syn.* exchange rate.

foreign fund *See* specialized fund.

Form 10K An annual audited report that covers essentially all the information contained in an issuing company's original registration statement. A Form 10K is due within 90 days of year end.

Form 10Q A quarterly report containing a corporation's unaudited financial data. Certain nonrecurring events that arise during the quarterly period, such as significant litigation, must be reported. A Form 10Q is due 45 days after the end of each of the first three fiscal quarters.

forward pricing The valuation process for mutual fund shares, whereby an order to purchase or redeem shares is executed at the price determined by the portfolio valuation calculated after the order is received. Portfolio valuations occur at least once per business day.

401(k) plan A tax-deferred defined contribution retirement plan offered by an employer.

403(b) plan A tax-deferred annuity retirement plan available to employees of public schools and certain nonprofit organizations.

fourth market The exchange where securities are traded directly from one institutional investor to another without a brokerage firm's services, primarily through ECNs.

fractional share A portion of a whole share of stock. Mutual fund shares are frequently issued in fractional amounts. Fractional shares used to be generated when corporations declared stock dividends, merged or voted to split stock, but today it is more common for corporations to issue the cash equivalent of fractional shares.

fraud The deliberate concealment, misrepresentation or omission of material information or the truth, so as to deceive or manipulate another party for unlawful or unfair gain.

FRB *See* Federal Reserve Board.

Freddie Mac *See* Federal Home Loan Mortgage Corporation.

free credit balance The cash funds in customer accounts. Broker/dealers must notify customers of their free credit balances at least quarterly.

freeriding Buying and immediately selling securities without making payment. This practice violates the SEC's Regulation T.

freeriding and withholding The failure of a member participating in the distribution of a hot issue to make a bona fide public offering at the public offering price. This practice violates the NASD Conduct Rules. *Related item(s):* hot issue.

front-end fee The expenses paid for services rendered during a direct participation program's organization or acquisition phase, including front-end organization and offering expenses, acquisition fees and expenses, and any other similar fees designated by the sponsor.

front-end load (1) A mutual fund commission or sales fee that is charged at the time shares are purchased. The load is added to the share's net asset value when calculating the public offering price. *Related item(s):* back-end load.

frozen account An account requiring cash in advance before a buy order is executed and securities in hand before a sell order is executed. An account holder under such restrictions has violated the SEC's Regulation T.

Full Disclosure Act *See* Securities Act of 1933.

full power of attorney A written authorization for someone other than an account's beneficial owner to make deposits and withdrawals and to execute trades in the account. *Related item(s):* limited power of attorney.

full trading authorization An authorization, usually provided by a full power of attorney, for someone other than the customer to have full trading privileges in an account. *Related item(s):* limited trading authorization.

fully registered bond A debt issue that prints the bondholder's name on the certificate. The issuer's transfer agent maintains the records and sends principal and interest payments directly to the investor. *Related item(s):* registered; registered as to principal only.

functional allocation A sharing arrangement whereby the investors in an oil and gas direct participation program are responsible for intangible costs and the sponsor is responsible for tangible costs; revenues are shared. *Related item(s):* sharing arrangement.

fundamental analysis A method of evaluating securities by attempting to measure the intrinsic value of a particular stock. Fundamental analysts study the overall economy, industry conditions and the financial condition and management of particular companies. *Related item(s):* technical analysis.

funded debt All long-term debt financing of a corporation.

funding An ERISA guideline stipulating that retirement plan assets must be segregated from other corporate assets.

fund manager *See* portfolio manager.

funds statement The part of a corporation's annual report that analyzes why working capital increased or decreased.

fungible Interchangeable, owing to identical characteristics or value. A security is fungible if it can be substituted or exchanged for another security.

G

GDP *See* gross domestic product.

general account The account that holds all of an insurer's assets other than those in separate accounts. The general account holds the contributions paid for traditional life insurance contracts. *Related item(s):* separate account.

general obligation bond (GO) A municipal debt issue backed by the full faith, credit and taxing power of the issuer for payment of interest and principal. *Syn.* full faith and credit bond. *Related item(s):* double-barreled bond; revenue bond.

general partner (GP) An active investor in a direct participation program who is personally liable for all debts of the program and who manages the business of the program. The GP's duties include: making decisions that bind the partnership; buying and selling property; managing property and money; supervising all aspects of the business; and maintaining a 1 percent financial interest in the partnership. *Related item(s):* limited partner.

general partnership (GP) An association of two or more entities formed to conduct a business jointly. The partnership does not require documents for formation, and the general partners are jointly and severally liable for the partnership's liabilities. *Related item(s):* limited partnership.

General Securities Principal *See* Series 24.

General Securities Representative *See* Series 7.

generic advertising Communications with the public that promote securities as investments, but that do not refer to particular securities. *Syn.* institutional advertising.

Ginnie Mae *See* Government National Mortgage Association.

Glass-Steagall Act of 1933 Federal legislation that forbids commercial banks to underwrite securities and forbids investment bankers to open deposit accounts or make commercial loans. *Syn.* banking act.

GNMA *See* Government National Mortgage Association.

GNP *See* gross domestic product.

GO *See* general obligation bond.

good delivery A term describing a security that is negotiable, in compliance with the contract of the sale and ready to be transferred from seller to purchaser.

good faith deposit A deposit contributed by each syndicate involved in a competitive bid underwriting for a municipal issue. The deposit ensures performance by the low bidder. The amount required to be deposited is stipulated in the official notice of sale sent to prospective underwriters; it is usually 2 percent of the par value.

good till canceled order (GTC) An order that is left on the specialist's book until it is either executed or canceled. *Syn.* open order.

goodwill An intangible asset that represents the value that a firm's business reputation adds to its book value.

Government National Mortgage Association (GNMA) A wholly government-owned corporation that issues pass-through mortgage debt certificates backed by the full faith and credit of the US government. *Syn.* Ginnie Mae.

government security A debt obligation of the US government, backed by its full faith, credit and taxing power, and regarded as having no risk of default. The government issues short-term Treasury bills, medium-term Treasury notes and long-term Treasury bonds. *Related item(s):* agency issue.

GP *See* general partner; general partnership.

green shoe option A provision of an issue's registration statement that allows an underwriter to buy extra shares from the issuer (thus increasing the size of the offering) if public demand proves exceptionally strong. The term derives from the Green Shoe Manufacturing Company, which first used the technique.

gross domestic product (GDP) The total value of goods and services produced in a country during one year. It includes consumption, government purchases, investments, and exports minus imports.

gross income All income of a taxpayer, from whatever source derived.

gross proceeds The total of the initial invested capital in a direct participation program contributed by all of the original and additional limited partners.

gross revenue pledge The flow of funds arrangement in a municipal revenue bond issue indicating that debt service is the first payment to be made from revenues received. The pledge is contained in the trust indenture. *Related item(s):* net revenue pledge.

gross revenues All money received by a business from its operations. The term typically does not include interest income or income from the sale, refinancing or other disposition of properties.

group net order In a municipal bond underwriting, an order received by a syndicate member that is credited to the entire syndicate. Takedowns on these orders are paid to members according to their participation in the syndicate. *Related item(s):* designated order; member-at-the-takedown order; presale order.

growth fund A diversified common stock fund that has capital appreciation as its primary goal. It invests in companies that reinvest most of their earnings for expansion, research or development. *Related item(s):* diversified common stock fund; mutual fund.

growth industry An industry that is growing faster than the economy as a whole as a result of technological changes, new products or changing consumer tastes.

growth stock A relatively speculative issue that is believed to offer significant potential for capital gains. It often pays low dividends and sells at a high price/earnings ratio.

GTC *See* good till canceled order.

guaranteed bond A debt obligation issued with a promise from a corporation other than the issuing corporation to maintain payments of principal and interest.

guaranteed dollar annuity *See* fixed annuity.

guaranteed stock An equity security, generally a preferred stock, issued with a promise from a corporation other than the issuing corporation to maintain dividend payments. The stock still represents ownership in the issuing corporation, but it is considered a dual security.

guardian A fiduciary who manages the assets of a minor or an incompetent for that person's benefit. *Related item(s):* fiduciary.

H

HALT A message on the Consolidated Tape indicating that trading in a particular security has been stopped. *Related item(s):* trading halt.

head and shoulders On a technical analyst's trading chart, a pattern that has three peaks resembling a head and two shoulders. The stock price moves up to its first peak (the left shoulder), drops back, then moves to a higher peak (the top of the head), drops again but recovers to another, lower peak (the right shoulder). A head and shoulders top typically forms after a substantial rise and indicates a market reversal. A head and shoulders bottom (an inverted head and shoulders) indicates a market advance.

hedge An investment made in order to reduce the risk of adverse price movements in a security. Normally, a hedge consists of a protecting position in a related security. *Related item(s):* long hedge.

HH savings bond *See* Series HH bond.

high The highest price a security reaches during a specified period of time. *Related item(s):* low.

holder The owner of a security. *Related item(s):* long.

holding company A company organized to invest in and manage other corporations.

holding period A time period signifying how long the owner possesses a security. It starts the day after a purchase and ends on the day of the sale.

hold in street name A securities transaction settlement and delivery procedure whereby a customer's securities are transferred into the broker/dealer's name and held by the broker/dealer. Although the broker/dealer is the nominal owner, the customer is the beneficial owner. *Related item(s):* transfer and hold in safekeeping; transfer and ship.

horizontal spread The purchase and sale of two options on the same underlying security and with the same exercise price but different expiration dates. *Syn.* calendar spread; time spread. *Related item(s):* spread.

hot issue A new issue that sells or is anticipated to sell at a premium over the public offering price. *Related item(s):* free-riding and withholding.

house maintenance call *See* margin maintenance call.

house maintenance requirement *See* margin maintenance requirement.

Housing Authority bond *See* New Housing Authority bond.

HR-10 plan *See* Keogh plan.

hypothecation Pledging to a broker/dealer securities bought on margin as collateral for the margin loan. *Related item(s):* rehypothecation.

I

IDB *See* industrial development bond.

IDC *See* intangible drilling cost.

IDR *See* industrial development bond.

identified security The particular security designated for sale by an investor holding identical securities with different acquisition dates and cost bases. This allows the investor to control the amount of capital gain or loss incurred through the sale.

immediate annuity An insurance contract purchased for a single premium that starts to pay the annuitant immediately following its purchase. *Related item(s):* annuity.

immediate family A parent, mother-in-law or father-in-law, husband or wife, child, or sibling or another relative supported financially by a person associated with the securities industry.

immediate or cancel order (IOC) An order that instructs the floor broker to execute it immediately, in full or in part. Any portion of the order that remains unexecuted is canceled.

income bond A debt obligation that promises to repay principal in full at maturity. Interest is paid only if the corporation's earnings are sufficient to meet the interest payment and if the board of directors declares the interest payment. Income bonds are usually traded flat. *Syn.* adjustment bond. *Related item(s):* flat.

income fund A mutual fund that seeks to provide stable current income by investing in securities that pay interest or dividends. *Related item(s):* mutual fund.

income program A limited partnership that buys and markets proven reserves of oil and gas: it buys the value of the oil in the ground. *Related item(s):* developmental drilling program; exploratory drilling program.

income statement The summary of a corporation's revenues and expenses for a specific fiscal period.

index A comparison of current prices to some baseline, such as prices on a particular date. Indexes are frequently used in technical analysis. *Related item(s):* average.

index option A security representing the right to receive, in cash, the difference between the underlying value of a market index and the strike price of the option. The investor speculates on the direction, degree and timing of the change in the numerical value of the index. *Related item(s):* capped index option.

indication of interest (IOI) An investor's expression of conditional interest in buying an upcoming securities issue after the investor has reviewed a preliminary prospectus. An indication of interest is not a commitment to buy.

individual retirement account (IRA) A retirement investing tool for employed individuals that allows an annual contribution of 100 percent of earned income up to a maximum of $2,000. Some or all of the contribution may be deductible from current taxes, depending on the individual's adjusted gross income and coverage by employer-sponsored qualified retirement plans. *Related item(s):* Keogh plan; nonqualified retirement plan; qualified retirement plan; simplified employee pension plan.

industrial development bond (IDB) A debt security issued by a municipal authority, which uses the proceeds to finance the construction or purchase of facilities to be leased or purchased by a private company. The bonds are backed by the credit of the private company, which is ultimately responsible for principal and interest payments. *Syn.* industrial revenue bond.

industrial revenue bond (IDR) *See* industrial development bond.

industry fund *See* sector fund.

inflation A persistent and measurable rise in the general level of prices. *Related item(s):* deflation.

inflation risk *See* purchasing power risk.

initial margin requirement The amount of equity a customer must deposit when making a new purchase in a margin account. The SEC's Regulation T requirement for equity securities is currently 50 percent of the purchase price. The NYSE and NASD's initial minimum requirement is a deposit of $2,000 but not more than 100 percent of the purchase price. *Related item(s):* margin; margin call.

initial public offering (IPO) A corporation's first sale of common stock to the public. *Related item(s):* new issue market; public offering.

in-part call The redemption of a certain portion of a bond issue at the request of the issuer. *Related item(s):* in-whole call.

inside information Material information that has not been disseminated to, or is not readily available to, the general public.

inside market The best (highest) bid price at which an OTC stock can be sold, and the best (lowest) ask price at which the same stock can be bought in the interdealer market. *Related item(s):* affiliate; control person.

insider Any person who possesses or has access to material nonpublic information about a corporation. Insiders include directors, officers and stockholders who own more than 10 percent of any class of equity security of a corporation.

Insider Trading Act *See* Insider Trading and Securities Fraud Enforcement Act of 1988.

Insider Trading and Securities Fraud Enforcement Act of 1988 Legislation that defines what constitutes the illicit use of nonpublic information in making securities trades and the liabilities and penalties that apply. *Syn.* Insider Trading Act. *Related item(s):* Chinese wall; insider.

institutional account An account held for the benefit of others. Examples of institutional accounts include banks, trusts, pension and profit-sharing plans, mutual funds and insurance companies.

institutional investor A person or an organization that trades securities in large enough share quantities or dollar amounts that it qualifies for preferential treatment and lower commissions. An institutional order can be of any size. Institutional investors are covered by fewer protective regulations because it is assumed that they are more knowledgeable and better able to protect themselves.

insurance covenant A provision of a municipal revenue bond's trust indenture that helps ensure the safety of the issue by promising to insure the facilities built. *Related item(s):* maintenance covenant; rate covenant.

intangible asset A property owned that is not physical, such as a formula, a copyright or goodwill. *Related item(s):* goodwill.

intangible drilling cost (IDC) In an oil and gas limited partnership, a tax-deductible cost; usually this is for a non-physical asset, such as labor or fuel, which does not depreciate. The cost may be expensed in the year incurred, or deductions may be amortized over the life of the well. *Syn.* intangible drilling development expense.

intangible drilling development expense *See* intangible drilling cost.

interbank market An unregulated, decentralized international market in which the various major currencies of the world are traded.

interest The charge for the privilege of borrowing money, usually expressed as an annual percentage rate.

interest coverage ratio *See* bond interest coverage ratio.

interest rate option A security representing the right to buy or sell government debt securities. The federal deficit has created a large market in securities that are sensitive to changes in interest rates; the investor can profit from fluctuations in interest rates and can hedge the risks created by the fluctuations.

interest rate risk The risk associated with investments relating to the sensitivity of price or value to fluctuation in the current level of interest rates; also, the risk that involves the competitive cost of money. This term is generally associated with bond prices, but it applies to all investments. In bonds, prices carry interest risk because if bond prices rise, outstanding bonds will not remain competitive unless their yields and prices adjust to reflect the current market.

Internal Revenue Code (IRC) The legislation that defines tax liabilities and deductions for US taxpayers.

Internal Revenue Service (IRS) The US government agency responsible for collecting most federal taxes and for administering tax rules and regulations.

interstate offering An issue of securities registered with the SEC sold to residents of states other than the state in which the issuer does business.

in-the-money The term used to describe an option that has intrinsic value, such as a call option when the stock is selling above the exercise price or a put option when the stock is selling below the exercise price. *Related item(s):* at-the-money; intrinsic value; out-of-the-money.

intrastate offering An issue of securities exempt from SEC registration, available to companies that do business in one state and sell their securities only to residents of that same state. *Related item(s):* Rule 147.

intrinsic value The potential profit to be made from exercising an option. A call option is said to have intrinsic value when the underlying stock is trading above the exercise price. *Related item(s):* time value.

inverted yield curve A chart showing long-term debt instruments having lower yields than short-term debt instruments. *Syn.* negative yield curve. *Related item(s):* flat yield curve; normal yield curve.

invested capital *See* capitalization.

investment adviser (1) Any person who makes investment recommendations in return for a flat fee or a percentage of assets managed. (2) For an investment company, the individual who bears the day-to-day responsibility of investing the cash and securities held in the fund's portfolio in accordance with objectives stated in the fund's prospectus.

Investment Advisers Act of 1940 Legislation governing who must register with the SEC as an investment adviser. *Related item(s):* investment adviser.

investment banker An institution in the business of raising capital for corporations and municipalities. An investment banker may not accept deposits or make commercial loans. *Syn.* investment bank.

investment banking business A broker, dealer or municipal or government securities dealer that underwrites or distributes new issues of securities as a dealer or that buys and sells securities for the accounts of others as a broker. *Syn.* investment securities business.

investment company A company engaged in the business of pooling investors' money and trading in securities for them. Examples include face-amount certificate companies, unit investment trusts and management companies.

Investment Company Act Amendments of 1970 Amendments to the Investment Company Act of 1940 requiring a registered investment company that issues contractual plans to offer all purchasers withdrawal rights and purchasers of front-end load plans surrender rights. *Related item(s):* Investment Company Act of 1940.

Investment Company Act Amendments of 1975 Amendments to the Investment Company Act of 1940 requiring, in particular, that sales charges relate to the services a fund provides its shareholders. *Related item(s):* Investment Company Act of 1940.

Investment Company Act of 1940 Congressional legislation regulating companies that invest and reinvest in securities. The act requires an investment company engaged in interstate commerce to register with the SEC.

investment grade security A security to which the rating services (Standard & Poor's, Moody's, etc.) have assigned a rating of BBB/Baa or above.

investment objective Any goal a client hopes to achieve through investing. Examples include current income, capital growth and preservation of capital.

investment pyramid A portfolio strategy that allocates investable assets according to an investment's relative safety. The pyramid base is composed of low-risk investments, the mid portion is composed of growth investments and the pyramid top is composed of speculative investments.

investment value The market price at which a convertible security (usually a debenture) would sell if it were not converted into common stock. *Related item(s):* conversion value; convertible bond; debenture.

investor The purchaser of an asset or security with the intent of profiting from the transaction.

invitation for bids A notice to securities underwriters soliciting bids for the issuing of a bond issue. These notices are published in *The Bond Buyer, Munifacts,* newspapers and journals.

in-whole call The redemption of a bond issue in its entirety at the option of the issuer, as opposed to its redemption based on a lottery held by an independent trustee. *Related item(s):* in-part call.

IOC *See* immediate or cancel order.

IOI *See* indication of interest.

IPO *See* initial public offering.

IRA *See* individual retirement account.

IRA rollover The reinvestment of assets that an individual receives as a distribution from a qualified tax-deferred retirement plan into an individual retirement account within 60 days of receiving the distribution. The individual may reinvest either the entire sum or a portion of the sum, although any portion not reinvested is taxed as ordinary income. *Related item(s):* individual retirement account; IRA transfer.

IRA transfer The direct reinvestment of retirement assets from one qualified tax-deferred retirement plan to an individual retirement account. The account owner never takes possession of the assets, but directs that they be transferred directly from the existing plan custodian to the new plan custodian. *Related item(s):* individual retirement account; IRA rollover.

IRC *See* Internal Revenue Code.

irrevocable stock power *See* stock power.

issued stock Equity securities authorized by the issuer's registration statement and distributed to the public. *Related item(s):* outstanding stock; treasury stock.

issuer The entity, such as a corporation or municipality, that offers or proposes to offer its securities for sale.

J

joint account An account in which two or more individuals possess some form of control over the account and may transact business in the account. The account must be designated as either tenants in common or joint tenants with right of survivorship. *Related item(s):* tenants in common; joint tenants with right of survivorship.

joint life with last survivor An annuity payout option that covers two or more people, with annuity payments continuing as long as one of the annuitants remains alive.

joint tenants with right of survivorship (JTWROS) A form of joint ownership of an account whereby a deceased tenant's fractional interest in the account passes to the surviving tenant(s). It is used almost exclusively by husbands and wives. *Related item(s):* tenants in common.

joint venture The cooperation of two or more individuals or enterprises in a specific business enterprise, rather than in a continuing relationship—as in a partnership.

JTWROS *See* joint tenants with right of survivorship.

junior lien debt A bond backed by the same collateral backing a previous issue and having a subordinate claim to the collateral in the event of default. *Related item(s):* closed-end covenant; open-end covenant.

K

Keogh plan A qualified tax-deferred retirement plan for persons who are self-employed and unincorporated or who earn extra income through personal services aside from their regular employment. *Syn.* HR-10 plan. *Related item(s):* individual retirement account; nonqualified retirement plan; qualified retirement plan.

Keynesian economics The theory that active government intervention in the marketplace is the best method of ensuring economic growth and stability.

know your customer rule *See* Rule 405.

L

lagging indicator A measurable economic factor that changes after the economy has started to follow a particular pattern or trend. Lagging indicators are believed to confirm long-term trends. Examples include average duration of unemployment, corporate profits and labor cost per unit of output. *Related item(s):* coincident indicator; leading indicator.

last in, first out (LIFO) An accounting method used to assess a corporation's inventory in which it is assumed that the last goods acquired are the first to be sold. The method is used to determine cost basis for tax purposes; the IRS designates last in, first out as the order in which sales or withdrawals from an investment are made. *Related item(s):* average basis; first in, first out; share identification.

leading indicator A measurable economic factor that changes before the economy starts to follow a particular pattern or trend. Leading indicators are believed to predict changes in the economy. Examples include new orders for durable goods, slowdowns in deliveries by vendors and numbers of building permits issued. *Related item(s):* coincident indicator; lagging indicator.

LEAPS® *See* long-term equity option.

lease rental bond A debt security issued by a municipal authority to raise funds for new construction with the understanding that the finished structure will be rented to the authority and that the rental payments will finance the bond payments.

legal list The selection of securities a state agency (usually a state banking or insurance commission) determines to be appropriate investments for fiduciary accounts such as mutual savings banks, pension funds and insurance companies.

legal opinion of counsel The statement of a bond attorney affirming that an issue is a municipal issue and that interest is exempt from federal taxation. Each municipal bond certificate must be accompanied by a legal opinion of counsel. *Related item(s):* ex-legal; qualified legal opinion; unqualified legal opinion.

legislative risk The potential for an investor to be adversely affected by changes in investment or tax laws.

letter of intent (LOI) A signed agreement allowing an investor to buy mutual fund shares at a lower overall sales charge, based on the total dollar amount of the intended investment. A letter of intent is valid only if the investor completes the terms of the agreement within 13 months of signing the agreement. A letter of intent may be backdated 90 days. *Syn.* statement of intention.

level debt service A schedule for debt repayment whereby principal and interest payments remain essentially constant from year to year over the life of the issue. *Related item(s):* decreasing debt service.

level load A mutual fund sales fee charged annually based on the net asset value of a share. A 12b-1 asset-based fee is an example of a level load. *Related item(s):* back-end load; Class C share; Class D share; front-end load.

Level One The basic level of Nasdaq service; through a desktop quotation machine, it provides registered representatives with up-to-the-minute inside bid and ask quotations on hundreds of over-the-counter stocks. *Related item(s):* National Association of Securities Dealers Automated Quotation System.

Level Two The second level of Nasdaq service; through a desktop quotation machine, it provides up-to-the-minute inside bid and ask quotations and the bids and askeds of each market maker for a security. *Related item(s):* National Association of Securities Dealers Automated Quotation System.

Level Three The highest level of Nasdaq service; through a desktop quotation machine, it provides up-to-the-minute inside bid and ask quotations, supplies the bids and askeds of each market maker for a security and allows each market maker to enter changes in those quotations. *Related item(s):* National Association of Securities Dealers Automated Quotation System.

leverage Using borrowed capital to increase investment return. *Syn.* trading on the equity.

liability A legal obligation to pay a debt owed. Current liabilities are debts payable within 12 months. Long-term liabilities are debts payable over a period of more than 12 months.

LIBOR *See* London Interbank Offered Rate.

life annuity/straight life An annuity payout option that pays a monthly check over the annuitant's lifetime.

life annuity with period certain An annuity payout option that guarantees the annuitant a monthly check for a certain time period and thereafter until the annuitant's death. If the annuitant dies before the time period expires, the payments go to the annuitant's named beneficiary.

life contingency An annuity payout option that provides a death benefit during the accumulation stage. If the annuitant dies during this period, a full contribution is made to the account, which is paid to the annuitant's named beneficiary.

LIFO *See* last in, first out.

limited liability An investor's right to limit potential losses to no more than the amount invested. Equity shareholders, such as corporate stockholders and limited partners, have limited liability.

limited partner (LP) An investor in a direct participation program who does not participate in the management or control of the program and whose liability for partnership debts is limited to the amount invested in the program. *Related item(s):* general partner; participant; passive investor.

limited partnership (LP) An association of two or more partners formed to conduct a business jointly and in which one or more of the partners is liable only to the extent of the amount of money they have invested. Limited partners do not receive dividends but enjoy direct flow-through of income and expenses. *Related item(s):* flow-through; general partnership.

limited partnership agreement The contract between a partnership's limited and general partners that provides the guidelines for partnership operation and states the rights and responsibilities of each partner.

limited power of attorney A written authorization for someone other than an account's beneficial owner to make certain investment decisions regarding transactions in the account. *Related item(s):* discretion; full power of attorney.

limited tax bond A general obligation municipal debt security issued by a municipality whose taxing power is limited to a specified maximum rate.

limited trading authorization An authorization, usually provided by a limited power of attorney, for someone other than the customer to have trading privileges in an account. These privileges are limited to purchases and sales; withdrawal of assets is not authorized. *Related item(s):* full trading authorization.

limit order An order that instructs the floor broker to buy a specified security below a certain price or to sell a specified security above a certain price. *Syn.* or better order. *Related item(s):* stop limit order; stop order.

limit order book *See* specialist's book.

liquidation priority In the case of a corporation's liquidation, the order that is strictly followed for paying off creditors and stockholders:
1. unpaid wages
2. taxes
3. secured claims (mortgages)
4. secured liabilities (bonds)
5. unsecured liabilities (debentures) and general reditors
6. subordinated debt
7. preferred stockholders
8. common stockholders

liquidity The ease with which an asset can be converted to cash in the marketplace. A large number of buyers and sellers and a high volume of trading activity provide high liquidity.

liquidity ratio A measure of a corporation's ability to meet its current obligations. The ratio compares current assets to current liabilities. *Related item(s):* acid-test ratio; current ratio.

liquidity risk The potential that an investor might not be able to sell an investment as and when desired. *Syn.* marketability risk.

listed option An option contract that can be bought and sold on a national securities exchange in a continuous secondary market. Listed options carry standardized strike prices and expiration dates. *Syn.* standardized option. *Related item(s):* OTC option.

listed security A stock, a bond or another security that satisfies certain minimum requirements and is traded on a regional or national securities exchange such as the New York Stock Exchange.

LMV *See* current market value.

loan consent agreement An optional contract between a brokerage firm and a margin customer that permits the firm to lend the margined securities to other brokers; the contract is part of the margin agreement. *Syn.* consent to lend agreement.

locked market The situation created when there is no spread between the bid and the ask on the same security; that is, one market maker bids for a stock at the same price that another market maker quotes its ask price. This violates the NASD Conduct Rules. *Related item(s):* crossed market.

LOI *See* letter of intent.

London Interbank Offered Rate (LIBOR) The average of the interbank-offered interest rates for dollar deposits in the London market, based on the quotations at five major banks.

long The term used to describe the owning of a security, contract or commodity. For example, a common stock owner is said to have a long position in the stock. *Related item(s):* short.

long hedge Buying puts as protection against a decline in the value of a long securities or actuals position. *Related item(s):* hedge.

long market value (LMV) *See* current market value.

long straddle An option investor's position that results from buying a call and a put on the same stock with the same exercise price and expiration month. *Related item(s):* short straddle; spread; straddle.

long-term equity option An option contract that has a longer expiration than traditional equity option contracts. The most common long-term equity option is the CBOE's Long-term Equity AnticiPation Security (LEAPS®).

long-term gain The profit earned on the sale of a capital asset that has been owned for more than 12 months. *Related item(s):* capital gain; capital loss; long-term loss.

long-term loss The loss realized on the sale of a capital asset that has been owned for more than 12 months. *Related item(s):* capital gain; capital loss; long-term gain.

loss carryover A capital loss incurred in one tax year that is carried over to the next year or later years for use as a capital loss deduction. *Related item(s):* capital loss.

low The lowest price a security or commodity reaches during a specified time period. *Related item(s):* high.

LP *See* limited partner; limited partnership.

M

M1 A category of the money supply that includes all coins, currency and demand deposits—that is, checking accounts and NOW accounts. *Related item(s):* M2; M3; money supply.

M2 A category of the money supply that includes M1 in addition to all time deposits, savings deposits and noninstitutional money-market funds. *Related item(s):* M1; M3; money supply.

M3 A category of the money supply that includes M2 in addition to all large time deposits, institutional money-market funds, short-term repurchase agreements and certain other large liquid assets. *Related item(s):* M1; M2; money supply.

maintenance call *See* margin maintenance call.

maintenance covenant A provision of a municipal revenue bond's trust indenture that helps ensure the safety of the issue by promising to keep the facility and equipment in good working order. *Related item(s):* insurance covenant; rate covenant.

maintenance requirement *See* margin maintenance requirement.

Major Market Index (MMI) A market indicator designed to track the Dow Jones industrials. It is composed of 15 of the 30 Dow Jones industrials and five other large NYSE-listed stocks. *Related item(s):* index.

make a market To stand ready to buy or sell a particular security as a dealer for its own account. A market maker accepts the risk of holding the position in the security. *Related item(s):* market maker.

managed underwriting An arrangement between the issuer of a security and an investment banker in which the banker agrees to form an underwriting syndicate to bring the security to the public. The syndicate manager then directs the entire underwriting process.

management company An investment company that trades various types of securities in a portfolio in accordance with specific objectives stated in the prospectus. *Related item(s):* closed-end management company; diversified management company; mutual fund; nondiversified management company.

management fee The payment to the sponsor of a direct participation program for managing and administering the program. The fee is capped at about 5 percent of the program's gross revenues.

manager of the syndicate *See* underwriting manager.

managing partner The general partner of a direct participation program that selects the investments and operates the partnership.

managing underwriter *See* underwriting manager.

mandatory call The redemption of a bond by an issuer authorized in the trust indenture and based on a predetermined schedule or event. *Related item(s):* catastrophe call; partial call.

margin The amount of equity contributed by a customer as a percentage of the current market value of the securities held in a margin account. *Related item(s):* equity; initial margin requirement; margin call; Regulation T.

margin account A customer account in which a brokerage firm lends the customer part of the purchase price of securities. *Related item(s):* cash account; Regulation T.

margin call The Federal Reserve Board's demand that a customer deposit a specified amount of money or securities when a purchase is made in a margin account; the amount is expressed as a percentage of the market value of the securities at the time of purchase. The deposit must be made within one payment period. *Syn.* Fed call; federal call; federal margin; Reg T call; T call. *Related item(s):* initial margin requirement; margin.

margin deficiency *See* margin maintenance requirement.

margin department The department within a brokerage firm that computes the amount of money clients must deposit in margin and cash accounts. *Syn.* credit department.

margin excess *See* excess equity.

margin maintenance call A demand that a margin customer deposit money or securities when the customer's equity falls below the margin maintenance requirement set by the broker/dealer or by the NASD or NYSE. *Syn.* house maintenance call; maintenance call; NASD/NYSE maintenance call.

margin maintenance requirement The minimum equity that must be held in a margin account, determined by the broker/dealer and by the NASD or NYSE. The amount of equity required varies with the type of security bought on margin, and the broker/dealer's house requirement is usually higher than that set by the NASD or NYSE. *Syn.* house maintenance requirement; maintenance requirement; NASD/NYSE maintenance requirement.

margin risk The potential that a margin customer will be required to deposit additional cash if his security positions are subject to adverse price movements.

margin security A security that is eligible for purchase on margin, including any registered security, OTC margin stock or bond or Nasdaq National Market security. A firm is permitted to lend money to help customers purchase these securities, and may accept these securities as collateral for margin purchases. *Syn.* eligible security. *Related item(s):* nonmargin security; OTC margin security.

markdown The difference between the highest current bid price among dealers and the lower price that a dealer pays to a customer.

marketability The ease with which a security can be bought or sold; having a readily available market for trading.

market letter A publication that comments on securities, investing, the economy or other related topics and is distributed to an organization's clients or to the public. *Related item(s):* sales literature.

market maker A dealer willing to accept the risk of holding a particular security in its own account to facilitate trading in that security. *Related item(s):* make a market.

market NH *See* not held order.

market not held order *See* not held order.

market-on-close order An order that specifies it is to be executed at the close. The order will be executed at the closing price. *Syn.* at-the-close order. *Related item(s):* at-the-opening order.

market order An order to be executed immediately at the best available price. A market order is the only order that guarantees execution. *Syn.* unrestricted order.

market-out clause The standard provision of a firm commitment underwriting agreement that relieves the underwriter of its obligation to underwrite the issue under circumstances that impair the investment quality of the securities.

market risk The potential for an investor to experience losses owing to day-to-day fluctuations in the prices at which securities can be bought or sold. *Related item(s):* systemic risk.

market value The price at which investors buy or sell a share of common stock or a bond at a given time. Market value is determined by buyers' and sellers' interaction. *Related item(s):* current market value.

mark to the market To adjust the value of the securities in an account to the current market value of those securities; used to calculate the market value and equity in a margin account.

markup The difference between the lowest current offering price among dealers and the higher price a dealer charges a customer.

markup policy *See* NASD 5 percent markup policy.

married put The simultaneous purchase of a stock and a put on that stock specifically identified as a hedge.

material information Any fact that could affect an investor's decision to trade a security.

maturity date The date on which a bond's principal is repaid to the investor and interest payments cease. *Related item(s):* par; principal.

maximum loan value The percentage of market value a broker/dealer is permitted to lend a margin customer for the purchase of securities. Loan value is equal to the complement of the Regulation T requirement: if Reg T were 65 percent, the maximum loan value would be 35 percent. *Syn.* loan value.

maximum market value The market value to which a short sale position may advance before a margin maintenance call is issued. Maximum market value is set by the NASD/NYSE, and currently equals the credit balance divided by 130 percent. *Syn.* maximum short market value.

MBIA *See* Municipal Bond Investors Assurance Corp.

member-at-the-takedown order In a municipal bond underwriting, a customer order submitted by one syndicate member, who will receive the entire takedown. Member-at-the-takedown orders receive the lowest priority when the securities of the issue are allocated. *Syn.* member order. *Related item(s):* designated order; group net order; presale order.

member firm A broker/dealer in which at least one of the principal officers is a member of the New York Stock Exchange, another exchange, a self-regulatory organization or a clearing corporation.

member order *See* member-at-the takedown order.

mini-max underwriting A form of best efforts underwriting in which the issuer sets a floor and a ceiling on the amount of securities to be sold. *Related item(s):* underwriting.

minimum margin requirement *See* margin maintenance requirement.

minus tick A security transaction's execution price that is below the previous execution price, by a minimum amount. A short sale may not be executed on a minus tick. *Syn.* down tick. *Related item(s):* plus tick; plus tick rule; short sale; tick; zero-minus tick.

modern portfolio theory (MPT) A method of choosing investments that focuses on the importance of the relationships among all of the investments in a portfolio rather than the individual merits of each investment. The method allows investors to quantify and control the amount of risk they accept and return they achieve.

monetarist theory An economic theory holding that the money supply is the major determinant of price levels and that therefore a well-controlled money supply will have the most beneficial impact on the economy.

monetary policy The Federal Reserve Board's actions that determine the size and rate of the money supply's growth, which in turn affect interest rates. *Related item(s):* fiscal policy.

money market The securities market that deals in short-term debt. Money-market instruments are very liquid forms of debt that mature in less than one year. Treasury bills make up the bulk of money-market instruments.

money-market fund A mutual fund that invests in short-term debt instruments. The fund's objective is to earn interest while maintaining a stable net asset value of $1 per share. Generally sold with no load, the fund may also offer draft-writing privileges and low opening investments. *Related item(s):* mutual fund.

money supply The total stock of bills, coins, loans, credit and other liquid instruments in the economy. It is divided into four categories—L, M1, M2 and M3—according to the type of account in which the instrument is kept. *Related item(s):* M1; M2; M3.

Moody's Investors Service One of the best known investment rating agencies in the United States. A subsidiary of Dun & Bradstreet, Moody's rates bonds, commercial paper, preferred and common stocks, and municipal short-term issues. *Related item(s):* bond rating; Standard & Poor's Corporation.

moral obligation bond A municipal revenue bond for which a state legislature has the authority, but no legal obligation, to appropriate money in the event the issuer defaults.

mortgage bond A debt obligation secured by a property pledge. It represents a lien or mortgage against the issuing corporation's properties and real estate assets.

moving average chart A tool used by technical analysts to track the price movements of a commodity. It plots average daily settlement prices over a defined period of time (for example, over three days for a three-day moving average). *Related item(s):* bar chart; point-and-figure chart.

MSRB *See* Municipal Securities Rulemaking Board.

multiplier effect The expansion of the money supply that results from a Federal Reserve System member bank's being able to lend more money than it takes in. A small increase in bank deposits generates a far larger increase in available credit.

municipal bond A debt security issued by a state, a municipality or another subdivision (such as a school, a park, a sanitation or another local taxing district) to finance its capital expenditures. Such expenditures might include the construction of highways, public works or school buildings. *Syn.* municipal security.

municipal bond fund A mutual fund that invests in municipal bonds and operates either as a unit investment trust or as an open-end fund. The fund's objective is to maximize federally tax-exempt income. *Related item(s):* mutual fund; unit investment trust.

Municipal Bond Investors Assurance Corp. (MBIA) A public corporation offering insurance as to the timely payment of principal and interest on qualified municipal issues. Issues with MBIA insurance are generally rated AAA by Standard & Poor's.

municipal note A short-term municipal security issued in anticipation of funds from another source. *Related item(s):* municipal security.

Municipal Securities Rulemaking Board (MSRB) A self-regulatory organization that regulates the issuance and trading of municipal securities. The Board functions under the Securities and Exchange Commission's supervision; it has no enforcement powers. *Related item(s):* Securities Acts Amendments of 1975.

municipal security *See* municipal bond.

Munifacts A news wire service for the municipal bond industry; a product of *The Bond Buyer*.

mutual fund An investment company that continuously offers new equity shares in an actively managed portfolio of securities. All shareholders participate in the fund's gains or losses. The shares are redeemable on any business day at the net asset value. Each mutual fund's portfolio is invested to match the objective stated in the prospectus. *Syn.* open-end investment company; open-end management company. *Related item(s):* asset allocation fund; balanced fund; contractual plan; net asset value.

mutual fund custodian A national bank, a stock exchange member firm, a trust company or another qualified institution that physically safeguards the securities a mutual fund holds. It does not manage the fund's investments; its function is solely clerical.

N

naked The position of an option investor who writes a call or a put on a security he does not own. *Syn.* uncovered.

naked call writer An investor who writes a call option without owning the underlying stock or other related assets that would enable the investor to deliver the stock should the option be exercised. *Syn.* uncovered call writer. *Related item(s):* naked put writer.

naked put writer An investor who writes a put option without owning the underlying stock or other related assets that would enable the investor to purchase the stock should the option be exercised. *Syn.* uncovered put writer. *Related item(s):* naked call writer.

narrow-based index An index that is designed to reflect the movement of a market segment, such as a group of stocks in one industry or a specific type of investment. Examples include the Technology Index and the Gold/Silver Index. *Related item(s):* broad-based index; index.

Nasdaq *See* National Association of Securities Dealers Automated Quotation System.

Nasdaq National Market (NNM) The most actively traded over-the-counter stocks quoted on Nasdaq. Trades in these stocks are reported as they occur.

Nasdaq 100 An index of the largest 100 nonfinancial stocks on Nasdaq, weighted according to capitalization.

NASD 5 percent markup policy A guideline for reasonable markups, markdowns and commissions for secondary over-the-counter transactions. According to the policy, all commissions on broker transactions and all markups or markdowns on principal transactions should equal 5 percent or should be fair and reasonable for a particular transaction. *Syn.* markup policy.

NASD Regulation, Inc. Branch of the NASD organized in 1996 to supervise member broker/dealers, enforce laws and ethical standards and mete out disciplinary action.

National Association of Securities Dealers Automated Quotation System (Nasdaq) The nationwide electronic quotation system for up-to-the-minute bid and asked quotations on approximately 5,500 over-the-counter stocks.

National Quotation Bureau The publisher of compiled quotes from market makers in over-the-counter stocks and bonds. The daily *Pink Sheets* report stock quotes and the daily *Yellow Sheets* report corporate bond quotes. *Related item(s): Pink Sheets; Yellow Sheets.*

National Securities Clearing Corporation (NSCC) An organization that acts as a medium through which member brokerage firms and exchanges reconcile accounts with each other.

NAV *See* net asset value.

NAV of fund The net total of a mutual fund's assets and liabilities; used to calculate the price of new fund shares.

NAV per share The value of a mutual fund share, calculated by dividing the fund's total net asset value by the number of shares outstanding.

negotiability A characteristic of a security that permits the owner to assign, give, transfer or sell it to another person without a third party's permission.

negotiable certificate of deposit (CD) An unsecured promissory note issued with a minimum face value of $100,000. It evidences a time deposit of funds with the issuing bank and is guaranteed by the bank.

negotiated underwriting A form of underwriting agreement in which a brokerage firm consults with the issuer to determine the most suitable price and timing of a forthcoming securities offering. *Related item(s):* competitive bid underwriting.

net asset value (NAV) A mutual fund share's value, calculated once a day, based on the closing market price for each security in the fund's portfolio. It is computed by deducting the fund's liabilities from the portfolio's total assets and dividing this amount by the number of shares outstanding. *Related item(s):* mutual fund.

net change The difference between a security's closing price on the trading day reported and the previous day's closing price. In over-the-counter transactions, the term refers to the difference between the closing bids.

net current asset value per share The calculation of book value per share that excludes all fixed assets. *Related item(s):* book value per share.

net debt per capita A measure of the ability of a municipality to meet its debt obligations; it compares the debt issued by the municipality to its property values.

net debt to assessed valuation A measure of the financial condition of a municipality; it compares the municipality's debt obligations to the assessed value of its property. *Related item(s):* net debt to estimated valuation.

net debt to estimated valuation A measure of the financial condition of a municipality; it compares the municipality's debt obligations to the estimated value of its property. *Related item(s):* net debt to assessed valuation.

net direct debt The amount of debt obligations of a municipality, including general obligation bonds and notes and short-term notes. Self-supported debt from revenue bond issues is not included in the calculation.

net domestic product A measure of the annual economic output of a nation adjusted to account for depreciation. It is calculated by subtracting the amount of depreciation from the gross domestic product. *Related item(s):* gross domestic product.

net fixed assets per bond A measure of a bond's safety; it is a conservative measure because it excludes intangible assets, working capital and accumulated depreciation.

net income to net sales *See* net profit ratio.

net interest cost (NIC) A means of evaluating the competitive bids of prospective bond underwriting syndicates. It calculates the coupon interest to be paid by the issuer over the life of the bond. *Related item(s):* true interest cost.

net investment income The source of an investment company's dividend payments. It is calculated by subtracting the company's operating expenses from the total dividends and interest the company receives from the securities in its portfolio.

net investment return The rate of return from a variable life insurance separate account. The cumulative return for all years is applied to the benefit base when calculating the death benefit.

net operating profits interest A sharing arrangement in an oil and gas direct participation program whereby the general partner bears none of the program's costs but is entitled to a percentage of profits after all royalties and operating expenses have been paid. *Related item(s):* sharing arrangement.

net proceeds The amount of money received from a direct participation program offering less expenses incurred, such as selling commissions, syndicate fees and organizational costs.

net profit margin *See* net profit ratio.

net profit ratio A measure of a corporation's relative profitability. It is calculated by dividing aftertax income by net sales. *Syn.* net income to net sales; net profit margin; net profits to sales; profit after taxes; profit ratio.

net profits to sales *See* net profit ratio.

net revenue pledge The flow of funds arrangement in a municipal revenue bond issue pledging that operating and maintenance expenses will be paid before debt service. The pledge is contained in the trust indenture. *Related item(s):* gross revenue pledge.

net tangible assets per share *See* book value per share.

net total debt The sum of the debt obligations of a municipality, calculated by adding the municipality's net direct debt to its overlapping debt. *Related item(s):* net direct debt; overlapping debt.

Network A A Consolidated Tape reporting system that provides subscribers with information on transactions in NYSE-listed securities. *Related item(s):* Consolidated Tape.

Network B A Consolidated Tape reporting system that provides subscribers with information on transactions in AMEX-listed and certain regional securities. *Related item(s):* Consolidated Tape.

net worth The amount by which assets exceed liabilities. *Syn.* owners' equity; shareholders' equity; stockholders' equity.

new account form The form that must be filled out for each new account opened with a brokerage firm. The form specifies, at a minimum, the account owner, trading authorization, payment method and types of securities appropriate for the customer.

new construction program A real estate direct participation program that aims to provide capital appreciation from building new property.

New Housing Authority bond (NHA) A municipal special revenue bond backed by the US government and issued by a local public housing authority to develop and improve low-income housing. *Syn.* Housing Authority bond; Public Housing Authority bond.

new issue market The securities market for shares in privately owned businesses that are raising capital by selling common stock to the public for the first time. *Syn.* primary market. *Related item(s):* initial public offering; secondary market.

New Issues Act *See* Securities Act of 1933.

New York Stock Exchange (NYSE) The largest stock exchange in the United States.

New York Stock Exchange Composite Index Index of common stocks listed on the NYSE, based on the price of each stock weighted by its total value of shares outstanding. *Syn.* NYSE Index.

NH *See* not held order.

NHA *See* New Housing Authority bond.

NIC *See* net interest cost.

NNM *See* Nasdaq National Market.

no-load fund A mutual fund whose shares are sold without a commission or sales charge. The investment company distributes the shares directly. *Related item(s):* mutual fund; net asset value; sales load.

nominal owner The person in whose name securities are registered if that person is other than the beneficial owner. This is a brokerage firm's role when customer securities are registered in street name.

nominal quote A quotation on an inactively traded security that does not represent an actual offer to buy or sell, but is given for informational purposes only. *Related item(s):* bona fide quote; firm quote.

nominal yield The interest rate stated on the face of a bond that represents the percentage of interest the issuer pays on the bond's face value. *Syn.* coupon rate; stated yield. *Related item(s):* bond yield.

nonaccredited investor An investor not meeting the net worth requirements of Regulation D. Nonaccredited investors are counted for purposes of the 35-investor limitation for Regulation D private placements. *Related item(s):* accredited investor; private placement; Regulation D.

nonaffiliate A buyer of an unregistered public offering security who has no management or major ownership interest in the company being acquired. Nonaffiliates may sell this stock only after a specified holding period.

noncompetitive bid An order placed for Treasury bills in which the investor agrees to pay stop out price and in return is guaranteed that the order will be filled.

noncumulative preferred stock An equity security that does not have to pay any dividends in arrears to the holder. *Related item(s):* convertible preferred stock; cumulative preferred stock; preferred stock.

nondiscrimination In a qualified retirement plan, a formula for calculating contributions and benefits that must be applied uniformly so as to ensure that all employees receive fair and equitable treatment. *Related item(s):* qualified retirement plan.

nondiversified investment company A management company that does not meet the diversification requirements of the Investment Company Act of 1940. These companies are not restricted in the choice of securities or by the concentration of interest they have in those securities. *Related item(s):* diversified investment company; management company; mutual fund.

nonequity option A security representing the right to buy or sell an investment instrument other than a common stock at a specified price within a specified time period. Examples of such investment instruments include foreign currencies, indexes and interest rates. *Related item(s):* equity option; foreign currency option; index option; interest rate option; option.

nonmargin security A security that must be purchased in a cash account, that must be paid for in full, and that may not be used as collateral for a loan. Examples include put and call options, rights, insurance contracts and new issues. *Related item(s):* margin security.

nonqualified retirement plan A corporate retirement plan that does not meet the standards set by the Employee Retirement Income Security Act of 1974. Contributions to a nonqualified plan are not tax deductible. *Related item(s):* qualified retirement plan.

nonrecourse financing Debt incurred for the purchase of an asset which pledges the asset as security for the debt but that does not hold the borrower personally liable. *Related item(s):* recourse financing.

nonsystematic risk Company-specific risk.

normal yield curve A chart showing long-term debt instruments having higher yields than short-term debt instruments. *Syn.* positive yield curve. *Related item(s):* flat yield curve; inverted yield curve; yield curve.

note A short-term debt security, usually maturing in five years or less. *Related item(s):* Treasury note.

not held order (NH) An order that gives the floor broker discretion as to the price and timing of the order's execution. Not held orders are often entered for large amounts of a security. *Syn.* market NH; market not held order.

notification *See* registration by filing.

NSCC *See* National Securities Clearing Corporation.

numbered account An account titled with something other than the customer's name. The title might be a number, symbol or special title. The customer must sign a form designating account ownership.

NYSE *See* New York Stock Exchange.

NYSE Composite Index *See* New York Stock Exchange Composite Index.

NYSE maintenance call *See* margin maintenance call.

NYSE maintenance requirement *See* margin maintenance requirement.

O

OBO *See* order book official.

OCC *See* Options Clearing Corporation.

OCC Disclosure Document *See* options disclosure document.

odd lot An amount of a security that is less than the normal unit of trading for that security. Generally, an odd lot is fewer than 100 shares of stock or five bonds. *Related item(s):* round lot.

odd-lot theory A technical analysis theory based on the assumption that the small investor is always wrong. Therefore, if odd lot sales are up—that is, small investors are selling stock—it is probably a good time to buy.

offer Under the Uniform Securities Act, any attempt to solicit a purchase or sale in a security for value. *Related item(s):* bid; public offering price; quotation, ask.

offering circular An abbreviated prospectus used by corporations issuing less than $5 million of stock. The SEC's Regulation A allows these offerings an exemption from the full registration requirements of the 1933 act. *Related item(s):* Regulation A.

official notice of sale The invitation to bid on a municipal bond issue; the invitation is sent to prospective underwriters and specifies, among other things, the date, time and place of sale, description of the issue, maturities, call provisions and amount of good faith deposit required.

official statement (OS) A document concerning a municipal issue that must be provided to every buyer. The document is prepared by the underwriter from information provided by the issuer; typically included are the offering terms, descriptions of the bonds and the issuer, the underwriting spread, fees received by brokers, initial offering price and tax status.

OID *See* original issue discount bond.

oil and gas direct participation program A direct participation program formed to locate new oil and gas reserves, develop existing reserves or generate income from producing wells. A high return is the primary objective of such a program. *Syn.* oil and gas limited partnership.

oil depletion allowance An accounting procedure that reduces the taxable portion of revenues from the sale of oil to compensate for the decreased supply of oil in the ground. Depletion is the natural resource counterpart of depreciation.

omnibus account An account opened in the name of an investment adviser or a broker/dealer for the benefit of its customers. The firm carrying the account does not receive disclosure of the individual customers' names or holdings and does not maintain records for the individual customers. *Syn.* special omnibus account. *Related item(s):* introduced account.

open-end covenant A provision of a bond's trust indenture allowing the issuer to use the same collateral backing a bond as collateral for future bond issues. As a result, new creditors have the same claim on the collateral as existing creditors. *Related item(s):* closed-end covenant; junior lien debt.

open-end investment company *See* mutual fund.

opening purchase Entering the options market by buying calls or puts. *Related item(s):* closing sale; opening sale.

opening sale Entering the options market by selling calls or puts. *Related item(s):* closing purchase; opening purchase.

open-market operations The buying and selling of securities (primarily government or agency debt) by the Federal Open Market Committee to effect control of the money supply. These transactions increase or decrease the level of bank reserves available for lending.

open order *See* good till canceled order.

operating expenses (1) The day-to-day costs incurred in running a business. (2) In an oil and gas program, any production or leasehold expense incurred in the operation of a producing lease, including district expense, direct out-of-pocket expenses for labor, materials and supplies and those shares of taxes and transportation charges not borne by overriding royalty interests.

operating income The profit realized from one year of operation of a business.

operating ratio The ratio of operating expenses to net sales; the complement to the margin of profit ratio.

operations and maintenance fund The account from which are paid current operating and maintenance expenses on a facility financed by a municipal revenue bond. *Related item(s):* flow of funds.

operator The person who supervises and manages the exploration, drilling, mining, production and leasehold operations of an oil and gas or mining direct participation program.

option A security that represents the right to buy or sell a specified amount of an underlying security—a stock, bond, futures contract, etc.—at a specified price within a specified time. The purchaser acquires a right, and the seller assumes an obligation.

option agreement The document a customer must sign within 15 days of being approved for options trading. In it the customer agrees to abide by the rules of the options exchanges and not to exceed position or exercise limits.

option contract adjustment An adjustment made automatically to the terms of an option on the ex-dividend date when a stock pays a stock dividend or if there is a stock split or a reverse split.

options account A customer account in which the customer has received approval to trade options.

Options Clearing Corporation (OCC) The organization that issues options, standardizes option contracts and guarantees their performance. The OCC made secondary trading possible by creating fungible option contracts.

options disclosure document A publication of the Options Clearing Corporation that outlines the risks and rewards of investing in options. The document must be given to each customer at the time of opening an options account, and must accompany any options sales literature sent to a customer. *Syn.* OCC Disclosure Document.

order book official (OBO) The title given to a specialist or market maker employed on the Pacific, Philadelphia and Chicago Board Options exchanges.

order department The department within a brokerage firm that transmits orders to the proper market for execution and returns confirmations to the appropriate representative. *Syn.* order room; wire room.

order memorandum The form completed by a registered rep that contains customer instructions regarding an order's placement. The memorandum contains such information as the customer's name and account number, a description of the security, the type of transaction (buy, sell, sell short, etc.) and any special instructions (such as time or price limits). *Syn.* order ticket.

order room *See* order department.

order ticket *See* order memorandum.

ordinary income Earnings other than capital gain.

organization and offering expense The cost of preparing a direct participation program for registration and subsequently offering and distributing it to the public; the cost includes sales commissions paid to broker/dealers.

original issue discount bond (OID) A corporate or municipal debt security issued at a discount from face value. The bond may or may not pay interest. The discount on a corporate OID bond is taxed as if accrued annually as ordinary income. The discount on a municipal OID bond is exempt from annual taxation; however, the discount is accrued for the purpose of calculating cost basis. *Related item(s):* zero-coupon bond.

OTC Bulletin Board An electronic quotation system for equity securities that are not listed on a national exchange or included in the Nasdaq system.

OTC margin security A security that is not traded on a national exchange but that has been designated by the Federal Reserve Board as eligible for trading on margin. The Fed publishes a list of such securities. *Related item(s):* margin security.

OTC market The security exchange system in which broker/dealers negotiate directly with one another rather than through an auction on an exchange floor. The trading takes place over computer and telephone networks that link brokers and dealers around the world. Both listed and OTC securities, as well as municipal and US government securities, trade in the OTC market.

OTC option An option contract that is not listed on an exchange. All contract terms are negotiated between buyer and seller. *Syn.* nonstandard option. *Related item(s):* listed option.

out-of-the-money The term used to describe an option that has no intrinsic value, such as a call option when the stock is selling below the exercise price or a put option when the stock is selling above the exercise price. *Related item(s):* at-the-money; in-the-money; intrinsic value.

outstanding stock Equity securities issued by a corporation and in the hands of the public; issued stock that the issuer has not reacquired. *Related item(s):* treasury stock.

overbought A technical analysis term for a market in which more and stronger buying has occurred than the fundamentals justify. *Related item(s):* oversold.

overlapping debt A condition resulting when property in a municipality is subject to multiple taxing authorities or tax districts, each having tax collection powers and recourse to the residents of that municipality. *Related item(s):* coterminous.

overriding royalty interest A sharing arrangement whereby a person with a royalty interest in an oil and gas direct participation program takes no risks but receives a share of the revenues; the share is carved out of the working interest without liability for any costs of extraction. *Related item(s):* sharing arrangement.

oversold A technical analysis term for a market in which more and stronger selling has occurred than the fundamentals justify. *Related item(s):* overbought.

P

paid-in capital *See* capital surplus.

paid-in surplus *See* capital surplus.

par The dollar amount the issuer assigns to a security. For an equity security, par is usually a small dollar amount that bears no relationship to the security's market price. For a debt security, par is the amount repaid to the investor when the bond matures, usually $1,000. *Syn.* face value; principal; stated value. *Related item(s):* capital surplus; maturity date.

parity In an exchange market, a situation in which all brokers bidding have equal standing and the winning bid is awarded by a random drawing. *Related item(s):* precedence; priority.

parity price of common The dollar amount at which a common stock is equal in value to its corresponding convertible security. It is calculated by dividing the convertible security's market value by its conversion ratio.

parity price of convertible The dollar amount at which a convertible security is equal in value to its corresponding common stock. It is calculated by multiplying the market price of the common stock by its conversion ratio.

partial call The redemption by an issuer of a portion of an outstanding bond issue prior to the maturity date. *Related item(s):* catastrophe call; mandatory call.

participant (1) A person who advises stockholders in a proxy contest. (2) The holder of an interest in a direct participation program. *Related item(s):* limited partner.

participating preferred stock An equity security that offers the holder a share of corporate earnings remaining after all senior securities have been paid a fixed dividend. The payment is made in addition to the fixed dividend stated on the certificate, and may be cumulative or noncumulative. *Related item(s):* convertible preferred stock; cumulative preferred stock; noncumulative preferred stock; preferred stock.

participation The provision of the Employee Retirement Income Security Act of 1974 requiring that all employees in a qualified retirement plan be covered within a reasonable time of their dates of hire.

partnership A form of business organization in which two or more individuals manage the business and are equally and personally liable for its debts.

partnership account An account that empowers the individual members of a partnership to act on the behalf of the partnership as a whole.

partnership management fee The amount payable to the general partners of a limited partnership, or to other persons, for managing the day-to-day partnership operations. *Syn.* program management fee; property management fee.

par value The dollar amount assigned to a security by the issuer. For an equity security, par value is usually a small dollar amount that bears no relationship to the security's market price. For a debt security, par value is the amount repaid to the investor when the bond matures, usually $1,000. *Syn.* face value; principal; stated value. *Related item(s):* capital surplus; discount bond; premium bond.

passive income Earnings derived from a rental property, limited partnership or other enterprise in which the individual is not actively involved. Passive income therefore does not include earnings from wages or active business participation, nor does it include income from dividends, interest and capital gains. *Related item(s):* passive loss; unearned income.

passive investor *See* limited partner.

passive loss A loss incurred through a rental property, limited partnership or other enterprise in which the individual is not actively involved. Passive losses can be used to offset passive income only, not wage or portfolio income. *Related item(s):* passive income.

pass-through certificate A security representing an interest in a pool of conventional, VA, Farmers Home Administration or other agency mortgages. The pool receives the principal and interest payments, which it passes through to each certificate holder. Payments may or may not be guaranteed. *Related item(s):* Federal National Mortgage Association; Government National Mortgage Association.

pattern A repetitive series of price movements on a chart used by a technical analyst to predict future movements of the market.

payment date The day on which a declared dividend is paid to all stockholders owning shares on the record date.

payment period As defined by the Federal Reserve Board's Regulation T, the period of time corresponding to the regular way settlement period established by the NASD.

payout stage *See* distribution stage.

payroll deduction plan A retirement plan whereby an employee authorizes a deduction from his check on a regular basis. The plan may be qualified, such as a 401(k) plan, or nonqualified.

P/E *See* price/earnings ratio.

peak The end of a period of increasing business activity throughout the economy, one of the four stages of the business cycle. *Syn.* prosperity. *Related item(s):* business cycle.

pension plan A contract between an individual and an employer, a labor union, a government entity or another institution that provides for the distribution of pension benefits at retirement.

P/E ratio *See* price/earnings ratio.

percentage depletion A method of tax accounting for a direct participation program whereby a statutory percentage of gross income from the sale of a mineral resource is allowed as a tax-deductible expense. Percentage depletion is available to small producers only and not to purchasers of producing interests.

periodic payment plan A mutual fund sales contract in which the customer commits to buying shares in the fund on a periodic basis over a long time period in exchange for a lower minimum investment.

person As defined in securities law, an individual, a corporation, a partnership, an association, a fund, a joint stock company, an unincorporated organization, a trust, a government or a political subdivision of a government.

personal income (PI) An individual's total earnings derived from wages, passive business enterprises and investments. *Related item(s):* disposable income.

phantom income In a limited partnership, taxable income that is not backed by a positive cash flow. *Related item(s):* crossover point.

Pink Sheets A daily publication compiled by the National Quotation Bureau and containing interdealer wholesale quotations for over-the-counter stocks. *Related item(s): Yellow Sheets*.

pipeline theory *See* conduit theory.

placement ratio A ratio compiled by *The Bond Buyer* indicating the number of new municipal issues that have sold within the last week.

plan custodian An institution retained by a contractual plan company to perform clerical duties. The custodian's responsibilities include safeguarding plan assets, sending out customer confirmations and issuing shares. *Related item(s):* custodian; mutual fund custodian.

plus tick A security transaction's execution price that is above the previous execution price, by a minimum amount. *Syn.* up tick. *Related item(s):* minus tick; plus tick rule; tick; zero-plus tick.

plus tick rule The SEC regulation governing the market price at which a short sale may be made. No short sale may be executed at a price below the price of the last sale. *Syn.* up tick rule. *Related item(s):* minus tick; short sale; tick; zero-plus tick.

point A measure of a bond's price; $10 or 1 percent of the par value of $1,000. *Related item(s):* basis point.

point-and-figure chart A tool used by technical analysts to track the effects of price reversals, or changes in the direction of prices, of a commodity over time. *Related item(s):* bar chart; moving average chart.

POP *See* public offering price.

portfolio income Earnings from interest, dividends and all nonbusiness investments. *Related item(s):* earned income; passive income; unearned income.

portfolio manager The entity responsible for investing a mutual fund's assets, implementing its investment strategy and managing day-to-day portfolio trading. *Syn.* fund manager.

position The amount of a security either owned (a long position) or owed (a short position) by an individual or a dealer. Dealers take long positions in specific securities to maintain inventories and thereby facilitate trading.

position limit The rule established by options exchanges that prohibits an investor from having a net long or short position of more than a specific number of contracts on the same side of the market.

positive yield curve *See* normal yield curve.

power of substitution *See* stock power.

precedence In an exchange market, the ranking of bids and offers according to the number of shares involved. *Related item(s):* parity; priority.

preemptive right A stockholder's legal right to maintain her proportionate ownership by purchasing newly issued shares before the new stock is offered to the public. *Related item(s):* right.

preferred dividend coverage ratio An indication of the safety of a corporation's preferred dividend payments. It is computed by dividing preferred dividends by net income.

preferred stock An equity security that represents ownership in a corporation. It is issued with a stated dividend, which must be paid before dividends are paid to common stockholders. It generally carries no voting rights. *Related item(s):* callable preferred stock; convertible preferred stock; cumulative preferred stock.

preferred stock fund A mutual fund whose investment objective is to provide stable income with minimal capital risk. It invests in income-producing instruments such as preferred stock. *Related item(s):* bond fund.

preliminary prospectus An abbreviated prospectus that is distributed while the SEC is reviewing an issuer's registration statement. It contains all of the essential facts about the forthcoming offering except the underwriting spread, final public offering price and date on which the shares will be delivered. *Syn.* red herring.

premium (1) The amount of cash that an option buyer pays to an option seller. (2) The difference between the higher price paid for a security and the security's face amount at issue. *Related item(s):* discount.

premium bond A bond that sells at a higher price than its face value. *Related item(s):* discount bond; par value.

prerefunding *See* advance refunding.

presale order An order communicated to a syndicate manager prior to formation of the underwriting bid of a new municipal bond issue. If the syndicate wins the bid, the order takes the highest priority when orders are filled. *Related item(s):* designated order; group net order; member-at-the-takedown order.

price/earnings ratio (P/E) A tool for comparing the prices of different common stocks by assessing how much the market is willing to pay for a share of each corporation's earnings. It is calculated by dividing the current market price of a stock by the earnings per share.

price risk The potential that the value of a currency or commodity will change between the signing of a delivery contract and the time delivery is made. The futures markets serve to manage price risk.

price spread *See* vertical spread.

primary distribution *See* primary offering.

primary earnings per share *See* earnings per share.

primary market *See* new issue market.

primary offering An offering in which the proceeds of the underwriting go to the issuing corporation, agency or municipality. The issuer seeks to increase its capitalization either by selling shares of stock, representing ownership, or by selling bonds, representing loans to the issuer. *Syn.* primary distribution.

prime rate The interest rate that commercial banks charge their prime or most creditworthy customers, generally large corporations.

principal A person who trades for his own account in the primary or secondary market. Also, a dealer.

principal transaction A transaction in which a broker/dealer either buys securities from customers and takes them into its own inventory or sells securities to customers from its inventory. *Related item(s):* agency transaction; agent; broker; dealer; principal.

priority In an exchange market, the ranking of bids and offers according to the first person to bid or offer at a given price. Therefore, only one individual or firm can have priority. *Related item(s):* parity; precedence.

prior lien bond A secured bond that takes precedence over other bonds secured by the same assets. *Related item(s):* mortgage bond.

private placement An offering of new issue securities that complies with Regulation D of the Securities Act of 1933. According to Regulation D, a security generally is not required to be registered with the SEC if it is offered to no more than 35 nonaccredited investors or to an unlimited number of accredited investors. *Related item(s):* Regulation D.

productive well An oil or gas well that produces mineral resources that can be marketed commercially. *Related item(s):* dry hole.

profitability The ability to generate a level of income and gain in excess of expenses.

profit ratio *See* net profit ratio.

profit-sharing plan An employee benefit plan established and maintained by an employer whereby the employees receive a share of the business's profits. The money may be paid directly to the employees or deferred until retirement. A combination of both approaches is also possible.

progressive tax A tax that takes a larger percentage of the income of high-income earners than that of low-income earners. An example is the graduated income tax. *Related item(s):* regressive tax.

project note (PN) A short-term municipal debt instrument issued in anticipation of a later issuance of New Housing Authority bonds. *Related item(s):* New Housing Authority bond.

property dividend A distribution made by a corporation to its stockholders of securities it owns in other corporations or of its products. *Related item(s):* dividend.

prospectus *See* final prospectus.

Prospectus Act *See* Securities Act of 1933.

proxy A limited power of attorney from a stockholder authorizing another person to vote on stockholder issues according to the first stockholder's instructions. To vote on corporate matters, a stockholder must either attend the annual meeting or vote by proxy.

proxy department The department within a brokerage firm that is responsible for sending proxy statements to customers whose securities are held in the firm's name, and for mailing financial reports received from issuers to their stockholders.

prudent man rule A legal maxim that restricts discretion in a fiduciary account to only those investments that a reasonable and prudent person might make.

Public Housing Authority bond (PHA) *See* New Housing Authority bond.

publicly traded fund *See* closed-end investment company.

public offering The sale of an issue of common stock, either by a corporation going public or by an offering of additional shares. *Related item(s):* initial public offering.

public offering price (POP) (1) The price of new shares that is established in the issuing corporation's prospectus. (2) The price to investors for mutual fund shares, equal to the net asset value plus the sales charge. *Related item(s):* ask; bid; mutual fund; net asset value.

public purpose bond A municipal bond that is exempt from federal income tax as long no more than 10 percent of the proceeds benefit private entities.

Public Securities Association (PSA) An organization of banks and broker/dealers that conduct business in mortgage-backed securities, money-market securities and securities issued by the US government, government agencies and municipalities.

purchasing power risk The potential that, due to inflation, a certain amount of money will not purchase as much in the future as it does today. *Syn.* inflation risk.

put (1) An option contract giving the owner the right to sell a certain amount of an underlying security at a specified price within a specified time. (2) The act of exercising a put option. *Related item(s):* call.

put bond A debt security requiring the issuer to purchase the security at the holder's discretion or within a prescribed time. *Syn.* tender bond.

put buyer An investor who pays a premium for an option contract and receives, for a specified time, the right to sell the underlying security at a specified price. *Related item(s):* call buyer; call writer; put writer.

put spread An option investor's position in which the investor buys a put on a particular security and writes a put on the same security but with a different expiration date, exercise price, or both.

put writer An investor who receives a premium and takes on, for a specified time, the obligation to buy the underlying security at a specified price at the put buyer's discretion. *Related item(s):* call buyer; call writer; put buyer.

pyramiding A speculative strategy whereby an investor uses unrealized profits from a position held to increase the size of the position continuously but by ever-smaller amounts.

Q

qualification *See* registration by qualification.

qualified legal opinion The statement of a bond attorney affirming the validity of a new municipal bond issue but expressing reservations about its quality. *Related item(s):* legal opinion of counsel; unqualified legal opinion.

qualified retirement plan A corporate retirement plan that meets the standards set by the Employee Retirement Income Security Act of 1974. Contributions to a qualified plan are tax deductible. *Syn.* approved plan. *Related item(s):* individual retirement account; Keogh plan; nonqualified retirement plan.

quick assets A measure of a corporation's liquidity that takes into account the size of the unsold inventory. It is calculated by subtracting inventory from current assets, and it is used in the acid-test ratio. *Related item(s):* acid-test ratio.

quick ratio *See* acid-test ratio.

quotation The price or bid a market maker or broker/dealer offers for a particular security. *Syn.* quote. *Related item(s):* ask; bid; bond quote; stock quote.

quote *See* quotation.

R

RAN *See* revenue anticipation note.

random walk theory A market analysis theory that the past movement or direction of the price of a stock or market cannot be used to predict its future movement or direction.

range A security's low price and high price for a particular trading period, such as the close of a day's trading, the opening of a day's trading, or a day, month or year. *Syn.* opening range.

rate covenant A provision of a municipal revenue bond's trust indenture that helps ensure the safety of the issue by specifying the rates to be charged the user of the facility. *Related item(s):* insurance covenant; maintenance covenant.

rating An evaluation of a corporate or municipal bond's relative safety, according to the issuer's ability to repay principal and make interest payments. Bonds are rated by various organizations, such as Standard & Poor's and Moody's. Ratings range from AAA or Aaa (the highest) to C or D, which represents a company in default.

rating service A company, such as Moody's or Standard & Poor's, that rates various debt and preferred stock issues for safety of payment of principal, interest or dividends. The issuing company or municipality pays a fee for the rating. *Related item(s):* bond rating; rating.

ratio writing An option hedge position in which the investor writes more than one call option for every 100 shares of underlying stock that the investor owns. As a result, the investor has a partly covered position and a partly naked position.

raw land program A real estate direct participation program that aims to provide capital appreciation by investing in undeveloped land.

real estate investment trust (REIT) A corporation or trust that uses the pooled capital of many investors to invest in direct ownership of either income property or mortgage loans. These investments offer tax benefits in addition to interest and capital gains distributions.

real estate limited partnership A direct participation program formed to build new structures, generate income from existing property or profit from the capital appreciation of undeveloped land. Growth potential, income distributions and tax shelter are the most important benefits of such a program.

realized gain The amount a taxpayer earns when he sells an asset. *Related item(s):* unrealized gain.

reallowance A portion of the concession available to firms that sell shares in an offering but are not syndicate or selling group members.

recapitalization Changing the capital structure of a corporation by issuing, converting or redeeming securities.

recapture The taxation as ordinary income of previously earned deductions or credits. Circumstances that may cause the IRS to require this tax to be paid include excess depreciation, premature sale of an asset or because a previous tax benefit is now disallowed.

recession A general economic decline lasting from 6 to 18 months.

reciprocal immunity *See* doctrine of mutual reciprocity.

reclamation The right of the seller of a security to recover any loss incurred in a securities transaction owing to bad delivery or other irregularity in the settlement process.

reclassification The exchange by a corporation of one class of its securities for another class of its securities. This shifts ownership control among the stockholders and therefore falls under the purview of the SEC's Rule 145. *Related item(s)*: Rule 145.

record date The date a corporation's board of directors establishes that determines which of its stockholders are entitled to receive dividends or rights distributions.

recourse financing Debt incurred for the purchase of an asset and that holds the borrower personally liable for the debt. *Related item(s)*: nonrecourse financing.

recovery *See* expansion.

redeemable security A security that the issuer redeems upon the holder's request. Examples include shares in an open-end investment company and Treasury notes.

redemption The return of an investor's principal in a security, such as a bond, preferred stock or mutual fund shares. By law, redemption of mutual fund shares must occur within seven days of receiving the investor's request for redemption.

redemption notice A published announcement that a corporation or municipality is calling a certain issue of its bonds.

red herring *See* preliminary prospectus.

refinancing Issuing equity, the proceeds of which are used to retire debt.

refunding Retiring an outstanding bond issue at maturity using money from the sale of a new offering. *Related item(s)*: advance refunding.

regional exchange A stock exchange that serves the financial community in a particular region of the country. These exchanges tend to focus on securities issued within their regions, but also offer trading in NYSE- and AMEX-listed securities.

regional fund *See* sector fund.

registered Describes a security that prints the owner's name on the certificate. The owner's name is stored in records kept by the issuer or a transfer agent.

registered as to principal only The term describing a bond that prints the owner's name on the certificate, but that has unregistered coupons payable to the bearer. *Syn.* partially registered. *Related item(s)*: coupon bond; fully registered bond; registered.

registered options principal (ROP) The officer or partner of a brokerage firm who approves in writing accounts in which options transactions are permitted.

registered principal An associated person of a member firm who manages or supervises the firm's investment banking or securities business. This includes any individual who trains associated persons and who solicits business.

Unless the member firm is a sole proprietorship, it must employ at least two registered principals, one of whom must be registered as a general securities principal and one of whom must be registered as a financial and operations principal. If the firm does options business with the public, it must employ at least one registered options principal.

registered representative (RR) An associated person engaged in the investment banking or securities business. According to the NASD, this includes any individual who supervises, solicits or conducts business in securities or who trains people to supervise, solicit or conduct business in securities.

Anyone employed by a brokerage firm who is not a principal and who is not engaged in clerical or brokerage administration is subject to registration and exam licensing as a registered rep. *Syn.* account executive; stockbroker. *Related item(s)*: associated person of a member.

registrar The independent organization or part of a corporation responsible for accounting for all of the issuer's outstanding stock and certifying that its bonds constitute legal debt.

registration by coordination A process that allows a security to be sold in a state. It is available to an issuer that files for the security's registration under the Securities Act of 1933 and files duplicates of the registration documents with the state administrator. The state registration becomes effective at the same time the federal registration statement becomes effective.

registration by filing A process that allows a security to be sold in a state. Previously referred to as *registration by notification*, it is available to an issuer who files for the security's registration under the Securities Act of 1933, meets minimum net worth and certain other requirements, and notifies the state of this eligibility by filing certain documents with the state administrator. The state registration becomes effective at the same time the federal registration statement becomes effective.

registration by notification *See* registration by filing.

registration by qualification A process that allows a security to be sold in a state. It is available to an issuer who files for the security's registration with the state administrator, meets minimum net worth, disclosure and other requirements and files appropriate registration fees. The state registration becomes effective when the administrator so orders.

registration statement The legal document that discloses all pertinent information concerning an offering of a security and its issuer. It is submitted to the SEC in accordance with the requirements of the Securities Act of 1933, and it forms the basis of the final prospectus distributed to investors.

regressive tax A tax that takes a larger percentage of the income of low-income earners than that of high-income earners. Examples include gasoline tax and cigarette tax. *Related item(s):* progressive tax.

Reg T *See* Regulation T.

Reg T call *See* margin call.

regular way A settlement contract that calls for delivery and payment within a standard payment period from the date of the trade. The NASD's Uniform Practice Code sets the standard payment period. The type of security being traded determines the amount of time allowed for regular way settlement. *Related item(s):* cash transaction; settlement date.

regulated investment company An investment company to which Subchapter M of the Internal Revenue Code grants special status that allows the flow-through of tax consequences on a distribution to shareholders. If 90 percent of its income is passed through to the shareholders, the company is not subject to tax on this income.

Regulation A The provision of the Securities Act of 1933 that exempts from registration small public offerings valued at no more than $5 million worth of securities issued during a twelve-month period.

Regulation D The provision of the Securities Act of 1933 that exempts from registration offerings sold to a maximum of 35 nonaccredited investors during a twelve-month period. *Related item(s):* private placement.

Regulation T The Federal Reserve Board regulation that governs customer cash accounts and the amount of credit that brokerage firms and dealers may extend to customers for the purchase of securities. Regulation T currently sets the loan value of marginable securities at 50 percent and the payment deadline at two days beyond regular way settlement. *Syn.* Reg T. *Related item(s):* Regulation U.

Regulation U The Federal Reserve Board regulation that governs loans by banks for the purchase of securities. Call loans are exempt from Regulation U. *Related item(s):* broker's loan; call loan; Regulation T.

rehypothecation The pledging of a client's securities as collateral for a bank loan. Brokerage firms may rehypothecate up to 140 percent of the value of their customers' securities to finance margin loans to customers. *Related item(s):* hypothecation.

reinstatement privilege A benefit offered by some mutual funds, allowing an investor to withdraw money from a fund account and then redeposit the money without paying a second sales charge.

REIT *See* real estate investment trust.

rejection The right of the buyer of a security to refuse to accept delivery in completion of a trade because the security does not meet the requirements of good delivery.

renewal and replacement fund The account that is used to fund major renewal projects and equipment replacements financed by a municipal revenue bond issue. *Related item(s):* flow of funds.

reoffering price The price or yield at which a municipal security is sold to the public by the underwriters.

reorganization department The department within a brokerage firm that handles transactions that represent a change in the securities outstanding, such as trades relating to tender offers, bond calls, preferred stock redemptions and mergers and acquisitions.

repo *See* repurchase agreement.

repurchase agreement A sale of securities with an attendant agreement to repurchase them at a higher price on an agreed-upon future date; the difference between the sale price and the repurchase price represents the interest earned by the investor. Repos are considered money-market instruments, and are used to raise short-term capital and as instruments of monetary policy. *Syn.* repo. *Related item(s):* reverse repurchase agreement.

reserve maintenance fund The account that holds funds that supplement the general maintenance fund of a municipal revenue bond issue. *Related item(s):* flow of funds.

reserve requirement The percentage of depositors' money that the Federal Reserve Board requires a commercial bank to keep on deposit in the form of cash or in its vault. *Syn.* reserves.

residual claim The right of a common stockholder to corporate assets in the event that the corporation ceases to exist.

A common stockholder may claim assets only after the claims of all creditors and other security holders have been satisfied.

resistance level A technical analysis term describing the top of a stock's historical trading range. *Related item(s):* breakout; support level.

restricted account A margin account in which the equity is less than the Regulation T initial requirement. *Related item(s):* equity; initial margin requirement; margin account; retention requirement.

restricted security An unregistered, nonexempt security acquired either directly or indirectly from the issuer, or an affiliate of the issuer, in a transaction that does not involve a public offering. *Related item(s):* holding period; Rule 144.

retained earnings The amount of a corporation's net income that remains after all dividends have been paid to preferred and common stockholders. *Syn.* earned surplus; reinvested earnings.

retention requirement The provision of Regulation T that applies to the withdrawal of securities from a restricted account. The customer must deposit an amount equal to the unpaid portion of the securities being withdrawn, in order to reduce the debit balance. The retention requirement is the reciprocal of the initial margin requirement. *Related item(s):* restricted account.

retirement account A customer account established to provide retirement funds.

retiring bonds Ending an issuer's debt obligation by calling the outstanding bonds, by purchasing bonds in the open market, or by repaying bondholders the principal amount at maturity.

return on common equity A measure of a corporation's profitability, calculated by dividing aftertax income by common shareholders' equity.

return on equity A measure of a corporation's profitability, specifically its return on assets, calculated by dividing aftertax income by tangible assets.

return on investment (ROI) The profit or loss resulting from a security transaction, often expressed as an annual percentage rate.

revenue anticipation note (RAN) A short-term municipal debt security issued in anticipation of revenue to be received.

revenue bond A municipal debt issue whose interest and principal are payable only from the specific earnings of an income-producing public project. *Related item(s):* double-barreled bond; general obligation bond; municipal bond; special revenue bond.

reverse repo *See* reverse repurchase agreement.

reverse repurchase agreement A purchase of securities with an attendant agreement to resell them at a higher price on an agreed-upon future date; the difference between the purchase price and the resale price represents the interest earned by the investor. The purchaser initiates the deal. *Syn.* reverse repo. *Related item(s):* repurchase agreement.

reverse split A reduction in the number of a corporation's shares outstanding that increases the par value of its stock or its earnings per share. The market value of the total number of shares remains the same. *Related item(s):* stock split.

reversionary working interest A sharing arrangement whereby the general partner of a direct participation program bears none of the program's costs and does not share in revenues until the limited partners receive payment plus a predetermined rate of return. *Syn.* subordinated interest; subordinated reversionary working interest. *Related item(s):* sharing arrangement.

right A security representing a stockholder's entitlement to the first opportunity to purchase new shares issued by the corporation at a predetermined price (normally less than the current market price) in proportion to the number of shares already owned. Rights are issued for a short time only, after which they expire. *Syn.* subscription right; subscription right certificate. *Related item(s):* preemptive right; rights offering.

right of accumulation A benefit offered by a mutual fund that allows the investor to qualify for reduced sales loads on additional purchases according to the fund account's total dollar value.

rights agent An issuing corporation's agent who is responsible for maintaining current records of the names of rights certificate owners.

rights offering An issue of new shares of stock accompanied by the opportunity for each stockholder to maintain a proportionate ownership by purchasing additional shares in the corporation before the shares are offered to the public. *Related item(s):* right.

risk arbitrage The purchase of stock in a company that is being acquired and the short sale of stock in the acquiring company, in order to profit from the anticipated increase in the acquired corporation's shares and decrease in the acquiring corporation's shares.

riskless and simultaneous transaction The buying or selling by a broker/dealer of a security for its own account so as to fill an order previously received from a customer. Although the firm is technically acting as a principal in the trade, the transaction is relatively riskless because the purchase and sale are consummated almost simultaneously. *Syn.* riskless transaction.

ROI *See* return on investment.

rollover The transfer of funds from one qualified retirement plan to another qualified retirement plan. If this is not done within a specified time period, the funds are taxed as ordinary income.

ROP *See* registered options principal.

round lot A security's normal unit of trading, which is generally 100 shares of stock or five bonds. *Related item(s):* odd lot.

royalty interest The right of a mineral rights owner to receive a share in the revenues generated by the resource if and when production begins. The royalty interest retained is free from production costs.

Rule 144 SEC rule requiring that persons who hold control or restricted securities may sell them only in limited quantities, and that all sales of restricted stock by control persons must be reported to the SEC by filing a Form 144, "Notice of Proposed Sale of Securities." *Related item(s):* control security; restricted security.

Rule 145 SEC rule requiring that, whenever the stockholders of a publicly owned corporation are solicited to vote on or consent to a plan for reorganizing the corporation, full disclosure of all material facts must be made in a proxy statement or prospectus that must be in the hands of the stockholders before the announced voting date. *Related item(s):* reclassification.

Rule 147 SEC rule that provides exemption from the registration statement and prospectus requirements of the 1933 act for securities offered and sold exclusively intrastate.

Rule 15c2-1 SEC rule governing the safekeeping of securities in customer margin accounts. It prohibits broker/dealers from (1) using a customer's securities in excess of the customer's aggregate indebtedness as collateral to secure a loan without written permission from the customer, and (2) commingling a customer's securities without written permission from the customer. *Related item(s):* rehypothecation.

Rule 405 NYSE rule requiring that each member organization exercise due diligence to learn the essential facts about every customer. *Syn.* know your customer rule.

Rule 415 SEC rule governing shelf offerings. The rule allows an issuer to sell limited portions of a new issue over a two-year period. *Related item(s):* shelf offering.

Rule 504 SEC rule providing that an offering of less than $1,000,000 during any twelve-month period may be exempt from full registration. The rule does not restrict the number of accredited or nonaccredited purchasers.

Rule 505 SEC rule providing that an offering of $1,000,000 to $5,000,000 during any twelve-month period may be exempt from full registration. The rule restricts the number of nonaccredited purchasers to 35 but does not restrict the number of accredited purchasers.

Rule 506 SEC rule providing that an offering of more than $5,000,000 during any twelve-month period may be exempt from full registration. The rule restricts the number of nonaccredited purchasers to 35 but does not restrict the number of accredited purchasers.

Rule G-1 MSRB rule that classifies as municipal securities dealers any separately identifiable departments of banks that engage in activities related to the municipal securities business. *Related item(s):* separately identifiable department or division.

Rule G-2 MSRB rule that sets professional qualification standards.

Rule G-3 MSRB rule governing the classification of municipal securities principals and representatives.

Rule G-4 MSRB rule that statutorily disqualifies members who have violated securities laws or regulations.

Rule G-5 MSRB rule governing disciplinary actions by regulatory agencies, including the SEC and other SROs.

Rule G-6 MSRB rule governing the fidelity bond requirements for member broker/dealers.

Rule G-7 MSRB rule governing the documentation that must be kept on each associated person.

Rule G-8 MSRB rule outlining the requirements for maintaining books and records.

Rule G-9 MSRB rule governing the preservation of books and records.

Rule G-10 MSRB rule requiring that an investor brochure be delivered in response to a customer complaint.

Rule G-11 MSRB rule governing the priority given to orders received for new issue municipal securities.

Rule G-12 MSRB rule governing the uniform practices for settling transactions between municipal securities firms.

Rule G-13 MSRB rule requiring broker/dealers to publish only bona fide quotations for municipal securities unless the quotations are identified as informational.

Rule G-14 MSRB rule prohibiting fictitious, deceptive or manipulative reports of municipal securities sales and purchases.

Rule G-15 MSRB rule governing the confirmation, clearance and settlement of customer municipal securities transactions.

Rule G-16 MSRB rule requiring inspections to be conducted every 24 months, to verify compliance.

Rule G-17 MSRB rule that sets ethical standards for conducting municipal securities business.

Rule G-18 MSRB rule requiring firms to make an effort to obtain the best price when executing municipal securities transactions for customers.

Rule G-19 MSRB rule governing discretionary accounts and the suitability of municipal securities recommendations and transactions.

Rule G-20 MSRB rule that sets a limit on the value of gifts and gratuities given by municipal securities firms.

Rule G-21 MSRB rule governing the advertising of municipal securities.

Rule G-22 MSRB rule requiring disclosures to customers of control relationships between municipal firms and issuers.

Rule G-23 MSRB rule that seeks to minimize conflicts of interest arising out of the activities of financial advisers that also act as municipal underwriters to the same issuer.

Rule G-24 MSRB rule prohibiting the misuse of confidential information about customers obtained by municipal securities firms acting in fiduciary capacities.

Rule G-25 MSRB rule prohibiting the improper use of assets by municipal securities firms and their representatives.

Rule G-26 MSRB rule governing municipal customer account transfers.

Rule G-27 MSRB rule requiring each municipal securities firm to designate a principal to supervise its municipal securities representatives.

Rule G-28 MSRB rule governing employee accounts held at other municipal securities firms.

Rule G-29 MSRB rule governing the availability of MSRB regulations.

Rule G-30 MSRB rule requiring prices and commissions charged by municipal securities firms to be fair and reasonable.

Rule G-31 MSRB rule prohibiting a municipal securities professional from soliciting business from an investment company portfolio in return for sales of that fund to its customers.

Rule G-32 MSRB rule requiring that customers receive a copy of the preliminary or final official statement when purchasing a new municipal issue.

Rule G-33 MSRB rule governing the calculation of accrued interest on municipal bonds using a 360-day year.

Rule G-34 MSRB rule requiring a managing underwriter to apply for a CUSIP number for a new municipal issue.

Rule G-35 MSRB rule governing the rules for arbitration to settle disputes between parties engaged in the municipal securities business.

Rule G-36 MSRB rule requiring the underwriter of a new municipal issue to file the final official statement with the MSRB.

Rule G-37 MSRB rule prohibiting municipal securities dealers from underwriting securities issued under the authority of a public official to whom an associated person of the dealer has contributed money.

Rule G-38 MSRB rule requiring municipal securities firms to disclose relationships with consultants hired to obtain business from municipal issuers.

S

sale *See* sell.

sales charge *See* commission.

sales literature Any written material a firm distributes to customers or the public in a controlled manner. Examples include circulars, research reports, form letters, market letters, performance reports and text used for seminars. *Related item(s):* advertisement; market letter.

sales load The amount added to a mutual fund share's net asset value to arrive at the offering price. *Related item(s):* mutual fund; net asset value; no-load fund.

Sallie Mae *See* Student Loan Marketing Association.

S&P *See* Standard & Poor's Corporation.

S&P 100 *See* Standard & Poor's 100 Stock Index.

S&P 500 *See* Standard & Poor's Composite Index of 500 Stocks.

savings bond A government debt security that is not negotiable or transferable and that may not be used as collateral. *Related item(s):* Series EE bond; Series HH bond.

scale A list of each of the scheduled maturities in a new serial bond issue. The list outlines the number of bonds, maturity dates, coupon rates and yields. *Related item(s):* writing a scale.

SEC *See* Securities and Exchange Commission.

secondary distribution (1) A distribution, with a prospectus, that involves securities owned by major stockholders (typically founders or principal owners of a corporation). The sale proceeds go to the sellers of the stock, not to the issuer. *Syn.* registered secondary distribution.
(2) A procedure for trading very large blocks of shares of stock whereby the trade is executed off the floor of an exchange after the market closes.

secondary market The market in which securities are bought and sold subsequent to their being sold to the public for the first time. *Related item(s):* new issue market.

secondary offering A sale of securities in which one or more major stockholders in a company sell all or a large portion of their holdings; the underwriting proceeds are paid to the stockholders rather than to the corporation. Typically such an offering occurs when the founder of a business (and perhaps some of the original financial backers) determine that there is more to be gained by going public than by staying private. The offering does not increase the number of shares of stock outstanding. *Related item(s):* secondary distribution.

sector fund A mutual fund whose investment objective is to capitalize on the return potential provided by investing primarily in a particular industry or sector of the economy. *Syn.* industry fund; specialized fund.

secured bond A debt security backed by identifiable assets set aside as collateral. In the event that the issuer defaults on payment, the bondholders may lay claim to the collateral. *Related item(s):* debenture.

Securities Act of 1933 Federal legislation requiring the full and fair disclosure of all material information about the issuance of new securities. *Syn.* Act of 1933; Full Disclosure Act; New Issues Act; Prospectus Act; Trust in Securities Act; Truth in Securities Act.

Securities Acts Amendments of 1975 Federal legislation that established the Municipal Securities Rulemaking Board. *Related item(s):* Municipal Securities Rulemaking Board.

Securities and Exchange Commission (SEC) Commission created by Congress to regulate the securities markets and protect investors. It is composed of five commissioners appointed by the President of the United States and approved by the Senate. The SEC enforces, among other acts, the Securities Act of 1933, the Securities Exchange Act of 1934, the Trust Indenture Act of 1939, the Investment Company Act of 1940 and the Investment Advisers Act of 1940.

Securities Exchange Act of 1934 Federal legislation that established the Securities and Exchange Commission. The act aims to protect investors by regulating the exchanges, the over-the-counter market, the extension of credit by the Federal Reserve Board, broker/dealers, insider transactions, trading activities, client accounts and net capital. *Syn.* Act of 1934; Exchange Act.

Securities Investor Protection Corporation (SIPC) A nonprofit membership corporation created by an act of Congress to protect clients of brokerage firms that are forced into bankruptcy. Membership is composed of all brokers and dealers registered under the Securities Exchange Act of 1934, all members of national securities exchanges and most NASD members. SIPC provides brokerage firm customers up to $500,000 coverage for cash and securities held by the firms (although cash coverage is limited to $100,000).

security Other than an insurance policy or a fixed annuity, any piece of securitized paper that can be traded for value. Under the Act of 1934, this includes any note, stock, bond, investment contract, debenture, certificate of interest in a profit-sharing or partnership agreement, certificate of deposit, collateral trust certificate, preorganization certificate, option on a security, or other instrument of investment commonly known as a *security*.

segregation Holding customer-owned securities separate from securities owned by other customers and securities owned by the brokerage firm. *Related item(s):* commingling.

selection risk The potential for loss on an investment owing to the particular security chosen performing poorly in spite of good overall market or industry performance.

self-regulatory organization (SRO) One of eight organizations accountable to the SEC for the enforcement of federal securities laws and the supervision of securities practices within an assigned field of jurisdiction. For example, the National Association of Securities Dealers regulates the over-the-counter market; the Municipal Securities Rulemaking Board supervises state and municipal securities; and certain exchanges, such as the New York Stock Exchange and the Chicago Board Options Exchange, act as self-regulatory bodies to promote ethical conduct and standard trading practices.

sell To convey ownership of a security or another asset for money or value. This includes giving or delivering a security with or as a bonus for a purchase of securities, a gift of assessable stock, and selling or offering a warrant or right to purchase or subscribe to another security. Not included in the definition is a bona fide pledge or loan or a stock dividend if nothing of value is given by the stockholders for the dividend. *Syn.* sale.

seller *See* writer.

seller's option A settlement contract that calls for delivery and payment according to a number of days specified by the seller. *Related item(s):* buyer's option.

selling away An associated person engaging in private securities transactions without the employing broker/dealer's knowledge and consent. This violates the NASD Conduct Rules.

selling concession *See* concession.

selling dividends (1) Inducing customers to buy mutual fund shares by implying that an upcoming distribution will benefit them. This practice is illegal. (2) Combining dividend and gains distributions when calculating current yield.

selling group Brokerage firms that help distribute securities in an offering but that are not members of the syndicate.

sell-out The procedure that the seller of a security follows when the buyer fails to complete the contract by accepting delivery of the security. The seller closes the contract by selling the security in the open market and charging the account of the buyer for transaction fees and any loss caused by changes in the market. *Related item(s):* buy-in.

sell stop order An order to sell a security that is entered at a price below the current market price and that is triggered when the market price touches or goes through the sell stop price.

senior lien debt A bond issue that shares the same collateral as is backing other issues but that has a prior claim to the collateral in the event of default.

senior registered options principal (SROP) The principal responsible for developing and enforcing a program for supervising customer options accounts. The SROP must review accounts for compliance with suitability rules and must approve all customer correspondence.

senior security A security that grants its holder a prior claim to the issuer's assets over the claims of another security's holders. For example, a bond is a senior security over common stock.

SEP *See* simplified employee pension plan.

separate account The account that holds funds paid by variable annuity contract holders. The funds are kept separate from the insurer's general account and are invested in a portfolio of securities that match the contract holders' objectives. *Related item(s):* accumulation unit; annuity; general account.

separately identifiable department or division A department of a bank that engages in the business of buying or selling municipal securities under the direct supervision of an officer of the bank. Such a department is classified by the Municipal Securities Rulemaking Board as a municipal securities dealer, and must comply with MSRB regulations. *Related item(s):* Rule G-1.

Separate Trading of Registered Interest and Principal of Securities (STRIPS) A zero-coupon bond issued and backed by the Treasury Department. *Related item(s):* zero-coupon bond.

SEP-IRA *See* simplified employee pension plan.

serial bond A debt security issued with a maturity schedule in which parts of the outstanding issue mature at intervals until the entire balance has been repaid. Most municipal bonds are serial bonds. *Related item(s):* maturity date; series bond.

series Options of the same class that have the same exercise price and the same expiration date. *Related item(s):* class; type.

Series 6 The investment company/variable contract products limited representative license, which entitles the holder to sell mutual funds and variable annuities and is used by many firms that sell primarily insurance-related products. The Series 6 can serve as the prerequisite for the Series 26 license.

Series 7 The general securities registered representative license, which entitles the holder to sell all types of securities products, with the exception of commodities futures (which requires a Series 3 license). The Series 7 is the most comprehensive of the NASD representative licenses and serves as a prerequisite for most of the NASD's principals examinations.

Series 24 The General Securities Principal License, which entitles the holder to supervise the business of a broker/dealer. A Series 7 or a Series 62 qualification is a prerequisite for this license.

Series 63 The uniform securities agent state law exam, which entitles the successful candidate to sell securities and give investment advice in those states that require Series 63 registration. *Related item(s):* blue-sky laws; Uniform Securities Act.

series bond A debt security issued in a series of public offerings spread over an extended time period. All the bonds in the series have the same priority claim against assets. *Related item(s):* serial bond.

Series EE bond A nonmarketable, interest-bearing US government savings bond issued at a discount from par. Interest on Series EE bonds is exempt from state and local taxes. *Related item(s):* savings bond; Series HH bond.

Series HH bond A nonmarketable, interest-bearing US government savings bond issued at par and purchased only by trading in Series EE bonds at maturity. Interest on Series HH bonds is exempt from state and local taxes. *Related item(s):* savings bond; Series EE bond.

settlement The completion of a trade through the delivery of a security or commodity and the payment of cash or other consideration.

settlement date The date on which ownership changes between buyer and seller. The NASD's Uniform Practice Code standardizes settlement provisions. *Related item(s):* cash transaction; regular way.

75-5-10 test The standard for judging whether an investment company qualifies as diversified under the Investment Company Act of 1940. Under this act, a diversified investment company must invest at least 75 percent of its total assets in cash, receivables or invested securities and no more than 5 percent of its total assets in any one company's voting securities. In addition, no single investment may represent ownership of more than 10 percent of any one company's outstanding voting securities. *Related item(s):* diversified management company.

share identification An accounting method that identifies the specific shares selected for liquidation in the event that an investor wishes to liquidate shares. The difference between the buying and selling prices determines the investor's tax liability.

sharing arrangement A method of allocating the responsibility for expenses and the right to share in revenues among the sponsor and limited partners in a direct participation program. *Related item(s):* carried interest; disproportionate sharing; functional allocation; net operating profits interest; overriding royalty interest; reversionary working interest.

shelf offering An SEC provision allowing an issuer to register a new issue security without selling the entire issue at once. The issuer can sell limited portions of the issuer over a two-year period without reregistering the security or incurring penalties. *Related item(s):* Rule 415.

short The term used to describe the selling of a security, contract or commodity that the seller does not own. For example, an investor who borrows shares of stock from a broker/dealer and sells them on the open market is said to have a *short position* in the stock. *Related item(s):* long.

short against the box The term used to describe the selling of a security, contract or commodity that the seller owns but prefers not to deliver; frequently this is done to defer taxation.

short-interest theory A technical analysis theory that examines the ratio of short sales to volume in a stock. Because the underlying stock must be purchased to close out the short positions, a high ratio is considered bullish.

short sale The sale of a security that the seller does not own, or any sale consummated by the delivery of a security borrowed by or for the account of the seller. *Related item(s):* plus tick rule.

short straddle An option investor's position that results from selling a call and a put on the same stock with the same exercise price and expiration month. *Related item(s):* long straddle; spread; straddle.

short-term capital gain The profit realized on the sale of an asset that has been owned for twelve months or less. *Related item(s):* capital gain; capital loss; short-term capital loss.

short-term capital loss The loss incurred on the sale of a capital asset that has been owned for twelve months or less.

Related item(s): capital gain; capital loss; short-term capital gain.

simplified arbitration An expedient method of settling disputes involving claims not exceeding $25,000, whereby a panel of arbitrators reviews the evidence and renders a decision. All awards are made within 30 business days. *Related item(s):* arbitration.

simplified employee pension plan (SEP) A qualified retirement plan designed for employers with 25 or fewer employees. Contributions made to each employee's individual retirement account grow tax deferred until retirement. *Related item(s):* individual retirement account.

single account An account in which only one individual has control over the investments and may transact business.

sinking fund An account established by an issuing corporation or municipality into which money is deposited regularly so that the issuer has the funds to redeem its bonds, debentures or preferred stock.

SIPC *See* Securities Investor Protection Corporation.

SLD A message on the Consolidated Tape indicating that the sale being reported was not reported on time and is therefore out of sequence.

SLMA *See* Student Loan Marketing Association.

SMA *See* special memorandum account.

solvency The ability of a corporation both to meet its long-term fixed expenses and to have adequate money for long-term expansion and growth.

special assessment bond A municipal revenue bond funded by assessments only on property owners who benefit from the services or improvements provided by the proceeds of the bond issue. *Related item(s):* revenue bond.

specialist A stock exchange member who stands ready to quote and trade certain securities either for his own account or for customer accounts. The specialist's role is to maintain a fair and orderly market in the stocks for which he is responsible. *Related item(s):* specialist's book.

specialist's book A journal in which a specialist records the limit and stop orders that he holds for execution. The contents of the journal are confidential. *Syn.* limit order book. *Related item(s):* specialist.

specialized fund *See* sector fund.

special memorandum account (SMA) A notation on a customer's general or margin account indicating that funds are credited to the account on a memo basis; the account is used much like a line of credit with a bank. An SMA preserves the customer's right to use excess equity. *Syn.* special miscellaneous account.

special revenue bond A municipal revenue bond issued to finance a specific project. Examples include industrial development bonds, lease rental bonds, special tax bonds and New Housing Authority bonds. *Related item(s):* revenue bond.

special situation fund A mutual fund whose objective is to capitalize on the profit potential of corporations in nonrecurring circumstances, such as those undergoing reorganizations or being considered as takeover candidates.

special tax bond A municipal revenue bond payable only from the proceeds of a tax on certain items, rather than an ad valorem tax. *Related item(s):* revenue bond.

speculation Trading a commodity or security with a higher than average risk in return for a higher than average profit potential. The trade is effected solely for the purpose of profiting from it and not as a means of hedging or protecting other positions.

speculator One who trades a commodity or security with a higher than average risk in return for a higher than average profit potential. *Related item(s):* speculation.

split offering A public offering of securities that combines aspects of both a primary and a secondary offering. A portion of the issue is a primary offering, the proceeds of which go to the issuing corporation; the remainder of the issue is a secondary offering, the proceeds of which go to the selling stockholders. *Syn.* combined distribution. *Related item(s):* primary offering; secondary offering.

sponsor A person who is instrumental in organizing, selling, or managing a limited partnership.

spousal account A separate individual retirement account established for a nonworking spouse. Contributions to the account made by the working spouse grow tax deferred until withdrawal. *Related item(s):* individual retirement account.

spread In a quotation, the difference between a security's bid and ask prices.

spread order A customer order specifying two option contracts on the same underlying security and a price difference between them.

SRO *See* self-regulatory organization.

SROP *See* senior registered options principal.

$\frac{S}{S}$ A symbol on the Consolidated Tape indicating that the stock in question sold in 10-share units.

stabilizing Bidding at or below the public offering price of a new issue security. Underwriting managers may enter stabilizing bids during the offering period to prevent the price from dropping sharply.

stagflation A period of high unemployment in the economy accompanied by a general rise in prices. *Related item(s)*: deflation; inflation.

Standard & Poor's Composite Index of 500 Stocks (S&P 500) A value-weighted index that offers broad coverage of the securities market. It is composed of 400 industrial stocks, 40 financial stocks, 40 public utility stocks and 20 transportation stocks. The index is owned and compiled by Standard & Poor's Corporation. *Related item(s)*: index; Standard & Poor's Corporation; Standard & Poor's 100 Stock Index.

Standard & Poor's Corporation (S&P) A company that rates stocks and corporate and municipal bonds according to risk profiles and that produces and tracks the S&P indexes. The company also publishes a variety of financial and investment reports. *Related item(s)*: bond rating; Moody's Investors Service; rating; Standard & Poor's 100 Stock Index; Standard & Poor's Composite Index of 500 Stocks.

Standard & Poor's 100 Stock Index (S&P 100) A value-weighted index composed of 100 blue chip stocks. The index is owned and compiled by Standard & Poor's Corporation. *Related item(s)*: index; Standard & Poor's Corporation; Standard & Poor's Composite Index of 500 Stocks.

standby underwriter An investment banker that agrees to purchase any part of an issue that has not been purchased by current stockholders through a rights offering. The firm exercises the remaining rights, maintains a trading market in the rights, and offers the stock acquired to the public. *Related item(s)*: rights offering.

stated yield *See* nominal yield.

statutory disqualification Prohibiting a person from associating with a self-regulatory organization because the person has been expelled, barred or suspended from association with a member of an SRO; has had his registration suspended, denied or revoked by the SEC; has been the cause of someone else's suspension, barment or revocation; has been convicted of certain crimes; or has falsified an application or a report that he must file with or on behalf of a membership organization.

statutory voting A voting procedure that permits stockholders to cast one vote per share owned for each position. The procedure tends to benefit majority stockholders. *Related item(s)*: cumulative voting.

step-out well An oil or gas well or prospect adjacent to a field of proven reserves. *Related item(s)*: developmental drilling program.

stock ahead The term used to describe the inability of a specialist to fill a limit order at a specific price because other orders at the same price were entered previously.

stockbroker *See* registered representative.

stock certificate Written evidence of ownership in a corporation.

stock dividend *See* dividend.

stock loan agreement The document that an institutional customer must sign when the broker/dealer borrows stock from the customer's account; the document specifies the terms of the loan and the rights of both parties.

stock power A standard form that duplicates the back of a stock certificate and is used for transferring the stock to the new owner's name. A separate stock power is used if a security's registered owner does not have the certificate available for signature endorsement. *Syn.* irrevocable stock power; power of substitution. *Related item(s)*: assignment.

stock quote A list of representative prices bid and asked for a stock during a particular trading day. Stocks are quoted in points, where one point equals $1. Stock quotes are listed in the financial press and most daily newspapers. *Related item(s)*: bond quote.

stock split An increase in the number of a corporation's outstanding shares, which decreases its stock's par value. The market value of the total number of shares remains the same. The proportional reductions in orders held on the books for a split stock are calculated by dividing the stock's market price by the fraction that represents the split.

stop limit order A customer order that becomes a limit order when the market price of the security reaches or passes a specific price. *Related item(s)*: limit order; stop order.

stop order (1) A directive from the SEC that suspends the sale of new issue securities to the public when fraud is suspected or filing materials are deficient. (2) A customer order that becomes a market order when the market price of the security reaches or passes a specific price. *Related item(s)*: limit order; market order; stop limit order.

stopping stock The method used by a specialist to guarantee that a customer order will be executed at a specific price.

straddle An option investor's position that results from buying a call and a put or selling a call and a put on the same security with the same exercise price and expiration month. *Related item(s)*: long straddle; short straddle; spread.

straight-line depreciation An accounting method used to recover the cost of a qualifying depreciable asset, whereby the owner writes off the cost of the asset in equal amounts each year over the asset's useful life.

strike price *See* exercise price.

striking price *See* exercise price.

stripped bond A debt obligation that has been stripped of its interest coupons by a brokerage firm, repackaged and sold at a deep discount. It pays no interest but may be redeemed at maturity for the full face value. *Related item(s)*: zero-coupon bond.

stripper well An oil well that produces fewer than 10 barrels per day.

STRIPS *See* Separate Trading of Registered Interest and Principal of Securities.

Student Loan Marketing Association (SLMA) A publicly owned corporation that purchases student loans from financial institutions and packages them for sale in the secondary market, thereby increasing the availability of money for educational loans. *Syn.* Sallie Mae.

subject quote A securities quotation that does not represent an actual offer to buy or sell but is tentative, subject to reconfirmation by the broker/dealer. *Related item(s)*: bona fide quote; firm quote; nominal quote; workout quote.

subordinated debenture A debt obligation, backed by the general credit of the issuing corporation, that has claims to interest and principal subordinated to ordinary debentures and all other liabilities. *Related item(s)*: debenture.

subordinated debt financing A form of long-term capitalization used by broker/dealers, in which the claims of lenders are subordinated to the claims of other creditors. Subordinated financing is considered part of the broker/dealer's capital structure and is added to net worth when computing its net capital.

subordinated interest *See* reversionary working interest.

subordinated loan A loan to a broker/dealer in which the lender agrees to subordinate its claim to the claims of the firm's other creditors.

subordinated reversionary working interest *See* reversionary working interest.

subscription agreement A statement signed by an investor indicating an offer to buy an interest in a direct participation program. In the statement, the investor agrees to grant power of attorney to the general partner and to abide by the limited partnership agreement. The sale is finalized when the subscription agreement is signed by the general partner.

subscription amount The total dollar amount that a participant in a direct participation program has invested.

subscription right *See* right.

suitability A determination made by a registered representative as to whether a particular security matches a customer's objectives and financial capability. The rep must have enough information about the customer to make this judgment. *Related item(s)*: Rule 405.

Super Designated Order Turnaround System The computerized trading and execution system used by the New York Stock Exchange. *Syn.* SuperDot. *Related item(s)*: New York Stock Exchange.

SuperDot *See* Super Designated Order Turnaround System.

supply The total amount of a good or service available for purchase by consumers. *Related item(s)*: demand.

supply-side theory An economic theory holding that bolstering an economy's ability to supply more goods is the most effective way to stimulate economic growth. Supply-side theorists advocate income tax reduction insofar as this increases private investment in corporations, facilities and equipment.

support level A technical analysis term describing the bottom of a stock's historical trading range. *Related item(s)*: breakout; resistance level.

syndicate A group of investment bankers formed to handle the distribution and sale of a security on behalf of the issuer. Each syndicate member is responsible for the sale and distribution of a portion of the issue. *Syn.* underwriting syndicate. *Related item(s)*: Eastern account; Western account.

syndicate manager *See* underwriting manager.

systemic risk The potential for a security to decrease in value owing to its inherent tendency to move together with all securities of the same type. Neither diversification nor any other investment strategy can eliminate this risk. *Related item(s):* market risk.

T

T Consolidated Tape market identifier for trades of exchange-listed securities executed over the counter.

takedown The discount from the public offering price at which a syndicate member buys new issue securities from the syndicate for sale to the public. *Related item(s):* concession.

TAN *See* tax anticipation note.

Tape *See* Consolidated Tape.

taxability The risk of the erosion of investment income through taxation.

taxable gain The portion of a sale or distribution of mutual fund shares subject to taxation.

tax and revenue anticipation note (TRAN) A short-term municipal debt security to be paid off from future tax receipts and revenues.

tax anticipation note (TAN) A short-term municipal or government debt security to be paid off from future tax receipts.

tax basis The amount that a limited partner has invested in a partnership.

tax credit An amount that can be subtracted from a tax liability, often in connection with real estate development, energy conservation and research and development programs. Every dollar of tax credit reduces the amount of tax due, dollar for dollar. *Related item(s):* deduction.

tax-deferred annuity *See* tax-sheltered annuity.

tax-equivalent yield The rate of return a taxable bond must earn before taxes in order to equal the tax-exempt earnings on a municipal bond. This number varies with the investor's tax bracket.

taxes per capita *See* taxes per person.

taxes per person A measure of the tax burden of a municipality's population, calculated by dividing the municipality's tax receipts by its population. *Syn.* taxes per capita.

tax-exempt bond fund A mutual fund whose investment objective is to provide maximum tax-free income. It invests primarily in municipal bonds and short-term debt. *Syn.* tax-free bond fund.

tax-free bond fund *See* tax-exempt bond fund.

tax liability The amount of tax payable on earnings, usually calculated by subtracting standard and itemized deductions and personal exemptions from adjusted gross income, then multiplying by the tax rate. *Related item(s):* adjusted gross income.

tax preference item An element of income that receives favorable tax treatment. The item must be added to taxable income when computing alternative minimum tax. Tax preference items include accelerated depreciation on property, research and development costs, intangible drilling costs, tax-exempt interest on municipal private purpose bonds, and certain incentive stock options. *Related item(s):* alternative minimum tax.

tax-sheltered annuity (TSA) An insurance contract that entitles the holder to exclude all contributions from gross income in the year they are made. Tax payable on the earnings is deferred until the holder withdraws funds at retirement. TSAs are available to employees of public schools, church organizations and other tax-exempt organizations. *Syn.* tax-deferred annuity.

T-bill *See* Treasury bill.

T-bond *See* Treasury bond.

T-call *See* margin call.

TDA *See* tax-sheltered annuity.

technical analysis A method of evaluating securities by analyzing statistics generated by market activity, such as past prices and volume. Technical analysts do not attempt to measure a security's intrinsic value. *Related item(s):* chartist; fundamental analysis.

technician *See* chartist.

Telephone Consumer Protection Act of 1991 (TCPA) Federal legislation restricting the use of telephone lines for solicitation purposes. A company soliciting sales via telephone, facsimile or Email must disclose its name and address to the called party and must not call any person who has requested not to be called.

tenants in common (TIC) A form of joint ownership of an account whereby a deceased tenant's fractional interest in the account is retained by his estate. *Related item(s):* joint tenants with right of survivorship.

tender offer An offer to buy securities for cash or for cash plus securities.

term bond *See* term maturity.

term maturity A repayment schedule for a bond issue in which the entire issue comes due on a single date. *Syn.* term bond. *Related item(s):* maturity date.

testimonial An endorsement of an investment or service by a celebrity or public opinion influencer. The use of testimonials in public communications is regulated by the NASD.

third market The exchange where listed securities are traded in the over-the-counter market.

third-party account (1) A customer account for which the owner has given power of attorney to a third party. (2) A customer account opened by an adult naming a minor as beneficial owner. (3) A customer account opened for another adult. This type of account is prohibited.

30-day visible supply *See* visible supply.

tick A minimum upward or downward movement in the price of a security. *Related item(s):* minus tick; plus tick; plus tick rule.

Ticker Tape *See* Consolidated Tape.

TIGR *See* Treasury Investors Growth Receipt.

time deposit A sum of money left with a bank (or borrowed from a bank and left on deposit) that the depositing customer has agreed not to withdraw for a specified time period or without a specified amount of notice. *Related item(s):* demand deposit.

time spread *See* horizontal spread.

time value The amount an investor pays for an option above its intrinsic value; it reflects the amount of time left until expiration. The amount is calculated by subtracting the intrinsic value from the premium paid. *Related item(s):* intrinsic value.

timing risk The potential for an investor to incur a loss as a result of buying or selling a particular security at an unfavorable time.

T note *See* Treasury note.

tombstone A printed advertisement that solicits indications of interest in a securities offering. The text is limited to basic information about the offering, such as the name of the issuer, type of security, names of the underwriters and where a prospectus is available.

total capitalization The sum of a corporation's long-term debt, stock accounts and capital in excess of par.

trade confirmation A printed document that contains details of a transaction, including the settlement date and amount of money due from or owed to a customer. It must be sent to the customer on or before the settlement date.

trade date The date on which a securities transaction is executed.

trading authorization *See* full trading authorization; limited trading authorization.

trading halt A pause in the trading of a particular security on one or more exchanges, usually in anticipation of a news announcement or to correct an order imbalance. During a trading halt, open orders may be canceled and options may be exercised.

TRAN *See* tax and revenue anticipation note.

tranche One of the classes of securities that form an issue of collateralized mortgage obligations. Each tranche is characterized by its interest rate, average maturity, risk level and sensitivity to mortgage prepayments. Neither the rate of return nor the maturity date of a CMO tranche is guaranteed. *Related item(s):* collateralized mortgage obligation.

transfer agent A person or corporation responsible for recording the names and holdings of registered security owners, seeing that certificates are signed by the appropriate corporate officers, affixing the corporate seal and delivering securities to the new owners.

transfer and hold in safekeeping A securities buy order settlement and delivery procedure whereby the securities bought are transferred to the customer's name, but are held by the broker/dealer. *Related item(s):* hold in street name; transfer and ship.

transfer and ship A securities buy order settlement and delivery procedure whereby the securities bought are transferred to the customer's name and sent to the customer. *Related item(s):* hold in street name; transfer and hold in safekeeping.

Transportation Average *See* Dow Jones Transportation Average.

Treasury bill A marketable US government debt security with a maturity of less than one year. Treasury bills are issued through a competitive bidding process at a discount from par; they have no fixed interest rate. *Syn.* T bill.

Treasury bond A marketable, fixed-interest US government debt security with a maturity of more than 10 years. *Syn.* T bond.

Treasury Bond Receipt (TBR) One of several types of zero-coupon bonds issued by brokerage firms and collateralized by Treasury securities. *Related item(s):* Treasury receipt.

Treasury Investors Growth Receipt (TIGR) One of several types of zero-coupon bonds issued by brokerage firms and collateralized by Treasury securities. *Related item(s):* Treasury receipt.

Treasury note A marketable, fixed-interest US government debt security with a maturity of between 2 and 10 years. *Syn.* T note.

Treasury receipt The generic term for a zero-coupon bond issued by a brokerage firm and collateralized by the Treasury securities a custodian holds in escrow for the investor.

treasury stock Equity securities that the issuing corporation has issued and repurchased from the public at the current market price. *Related item(s):* issued stock; outstanding stock.

trendline A tool used by technical analysts to trace a security's movement by connecting the reaction lows in an upward trend or the rally highs in a downward trend.

triangle On a technical analyst's trading activity chart, a pattern that shows a narrowing of the price range in which a security is trading. The left side of the triangle typically shows the widest range, and the right side narrows to a point. *Syn.* pennant. *Related item(s):* ascending triangle; descending triangle.

trough The end of a period of declining business activity throughout the economy, one of the four stages of the business cycle. *Related item(s):* business cycle.

true interest cost (TIC) A means of evaluating the competitive bids of prospective bond underwriting syndicates. Each syndicate provides a calculation of the coupon interest to be paid by the issuer over the life of the bond, taking into account the time value of money. *Related item(s):* net interest cost.

trust agreement *See* trust indenture.

trustee A person legally appointed to act on a beneficiary's behalf.

trust indenture A legal contract between a corporation and a trustee that represents its bondholders that details the terms of a debt issue. The terms include the rate of interest, maturity date, means of payment and collateral. *Syn.* deed of trust; trust agreement.

Trust Indenture Act of 1939 The legislation requiring that all publicly offered, nonexempt debt securities be registered under the Securities Act of 1933 and be issued under a trust indenture that protects the bondholders.

Trust in Securities Act *See* Securities Act of 1933.

Truth in Securities Act *See* Securities Act of 1933.

TSA *See* tax-sheltered annuity.

12b-1 asset-based fees An Investment Company Act of 1940 provision that allows a mutual fund to collect a fee for the promotion or sale of or another activity connected with the distribution of its shares. The fee must be reasonable (typically ½ percent to 1 percent of net assets managed), up to a maximum of 8.5 percent of the offering price per share.

two-dollar broker An exchange member that executes orders for other member firms when their floor brokers are especially busy. Two-dollar brokers charge a commission for their services; the amount of the commission is negotiated.

type A term that classifies an option as a call or a put. *Related item(s):* class; series.

U

UGMA *See* Uniform Gifts to Minors Act.

UIT *See* unit investment trust.

uncovered *See* naked.

uncovered call writer *See* naked call writer.

uncovered put writer *See* naked put writer.

underlying securities The securities that are bought or sold when an option, right or warrant is exercised.

underwriter An investment banker that works with an issuer to help bring a security to the market and sell it to the public.

underwriting The procedure by which investment bankers channel investment capital from investors to corporations and municipalities that are issuing securities.

underwriting compensation The amount paid to a broker/dealer firm for its involvement in offering and selling securities.

underwriting discount *See* underwriting spread.

underwriting manager The brokerage firm responsible for organizing a syndicate, preparing the issue, negotiating with the issuer and underwriters and allocating stock to the selling group. *Syn.* manager of the syndicate; managing underwriter; syndicate manager. *Related item(s):* agreement among underwriters; syndicate.

underwriting spread The difference in price between the public offering price and the price an underwriter pays to the issuing corporation. The difference represents the profit available to the syndicate or selling group. *Syn.* underwriting discount; underwriting split.

underwriting syndicate *See* syndicate.

undivided account *See* Eastern account.

unearned income Income derived from investments and other sources not related to employment services. Examples of unearned income include interest from a savings account, bond interest and dividends from stock. *Related item(s):* earned income; passive income; portfolio income.

Uniform Gifts to Minors Act (UGMA) Legislation that permits a gift of money or securities to be given to a minor and held in a custodial account that an adult manages for the minor's benefit. Income and capital gains transferred to a minor's name are taxed at a lower rate. *Related item(s):* Uniform Transfers to Minors Act.

Uniform Securities Act (USA) Model legislation for securities industry regulation at the state level. Each state may adopt the legislation in its entirety or it may adapt it (within limits) to suit its needs. *Related item(s):* blue-sky laws; Series 63.

Uniform Transfers to Minors Act (UTMA) Legislation adopted in some states that permits a gift of money or securities to be given to a minor and held in a custodial account that an adult manages for the minor's benefit until the minor reaches a certain age (not necessarily the age of majority). *Related item(s):* Uniform Gifts to Minors Act.

unit A share in the ownership of a direct participation program that entitles the investor to an interest in the program's net income, net loss and distributions.

unit investment trust (UIT) An investment company that sells redeemable shares in a professionally selected portfolio of securities. It is organized under a trust indenture, not a corporate charter. *Related item(s):* fixed unit investment trust; unit of beneficial interest.

unit of beneficial interest A redeemable share in a unit investment trust, representing ownership of an undivided interest in the underlying portfolio. *Syn.* share of beneficial interest. *Related item(s):* unit investment trust.

unit refund annuity An insurance contract in which the insurance company makes monthly payments to the annuitant over the annuitant's lifetime. If the annuitant dies before receiving an amount equal to the account's value, the money remaining in the account goes to the annuitant's named beneficiary.

unqualified legal opinion The statement of a bond counsel affirming the compliance of a new municipal bond issue with municipal statutes and tax regulations, and expressing no reservations about its validity. *Related item(s):* legal opinion of counsel; qualified legal opinion.

unrealized gain The amount by which a security appreciates in value before it is sold. Until it is sold, the investor does not actually possess the sale proceeds. *Related item(s):* realized gain.

unsecured bond *See* debenture.

up tick *See* plus tick.

up tick rule *See* plus tick rule.

USA *See* Uniform Securities Act.

US government and agency bond fund A mutual fund whose investment objective is to provide current income while preserving safety of capital through investing in securities backed by the US Treasury or issued by a government agency.

Utilities Average *See* Dow Jones Utilities Average.

UTMA *See* Uniform Transfers to Minors Act.

Glossary

V

Value Line An investment advisory service that rates hundreds of stocks as to safety, timeliness and projected price performance. *Related item(s):* Value Line Composite Index.

Value Line Composite Index A market index composed of 1,700 exchange and over-the-counter stocks. *Related item(s):* index; Value Line.

variable annuity An insurance contract in which at the end of the accumulation stage, the insurance company guarantees a minimum total payment to the annuitant. The performance of a separate account, generally invested in equity securities, determines the amount of this total payment. *Related item(s):* accumulation stage; annuity; fixed annuity; separate account.

variable-rate demand note *See* variable-rate municipal security.

variable-rate municipal security A short-term municipal debt security issued when either general interest rates are expected to change or the length of time before permanent funding is received is uncertain. *Syn.* variable-rate demand note.

vertical spread The purchase and sale of two options on the same underlying security and with the same expiration date but with different exercise prices. *Syn.* money spread; price spread. *Related item(s):* spread.

vesting (1) An ERISA guideline stipulating that an employee must be entitled to his entire retirement benefits within a certain period of time even if he no longer works for the employer. (2) The amount of time that an employee must work before retirement or before benefit plan contributions made by the employer become the employee's property without penalty. The IRS and the Employee Retirement Income Security Act of 1974 set minimum requirements for vesting in a qualified plan.

visible supply (1) The disclosure, published in *The Bond Buyer*, of the total dollar amount of municipal securities known to be coming to market within the next 30 days. (2) All supplies of goods and commodities that are readily deliverable.

volatility The magnitude and frequency of changes in the price of a security or commodity within a given time period.

volume of trading theory A technical analysis theory holding that the ratio of the number of shares traded to total outstanding shares indicates whether a market is strong or weak.

voluntary accumulation plan A mutual fund account into which the investor commits to depositing amounts on a regular basis in addition to the initial sum invested.

voting right A stockholder's right to vote for members of the board of directors and on matters of corporate policy—particularly the issuance of senior securities, stock splits and substantial changes in the corporation's business. A variation of this right is extended to variable annuity contract holders and mutual fund shareholders, who may vote on material policy issues.

W

warrant A security that gives the holder the right to purchase securities from the warrant issuer at a stipulated subscription price. Warrants are usually long-term instruments, with expiration dates years in the future.

wash sale Selling a security at a loss for tax purposes and, within 30 days before or after, purchasing the same or a substantially identical security. The IRS disallows the claimed loss. *Related item(s):* bond swap.

Western account A securities underwriting in which the agreement among underwriters states that each syndicate member will be liable only for the sale of the portion of the issue allocated to it. *Syn.* divided account. *Related item(s):* Eastern account; syndicate.

when-, as- and if-issued security *See* when issued security.

when issued contract A trade agreement regarding a security that has been authorized but is not yet physically available for delivery. The seller agrees to make delivery as soon as the security is ready, and the contract includes provisions for marking the price to the market and for calculating accrued interest.

when issued security (WI) A securities issue that has been authorized and is sold to investors before the certificates are ready for delivery. Typically, such securities include new issue municipal bonds, stock splits and Treasury securities. *Syn.* when-, as- and if-issued security.

WI *See* when issued security.

wildcatting *See* exploratory drilling program.

Wilshire 5,000 Equity Index A value-weighted market indicator composed of 5,000 exchange-listed and over-the-counter common stocks. It is the broadest measure of the market. *Related item(s):* index.

wire room *See* order department.

workable indication The price at which a municipal securities dealer is willing to purchase securities from another municipal dealer. The price may be revised if market conditions change.

working capital A measure of a corporation's liquidity; that is, its ability to transfer assets into cash to meet current short-term obligations. It is calculated by subtracting total current liabilities from total current assets.

working capital ratio *See* current ratio.

working interest An operating interest in a mineral-bearing property entitling the holder to a share of income from production and carrying the obligation to bear a corresponding share of all production costs.

workout quote A qualified quotation whereby a broker/dealer estimates the price on a trade that will require special handling owing to its size or to market conditions. *Related item(s):* bona fide quote; firm quote; nominal quote; subject quote.

writer The seller of an option contract. An option writer takes on the obligation to buy or sell the underlying security if and when the option buyer exercises the option. *Syn.* seller.

writing a scale The process by which a syndicate establishes the yield for each maturity in a new serial bond issue in order to arrive at its competitive bid. *Related item(s):* scale.

Y

Yellow Sheets A daily publication compiled by the National Quotation Bureau and containing interdealer wholesale quotations for over-the-counter corporate bonds. *Related item(s):* Pink Sheets.

yield The rate of return on an investment, usually expressed as an annual percentage rate. *Related item(s):* current yield; dividend yield; nominal yield.

yield-based option A security representing the right to receive, in cash, the difference between the current yield of an underlying US government security and the strike price of the option. A yield-based option is used to speculate on or hedge against the risk associated with fluctuating interest rates; its strike price represents the anticipated yield of the underlying debt security.

yield curve A graphic representation of the actual or projected yields of fixed-income securities in relation to their maturities. *Related item(s):* flat yield curve; inverted yield curve.

yield to call (YTC) The rate of return on a bond that accounts for the difference between the bond's acquisition cost and its proceeds, including interest income, calculated to the earliest date that the bond may be called by the issuing corporation. *Related item(s):* bond yield.

yield to maturity (YTM) The rate of return on a bond that accounts for the difference between the bond's acquisition cost and its maturity proceeds, including interest income. *Related item(s):* bond yield.

YTC *See* yield to call.

YTM *See* yield to maturity.

Z

zero-coupon bond A corporate or municipal debt security traded at a deep discount from face value. The bond pays no interest; rather, it may be redeemed at maturity for its full face value. It may be issued at a discount, or it may be stripped of its coupons and repackaged.

zero-minus tick A security transaction's execution price that is equal to the price of the last sale but lower than the last different price. *Related item(s):* minus tick; plus tick; zero-plus tick.

zero-plus tick A security transaction's execution price that is equal to the price of the last sale but higher than the last different price. *Related item(s):* minus tick; plus tick; plus tick rule; zero-minus tick.

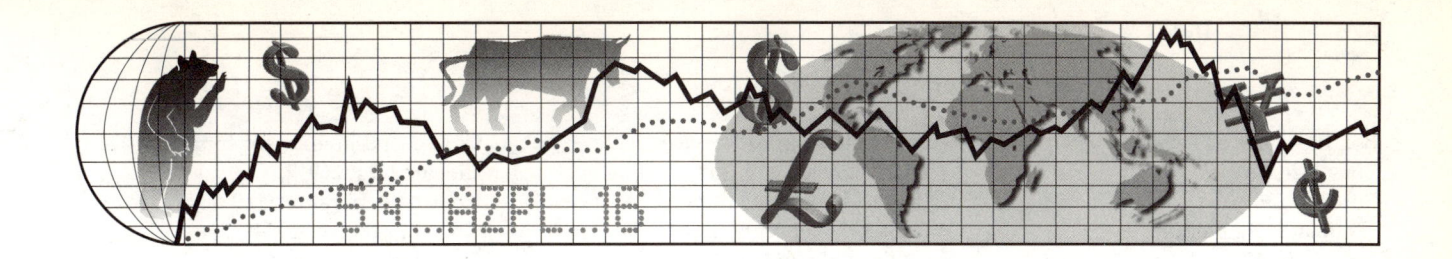

Index

Numerics
5 Percent Markup Policy, **430**
90-second reporting, **435**

A
Acceptance, waiver and consent (AWC), **728**
Account
    cash, **290**
    combined, **343**
    corporate, **297**
    custodial, **297**
    discretionary, **299**
    fiduciary, **297**
    joint, **296**
    margin, **290**, **315**
    MSRB requirements, **293**
    multiple, **291**
    NASD requirements, **292**
    new, **286**
    numbered, **291**
    NYSE requirements, **292**
    other brokers' employee's, **292**
    partnership, **296**
    prohibited, **382**
    record, **292**
    registration, **295**
    restricted, **324**
    retirement, **291**
    single, **295**, **301**
    special situations, **291**
    transfer, **291**
    types of, **295**
    Uniform Gifts to Minors Act (UGMA), **301**, **302**
Account executive's number, **451**

Account number, **451**
Accounts payable, **626**
Accounts receivable, **625**
Accredited investor, **575**
Accrued interest, **461**, **674**
Accrued taxes, **626**
Accrued wages payable, **626**
Accumulation phase, **557**
Accumulation plan, **512**
Accumulation unit, **557**
Active and passive management, **670**
Active market, **424**
Ad valorem tax, **152**
Additional disclosure, **487**
Additional issue, **365**
Adjustment, **265**
Advance, **616**
Advertising, **360**, **738**
Aftermarket sales, **361**
Agency issue, **83**, **674**
Agency security fund, **492**
Agency transaction, **165**
Agent, **403**
All or none order (AON), **372**, **417**
Allocation priority, **147**
Alpha, **669**
Alternative minimum tax, **674**, **684**
Alternative order, **417**
American Depositary Receipts, **33**
American Stock Exchange, **421**
American style, **190**
Amount, **451**
Analysis, **601**
Annuitization, **557**
Annuity phase, **557**
Annuity unit, **557**
Antireciprocal rule, **163**

Approval, **290**, **499**
Arbitration, **726**, **737**
Assessments, **718**
Asset, **380**, **625**
Asset allocation, **669**
Asset allocation fund, **491**
Asset-based fee, **498**
Assignment, **463**
Assumed interest rate, **558**
At-the-money, **198**, **200**
At-the-open order, **417**
Auction market, **401**
Automatic exercise, **262**
Average basis, **509**
Awarding the issue, **144**
Awards, **732**

B
Backdating, **501**
Back-end load, **498**
Backing away, **428**
Balance of payment, **612**
Balance sheet, **624**, **628**
Balanced fund, **491**
Bankers' acceptance, **101**
Basic earnings per share, **637**
Basis, **508**
Basis of compensation, **167**
Bearish breakout, **619**
Beneficial owner, **317**
Beneficiary, **541**
Best effort, **372**
Best execution, **165**
Beta, **664**, **669**
Bid, **427**
Blind pool, **594**
Blue-skying, **365**

825

Index

Board of directors, 483
Bona fide, 161
Bond, 44, 365
    bank eligible, 140
    basis, 49
    bearer, 46
    book-entry, 47
    calling, 52
    collateral trust, 67
    contract, 134
    convertible, 71
    corporate, 66, 71, 109
    coupon, 46
    double-barreled, 126
    General Obligation, 151
    guaranteed, 68
    income, 68
    Industrial Development Revenue (IDR), 128
    lease rental, 129
    moral obligation, 130
    mortgage, 66
    municipal, 122
    New Housing Authority (NHA), 129
    New York Stock Exchange (NYSE), 71
    premium, 47
    prior lien, 67
    put, 55
    rating, 157
    revenue, 154
    secured, 66
    special assessment, 129
    special tax, 129
    treasury, 81
    unsecured, 68
    yield, 56, 58
    zero-coupon, 69
Bond certificate, 46
Bond delivery, 151
Bond discount, 47
Bond fund, 492
Bond interest, 44
Bond issuer, 44
Bond par, 47
Bond ratio, 635
Bond redemption, 630
Bond yield, 50
Bondholders, 44
Book value, 5, 637
Borrowing, 652
Bought, 451
Breakeven, 198, 200
Breakpoint, 500, 651
Broker, 398
Broker loan rate, 103
Broker's broker, 163
Brokerage support services, 447
Broker-dealer, 317, 398
Broker-dealer registration, 719
Broker-dealer regulations, 163
Bullish breakout, 619
Business cycle, 602
Buy stop order, 409
Buyer, 193, 214
Buying power, 327

C

Calendar spread, 235
Call, 191, 209, 210, 244
    covered, 225
    effects of, 53
    long, 191
    money rate, 104
    premium, 52
    protection, 53
    provision, 154
    short, 191
Call risk, 663
Cancellation, 503
Capacity, 452
Capital asset pricing model (CAPM), 668
Capital gain, 506, 675
Capital growth, 583, 659
Capital in excess of par, 628
Capital market financing, 365
Capital risk, 662
Capital stock at par, 627
Capital structure, 629
Capitalization, 628
Capitalization ratio, 635
Capped index option, 253
Capping, 655
Carried interest, 591
Cash and equivalents, 625
Cash flow, 583, 592
Cash settlement, 456
Cash trade, 27
Cashiering department, 448
CD rate, 104
Centralized management, 574
Certificate negotiability, 463
Certificate of deposit, 102
Certificate of limited partnership, 575
Charges, 454
Charting stocks, 616
Chicago Board of Options Exchange (CBOE), 263
Chinese wall, 702
Circuit breaker, 402
Class, 190
Clerical personnel, 721
Closed-end fund, 492, 498
Closed-end investment company, 476
Closing, 221, 269
Code of Arbitration, 719, 731
Code of procedure, 719, 726
Coincident indicator, 605
Collateralized Mortgage Obligation, 89
Collection ratio, 156
Combination, 234, 249
Combination fund, 490
Combination privilege, 502
Combined distribution, 366
Commercial paper, 102, 104
Commission, 164, 451, 720, 736
Commission house broker, 400
Common stock, 3
common stock, 3
Common stock ratio, 635
Communication, 541
Compensation, 737
Competing facilities, 154
Competitive bid, 137, 370
Conduct rules, 718
Conduit theory, 506
Confidentiality, 653
Confirmation, 151, 165, 166, 453
Conflict of interest, 167
Consolidated Tape, 396, 423
Consolidation, 380, 617
Constant dollar plan, 668
Constant dollars, 604
Constant ratio plan, 668
Consumer Price Index (CPI), 604
Contemporaneous cost, 432
Contested offer, 727
Continuing education, 720
Continuity of life, 574
Continuous public offering security, 481
Contract, 190, 258
Contracting, 602
Convertible security, 72, 402, 630
Coordination, 358, 706
Corporate analysis, 624
Corporate bond, 91, 674
Corporate book inspection, 9
Corporate debt, 51
Corporate officer, 721
Corporate retirement plan, 538
Corporate tax, 684
Cost, 494
Cost basis, 510, 675
Coterminous, 125
Coverage ratio, 156
Credit, 316, 395
Credit agreement, 317
Credit call spread, 238
Credit department, 448
Credit put spread, 241

Credit register (CR), **337**
Credit risk, **663**
Criminal penalty, **654**
Crossing orders, **406**
Currency risk, **33**
Current assets, **625**
Current income, **658**
Current long-term debt, **626**
Current yield, **20, 56, 638**
CUSIP number, **21, 451**
Custodian, **302, 484**
Custodian bank, **33**
Customer
    death, **300**
Customer account, **163**
Customer account statement, **453**
Customer services agent, **485**
Cyclical industry, **622**

D

Dated date, **90**
Day order, **416, 417**
Dealer, **398**
Dealer paper, **102**
Death
    customer, **300**
Death of a minor, **303**
Death of an account holder, **300**
Debenture, **68**
Debit call spread, **236**
Debit put spread, **241**
Debit register (DR), **322**
Debt limit, **152**
Debt per capita ratio, **156**
Debt ratio, **156**
Debt retirement, **51**
Debt service account, **155**
Debt service ratio, **637**
Debt service reserve fund, **155**
Debt statement, **153**
Debt trend ratio, **156**
Debt-to-equity ratio, **635**
Declaration, **631**
Declaration date, **26**
Decline, **616**
Decreased income, **12**
Deduction, **592**
Defensive industry, **622**
Deferring a decision, **209, 214**
Defined benefit, **538**
Defined contribution, **538**
Deflation, **604**
Delisting, **400**
Delivery, **449**
Delivery instructions, **289**
Denomination, **97**
Department of enforcement, **727**

Depletion, **592**
Depletion allowance, **586**
Depreciation, **592, 628**
Depression, **602**
Description, **451**
Designated order, **147**
Developmental, **587**
Diagonal spread, **236**
Digits & vol deleted, **424**
Direct paper, **102**
Direct participation program, **571, 741**
Disciplinary action, **721**
Disciplinary hearing, **737**
Disclosure, **144, 164, 165, 300, 432, 452, 453, 742**
Discount rate, **103, 104, 610**
Discretionary authority, **299**
Disintermediation, **612**
Disproportionate sharing, **591**
Distribution, **506**
District, **718**
Diversification, **477, 659, 667, 668**
Diversifying holdings, **209**
Dividend, **19, 28, 329, 630**
    cash, **19**
    stock, **19**
    yield, **20**
Dividend department, **26, 448**
Dividend distribution, **26, 506**
Dividend exclusion, **684**
Dividend income, **674**
Dividend payout ratio, **638**
Dividend record date, **27**
Dividends per share, **638**
Do not reduce (DNR) order, **415**
Dollar amount, **431**
Dollar bond, **160**
Dollar cost averaging, **512, 668**
Don't know procedure, **460**
Donating securities, **301, 682**
Double auction market, **401**
Dow theory, **619**
Dual-purpose fund, **492**
Due bill, **28**
Due diligence, **143, 360**
Duration, **665**

E

Earned income, **673**
Earnings per share (EPS), **634, 637**
Eastern account, **142**
Economic indicator, **604**
Economic justification, **154**
Economic viability, **592**
Economics, **601**
Education IRA, **531**
Effective date, **367**

Efficient market theory, **620**
Employment contract, **651**
Equipment leasing program, **591**
Equipment trust certificate, **67**
Equity (EQ), **322, 337**
Erroneous report, **451**
Estate tax, **683**
Ethics, **647**
Eurocurrency, **106**
Eurodollar, **106**
European style, **190**
Eurosecurity, **107**
Excess equity, **326, 327, 328, 329, 340**
Excess reserves, **610**
Excessive trading, **651**
Exchange rate, **107**
Exchanges, **510**
Ex-date, **27**
Ex-dividend date, **26, 507**
Execution, **409, 450**
Exempt issuer, **376**
Exempt security, **376**
Exempt transaction, **376**
Exemption, **70**
Exercise, **191, 252, 269**
Existing property, **585**
Expansion, **602**
Expense ratio, **494**
Expiration, **191, 252, 258, 261, 269**
Exploratory program, **587**
Extension, **457**

F

Face-amount certificate company, **474**
Fail to deliver, **464**
Failure to act, **732**
Fair dealing, **650**
Family of funds, **502**
Federal Farm Credit Bank, **85**
Federal funds, **611**
Federal funds rate, **103, 610**
Federal Home Loan Mortgage
    Corporation (Freddie Mac), **85**
Federal National Mortgage Association
    (Fannie Mae), **86**
Federal Open Market Committee
    (FOMC), **610**
Federal Reserve Board, **609**
Fidelity bond, **700**
Fiduciary responsibility, **302**
Filing, **358, 706**
Filing requirement, **741**
Fill or kill (FOK) order, **417**
Filling an order, **399**
Final prospectus, **360**
Financial adviser, **167**
Financial leverage, **630**

Financial report, 486
Financial statement, 395, 624
Fingerprinting, 716
Firewall, 702
Firm commitment, 144, 371
Firm element, 720
Firm quote, 427
First In, First Out, 509
Fixed assets, 625
Fixed dollar, 513
Fixed percentage, 513
Fixed public offering price, 430
Fixed rate, 16
Fixed share, 513
Fixed time, 513
Floor broker, 263
Flow of funds, 154, 155
Foreign associate, 721
Foreign currency market, 106
Foreign currency option, 257
Foreign security, 33, 675
Foreign stock fund, 491
Forward pricing, 497
Front-end load, 498
Front-running, 655
Frozen account, 458
Full faith and credit issue, 125
Functional allocation, 591
Fund yield, 507
Fundamental analysis, 622
Funding, 541

G

General obligation issue, 125
General partner, 580
General securities principal license (Series 24), 722
General securities representative license (Series 7), 722
Generic advertising (Rule 135a), 739
Gift tax, 683
Glass-Steagall Act of 1933, 140
Good delivery, 461, 462
Good till canceled order, 416, 417
Government agency issue, 50
Government assisted housing, 585
Government National Mortgage Association (Ginnie Mae), 84
Gross domestic product (GDP), 602
Group net order, 147
Growth fund, 490
Growth industry, 623
Growth portfolio managers, 670

H

Head and shoulders bottom, 618
Hearing, 729

Historic rehabilitation, 586
Hold, 290
House minimum, 325
Hypothecation, 317, 346

I

Immediate or cancel order, 417
Inactively traded stock, 431
Income, 588
Income fund, 490
Income statement, 633
Income tax, 672
Increasing return, 210, 214
Indenture, 134
    closed-end, 67
    open-end, 67
Index, 616
Index arbitrage, 401
Index fund, 490
Index option, 251
Individual retirement account, 528
Individual retirement account (IRA) rollovers, 530
Industry analysis, 622
Industry standard, 373
Inflation, 662
Informer bounty, 702
Inherited securities, 682
Initial requirements, 320
Initiation of proceedings, 731
Inside market, 436
Insider Trading and Securities Fraud Enforcement Act of 1988, 701
Intangible drilling costs (IDCs), 586
Interbank Market, 107
Interest expense, 633
Interest income, 673
Interest rate, 103, 612
Interest rate comparison, 157
Interest rate option, 257
Interest rate risk, 662
Interest rate summary, 103
Interest-Only CMO (IO), 96
Intermarket Trading System (ITS), 422
Internal rate of return, 592
International market, 422
In-the-money, 198, 200
Intrastate offering, 378
Intrinsic value, 198, 200, 206
Inventory, 431, 625
Inverse relationship, 61
Inverted head and shoulders, 618
Investigation, 726
Investment adviser, 484
Investment Advisers Act of 1940, 699
Investment banking, 364
Investment company, 741

Investment Company Act of 1940, 698
Investment company products, 473
Investment company security, 515
Investment fund, 489
Investment grade, 49
Investment objective, 489
Issuance, 29
Issuer, 123, 365
Issuing security, 630

J

Joint life with last survivor, 561
Joint Tenants with Right of Survivorship (JTWROS), 296
Junior security, 10

K

KEOGH (HR-10) plan, 535
Keynesian theory, 606
Know your customer rule, 658

L

Laffer curve, 607
Lagging indicator, 605
Last-in, first-out (LIFO), 564
Late receipt of information, 27
Leading indicator, 604
Legal opinion, 135
Legal recourse, 754
Legal transfer, 463
Legend stock, 378
Legislative risk, 664
Lending, 652
Letter of intent, 500, 501
Letter stock, 378
Level 1, 434
Level 2, 434
Level 3, 434
Leverage, 316, 635
Liabilities, 626
Life income option, 561
Life with period certain, 561
Limit order, 407, 408
Limited liability, 9
Limited ownership, 17
Limited partnership, 572, 575, 580
Limited principal license, 722
Liquidation, 68
Liquidity, 51, 97, 100, 628, 659
Liquidity ratio, 636
Liquidity risk, 663
Listed option, 261
Loan, 346
Loan consent form, 317
Loan value, 329
Location, 396, 397
Locking in a stock price, 210

Index

Long margin accounting, 322
Long market value (LMV), 322
Long sale, 418
Long straddle, 247
Long-term Equity AnticiPation Securities (LEAPS), 191
Long-term liability, 626
Loss, 675
Low priority, 12

M

M1, 609
M2, 609
M3, 609
Mailing instructions, 290
Maintenance, 155
Maintenance call, 325, 340
Maintenance requirement, 324
Maloney Act, 698
Management investment company, 475
Manager's fee, 373
Manipulative devices, 649
Margin, 482
Margin accounting, 322
Margin call, 321
Margin department, 448
Margin expenses, 683
Margin requirement, 337
Market
    exchange, 396
    fourth, 396
    inside, 397
    listed, 396
    over-the-counter, 396, 397
    securities, 395
    third (OTC-listed), 396
Market arbitrage, 402
Market attitude, 193, 196
Market average, 616
Market breadth, 616
Market maker, 263, 396, 402, 426
Market maker report, 435
Market order, 407
Market risk, 12, 663
Market value, 5, 326
Marketability, 374
Marketability risk, 663
Marketing, 496
Market-on-close order, 417
Market-out clause, 371
Marking to the market, 322
Markup, 164, 432
Matching, 655
Maturity
    agency issue, 83
    balloon, 45, 124
    serial, 45, 123

    T bill, 80
    T note, 80
    term, 45, 123
    Treasury bond, 81
Maturity structure, 123
Maturity value, 17
Maximum gain, 210, 214
Maximum loss, 214
Mediation, 732
Member firm, 736
Member order, 148
Merger, 380
Mini-max, 372
Minimum maintenance, 324
Minor Rule Violation (MRV), 728
Misrepresentation, 652
Missing coupon, 462
Modern portfolio theory, 620, 668
Monetarist theory, 607
Monetary policy, 608
Money, 608
Money market, 100
Money market financing, 365
Money-market fund, 492
Multiplier, 252
Municipal bond, 91
Municipal bond analysis, 157
Municipal bond insurance, 157
Municipal issue, 50, 125
Municipal note, 132
Municipal securities, 44
Municipal Securities Rulemaking Board (MSRB), 171
Municipal security, 674, 684
Municipal trading, 160
Munifacts, 139
Mutual fund, 477, 488, 496

N

N1-A prospectus, 481
NASD CUSIP regulations, 467
Nasdaq
    national market stocks, 25
Nasdaq National Market (NNM), 25
Nasdaq quotation service, 434
National Association of Securities Dealers (NASD), 423, 717
Negotiability, 21
Negotiable CD, 103
Negotiated market, 426
Negotiated underwriting, 137, 370
Net amount, 451
Net asset value (NAV), 497
Net debt to assessed valuation ratio, 156
Net debt to estimated valuation ratio, 156

Net direct debt, 153
Net gain, 509
Net income after taxes, 633
Net investment income, 506
Net loss, 509
Net operating profits interest, 590
Net overall debt, 153
Net revenue pledge, 155
Net tangible asset value, 637
Net total debt, 153
Network A, 423
Network B, 423
New construction, 584
New issue, 356, 365
New York Stock Exchange (NYSE), 399, 735
New York Stock Exchange SuperDot, 422
No-load terminology, 499
Nominal owner, 317
Nominal quote, 429
Nominal yield, 56
Nondiscrimination, 541
Nondiversification, 477
Nonequity option, 251
Nonnegotiable CD, 102
Nonqualified retirement plan, 526
Nonrecourse loan, 576
Nonrequired cash deposit, 329
Non-targeted material, 743
Normal investment practice, 383
Not held order, 417
Notes payable, 626
Notification, 358, 649, 706
Numbered account, 653

O

Obligation, 191
Obligation to buy, 191
Obligation to sell, 191
Odd-lot theory, 620
Offer, 427
Offer of settlement, 727
Offering size, 374
Offerings, 365
Official notice of sale, 138
Official statement, 134, 153
Oil and gas partnership, 586
Open-end company, 480
Open-end fund, 498
Open-end investment company, 477
Open-market operations, 610
Operating income, 633
Operations, 155
Option, 189, 261, 741
option
    sales personnel, 723

Option agreement, 264
Option exercise, 218
Option premium, 206
Option transaction, 209
Options Clearing Corporation (OCC), 263
Options disclosure document, 264
Order allocation, 147
Order book, 403
Order book official, 263
Order department, 448
Order memorandum, 449
Order period, 147
Order room, 448
Order routing system, 263, 422
Order ticket, 449
Out-of-the-money, 198, 200
Outside business (independent) activity, 649
Overdelivery, 462
Overlapping debt, 125, 153
Overriding royalty interest, 590
Over-the-Counter (OTC) market, 425
Ownership rights, 6

P

Painting the tape, 654
Par value, 5
Parity, 74, 401
Partial delivery, 462
Participation, 540
Partnership agreement, 575, 576
Passive income, 574, 673
Passive loss, 574
Pass-through certificate, 85
Payable date, 27
Payment, 151
Payment instructions, 289
Payment method, 289
Peak, 602
Penalties, 738
Penny Stock Cold Calling Rules, 704
Performance, 493
Periodic payment plan, 745
Planned Amortization Class CMO (PAC), 96
Pledging, 347
Plus tick, 419
Portfolio income, 673
Portfolio insurance, 254
Portfolio management, 667
Portfolio turnover, 494
Position limit, 262
Position trading, 398
Power of attorney, 289, 298
Precedence, 401
Preemptive right, 9

Preferred stock, 3
Preferred stock ratio, 635
Pre-hearing conference, 728
Premium, 257
Prepaid expenses, 625
Prerefunding, 54
Presale order, 147
Preservation of capital, 658
Price, 73, 451
Price dynamic, 396, 397
Price level, 604
Price spread, 235
Price volatility, 669
Price-earnings ratio, 638
Pricing, 47, 367, 496
    T bill, 80
    T note, 81
    Treasury bond, 81
Pricing system, 396, 397
Primary earnings per share, 637
Primary offering, 366
Prime rate, 103, 104
Principal, 403
Principal capacity, 372
Principal transaction, 164
Principal-Only CMO (PO), 95
Priority, 401
Private placement, 366, 377
Private placement memorandum, 575
Private purpose bond, 674
Private transaction, 649
Proceeds transaction, 431
Processing orders, 448
Program trading, 401
Prospectus, 486
Protection, 209, 210, 214, 224
Protective covenant, 70, 128
Proxy, 8, 448, 459
Public offering, 366
Public offering requirements, 481
Purchases and sales department, 448
Put, 191, 213, 214, 244
    covered, 226
    long, 191
    short, 191

Q

Qualification, 358, 707
Qualified institutional buyer, 380
Qualified quote, 428
Quantity, 451
Quick asset, 636
Quotation, 160, 162, 427
Quotation size, 429
Quotation spread, 429
Quote, 404, 427
Quote machine, 437

R

Random walk theory, 620
Rating, 48
Ratio, 73
Ratio call, 227
Raw land, 584
Real Estate Investment Trust (REIT), 34
Real estate partnership, 583
Receipt, 449
Recession, 602
Reciprocal dealing, 163
Reclassification, 380
Recognized quotation, 428
Recommendation, 163, 647, 742
Record date, 27
Recourse loan, 576
Redemption, 51, 503
Reducing order, 414
Refunding, 54
Reg T, 324
Reg T payment, 457
Regional exchanges, 422
Registered, 46
Registered owner, 34
Registered principal, 722
Registered representative, 722
Registered trader, 400
Registration, 394, 480, 737
    associated person, 719
Regressive tax, 672
Regular way settlement, 456
Regulation A, 377
Regulation D, 377
Regulation T, 317
Regulatory element, 720
Reinvestment of distributions, 507
Reinvestment risk, 663
Renewal and replacement fund, 155
Reorganization department, 448
Repeat prices omitted, 424
Repurchase agreement, 101
Research report, 652
Reserve maintenance fund, 155
Reserve requirement, 611
Reset date, 16
Residual claims to assets, 10
Resistance level, 618
Restricted, 378
Restricted equity, 340
Retained earnings, 628, 634
Retirement plan, 525
Return, 19
Revenue bond, 127
Revenue source, 154
Reversal, 617
Reverse repurchase agreement, 101
Reverse split, 10

Reversionary working interest, **590**
Right, **191**
Right to buy, **191**
Right to sell, **191**
Rights agent, **31**
Rights of accumulation, **500**, **501**
Risk, **662**
Risk arbitrage, **402**
Riskless and simultaneous transaction, **431**
Roth IRA, **531**
Rule 144, **378**
Rule 144a, **380**
Rule 145, **380**
Rule 147, **378**
Rule 415, **366**
Rule G-1, **172**
Rule G-10, **173**
Rule G-11, **173**
Rule G-12, **173**
Rule G-13, **174**
Rule G-15, **174**
Rule G-16, **174**
Rule G-17, **175**
Rule G-18, **175**
Rule G-19, **175**
Rule G-2, **172**
Rule G-20, **175**
Rule G-21, **175**
Rule G-22, **175**
Rule G-24, **176**
Rule G-25, **176**
Rule G-27, **176**
Rule G-28, **176**
Rule G-29, **176**
Rule G-3, **172**
Rule G-30, **177**
Rule G-31, **177**
Rule G-32, **177**
Rule G-33, **177**
Rule G-37, **177**
Rule G-39, **177**
Rule G-6, **173**
Rule G-7, **173**

S

Safety, **100**
Sale date, **163**
Sales charge, **497**
Sales charge percentage, **499**
Sales load, **494**
Sanctions, **729**
SEC registration, **481**
Secondary offering, **366**
Sector fund, **490**
Securities Act of 1933, **356**, **376**, **381**

Securities Acts Amendments of 1975, **701**
Securities and Exchange Commission, **361**, **394**, **716**
Securities Exchange Act of 1934, **356**, **381**, **394**, **696**
Securities Investor Protection Corporation (SIPC), **699**
Security
 agency, **79**
 debt, **43**
 equity, **1**, **2**
 exempt, **319**
 issuing, **355**
 marginable, **318**
 money market, **100**
 municipal, **121**, **137**, **151**, **171**, **178**
 registration, **134**, **357**
 safety, **50**
 tracking, **22**, **109**
 U.S. government, **50**, **79**
 zero-coupon municipal, **166**
Self-Regulatory Organizations, **717**
Self-supporting debt, **153**
Sell order ticket, **420**
Sell stop order, **409**
Seller's option contract, **456**
Selling away, **649**
Selling concession, **145**, **373**, **374**
Selling dividends, **507**, **651**
Selling group, **369**
Selling price, **431**
Separate Trading of Registered Interest and Principal of Securities (STRIPS), **82**
Series, **46**, **190**
Series 27, **723**
Series 4, **722**
Series 53, **723**
Series 8, **723**
Series 8 (Sales Supervisor), **723**
Settlement, **261**, **727**
Settlement date, **451**
Settlement dates and terms, **456**
Share identification, **509**
Shared account, **653**
Shareholders' equity, **627**
Shareholders' right to vote, **482**
Sharing arrangement, **590**
Shelf offering, **366**
Short against the box, **683**
Short interest theory, **620**
Short market value (SMV), **337**
Short sale, **337**, **418**
Short straddle, **248**
Shorting bonds, **420**
Short-term capital gain, **269**
Signature, **463**

Signature guarantee, **463**
Signature requirement, **463**
Simplified arbitration, **732**
Simplified employee pension plans (SEPs), **532**
Simplified Employee Pensions (SEP-IRAs), **532**
Sinking fund, **52**
Size, **405**, **429**
Small offering, **377**
Sold, **451**
Special Memorandum Account (SMA), **327**, **345**
Special situation fund, **490**
Special situation stock, **623**
Specialist, **400**, **402**
Specialized fund, **490**
Specified program, **594**
Speculating, **108**
Speculation, **209**, **210**, **213**, **214**, **660**
Split, **28**
Split offering, **366**
Spot check, **741**
Spread, **234**, **427**, **429**
Spread breakdown, **145**
Stabilizing, **367**
Standard deviation, **665**
Standby underwriting, **31**, **371**
State registration, **358**, **721**
Statute of limitations, **733**, **754**
 arbitration, **733**
Statutory disqualification, **723**
Stock, **365**
 adjustable-rate preferred, **16**
 approval, **29**
 authorized, **3**
 benefits, **11**
 callable preferred, **18**
 certificate, **20**
 common, **11**
 convertible preferred, **18**
 cumulative preferred, **17**
 dividend, **73**
 exchange-listed, **23**
 growth, **11**
 income, **11**
 issued, **4**
 long, **11**
 nonvoting common, **9**
 offering, **29**
 outstanding, **4**
 over-the-counter (Non-Nasdaq), **24**
 participating preferred, **18**
 preferred, **16**, **17**
 rights, **29**
 risks, **12**
 sale, **329**

short, **11**
split, **10, 73**
straight, **17**
treasury, **4**
types of, **3**
value, **5**
warrant, **31**
Stock ahead, **408**
Stock fund, **490**
Stock holding period, **270**
Stock market, **611**
Stock record department, **448**
Stock split, **416, 630**
Stop limit order, **407, 410**
Stop order, **407, 408**
Stopping stock, **405**
Straddle, **234, 247**
Strategy, **258**
Street name, **317**
Strike price, **257**
Subject quote, **428**
Subordinated debenture, **68**
Subscription agreement, **575, 576**
Subscription right, **29**
Suitability, **97**
Summary prospectus, **481**
Supply side economics, **607**
Support level, **618**
Surplus fund, **155**
Syndicate, **367, 369**
Syndicate account, **142, 145**
Syndicate agreement, **141**
Syndicate bid, **143**
Syndicate contract, **141**
Syndicate letter, **141**
Syndicate manager fee, **145, 373**
Syndicator, **575**
Systematic risk, **254, 663**

T

Takedown, **145**
Targeted Amortization Class CMO (TAC), **96**
Targeted material, **743**
Tax, **659**
Tax basis, **593**
Tax benefit, **122**
Tax bracket, **673**
Tax consequence, **365**
Tax credit, **593**
Tax deduction, **584**
Tax preference, **684**
Tax rules, **269**
Taxable on receipt, **675**

Taxation, **69, 97, 160, 170, 303, 494, 506, 508, 510, 563, 647**
   agency issue, **84**
   GNMA certificates, **85**
Taxes per person ratio, **156**
Tax-exempt bond fund, **492**
Tax-exempt commercial paper, **102**
Tax-free bond fund, **492**
Technical analysis, **615**
Technical market theory, **619**
Tender offer, **55**
Termination, **499, 721**
Testimonials, **746**
The Bond Buyer, **138**
Time spread, **235**
Time value, **206**
Time-sensitive order, **416**
Timing risk, **662**
Tombstones (Rule 134 Advertisements), **740**
Total debt, **153**
Trade confirmation, **451**
Trade date, **451**
Trade settlement, **449**
Trading, **258, 261, 393**
Trading authorization, **289**
Trading halt, **397**
Trading hours, **396**
Trading post, **403**
Trading volume, **616**
Tranche, **94**
Transaction, **449**
Transfer, **290, 380**
Transfer agent, **21, 485**
Transfer of ownership, **20**
Transfer procedure, **21**
Treasury bill, **80, 111**
Treasury bond, **111**
Treasury note, **80, 111**
Treasury receipt, **82**
Trend, **616**
Trigger, **409**
Trust indenture, **70**
Trust Indenture Act of 1939, **356, 698**
Trustee, **70**
Two-dollar broker, **400**

U

U.S. government fund, **492**
U.S. government security, **674**
Uncontested offer, **727**
Underdelivery, **462**
Underwriter, **365, 485**
Underwriter's counsel, **136**
Underwriting, **364, 369, 370**

   compensation, **373**
Underwriting fee, **373**
Underwriting manager, **369**
Underwriting risks, **371**
Underwriting sequence, **367**
Underwriting syndicate, **141**
Uniform practice code, **718**
Unit Investment Trust, **474**
Unregistered, **378**
Unsuitable trade, **662**

V

Valuation, **108**
Valuation ratio, **637**
Value portfolio managers, **671**
Valuing fund shares, **508**
Variable annuity, **549**
Variable rate municipal, **132**
Vertical spread, **235**
Vesting, **541**
Volume report, **435**
Voluntary accumulation plan, **512**
Voting
   calculating, **7**
   cumulative, **7**
   statutory, **7**
Voting rights, **6**

W

Warrants, **29**
Wash sale, **676**
Western account, **142**
When-, As- and If-Issued Contracts, **457**
Wildcatting, **587**
Wire room, **448**
Withdrawal plan, **513, 514**
Withholding tax, **509**
Working capital, **636**
Workout quote, **428**
Worksheet, **141**
Wrap account, **699**
Writer, **193**

Y

Yield, **97, 451**
Yield curve, **61**
Yield to call, **59**

Z

Zero-Coupon Bond, **69**
Zero-Coupon Municipal Securities, **166**
Zeros, **69**
Zero-Tranche CMO, **96**

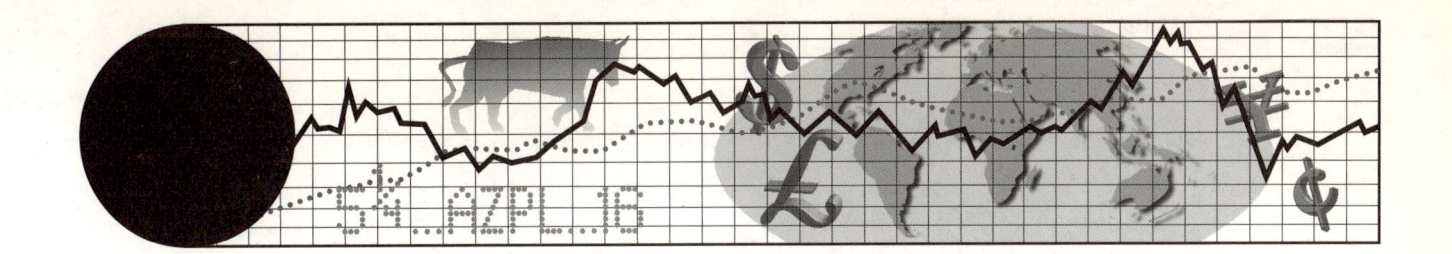

HotSheets

Equity Securities HotSheet

Stock Classifications:
- Authorized: number of shares corporation is permitted to issue
- Issued: has been sold to the public
- Treasury: repurchased by corporation; no voting rights, receives no dividends, cannot be traded on the open market
- Outstanding: number of shares held by the public
- Treasury = issued – outstanding
- Outstanding = issued – treasury

Stock Valuations:
- Par: assigned accounting value
- Book: liquidation or net worth value
- Market: value determined by supply and demand

Preemptive Rights:
- Allow shareholders to maintain proportionate interest

Voting Rights:
- Directors, issuance of convertible bonds or preferred stock; *not* on dividend payment or amount

Stock Splits:
- Forward: more shares, less value per share, same total value before and after
- Reverse: less shares, more value per share, same total value before and after

Preferred Stock:
- Par value = $100
- Stated (fixed) dividend rate
- Priority over common stock in liquidation and dividend payment
- Typically no voting rights

Current Yield:
- Annual dividends divided by current market price

Rights:
- 30–45 day duration
- Exercise price is below market on issuance
- Trade as a separate security
- Available to existing shareholders only
- One right per share outstanding

Warrants:
- Long term
- Exercise price above market when issued
- Trade as separate security
- Offered as sweeteners

ADRs:
- No preemptive rights
- Dividends in dollars
- No voting rights

REITs:
- Not a limited partnership
- Not an investment company
- Pass through income, not losses
- 75% of income must come from real estate
- Must distribute 90% or more of income to shareholders to avoid taxation as a trust
- Trade on exchanges or OTC

Dividends:
- Ex-date 2 business days prior to record date
- Ex-date set by NASD or Exchange
- Price of stock reduced at the opening by the amount of the dividend

Debt Securities HotSheet

Maturities:
- Term: matures at one date in the future
- Serial: matures over period of years; Balloon: large lump payment at end; Series: spread out issue, not a maturity

Investment Grade:
- Baa or BBB and above; based on default risk; ability to pay interest and principal when due

Call Features:
- Called by issuer when interest rates are falling; no interest after call
- Issuer cannot call during call protection period

Interbank Market:
- Establishes rates of exchange for foreign currency; decentralized; unregulated

Bond Yields:

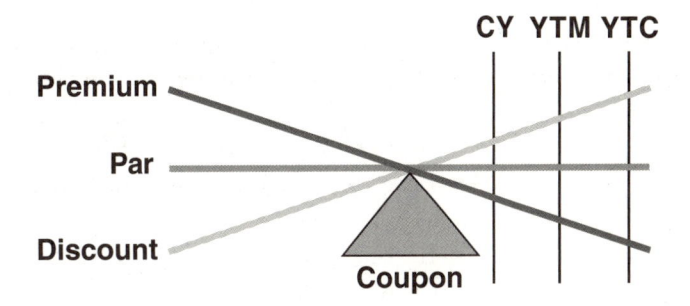

```
                              CY  YTM YTC
   Premium ─────────────────╲  │   │   │
                             ╲ │   │   │
   Par ═══════════════════════╳═══════════
                             ╱ │   │   │
   Discount ─────────────────╱  │   │   │
                          ▲
                        Coupon
```

Refunding:
- Refinancing at a lower rate
- Pre-refunded bonds are Triple A rated, considered defeased, funds escrowed in Treasuries

Corporate Bonds:
- Called *funded debt* if 5 or more years to maturity
- **Secured:** mortgage, collateral trust (backed by securities), equipment trust certificates
- **Unsecured:** backed by full faith and credit, debentures and subordinated debentures

Trust Indenture:
- Covenants between issuer and trustee for the benefit of bondholders

Convertibles:
- Par / conversion price = conversion ratio
- Market price / conversion ratio = parity price of common
- Conversion ratio × common stock price = parity price of bond

Governments:
- Bills quoted at a discount; notes and bonds in 32nds; notes and bonds are callable, bills are not
- Treasury STRIPS are backed in full by the US government

- TIPs provide inflation protection, safety of principal
- Interest is taxed at federal level, exempt from state and local taxation

Agencies:
- Ginnie Maes are backed in full by US government
- Interest fully taxable on mortgage-backed securities

CMOs:
- Corporate instrument with tranches; taxable monthly interest
- PACs protect from prepayment risk
- TACs— no protection from extension risk; subject to interest rate risk

Money Markets:
- Commercial paper: most heavily traded; corporate issue; issued at a discount, 270-day max maturity
- Negotiable CD: minimum face of $100,000, trade with accrued interest
- BAs: time draft, letter of credit for foreign trade; 270-day max maturity

Interest Rates:
- Fed funds rate most volatile, established by market; discount rate set by FRB; short-term rates more volatile than long-term rates

Rate Changes and Bond Prices:
- Long-term bonds react more than bonds to interest rate changes
- Discounts react more than premiums to rate changes
- In comparing two discount bonds, the one with the deeper discount (lower coupon) will react more
- Long-term zeroes react the most to rate changes

Savings Bonds:
- EE bonds issued at 50% of face value; interest is added to value of bond; investors can defer tax until maturity or redemption
- HH bonds issued at face value and pay fixed rate of interest which is taxable in year of receipt; can only be obtained in exchange for EE bonds
- I bonds have a fixed rate of interest plus inflation-adjusted rate; interest is added to the value of bond; taxable on redemption are used to pay tuition etc. at eligible colleges.

TIPS:
- Issued with fixed rate, principal is adjusted for inflation

Insurance of Government Securities:
- T-bills and T-notes are sold at auction
- Competitive bids by primary dealers are not always filled
- Non-competitive bids are always filled
- Competitive bid made in yield
- All winning bids filled at stop out price
- Agency securities sold through underwriting groups

Accrued Interest:
- Corp. and Muni–30/360
- T-notes and T-bonds—actual days
- Prior interest payment date up to but not including SD

Municipal Securities HotSheet

GOs:
- "Full faith and credit bonds"
- Backed primarily by taxes
- Generally safer than revenues
- Voter approval required
- Debt limits may restrict issuance
- Generally competitive bid underwriting
- Generally firm commitment underwriting
- Generally serial maturities with basis quotes
- Analysis based on taxes, debt statement, ratios, demographics

Revenues:
- Self-supporting bonds
- Backed by user fees
- Generally less safe than GOs
- No voter approval, may be subject to additional bonds test
- Feasibility study to determine economic viability
- Generally negotiated underwriting
- May be serial maturities with basis quotes or term maturities with dollar quotes
- Analysis based on feasibility study, debt service coverage ratio

IDRs:
- Backed by corporations; leaseback payments; interest may be taxable

PGDM:
- Presale, Group, Designated, Member: order allocation priority in syndicate letter

Bond Buyer:
- Mostly primary market info
- Includes 30-day visible supply, placement ratios, official notices of sale

Munifacts:
- Wire service, provides general information relevant to muni market
- Owned by the *Bond Buyer*

Spread:
- Compensation to syndicate
- Smallest portion is manager's fee
- Largest portion is takedown (concession plus additional takedown)

Three Years:
- Required time for keeping advertising records
- 2 years in readily accessible location
- Advertising may be approved by muni or general securities principal

90 Days:
- Muni apprenticeship period; no commissions, no dealing with customers

Confirmations:
- No later than settlement date for final confirmations

Unqualified:	• Most desirable legal opinion; no reservations by bond counsel
$100:	• Maximum gift allowed to persons other than employees
TIC:	• Includes time value of money; NIC method more commonly used for determining winning bid
Commissions:	• Markups/commissions must be fair and reasonable; no 5% guideline for MSRB
Tax-Equivalent Yield:	• Muni yield / (100% − Investor's tax bracket)
Tax-Free Equivalent Yield:	• Corp yield × (100% − Investor's tax bracket)
Rule G-37:	• 2-year prohibition on municipal securities business • Exemption allowed for contributions of $250 or less by municipal finance professionals

Options HotSheet

Options Chart:

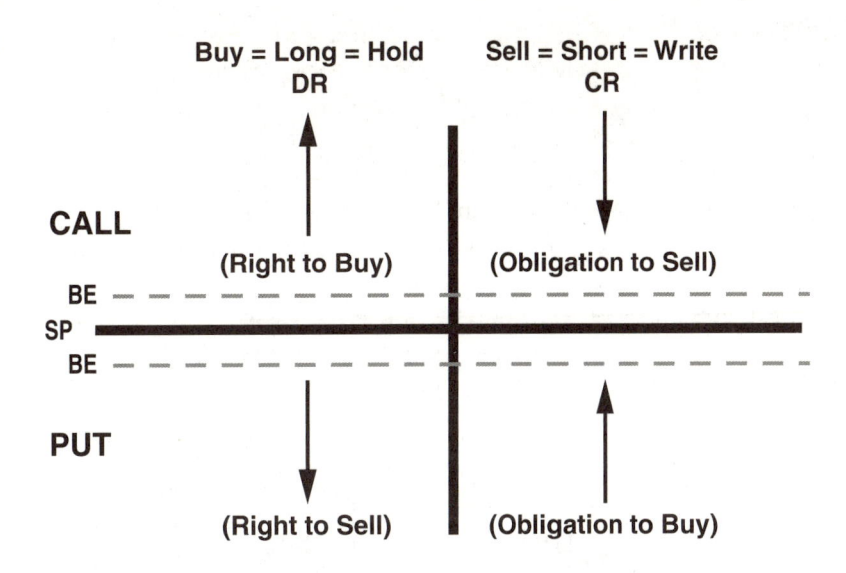

```
                Buy = Long = Hold        Sell = Short = Write
                      DR                         CR
                       ↑                          ↓
   CALL
                  (Right to Buy)           (Obligation to Sell)
      BE  - - - - - - - - - - - - |- - - - - - - - - - - -
      SP _____|_____
      BE  - - - - - - - - - - - - |- - - - - - - - - - - -
   PUT
                  (Right to Sell)          (Obligation to Buy)
                       ↓                          ↑
```

Single Options:

Position	Maximum Gain	Maximum Loss
Long Call	Unlimited	Premium
Short Call	Premium	Unlimited
Long Put	Strike price – Premium	Premium
Short Put	Premium	Strike price – Premium

Breakevens:
- Calls: SP + Premium
- Puts: SP – Premium

Intrinsic Value:
- Calls: Market price – SP (Call Up)
- Puts: SP – Market price (Put Down)

Hedging:
- Best or full protection = Buy an option
- Partial protection, improve rate of return, earn income: sell an option
- Long stock position: Risk is down: buy puts
- Short stock position: Risk is up: buy calls

Long Stock, Long Put:
- BE: Do T-chart: Stock price + Premium
- Max gain: Unlimited
- Max loss: (Stock price – Strike price) + Premium

Long Stock, Short Call:	• BE: Do T-chart: Stock Price – Premium • Max gain: (Strike price – Stock price) + Premium • Max loss: Stock price – Premium
Short Stock, Short Put:	• BE: Do T-chart: Stock price + premium • Max gain: (Stock price – Strike price) + Premium • Max loss: Unlimited
Short Stock, Long Call:	• BE: Do T-chart: Stock price – Premium • Max gain: Stock price – Premium • Max loss: (Strike price – Stock price) + Premium
Spreads:	• Debits = Widen = Exercise • Credits = Narrow = Expire

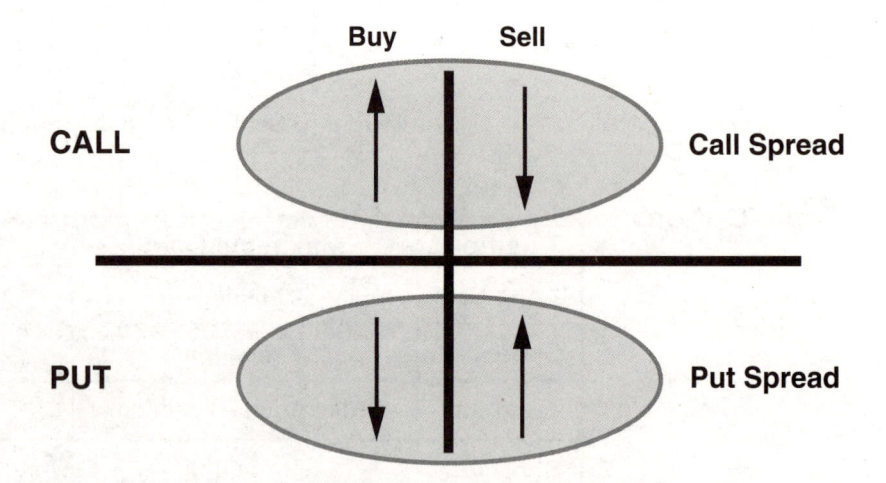

```
                    Buy    Sell
                     ↑      ↓
   CALL         (       |       )    Call Spread
   ────────────────────┼────────────────────
   PUT          (       |       )    Put Spread
                     ↓      ↑
```

Do T-chart to determine net position

Credit Spreads:	• Max gain = Initial net credit • Max loss = Difference in strike prices minus the net credit
Debit Spreads:	• Max gain = Difference in strike prices minus the net debit • Max loss = Initial net debit
Spread Breakevens:	• CAL: For call spreads add net premium to lower strike price • PSH: For put spreads subtract net premium from higher strike price
Market Attitude for Spreads:	• Investor is bullish if long the lower strike price
Straddles:	• Long straddles—expect sharp move in price but uncertain of direction • Short straddles—expect little or no movement in stock price

- Same SP and expiration

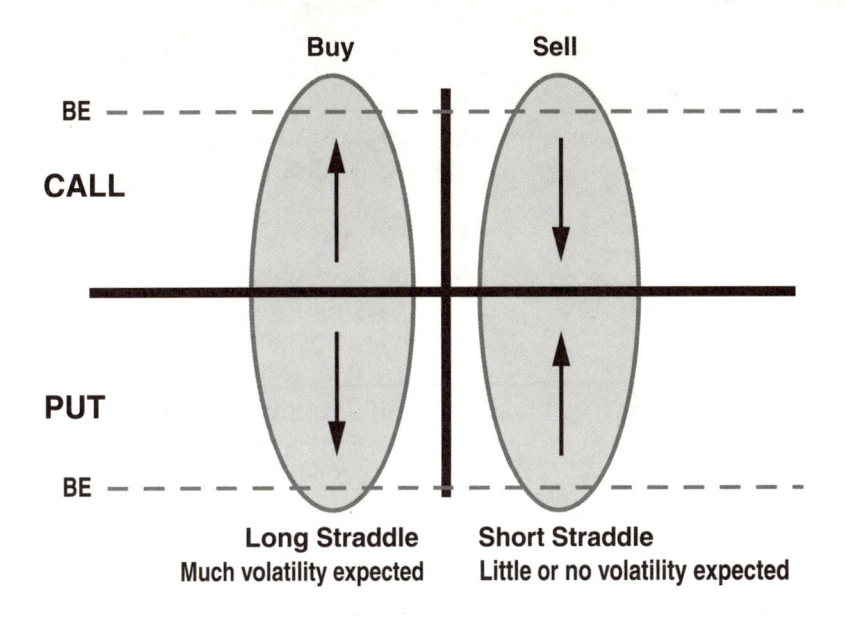

```
              Buy        Sell
BE  - - - - - ⭕ - - - - - - -
              ↑
CALL          
              ↓   ⭕
                  ↓
━━━━━━━━━━━━━━━━━┿━━━━━━━━━━━
                  
PUT           ⭕   
              ↓   ↑
BE  - - - - - - - ⭕ - - - - -
                  
         Long Straddle      Short Straddle
     Much volatility expected   Little or no volatility expected
```

Breakevens:
- Call: SP + Both premiums
- Put: SP − Both premiums

Options Concepts:
- A **call option buyer** has the right to purchase the underlying security for a specified price within a specified time frame.
- A **call option seller** is obligated to sell the underlying security for a specified price within a specified time frame if exercised.
- A **put option buyer** has the right to sell the underlying security for a specified price within a specified time frame.
- A **put option seller** is obligated to purchase the underlying security for a specified price within a specified time frame if exercised.
- Because of the **leverage** option contracts offer investors, they may be used to protect investment portfolio positions or to speculate on the direction of the underlying security.
- An **option contract** has a relatively short life span. Time remaining to expiration is important in determining the option's value. The amount by which the contract is in-the-money is also critical. Initial transactions in options are opening purchases or sales. Once a position is established, a closing sale or purchase (offsetting transaction), or the expiration or exercise of the contract, ends the position.
- Option transactions may be straightforward, such as the opening purchase or sale of a call or put. They may be coupled with other portfolio securities or other option contracts in order to use more complicated investment strategies.

The Four Basic Option Transactions:

- LONG CALL
  Max gain: unlimited
  Max loss: premium paid
  Breakeven: strike price + premium
- SHORT CALL
  Max gain: Premium received
  Max loss: Unlimited
  Breakeven: Strike price + Premium
- LONG PUT
  Max gain: Strike price – Premium paid
  Max loss: Premium paid
  Breakeven: Strike price – Premium
- SHORT PUT
  Max gain: Premium received
  Max loss: Strike price – Premium received
  Breakeven: Strike price – Premium

Customer Accounts HotSheet

New Account Forms:
- Required for all accounts
- Birthdate required
- Customer signature not required for cash accounts; is required for margin accounts
- Signed by representative and approving principal
- Identity verification required

Account Approval:
- By principal, either prior to or promptly after the first transaction

Trading Authorization:
- Limited—third party can trade only
- Full—third party can trade and withdraw cash and securities

Fiduciary Accounts:
- Subject to prudent man rule or legal list
- All require written legal document, except UGMA/UTMA
- Margin accounts permitted only if authorized in document
- No short sales, naked options

Account Transfers:
- Verify positions within three business days; then freeze the account; three more business days to transfer

Accounts for Other Broker/Dealer Employees:
- NYSE—permission first, prior written notification, duplicate statements and confirms
- MSRB—prior written notification, duplicate confirms
- NASD—prior written notification, duplicate confirms request only

Joint Accounts:
- All signatures required to open
- Any party can trade
- Distributions payable to all
- Each owns undivided interest

JTWROS:
- Equal ownership interest
- Passes to remaining tenant at death; no probate

TIC:
- Unequal interests OK
- Passes by will to heirs, not to remaining tenant(s)

Discretionary:
- Authority from customer must be in writing
- Account must be approved before the first trade
- Principal must review discretionary accounts frequently for churning
- Time and price not discretionary

UGMA:
- Cash accounts only
- Minor is beneficial owner; minor's Social Security number on account
- One minor, one custodian
- No short sales, no uncovered options, no margin

Margin Accounts HotSheet

Long and Short T-Charts:

LMV	DR		CR	SMV
	EQ			EQ

Account Status:

Excess Equity — Creates SMA

━━━━━━━━━━━━━━━━━━━━━━━━━━━━━━ Reg T

Restricted Status
Buy—Pay 50%
Sell—50% retention
Withdraw securities—Deposit 50%

━━━━━━━━━━━━━━━━━━━━━━━━━━━━━━ Min. Maintenance

Maintenance Call
Deposit Cash
Deposit Securities
Sell Securities in an Account

Market Value at Maintenance:
- Long account: DR / .75
- Short account: CR / 1.30

Margin Agreement:
- Credit agreement: required; investor pays variable rate interest on money borrowed
- Hypothecation agreement: required; investor pledges securities to broker/dealer
- Loan consent form: optional; if signed, broker/dealer may loan customer margin securities for short sales

Reg T Exemptions:
- Government securities, municipals, corporate debt are subject to SRO requirements only

SMA in Long Account:
- Increased by:
  – increase in market value of securities in account
  – nonrequired cash deposit ($1 for $1)
  – sale of securities (50% of sales proceeds to SMA)
- Decreased by:
  – purchase of securities or withdrawal of cash, not market value decline

SMA Buying Power:
- $1 of SMA buys $2 of stock (2 to 1)

Maintenance Call:
- Must be met promptly; $1,000 exemption

Initial Requirement:
- Reg T or $2,000, whichever is greater (exception for long account: 100% of purchase price if less than $2,000)

Issuing Securities HotSheet

Act of 1933:
- Requires registration of all nonexempt issues
- Requires full and fair disclosure of new issues
- The "Paper Act"

Exempt Securities:
- Commercial paper, banker's acceptances with maturities of less than 270 days

Exempt Issuers:
- US govt., municipalities, nonprofits/charities/churches, banks

Reg A:
- $5 million or less in 12 months; offering circular for disclosure

Rule 147:
- Home office in state; 80% of business and assets in state
- Only state residents can buy, no resale to non-residents for 9 months

Reg D (Private Placements):
- No more than 35 non-accredited investors
- Unlimited accredited investors
- Institutions, broker/dealers, individuals with income of more than $200,000 single, $300,000 married in last two years, officers and directors of the issuer
- Sign investment letter, hold for one year
- Private placement memorandum for disclosure

Rule 144:
- One-year hold on restricted securities, insiders or non-insiders
- Volume limitations apply to all control stock sales
- Limits for 90 days are greater of 1% of outstanding voting stock or average of preceding 4 weeks trading volume
- Must file Form 144 with SEC no later than sale date
- Insiders can't sell short; short-swing profits must be disgorged
- Form 144 good for 90 days

Rule 144a:
- No holding period on unregistered securities sold to institutional investors

Rule 145:
- Proxy statement required to inform shareholders of mergers, acquisitions, reclassifications

Prospectus Delivery:
- Final prospectus no later than confirmation of sale
- 40 days for non-Nasdaq subsequent primary; no extended delivery requirement for listed or Nasdaq subsequent primary
- 25 days for listed IPOs and Nasdaq
- 90 days for Pink Sheet, OTCBB IPOs

Cooling-Off Period:
- Minimum of 20 days
- No advertising, sales literature, orders, offers
- Tombstones, red herrings, indications of interest are OK

Underwriting:
- Must be NASD members to underwrite corporate securities
- Firm commitment = principal capacity; underwriters have risk
- Best efforts = agent capacity; issuer has risk
- Syndicate members have liability; selling group members do not

Stabilizing:
- One bid, at or below public offering price, only in underwriting period
- Must be stated in prospectus

Freeriding/Withholding:
- Firms/reps, financially supported persons cannot buy hot issues
- Nonsupported family and officers of financial institutions may if prior history and insubstantial amount

Trading Securities HotSheet

Act of 1934:	• **People Act;** regulates exchanges and OTC trading activity
Securities Markets:	• **Exchanges**: listed securities, auction market • **OTC**: unlisted securities, negotiated transactions • **Third market**: listed securities traded OTC, negotiated trades, trades reported in 90 seconds • **Fourth market**: institutions trading direct through Instinet service
NYSE Trade Rule:	• Priority, precedence, and parity: determines which order executed first
Specialist:	• Maintains an orderly market; acts as agent and principal, priority to customer orders • Holds book of stop and limit orders; sets opening quote
Order Chart:	• Orders placed below the current market are adjusted for cash dividends (BLISS) unless marked DNR (do not reduce) • All orders are adjusted for stock splits and stock dividends
Stop Orders:	• **Buy stop** triggered at or above order price, executed at next available price. • **Sell stop** triggered at or below order price, executed at next price.
Stop Limit:	• Once stock trades at or through stop price, becomes a limit order to buy or sell
Time-Sensitive Orders:	• FOK: execute all immediately or cancel entire order • AON: execute all, immediacy is not important; hold as GTC on book until filled • IOC: execute whatever is available now, remainder is cancelled
Short Sale Rules:	• Must be executed on plus tick or zero-plus tick for exchanges, OTC has down bid rule • Inside bid = down bid • A legal short sale must be executed at least $.01 above bid if bid is a down bid • Short sale order tickets must be marked
Order Routing:	• SuperDot for NYSE
Non-Nasdaq:	• Quotes not firm unless priced • Three-quote rule generally applies • Corporate bonds on Yellow Sheets

5% Policy:
- Guide for OTC nonexempt (not munis or govs)
- For markups, markdowns, commission

Nasdaq Levels:
- Level 1: Inside quote (basis for markup/markdown)
- Level 2: Displays quotes of all market makers
- Level 3: Market makers enter quotes (interactive level)

SuperMontage:
- Order display and execution system for Nasdaq
- Shows trading interest at 5 levels on each side of the market

Brokerage Support Services HotSheet

OPMC:	• Order routing through broker/dealer is: – Order department – Purchases & Sales department – Margin department – Cashier department
Order Tickets:	• Must be approved by principal no later than the end of the trade date
Errors:	• Report first to principal • Reporting errors binding on customer at executed price • Errors of execution are not binding on customer
Confirmations:	• Customer: No later than settlement date • Broker/dealer-to-broker/dealer: No later than T+1 • Must disclose agent or principal • Commissions must be disclosed; markups/downs are disclosed for Nasdaq trades
Customer Statements:	• Minimum of quarterly; monthly statements for active accounts
Financial Disclosure:	• Customers entitled to most recent balance sheet upon written request
Settlement Dates:	• Regular way: Corps and Munis: T+3; Governments: T+1 • Cash settlement: same day • Reg T settlement: T+5 • Seller's option: no sooner than first day after regular way; no later than the date identified in the contract • When issued: determined by Uniform Practice Committee
Frozen Accounts:	• If no extension granted from SRO, 90 day freeze applies • Amounts of less than $1,000 can be ignored
Bonds Traded Flat:	• No accrued interest • Income (adjustment bonds), defaulted bonds, zeros
Invalid Signatures:	• Deceased persons, minors, persons declared legally incompetent

Investment Company Products HotSheet

Investment Company Act of 1940:	• Defines and regulates investment companies • Three types: face amount certificate, UIT, management company
Open-End Company:	• Mutual fund; continuous primary offering • Redemption in seven calendar days • Price by formula in prospectus • Fractional shares
Closed-End Company:	• Trade in secondary market; issues debt and equity • Fixed number of shares • Sold with prospectus in IPO only
Diversified Status:	• 75% invested in other companies • Max of 5% in any one company • Can own no more than 10% of a target company's voting stock • Status applies to open- and closed-end companies
Registration Requirements:	• Minimum $100,000 capital, 100 investors • Clearly defined investment objective • Asset to debt ratio not less than 3-to-1 (300%)
Prohibited Investing:	• No purchases on margin; no short sales
Shareholder Votes:	• Change investment objective; change sales load policy; change fund classification
Shareholder Reports:	• Annual audited report, semiannual unaudited report (two per year)
Sector Funds:	• Minimum of 25% of assets in area of specialty; more aggressive
Money-Market Funds:	• No load, fixed NAV, check-writing privileges, daily interest
Performance History:	• One, five, 10 years (or fund's life if less than 10 years)
Sales Charge %:	• (POP − NAV) ÷ POP (NASD maximum of 8.5% of POP)
POP Calculation:	• NAV ÷ (100% − SC%)

12b-1 Charges:	• Distribution fee approved annually and charged quarterly; cannot be described as no-load fund if exceeds 0.25%
8½% Sales Charge:	• Only if fund offers reinvestment at NAV; rights of accumulation; breakpoints
Letter of Intent:	• Must be in writing; maximum 13 months; can be backdated 90 days
Conduit Theory:	• IRC subchapter M: fund is regulated investment company if it distributes a minimum of 90% of net investment income • Fund taxed only on retained earnings
Ex-dividend Date:	• Determined by BOD; typically business day after record date
Calculating Yield:	• Annual dividends ÷ POP; capital gains distributions are not included
Dollar Cost Averaging:	• Effective if average cost per share is lower than average price per share • No guarantees

Retirement Plans HotSheet

Nonqualified Plans:
- Nondeductible contributions; can be discriminatory
- Examples are payroll deduction; deferred compensation
- Risk of deferred compensation is employer failure

IRAs:
- Maximum contribution is $3,000, or 100% of earned income
- Spousal IRA allows $6,000 between spouses filing joint returns, split between two accounts
- No life insurance or collectibles as investments
- 10% penalty, plus applicable ordinary income tax on withdrawals before age 59½
- 6% excess contribution penalty
- 50% insufficient distribution penalty (insufficient if after 70½)
- One rollover allowed each 12 months to be completed within 60 days
- Unlimited trustee-to-trustee transfers
- Contributions are immediately vested

SEPs:
- Qualified plan; allows employers to contribute money to employee IRAs
- Contribution max = $40,000
- Contributions are immediately vested

Roth IRAs:
- New IRA that allows after-tax contributions, possible tax-free distributions
- Maximum contribution of $3,000 per individual, $6,000 per couple
- Does not require distributions to begin at age 70½

Education IRAs:
- New IRA: allows after-tax contributions for children under age 18
- Maximum contribution is $2,000 per year
- Tax-free distributions if funds are used for education
- Contributions may be made by any adult

Keoghs (HR-10 Plans):
- Available to self-employed persons, owners of unincorporated businesses, and professional practices
- Contribution max is lesser of 20% of gross for employer (25% for employee) or $40,000
- All employees must participate if age 21 or older, employed more than one year, work more than 1,000 hours per year
- Life insurance may be held within the plan

TSAs (403(b) Plans):
- Available to employees of nonprofit organizations
- Typically funded by elective employee salary reductions; usually no cost basis

Pension Plans:	• Require annual contribution • Defined benefit: based on formula factoring age, salary, years of service; calculated by actuary; favor older key employees • Defined contribution: simpler to administer, contribution is typically a percent of salary
Profit-Sharing Plans:	• Annual contribution not required; great investment and contribution flexibility
Withholding Rule:	• 20% withholding applied to distributions from qualified plans made payable to participant
ERISA:	• Protects participants in corporate (private) plans, not public plans • Rules for funding, vesting, nondiscrimination, participation, communication

Variable Annuities HotSheet

Fixed Annuity:
- Guaranteed rate of return; insurance company has investment risk
- Subject to purchasing power risk
- Fixed income guaranteed for life; not a security

Variable Annuity:
- Rate of return dependent on separate account performance
- Investor has investment risk; sold with prospectus
- Can keep pace with inflation
- Variable income guaranteed for life; principal is not guaranteed

Accumulation Phase:
- Investor pays money to insurer; units vary in number and in value

Annuity Phase:
- Investor receives payments from insurer; fixed number of units; vary in value

Purchase Methods:
- **Periodic deferred**: paid in installments; payouts taken later
- **Single premium immediate**: lump-sum payment; payouts begin immediately, no accumulation period
- **Single premium deferred**: lump-sum payment; payouts taken later

Payout Methods:
- Lump sum or random withdrawals
- Annuitization (monthly income guaranteed for life)
- **Life income**: no beneficiary, largest monthly payment
- **Life with period certain**: minimum guaranteed period
- **Joint life w/last survivor**: annuity on two lives; smallest month

AIR:
- Used to determine monthly income
- Income goes up from previous month if separate account performance is greater than AIR
- Income stays the same as previous month if separate account performance is equal to AIR
- Income falls from the previous month if separate account performance is less than the AIR

Taxation:
- Monthly income: part return of cost basis, part taxable; proportion determined by exclusion ratio
- Lump sum/random withdrawals: LIFO applies; earnings withdrawn first, taxable as ordinary income; no tax on remainder because it is a return of cost basis

Regulated by:
- Act of 1933; Act of 1934, Investment Company Act of 1940; Investment Advisers Act of 1940, State Insurance Departments; Federal insurance law

Max Sales Charge:
- 8½%

Direct Participation Programs HotSheet

DPPs:
- Not investment companies
- Distribute proportionate share of losses, gains, income

DPP: *Real Estate*
- Raw land
- Existing property, least risky
- Tax credits from government assisted housing programs

Oil & Gas
- Exploratory, most risky (high IDC write-offs)
- Income Programs, least risky (provide depletion allowances)

Sharing Arrangements:
- Most common is functional allocation

Limited Partners:
- No management
- Limited liability
- Passive investors only
- Can sue GP

General Partners:
- Active management
- Fiduciary responsibility
- Cannot borrow, compete, or commingle

Syndicator:
- Distributes partnership interests
- Compensation max is 10%

Documentation:
- Certificate of Limited Partnership: identifies GP and LPs
- Partnership Agreement: rules of "the club"; empowers GP to manage
- Subscription Agreement: application for membership; effective when signed by GP; discloses income, net worth, understanding of risk

Partnership Democracy:
- Special vote for switching GPs, dissolving partnership

Taxation:
- Passive loss can only be used to shelter passive income
- LPs provide pass-through of all income, losses, gains to partners

Reason to Invest:
- Economic viability is first concern

Methods of Analysis:
- Cash flow analysis and internal rate of return computations

Liquidation Priority:
- 1. Secured creditors
- 2. Other creditors
- 3. Limited partners
- 4. GP(s)

Economics & Analysis HotSheet

Business Cycle:	• **Expansion**: low unemployment, increased business activities • **Peak** • **Contraction**: falling stock markets, rising inventories, decreasing GDP • **Trough**: (Recession = 6 months of declining GDP; Depression = 6 quarters of declining GDP) accompanied by high unemployment
CPI:	• Measures inflation through comparison of constant dollars
Leading Indicators:	• Money supply; building permits; number of unemployment claims; orders; stock prices
Coincident Indicators:	• Personal income; GDP; industrial production
Lagging Indicators:	• Duration of unemployment; corporate profits; commercial loans outstanding
Economic Theories:	• **Keynes**: aggregate demand; government intervention encouraged • **Friedman**: monetarist theory; quantity of money determines price levels • **Laffer**: supply-side economics; government should reduce spending and taxes
Money Supply:	• M1 = currency and demand deposits • M2 = M1 + money markets, savings accounts, overnight repos • M3 = M2 + large time deposits, longer repos
Fiscal Policy:	• Taxation; spending by Congress and president
Monetary Policy:	• FRB's tools: discount rate, reserve requirement (greatest impact) and FOMC (most used)
Technical Analysis:	• Charting; market timing; price predictions based on trends
Technical Theories:	• **Dow theory**: confirms end of market trends; changes in stock prices reflected by indexes • **Odd-lot theory**: do the opposite of the small investor • **Short interest theory**: large amount of short interest is bullish • **MPT**: focuses on portfolio relationships; efficient markets • **Random walk**: direction of stock market or prices is unpredictable
Fundamental Analysis:	• Study of a company's prospects based on overall economy, financial statements

Industry Analysis:
- Defensive: food, tobacco, pharmaceuticals, utilities
- Cyclical: heavy machinery
- Growth: technology (low dividend payouts)

Balance Sheet:
- Assets – liabilities = net worth;
- Assets = liabilities + net worth
- Used to compute capitalization and liquidity ratios

Income Statement:
- Summarizes revenues and expenses to determine efficiency and profitability

Ratios:
- Capitalization: debt/equity; bond ratio; common stock ratio
- Liquidity: current ratio; acid-test ratio
- Valuation: PE ratio; current yield; dividend payout ratio
- Working capital: current assets – current liabilities

Ethics, Recommendations & Taxation HotSheet

Private Transactions:
- Not allowed without broker/dealer's knowledge and consent; prior written notice and disclosure of compensation required
- Passive investments not subject to this requirement

Gift Limit:
- No more than $100 cash per year to employees of other member firms; both NASD and MSRB rule

Selling Dividends:
- Prohibited practice due to tax liability

Breakpoint Sales:
- Encouraging customer to purchase below the opportunity for a discount; prohibited practice

Research Reports:
- Must disclose if prepared by someone outside firm

Shared Accounts:
- Allowable only if firm grants prior written approval; sharing only in proportion to contribution

Prohibited Trading Practices:
- **Painting the Tape**: party sells with agreement from buyer that repurchase will occur the same day
- **Matching**: broker/dealer stages a hot market by simultaneous purchases and sales
- **Front running**: broker/dealer order placed ahead of customer order for better price
- **Capping**: exerting selling pressure to keep stock prices from rising

Investment Objectives:
- Preservation of capital; safety = government securities or Ginnie Maes
- Growth = common stock or common stock mutual fund
- Balanced or moderate growth = blue-chip stocks
- Aggressive growth = technology stocks or sector funds
- Income = bonds (but not zero-coupons); preferred stock and utilities also provide income
- Tax-free income = municipal bonds or muni bond funds
- High-yield income = corporate bonds or corporate bond funds
- Liquidity = money market funds; (DPPs, CDs, real estate, and annuities are illiquid)

Investment Risks:
- **Purchasing power risk**: inflation
- **Reinvestment risk**: mortgage-backed securities and callable bonds are susceptible
- **Market risk**: also called systematic risk; diversification does not reduce
- **Credit risk**: risk of issuer's default causing loss of principal
- **Liquidity risk**: also called marketability risk; risk that investor cannot convert to cash quickly and at a fair price

CAPM:	• Determines risk and reward from total portfolio; basis of modern portfolio theory
Beta:	• Overall market has beta of 1; S&P 500 is benchmark; beta higher than 1 is more volatile, aggressive
Foreign Stock:	• Income taxed by country of investor's citizenship; typically 15% withholding on foreign distributions
Wash Sales:	• Loss disallowed if substantially identical security purchased 30 days before or after sale for loss
Bond Cost Basis:	• Amortize all premiums; secondary market discounts are subject to taxation as ordinary income
Gifted/Inherited Stock:	• For gifts, cost basis is giver's original basis; heirs' cost basis is MV on date of death
Dividend Exclusion:	• 70% exclusion on corporate dividends; no dividend exclusion for individuals

US Government and State Rules & Regulations HotSheet

Act of 1933:
- The Paper Act
- Nonexempt issuers must file registration statements with the SEC
- Requires use of prospectus when selling new issues
- Requires full and fair disclosure of new issues
- Regulates primary market activity (issuing and underwriting)

Act of 1934:
- The People Act; regulates secondary market activity
- Created the SEC
- Requires registration of all reps and firms that trade securities for the public
- Oversees exchanges and OTC market
- Regulates extension of credit
- Prohibits fraudulent trading activities
- Regulates insider transactions, short sales, proxies, and client accounts
- Prohibits use of inside information
- No security is exempt from antifraud provisions (even if exempt from 1933 registration)

Maloney Act:
- Chartered the NASD as the SRO of the OTC

Trust Indenture Act of 1939:
- Regulates senior corporate securities (bonds)
- Requires trust indenture/trustee for issues of more than $5 million in 12 months
- Trust indenture is covenant between issuer and trustee for protection of bondholders

Investment Advisers Act of 1940:
- Requires registration of persons who receive fees for giving investment advice

Investment Company Act of 1940:
- Regulates and defines investment companies
- Three types of investment companies: face amount certificate companies; unit investment trusts; management companies
- Requires clearly stated investment objectives
- Minimum of $100,000 assets, 100 shareholders

Insider Trading Act of 1988:
- Tippers and tippees are guilty
- Penalties up to greater of $1,000,000 or 3 × profit made/loss avoided
- Broker/dealers must have written supervisory procedures
- Chinese Walls prohibit sensitive information passed between departments of broker/dealers

Penny Stock Cold Calling Rule:
- Persons that buy non-Nasdaq stock of less than $5 must sign suitability statements before transactions
- Firms required to provide monthly statements of penny stock accounts regardless of activity
- Customers receive disclosure of risk and commissions made by rep firm
- Customers who opened account more than 12 months before, or made three different penny stock transactions with the firm

Uniform Securities Act (USA):
- Blue-sky laws—coordination, filing, qualification for registering securities
- Requires registration of securities, broker/dealers, and reps at state level

Other SEC & SRO Rules & Regulations HotSheet

NASD Manual:
- **Conduct Rules**: fair and ethical dealing with the public
- **Uniform Practice Code**: standardizes practices between broker/dealers (DKs, settlements, ex-dates)
- **Code of Procedure** (**COP**): handles complaints, disciplinary action; Department of Enforcement investigates
- **Code of Arbitration**: handles monetary disputes between BDs or within the industry

Principals:
- Minimum of two per firm; manage, train, and supervise
- Approve all accounts and client transactions

Felony Conviction:
- May be disqualified for 10 years

Code of Procedure:
- Respond to DOE notice within 25 days
- DOE can administer any penalty other than jail
- Decision final after 45 days

Minor Rule Violation:
- Maximum fine $2,500
- Appeal within 25 days of decision date

Code of Arbitration:
- Between members, with public only with written consent
- Decisions are final and binding on all parties
- Awards after 30 days
- Simplified is $25,000 for public and industry
- 6-year statute of limitations

NYSE Rules:
- Prior permission for outside employment; no transfer of registration

NASD Communications:
- Advertising = nontargeted communications; sales literature = targeted communications
- Both must be approved by principal before use; filed for 3 years, 2 years easily accessible
- Investment company material must be filed with NASD within 10 days of use
- 1st year firms must file with NASD 10 days before first use
- Generic advertising is OK if product or service offered is available
- Name of member required except on recruitment ads
- Testimonials OK with disclosure of compensation

Recommendations:
- Must be suitable; disclose current price; potential conflicts of interest
- "Past performance does not guarantee future results"

Investment Company Recommendations:
- Advertising/sales literature must disclose performance history for a 10-year period unless new fund
- Advertise based on highest charge: no breakpoint
- Yield = Annual dividend/POP

Telephone Consumer Protection Act:
- Must call noncustomers at home between 8 am and 9 pm
- Firms must maintain *Do-Not-Call* list and written procedures
- Not applicable to nonprofit organizations